HOST OF PARADOX

A QUALMISH DISCLOSURE

JOHN RIXEY MOORE

BETTIE YOUNGS BOOKS

Disclaimer: This is a true story, and the characters and events
are real. However, in some cases, the names have been altered,
but the overall chronology is an accurate depiction of the author's
experience.

Cover photo by Bill Phalen
Cover design by Roy Samuelson and Sean Akers
Photo of John Rixey Moore by Nicholas Paulos

BETTIE YOUNGS BOOK PUBLISHERS
www.BettieYoungsBooks.com
info@BettieYoungsBooks.com

Bettie Youngs Books are distributed worldwide. If you are unable to
order this book from your local bookseller, Espresso, or online, you
may order directly from the publisher.

Library of Congress Control Number: 2011942502

ISBN: 978-1-936332-37-3
ePub ISBN: 978-1-936332-33-5

Printed in the United States of America

What Others Are Saying about This Book . . .

Some men lead an exciting, stimulating life of high adventure. John Rixey Moore has somehow packed at least three of these lives into one.
—Andy Shrader, writer, the Antarctic feature film script, *Ice Men*

An epic tale.
—Steve Hudis, producer, IMPACT Motion Picture

John Moore takes you on a ride that grabs you and does not let you go.
—David Hadley, actor, "China Beach," "Quantum Leap"

A compelling story told with extraordinary insight, disconcerting reality, and engaging humor. A most amazing saga!
—Ron Russell, author, *Don Carina*

John captures his endlessly terrifying journeys through multiple reconnaissance missions in Vietnam by putting you into his own intimate experience, with sensory descriptions more realistic than virtual reality, perfectly seasoned with deep thoughtfulness, a disarming wit, and an unexpected charm.
—Roy Samuelson, actor, voice of Intel, ford.com, Wonka

Moore plunges us deep into the jungles of Southeast Asia as we walk, crawl, and sweat with him on excruciatingly dangerous missions, just hoping to get back alive! The mind-expanding discourse about life on the edge, the emotional tension it engenders, and the places it takes you, shows the author's penchant for paradox and is a testament to what a compelling writer he is.
—Clif Potts, actor, "Once an Eagle," "Silent Running," "Wild Hearts"

Intensely personal and perceptive. You'll never forget this book!
—Leon Logothetis, host, producer, best-selling author, *Amazing Adventures of a Nobody*

John Moore fills this memoir with craft, immediacy, and authenticity. Simply the best Vietnam narrative I have ever read.
—Tom Perry, Producer

War is the health of the state.

Randolph Bourne

TABLE OF CONTENTS

DEDICATION

Having no children of my own I can only guess at the depths of parental bonds. Indeed life has more than once given me painful lessons of this ignorance. I dedicate this book to the loving memory of my parents, Joseph and Lloyd (named for her famous father), who did an admirable job of launching their offspring onto the path of decency and humble wonder and who must have dwelt in a private hell of anxiety while the events described herein were taking place on the other side of the world.

I wish further to share this acknowledgement with their grandchildren, my nephew Joseph and niece Susanne, and thereby join with their parents in the edgy hope that the world they are entering will soon shake itself free from the bloody legacy of military adventurism, religious dogma, and government interference with the free comportment of their lives.

FOREWORD

It took an eternity of hot, stupefying seconds in a chaos of automatic rifle fire to splinter the wood around my head and thump into the bodies of my companions for me to accept the fact that there really were people who wanted to kill me. What came next was a delirium of such sustained violence that the language to describe it all lies beyond reach, the kind of night men dream about in after years, waking in a cold sweat to a surge of gratitude that it was only a dream.

The surreal confusion of my first firefight left me stunned, wounded, and filled, if that's the word, with a windblown emptiness within, a breathless pain, and a sense of unnatural fragility, like hollow glass. My mind became a bloody vacancy and cold, like a cellar in which there had been a burial.

In the presence of real mortality for the first time, I felt neither pain nor hatred, nor conscious relief at being spared, just a sense of enormous space and time suspended in a state of emotionally anesthetized detachment, yet intensely aware, and mixed with a terrible new fear rising across the empty field of that last enormous, unanswerable question.

In the year 1525, King Francis I of France led his troops into an indefensible position in some fruit orchards outside Pavia in Italy, and in the subsequent battle lost his army and got himself taken prisoner. That night, in a long letter rambling through the tangled thickets of 16th century prose, a disorderly jumble of subordinate clauses and dangling participles, the captive King wrote his mother to explain how the unthinkable had happened, pouring out all his grief and rage and humiliation and his unconquerable will to survive. By the time his mother, her royal counselors, and ladies in waiting had passed the letter around and commented and gossiped about it, the message had been reduced to a single sentence: "All is lost but honor." An early sound-bite.

The Vietnam metaphor is analogous, both in the envelopment and disenfranchisement of the army and in the effort on the part of those who placed themselves in charge of public sentiment to minimize the errors and reduce the record of suffering with ill-informed generalities and pithy diminutives. Unfortunately it will likely be to these abridged and sadly devitalized summaries that future historians who might choose to examine the events will turn.

Yet for me and thousands of other veterans, our clear and present memories of the Brutal Absurdity refuse to die. I begin to write about it and find my words going shrill, my body trembling with forty-five-year-old frustration. Old injustices still march through my dreams, nurtured somehow within me in a place full of sadness and suppressed anger. There is still something unsettled there, a smothered antagonism, a source of private irritation. Yet I choose to make the effort to record my experiences in part to see whether memory can engender understanding, bring some light to the weltering chaos of the past, and in part to record some of its images for a generation that is unlikely to learn more about certain aspects of the conflict that have been kept secret than can be gleaned from the abbreviated accounts to be found in textbooks.

The sad fact is that after some sixty generations of popularity as a substitute for political and economic diplomacy, war remains a fundamentally non-transferable experience. The literary records of most wars can be seen as a series of anxious, sometimes coldly objective, and occasionally inspired attempts to evoke a response that might have some degree of adequacy to the unparalleled situation in which the individual authors were involved. The problem for the writer trying to describe any direct experience of war is the utter incredibility of events, and thus their essential incommunicability in their own terms. The memoirist who writes about the personal experience of war nibbles at the corner of an impossibly obtuse canvas, for language does not contain the material to fully convey the subject's pertinacious, writhing images, thus leaving the gap incompletely spanned. Unprecedented meaning must then sort through precedent motifs. Thus, one searches for an un-impoverished system of symbols capable of conveying to a contemporary audience the rich and terrible complications of first-hand participation in an unimaginably violent event. And, popular images aside, on a visceral level it is truly unimaginable.

Photographs that depict the subject have been widely available since the 19th century, and modern films lend a certain spurious animation to the images, but these efforts can only simulate a kind of symbolic version of events. Nothing short of direct experience can fully imprint the thunderous living nightmare that bursts upon its victim with horrifying intimacy, nor the baleful and relentless weight it places forever after upon one's values, habitudes and altered perceptions. Nothing but a dose of its live-action terrors can impart its awesome atavistic power, its sudden impenetrable noise, its indelible sights and smells, or its terrible silences.

It is a realm in which mortal fear becomes much more than one of nature's warning signs. Fear can grow into a monstrous living breathing thing that, like a malevolent home invader, can move in and take over one's very being, filling even those hidden places where we keep our silent hopes and dreams. It must be kept at bay by whatever means an individual can master, for its unguarded legacy is death.

A few minutes of modern ground warfare teaches that personal heroism is but a pliable abstraction, often making no difference in a day's outcome, partially because technological advances in weaponry have made the weapons themselves the principal actors, and the men, often reduced in the planners' minds merely to the commodity that measures the weapons' effectiveness. Thus what every combat veteran knows but finds hard to voice aloud is that death and injury is entirely random, and success is only partly related to one's talents. The temporarily useful but irrational belief that one is invincible and indestructible because one is uniquely intelligent, agile, skillful, or even lucky is self-delusion that rarely survives one's first firefight. Then the terror and the despair are the deeper for the fall from such happy delusions.

The record is further complicated by the fact that, in the end, there have always been two wars: the one the civilians "remember" and the one that disillusioned young men have fought; and this quiet conflict between historical reality and hearth-side expectations often serves to drive the veteran to silence for a host of personal reasons, but partly to avoid the haunting memories and partly in reluctance to challenge the prevailing view at home.

Besides, the roots of healing are in forgetting. Selectively forgetting means that after a ten or fifteen-year silence following a war, a revival of historical interest in it once more somehow renders the fighting and the sacrifice purifying. By then, in their nostalgic retelling, the veterans, insulated by time and fraught with the limitations of language, tend in relating their experiences to depict themselves as having somehow been in control of their little share of events. They forget, or simply abbreviate, the mind-numbing chaos of the actual fighting, and thus the following generation goes off to subsequent war in the shadow of their fathers' rather diluted and misguiding accounts, with much of their fathers' somewhat glorified pre-war expectations intact. This brings into sharp relief a tragic generational legacy in which the innocent must once again learn from each other and not from those who have lived through the monstrous extravagance, from which backing out is always decreed somehow impossible, while thousands of distant voices scream that going forth is fruitless, futile, and immoral.

My mental equipment as a private school boy who went straight from academe to the military and then to war was as useful for confronting the shock of the experience as the imitation armor and dummy shield of an actor in a pageant. In addition, I knew nothing about Vietnam or its history. I did not know that the French had taken the country in 1887, after twenty years of trying, though I had a hazy recollection that one of the peninsulas in the Southeast Asian region was referred to in some school books as French Indochina. The map image was shaped vaguely like a shrimp and colored pink.

I did not know that the United States had once supported Ho Chi Minh against the Japanese during the Second World War, though I was dimly aware of his name as a participant in reports of Allied conferences on obscure border disputes and air-drop support for now-forgotten guerrilla actions in a faraway jungle–and even that some considered him at the time to be a tactical genius. Nor did I know that after the war this little country that thought it was finally free of colonialism was handed back to the French by occupying British forces, with the grinning consent of the Americans, and that Ho Chi Minh then began fighting to drive the French out again, in an effort that lasted from 1946 until his ragtag army overran them at Dien Bien Phu in 1954, despite direct American support for the Foreign Legion.

I did not know that free elections scheduled by the Geneva Conference for 1956, the year before I started high school, were blocked because it was known that Ho Chi Minh would win; and I was likewise ignorant of the fact that our government backed a corrupt and oppressive leader in the South, Ngo Dinh Diem, and later participated in his overthrow and assassination in 1963, by which time I was a student in college.

I did not know that the Johnson administration's impenetrable determination to involve our country in a Southeast Asian war had led the gnomes in Washington, with base motive or enfeebled intellect and a tragic misapprehension of the merits of statistical analysis, to fabricate the infamous Gulf of Tonkin incident in order to create an ostensible excuse for the commitment of our troops to ground operations in a tiny, backward, agrarian nation of no identifiable strategic or economic value to ourselves. I did not know about U.S. government-sanctioned assassination programs, like Phoenix, which by the time of my arrival in-country when I would become an unwitting operative in the project, had called for "neutralizing" eighteen hundred civilian Viet Cong cadre a month. I had not heard of our clandestine adventurism into Cambodia, Project Gamma, or Project Cherry, tasked with the elimination of Cambodian officials suspected of collaborating with the North Vietnamese or the KGB; nor did I know about Project Oak, targeted against suspected South Vietnamese government collaborators.

Not even by 1968, when the war and my life converged, and I was serving in the Special Forces, had I heard about our secret plans to invade Laos and Cambodia and to assassinate Prince Sihanouk in an insidious operation appropriately known as Dirty Tricks. Some of these plans were contingencies based on events that ultimately did not happen. Others, like Phoenix, were very much alive, and by the time I was in the program, vandals ran the South Vietnamese government, and even the ancient pottery had been looted long before. I did not know these things, but the U.S. government did, and over the years that I was a schoolboy and largely ignorant of world events, the government applied its might in Vietnam, then doubled the might, and thus, by the time I arrived in the country, had squared the error.

War is a political, social, and psychological disaster. Aside from often interim shifts to lines upon maps and certain cultural cross-pollination, it is also a perceptual and rhetorical scandal from which total recovery is unlikely. As the person who experienced the events of these memoirs, my journey has been from an academic incubator of insulated global naïveté, where I held the woefully common misapprehension that adults in positions of authority know what they're doing, through an abrupt childhood's end, and into the community of world initiates, whose constant companion is wry skepticism, whose dark crystal of personal ideals is now well-insulated by a heavy concretion of instructive unpleasantness, and who are therefore somewhat better equipped to function in a culture whose leadership lies to them instinctively and without apparent motive.

Not the least of the hazards on this reluctant odyssey was the difficulty of piercing the barrier of romantic optimism about human nature woven into the fabric of my upbringing and implicit in the notion that we are in the right, that we are always the good guys, and that we are the special providence of an immortal, omnipotent, omniscient, humane, universal, anthropomorphic, English-speaking, Anglo-Saxon, pro-American God, who is always deliberately on our side. I am the product of a generation that believed in the country, and in national service, and in the merits of certain sacrifices for the greater good.

By an accident of generational timing, my family has produced sons for each of the country's wars since before the American Revolution, and despite the dubious and much debated rationale for our Vietnam adventurism, I was expected to do my part. In view of the then policy of selective service, I saw the military as not so much the adventure that some of my companions did, but rather as an inescapable task. As I have always been averse to conflict and strife, but have lacked the courage to be a pacifist, I saw no alternative to the draft but to enlist. Besides, with a conscription rating of 1-A, I could not leave the country even to visit my parents who were living in England at the time, nor could I look for a job, as employment in the shadow of the draft was highly unlikely. I was trapped into an act of ostensible patriotism.

Once the decision was made, there was no turning back. I enlisted under the provisions of what at the time was called the College Option Plan, whereby college graduates entered Basic Training on a fast track to Officers Candidate School. However, during the first eight to ten weeks of training I came to realize that fresh young lieutenants were often less respected than sergeants, and, alarmingly, that their life expectancy in Vietnam was running at some fifteen to twenty minutes. I therefore decided to throw the dice again and gamble my future on an application for the Special Forces (Green Berets). It seemed that if Vietnam lay in my future, at least in SF I would be with the best-trained force in the world at the time. Besides, I had grown up in Venezuela, and my parents were now living in Germany. I was okay in Spanish, the Special Forces required a second language, and they maintained Groups in both Panama and Germany. It appeared that my qualifications were most suited for assignment to either of those countries. I applied, was duly accepted, and ultimately became an airborne Ranger, was the honor graduate from the Jungle School in Panama, and received rapid promotion, due in part to the fact that I was reasonably athletic, held a university degree, and had resisted the pressure to become an officer, all while the war was tearing holes in the ranks above me.

When orders finally came for me to report for transportation to the Republic of Vietnam, it was, of all the postings available, the one for which I was least qualified. I, like countless men before me throughout history, worried about how I would act under fire. The reality, when it comes, except perhaps in the cases of a few lunatics, is far more terrifying, sober, and sickening than can be imagined in advance, and the acts less noble. They're often instinctive, ill-considered, and irrational, and the person you were going in seldom, if ever, survives the initiation.

Ultimately, space and time are not the real measure of distance, and along with the inevitable divestiture the war brought of my privileged innocence, its baneful influence controls still many of my thoughts and acts, directly or indirectly. I am still close to much of it: To this day, I prefer to sit with my back to a wall or corner, with flanks visible–not a compulsion or a need, simply a mild vestigial preference born on the edge of an invisible abyss of prolonged destruction in a distant jungle long ago. I have a lingering aversion to the formal carving of meat dishes, lest it reawaken my hand to the haunting scrape of a blade against bone. I seem to be the only person who actually turns around to check the location of emergency exits on airplanes; I never like to carry things in such a way that one arm does not remain free; and I catnap on my back, a habit learned in the field, as that position more than any other enables you to see the most of your surroundings when you first open your eyes. Whenever I arrange to meet someone, I feel a residual inclination to go, not to the place agreed upon, but rather to a position from which the place can be observed. I have a lingering inclination to crush all empty drink cans so that the long-gone enemy cannot make them into hand grenades, and I cannot pass under an elevated train without the sound sending the cold toes of lizards up my back.

When the mind loses its grasp upon the particulars of specific resonant events, as they become unclear, obscured by the accretion of time, it seems that habits conceived therein are stored elsewhere, for they persist long after the things that were the root cause are forgotten. After enough time spent in peril in wild country, men can develop strong principles. They learn to suppress emotion, often for years, sometimes for the rest of their lives, so that when the accumulation of pressure within demands release, it can explode in a violence of mirth or anger over little things which those who have enjoyed lives in shelter find hard to fathom.

As with thousands of other veterans I'm sure, there are many incidental smells, sounds, and daily events that are imbued with the power to bring on a blind rush of memory. One of these, thankfully seldom encountered these days, is the rancid odor of fish oil known as *Nuoc*

Mam, much used in Vietnamese cooking, which for me emits ghostly tendrils of raw, nauseating despair.

More generally, and aside from occasional possession by a wild and entirely illogical unrest–the same sort of unrest, I imagine, that migratory creatures feel in captivity when the season of their movement is at hand–I retain the loose habit of endurance, a determined persistence in seeing things through somehow, anyhow, often without finesse and satisfied with the main points of the situation. I harbor still an inordinate lack of patience with people involved in a team effort who do not pull their share–motor traffic being the province of the most consistently outrageous offenders.

I returned home with the operative conviction that life itself, no matter how sacred we try to make it, is cheap as dirt and that, ultimately, it is difficult to overstate the unimportance of practically everything. That being said, I learned that perpetual fear and loathing, like perpetual optimism, is a force multiplier and must be consciously managed, just as doubt and resentment must be–a valuable lesson, found too late in the sour mash of bitter experience only after I had become a timid plaything of the enormous forces that comprised the great jumbled paradox of the Vietnam War.

In a true paradox, opposites do not negate each other; they cohere in mysterious alchemy at the very heart of reality. In fact they need each other, just as breathing has equal and opposite phases. Just as absence has the power to diminish mediocre passions while increasing great ones, so does the wind both fan fire and blow out candles. Water, the world's best-known fire extinguisher, is composed of two of the world's most flammable gasses, hydrogen and oxygen. The 360th degree is also the 0. Yet, in a culture that prefers either-or thinking, we have difficulty holding opposites together conceptually. We use light to chase out the dark, massed force and weapons to suppress violence, citizens of a nation at peace to fight a war nobody understands in a country of no significant value to the rest of the world. We want victory without sacrifice, and the Faustian bargains we made in Southeast Asia always failed to supply the balance.

Considering the broader currents of history, Vietnam, if it is remembered at all, will be seen as a minor thing. Much of the study of history is a matter of comparison, of relating what happened in one area with what was happening in another and how it resulted from something that happened before. To view a period in isolation is to miss whatever message it has to offer, just as taking a quotation out of context is to skew the understanding, yet the Vietnam debacle began without clear outside cause, and at its conclusion, America's rush to bury its mistake seems to have produced a generation of politicians who've missed its lessons. It is perhaps too early to tell what long-term effects, if any, the Vietnam War will have on our culture. To date, it seems to have produced certain scattered regions of limited economic improvements in that country, though its effect on our own continues to beggar debate.

After enough years for the fire of passion to cool, with it dies what was once believed to be the light of truth. Who is able to say now whether Hector or Achilles was right, Agamemnon or Priam, when they fought over the beauty of a woman who is now dust? The massive—even today not accurately estimable—blood sacrifice of WWI, a war to which some today are still linked by living memory of family loss, was a hemorrhage from which Britain and France, still weakened by the Napoleonic war, never fully recovered and which brought on the Bolshevik Revolution in Russia. These conflicts of the past century still resonate, as the last of their generation dies away. We view the devastation of Hiroshima with horror. Yet such things happened regularly in the ancient world. The Assyrians destroyed every major city in their region many times over, the body counts far exceeding that of Hiroshima. The Aztecs had to open a human chest *every day* just to make sure the sun came up, and Tamerlane made enormous pyramids of the skulls of those destroyed in his westward march. The tide of civilization was turned back again and again by the march of the barbarians, and unhappily, some of the barbarians came from within.

An old foolishness is not improved with age, nor are hostilities dignified by the fact that they happened long ago. Once my generation has died off, should this sacrificial incident in the late twentieth century American pageant be reviewed at all, there will be no one left with the emotional investment to see the cleansing value in remembering it.

In this our current age where the misuse of expletive is common, truly terrible words have been robbed of their meaning. (What now can be said of the world-changing achievements of the past when someone can have an "incredible" party, or enjoy a "truly awesome" slice of pizza?) We live in a time when the effort to garnish the ordinary has so impoverished the language that the nature of modern conflict has outgrown our "corrected" New Age sensibilities, and our softened lexicon can not provide for the full scale of its horrors and its waste. When words of power are squandered on the commonplace, we distort the record.

Today, the word "survivor" is a term embraced by Americans claiming triumph over a host of humiliations ranging from incest to smoke in the workplace. It is hoped the reader will find that the eager self-love with which it is breathed into talk show microphones has not entirely diluted the word's power. For the thousands of men and women who are today the passing remnants of the national humiliation of Vietnam, I hope that for the rest of their days, when life affords them a quiet moment to flick pebbles into the pool of memory, they will always regard their own existence with ever-renewed rings of humble wonder.

JRM
Pine Mountain, CA
June, 2012

ACKNOWLEDGEMENTS

I am deeply indebted to the members of the Wednesday night Writer's Group of Studio City, California for their long support and kind critique of this project during the sometimes distressing effort to chip from my memory the images that are now contained in the accounts of *Hostage of Paradox* and a second book, *Company of Stone*. It was the safe support found in the group's membership that encouraged me to write after I had joined them as a reader, and it was they, with consistent guidance, who continued alongside, greasing the training wheels through wobbly tentative drafts of the manuscripts.

In particular I have been greatly helped by James and Dallas Mathers, founders of the group and the ones who established its culture; the unusually talented Clif Potts, close friend and one who believed in the worth of my story months before I did, and the versatile Debra Rogers, actor, writer, and insightful critic; to Brennan Byers for sneaking it to a wider audience before I'd had a chance to suppress the effort with false modesty, Dave Hadley with his personal enthusiasm and ferret-like nose for type-os and cumbrous wording; to Sean Akers, Film Producer and publisher; and especially to the profluent Roy Samuelson, computer prodigy and publication Sherpa, voiceover star, and great friend, whose macroscian influence lives in quiet anonymity throughout the formatting of this effort. The reader may recognize some of these names for their many performance credits in film and television. Their literary talents are, for the present, less well known. Whatever adventures may come from the circulation of these books will be a shared legacy of theirs.

Lastly, I must acknowledge my publisher, Bettie Youngs Books. Bettie's personal insight and delightful friendship are singularly responsible for bringing this memoir to print. Her sharp eye for detail has guided the necessary refinements in presenting a work worthy of wider audience attention, and for that I am extremely grateful. I'd also like to thank her talented staff for their work on this book, most especially Mark A. Clements, whose many insightful suggestions have served to clarify much of the language and have resulted in a greatly improved book.

My gratitude for and to all these extraordinary people surpasses the limitations of language. Thank you all.

Any opinions or offensive criticisms which the reader may find poorly disguised beneath the descriptions in this book are entirely my own.

AUTHOR'S NOTE

Many people believe that North and South Vietnam were one country divided, the way Korea has been, but such was never the case, except briefly under French administration. North Vietnam itself had originally been two countries, Annam and Tonkin, and their civilization derived largely from China. South Vietnam had formerly been known as Champa, and like Cambodia's, its civilization came from India. Before France moved into the situation, the two countries had been fighting for nearly 2000 years.

Champa had always been a relatively rich agricultural region, its crops a challenge to less fertile northern countries. Both Amman and Tonkin, usually with assistance from China, had long attempted to dominate Champa. The Vietnam War—our Vietnam War—was simply another move in the same continuing effort.

In Vietnam, after taking over the hemorrhagic venture from the French, the United States played the wrong game. Our troops were not perceived as liberators but as foreigners. They looked and acted just like the French, and to a lesser degree, like the Japanese and the Chinese, other foreigners whom the Vietnamese had learned to hate and had thrown out of their country. Worse than that, the Americans turned the friendly Vietnamese into oppressive foreigners, too, by putting them into the same uniforms worn by the French, and into the same palace used by the French Governor General, and by using the same flag flown by the French puppet regime under the hated Bao Dai. Then we fed and supplied them so that they didn't need the support of the Vietnamese populace, thus further deepening the separation and popular resentment.

The Viet Cong in the South and the communists in the northern capitol of Hanoi, for all their ideological differences, had one thing going for them. They were not foreigners. In addition, they were viewed by many as the protectors of the nationalist pride that had motivated generations of Vietnamese against foreign invaders.

The war we fought did not start in the minds of evil plotters in Hanoi so much as in the hearts of oppressed and frightened southerners who had defeated the French in 1946-54, but then discovered that Hanoi was out to get them. They had the choice of submitting and of being punished, or of heading into the jungle again to dig up the cached weapons that had served them against the French. Americans would have done the same thing, as they did in 1775. That is what the southern Vietnamese rebels did in 1957, and then Hanoi had to come help them a few years later, when the Americans began to give Saigon massive military aid and logistical support.

Had the Saigon government that we supported been any good, it would in all likelihood never have triggered the Viet Cong rebellion. However, from the start the United States thought of Vietnam as a military struggle rather than the political, ideological conflict that it actually was. We poured in weapons so that Diem and his regime of henchmen could kill their political opponents, we supported a military coup when Diem not surprisingly lost the support of his people, and we poured in more weapons along with our own troops when the resulting junta failed to get popular support.

In 1969, David Halberstam wrote in his prize-winning *The Best and the Brightest* that the use of U.S. air power at the Bay of Pigs "would only have prolonged and deepened the tragedy without changing the outcome." President Lyndon Johnson's massive build-up of our armed forces in Vietnam prolonged and deepened that tragedy without changing the outcome. Vietnam was a political struggle, and it was a mistake of historical importance for the U.S. to have sent in its enormous military might, who gave so much blood and so many years to prolonging the tragedy without changing the outcome.

In May of 1967, William Colby, head of the CIA's Far East Division of Clandestine Services, launched Project Phoenix. This was a comprehensive attack against the Viet Cong infrastructure that soon turned into a straight-forward assassination program of suspected Viet Cong and their sympathizers, often as a simple bullet in the head while the target slept. Under the umbrella of this program the CIA established a network of interrogation centers, about which little is known to this day. According to Colby's testimony in 1971, Phoenix "neutralized" (read "killed") 20,587 suspected VC in 2 ½ years. The South Vietnamese government put the figure at 40,994. Both reports represent agendas, so the truth may never be accurately known. In any case, both claim a lot of neutralizing.

Special Forces got missions directly from the Pentagon's Office of Special Activities as well as from the CIA, with whom we always enjoyed a special relationship. (President John Kennedy had created the Special Forces so that he would have a highly trained and specialized force of discretionary operatives that he could dispatch anywhere in the world from his bedside phone, thus circumventing the Congress, whose approval would take longer than the immediacy of such requirements would allow, and in any case, whose deliberations would inevitably result in compromise of the mission. Thus, Special Forces shared certain interests in common with the Central Intelligence Agency. The very nature of the missions meant that much of the training had to be in secret, even conducted at times outside the country, and though the elite nature of the force became celebrated, the truth of its activities around the world remains largely unknown.) The 5th Special Forces Group, of which I was a member, was often used, among other intelligence gathering operations, as the agents of policy for the Phoenix program. We occupied a unique and independent niche, reporting ostensibly only to General Creighton Abrams (though the relationship soured) and bypassing the Army's regional chain of command. The War Powers Act, which required Congress to be notified of military engagements by U.S. armed forces, did not apply to the CIA, which could "borrow" Army resources for military action that was then not reported to Congress. Thus, we were outlaws, and the secrecy of our operations filled me with a dread that was equal parts boundlessness and constriction.

We were part of the inscrutable puzzle known to those who knew of it at all as SOG (Variously called Special Operations Group or Studies and Observations Group. I never did sort out the cover name. It was an organization that did not officially exist, so confusion over the actual name probably served a purpose at the time, too). Military Assistance Command, Vietnam Studies and Observations Group (MACV-SOG) was actually a cover for a high-command warfare task force that engaged in highly classified clandestine operations throughout Southeast Asia. We were funded, equipped, and often directed by CIA requirements, usually in the conduct of small-unit long range reconnaissance, interdiction, and/or assassination missions into Laos, Cambodia, North Vietnam, and even to ports around the world from which supplies to the enemy might be moving. SOG teams prowled the tri-border area and much of the trackless jungle around it in search of POW camps that held Americans and to observe the enemy's movements. We were inserted deep enough into the wilderness to watch and count both human and vehicular traffic on the Ho Chi Minh trail, and to dog, and be dogged by, insurrectionists who came across the border to raid in South Vietnam, and who then tried to sneak back out of the country, usually westward into Cambodia and Laos or to the north. Our teams snatched NVA officers and men, even East German, Russian, or Red Chinese advisors for clandestine interrogations, then sometimes dumped them back in the jungle, always seeking information in places and in ways the bad guys did not expect. Both the range and the nature of these missions made the work extremely dangerous.

To simply list some of the activities of these operations is to say nothing of their reality. In the field, your very life depended upon the ability to constantly manage your resources and to refine your senses. You could never relax in the jungle, even as its character changed. Never. Even though you might keep up your guarded movement from before dawn until dusk without enemy contact, without even hearing a single non-jungle sound, in the fierce, relentless game of hide-and-seek you were utterly worn out with nervous strain by the approach of dark. Even there it continued, for it was not safe to sleep. Your awareness had to be kept on trickle charge, hovering through each long night in a guarded limbo of consciousness.

Because we were sent into remote places known to be areas in which the enemy was operating, and due to the limited visibility in jungle terrain, contact with the enemy, though thankfully rare, was usually sudden, violent, and at very close range, with the chances of extraction greatly reduced—in some cases to zero—in the event that the radio were damaged in the action. These were politically deniable missions, and due to their sensitive nature and the need for extraordinary stealth in remote and trackless wilderness, a compromised operation was often known only by its failure to come up on the assigned frequencies at certain pre-arranged intervals. In such cases retrieval of the bodies was rare. There could be no official recognition for either success or failure, and where the reward for success was to be sent out again, the price of failure was usually an inaccessible and anonymous death.

By the time I was assigned to this program I learned that my unit had taken 100% casualties over the previous two years, a statistic as deeply disturbing as operationally unverifiable, and the report did nothing to support my initially naïve hopes of survival. I entered this strange and frightening shadow world of international snooping and hidden agendas as unprepared as a schoolboy, despite some two full years of Special Forces training, though (of course) not in the specialized long distance reconnaissance work into which I would soon be drawn by age, rank, and the attrition of more qualified personnel.

I have read that the direct cost of the Vietnam war was some $2 million an hour, though the price for real estate in Southeast Asia, where the world's largest super power was killing or seriously wounding some one thousand noncombatants a week while trying to pound a tiny, backward country into submission on an issue whose merits were widely disputed, is harder to measure. In light of the Johnson administration's tremendous infusion of troops and materiel after some twenty years of relative stalemate, it is impossible to justify.

MACV, the overall command organization trying to prosecute the war in Vietnam, was located at the Tan Son Nhut airport in Saigon. MACV was a 320-man unified command whose title rang with excruciating irony and whose immediate boss was the Commander in Chief of the Pacific Command (CINCPAC), based in distant Hawaii. CINCPAC, in turn, answered directly to the Secretary of Defense, a self-styled intellectual civilian with bad eyesight who himself had only 2 years of WW II supply service before going to Ford Motor Company and thence to the Pentagon in remote Washington, DC, 12,500 miles from the Area of Operation. With this attempt at remote control of a hot shooting war conducted from the scented bosom of illusion in Washington, it was inevitable that mistakes of both tactics and timing would characterize the whole effort.

If it was Churchill who said that the distinction between politics and strategy diminishes as the point of view is raised, Vietnam served as confirmation of Sir Winston's famous insight. There is less alertness to the role of accident, less concern for field intelligence, and less thought given to the mysteries of irreducible fortune as one moves up the structure of command.

Thus things didn't always go according to CIA dictates. In late June of 1967, a major three-way debate arose between the CIA, the Chairman of the Board of National Estimates, and the Pentagon regarding the North Vietnamese Order of Battle—in civilian terms, the size of the enemy's forces. The gap was irreconcilable. Military estimates placed the number at 270,000, while the CIA's main analyst called this "ridiculously low"—more like 600,000, he said.

By September of that year the military had compromised to 300,000 and continued to manipulate the numbers and categories in the debate. When the CIA analyst proved the VC had more men in one category, the military reduced those of another category by a similar amount. On September 11, Director of Central Intelligence Richard Helms ordered the CIA station in Saigon to accept the military's figure of 299,000. It soon went down to 248,000. Thus could the Pentagon, half a world away from the action, prove that America was winning the war. Helms knew the numbers were phony, but he also knew what numbers President Johnson wanted. In January 1968, the Tet Offensive made the debate moot.

Of course none of this internecine bickering nor the rarified theoretical dialectics of high command meant a thing to those of us in the field, where we slogged through the sweltering pteridophyte ooze far beyond ideological sanction, often beyond any timely help or support, where the war came down to your own survival, to that of your companions, to drinking water with little zoos in it, and where the only imperative was to live long enough each day to establish goals worth living for through the next. Those who have been shot at and who must dwell in circumstances that forge comradeship born of shared distress far beyond the point of screaming are not candidates for the merits of political theory, pliable abstractions, or patriotic sloganeering.

We must remember that the state of the world is, and always has been, manipulated by those who benefit most from conflict. We owe it to ourselves and to our children to examine the record of history and to ask of those who seek high office how they would weigh the force of history's lessons against interim political opportunity.

1

Time hung like a drop that would not fall. I squirmed against the fabric of the aircraft seat, tried to stretch my legs as much as the restricted angle from the cushion to the space under the seat in front of mine would allow, and felt yet again in the weight of passing hours a grim and wearing accrual of inertia. My thoughts thronged with home images and disrupted associations, as they hurled themselves in undigested worry against a threatening host of vague foreboding that awaited my arrival in a mysterious jungle on the other side of the Pacific Ocean.

I remembered the exact moment that my seat on this flight became inevitable. Just a month before, I stood in what would turn out to be the last of many morning formations at Fort Bragg, North Carolina. Moments after I had reported my platoon present or accounted for, Sergeant Major Fant stepped forth and began handing down the day's orders. Fant, with his chiseled features and immaculately tailored uniform, could have stepped out of a Special Forces recruitment poster. He was the quintessential Green Beret. Handsome, professional, and a combat veteran whose service in Vietnam was behind him, he was the ranking NCO of the company and, if not exactly the commanding officer, was unquestionably the psychological head of the unit.

At the end of the day's mundane list of assignments, he shifted his cold green eyes, pointed directly and unmistakably at me, and said one word: "Vietnam." I knew right then that whatever might come of this unwelcome news, my life would never be the same.

Now I was irretrievably, depressingly, on the way. Despite over three years in the Army, I had resisted the military's efforts to wear down my sense of independence enough to maintain a vestige of individualism–or at least of what I regarded as the remnants of my old pre-conditioned self. Though most of the men I served with in Special Forces were "lifers", that is, guys who saw the military as a career, there were some like me whose private reaction to official attempts at imposing service protocols beyond obeying orders was essentially that of civilians in uniform. Yet now, trapped in an airplane, bound to a common fate with so many others, I began to feel slender layers of myself slipping quietly away beneath the hopelessness and the uniformity. I had become anonymously undifferentiated from the others. I knew I had been reduced by training and equipment to a quasi-mechanical, interchangeable part in the whole monstrous enterprise, a reflection of the success of human mass production and the equipping of armies.

Trapped within the ferocious indifference of such huge logistical processes, the borders of my former familiar world lost their definition. The way I thought of myself began taking on a nebulous and transparent edge. It occurred to me that I had somehow, through some process I could not name, at some undetected moment—perhaps when I had climbed the ladder to the aircraft—been transmogrified into one of history's nameless GIs. I had not thought of myself in just that way before, not even after nearly four years in the military. Of course there had been many joking references to the term "GI" over the years, but in a moment of painful existential alarm I came to see that I was being herded onto the pages of America's history of war as just another G.I: Government Issue; One Each; Olive Drab. Utterly expendable, instantly replaceable, and with vestigial individualism suppressed beneath the time-tested rites of military protocol, I had become all but lost in a faceless abstraction of serial numbers.

Over time, a tour in the military succeeds in drawing solitaries together and dissolving their singularities in the face of shared challenges. The child I once had been drew inexorably nearer the edge of the void, saw the blackness there, and somewhere during the night, fell slowly adrift among the shifting fragments of paradigm. Like some hapless mariner from another time, I was the unwilling hostage of enormous forces, which now converged toward that dark region near the margin of ancient maps labeled, "Here bee strange beests."

The barracks rumor and apocrypha that preceded the flight had supercharged the air, and despite my efforts to ignore scuttlebutt, I was slowly burying myself in morbid images of my own death, which warped and writhed before me, demanding attention and capturing my imagination in a paralyzing collision of mind and heart. I had a book along, but could not keep these thoughts from their insistent intrusion on any reading. For hours I stared out the window at the endless steel-grey sea until even that was swallowed whole by an insidiously deepening night. The darkness quickly closed about me like some implacable malevolent force with a brooding and inscrutable intention of its own .

I don't think I feared the fact of death, which, as the ultimate unknowable, I found hard to expect as a reality, but I worried about the method of it. How would I face it? Would it be a quick flashing blind shot through the head, or might my end instead come in a screaming agony of dismemberment in some dark, blood-spattered corner of jungle while my companions looked on with helpless indifference?

Yet from time to time my efforts to suppress the furtive parade of these images brought forth prolonged seizures of another naïve certainty that, no, I would be fine after all. That sort of violent end only happens to other people. I'm too, what?–agile, decent, free of malice, educated, well trained, or just plain lucky (fill in the blank)–to die in Vietnam.

I thought about my life and how little of it I could have foreseen, and in my yearning for things now gone and perhaps forever out of reach, I tried to read through memory's secondhand images the shapes of the roads that had led me to this moment, this dreaded flight, and wondered for all my will and intent how much of it was really my own doing. I could not know it at the time of course, but I was traveling toward a forced education on the subject of fate by a protracted intimacy with both the quick and the dead.

It was July 27/28, 1968, somewhere beyond the international dateline and farther from home than I had ever been. My twenty-fifth birthday had come and gone the day before, during through-processing at Fort Lewis, Washington. Some birthday present.

The flight was long and oppressive. The tedium lay not so much in the duration as in the dull, kinetic threat that lay somewhere ahead in the night. It was difficult not to think about it. Vietnam and whatever dangers it held waited out there in the dark, an immutable beast, ancient, and humped out of the sea like the abrupt landscape on a Chinese scroll, its smoky yellow eyes fixed upon me.

We were being transported in a converted air freighter, chartered by the government from the Flying Tiger Line, and fitted with seats as a troop carrier. It had even been equipped with a few apprentice air hostesses, who floated incongruously along the corridor with self-conscious cheer in a cautious pantomime of tentative assistance, their crisp and colorful clothing whispering among us with excruciating irony. With their curiously reserved attentions, they seemed like glamorous technicians in some experimental botanical laboratory, tending to the needs of rare, poisonous vines. Yet, it was they who belonged in the rarified atmosphere of soft lighting, automated temperature control, and scented air. We, citizens masquerading as soldiers, misconstrued in the government-issued clothes and hermetically sealed in an aluminum chrysalis far above the oxygen, were simply passing through the elaborate metaphor.

I had a left-side window seat where, unable to read for the endless hours, I stared out across an empty burnished sea that stretched away so far to the south that it blended into nothingness in misty layers of vapor along the curvature of the earth itself. The engines filled the cabin with their continual drone, while outside my window the seascape passed slowly behind us in ponderous silence.

As the day began to fade, the scale of the view, the very breadth of its panorama, rather than having the effect of freeing my spirit from the confines of an aircraft full of uniforms and uncertain destiny, instead began to press in upon me with the full weight of my own insignificance. My sense of aloneness deepened. I tried to send my mind loping back along the years of my life in search of sunny memories from any time not freighted by dread. A few scenes of home and of younger days came gamely forth, but the comfort I hoped for, the sense of self I sought there, was not in them. The heavy uncertainty of my situation, the looming presence of whatever lay ahead, pressed in upon all my efforts to think about other things like a low-intensity headache. I could not escape the feeling that something profoundly unpleasant had already singled me out from the crowd and was waiting now somewhere in the night, patiently tapping its claws.

In the long, crowded solitude my gnawing fear gave way periodically to grapple with a growing curiosity about the coming day and what I would find there. Like struggling creatures, neither fear nor my curiosity could prevail, and neither would withdraw.

Outside, the starlit ocean seemed oddly tipped beneath the encroaching gloom, as though its conjectural lines of longitude gathered ahead like drawstrings. Behind us and a little to the south, a red moon rising slow in the east came up through layered clouds like a crooked smile, and as a deeper darkness closed in around us, lightning began to stitch up its distant folds with pale fire.

In the momentary light that flashed through the clouds of a distant storm I thought I glimpsed the Beast of my imagination. A vein pulsed out there, and almost imperceptibly, two ominous plates moved together, dusky tiles of armor in the fierce cold flicker. As we rushed on toward some distant collected point of fury beneath the vast and relentless sky the whole cloak of night came down upon my tiny hopes and fears.

We were retracing the route taken far below us in 1942 by men just like ourselves who rode in rolling, sweltering troop ships. Many of them had been bundled into eternity in the first quick chaotic moment they stepped ashore, and during the hours of that night with nothing to see out the window, I wondered again what our own arrival would be like:

We would probably land at night, I thought, likely drawing fire on the runway. Then, under covering perimeter fire, we would be hurried into underground bunkers by way of a trench dug into the earth alongside the runway, and would undergo our first briefings there, perhaps with moist dirt, loosened by incoming rounds, sifting down through overhead logs. Indoctrination by newsreel tends to animate the expectations of those who are faced with the prospect of a featured role in one.

Through the night the flight attendants practiced their professional smiles on those who were awake. They had to. This was not the sort of duty anyone with any airline seniority would have taken. Despite occasional rousing outbursts among a group of men seated near the front of the plane, there was little talk. An atmosphere of quiet introspection seemed to prevail; or perhaps that was simply my own contribution to the stillness.

Self-conscious conversation and easy teasing drifted between the girls and some of the men. A pang of envy for the girls' attentions sagged through me, and in that strange aquarium world of silences and undercurrents, it shifted again my alternating awareness of their presence. Inept at talking to girls anyway, I could think of nothing to say and so drifted in private twilight for hours, while struggling with an undeniable urge to memorize their movements as diminishing remnants of all romantic fantasy. By the time the long flight ended, I had not spoken a word to any of them, hoping that silence at least had the virtue of a certain colorless dignity, which is the only substitute for constructive ideas on unhappy days.

2

During the afternoon of the following day we made a fuel stop on the Japanese island of Okinawa in clear weather. We descended through a wispy layer of cloud, and long before the shoreline shot under the wing, we descended low enough for our growing shadow to jump nervously over the waves, where the harsh Pacific sunlight sent sparkling crescent spangles chasing themselves along the arcing fan-shaped crests of shallow brown water. Just as it appeared that we were too low to be without a landing surface, the shadow of the wing leapt across a thick band of shoring trees, and in seconds the main gear tugged at an unseen runway with distant chirps, then began rumbling steadily as the struts absorbed the unevenness of the pavement. Inside, equipment rattled and buzzed as a few of the men clapped in weary celebration. We taxied onto a broad, empty ramp, and for the first time in a day and a night, the engines whined down to silence.

Outside my window, the black shadow inside a large hangar that served as the terminal building yawned across the concrete glare, full of obscure promise. We were allowed to disembark for a welcome stretch, and with the general clattering of unlatching seat belts, began crowding the aisle all at once like airline passengers everywhere.

When I stepped into the sunlight, the heat and humidity hit me like a fist. The steamy air entered my clothes and hair before I could breathe. Sweat sprang from my skin and started to roll down my sides while I was still on the ladder. The place seemed to have been baked still. Even the airport equipment—tugs, tractors, and portable stairways—lay in a state of hushed suspension, their shadows cowering beneath them.

I walked stiffly and quickly as possible toward the welcoming shade of the terminal's wide entryway. Inside, many dozens of people, a mix of Asian and Western, milled about beneath a tall, arched roof, which appeared doubtfully supported by an angular confusion of long–unpainted trusses and narrow girders, much the way I imagined the interior of a dirigible. High shuttered skylights permitted ladders of sunshine to fall upon dusty islands of broken linoleum on the floor. The muggy air trapped the smell of cooking grease mixed with jet fuel from outside, cigarette smoke, and an occasional whiff of tired cologne.

As I strolled through the banded interior light, I became aware of the familiar cadence of scratchy rock-n-roll music that fell wearily from a tinny public address system high in the rafters. It strained to lend a cheerful backbeat to the atmosphere, but the words drowned in the hollow oceanic hum of language, electric fans, and shuffling that echoed within the cavernous building. The effect was like an audible toothache.

The broad concourse was lined with American-style grilled food stands, complete with side orders of discarded paper, snack wrappers, and spilled catsup. There were travel booths, and a tailor shop manned by a tiny impeccable Japanese who would not have seemed any more out of place surrounded by coconuts.

Incongruously cheerful soft drink machines, a few with a short in their lighting systems, so that they beckoned in uncertain solicitation like inexperienced bar girls [Hey, soldier, (wink)…want uh, …(wink) one of these?] lined the outer walls or stood back to back as though for mutual protection in the center of the open space.

The place was evidently one of the many backwater crossroads in the Pacific. It may even have been the prototype, the Mother Hangar, with its vaguely military undertone and shabby imitation of civilian amenities. Yet even with paint on the walls, it bore a kind of frontier practicality that served well its function as an anonymous juncture for countless private lives and un-pronounceable destinations. Everything about it seemed designed to please the foreigner, yet based on second-hand information. Rumor engineering. Even the milling crowd, in a mixture of uniform and mufti, was in busy parody of "real" travelers elsewhere. A lot of unfamiliar triphthong began to fall among the broad American vowels.

Proceeding down the concourse, I suddenly noticed a muddy tangle of green-booted feet and assorted weaponry spilling out from the space between two large vending machines that stood against the wall. As I came closer, I saw that they belonged to a small assembly of weary, moon-faced Asians in dirty combat dress accompanied by a bone-tired Caucasian, also in faded American-style combat fatigues. They seemed out of place in this self-conscious atmosphere of civility, and both the worn condition of their equipment and the weariness in their eyes were alarming. I hesitated to approach.

The Asians sprawled on the floor in jumbled postures of exhaustion with their backs to the nook formed by the wall and the machines and looked up at me with impenetrable black eyes. They seemed like dangerous children, yet whose youth was somehow gone. The Caucasian had sun-bleached blond hair, a drooping yellow moustache and dark, ruddy skin. All of them were browned by too much sun and further darkened by dirt. The whole group was dusted with a fine powder of red earth, which had clotted conspicuously between the lugs on the soles of their American issue jungle boots and in the creases of their clothes. Their worn combat fatigues were sweat stained and frayed, with streaks of peril still trapped in the fabric. Their dull grey weapons, without the customary sheen of garrison oil, had the sudden, cold practicality of power tools, and it unnerved me unexpectedly.

I was unprepared for them and resisted the perverse disequilibrium of the very element that the quaint civility of the building was meant to exclude. Apprehension seeped across the floor and into the soles of my feet. They were evidently fresh from some combat operation, but where? Surely not here on Okinawa. There was something about their equipment and guarded demeanor that belied any common training mission. These guys were old in ways I didn't want to know about. They seemed aware of their displacement and huddled together by instinct, or habit, in the one place where they were protected on three sides.

The blond man crouched and delivered an armload of canned Cokes to his team's dirty fingers like a mother bird returning to her nest of chicks. As I came nearer, he shifted his weight slightly and settled for a moment his steady gaze upon me. In an instant I knew that I had crossed an unseen threshold, had broken some kind of proximity barrier. The face itself was without expression, but in that second his deep red eyes poured out a long, steady charge of wasted horror. Suddenly all normal sound seemed to drain out of the air, leaving an eerie silence. He was only a few feet away, but those bloody eyes looked back at me over a distance I knew I did not want to cross. At that moment something opened in me like a window shade unexpectedly rattling up in a dark room, and whole sections of my experience suddenly went trivial.

My mouth let out an unintended "…Oh."

Later, I asked a guy in uniform about them and was told they were a Special Forces Long Range Reconnaissance team just in from an operation in Vietnam and staging in the transportation loop back to some mysterious-sounding place I had never heard of in-country. It surprised me to learn that the sweep of Special Forces operations in Vietnam went outside the county. I felt somehow oddly, too, that I had escaped a brush with danger, that I had stolen a glimpse across some forbidden frontier of mortality.

"Place is prob'ly a cover name, anyway," he added for clarity. "I tell ya, Sergeant, you don' wanna go where they're goin'."

Hell, man, I thought, I don't want to go where they've already been.

After a string of brief departure delays, each of which came like a spoonful of consolation, we departed for the last leg of the flight on to Vietnam. Much later and far away to the southwest, long after another twilight had drifted down upon us in a mist of smoky purple light, the blond man's eyes still breathed out their message to me like a cold sigh from the pit. They had shifted the dimensions of things somehow, leaving a number of puzzling margins. I began to wonder if our belief in the eternal nature of the soul might be simply an escape clause in our contract with mortality.

In a jumble of vicarious emotions, I sank again into discomforting ruminations, and by the time the aircraft finally began its long-anticipated descent, that awful, impalpable Thing that claimed possession had grown to fill the darkness outside my window. As we approached the mainland, a few tiny scattered lights pricked the blackness ahead. I was surprised to realize that there might still be families who could simply be sitting with a lighted window open to the night in a war zone, not realizing that from fifty miles away out over the South China Sea, other eyes could see its tiny amber beam. It was not until much later that I remembered how few lights there had actually been to announce the presence of a whole country.

The airplane continued to sink, and as the whine of the flap motors came on, a guy whose loud comments and good natured sarcasm had entertained us from time to time throughout the flight, stood up and yelled,

"I don't know about you guys, but I'm *scared*!"

It was exactly the right thing to say. Spontaneous laughter erupted throughout the plane. It burst the intangible meniscus of solitude and rolled forward in waves until it broke against the bulkhead and washed back again, gradually diminishing into moist coughs that muttered off beneath the sound of the engines, which seemed somehow louder now that they were throttled back.

The fatalistic thump of the wheels on the runway at Cam Ranh Bay remain frozen in time. As an isolated event, it could have been a slightly harder than normal landing anywhere, but the moment vibrates in me still with a lasting poignancy. It was two-thirty in the morning. Zero Two Thirty. Deep night. As the aircraft coasted to a stop, and the engines sighed, decanting their spent force, I could see from the window that we were a long way from any buildings. Those structures, delineated by the scattered light from their distant windows, seemed surprisingly modern, yet crouched and furtive in the dim initial landscape. I strained to hear any shots. There were none.

When the doors opened, the humid night air that rushed in to replace our artificial atmosphere was freighted with the smell of the sea and redolent of wet earth and that peculiar tension between genesis and rot that all jungles give off. A spontaneous fog formed along the ceiling of the plane and swirled from the air vents. Suddenly, the salt air reminded me that this place had once been a French coastal resort, a place for vacations, and that at least a part of it was still being used as an in-country R&R center. This thought served to drain a reservoir of immediate fears I had been holding in reserve for this moment, and I crowded into the aisle with the others. When my turn came, I stepped out onto the platform, into the surprisingly mild Southeast Asian night and breathed in the heavy, perfumed air.

The runway was puddled with recent rain, and fragments of the night sky reflected up from the patches of water as from scattered glass. As we walked unsteadily toward a dark row of waiting busses, some of the men stepped almost daintily around the little pools. It struck me as a quaint affectation, given all that was probably at stake for each of us. We were like children who had wandered into some vast and forbidden temple, and we trod as though afraid to leave a trace of our indiscretion. I for one didn't want to be singled out for any reason, even a footprint.

Somewhere beyond a distant ridge line that rose against the star light, artillery cleared its throat, and the sound, once distinguished from thunder, was oddly thrilling.

Through the grilled windows of the armored bus that drove us toward the processing station, I saw in the dim wash of light from distant buildings that the pavement was new. The concrete had evidently been put in so fast that little sand dunes remained trapped between the taxiways. The tall, abrupt edges of surrounding jungle, haunted with deep shadows, leaned forth, as its population of angry monkeys screeched their raucous frustration at us, too outraged to withhold comment and too curious to leave. Behind their cries there was only the soft jungle chorus of chirps and croaks against the deep background murmur of the heavy, alien night.

As we stepped down from the busses and into the harsh florescence of the station, the familiar pattern of military bureaucracy which quickly revolved around our in-processing, unchanged even in this foreign place, suddenly took on a comforting familiarity. Here at least was an event governed by rules I understood. I was logged into the country and the unknown destiny it held with surprising informality. Then, as the friendly, if somewhat routine-numbed, clerk removed the top sheet of my stapled packet of orders, the worn manila envelope containing the rest was handed back to me with the vaguely indulgent resolve that a condemned prisoner might expect with his last meal. I was given a barrack number and invited to find the building and select a bunk and then to go into the mess hall for as much breakfast as I wanted.

I hefted my duffle bag, and after a brief walk back outside through pools of window-cast light on duckboards that ran between the painted plywood buildings, I located the transit barrack to which I had been assigned and stepped in. The still interior air carried the soft sounds of slumber from dark rows of beds. It was difficult to make out anything beyond the colored geometric patterns behind my light-stunned retinas. The silence was conspicuously compact, as if deliberately assembling itself for the nerve flash caused by any small sound I might make.

Fearing the release of unknown demons from the sleepers, should I blunder noisily into something unseen, I tiptoed as quietly as paratroop boots on linoleum would allow and groped carefully among the steel bunks. I felt like a zookeeper unsure if the cages are locked. As my eyes adjusted slightly to the dark, the thin, powdery light that drifted through a row of screened windows just under the eaves in the walls seemed to dust the upper berths and their spilling cargo with a vague vulnerability. I wondered fleetingly just how secure these wooden buildings really were.

I soon found a lower bunk, somewhat aloof from the occupied beds, and carefully rolled out the narrow mattress to assert my temporary claim. I heaved my heavy duffle onto the mattress and winced at the symphony of tortured wire springs that resulted. As I stood for a tense moment awaiting a barrage of curses, a whispered voice behind me invited me to join him for breakfast. I turned to see the dull glint of collar brass against a black silhouette which moved slightly in the dark. From his head gear I saw that he was one of the few other Green Berets in our shipment.

His name, I learned as we stepped back into the night, was Steve Anderson. Two ranks below me and two inches taller, he strode noisily along with a loping nonchalance that defied all courtesy to the sleepers, as we clumped along the duckboards toward the bright rectangle of light that spilled across our path from the messhall a few buildings down. He talked easily, quickly revealing his gregarious nature and the kind of personality that biographers would call "irrepressible." He had deep-set blue eyes and a ready good humor, and he bore a vague resemblance to the Hollywood actor Keenan Wynn. I liked him immediately.

Together we pushed aside a pair of wide screen doors and passed into the bright light of the empty messhall, where we were instantly rewarded by the warm, heady aroma of fresh bacon and hot syrup, along with a confusion of other breakfast smells, heavy with coffee and browning toast. Suddenly, I was ravenous.

While lingering over a meal with multiple courses, Steve and I took advantage of our mutually uncritical ears to exchange some of our more immediate concerns for impending events. I soon learned that he was not, in fact, trained for Special Operations. He was a Clerk/Typist, assigned to Special Forces Headquarters in Nha Trang for a year. It was decidedly soft, rear-echelon duty, and he knew it. He felt safe. I felt safe for him. I felt safe *with* him. (Look at this, will you? In-country less than two hours, and I'm already hanging around with guys who've almost already made it.) That breakfast was the beginning of a friendship that, at least once in the coming months, would save my life and would eventually outlast the war itself.

When we finally tired of talking and headed back to the barrack to sleep, there was little left of the night. The air was muggy, heavy with botany, the *poip-poip* of tree frogs, and intermittent lurches of hot wind. The low rumble of artillery came from the hills to the west, just to remind me that the breakfast was a teaser. The silent earth that memorable first night seemed to murmur of great mysteries but in a voice too vast and deep for me to catch the sound, while the trees beyond the buildings to the north whispered soft cautions in the deceptive serenity. Overhead, a splay of stars lay unfurled across the sky like a flung bolt of lace.

_3_

The morning began with more of the unaccustomed informality of the night before as a crisp, shiny corporal, instead of bellowing from the entrance as I would have expected, strolled casually among the grove of metal beds, quietly harvesting our wavering fronds of sleep with practiced authority. Yet I felt a stab of irritation at his privileged garrison duties and the practiced finesse with which he went about them, born no doubt of long confidence that his job was a safe one.

His demeanor of almost prissy piety and his even beach tan tended to set my own feelings out of context, and I had trouble placing him in the moment. With his polished brass and creased fatigues, he was not even dressed for the kinds of surprises that troubled my expectations. He was too casual, too nonchalant in the way he went about his rounds. It seemed that he was being deliberately presented to our wondering attention as a fashion statement, a sample offered by the cadre as proof of confidence in their own safe, risk-free assignments. His passage was greeted with the familiar benediction of rustling sheets, a muffled litany of epithets, and the curious mechanical concert of release and latch that always seems to accompany the transfer of weight from springs to knee joints, all along the rows of beds.

As most of the other men in the room were holdovers from previous days, and were by now scheduled on local time, Steve and I took advantage of their absence at breakfast to indulge in the surprising hot water showers and the rare opportunity of starting a day without the customary military herding. I relaxed and hoped that I might be detained for several days in this nice, surprisingly safe place with its good food, casual protocol, and hot water.

After clumping back to my bunk, wet feet in unlaced boots and torso wrapped in a towel, the sudden roaring clatter of very low helicopter rotors drew my attention through the screen windows. To my surprise, the world outside was not one of fetid jungle, pressed upon a tiny isolated processing station, surrounded by a jumble of barbed wire. (Where did that idea come from, anyway?) We were in the middle of a modern military city, built upon the old French settlement, with paved streets, permanent buildings, and neat palm trees with white-painted stems. From these windows I couldn't even see any jungle.

Of course! How could I have failed to remember the universal American custom of civilizing through construction engineering? After all, I had grown up in American-built oil drilling camps in Venezuela, and the U.S. presence in Vietnam had been at least acknowledged since the fifties–plenty of time to have built towns all over the country. I smiled at my innocence as I stood there like a wet goldfish staring out at the world from its bowl.

The worn tropicality of French colonial architecture combined with the gleaming functionality of contemporary American plumbing was a fraternal tribute to the unrelenting march of the pioneer spirit. I turned away from the transoms feeling once again the foolishness of having wasted brain time chasing down labyrinths of misguided apprehension.

With new enthusiasm for what promised—given the usually ponderous bureaucracy of processing, and considering the number of men still being held over from previous shipments in our barrack alone—to be the first of possibly several secure days in this comfortable rearward area, I decided to indulge myself in the luxury of any postponement. I quickly finished dressing and headed back to the messhall just for the pure, exalted benediction of a leisurely cup of coffee.

It was to be my last such moment for a long while. The compound had an extensive PA system through which general orders echoed throughout the day. Sometime before midmorning, to my disappointing surprise, the classification given to the shipment of souls to which I was attached was loudly directed to assemble in the center of the compound for unit assignments. The syllables came sharp as cracks s in porcelain through the humid air.

So there was to be no respite after all. From the doorways and around the corners of the buildings, and with differing degrees of enthusiasm, men began to converge on the company square, where we formed ourselves loosely into ranks along several lengths of Marsden matting, the perforated steel plates used since the forties for building temporary runways and repairing damaged roads.

Before us stood a wooden platform, elevated slightly above the sandy ground on over-strength sleepers and covered by a finished plywood sunroof. A edgy expectation spread among us as we waited for the cadre officer to show up.

Very soon, as we stood in the open, the Southeast Asian day gave birth to its heat, asserting itself with an almost conscious vengeance as the first hot breath of morning pressed down upon us in leaden waves. In the sudden, unbearably heavy air, I felt the burn of the sun inside my clothes, the fabric of my uniform became warm to the touch, and the steel plates underfoot began to radiate heat into the soles of my boots.

I glanced around at the others and saw that their eyes had receded into the moist folds of their faces, seeking shade. The skin on their arms looked greasy, uniforms were becoming darkly streaked, and everyone seemed to have shrunk slightly, transformed by an alchemy of heat and moisture into a formation of glistening mannequins. A trickle of sweat began between my shoulder blades and coursed diagonally downward to disappear into my beltline off to one side, and I spent long moments speculating on this gravitational improbability in an effort not to think about where I was.

Behind me, a guy from some infantry unit was complaining loudly that he didn't deserve to be there because he'd had part of a finger blown off on a previous tour and that coming back again wasn't fair. Personally, I couldn't have agreed more. (No lie, GI.) He held up the spread of his hand to show us the stump. He was missing the outer joint of one finger, sure enough. It was an object lesson in what not to have happen.

We continued to wait the arrival of whatever official would be reading us our assignments. The heat grew. I began to wonder if being made to stand out in the oppressive heat was actually part of our acclimatization and silently cursed whoever was responsible. From another row, the familiar casual slur of the Appalachian Mountains rose and fell in lilting dialog with a soft but throaty southwestern twang, gravelly from hard use in prairie windstorms. They were evidently discussing the relative merits of demanding topsoils, an ironic form of nostalgia for home. I tried to listen. Any exercise to get my mind off the heat, but whole phrases fell away in the tortured air, and only fragments made it to my ear in the front row, arriving like images seen through the windows of a passing train:

"Man, the punkin' vines grow so fast down thar they wear the melons out draggin' em"; and:

"Well, we gotta' hard cuss gourd seed to get it up outta the ground a'tall, mosta' the time."

Later: ..."Man, it's getting' hotter'n th' inside of a cow, ain't it?"

"Hell. A healthy cow's only 101."

"Yeah? What about one's not feelin' too good?"

After a while, word went around that several Special Forces guys from a previous shipment had been assigned to conventional infantry units in order to fill certain quotas, and the news struck me. Suddenly a rumor became excruciatingly personal. I was having trouble enough with seeing in everything a potential for invidious change; trying to find evidence for comforting futures in even quite ordinary information.

Time that had not come yet–an anomaly in itself–was taking on a fierce reality for me, and I told myself I was not about to accept orders to some ordinary "leg" outfit after months of highly specialized and often clandestine training in unconventional, small-unit warfare, without making the point noisily.

Yet I knew that, in the event, I'd be helpless. The few other Special Forces guys in the formation revealed by a telling little glossary of head shakes and furtive glances that they were concerned, too. We moved instinctively together, forcing some of the other men to adjust the lines.

By the time an officer appeared in the bright shade of the covered platform, a yellow simmer of glaring haze had settled over the place like a pot lid. Our conversations, grown ragged and barely audible in the freighted air, died out entirely as we united in a complicity of expectant silence.

The officer was all cold, sea-green, Robespierrian sobriety. Accompanied by polished assistants, he stood before us holding in his hands the power of life and death in the form of individual order sheets. He was tall, or seemed so from where we squinted up at him, and his sharp features, peaked in almost comic rivalry between campaign cap and nose, did not seem to know the meaning of teamwork. When he spoke, his face softened in unexpected contrast with his bearing, and from his eyes and mouth came conflicting messages, with a hint of clinical foreboding.

He began with a strenuous cheerfulness, to tell us a bit about the country as though to gild the clouds of fate, his voice rendered smooth by a heavy coating of patronizing disparagement, and he gestured offhandedly with the pack of orders as though they were of little consequence to the proceedings. I appreciated his gameful effort, but nothing he was saying was as important just then as my extreme discomfort in the relentless solar furnace in which we stood. I began to hear through my brain the electric winds of an emptying universe, and found myself desperately navigating my inner list of potential assignments in an effort to place a finger on the pulse of my options. Nothing in my training or orientation lectures in the States had prepared me for the possibility that I might arrive in-country only to be assigned to some conventional outfit full of people I didn't know or trust, whose mission I didn't understand, and whose operations in any case were to be conducted in a place where the temperature soared daily to over 100, with 100% humidity.

Every few minutes as we stood there, the assignment officer's words, along with all other sounds of natural origin, were crushed beneath the excruciating howl of aircraft engines, as C-130 transports climbed out alarmingly low overhead from the nearby airport, with Jet Assisted Take-Off bottles (JATOs) screaming in their struggle up through the muggy air. We pulled our heads into our shoulders and covered our ears as the sound beat down upon us in waves. Even the ground shook with the unbearable noise of their low level passing. Afterwards, the exhaust fumes settled upon us, an oily smell of kerosene and a mix of something like fire cracker powder and Band-Aids.

The first time one of these giants swept over our little formation, while we cringed in childlike defense from the concussive vibrations, the officer tried to race the crescendo to his next point by yelling with such mounting force that it carried him up onto his toes. As he surrendered the fruitless effort, his tinny voice flailing with shrill fists against the falling wall of noise, his right hand rose as though to order divine retribution to stand by, as his large eyes looked heavenward, in smiling recognition of the absurd competition, before retiring into a few moments of impenetrable mutterings, all inaudible.

I told myself that, like the rest of the cadre here, he, too was enjoying the fact that he was spending his year in a comfortable, safe, rear echelon assignment at the expense of those of us who were only passing through his little fiefdom and were doubtless going to be sent out into the scary jungle where the bad guys were lurking. I added that to my resentments. He put me in mind of an amateur comedian who, detected in the rear half of a stage cow, still makes an effort to maintain the deception.

During a lull between air operations, he asked in his waning voice if there were any parachute riggers in the formation. "Yes, sir," said the voice of Sgt. Heuel, one of the Green Berets in my group, and I turned to see his open hand rise slowly against the yellow sky. According to the papers the officer was holding, Cam Ranh Bay was allocated two parachute packers and, up until that very moment, had exactly none.

Heuel was to stay there in Cam Ranh to comprise 50% of the installation's parachute maintenance function. We all knew that nobody was doing any jumping anywhere in Vietnam, and we couldn't believe his luck. Heuel couldn't either. All that special warfare training was going to spend a year lounging on the beach. He was immediately directed to come to the dais for the paper orders, then to fall out and get his gear. On his way past, he pranced over to me, his face flushed and voice pitched with contained hysteria.

"I haven't packed a chute in three years!" he hissed delightedly through a grin that resembled a parade of Chicklets. Then he hopped away with shoulders hunched, a picture of impish glee, clutching his orders like a passport to El Dorado. I envied him both the cushy assignment and his freedom from the cloying weight of uncertainty with its ponderous freight of distasteful alternatives.

The air exploded with another heavy C-130 take-off. It roared overhead, all four engines clawing for altitude, shaking the broiled morning air, its JATO bottles screeching painfully. I looked up and saw that the airplane was painted an unusual flat black and that it showed no national or unit markings. The sheenless paint seemed actually to absorb light from the pale sky, like a howling black hole in the atmosphere. It looked ominous, and I felt an instinctive chill when its shadow passed over me. As the airplane climbed rapidly away, retrieving its thunder, it drew nervous comments into the vacuum of stunned air that followed it:

"Yeah, that's one'a them Sneaky Petes," said a voice nearby. "You don't want to go where that's goin'!" (Where had I heard that before?) "Spooks. Nobody knows what those guys are up to, but that there's a one-way trip, man."

While I was hoping I would never have to find out what those black C-130s were up to, my name was called, and I was relieved of the rumored assignment to a conventional infantry outfit by orders to report to Special Forces headquarters in Nha Trang, as I should have expected. With a few muttered goodbyes and a final glance back at our diminished formation, I fell out to retrieve my bag and report for transportation back to the airport.

Through-processing to the interior of the country at the air station was conducted with the same lack of cumbrous military protocol that had surprised me the night before. My papers were passed back and forth along a segregated bazaar of authority, free of the customary accumulation of tedium to which I had grown accustomed, until a pleasant junior enlisted guy glanced at my orders, smiled, and waved me languorously through, as though he were checking invitations to a party.

I was soon shouldering my duffle across a simmering tie-down ramp toward the loading door of a worn C-7 Caribou transport. The heat burned through the wool of my beret and attacked my scalp, and the sun blasted off the concrete in every direction. I could barely keep my eyes open against its glare. It burned my face and arms, and it baked my feet through the toes of my boots. Sweat oozed from beneath the beret and joined that which soaked the khaki uniform, which clung to me in a hot mephitic damp. I decided that dark green wool was not the material of choice for head gear in Southeast Asia. I also resolved to get my hands on a pair of the dark glasses that I'd seen all the helicopter pilots wear.

As I approached the aircraft I noted that its green camouflage paint was faded to a powdery mold that was extensively chipped along its rows of rivets. The tires were worn smooth and the engine cowls streaked with fresh rivulets of black oil. Dried mud and stone chips splashed its sides. It smelled of hot grease. For some reason, I had never seen a Caribou before, and despite its patched and shabby make-up, it was a distinctly elegant-looking medium cargo plane that stood astride its slanted black shadow on long legs, its high wings lending it the slightly humped and purposeful aspect of an insect poised to leap. As in all well-designed aircraft, the harmony of its lines of form and lines of function were pleasing to the eye and oddly reassuring. I had the peculiar feeling that, like me, it was uncomfortable in war paint. I liked it. Surely it would only take me to a good place.

The high tail of the airplane rose darkly against a line of fleecy rain clouds which were assembling themselves as though crowding forth to witness my departure from the safety of this rearward base. Their dark scrumbled undersides, vaporous and gray with un-fallen drizzle, hinted ominously, yet spread apart in measured intervals as deliberate as 18th century prose sent by smoke signal, they reminded me of an English sky piled above the landscapes of John Constable, their symmetry offering poignant contrast to my own anxious confusion of curiosity and dread.

I stepped up the loading ramp and into the welcome shade of the Caribou's hollow interior, added my duffle bag to a pile of others, then found a webbed canvas seat along the left-side, slightly aft of center, and settled in among the other men. The seats were all slung along the curvature of the fuselage so that we sat facing each other with our backs to the bare aluminum walls of the aircraft. I looked around at the other passengers. They appeared to be a mixture of replacements and veterans, each, judging by the assortment of uniforms and ranks, headed somewhere on differing orders. I exchanged a few nods and felt again the discomforting realization I had experienced on the long flight to Okinawa that my private destiny had begun to intersect with incomprehensibly larger events.

This was a catch-all flight, pollinating the airfields along its circuit with general cargo from equipment to people, wherever their orders converged with its own. Around me were men in various stages of wear, from the newly-arrived, with their skin like veal, to the sunken, introspective veterans whose unfathomable experiences seemed to cling to them in weary lines of solemnity.

Strapped in across from me was a tall, thin kid in worn combat fatigues; one of those soldiers whose weariness had obviously gone far beyond physical exhaustion, into that state where no amount of sleep would ever give him the kind of rest he needed. He had probably been a teenager when he was sent to Vietnam, but he no longer looked it. He was old now, clean through.

He had a small cross sketched in ballpoint on his sun-bleached flak jacket and another, less obtrusive, on his helmet cover band. The once camouflaged helmet canvas was faded almost chino white, and on the side of it away from the polished young officer who had taken the seat next to him was a crude calendar drawn in ink with many squares crossed off. Next to that was scripture, sort of: "Yay, though I walk through the valley of the shadow of death, I shall fear no evil, for I am the meanest motherfucker in the val-." For some reason the inscription was unfinished.

He looked out of place, even among our transitional eclecticism, and watching him made me more conscious of my own newness. For one thing, his skin was deeply tanned, but when he pushed his helmet back I saw that his forehead was the color of suet. Was he really in a combat area so much that he seldom removed his helmet? His hair was dark and was plastered to his head, greased there by the sweat band. I could see from the worn condition of his boots and equipment that he had spent plenty of time in the boonies, humping the gear. His eyes were bloodshot and puffy, the lower lids sagging slightly at the corners like a dog's. They were dim with fatigue, vacant and inscrutable, like the windows of a limousine. I couldn't see in, but I knew whatever was inside could see out. His face was drawn and streaked with dirt. I was to learn later that when people in that condition smile you have to accept it as a token.

He fished a crushed pack of cigarettes out of his pocket and shook out a bent one. He appeared to be looking past it when he found the end with a military issue Zippo lighter, which he snapped closed afterward with a sharp metallic click, but then he simply dropped his hand and let the cigarette smolder, neglected between his fingers while he stared at the deck plates.

Sitting next to him, one of the new arrivals, a Lieutenant in a damp but still creased and tailored Class A travel uniform like mine, who had evidently also been watching him, asked him innocently enough, "How long you been in-country?"

There was a pause. The kid half lifted his head; surely that question could not be serious. He took a long drag before responding. The weight dripped from him, and words I had never heard spoken to an officer came slowly.

"All...fuckin'...day," he said.

The old Caribou, rattling and buzzing with the odd harmonic vibrations that machines often produce in an effort to inspire our analogies to living things, seemed to gallop and plunge over the pavement joints in the long runway until the wings took on an intelligence of their own, as if some disembodied presence had joined the enterprise, and then we slipped smoothly into a different set of laws. The captured ground air inside, laden with the smells of musty equipment and perspiration, was quickly replaced by a cooler element that whistled into the fuselage through dozens of tiny non-regulation openings as we climbed northward over the featureless coastal terrain.

I twisted around in the seat to look out the porthole window behind me. Below us stretched an endless jungle, which had seen in its relentless accumulation unguessable millennia; passive in fact, but sinister by reputation, and the rumor was good enough for me. I had heard enough stories about it to decide that the plural of "anecdote" may as well be "data." I determined to keep alert for anything, real or imaginary, which might serve to inscribe a warning on the tabula rasa of coming events.

North to Nha Trang, which the native aides pronounced with an odd little click in the throat. The place names alone carried an uncomfortably exotic bi-syllabic inscrutability, with none of the familiar melody of romance language. It was all becoming truly foreign, and we, as I was beginning to see unequivocally, were the outsiders.

North. Even the direction of our flight dragged a connotation of unspoken reverence through the mind, leaving a soft furrow of silence. North was where the bad guys were. The Source, from which the roots of all despair and hope began their climb upon the spreading trellis of my foreboding. North was where the Beast was waiting.

The flight was surprisingly brief, as Nha Trang was only a short distance up the coast. We had barely leveled out when the deck angle of the aircraft suddenly canted sharply forward, and we went light in our seats for a long moment as we began an abrupt descent over a high ridge line that rose spectacularly close to our altitude before plunging sharply down to a rolling arboreal sea of double and triple jungle canopy that broke in waves against its foothills.

As we slid downward over the sloping alluvial plain, cut here and there by a feeble thread of road scratched into the red earth, or by a loop of chocolate-colored river, it was impossible to see any evidence of human habitation. There were no signs of villages in the fathomless green sea of trees, no isolated huts, no clearings, just an unbroken primordial wasteland, bulging and coiling back upon itself in steaming carboniferous undulations without end, disappearing at last far to the west in pale blue layers of mist. About twenty kilometers off the wing, a cloudburst hung like a broken bag in the sky, and beyond it, a slanting line of grey showers, suspended like wet laundry, was moving slowly northward. Were people really out there somewhere, hunting each other in the rain?

The engines continued to relax steadily, as the trees rushed upward. The temperature rose sharply, and the men around me began to shift in their seats and to glance furtively about, stirring with a subtle telegraphy of imminence. We were down to well within small arms range of the ground with no evident reason for it, when suddenly the first shabby houses with corrugated tin roofs and dirt packed streets began to rush past, emerging from their jungle setting abruptly, like a child's toys in high grass.

Without the graduated encroachment upon the forest one might expect to see along the edges of a major settlement in more developed countries, here the jungle abruptly ceased, and the folds of its long green curtain, as though suddenly checked, splayed here and there against a sprawl of low buildings and open storage depots. The clearings seemed to have been hastily cut at random along the foot of a broad valley by the sea. From the air, the place reminded me of a river mouth, where, mounting like silt, a century or more of pulverized civilization had been deposited in a jumble, having floated from the darker interior of the country, then had collapsed and been abandoned. Now, the relentless press of trees, was quietly inching forward, determined to obliterate the feeble human effort and restore the wilderness to the way it was before.

We banked low over the city, descending across a wide beach with dark cinnamon sand, on which a lot of tanned Caucasians were sunning themselves and playing in the waves like Mediterranean tourists. This paradoxical holiday scene tilted away from the top of my window as we banked out over the sea beyond the pattern of shore bound waves. Then our turn steepened, and as we rolled out for the approach, the shore line returned. We passed over a row of weathered concrete buildings, four or five stories high, which stood in forlorn prominence above a confusion of tattered hovels that crowded the crumbling pavement of a wide beachfront boulevard lined with date palms. As we descended low over them, I saw that their balustraded balconies and breezy colonial terraces were broken and empty. They resembled old bureaus, abandoned with their drawers left open, and were festooned in coils of rusting barbed wire, their unpainted walls streaked like tears and crowned with rows of green sandbags. They seemed to stare out at the sea with sad eyes, their former glory as quiet French resort hotels now long past. It must have been lovely once.

On the ground, after we had taxied to a stop, the rear cargo door sucked open, and the heat poured in like a religious conviction. The life of a bustling Southeast Asian city with a large American presence asserted itself immediately upon all the senses. Along with a few other men who were getting off here, I stepped again into the boiled glare and breathed in the stifling effluvium of jet fumes, sun baked tar, and the ever-present hint of vegetable rot, all accompanied by the roar of aircraft and the clatter of ground traffic. It was even hotter here than it had been in Cam Ranh. The heat and humidity fell upon me like a blanket. Breathing became difficult. The air that beat up in waves from the pavement could have risen from the vents of a furnace.

The air-conditioning in the reception station was a shock, even after the deceptive shade of the airport breezeway had teased us. It must have been set at about half the outside temperature. It dried the air and was cold enough to raise goose bumps on my arms. I luxuriated in it for what I knew would be a short stay, feeling conspicuous in my stateside uniform, surrounded by faded green fatigues and worn jungle boots, deep tans, and elaborate, non-regulation moustaches.

The general informality of duty in this strange new place was evident everywhere in the casual manner of dress and in the attitude of the processing personnel, though these small freedoms from petty military protocol seemed hardly adequate compensation for the oppressive climatic environment.

Too soon, my duffle and I were driven in an open Jeep through the crowded hard-pack streets of Nha Trang to Special Forces Headquarters, Republic of Vietnam. The ride was a noisy obstacle course of scurrying street urchins, ancient bicyclists wearing incongruously stylish dark glasses, and weary pedestrians in conical straw hats right out of period travel posters. Here and there pairs of young women dressed in their colorful ao dai dresses drifted like slender ghosts amid the dingy mass, but most people hurried past in the traditional loose cotton trousers that can only be described as pajamas.

The traffic was a surprise. Despite a general appearance of decomposition, this was a busy Asian metropolis with one foot in a sleepy colonial past and the other in the cacophonous din of modern technology and choking on a blue haze of diesel smoke. The main streets were crowded with old Citroens, painted busses with windows full of elbows, haggard vendors calling through the dust, and the piercing buzz of small-bore Honda motorbikes. There appeared to be no rules of the road. The throng jostled and shouted, tooted, swerved and swore, in a moving press of humanity and machines through which we crept in a vacuum of disregard.

On pedestals at some of the intersections, little native traffic cops dressed in khaki and wearing white utility belts, oversized white military hats and dark glasses, their hips weighed down with heavy American side arms, conducted an invisible symphony to the indifferent mass. These, I was to learn, were the indolent and officious Quan Canh, white-uniformed police, called QC, or as my American driver referred to them, "White Mice."

The people were all surprisingly small in stature and most seemed old, the deep lines in their squinting faces grooved there by the thin difference between chaotic living and its alternative. The dark eyes of the few who noticed us regarded our slow passage among them with a mixed air of watchful suspicion and endless patience. Despite its pace and evidently large population, the city seemed bleak and neglected; a lost remnant of civilization in tropical isolation, tired of foreigners and accustomed to damage, whose citizens were all just passing through without taking much notice of it. More like a coastal village, uncomfortable with the extended new dimensions the Barbarians had graded and built with their confusing technology than a prominent city whose name rated darker letters on the map, the town appeared to have been pounded into existence from the very ground itself.

Broken masonry, rubble, and closely-packed structures, some of them built entirely of discarded U.S. government packing crates, peered sidelong and squinting, as one does in sudden light, gray and dirty in the dust-laden haze of mid day. The place held a kind of nameless disquiet that I was beginning to see occurred everywhere, born of silence, veiled looks and closed houses. Angular planes of sunlight falling across the fractured walls and drooped awnings did nothing to relieve the feeling that the crude hovels were huddled together for reassurance.

Once through the gates at the Headquarters compound–an oasis of painted palm stems, paved streets and permanent buildings on mowed lawns, where the hot breeze hummed with the sound of air-conditioners–I was struck by the feeling of being suddenly "inside"; safe, the way early American pioneers must have felt on arrival at a log stockade. My feeling of splendid isolation faded, though, when I stepped into the frigid, antiseptic reception office of the HQ building. There, an overweight NCO with a waxed moustache sat behind the counter, too preoccupied with examining the inside of his mouth in a pocket mirror to deal with my arrival. Finally, with a gruff and dismissive air, he instructed me to wait.

Not wishing to alienate someone who, for all I knew, had the power to tweak my fate, I entertained myself quietly for several minutes by examining a collection of carefully preserved nickel-plated Viet Cong weapons of Chinese origin displayed on the walls. They were of course entirely bogus in their shiny new coatings and artistic array. They reminded me that the attention lavished upon the plantings, the grounds, the Jeeps of Generals, and other visible details of headquarters installations by those with the leisure time for such denominational irrelevancies was for the purely symbolic benefit of visiting dignitaries and others who never ventured into the field, of whom this fatuous processing NCO was clearly one. The rifles gleamed with the antiseptic aesthetic of fishing trophies. Regardless of how they may have been acquired, their true purpose had been glazed over. They were decorations now.

When the clerk at last put his little mirror away and turned his august attention to me, it was at first with a supercilious air of dismissal. With tight lips and a slight flaring of his nostrils while staring at the empty space beside me as though I had arrived with an invisible double, he extended his pink and manicured hand for my papers and wriggled his fingers in a little semaphore of impatience. I had an impulse to kick the chair out from under him. Clearly, I was detaining a superior person. I felt a flash of irritation at being in the presence of someone so free of dangers that he would be allowed to develop this attitude. I stepped over and handed him my orders packet, wishing I could have surprised him instead with a fresh stool sample on a dish.

He looked up the moment he felt the papers touch his hand, his unblinking eyes boring into what he must have imagined to be my vulnerability. A quick perusal of the papers, however, brought about a noticeable transformation in his attitude. In fact, he seemed to place an undue value on my worth as a replacement, and this carried implications I did not want to think about. What was going on that a single replacement was so interesting? Did my papers carry a secret code which designated me for some special assignment of which I alone was ignorant?

I was again struck by a feeling of unspecified vulnerability as he tore more copies from the stapled packet of my orders, making officious snapping noises with the pages. I speculated despairingly about the bureaucratic sorcery that had produced whatever fateful assignment would be revealed when the remaining copies of my orders had become so thin that I could see light through the last pages. In what isolated, twittering jungle might I be when the very last copy was handed back to me? I wondered briefly if the manufacturers of the staplers had been instructed to demonstrate their product's resistance to such abuse when they bid for the government contract.

He handed back the packet, smiling without warmth, his thin lips jabbing the folds of his jowls, and I was suddenly struck by the thought that he looked older than he probably was. He instructed me to report to the Transient's section of the compound for assignment to a bunk and to draw combat fatigues. His chin was still tucked back into his neck, but there was nothing aggressive about him anymore. It seemed suddenly only the mannerism of one who used suspicion instead of understanding to give himself a reputation for shrewdness.

"Thank you," I said evenly, the words like little stones dropped into the charged air between us. I hefted my bag and left him standing there alone in his refrigerated office, wearing his unctuous vocational smile.

Back outside, half blinded by the pitiless glare from both the ground and the sky, I trudged beneath the brutal brass eye of the sun across the sandy compound to the Transient Office. There I met a tall Sergeant who unfolded from behind his desk in friendly greeting. He was surprisingly pale and thin as a naked chicken, with a mist of grey hairs hovering about his skull like a magnetic field. His head, round as a knob, prominent nose and large Adam's apple lent him an air of displacement, like some character from literature, or some personified halcyon bird trapped in this new reality. His deep-set eyes, pale blue and compassionate, held an expression of benign curiosity, and although he appeared to regard me without judgment, I noticed a brisk travel of thought behind his eyes when I handed him my packet of orders.

As he began to scan the pages, I tried to amuse myself by imagining that he had probably played the triangle in his high school band. It became quickly evident, though, that he too was disconcertingly glad to read the secrets hidden in the codified confusion of numbers and abbreviations which elaborated the few phrases of clear language on my orders.

After stripping another of the manifold layers of discomforting illusion from my thinning packet of orders, he directed me out to his demesne with a sweeping, almost theatrical gesture to a side doorway. Despite the friendly camaraderie with which he had greeted me, there appeared an air of sadness about him as I left, as though he had just received some bad news. Was he sending another lamb to slaughter? I felt grateful for the contrast he presented to the officious headquarters clerk I had visited just before, yet when he handed me my bunk assignment his demeanor spoke to me almost aloud, like an embodied sigh.

I still had no idea what most of the numbers and abbreviations on my orders designated, but the shift in attitude by the last two clerks who read them was a bit unsettling. I shouldered my bag again and stepped out of the office, back onto the light-soaked sand. Following the Sergeant's directions, and squinting hard with stunned retinas in the apocalyptic afternoon sun, walked along some duckboards toward the Transients barrack. This proved to be nothing more than a double row of bunks in the open shadow beneath a large community tent.

The long, sagging structure was erected over a wooden deck, which offered some slight elevation off the blinding ground, and in view of the extreme heat, the heavy fabric side panels of the tent were mercifully rolled up. Nonetheless, the broiling tropical air trapped beneath the tent was heavy with the smell of oil-impregnated canvas, and to move through it was to press one's face through a heady miasma of chemical-laden gas. It was better to crouch or simply to sit down, which I quickly did as soon as I found my bunk number—along the right side, about a third of the way in. The air was much easier to breathe where it was free to move below the captured bubble of pungent heat and beneath the complex of fire-retardant chemical smells. I sat there for several minutes trying to catch my breath, sweating on the edge of a thin government mattress and blinking out at the rim of a new world.

The heat was beyond my experience. I had sweated completely through my tired khakis by the time a few of the other guys assigned to the tent came over and directed me to a little NCO club at the northwest corner of the compound where I could get something cold to drink. I thanked them, and as I was on my own with no specific orders to be any place in particular, immediately made my way toward the western edge of the enclosure and turned north along the rambling fortifications of piled sandbags until I came to a painted shack set on low piling in an angle of the perimeter.

A number of other men, most in newly-issued fatigues, were standing around in the shade of the hut, talking and holding beer cans with voluptuous drops of condensation running between their fingers. I recognized a few people from Ft. Bragg, and the reunion made me feel a little less the uncanny foreignness of the place. I nodded at the faces and went up a stile of short wooden steps and into the "club."

The air-conditioning hit me almost as hard as the heat had earlier as I entered the little 15' x 15' room and adjusted to the reduced light. Too timid of my own expectations to drink anything alcoholic, I ordered two orange sodas, and when I turned around, a polished boot shoved an empty chair my way as invitation to sit at a small table.

I looked up at the occupant and was surprised to see the guarded smile of a Staff Sergeant I had known at Fort Bragg and who had always treated me as considerably more subordinate to himself than the single rank separating us would have warranted. I grinned to find a familiar face, even his.

"Hello, Moore," he said without stirring or offering his hand.

"Well hello, Sergeant Westerfield," I said taking the chair and hoping he wouldn't detect my mixed feelings. "What're you doing here?"

He made a noise of mild derision through his nose.

"When did you get here?" I asked, trying to catch the tail of his mood.

"Couple days ago."

At a glance I could tell that it was true. His fatigue uniform was newly issued, and the bright yellow thread of his chevrons was as yet unfaded by laundering. The skin on the high points of his face was flushed with new sunburn.

He kept eye contact in a way that made him seem genuinely glad for familiar company, even mine, and I could tell he wasn't any happier about being there than I was. At least that gave us something in common for a change.

"D'you know where you're going?" he asked.

"No. Just got here today. You?"

"Not yet."

I sipped the sweet aerated syrup and remarked that it tasted like a foot that's gone to sleep. The comment started a conversation during which he surprised me by admitting some of his fears about being in a combat zone, while revealing a philosophical side of his nature that was unexpected. At least I wasn't alone in my crippling preoccupations about what the year might bring. His point was that, on the whole, he had enjoyed his life, and if he was nearing the end of it, at least this was no worse than any number of other ways a man might die.

Though it was of some small comfort to know my own reservations were shared, it soon became evident that his deep fatalism, cloaked in the distracted charm of specious erudition, lay coiled like a cobra just beneath the surface of his words. He was disconcertingly morose, and it ate away at my mood quickly. I began gulping the drinks more quickly than I had wanted to and soon left the cool air to return to the Transients tent, grateful for the solitude, even in the crushing heat. I never learned where Sergeant Westerfield was assigned and never saw him again.

A note was on my bunk instructing me to draw my equipment and clothing from Supply. Following directions to a nearby Quonset hut, I was issued all new field gear, which enabled me at last to change out of my stained, rumpled, and by now sweat-rancid Class A khaki uniform for the heavy olive drab fatigues that I would live in for the rest of my time in Vietnam—all too possibly for the rest of my life.

The synthetic fabric of the new combat dress was treated for flame and gas resistance, which imparted a slightly oily texture to the cloth, made it heavy and a little stiff, thus greatly reducing its ability to breathe until it had been washed many times. This effective barrier to the passage of even warm air, coupled with its dark color, converted it into an instant sauna. On that afternoon, it was the most uncomfortably hot clothing I had ever worn anywhere in the world. I felt sheathed in lead and wondered why they bothered to impregnate the cloth in the first place if the chemicals would soon wash out anyway.

I chose not to have any insignia of rank sewn onto any but one of the shirts, but was told that name labels were required for "home" dress in the compound. Having the name tags sewn on the shirts left me feeling conspicuous and somehow more vulnerable. This was not a country in which I had any wish to be singled out. I sensed the un-spoken loom of danger as a conscious presence everywhere, and even though everyone in the military wears a name tag in normal duty, here in this realm of storied hazards, the new cloth labels increased my sense of being somehow nominated. I remembered that the ancient Egyptians held the belief that to pronounce the name of the dead was to give them life, to summon them from the realm of shadows, yet here I had the odd feeling that by giving life to my name the labels might awaken the ancient shades to opposite effect.

I carried everything back to my bunk, cradling the folds in sun-burned arms while inhaling the fabric's newness. A little later, while bent over in an effort to pack the crisp clothing into my bag, the per-spiration literally poured out of my sleeve in a stream. I was shocked to realize that a human body, especially my own, could purge itself of fluid through the skin at such a rate.

As I was packing my new clothes into the duffle, another guy, who by the worn condition of his field tunic and his deep tan, I took to be an outbound transient, stopped at the foot of my bunk and, pointing to the small pile of government issue olive drab underwear there said, "You might's well shit-can them things."

"What do you mean?" I asked.

"Them undies."

"Why?"

"Nobody wears 'em. They're hot as hell; they're cut too full, so they bunch up in yer ass; they're uncomfortable and can start a fungus when you're out in th' boonies…An' besides, if anything happens to ya, they're just one more layer the medics gotta cut through to get to ya."

All of that, every reason, made perfect sense to me. I thanked him and repacked, placing all but one pair in the bottom of the bag. There they stayed. Except for sleeping, I never wore them from that day until I left the country. In that place where small pleasures were prized, the marginal freedom of movement that resulted was almost refreshing.

By the time I got my new clothes packed, found the laundry ser-vice for the old ones, and tried to organize my little corner of the plat-form, the afternoon heat began at last to give way to evening. Activity in the tent picked up as people came in from various activities to clean up and stow things for the night. Some were new to the country like me, others were transiting out of the country with their lives, and still others were moving through to different assignments in-country. Everyone I spoke to was helpful in explaining where various buildings were and what was expected of anyone who was, as yet, unassigned. The consensus appeared to be that, until some specific orders came through, I was pretty much on my own and that the time should be enjoyed, so I decided to begin working the stiffness out of my newly-issued jungle boots by hiking back over to the little clubhouse on the perimeter to enjoy the air-conditioning and to see if there was anyone else there I knew.

With the day's work done, the crowd by the steps of the clubhouse shed was a little larger, and a dozen or more men had spilled over onto the sandbagged top of the perimeter's large corner bunker. These bunkers were positioned so as to have interlocking fields of fire all along the landward perimeter, which overlooked an expanse of rice paddies, beyond which spread a wide valley of dense medium height growth of the sort called in the American southwest by the Spanish name "chaparral." Though not very high, this foliage was thick, certainly heavy enough to conceal a sniper well within rifle range of this corner of the compound and therefore also of the shed, where the men were grouped so casually. The bunkers were set into a low embankment and constructed so that their outward-facing sides were perhaps six feet high, but the tops were only a few layers of sandbags above the elevated level of the inner compound itself, and were thus easy to step up onto.

Several men lounged in beach chairs set atop the bags, while others stood in groups, smoking and enjoying the easing temperature. In view of the open low ground just beyond our perimeter, and the fact that these guys were bunched together in what appeared to be clear silhouette against the sky, I hesitated to join them. Nonetheless, it seemed by their carefree attitudes and the fact that none of them was armed, that this was a completely ordinary place to be having a beer at the end of the day, and I had to conclude that they must know what they were doing. After all, judging by the tans, non-regulation moustaches, and many faded fatigues, most of this group had survived here for a long time.

Had it not been for the congested coils of strung razor wire, the light stanchions, and piled sandbags, the scene might have been one of any casual drinking party at some remote posting, but the presence of all the defensive construction served to lend the gathering an ironic vulnerability. Although the compound appeared well designed against direct infantry assault, it was built on the edge of open and presumably hostile ground, and these men as well as the defensive equipment clearly seemed to constitute a target-rich environment for anyone outside the wire.

The men were directing their attention across the open ground and water-filled rice fields beyond. I guessed that the valley, despite its potential for concealment, was regarded as a buffer zone between our western perimeter and a dark stand of trees that crowded the foothills and steep ravines of a mountain which dominated the skyline a mile or so away.

Large flood lights were mounted every few yards along our necklace of sandbagged dugouts, and they were all aimed outward, across the fields. I moved over near where the beach chairs were being set up on the roof of the corner bunker and noted the lower ground where the paddies lay, then checked behind me and confirmed that, sure enough, from beyond the wire, we all stood exposed against the sky. I assumed this meant the area was secure, or at least dependably quiet of any enemy action, but I moved away and stood back from the others just the same.

A few Vietnamese rice farmers were out in the paddies, bent to their ancient task in the slanted evening light. With their faces hidden beneath conical straw hats, their tiny legs dangling from rolled trousers gave them the appearance of strange aquatic birds as they dipped daintily among the watery furrows. I felt compelled to stop and survey the ironic panorama just as a burst of nearby laughter released an elliptic flock of wildfowl, which sprang from their cover and wheeled away in painted flashes, like scraps of colored paper against the deep green background of the mountain. They rose across the paddies, flickering away into nothingness, to become lost in the pale carnelian sky.

The whole scene was so peaceful that I was struck by the contrast. Just yards away, an ancient culture was playing out the timeless ritual of farming the region's only staple product by hand, while we, the most technologically advanced culture in the world, stood around watching, entertained like children at a zoo.

I turned and went into the shack, got a soda, and returned to join the others, thinking that the simple aluminum cans we were drinking from alone represented manufacturing processes and an industrial infrastructure beyond a native farmer's imagining. Besides despising us as invaders, I wondered what myth conceptions our presence in their country suggested to our reluctant hosts. Did the farmers see our drink cans as symbols of some alien liturgy, of which we, in the green uniformity of our dress and our descent from roaring helicopters, were its priests?

I soon learned that the object of the men's attention was the mountain beyond the paddies. Mount Ngui Koto. According to the comments around me, the mountain had long been a known Viet Cong R&R center, but we had always left each other alone. From time to time, though, usually just after or just before some visiting official from the States was due to arrive for a "fact finding" (publicity) visit, someone decided that it was undignified to have the bad guys lounging around almost within 81mm mortar range of Special Forces HQ, and presumably looking back at us through heavy lenses. For this reason, the next in a series of ritual napalm attacks on the top of Mt. Ngui Koto was due to start at any minute. The mountain, which seemed to me uncomfortably close in view of this information, took on a new significance.

The sun was dissolving in a hazy yellow wash that settled among the forested slopes of the mountains as the swift tropical night raced in from the east carrying the sound of distant aircraft engines adrift on a slight breeze. I re-assumed a place apart from the others and watched with growing curiosity.

Four C-130s appeared in the distance, stacked in echelon formation, each flying above and behind the plane ahead, quite high over the crumpled line of the ridge. They approached slowly, like tiny black insects droning faintly on the evening air. As they closed on the peak, I heard that this was going to be another "Hollywood" drop, which wouldn't accomplish anything, as the targets could monitor our frequencies and were all safely underground in their caves, but everyone agreed that we had great conditions for the spectacle.

In a few minutes, the first 55-gallon drums of jellied gasoline began to fall from the rear cargo doors of the lead plane; black specks, clearly visible in their slow, tumbling descent against the delicate pink sky. Before the first dots hit the ground, the second string began falling, and then the third, in a series of gracefully arcing seams.

Then the mountaintop erupted in a spectacular splash of orange and red flame, flashing in a roiling bloom of consecutive fires so bright that it lit the smiling faces of the men around me and twinkled along their beer cans, before being swallowed by its own dense, black smoke. I was instantly captivated by the show, mesmerized by the destructive beauty of the colors, the burgeoning swell of the serried explosions, and by the silent dance of green and yellow lambencies flickering within the smoke. The distance withheld all sound, thus lending the spectacle a surreal quality, as though it could not really be happening–like a disaster unfolding in slow motion. The conspicuous absence of any noise enhanced the fascination.

After an initial stunned delay, approving "Ahs" and "Oohs" burst from our gallery, as though we were some prompted studio audience. Then, as I watched enraptured the huge gouts of flame spilling down from Ngui Koto's crest rocks, the sound came rumbling toward us across the valley of paddies. Though deep, rather like a growl, it arrived ragged and hollowed out by the trip, sounding vaguely artificial and not really up to what we had seen.

Yet there was an awesome power in the spectacle and in its thunderous silences, even at this distance, like some ancient religious display. It seemed almost to hold a moral force, and I recoiled involuntarily at its unspoken warning to stand back before the supremacy of its inevitable prerogative, such that in response perhaps to some dim atavistic urge, some impulse smuggled down though the generations in the baggage of inherited superstition and fear, I felt a momentary urge to pray to it.

At last, with the final detonations grumbling on the evening air, a heavy pall of petroleum smoke rolled upward in a plump black column, perhaps a thousand feet into the air above the peak, spreading like spilled wine over a tablecloth. There it slowed and pooled gently against the atmosphere, darkening the whole sky, while a profound silence settled again over the smoldering mountain and the quiet paddies.

As the formation of aircraft continued on, holding altitude with an air of nonchalance, the conflagration on the mountain quickly subsided into isolated brush fires. Its dark cloud of smoke, smudged by the breezes aloft, drifted toward us, until by nightfall it had crossed the whole width of the valley.

When it became evident that the show was over, that there was to be no second pass, the men around me began to step down from the sandbags, muttering their disappointment at the brevity of the one-act performance and talking about their plans for the evening. As I was beginning to feel hungry, having just been treated to an expensive dinner show at the end of a long day, I trudged back to the Transient area for the third time, my stiff new jungle boots rubbing the bones of my feet.

Later, after a dinner in the common messhall, a meal as satisfying for its quality as for its density and weight, I walked back to the perimeter for another look out across the rice paddies, my steps whispering softly in the sand. The club shack, half hidden in the shadows behind the security lights at the angle of the perimeter, was dark within, the corner of the compound deserted. All was eerily quiet. I stood still and listened to the night. I realized that for the first time since arriving in-country I could hear no aircraft, no machinery of any kind.

The sand all about was gouged and cupped with thousands of footprints which seemed to echo the pervading silence. The ground beyond the wire had taken on a lunar aspect where our floodlights, busy with strange insects, cast a bleaching glare over the rumpled surface and out to the scrub on the far side of the rice fields, the bulbs down the line so fierce they left after images. In the deep shadows beyond their reach, all was still.

A lone white heron stood stark and motionless in the shallow paddy at the edge of the light with legs like tiny stilts balanced on their own reflections. There was no breeze to ruffle the surface. Far away a dog barked twice, two scratches in the silence. Then the quiet healed over and there was nothing but the starlit rice paddy and the motionless bird.

I stood for some time, hiding myself in the darkness behind the back spill of the lights, watching and listening. No moon emerged to break the spell on the petrified landscape. Furrowed patches of starlight lay upon the paddies, and the mountain beyond stood dark and silent against the sky. The fires at its crest were out. The night had smothered all but faint evidence of human antagonism, for a veil of smoke still hung in a thin oleaginous smear across the stars.

Suddenly, a squawk from the jungle pierced the indelible hush, faint but sharp and poignant. Then the silence sealed itself again. The cry sent a little scurry of alarm through me. I wondered if it was really from a bird. In western films the Indians could always sneak up on wagon camps by fooling the Whites with bird calls. I wondered anew what might happen to me in the dim, incalculable months ahead, wondered again if my life would be ended somewhere in this country.

My fear of death itself remained muddy and less substantial than the insistent feeling of insidious vulnerability that had been haunting me ever since I was deposited in the country. Perhaps this was due to my sense of being displaced in the stunning heat, the strange primordial landscapes, and the overwhelming presence everywhere on the ground and in the air of the equipment for war, with its aura of singular purpose and vague impatience. Speculating on death itself was fruitless anyway, not only because I didn't need another reason to feel depressed, but because what lay beyond was unknown and unknowable. Even so, my continuing anxiety over the method of it was real, and I did not want my natural fear of an agonized and lingering end to haunt my behavior through whatever challenges lay ahead.

It was then that I decided to grow a moustache. It might alter my appearance just enough to ease the initial shock of recognition in the event that I would be returned home in a box and my parents be called upon to make the final identification.

Back in the tent sometime late that night, the faint slumbering sounds around me were shattered by sudden rain, which came out of the blackness with astonishing abruptness. It fell hard and steadily without wavering in intensity. It sounded like a sewing machine on the tent canvas. A hot gust pressed against my skin as the incredible downdraft changed the air pressure, sucking past in a mild vacuum. The dense oiled cloth shivered as the water bounced heavily upon it to cascade off the rolled side curtains and splash loudly on the ground, launching the ancient smell of dust. After a while, I got up and moved barefoot across the cool boards to the entrance and stared into the night.

The mountains were invisible behind the grille of rain, but I knew they were out there, watching. I had the feeling they resented us, that they had turned against us and now laughed at the smallness of our numbers and at the intrusion of our pointless presence. I could feel it in my stomach. They stood over us, grim and foreboding, conscious of every move and knowing that each thing we did was of little purpose. Men were foolish and were made only so that they should die, while mountains and rivers went on forever and did not notice the passing of time.

5

I was startled awake the next day by the low passage of a helicopter. The sudden arrival of its engine and the alarming chatter of the rotor beating the air into a rippled sheet of sound directly overhead jerked me from a viscous sleep that left me momentarily disoriented. As the engine noise and the chopping waves of air pressure receded, I lay there for a few minutes, initially disoriented, taking in the tent and the lumps that were beginning to stir on the other cots. I realized that ever since my arrival there had been only brief intervals of silence from the air. Aircraft of all kinds, but especially helicopters, seemed constantly overhead, and the sounds of their passing lent a nervous background energy to even mundane events on the ground.

The morning dawned breezy and clear, with fleecy little clouds chasing each other out of the mysterious green hills and a deceptive promise of cooler conditions on the ground. Everywhere outside our tent the damp sand was delicately pitted from the recent rainfall. Inside, sharp shadows cast by the angled morning light among the bunks seemed to be the hardest objects in the space, and I felt for a moment the same pang of irony that had occurred to me in the terminal at Okinawa—that the customary purpose of edifices had become muddled with the surrounding atmosphere, and each was exploring without permission the other's dimension.

I soon learned it was the beginning of a weekend, and the information surprised me. I realized I had lost track of the days. How long ago had I left the States? I also learned that even in a war zone, the Headquarters village likes to celebrate a weekend the way it does at home, with leisurely meals and extended sack time. After a large breakfast, then, I took advantage of this crease in the continuum and set out to explore the compound, which proved to be much larger than my limited movements of the day before had revealed.

About a hundred meters to the south of the tent, I strolled past a fenced section restricted to the use of former Viet Cong, who for one reason or another (usually money), had come over to our side, at least for a while. They were known as PRUs, Provincial Reconnaissance Units. Notoriously ruthless and untrustworthy, some had long been content to work for the side that provided the more comfortable living conditions. Others were true idealists, with their own dark agendas, and I had already heard horrible stories of what happened to their American advisors on patrols when one or two of these people had "turned" in the field. So, I thought in a moment of naïve humor, this was the "Enemy House" at the zoo. Then, a few steps later, I saw them.

They were scary, their sinister, impenetrable faces watchful and closed. None returned my thin smiles of greeting. Here was a camp full of professional killers, and though they looked like boys, their furtive glances through the wire fencing, cold and full of somber alertness, gave the indelible impression of a vulturine capacity to wait. It caused the ancient animal deep within me to shiver involuntarily. I skirted their compound and hurried on, feeling as though I was passing a haunted house.

Beyond their wire, I encountered a small artillery battery of three 155s, their long, dark barrels elevated menacingly against the sky to the west. A few bored-looking G.I.s sat on the gun control platforms with their shirts off, sunning themselves, all biceps and tattoos, their cigarettes dancing precariously as they talked quietly together and their fingers moving among the folds of their greasing rags. I nodded in passing and continued on, away from the guns and into a small grove of trees, in whose dappled shadows the concrete neighborhood of the permanent American cadre appeared to be seeking refuge.

Here, the men slept in solid reinforced cinderblock buildings surrounding an open community center, like a small town square, containing an open-air circular bar beneath a thatched roof and fronted by well-engineered concrete bunkers. The heavy thump of American music, trapped in undernourished air between the low buildings, drew me into the shaded center, where "Black Is Black," by Los Bravos, played from speakers mounted in the upper corners of the club. The air was too heavy and the atmosphere too foreign for the song, though, so the familiar associations it engendered seemed to hang at the periphery of the place like guests at the wrong address.

Several people, some dressed in surprising Hawaiian shirts, were milling around and laughing, in evident preparation for a large party, which, judging from the practiced familiarity with which the guy behind the bar scooped ice and arranged his bottles, seemed to be a Saturday ritual.

With uninvited expertise, someone slid a wet bottle of beer to me down the curved mahogany bar, and it stopped so near my hand that

I had to smile at life's imitation of art. How often had I seen that trick in western movies? There seemed an almost portentous grace in the ironic idiom of the gesture. I took up the bottle, stood by the bar, and surveyed the square.

Four benches stood in shifting shadow beneath the palms. The ground was scuffed and foot-worn in half circles around them like the beaten dirt at the range of a tethered dog. Broken sunlight moved on the dusty ground beneath the husking fronds of the trees.

Several plump domestic farm geese emerged incongruously from the shade and, muttering softly, waddled confidently toward the bar. I learned that they were part of an old Special Forces trick of using geese for watchdogs, as they are easily disturbed, and their raucous cries are readily distinguished from all other sounds, especially at night. These particular birds, though, bore the signs of easy duty. With their comically rolling gait and strange watchfulness, they were clearly well fed and quite used to human company. I enjoyed their bold approach as the barman tossed them some chips.

By the time about half the beer remained in the bottle, it had begun to sour and tasted like pennies. The sound system began pushing out "We Gotta' Get Outta' This Place," by Eric Burdon and The Animals, which I took as a sign that my presence might soon be seen as presumptuous. I thanked the man behind the bar and left to resume my exploration.

I soon arrived at the gate on the southern perimeter of the U.S. compound. Beyond it passed the bustle of local civilian life, busy but unhurried, with both foot and pedal traffic, all impacted with the nameless disquiet I had felt with each of my brief exposures to Vietnamese culture. Women, young and old, passed with baskets slung on their arms or bundles balanced on their heads, as bicyclists wearing white short sleeved shirts and khaki pith helmets wove their way among them.

I hesitated, wondering if the alien world outside the compound was off limits or even safe to enter. The fact that the gate was wide open, and the sentry was engrossed in a curled paperback novel much the worse for pocket wear, encouraged me to continue. I nodded to the top of the guard's head and stepped out into the exotic, forbidden, and closed life of Vietnam.

The air smelled of rotting vegetation, jungle underbrush and earth, with a faint mix of bus fumes and sewage, complicated by my own perspiration and the chemicals in my newly issued clothes. The hard-packed dirt road that ran toward the sea along our southern perimeter passed through the shade of several large fluted banyan trees and was busy with dozens of small brown entrepreneurs. A mist of red dust, launched by foot traffic and cycle tires, filled the air and settled upon everything like dried smog, coloring the vegetation, the vendors and their wares. Its dark talcum soon lay on my clothes. It found its way into my hair and nose, and it clung to my wet skin in a layer of thin mud. Bits of paper tumbled and clutched and rattled briefly in the lower branches of the roadside growth, then loped on again. Beyond the verge, the interlaced lower branches of the jungle filtered the sun through slanted dust-filled beams of yellow light.

I prepared a face for the natives to judge; not a brave or confident one but not a fearful one either. I tried to look well-meaning and slightly apologetic, like a nice person who has been swept up by forces beyond his control and set down in a place he knows he doesn't belong. It didn't matter, though, because the only people who noticed me were the merchants, whose singular agenda kept them ever vigilant for prospects.

Some people sold exotic-looking speckled fruit from cyclos, and particularly risky-looking meat hung from strings, their displays alive with flies and their voices high with impassioned, competitive gibberish. Many called out to me with vaguely familiar Pidgin-English epithets, while others simply regarded my passage wordlessly, with the calm, horizontal look of settled purpose with which a person might watch the shore from a slowly sinking boat.

I passed through eloquent, often unfamiliar, odors and walked around the more aggressive hawkers of black market U.S. goods. Any acknowledgment of their presence, any innocent signal of greeting, was instantly and loudly interpreted as commercial interest and sent the vendor back to his goods expectantly, in a comical pretense of sudden gravity. Their childlike disappointment when I failed to follow was almost tangible.

An old woman, her small black eyes staring ahead from a dark face deeply lined with care, suddenly halted in her progress, gathered up her loose trouser leg and squatted beside the road. There she released a stream of urine into the red dust, then rose and continued on her way, apparently only mildly inconvenienced by the delay. I began to appreciate the practicality of the national costume.

One old man had a vehicle-cleaning business established under a grove of thorn trees beside the dirt road where it met the shorefront pavement. It was a kind of intersection between road and path, a well-conceived location indeed. His worn plywood sign, propped against a water can, declared confidently in bold red hand-painted English:

CA

RWAS

HIN

G HE

RE

He and a young boy were vigorously scrubbing a jeep, while its American driver stood approvingly aside in odd parody of some sub-urban weekender far away. The advertising, though, failed to mention a truly unique aspect of the service, which was the optional use of hot water. Nearby, two bubbling water cans rattled gently atop a crude brazier, from which blue smoke broke fast in a kind of running crouch. An old woman raked at the flames with evident apprehension, as one might goad a small dragon. Perhaps she disapproved of her role as Plant Manager in the family enterprise.

Farther along the road, nearer the crowded beach, I came across a scene that arrested my attention for a long time. As I looked at it, there gradually followed one of those flame-lit revelations which alters the natural order of things forever and replaces it with some searing in-ner vision that accompanies us to the end of our lives: Beginning in a ditch beside the road was a small rectangular clearing, containing an open thatched dwelling which consisted entirely of dried palm fronds supported by slender, hand-cut poles. With the single exception of one mud corner that contained the blackened mouth of a tiny oven, the crude structure had no walls.

It was obvious that the family was home. So were a gray cow and a few bony dogs and some chickens that scuffled about under foot, all crowded into the splintered shadow of the fronds. Two sagging hammocks drooped between the dubious uprights, lending the place its only relief from harsh lines. Close to the edge of the clearing was a small garden scratched into the desiccated soil and sprinkled over with a scattered eruption of sickly plants.

However, at the corner nearest the road, surrounded by finished masonry, and even featuring a stone archway, was the family grave plot. Its irony filled the air. That little family cemetery spoke more eloquently of our problems in Southeast Asia than all the political pontifications I had ever heard. It was uncomfortably obvious that these people were more interested in providing for the dead than for themselves. I stood there trying hard to reconcile what I was seeing, nagged by its significance, yet unable to articulate precisely the full implications it set free in my imagination.

From the direction of the crowded beach behind me, faint laughter and transistor radio music arrived on a thin tendril of sound, while a hot noon wind stalked through the thorn trees that surrounded the clearing. It pressed against my clothes, bearing the odor of dust and the breath of weeds and tangled brush. There was real loneliness in it, and aimlessness, as though its passing were only a sterile duty, lacking even the beneficent promise of rain. Yet it chilled. I heard beyond it the black winds of chaos, and my hackles rose, as if someone had stepped upon my grave. These people might actually be anxious to die. Wow. I understood instinctively that what I was seeing evidenced something far more profound than the simple desire to escape their poverty. Paradigm shift.

Here was the deep philosophical inscrutability that had lain at the heart of Gen. MacArthur's warnings a generation ago never to get involved in a ground war in Southeast Asia. Here was the antithesis of the American experience, simple in its faith, holistic in its simplicity–the bureaucrat's requiem. We had been sent to fight, and perhaps to die, among people who placed such limited value on their own lives that they would live under thatchwork shelters while reserving their skill with stone for the dead. What sort of preparation for a ground war with Buddhists could one expect, then, of a government whose history of geographic isolation and seductive wealth had long produced some of the world's least subtle diplomats? What insights for winning the hearts and minds of any populace could be expected from a nation that doesn't even require its ambassadors to speak the language of the countries to which they are appointed?

I suddenly felt aware of how the tribal Judeans must have looked upon the Roman legions of occupation. I felt watched, the very eyes of ancient culture upon me, and fraught with conflicting existential notions, I turned and hurried back to the safety of the American compound and on to the Transient area, deep in its center, where I sat on my bunk in a silent and nameless disquiet. My little tour had created a vacuum into which rushed a multitude of trivial reflections as renewed misgivings about the whole war struggled for focus.

Later, while lying there trying to cull some distinct ideas from the collection of vague sensations that had been accumulating since I arrived, I was startled when the entrance to the tent suddenly filled with a dark figure. His features were indistinct against the outside light. He stood for a moment in the shadow, rolling his gaze about the room, his chin slightly elevated, like an animal sniffing the breeze.

"Sgt. John Moore in here?" he asked, more like an announcement than a query.

It was Steve Anderson, newly arrived and all but moved into the permanent barracks I had explored earlier! It was fun to see him again, and he immediately suggested that we go over to the main NCO Club, which he had already discovered, for a frosted deep-dish something-made-of-rum. Besides, he assured me, the air-conditioning in the place was downright legendary. It was good to have his upbeat nature around again. It pulled me from my introspective funk, and I did not need the extra incentive of the promised chill to tag along with enthusiasm.

We caught up on our first impressions of the compound as we left the tent area and walked toward the center of the headquarters village. Near the south end of the paved parade area, boisterous revelry began to float in upon our conversation through the afternoon shimmer in bursts of faint tumult, mixed with snatches of music, all emanating from an anonymous-looking building tucked among some office huts. Steve had already learned that the NCO in charge of the club was a famous scrounger, and rumor held that he had sent back home to his personal account over a million dollars from his various enterprises in Vietnam.

The place announced its popularity long before we got to the door. When we stepped into its dark and truly frigid interior, I was struck by an oasis of American culture. Country music twanged from a juke box, and the whole place was crowded with men drinking and pumping the handles of slot machines. The long bar, which went most of the length of the building, served as a rocky shore on which washed an ever-renewed green wave of servicemen, and behind the bar rose a mirrored forest of colored bottles whose terraces must have represented the distilled produce of every country on earth.

Filmy roseate light winked from the polished corners of things, adding to the surreal atmosphere. Men sat at low tables, their intense faces pink in the intimate glow of little candles flickering in red mood globes. Laughter competed for air superiority with laments from the jukebox. Nothing visible could ever have been on a legitimate military requisition form, and I began to realize that the NCOIC must deserve his reputation.

Steve pressed his way toward the bar as I stepped into a small, slightly less crowded room to the left that was ringed with slot machines. How in the world did he get those? Nobody knew and nobody cared. Around one machine in particular was gathered a small group of GIs and a few Vietnamese soldiers, their faces a study in fervor, while one man fed *piasters* into the machine, evidently spending on behalf of the whole group. Gambling by committee. With each pull of the knob, the group leaned inward, as though some result of equal importance to each of them might be affected by combined scrutiny.

I stepped over to watch and soon realized that I had become part of a long-standing practice in that room. One of the guys told me the machine had last paid off more than a year before, and the pot was now over $15,000. No wonder all the gaming rounders hung on each pull with ritualistic will.

Steve came back with a pair of planter's punches, and together we surveyed the room, cheerfully commenting on the fixed inward look of amiably tight men engaged in the ancient and solemn ceremony of revelry. Group drinkers seem mysteriously to find, almost at once, by a purely empiric but precise method, a common denominator of drunkenness to which everyone loyally adheres before descending, all together, to the next level.

Steve revealed that he was already ensconced in his new clerical job at Headquarters and that he had taken a look at my orders. He said it looked as though I was headed up north to the Da Nang area to a place called FOB 4. He didn't know yet exactly what that was, but it appeared to be a place from which we launched very long range missions of various kinds. He mentioned that a lot of stories were coming out of the FOBs. His use of the word "stories" sounded like a euphemism for something unpleasant. I didn't want to reveal the anxiety these suggestions caused me or to show my ignorance by asking what the letters actually stood for, but it occurred to me that perhaps this three-letter abbreviation meant something that would explain the subtle shift in attitude toward me that I had detected from each of the in-processing clerks the day before. Then he said, "Did you know you've been issued a Top Secret clearance?"

"...Er, no." It all sounded ominous.

Each bit of information attending my immediate future served only to feed further uncertainties. I was soon to learn that the initials FOB stood for Forward Operations Base (Sometimes also called Forward Observations Base), of which there were only four in the country, mine was to be #4, the farthest north. [I was also soon to learn what Steve had not told me–that the unit was reported (rumored?) to have taken 100% casualties for the previous two years.] I didn't even like the implications of the word "Forward."

On that afternoon with Steve, though, we decided that I would postpone worrying about it and just enjoy the air-conditioning and my friend's cheerful company. By the time we left the club, glasses were growing like mushrooms on the sills and in the shade of chairs.

Late that night, back in my bunk under the community tent and listening to the night sounds, a singular voice began to rise from one of the bunks at the end of the opposite row in a slow repetitive crescendo. One of the transients, a black soldier processing through, was talking to the enemy.

"Gon' git you, Charlie... Yeah... Gon' gitchu, Mistah Chah's."

I lay there listening to his rambling dementia for long minutes, hoping he would drop back into his troubled sleep, and let me get some rest. However, after some time, during which he drifted in and out of recognizable language, he got up from his cot and began to pace the central aisle between the bunks, muttering his private litany. His speech was deep with a ghetto undercurrent of pending violence.

"Ah'mone cutcho' haht out, Cha's."

As he neared my bunk, a shadow within a shadow, I could see in the dim light that filtered in through the tent flap that his large white eyes were the hard marbles of a man transfixed. One arm was outstretched, like a penalty call, and in his hand was an unsheathed bayonet. Yet there was something bogus about his manner, something revealing about his soft breathing. I wondered if he was just putting on a show for the new men. The need for attention, too, is a cruel master.

"...'mone cutcha. ...'mone gitcha, mistah Cha's." Over and over. Some of the other men began to stir. As he approached for the second time, I decided to speak to him. If he was simply acting, then by getting someone to notice, I reasoned that it would satisfy his purpose, and we could all go back to sleep—and if he really was teetering on the rim of enchantment, then I would at least be ready if he were startled enough to lunge with the knife.

Drawing up my knees in anticipation of the possible need to spring, I rose cautiously on one elbow and carefully drew out my own bayonet. My heart began to pound. I hoped my voice would sound steady.

"Take it easy, man," I said with calculated calm. "It's ok. We're all right here with you."

He hesitated for just a moment. The sound of my voice diminished into the corners of the tent like a dropped handful of birdshot. When he moved again it was to continue back to his own bunk, which he stole into wordlessly.

I don't know if he was faking or not, for I would learn soon enough that we all had strange dreams there, and in that place dreams were licensed as never before. But the event left me in a maze of impractical meditations and reckless conjecture, and I lay there for some time, listening to the vibrant silence that everyone liked to take for safety. Perhaps God was just making him write his litany on the blackboard a hundred times. The next day, nobody mentioned anything about the strange night, thus leaving the entire incident suspended within a nimbus of dim irrelevancy.

6

Through the next several days, I was subjected to something called "Orientation," a process which, so far as I could see, was designed to reduce me to a malleable state of hopeless depression. The only thing I actually learned was that, compared to the distant bureaucratic hierarchy in the Pentagon, this was a brotherhood of anarchy. At least I was temporarily safe within the localized activities of a large community, and as Steve settled into his clerical job at Headquarters, I saw less of him during the second half of that first week.

My orientation began when I was told by a senior sergeant, suitably inured by years of humorless discourse to qualify as a bearer of bad tidings, that I was slated for reconnaissance work, and I was quickly placed in the Special Forces RECONDO School for recon team leaders. It sounded mildly sinister but was presented without details. From the various ways I'd heard it used, "Recon" was a somewhat pliable abstraction, much-referenced within a HQ whose basic mission is intelligence-gathering, anyway. Of course I knew what reconnaissance meant in a general way, but I also knew that its practical application included multiple methods of assembling information—from satellites, aircraft, ground observation, electronic eavesdropping, the study of maps, and many other, more clandestine, operations. It was naggingly true that most of the scary war stories seemed to be coming in from the Recon teams, but my specialized training was in Weapons, not Intelligence, so unable to appreciate the full implications of this new development other than believing all knowledge is good, I just told myself there was a lot of misplaced hand-wringing and wishful thinking at any headquarters, so I began the RECONDO School not without reservations, but with no specific expectations either.

The training was familiar. The only thing that made any of it new was the searing heat. We were up, running several miles with full combat gear each morning in the dusty ocher haze, before the heat climbed to 100, though the humidity seldom fell below 100 at any time. There were wind sprints with full packs, full-load chin-ups when the slick sweat on our palms would cause us to lose our grips on the bar before completing the required number of repetitions, low crawl drills, and even a few merciful air-conditioned classroom lectures.

By lunchtime each day, the dirty perspiration ran from our necks and faces, black as oil. The water in our plastic canteens was warm and tasted of neoprene. Before drinking it in the early days, I would slush the first mouthful around to sluice the grit out of my teeth. Soon, though, I began to gulp it, dirt and all. People developed a mannerism of jerking the head abruptly to the side from time to time like a wet dog, and its purpose was similar to the dog's: to throw the sweat out of their eyes.

The school did, however, acclimatize us quickly to the Southeast Asian humidity. My clothes began to fade with each of the daily washings the training necessitated, until the cloth became marginally, and mercifully, cooler–well, slightly less stifling.

I began to wear my standard issue cotton tourniquet around my head as others did. When I first saw some of the guys wearing them that way, I thought it an affectation, but its practicality soon won out. It was as good a way as any to carry a large bandana; it served to break up the outline of one's head in the field; it absorbed much of the stinging perspiration that would otherwise be in my eyes, and it would be handy if I ever needed it for its designed purpose. My water intake began to normalize, and my perspiration level began to drop slightly.

After a week or two of this, my group was issued ammunition and sent out for our first night in the field. We loaded into venerable old Sikorsky S-1 helicopters for an over water flight out to Entre Island, at the entrance to Nha Trang, where we conducted a supervised reconnaissance of the old French tourists' landmark. The whole operation was not unlike a Boy Scout outing, except that we rode in open helicopters with the doors removed. I chose to sit in the door opening with my feet hanging outside. It was a thrill to ride along up there in the 100 mph breeze, with the sparkle of the South China Sea slipping by under my feet, and with nobody to tell me not to do it because it was dangerous.

Once on the ground we jumped off the choppers and fanned into the scrub growth near the crest of the island to set up a rambling perimeter around its slopes. I selected a position among the rocks of a stepped limestone outcropping that cut across one of the island's many steep trails. The location was too exposed for this to be a real combat operation, but it served well enough for a taste of sleeping outside in a region of unspecified threat from the enemy, sudden downpours, and insects in such astonishing variety that they defied classification.

I settled in along the rim of a deep stony crevasse with a more limited field of fire than I would have liked, but with the instinctive realization that this was only an exercise for green troops. Nonetheless, I made sure I had a round in the chamber of my temporarily-issued rifle, and when the night had risen up full, I looked along the perimeter to assure myself that I was not in the vicinity of any smokers. The glow of a cigarette can be seen from miles away.

I finally hunkered down among the rocks with a narrow ledge to sit on, another about right for an elbow, and with a third jammed into my ribs. I spent that first jungle night like a kid trying to sleep on a staircase, listening to the inscrutable pulse and yowl of insects, my thoughts a parade of absences.

The purpose of the exercise was never adequately explained, but the procedure was so familiar to me that I concluded the whole effort had been primarily just to get us out in the "boonies" for a night under the stars, come what may. We finished the experiment the following morning, but the choppers failed to return, and by late afternoon, after repeated futile radio calls for transport, we were all growing upset at the prospect of a second night on the island with no food. By then, the training cadre had long since dispensed with proper radio procedure and were screaming into the handset at the mainland air operations officer to dispatch the aircraft immediately. Apparently, after ferrying several dozen men out to this island off the coast, nobody thought to schedule the flights to retrieve us.

It was an afternoon of bright haze, the sunlight sourceless and uniform. I could sniff a sea change in the air. As the problem of our extraction was beyond my control, I found a comfortable place to sit with the rifle across my lap, among the spread of roots at the base of a large hardwood with a grand view of the sea, and resolved at least to enjoy the sunset over the water before the rain began. Some of the guys entertained themselves while we waited by dropping hand grenades from the cliffs into the sea to watch with loud approval the subsequent blossom of killed fish rise from the depths and spread upon the surface in glittering silver myriads.

At last, in the gathering gray of evening, the choppers finally returned for us, their blades stropping the air as they approached over the water like a gaggle of giant grasshoppers. Each machine maneuvered in turn down through the jungle cover to hover just off the ground with a single wheel balanced delicately on a rock ledge, like a dancer on point. The pilots were very good but were anxious to get away before the light failed, as the crowd of trees on the island afforded no clear landing zone. Some of them gestured angrily for us to hurry, but I couldn't hear their curses through the engine noise. With the rotor blades whipping the foliage in a violent local tornado, we used the tire as a step to climb into the machine through the roaring downdraft. Once loaded, each helicopter backed expertly out of the forest, then pivoted and headed for home. We were flown back to hot showers and a welcome meal.

While I was still in the messhall sorting through my expectations of the following day's training exercise, a staff clerk approached and casually handed me the orders for my combat assignment: FOB 4, Da Nang. I Corps, just as Steve had said. Whatever that meant, it seemed the die was finally cast. Most of the letters and numbers on the page were confusing, but I knew at least that I Corps was in the far North. I had been assigned to someplace up where the border between North and South Vietnam cut across the narrow waist of the country, a region where rumor had it that things were very "active" (read "dangerous"); a place where contact with the enemy was frequent, where incursions were common.

I had barely started RECONDO School, and aside from achieving some physical acclimatization, had learned virtually nothing about reconnaissance or the nature of operations in the dense Vietnamese jungle. My fate lay still hidden before me, enshrouded in a coffin of impenetrable abbreviations typed in regulation format on plain paper. How incidentally some momentous events come into our lives. A guy steps up and hands you a single sheet of paper on which are cryptic markings that draw you into a future you couldn't have imagined and from which there is no going back. Ever. Starting right then, the life you may once have known is gone.

In the morning, packed, and with yet another layer of my orders peeled away, I was taken to the airport in a Jeep, the corporal who drove me showing undue deference. He dropped me off at the entrance to a low building sided with corrugated metal, and I went inside where I was informed that my flight was already waiting.

When I started out toward the aircraft, the sight of it fell upon me with a silent scream. The black C-130 with no markings squatted like some monstrous winged toad about 70 yards away, an ominous twin shadow from which not one thing gleamed or glinted as metal should.

Its strangeness worked icy fingers within me. This was the very flight I'd been warned about back in Cam Ranh. I felt trapped in the prison light of the sun. So it was to be me, after all. In that instant the Beast stirred again, and I felt the glare of its hungry eyes upon me. I hesitated while the blood of heritage, death, and memory coursed through my heart.

While the bone-colored light around me rippled in the heat like drapery folds, I hoisted my bag, and then composing my face into an expression which I hoped would give me a look of rugged determination, began the long walk toward the gaping cargo ramp and all of its disquieting promise. I was bluffing though. I felt like a snail who has just learned the meaning of *escargot*.

7

The dark interior of the airplane was half full of crated industrial air-conditioning equipment, stacked nearly to the overhead, and the stifling captured air smelled of sun-baked metal and grease. I thought the cargo was surprisingly mundane for what one might have expected to find on board one of these mysterious black flights, but I consoled myself with the idea that the spooks needed air-conditioning as much as anybody.

Along the sides of the aircraft, in the few jungle-saturated webbed seats that were folded down where the windows should have been, sat about half a dozen stolid, boyish Vietnamese in unfamiliar uniforms—officers, judging by the pips on their shirt fronts—their faces devoid of expression. I wondered what they were doing on this airplane. Their sullen presence lent an air of foreboding to the mystery of our destination, for I had been lead to believe that these black flights were for operations so secret that even the Americans knew nothing about them but rumors.

Heavy duty equipment stamped with American corporate logos; adolescent foreign soldiers; and me. It seemed an odd load, especially for a flight that carried such an eerie reputation. I wondered if the markings on the crates weren't a cover of some kind.

The realization that I was to be the only American passenger quickened my acute sense of estrangement as I picked my way through their staring black gazes toward the wall of shipping crates forward of the seats, my footsteps on the metal deck unusually loud in the captive stillness of the interior. At least a load marked as air-conditioning supplies was less ominous than any number of other things might have been, like say, medical supplies or body bags. Besides, I felt urged toward the crates by a vague need for reassurance. They represented tangence with something that wasn't strictly military. I indulged a sudden impulse to climb up on top of the boxes, partially in order to escape the miasma of glum taciturnity which clung to the other passengers on the webbed seats, and partially just because I thought it would be more fun to ride on the cargo instead of the conventional strapped-in way. The airlines don't let you do that.

I wedged my bag under some cargo straps, then pulled myself up onto the boxes and lay down just under the orderly confusion of pipes, wires, and control cable channels that made up the ceiling of the fuselage. From my lofty vantage point, I looked down the length of the aircraft to the unbearably bright rectangle of outside light, in which the Loadmaster's fluid silhouette seemed almost ghostly in its flickering movements against the glare.

His slender frame came shimmering up the metal ramp, his effortless body movements belying busy eyes, which took in the position of everything in the dark hold. I was a little surprised to note that he wore the muted black chevrons of an ordinary Air Force Sergeant. Still, as a member of this crew, part of the mystery clung to him. Though he moved with an ageless grace, his deep blue eyes seemed to flash a shoal warning from some distant inner shore. His angular face was bisected by an enormously scruffy sand-colored moustache, which was probably a carefully-groomed handlebar when he was off duty but now blown into bushy disarray by his duties in the wind. His hair was sun-bleached too light to be called the brown it may once have been, yet it wasn't auburn enough to go with his sunburned skin. He was a blanched strawberry blond with a humorless dry smile, whose faded olive fatigues made him look surprisingly pink in contrast. Yet the youth had been sucked out of his eyes and much of the color drawn from his face, and when I noticed his cold, pale lips, I knew it was gone for good. Life had already made him old, and he would live it out old.

He stepped to one side and extracted a hand telephone from the maze of conduit near the ramp's lift controls. He spoke briefly into it. Then, turning to us, he raised his left hand and began moving it in a tight little circle over his head in the universal gesture for "spooling up" the engines. Though his movements seemed casual and economic, they were given a kinetic urgency by the low, sequential whine of a gas turbine as it began to feed life to each of the four engines, which in turn shattered our silence, building quickly to an excruciating high-pitched scream. The airplane shuddered as each engine started. The ramp was still down, presumably in the interest of comfort from the heat, but in through its opening came a world of tortuous sound. I clamped my hands over my ears. Then, with a slight lurch, the concrete outside began to back away from us.

The ramp came up as we taxied, closing with a soft hiss. It plunged us into darkness, and shut us off from the world, but at least our completed cocoon now enclosed a tolerable noise level and, amid the general buzzing and vibration, an atmosphere of common fate. In a few moments the Loadmaster flipped a switch, and a row of dim ceiling lights came on. They looked like the kind you might find in the corridors of a small-town motel, and I smiled at this incongruous semblance of service. Paradigm shift.

The eyes of the Vietnamese soldiers, now very white, darted about nervously in the filmy light. They looked like troubled Boy Scouts, and I wondered if this was their first ride in an airplane.

As the aircraft lurched heavily onto the runway, I gripped the tie-downs around me to keep from sliding foolishly off the cargo boxes in the unfamiliar side load. The engines suddenly came up to full power, and with the odd, wallowing rhythm of slightly non-synchronized props thrumming beneath their deafening whine, the giant C-130 lunged forward, hurling everything back against the straps. After a short run, it lifted off quickly, climbing out at a surprisingly steep angle, while I strained to hold my position atop the cargo with desperate nonchalance in a private little struggle of piled inertia. Since I had climbed up there as though I had done it many times before, I knew I would look as foolish as I felt if I slipped off the load and sprawled at the feet of the foreigners.

As it happened, we headed south, instead of up the coast toward Da Nang, where my orders directed me. We made several stops throughout the day, loading and discharging people and cargo at both paved runways and isolated jungle clearings. The Vietnamese soldiers got off at one of these, for which I was grateful, since I had quickly learned the impracticality of trying to ride atop the crates. Since I had been clinging precariously to the tie-down straps, I was relieved to be able to climb down as soon as the natives left, thus saving face while restoring the circulation in my arms.

All approaches and departures were abrupt and steep, and all landings hard. While yelling back and forth over the engine noise with the Loadmaster during one of the legs after I had become the only passenger, I came to realize the effect his clamshell life might have upon a person. Landing several times a day in remote outposts for which there was little or no dependable advance intelligence–some strips peaceful, but many unpredictably hot, that would suddenly erupt with mortar and rocket attacks as the aircraft approached; then out again, into the relative safety of altitude–had flipped him for months into extremes of risk and escape, heat and cold, and always on the cusp of the struggle between lift and the relentless agenda of gravity.

"These things is mortar magnets, man," he yelled over the din. "An' the gooks got all the LZs zero'd. No way to sneak in and out in one'a these. Nooo way."

A C-130 is big alright, and his words revealed the false security that rides with flight and speed. What goes up must, at least periodically, come down. Back down to the dark, ambiguous earth–the deep, pervasive "boonies," where secret almond eyes are focused on the co-ordinates of the intrusive foreigner's every move–diving repeatedly from the safety and the cool air of altitude down to the cloying, uncanny jungle mud, where they make the newsreels I'd seen, all fragmented and busy with blurry violence.

All of a sudden, I felt a shiver of terrible vulnerability in this loud aluminum shell, and for the first time in my life came to see an airplane as the ultimate trap. I had always enjoyed flying and regarded airplanes as almost magical in their power and indifference to distance, that great historical barrier to earthbound travel. The technical sophistication and national prestige which I had come to confuse with the airplane's wondrous capacity for delivering power evaporated. A fragment of inexpensive small-caliber ordnance delivered in the right place while we were low to the ground would bring down this multi-million dollar contraption in a massive helpless tangle in seconds.

I realized, too, that there is no bottom line in Nature; that in the end, nothing is accountable, and the world remains unmoved by our brief passing or the manner of our departure. Even the genteel vagueness of our commemorative captions reflects our naïveté. Expressions of clinical simplicity like, "...died in an airplane accident," convey nothing about the terrifying weightless fall, the explosive impact, or even about man's applied science for undoing, just as "KIA" says nothing of the fearsome hot chaos through which a person can pass in one of these machines. We need terms which give cataclysm some significance in human terms.

When I asked the Sergeant how things looked for this trip, he glanced quickly away and said, "We'll see when we get to Ban Me Thout." Another deeply foreign name, intense with bad feeling, instantly impacted with murky despair. If he was worried about Ban Me Thout, then so was I. Somewhere in the hills ahead of us, I felt the Beast creep closer, stirred by anticipation.

We were being hurled down the country as though in a camera, with long periods of droning darkness interrupted by bright snapshots of primitive locations, whenever the big eye of the loading door opened astern for brief periods of noisy activity, permitting glimpses of the outside world.

During the extended, lulling legs of the flight the Sergeant explained that the system of transport in the country was one of full round trips, which covered the entire length of South Vietnam. These aircraft, like the old Caribou in which I'd flown to Nha Trang a few weeks before, were on a constant nation-long round robin, carrying any and all cargo for their respective networks of command, some moving southward along the coast, and then northward, inland, while other flights covered the circuit the opposite way.

I began to understand why the air was constantly filled with the sound of aircraft. Aircraft of every description: large transports like this one, all kinds of smaller cargo planes, VIP twins and reconnaissance Bird Dogs, FACs, and helicopters. Lots and lots of helicopters. Everything with vertical take-off and land capability, ranging from the big twin-engined Chinook transports that the Marine Corps used (With the gaping mouth of their rear cargo opening, round at the top and flat across the bottom, they resembled gigantic insects being dragged backwards through the air, howling in protest.), down to the Army's fast little two-seater LOACH. In between, and by far the most numerous, were the Hueys–slicks, gunships, attack ships, people-movers of all kinds–and Cobras. The constant beating of their rotors formed a sharp, poignant base note for the rhythm of the whole conflict, and it was a sound in which I would come to invest lasting emotion.

Each time the C-130 landed, the loading ramp opened onto a new and unfamiliar landscape, each more primitive than the last. Once, it opened to a surprising rain storm, and the cold, damp air which rushed in was a shock. It brought with it the smell of trees and wet earth, mixed with something else, dense and unfamiliar, but a bit like charcoal. Loading and unloading was very fast here, as we never came to a full stop.

When he opened the ramp this time, the Loadmaster tossed two duffles of mail into the mud as we splashed past an earthen bunker bristling with antennas, and I saw in the sweep of misty landscape which fell away on all sides that we were high on a mountaintop, near the clouds, and that the rain-lashed runway was glistening red clay, hard-packed and rutted, with deeply eroded shoulders.

Just as we swung around and lurched back for the take-off run, two muddy men ran up and slung their rucksacks onto the ramp. The pilots were clearly anxious to get away, and the two guys barely made it, leaping onto the ramp from a dead run just as we began to pick up speed. They scrambled in and collapsed on the metal deck in a clatter of rain-soaked combat gear as the ramp started closing, scooping them up and spilling them forward. They landed in a heap and squirmed for hand holds as the ramp latched up, closing out the daylight.

With their tanned, unshaven faces turned upward, and chests heaving, the men peered about in the artificial darkness, tense, expectant, as though listening for something outside. Yet their red-rimmed eyes were fastened hard onto something inward, remote. After we had leveled off, they relaxed a little and made halfhearted attempts to blot their faces with filthy, wet sleeves. They were clearly glad to be on board, but the incalculable event from which they had come still had them. They probably thought they were smiling.

Some quirky Vietnamese who had boarded at another stop got off when we landed at Saigon, along with the two guys we had picked up on the mountain, and they all walked away from the giant airplane with practiced indifference, as though they had never seen it. I felt a flash of resentment at their collective ability to abandon our fateful conveyance without a thought. Then, recalling my own fears of entrapment earlier, I began to realize that, perhaps when you inch along the brink of your own extinction for long enough, you develop an economy of emotion in which you extend no attachment to transitory objects, regardless of their role in your temporary salvation. It was to prove a useful lesson.

Ton Son Nhut Airport at Saigon was a return to extensive modern facilities, with broad parking ramps, bright sunshine, a lot of vehicular activity around the aircraft, and an officious manner among the ground personnel. As my fellow travelers evaporated into its dazzling concrete confusion, the Sergeant, moving about in the manner of contained urgency with which one might await a late friend on some street corner, again refereed the exchange of people and goods with professional familiarity. He was good at his job. As often happens in the absence of alternatives or of a chance for relief, skill levels expand to meet the magnitude of responsibility. He off-loaded most of the heavy cargo here, and with it went the crates of air-conditioners.

Soon, a few clean-cut North American officers, who looked like recruitment posters for the laundry service, stepped into the shadow of the tail. They were joined by a cherubic Vietnamese officer with a broad perpetual grin, who wore starched jungle fatigues, a heavy frame nickel-plated American issue .45 caliber automatic in a polished leather shoulder holster across his chest, and a pair of large aviator glasses of fashionable hue. They chatted animatedly for a few moments, during which I could not escape noticing the ironic improbability of the group. The Americans resembled giants next to the toothy little Asian, and through the professional insincerity of their exchange, they became a metaphor for the larger relationship.

They came up the ramp all together, in odd parody of Gen. MacArthur's landing party at Leyte, and took seats in the webbing opposite mine. We all nodded amiably. Once wedged into the narrow seats, they settled into a kind of morphic parity, the tall men, shortened now, with elevated knees and large feet, and the Vietnamese, his plump body compressed and his round face bobbing like a doll's behind the enormous pistol which had ridden up to his chin, sat where he remained throughout the trip, grinning like an evil piece of garden sculpture strapped to a cannon.

After refueling and taking on a sled pallet, which was neatly packed with ammunition and food and tightly wrapped in an old tent canvas that reeked of oil and long confinement, we prepared to leave for the first leg of our long trek back to the north. This was the inland route. The idea of flying over so much hostile territory stirred my apprehensions, but now, too, I detected a subtle change in the Sergeant's manner. An undeniable preoccupation. Something was on his mind which formed a chink in the armor of his controlled impassivity.

The take-off from this modern runway was quick, due to our reduced weight, and the first landing, an hour or so later, was an uneventful touchdown on another paved runway. Here my countrymen disembarked, striding purposefully down the ramp and out into the sunshine with their pet Buddha, their movements a crisp concerto of whispering starch.

With their departure, I again became the only passenger. I suppose it was an opportunity to feel important, but it had the opposite effect. The aloneness in that expensive transportation now made me feel conspicuous. I didn't know why I was being singled out, but by some subtle and discomfiting alchemy, I was being changed from an anonymous molecule in the olive drab mass comprising the American presence in the country into a singular microbe on a specimen slide, where lines of immutable attention were converging upon me. I was being driven to the ball dressed in red pajamas.

The Sergeant became distinctly tense as he prepared for the departure this time. It was hard not to pick up on it, since I had been searching for valid signs in everything remotely noticeable from the start. I knew something was up for sure when, for the first time all day, he strapped on a side arm. then he took an M-16 from a recess near the back, checked the chamber with the charging handle, and replaced it in its brackets.

"Ban Me Thuot?" I asked, guessing the answer. He nodded slightly with painful eloquence, and busied himself with some incidental activity. From that moment, the next leg of the trip seemed very long. I could only sit and speculate about its worrisome outcome, while he engaged himself needlessly in checking and rechecking the tie-downs between long periods of wordless distraction.

Shortly before we began our approach into Ban Me Thout, he took a call from the cockpit on the inter-phone and immediately opened the ramp at several thousand feet. Just before my ears closed with the change in air pressure, the sucking sound it made reminded me of a refrigerator door. Then, in rushed a world of whistling sound carrying the cold air of altitude and the kerosene smell of engine exhaust. Beneath the tilting horizon of endless green below us was a rolling Cenozoic landscape, dark and wavering. Viewed through the distorting vapor of our exhaust stream, it seemed for a moment ironically laced with a mournful kind of poesy.

The Sergeant, framed against the sky with the wind tugging at his clothes, moved effortlessly around the open doorway without a safety line, so comfortable with the rolling and shaking of the ship that at first I didn't even think about his daring, and just marveled at his easy grace and control as he stepped out onto the ramp at some 1,500 feet and hunkered down to check out to the sides. He crouched there in that gale-sucking door, his hands resting on his hips, as though, he were just standing on a street corner somewhere, waiting. He knew he was good, too, an artist, and he probably knew that I was watching, but it wasn't for me at all; it was his, private. He was the man who was never going to fall out of any damn airplane.

The approach, as usual, was steep and short. There was a sudden power reduction, and we nosed over abruptly. The Sergeant sprang to the floor brackets and began loosening the quick-releases on the sled. In a few moments, we were down to treetop level, and things outside passed in a blur. He leaped behind the pallet with the ease of a cat and yelled for me to help him get it started. I jumped up and braced myself against the back of the musty load the way he showed me. Just as we hit the runway with a tremendous jolt, the aircraft groaned as though something had broken. It knocked me off balance as the Sergeant yelled, "Now!," and jerked the last release. We pushed, and the pallet took off down its grooves in the floor like an amusement park ride. I fell, sprawling among the abandoned shackles as it cleared the ramp, slammed onto the hard clay landing strip in a cloud of red dust, skidded for a moment, then capsized just before disappearing from view.

The airplane immediately pitched violently up and began a steep, accelerated climbing turn to the left. A few dun-colored tents and dusty structures spun past as I, with escalating terror, began to slide down the tilted deck toward the open door, scrabbling to grab hold of anything to keep me in the airplane.

After a few desperate moments, the aircraft reduced its angle of climb slightly, and the Sergeant and I were able to pick ourselves up, he from his practiced crouch and I from under the seat braces where I had managed a tenuous last-second hand hold. He moved aft to close the ramp, shutting out the whole event. We both collapsed onto the seats and leaned against the climb angle. Corks bobbing in the wake of the event, we were each coming off the jag from different places when he first looked over at me. His fierce smile was strained, and it quickly faded as though borrowed from some other context. I was still trying to get my breath, and my eyeballs pulsed with heartbeats when he looked back again. We stared at each other for the first time and began to giggle and groan from the relief and the fear and the cold.

When we finally landed at Da Nang, my destination, it was toward the end of the day, and the ramp opened onto long shadows. This was one of the biggest airports in the whole country, but as I waved goodbye to the Sergeant and stepped off the ramp, I saw that we had parked far from the life of the place, off by ourselves on a small concrete ramp near the periphery of the huge complex. Nearby was an open wire fence with brown grass crowding its posts, and beyond it was a sprinkling of squalid houses on sandy soil. Among them stood a few tired palms, motionless in the still tropic air, with clasped fronds bowed. When I came down the ramp I saw that nearby was parked another black C-130, but it was shut up tight, as though sleeping. Behind forested hills far to the west enormous billows of cloud soared upward into the shoreless void, their tops limned out in the declining sun, the high ground lost in their bases, grey and uncertain.

My name was called from a lone jeep parked about forty feet away. I looked over to see a slim figure with crossed arms, leaning casually against the grill with one foot on the bumper. As I approached him, his casual stance, suntanned skin, and faded clothes all combined to make a first impression that left a heavy stone in my mind. He was young, maybe a year or so older than myself, but it was hard to guess his age because, like others with time in-country I had seen, there was something ancient about him, remote in ways unrelated to distance. His appearance suggested a long time spent in the country, and his rain colored eyes carried the signature of loss and sadness. I had the feeling that his calm demeanor was a form of armor, a hand-beaten copper shield alloyed of grim resignation and the secret of death. A wide gulf suddenly yawned between us as the familiar rush of crushing loneliness returned.

Having arrived in the country with a large group of people, I had gradually been processed outward from each center to join ever smaller numbers, until now, all the others winnowed from my uneasy progress, the transportation was being sent for me alone. Were they simply husbanding their manpower, or was this mysterious operation to which I had been assigned so isolated and far from the chain of logistics that I had reached the very end–the last man in the last jeep?

The driver had close-cropped blondish hair, and his faded fatigues, with a wide sweat-soaked V down the front and dark crescents under each arm, showed no hint of name or rank. He canted forward off the bumper and, extending his hand in unconventional military greeting, introduced himself simply as my ride to FOB 4. There was a contained, quiet manner about him, and I liked his frugality with words, although any sign of reassurance would have been welcome. I sensed the same sort of remoteness that enclosed other veterans, that he held something essential within which his outward aspect of serenity masked, not just the ordinary reserve one exhibits to strangers, but something vital at the core of his nature, which had withdrawn to some deep place, there to live without light. His steady grey eyes took me in without apparent judgment, but they contained a strange hollowness, like a cold fireplace with the ashes shoveled out.

"Hop in," he said after a moment, turning toward the driver's side. It seemed somehow appropriate that my escort to this mysterious place would remain nameless. I lifted my duffle into the rear seat and climbed in beside him.

A pair of Phantom jets climbed steeply out nearby, then tilted northwest, their thunder crackling in painful syncope. I watched them go for a moment and wondered about their mission. They always seemed to fly in pairs.

We drove out of the airport and turned into the southern fringes of Da Nang. The city smelled of rot, dust, excrement, and diesel. Many of the buildings seemed to have been skillfully built, but that must have been long ago. Shattered masonry, some of it battle-scared and pocked with holes from a bewildering variety of calibers, stood over a meandering warren of shadowy makeshift hovels and wooden shelters assembled with wire. The place was a fertile, seething cornucopia of squalor. Pressed in upon the streets and staring blankly out at the crowd amid the rancid emanations of late afternoon, it seemed filled with secret murmurings and whispers; and in the wreckage everywhere, the strange dark weeds that always seem to grow in destroyed places.

Once, as we slowed in the polyglot press of pedestrians and trucks, I was startled by a seedy, cackling old man who bounded up to my elbow with malicious glee, his mouth reeking with the sour fumes of rancid fish oil, before dropping back into the throng with a hollow, excoriating laugh. From other faces, brought uncomfortably close by this exposure in an open jeep, came hollow eyes and soulless stares, looks from incomprehensible distances, and I felt upon my back a chilling malevolence that breathed out upon us from the shadows and the spaces between boards. If the eyes are, indeed, the windows of the soul, then I shuddered beneath the scrutiny of minds that, perhaps unable to tolerate the horrors of the present any longer, had retired, not into the surrounding hills, but into the ancient hills of the human past, into the old wilderness of self-preservation.

As we broke free of the city and gathered speed, my driver explained that things had been pretty quiet for the last few months, although a large influx of North Vietnamese regular battalions was known to be filtering into the hills to the west, in preparation for some major action. Nobody knew yet what they were planning, but the build-up was unprecedented, and some analysts expected a series of major attacks to be launched in conjunction with the coming national Tet (New Year) celebrations, as had happened on a limited, but still surprising, scale the year before. The consensus appeared to be that we could expect some sort of probing action soon, but nobody knew precisely where, or in what form, it might come.

It all sounded pretty ominous to me. The word "probing" alone carried such distasteful medical implications that I had no trouble placing its use in context. The whole idea of the North Vietnamese, or the "enemy," or the "VC," was still an abstraction for me, despite my three years beneath its shadow in the military and the constant efforts of the media to personify the terms as the embodiment of evil. I had no idea what the driver's information actually meant nor anything but pure imagination to connect any of it with my own private little life, yet I felt that to ask would reveal my ignorance and therefore, by extension, my unease, so I nodded thoughtfully and tried to put on a knowing expression.

We drove southward along a broken two-lane road that the driver explained was Highway 1, the rough shriveled artery running more or less north and south for the 400 mile length of this fraught and bifurcated country. I had heard of Highway One. "The Street of Tears" or "Street Without Joy," which was probably the more literal translation, but it wasn't a highway as Americans think of them. It was a ruptured tarmac thoroughfare, whose meandering progress along the sandy plain of coastland in this area was subject to hard use by heavy military equipment. Its shoulders slouched in wavy layers where the weight of loaded trucks and wheeled artillery had pressed its tarred coating, softened by relentless sun, outward toward the edges, like the folds in a pudding. Its potholes were deep and elongated by almost constant traffic, yet here and there, sections of old concrete curbing appeared along the sandy verge or peeked out from under the tar, lending forlorn testimony to its original construction by the hands of French engineers.

Our tires thrummed along the corrugations left by tracked vehicles as we passed one large American compound after another. Miles of tangled and rusted barbed wire, interlaced and piled high upon itself, surrounded storage depots, warehouses, tented field hospitals, motor pools, and engineer battalions whose outbuildings and jumbled perimeters frowned at one another with sullen purpose. We passed brightly colored signs which identified with cheerful irony and boastful slogans the entrance gates of construction units, supply depots, communications installations, and helicopter wings.

On the left side of the road, the open spaces declined gradually to a wide beach, where the sparkled blue South China Sea broke in measured riffles against the white sand. On the right side, trapped in waves of hallucinatory heat between the foreign construction, open sections of graded sand dunes, isolated and arbitrary, glared painfully in the bright sunlight, their slopes delicately scalloped by the searing on-shore breeze that carried off their tops like the spume from sea swells, the fraily shaped ledges at their backs shelving into the impenetrable prehistoric wilderness.

At one time, I glimpsed reminders that the whole area had been a broad crescent beach that stretched for miles along the coast, sweeping several hundred yards inland, before it disappeared beneath the dark tangled wall of jungle, but it had long since been expanded, bulldozed, bunkered, and wired into a gigantic suburb of industrial enclosures, all dedicated to the support of warfare, and subdivided according to specialties that had not even existed when the road was first built.

As we drove farther out of the city, the American presence became more scattered, more rural, each compound isolated within its own perimeter and therefore more starkly alone against the open landscape. I guessed that the purpose of this separation was to use the unobstructed furnace of sand for defensive fields of fire. It appeared that the location of these installations made a compromise between the advantages of open ground and those of closer proximity to immediate support.

We passed a modern hospital, four stories high, built on the beach in the center of a large treeless area. It had a single strand of barbed wire coiled like an expanded Slinky around it at some remove from the walls. Compared to the compounds we had passed, it was almost comically insecure, with a token perimeter that even an amateur insurrectionist could have walked through effortlessly. The building looked new, with fresh paint and large unprotected glass windows.

It bore a German name, written in tall Gothic letters painted in bright green across the facade in the manner of old European store fronts, which made the place stand out as such a cultural anomaly that I asked about it. The driver said it was a German hospital, just like it said, built and run for Vietnamese children by an order of Catholic women, and that they were not going to let a little thing like a shooting war interfere with their calling. Suddenly, its quaint display of barbed wire seemed less a naive deterrent than a deliberate snub–a calculated announcement to the rest of us who had moved in around them with our multi-billion dollar investment, our mobilized technology, and perpetual aircraft, that they were not going to play the game.

I looked back and watched it recede, defiant, ironic, and still as a Victorian photograph. I felt as though a nun had just given me the finger. In any other circumstance, I might have smiled at the paradox.

After swerving around broken pavement and dodging oncoming trucks that sped past us filled with sound and unknown purpose, the driver said, "There it is," in the manner of a man glad to be home. I looked ahead in the direction of his indistinct gesture.

On the left side of the road, a few hundred yards ahead, was an open compound containing a few unremarkable plywood buildings and one conspicuously large corrugated steel warehouse, all surrounded by a triple pile of razor wire, with wooden watch towers every fifty yards or so along its perimeter. There was no sign above the entrance, which was little more than a gap in the wire beside a tiny slouching guard shack covered with fine red dust. Here, after thousands of miles and halfway around the earth, was the place my cryptic orders referred to as "FOB 4." It was certainly unobtrusive for a place that engendered such a rich glossary of subtle reactions back at Headquarters.

The jumbled coils of perimeter wire followed the undulating contour of the sand all the way from the edge of the road out to the beach. There was, however, a singularly surprising feature. The camp was located at the very base of an extraordinary stone mountain which rose abruptly out of the ground, like the fantasy landscapes on Chinese scrolls. With small trees and scattered vegetation trapped on its ledges, it soared some two hundred feet above the buildings within the camp. The geology was striking, even spectacular, but I wondered at locating an installation—particularly one darkly rumored to be so important—at the foot of any terrain from which explosives could be so easily launched down into it.

Again I realized I still didn't know what FOB 4 did, nor even what the initials stood for. I had heard oblique references to our northernmost long-range reconnaissance base, and even that it had hidden ties to the CIA, but no one had explained it to me, and now that I was finally here, my ignorance felt uncomfortably magnified by what appeared to be degrees of artifice: the absence of unit identification at the gate; the simple, porous perimeter of barbed wire; the ominous proximity of the mountain. All this combined to deliver an initial impression of ordinariness, of mundane, unimportant activity deserving of no special defenses–odd for an outpost with a reputation of any kind. What was this place anyway? How had the central meaning of FOB 4 become lost in the jumble of military acronyms and spook speak that appeared like dropped stones in my short and guarded briefings and which had grown like a dark fungus among the roots of rumor in Nha Trang? Had I missed something I might actually have been told?

Naturally reticent by nature, particularly where levels of information equaled levels of dread, I must have missed a moment when I might have asked; or had the coded nature of my orders been so intimidatingly officious that I had somehow assumed the meanings of relevant abbreviations would become clear as I progressed through the tentacles of the bureaucratic octopus toward this final posting? I couldn't even remember.

Well, here it was, without sanctifying isolation, without even a secure perimeter, and it was too late to reveal my ignorance, as there would not be time enough to recover from whatever ill effects such questions were likely to have on my arrival. Since I didn't dare ask what the name of the place meant, I tried to load my words with tactical insight by observing, "That mountain seems kinda close," but my voice came out hitched to a squeak, presenting my words on a doily.

My companion told me that it was locally known as Marble Mountain and that it frequently served as a refuge for the Vietcong, who, after local forays and sabotage actions, would disguise themselves with shaven heads and the colorful robes of Buddhist monks, to hide in the many caves that honeycombed the interior of the huge rock. When I asked why we tolerated it, he told me that it was a mountain sacred to the Buddhists, with ancient pagodas carved within it, and that any attack on the place had to come with permission from the Saigon government. He further informed me that of course this policy was a joke generally acknowledged by everyone, since besides the fact that permission to go in there was never given, the bureaucratic delay in transmission and clearance from some distant air-conditioned office, literally hundreds of miles from any strategic relevance, made of any tactical urgency a cruel absurdity.

"Well, that sounds pretty stupid," I said, hoping that it sounded like a suggestion. Though his eyes measured the irony, his mouth hardened, and he muttered, "Welcome to the 'Nam, man," as he turned the wheel, and we swung through the gate, bucking over a grate of pipes that served as a cow guard by the entrance. He gestured acknowledgment to two dusty Asian soldiers as we slowed past the guard shack. While I wondered why the place needed a cow guard, the narrow black eyes if the men who waved us through regarded us steadily with malignant suspicion.

We headed toward the beach along the northern perimeter, driving fast beside the strands of wire in an effort to keep ahead of the enormous cloud of red dust the jeep generated from the fine-grained earth. We passed a large helipad on the right, paved with cracked tarmac. In the middle of it sat two old Sikorsky S-1s, their long rotor blades drooping like the wings of tired dragonflies, their subdued paint chipped and faded. I looked at them only briefly in my effort to take in this new place, but at a glance they appeared to be surprisingly primitive technology.

As we approached the first of the buildings, I looked up at the open watchtowers and was a bit disconcerted to see that each seemed to be manned by Asians. When I asked about that, the driver said, "Nungs. Chinese mercenaries. That's what we work with here. Some of 'em aren't bad."

That last comment stirred my doubts about the place. As I continued to take in the watchtowers and the looming presence of the strange mountain, he steered into the narrow shadow of an anonymous-looking plywood building and flipped the kill switch a second early so that the engine sighed into silence just as we stopped. He leaped easily out of the Jeep as though glad to be shed of the assignment.

"This is Admin," he said tonelessly, crossing behind the jeep. "We'll get you signed in, and you can meet the CO."

I followed him into the narrow entrance corridor, there to surrender the bottom copy of my orders at last.

8

The Colonel was a small man with nervous hands, which clasped and unclasped each other like desperate lovers. His watery blue eyes, busy in a web of deep tan lines, hurried over me without taking in the information. He seemed deeply fatigued and distracted. A little shorter than I, he held himself erect, which may have resulted from a combination of military habit and the subconscious effort to disguise the fact that he carried some weight in the haunch.

The pinched declivity of his worn face was slightly reminiscent of a rat in a fable. I was to learn there was disillusioned ambition there, barely concealed behind a practiced facade of impassivity, and a heavily egocentric outlook on the world, along with a gyroscopic intelligence, aimed at providing the navigational fixes required for the climb up humanity's pile.

I was presented to him, and he greeted me with complicated grace. Over the course of the next few weeks, I would be presented to him again with precisely the same results, despite the limited and highly specialized security elite of the camp. That was understandable, though, considering that our subsequent encounter would follow an event that could have supplanted a lot of preceding memory. Each subsequent encounter over the ensuing months would apparently be for the first time. After a while, a kind of shadow passed across his face, as though he were trying to place me.

I was assigned a temporary bunk in one of four identical frame buildings that stood abreast in the middle of the camp. The room, which served as a transit barrack for four men at a time, contained two double bunks with upper and lower berths. The high quality of the beds surprised me. They were solidly constructed and held well-made civilian type mattresses, not the roll-up stuffing pads I had grown to expect. It was evident that two of the beds were taken, so I dropped my gear onto a vacant lower to lay claim to it, and decided to go out and have a look around the camp. With eleven months remaining on my enlistment, I was curious about the place that would be, one way or the other, my home for the balance of my time in the military.

The house itself was sectioned and faced with plywood, painted a palesome color within, and stood on a poured concrete floor. It contained some eight rooms facing each other across a central corridor that opened to the outside at each end of the structure. My room formed the southwest corner, with windows opening in two directions. Just outside, a duckboard walkway led to a separate building about twenty feet away which contained a sizable bathroom facility with hot and cold running water and showers. Most convenient.

The opposite end of the house faced east toward the sea across a large open quadrangle of loose, sunbaked sand that comprised the center of the compound. From the east threshold you could see all the way down the spine of the camp to the sagging tiers of sandbags which topped the dunes and formed the highest level of the perimeter along the beach. The South China Sea lay tranquil and blue beyond, where a flat horizon stood against the sky in sharp contrast to the haphazard ramble of our defenses.

A long duckboard pier undulated along the hot sand down the center of the camp, leading from the area of my building toward the eastern end of the compound, where I would learn the mysterious reconnaissance team leaders lived near the beach in a line of small huts called "hootches." These were constructed of plywood with corrugated metal roofs that glared painfully bright in the sun, and were faced all around with seven-foot banquettes of weathered sandbags.

Nearby, on the left, was a curious sandbagged structure defiladed into the ground and topped with a hedgehog of long-range antennas. Low, and contoured by wind-blown sand which had accumulated on the piled bags in a scalloped calico, it lay humped and silent behind high chain-link fencing–the only part of the camp so protected. This was the Tactical Operations Center, the "TOC," a highly secure communications center. Though I knew what the letters stood for, at the time I could only guess at its real purpose. Its appearance hinted ominously of the reports about FOB 4. Both the size and array of antennas were too grandiose for a humble pile of sandbags. I began to see that extremely long range missions were probably being directed from this place.

Soon I would learn that some 8 to 10 men worked in the TOC–radio operators, code clerks, translators, and intelligence analysts, whose job it was to make sense of the mix of reports, photographs, and stolen artifacts supplied by spies and recon teams. Reports sometimes came in via radio in various stages of cryptography, by face-to-face meetings with U.S. operatives, and by "dead drops" in tree hollows, walls, and bridges–even in foreign ports.

About halfway along the boards, the camp messhall, painted an incongruous shallow-water green, dominated the ground on the right, and the camp's clubhouse, with its welcome refrigerators, hunkered in a sandy hollow across open ground on the left. Beyond the end of the boards, the area of the Recon teams also contained a large messhall for the Nungs (South Chinese mercenaries) and a series of platoon-sized tents, where some of the Nungs slept more or less in the open, as well as a few plywood barrack buildings, all interconnected by a meandering umbilical of duckboards.

I nosed into the clubhouse, where a lighted jukebox was thumping out Jeanie C. Riley's yelping delivery of "Ode to Billy Joe" with its odd clunking accompaniment. The room contained a large electric cooler in one corner and a curved wooden bar, with a few tables surrounded by government-issue metal chairs. It smelled, not surprisingly, of stale beer.

I nodded a tentative greeting to a few deeply tanned, sun-dried people who glanced back without speaking. The essential remoteness of all veterans I had met since arriving in country served to create a gulf of esoteric knowledge that separated us. I had landed in a new kind of brotherhood. Here an immensely intricate and arcane tribal life functioned beneath the surface requirements for mutual defense— one born of some hidden imperative—in which custom and tiny gestures were foreordained and vital. The enigma was evident even in the words of cautious welcome I received. It made me feel like a child pressing my face against the cold unyielding pane of adult knowingness.

After I returned to my room, a cadre Sergeant came and directed me to Supply for the purpose of completing my check-in and drawing additional gear. The supply depot, which stood about sixty yards west of my interim bunkhouse, was the most conspicuous building in the camp, both for its large size and its shiny corrugated steel siding. Besides a store of field equipment needed for long-range operations by small teams, and tons of freeze-dried LRRP (Long Range Reconnaissance Patrol) rations, it contained a variety of exotic electronic interdiction devices, both passive in the form of specialized radios, and active in the form of explosives, a stockpile of replacement clothing, both Chinese and American, and a sizable collection of captured Soviet- and Chinese- made weapons.

I was issued my basic combat equipment–clothing, web gear, one jungle hat, an extra pair of boots, insect repellant, and first aid kit containing bandaging, an assortment of different colored pills with their instruction sheet, and a half dozen or so little syrettes, each containing ¼ grain of morphine sulfate–along with some unconventional items, unique to the kinds of operations being run from this place: binoculars, a pocket camera, a coil of green rappelling rope and carabiner; a map case, two kinds of combat knives, a miniature signal flare pen gun with a dozen cartridges, penlight and strobe light, signal mirror, one each, and a day-glow orange panel, supposedly visible from the air. I was issued a black nylon windbreaker, a roll of muted green duct tape, two sticks of grease paint in different shades, and one of the most important items of all, an AN/URC-10 survival radio.

Most of this gear was brand new, but a few things had clearly seen hard use, and I found myself handling these with reservation, as though the previous owner's fatal energy might somehow be attached to them the way it is said that ghosts can impart a psychic sensibility to things. So it was with a rush of apprehension that I added each used item to the pile, unreasonably superstitious of somehow contaminating my own fortunes.

Besides a .45 cal. automatic pistol that was permanently issued in my name, I signed for a temporarily-issued M-1 carbine of WW II vintage, which was supposed to serve my needs until such time as a modern CAR-15 (Collapsible Automatic Rifle) could be obtained. I liked the little M-1 and had a good deal of experience with it over the previous few years. It was the primary weapon of U.S. foreign aid and had worked dependably for years, but it was no match for what the bad guys were using in accuracy, range, or rate of fire. I was anxious to replace it with a CAR for these purely practical reasons, and the Supply Sergeant assured me that one would be available in a few days.

Then I was shown a list of code words to choose from for the purpose of assigning all the equipment and was told that it would be my operational cover name while in-country. As I perused the list of names spaced down the page on the Sergeant's clipboard, I was again seized with a morbid disquiet. There was something disconcerting about even needing a code name. I had never been faced with the issue of selecting a name for myself. It presented a dilemma with something like ethical or moral implications. Besides, there was the question of what had happened to the men before me that these names should be available. I didn't want any tag that might be tinged with misfortune. If I had to do it, I wanted something lucky, something that had brought its previous owner through–a word, if possible, which held good fortune in the very shape of the letters.

I could see on the page where information had been erased under each name. Something was simply rubbed out, and a person was gone.

"What happened to these guys?" I heard myself ask.

The Sergeant looked quizzically at me for just a moment, and then, with a ghost of a smile at the corner of his mouth, said pleasantly,

"They're gone." Then, perhaps sensing my dilemma, he pointed to a name and added, "He was a good guy."

I looked at the word he indicated: Alkali.

"Alkali, eh?" I said aloud, testing the sound of it. The Sergeant was waiting. He had given me a hint. Maybe it counted for something that its previous owner had been a "good guy." The word might be difficult to make out in a bad radio transmission, but it did present an interesting symmetry on the page.

"...OK. Fair enough. Alkali," I said with forced resolve, hoping it made up for my hesitation; and so, for better or for worse, I became "Alkali," a word that has forever since leapt out at me from any context.

Despite the fact that I had seen no one in the area wearing a steel helmet, and that we had not used them in RECONDO training, I was issued one. He tossed it to me across the counter. Its faded camouflage cover still held long, hot days of sunlight trapped in the fabric, and the leather sweatband inside was seasoned up all black and greasy. It was probably more alive than the man who had last worn it, and it gave me an eerie feeling to hold it. I was glad when the Sergeant dropped a new sweatband and cover on my pile of issue, but when I got the equipment back to my room, I left the helmet under the bed and sneaked away from it, somewhat furtive and ashamed, a little afraid someone would see it and call after me, "Hey, numbnuts, you forgot something..."

There was to be a movie shown that night, and looking forward to the entertainment, I walked down the long sand pier to the club. A drink before dinner and just enough time after the meal to clean the carbine before the movie started seemed a good plan for my first evening in camp.

The day was darkening rapidly as I trudged past the high fence surrounding the TOC. A beaming vestige of sunlight lingered behind me, while far off toward the mountains, a western strip of overcast sky was muttering softly. The air was remarkably clear that evening, freeing the light and causing long darts of purple shadow to spring eastward from tiny irregularities in the ground. Even the occasional sand pebbles and crumbs of soil reposing on the boards sent their miniature semaphore toward the sea, from where a cooling onshore breeze carried the slap and hiss of waves upon the beach just beyond our eastern perimeter. It also carried the sounds of the club house juke box. I arrived at the club, stepped inside and began to move into the life of FOB 4.

The single room was crowded and surprisingly full of U.S. Marines visiting from a neighboring unit, which I was later to learn was the Third Marine Amtrac Division. They weren't allowed to drink on their own home base, and word was abroad that one of the first things a Special Forces Group installs is a generator to run cooling units. Besides the obvious benefits to food and the preservation of medical supplies provided by refrigeration, the implications that cold beer held for morale was irresistible to our neighbors, and they proved to be frequent visitors.

Buffalo Springfield's "For What It's Worth" blared from the jukebox, but the familiar metallic guitar and haunting lyrics, *"Somethin's happenin' here, and what it is ain't exac'ly clear..."* took on a disarming spookiness in this new place. The smoky air was full of loud banter, if a somewhat anxious camaraderie, whose occasional outbursts seemed somehow veiled by the odd air of remoteness that people often retain for a time after periods of intense emotion–or brushes with fate. All ranks were there, mixed in easy company. I glimpsed the Colonel through the standing crowd, responding to some joke with a controlled belly laugh, followed by a small, closing cough of feigned detachment.

But I quickly grew uncomfortable in the noise as I realized that if something threatening happened outside, not only would I be unable to hear it, I was almost at the opposite end of the compound from my weapon. I left the club and walked the few dozen yards to the messhall, where, at least away from the racket of music and talk, I took a seat at one of the community tables and enjoyed a hot meal that included, to my surprise, fresh milk and ice cream.

I remarked about the quality of the food to a guy nearby. He made a small noise through his nose and said,

"Yeah. The Mess Sergeant is a world-class scrounger. He's worked out this deal with an Air Force Supply guy. In exchange for some of our captured Viet Cong stuff, he goes out to the airport and backs up to the transports in a borrowed Air Force deuce-and-a-half and loads up with steaks, milk, booze, even ice cream."

I began to see that little happened exactly according to the book in a combat zone and resolved to feel entitled to a share in the superiority of our mess Sergeant if ever I found myself in a conversation on the subject with lesser men. After a dessert of vanilla ice cream and sliced peaches, I hurried back to my room, feeling that the duty in this place might hold at least a certain meretricious appeal.

I sat on the bunk and began disassembling the M-1. As I began to oil the parts, I felt that I had been flung about as far from the popular tenets of contemporary life as a person could get; how distant the world seemed, and how seamlessly I had come to be in harm's way. All I owned by which to be identified had come down to the specialized tools of combat operations. If anything happened to me, I would be defined entirely by a worn legacy of camouflaged web gear, a bayonet, a few hand grenades, and a rifle's serial number–whichever of these objects might remain. The roster of my assets sounded like a requiem.

When I was partly through the reassembly of the weapon, one of the other guys assigned to the room came down the corridor and leaned in to say that the movie was about to start. He didn't know what it was but evidently felt a kind of proprietorship concerning it, as he had flown in on the same chopper that delivered it the day before. I decided the carbine could wait until first thing in the morning, or at least until after the film, and I shoved a cloth containing the half-cleaned parts under the bunk, and with them, my earlier reservations about camp security. After all, it was clear that the unit had been operating here for quite some time, and the crusty old Colonel, despite his strange manner, didn't seem the sort who had made his rank at desk jobs.

Outside the messhall, a large U.S. Navy flood lamp was mounted atop a small shed used for projecting the movie against a clear space between the windows on the side of the building. In its bright pool of light a knot of people moved about, setting up chairs carried from the messhall or seeking a place to sit in the sand. The Americans brought drinks from the club, and their shadows, along with those of the insects diving at the bulb, swung enormously across the wall of the mess building as they set the chairs and positioned themselves for the show.

The Chinese squatted together oriental fashion on the dusty sand, down front near the "screen."

As I approached, it became evident that the whole concentration of people, as well as the projection shed itself, was visible from over the messhall roof to many points up the face of Marble Mountain and its alleged caves. Yet the easy movements of the men around the shed, the cheerful murmur of conversation, and the many glowing ciga-rettes, lent the gathering the nature of a casual and familiar ritual in the flood-lit open. I took this as further evidence that, appearances to the contrary, the camp enjoyed a degree of established security, and I relaxed at the prospect of enjoying the outdoor "theater."

Shortly after the film began, a few distant rifle shots cracked from the darkness high up on the mountain, and as the bullets whined past overhead, I ducked instinctively, tucking my head into my shoul-ders and realized with a start that we were being shot at. I crouched, searching the darkness for some cover, but nobody else seemed to pay it any mind. I asked someone about it and was told that the shooting was customary, but that nobody wanted to go up and eliminate this particular sniper, because he was a dependably poor shot and might be replaced by someone much better. Some thought he wasn't really try-ing. Nevertheless, it was disconcerting, and I half-watched with grow-ing discomfort the opening images of the film move across the wall.

The movie itself was disturbing. It turned out to be Truman Capote's "In Cold Blood." I couldn't understand why the Special Ser-vices people would circulate such a story of pointless violence to men who presumably needed an escape from it. Where shortly before I had begun to feel that conditions offered by this camp might be bearable, I turned away from the film and went back to my room, feeling hollow and nagged by a vague foreboding.

Two other men assigned to my room were on their bunks, trying to sleep, so I did not turn on the light and decided again to postpone reassembling my carbine until the morning. Across from my bunk, a Captain who had just arrived was stretched out on the lower bunk. He was a Ranger and had seen the Ranger tab on the sleeve of one of my shirts, so we spoke briefly, whispering our introductions and thereby acknowledging the unconventional training we had in common. He was old to the Army but, like me, brand new to the country and also like me, visibly uneasy. I felt that in a conversation born of loneliness, he was a little surprised to find that the first person with whom he had encountered much in common was a Sergeant.

He was a pleasant man, soft spoken, large in stature and good-looking, like a football player in a college brochure. I learned that he had left his family in Georgia just the week before. It was unusual for a field grade officer, an O-3, to be so open with his personal feelings, and I appreciated it not only for his honesty, but also because it affirmed my own profound disquiet. I had the feeling that we each took some small comfort in the other's presence. By the time I went out to take a shower, his words had helped me feel that at least my apprehension was shared, and that made me feel a little less alone in my featureless but growing dread.

When I came back into the room, I kicked off my rubber shower slippers and left them on the floor next to my duffel, and as quietly as possible, wearing only my skivvies, climbed into the bunk. It had been a long day filled with compounding anxieties, and I lay there for a while listening to the night sounds and wondering what job I might be assigned to do in this strange camp with its indistinct reputation. I thought that if my assignment permitted, it might be fun to go down and walk on the beach at some point in the morning. Soon though, in the later stages of exhaustion, there was no imaging, no dreaming, just a low succession of diminishing biological events. The night leaked its heat, while in the jungle beyond our southern perimeter an infinite army of insects sighed in mournful poignancy.

The first explosions flashed on my eyelids at what was later determined to be about 2:00 AM. The ground shuddered repeatedly at that instant. I sprang awake with my heart in my throat. The two other enlisted men in the room leapt out of bed and into the center of the room in an instantaneous contagion of shock. For one frozen moment, I heard only hoarse breathing and bare feet. Then, somewhere outside in the distance someone was yelling "In-comiiiing! In-comiiing!," the voice faltering with running.

"HOLY SHIT! LOOK! THEY'RE INSIDE!" screamed the guy who had been in the bunk over mine. They both grabbed their rifles and pistol belts and ran from the room, just as an enormous explosion went off immediately outside, blowing in our west window, and sending splinters, shrapnel, and bits of pulverized concrete clattering into the room. In its flash the shower building next door burst into flames. The air filled immediately with dust and the smell of cordite along with the anomalous odor of plowed earth. Deafening gunfire erupted everywhere, as shots fired from inside answered the more distant rattle from every direction outside.

In the flickering light of growing flames, I saw chunks of concrete and a bundled sheet on the floor. There the Ranger Captain knelt on his hands and knees, swinging his head back and forth, like a lost animal. I threw myself onto the floor and instinctively pulled the heavy mattress over me. A second later, something from outside bashed at the window screen just above my head. I looked up to see the blackened butt of a Chi-com AK-47 break through the screen, and a satchel charge with its fuse spitting red sparks tumbled into the room through the tear. It landed on the floor between the Captain and me.

"Get under the mattress!" I yelled and ducked my head.

In the next second the whole room flashed with the force of a tremendous detonation. The floor convulsed. My brain reeled as I felt the pressure wave, laden with metal particles, slam into the padding, and there was a sudden splash of sharp stinging in my bare feet.

Automatic rifle fire erupted through the plywood walls as splinters spun into the room and bullets cracked through the air from several directions at once in a horrifying and continuous exchange. Someone in the hallway just outside the room started blazing through magazines on full automatic and babbling curses in a frenzy of anger. In the momentary lulls, I heard empty casings clattering against a wall and onto the floor.

Suddenly, the room itself began to catch fire as hot fragments imbedded in the walls ignited. The Captain seemed to call out, but in the confusion of shouting and shooting, I couldn't understand what he was trying to say. A few rounds spit through the walls and dropped, spent and misshapen lead pellets in puzzling improbability, on the concrete floor.

I couldn't sort out the enormity of what was happening. Nothing made sense, and I could not think of what to do. With flames now springing in the room, it at last began to occur to me that anyone outside the house could see movement on the inside, and I realized that we had to get out of there. I pushed off the shattered and smoldering mattress and began to low-crawl over the hot fragments toward the door. The Captain kept calling incoherently, still on his knees in the middle of the room with one arm extended, now holding a Swedish K submachine gun.

Without conscious motive, I turned and crawled back to find him lunging feebly with his upper body, trying to get onto his feet. His skin shone wet in the fire light, but then I saw with horror that his entire back and legs had been blown open. Where his back had been was a jellied mass of exploded viscera, the flayed skin black and hanging in slimy tatters from his sides. Sections of his exposed ribs quivered with the muscular effort to move toward me. I couldn't believe what I was seeing. He continued reaching out with his weapon, like a man drowning. Was he offering it to me, or did he need me to pull him to safety with it?

I grabbed it and began to pull. He had it in a remarkable grip. As we struggled in the eerie flicker of the burning room, I realized that he was too heavy for me to drag free. I began to feel the real heat of the flames on my back and tried to get a better grip by grasping the man's wrist, but his skin was too slippery. When I reached over to pull with my other hand, much of the blood-slick skin of his forearm came off, and I fell back on the floor stunned and terrified, staring in disbelief over the heaving rack of my chest at a scene splattered with thick gobs of black blood, now running down the torn walls, carrying strings of meat and soapy white lumps. A slick, sebaceous tissue was strung thinly about in ghastly ribbons. How could this be happening? This was the kind of thing you might read about in a book or see in a film, but oh God, it was happening to me! What do I do? Where do I go?

The Captain fell forward, and I rolled and made for the doorway, leaving him face down in the middle of the burning room, still clutching his weapon. I ducked into the hallway and stood up, dazed and disoriented, ears ringing from the blast, wheezing with heavy pulmonary gasps, my temples pounding with a pressure that made me dizzy. I stood unsteadily for a moment and tried to wipe the gore from my hands, but could only smear the blood on my bare sides and underwear.

Then the shouts and sounds from outside registered again. M-16s were firing scattered bursts from all over the camp. From both close and farther away, their characteristic bark–a single, sharp POW! POW! was distinct. Most were firing on full automatic, where a burst of twenty rounds was gone in seconds: PTTTTTTTOW! They were being answered from everywhere inside the camp by Kalashnikovs, as sappers ran among the buildings. KA-CHOW! KA-CHOW! I knew the sound. The lower-pitched chugging of the Soviet weapons seemed very different from the way they had sounded when we were training on them with analytic detachment in North Carolina. Here, they cracked out in the dark with unmistakable deep-throated dread and chilling power. I stood frozen in an escalation of confusion beyond imagining, my mouth dry, heart racing, all sound strained through a ringing tinnitus, my eyes dazzled with blood-colored after-flashes.

In a few seconds I became aware of repeated puffs of wind on my face and loud popping sounds near my ears. Down the hall in the darkness, barely visible against the flicker of gunfire outside the far end of the hut, a man prone on the floor was shooting out through the front doorway from one of the end rooms, his bursts flashing in the black tunnel of the hallway, the ejected casings rattling emptily onto the floor. The silhouette of his head turned toward me.

"Whose the asshole standing up down there?!" he yelled. "Get down, you dumb fuck, can't you tell they're firing through the building?"

With a shock of comprehension, I dove into the next room and squirmed across the floor, stunned to realize what the popping sounds were. The room was brightly lit and seemed to reel in the exposing glare of a bare light bulb that swung wildly from its loosened wire in the middle of the ceiling. The window had been blown in, casement and all, and lay across the tousled beds. Overturned lockers swayed crazily in the careening shadows. The place had been hurriedly abandoned, and the jumbled bed sheets were smoking from hundreds of little burn holes.

Someone outside ran past the hole in the wall. There was a quick muzzle flash, then a sudden burst of automatic rifle fire tore through the room sending slivers of wood and dust fluttering into the smoky air. In a state of near abject panic in the lighted room, I wedged myself between two steel lockers which still stood near the doorway, but another burst sent me back onto the floor, where I lay breathless and wet with fear on the splinters, amid the bed legs and spilled clothing.

Helicopters began passing low overhead, the roar of the engines and the chatter of the M-60 door guns adding to the sodomy of noise and outcry. The hot downdraft of their passing blew dust and sand in through the open wall as bullets came through the ceiling and empty casings rattled across the roof.

Unable to escape the pendulating light and feeling terribly vulnerable in my underwear, with no weapon to defend myself, I knew I had to find some kind of protection—either solid cover or some kind of firearm, preferably both. With my heart pounding so hard I was afraid it could be heard from outside, I slithered on my stomach back into the open hallway and started squirming in the direction of the room where I knew at least one other American was firing.

The noise of constant shooting was relentless. Hot spent fragments on the floor burned my chest and pattered down on my bare back, stinging as they ricocheted off the walls on both sides. Everywhere, the floor was littered with wood splinters, sharp bits of metal, and hundreds of empty brass casings.

As I dragged myself along the floor toward the end room, bullets from a .30 caliber machine gun emplacement inside the TOC fence about 30 yards away were re-shaping the outline of the door at the end of the hall as though with an invisible axe, and they began splitting through the walls close above my head. The door frame was splintering into spinning fragments. The smell of pine wood came fresh and nostalgic through the smoke.

I became aware of a husky, repetitive and animalistic snorting sound from somewhere nearby—unworldly, chimeric, like the wheezing cry of something broken through a mis-weave in the weft of living things, and terrifyingly close. I knew it was closing on me. In a burst of panic, I leaped from the floor and tumbled into the end room to escape whatever living nightmare was bearing down upon me in the hall.

The room was empty. The guy who had yelled at me was gone. How had I failed to see that? The frightful breathing disappeared beneath a renewed eruption of nearby rifle fire. A deafening explosion detonated just outside in an orange flash. A hot wave of cordite, smoke and dust slammed into the building which lurched, cracking the studs and rafters. It knocked me off my knees. It burned in my eyes and held in my nostrils. Then I heard the adenoidal sound again and realized with a start that the breathing was my own. "Oh God, oh God," the voice repeated. It was the whimper of a little boy.

In the next flash I glimpsed a lone Swedish K, hung with three bandoliers of magazines, leaning in a corner by one of the beds. An image of the weapon registered for only a second in the intermittent light, and I lunged for it, grabbed it up in the darkness and suddenly panicked anew, unable to remember how to cock it. In fumbling them up, I became entangled in the straps of the bandoliers. As I struggled to make my fingers work to sort them, I noticed, with the sudden impatience inanimate objects sometimes show, a .45 automatic lying right in the middle of the bed by the window. It appeared on the blanket as though placed there by the hand of Providence. I snatched it up, and as I tried with sweating hands to cock the slide, a live round flipped out of the ejection port and skittered across the floor.

A sudden movement in the light of the fires outside flicked in my eye, and I looked up to see a dark figure in loin cloth and headband running along the side of the building next door, head down, with a rucksack in his hand. He appeared to look in my direction as he ran and prepared to sling the satchel. I pointed my arm on sheer impulse and squeezed the grip safety. The heavy pistol bucked in my hand as the shot flashed on the window screen, and it spat out a single casing.

The man's forward momentum was instantly converted. He spun around as though nicked by a train. He was thrown back against the other house, and in the next moment his satchel charge exploded. The entire corner of the building where he fell split open in the blast and caved inward. The roof above him lifted up in a shatter of broken boards, and when the hot concussion reached me it blew in the screen. It threw me back from the window onto the floor again, where I landed on my back without the pistol, my ears ringing and my skin stinging from ballistic sand.

My heart pounded violently as I tried to roll over and get my breath. The overdose reached it, robbing it of the next two contractions, clenching it like a fist and making me gasp before easing off, leaving me weak and drained. My mind blanked and splayed with the effort to concentrate, to accept that this hellish concatenation of murder and confusion was the real thing. My jaw muscles twitched uncontrollably, and it felt like valves were opening and closing in my stomach.

I scrabbled around on the floor feeling for the pistol but couldn't find it. Suddenly the room felt like a trap. The muzzle flash may have revealed my position to someone outside. I struggled with the realization that the shattered doorway might afford me a better chance to see what was going on. The building offered some cover, but bullets were splintering right through the plywood. It was a target in itself. With hands shaking, I managed to seat a long clip into the Swedish submachine gun and pull the charging lever to chamber the first round.

The doorway wasn't attracting the fire it had when the guy was firing from it earlier. What happened to him anyway? I began crawling slowly toward the opening, hugging my windfall "K," and hopelessly trussed in canvas straps. The hoarse breathing returned, and I fought to keep quiet. From the base of the door jamb, I peered outside, where constant rifle fire streaked the night with a bright cat's cradle of green and orange tracers.

I pulled myself forward and looked fearfully around the ruined doorframe into the dreamlike flashing darkness. On the threshold lay a naked man flapping feebly like a fish. Just beyond him in the sand were several dark mounds heaped together, inert, in a tangle of flung limbs.

Wheezing, eyes tearing, I pulled myself a little further along the floor on my elbows to the threshold slab. The naked man was motionless by the time I got my head out the door, his rigid legs splayed across the entrance. Protruding from the mush of his ruined throat was what looked like a torn section of ribbed appliance hose, and from it came a deep gurgling sound and a spray of dark blood. His gory fingers had evidently clawed at the horrible wound in disbelief, and now the dripping hands were frozen near his face in a grotesque parody of surprise. I stared terrified as his shoulders gave a little spasmodic jerk. His body emitted a long, rasping fart and became terribly still. Immediately there came the dark brown effluvium of the freshly slain–a sour, pervasive emanation which was different from anything I'd ever known. Seeing violent death at this range, like smelling it, required no previous experience. I instantly recognized the spastic convulsion and the rattle, which in his case was not loud, but deprecating and conciliatory, almost mannered.

I stared transfixed, death enthralled. Then I began to tremble, then to shake, and to moan again in a voice grainy with fear. Then the back of my throat opened, and I threw up on myself. The rotting puke smell rose above even the cordite, and with a fleeting incongruous detachment, I wondered why our excretions become so loathsome the moment they leave the body.

A loud burst from an AK on full-automatic came from close on my right, yanking me back. Instinctively, I half-rolled to the left and twisted, sliding my left arm through the slurry of vomit, to clear the K's magazine from the broken doorframe. I brought the little gun up just as a short, dark figure in black pajamas, muted with duct tape around his legs, came running full speed around the building, swinging a taped satchel. In utter panic, I fired a long, misdirected burst, which chipped a succession of shivers out of the house before I could move the chattering barrel out far enough to stop him. Then the deflected trajectory stitched him up the front, lifting him off his feet and throwing him back with astonishing force, leaving for a moment his splayed image suspended against the sky.

In those seconds the clip was empty. The weapon's sudden silence panicked me, as my finger was still hard on the trigger. I thought it must have jammed and began looking around desperately among the bodies for something else to shoot with, before coming to grips with the need just to reload. At least the ammunition was well-spent. Twisting around in my binding of bandolier straps, I fumbled another clip out of its canvas pocket and into the smoking recess at the base of the receiver, trying hard to concentrate on making my fingers perform the right movements and knowing that I had become a thing of tears and trembling.

The machine gun in the TOC compound was still covering the doorway in which I lay, and now it started up again with a withering tracery of fire that continued to shred pieces out of the wall just above my head, scattering scraps of wood over me. How did a machine gun get inside the TOC wire, firing into the camp? The gun must have already been in place when the first mortar rounds began to fall into the camp, as the bodies scattered around my position attested. I was desperate to get away from the concentrated fire but too terrified to move. I cowered there on the floor in a catatonic seizure of indecision, afraid to stay where so many men had been hit but unable to expose myself in any effort to take action before the nameless and terrifying aggressor outside.

Across the camp's open center, off to my right front about 40 yards away, a small group of Americans was engaging the sappers in the TOC from behind a berm of sandbags around a mortar pit near the center of the compound, and their exchange of tracer fire interlaced across the scene before me in incandescent streaks of orange and green. Every few moments one of the Americans, a tall man I thought I recognized from my visit to the club, stood up and threw a hand grenade, M-33s by the sound of them, across at the knot of intruders serving the machine gun. It was an extremely long shot, and he wasn't making the distance, though each throw seemed to get closer than the last, falling only yards short, sometimes bouncing off the chain link fencing of the TOC enclosure, to explode more or less harmlessly on open ground. In the flash of each detonation I could see the dark figures inside the TOC fence duck and scramble to swing their gun away from me in response.

During one of these exchanges, on blind impulse I scuttled across the dead man's legs and tried to flatten myself in the sand behind two of the dead bodies which had fallen together just beyond the concrete threshold. Away from the concentration of fire on the doorway at last, and burrowed head down, I could not tell if they had seen me from the TOC, and afraid that the muzzle flash would give away my position in case they hadn't, I was afraid to return any shots.

I thought that my survival depended on finding cover, and there was only one thing around with which to make some. In desperation, and with the K swinging wildly from the sling around my neck, I jumped up each time the machine gun turned back toward the mortar pit until I managed to drag three of the bodies together in a loose pile, their sprawled, inanimate limbs flaccid and uncooperative. Then, gasping from the effort of hauling their inert weight, I wriggled down in the sand behind them and cringed there, dry-mouthed, tear-sprung and shaking, breathing heavily with my face against the ground, gulping dust-filled clots of air, and prayed just to live out the endless concussive nightmare.

This was nothing like the movies–nothing so contained or organized. None of it made sense. From all directions, shouts and curses filtered through the shooting in a tossed word salad. People yelling warnings, pointing out targets of opportunity, crying, screaming in sudden pain, or swearing at the sheer magnitude of all that was happening, added their voices to those of the weapons.

At some point the mortars ceased to fall into the compound, but I didn't notice when. From somewhere, a voice broke into hysterical howling mixed with shuddering diminuendo groans. From everywhere the patter of fragments crackled against the buildings or scattered dully into the ground. I became used to being hit by them, some of them embedding themselves, burning into me like sparks, others bouncing off.

The roar of several low-flying Hueys began to criss-cross close overhead as they hosed a seemingly endless stream of arcing red tracer into the perimeter wire, while hot clouds of exhaust-laden dust swirled in their downdrafts. Humid, metallic sea-chill and warm vacuums sucked past together. At times the automatic rifle fire from both sides was so intense that it sounded like the continuous tearing of a blanket, and all that flying material in the air made the whole world seem to warble and shudder.

Under close, flat fire, the projectiles whipping in carried no warning, but in passing, some whined, some chirred through the air tonelessly, or sounded like a stick being jerked through water. The same principle governed all these sounds: the projectile's speed created a vacuum into which air rushed to close the gap, but it was all terrifying and relentless. There were times when I thought I could hear strange voices in it, or snatches of instrumental music. Everywhere fragments sang through the air, striking buildings, equipment, and people with abandon. Some pieces fizzled overhead like sparklers, whinnied, or whickered past. Some sighed, and once I heard a horrifying sound like a dog tearing at something. It drove me deeper into the uncanny earth, though my shins were pressed against something painfully hard that could not be fidgeted aside to make room for my legs or to get my feet down without contorting myself.

I don't know how long I waited and trembled there, my ears screaming, my whole being filled with pleadings, scrunched up in that hollow of dead men, every cell in my body shaking me with ravenous yearning for it to be over, for there are no clocks in combat. Time is seamless there. But irony is the attendant of hope, and the fuel of hope is innocence, and my tiny wishes counted for nothing against its ferocious indifference. There was no letup–none of the ebb and flow that battlefield historians talk about. The gates of Hell had slipped their hinges, giving voice and authenticity to the whole panorama of Dante's poetic nightmare, and I wondered if I would be found in the morning whole, or sane.

I was shaken from my twilight of helpless inertia by an enormous detonation and a brilliant flash. The ground shuddered and knocked the wind out of me. There was a heated wave of air, followed by frenzied shouting from the direction of the TOC. I looked over to see that the whole sandbagged bunker was beginning to burn, even as broken timbers and bits of debris were falling back to the ground. Fire leapt from a large hole in the ground where a wall of sandbags collapsed slowly into the orange flames as they rose and licked at the dark gray sky, sending strange phantoms of light and shadow writhing across the unearthly scene. Against its growing light, the enemy were clearly visible, their dark figures scuttling close to the ground like bottom fish.

Evidently aided by the backlight of the fires, the tall American finally began to find the range with his remarkable throwing arm, and his next toss blew a large hole in the chain link fencing, wounding some of the people on the machine gun. Between the fires and the first hint of graying dawn I could clearly see the moving shadows in the gun pit as they began to abandon their positions and to spill out through the opening in the fence, which was peeled back as it would have in a cartoon.

But the gun started up again with alarming fanaticism, giving sweeping cover to the little men who were coming through the ruined section of fence, some of them with their clothes burning. One turned toward me, just as the tall American stood again and threw a high, tumbling lob that came down right on the edge of the gun pit. The bodies of the gunners were blown out in a ragged blossom of yellow light. The man running toward my position dropped, momentarily startled, to one knee. In that instant, I saw the American's slowly-descending throwing arm hit by a bullet in the wrist, and he dropped from sight behind the far sandbags with a faint cry.

I took frantic aim at the dark little rifleman coming at me and opened up when he was about sixty feet away. Again, the first rounds were wild, but they surprised him, and he turned with desperate logic, stumbling as he pivoted. I fired again, the bullets kicking up jets of sand short of his scrambling heels, until the hot spatter found him and packed him with death. He collapsed forward in a heap like a thrown rag doll, hands still at his sides when his head thumped down.

A few survivors from within the fence responded to my shots and sent short rifle bursts toward me, but now, despite my terror of being seen, I was afraid to keep my head down for fear of not being able to see in case one of them rushed me again. Their bullets popped loudly close by my head or smacked into the shielding corpses, sending shivers through them. One of the bodies released a dreadful guttural groan from its open mouth.

As my private exchange with the TOC became a protracted firefight, the cadavers took repeated hits that caused them to twitch and jerk against me. I heard a bone break. At one point a torn, cold arm fell across my shoulder in deathly comradeship. It chilled and angered me, and I began to function in a bad dream state, fueled on the watery residue of exhaustion, and acting out an unfamiliar set of moves without any connection to their source. The space between subject and object disappeared, banged shut in a fast wash of adrenalin as all of life closed in. I had no conception of what was happening elsewhere, no thought or senses to spare for anything but what was happening right before my eyes, and with my throat, nostrils, and lungs burning in the smoke and the risen dust, and half blinded by the effort to blink away the tears, I fired singly and in short bursts at anything that moved near the TOC or in the open area before it, until I ran out of ammunition.

At some point the helicopters left and were replaced by a low flying C-47 that arced around the camp in extremely low orbits, pouring multiple streams of orange tracer all around the perimeter. The bright ribbons of fire hosed back and forth as flashes from the ground action winked along the aircraft's fuselage. We called it "Puff the Magic Dragon," and the spectacle of all that fire power was enough to sell the name.

Gradually, as the pale dawn tried to insinuate itself through the smoke and the dust, shots became sporadic and isolated. There were lulls as they finally died out altogether, and people began to rise hesitantly from cover here and there, blinking in the dim corona of hazy light, their faces pale and vacant, like tourists lost in a foundry.

At last I got painfully onto my knees and looked out upon a scene strewn with corpses, some jumbled together in clumps, others sprawled in amazing postures, many of them burning. Bodies wrenched too fast and violently into unbelievable contortion. I stared, uncomprehending, at the complete impersonality of group death, which left them lying anywhere and any way, hanging over barbed wire or thrown promiscuously on top of each other.

Something wasn't clear about it all, something monitored the images and withheld their essential information. I could not grasp what I was seeing, but from each, the message was the same: "Put yourself in my place."

All around, things were burning, and the air was full of mingling gray and black smoke that drifted close to the ground, occasionally obscuring the scene and carrying the acetyl odor of melting synthetics mixed with the familiar smell of burning wood. There were a few faint pops of isolated rifle fire from somewhere near the southwest corner of the perimeter, and then it was over.

I couldn't stop shivering. I tried to get up, but could not get my legs to work and rolled to look at them. My bare, swollen feet were brown and crusted with bloody sand, like some awful confectioner's glaze. Fresh dark blood seeped from dozens of small entry wounds in my lower legs, and as I watched the steady ooze with numb detachment, trying to place its significance, I was horrified to see a three-inch sliver of fresh bone protruding like a shattered pencil just above my right ankle, skewering the skin. I had not noticed or felt it before and was puzzled as to how it had come to be there. I touched it and realized that it wasn't my own.

Then, with dulled shock, I understood that I was staring at evidence of the Ranger captain's wounds. I reached down, pulled it straight out, and threw it away from me in disgust. Oddly, the childhood expression "icky" came to mind, but that sharp pull awakened my own senses as a crescendo of pain began to come on in a rising fugue of renewed assaults on my consciousness.

I felt a little faint and tried to objectify my comprehension of the sensation solely in terms of damaged synapses. I grasped for comfort in the quaintly scientific thought that if I could feel at all, my system must be working. I stared at my lacerated knees, and with wavering attention, noticed that the skin on the edges of the larger abrasions was dry, gray, and rolled into tiny spindles, like the shavings under a carpenter's bench. Courses of fresh blood from many puncture wounds cut rivulets through the sand which clung to my sweat-damp legs, absorbing the dust. I pulled a piece of sharp metal from the side of my right calf, releasing a new trickle of blood. I found that I had been grazed by two bullets. One had nicked a short furrow in my calf, and the other had been such a close miss that it left a deep purple streak along my ankle.

I still had the Swedish K around my neck by its sling, and I didn't want to let it go. I moved it carefully around to the side and rolled over onto my hands and toes in an effort to get upright and to clear my head, then got to my feet for a gratifying moment and hobbled unsteadily the few steps back to a badly shot-up wooden bench, just by the door to the building some six or seven feet away. My flame-cast shadow loomed up the bullet-pocked façade as I turned and eased onto the splintered seat in a festival of exhaustion.

It hurt to move, and as the fires and the dawn fought over how the shadows would fall, I sat for a long time, looking around at all the dead and listening to the crackling, malicious sound of burning timber, like demons' laughter. I waited for some thought that could explain all that had happened. Unable to summon an emotion worthy of the enormity, I simply sat there devoid of feeling, drained of sentiment, not even consciously grateful for having survived. Gradually, an emptiness opened within me, a hollow void from which the world appeared drained of color and forever changed.

A short distance away, still inside the TOC wire, one of the VC gunners burned brightly. The charcoal body, with its clothing and features gone, sat upright, rocking gently in the flames like a large black baby with one hand reaching. I was stunned, saddened, and confused by the new and excruciating reality, upon which I had exhausted all powers of adjustment. The Inscrutable Immutable was here. The Beast had risen from the heart of my fears to find me in this dreadful place, and I would keep on, or not, at its pitiless discretion. I had floated through the ruinous currents of the night as a dry leaf is swept through rapids, and I was spared simply because the ruin I rode upon was meant for greater things. Yet what I gave up to it I will never get back.

I don't know how long I sat there, stunned, in that grim, gathering dawn. My legs and feet were stinging, and my eyes burned in the acrid black volumes of smoke from dozens of fires that roiled between the buildings. It hugged the ground, moving confusedly this way and that on the conflicting air currents created by the fires. It seemed to be investigating our ruin, before hurrying on with its souvenirs of ash and sparks. The smoke was a frenzied looter, overburdened with armloads of glowing things which continuously spilled from its cinereous grasp and fell back to the ground.

There were a few isolated shots, carried on the heavy-laden breeze as distant pops, but everywhere the harsh crackle of burning served to intensify a pervasive silence. My ears whined a constant "A" note, isolating me in a tinny symphony of lingering echoes. Snapping tongues of flame from the ruins of the TOC fed smoke to the air around me in a swirling variety of shades. Black and brown, which bore the heavy odor of burning plastic; blues and grays, dragging in their veils the familiar smell of wood resins, all mixed with a heady pungency of oil and boiling grease that drifted in from somewhere else. Errant red signal smoke, whipped about in the troubled air, stirred with tendrils of yellow from canisters which must have been thrown to guide the medevac choppers. It all rose together, spreading like a sunset, to mingle with the exhaust of our destruction.

For a time the restless smoke seemed to be the only living thing. Spread before me as far as I could see was the night's harvest of death. Dark heaps lay clumped and sprawled, twisted like collapsed acrobats, and strung from the perimeter wire, across the open areas of the compound, fanning out into scattered points in the distance, and clumped together between the hootches and bunkers. Some were clustered near the corners of buildings, others in the open between the watch towers, where they had evidently cut the wire–places which were surprisingly exposed on open ground in the daylight, but which must have served each group some momentary tactical advantage under the cover of darkness.

I looked down at the shallow hollow where the magazines I had exhausted during the night lay scattered in the sand behind the pitiful shield I had made of my companions and realized how vulnerable a position it had actually been. The night itself had been my only real cover.

Near the TOC, a few of the corpses burned steadily. Others, partially blackened, gave off a dense white smoke, while little demons of flame still danced along their crusty ridges. The sickly sweetness of scorched meat, vaguely reminiscent of home barbeques, began to pervade the air, attended by a subtly different smell, sharp and metallic, which I soon realized was from boiling blood–distinct, abrupt, and insistent.

The human ruin was strewn all the way up to my feet, where a dead American I had not noticed in the night lay upon his back with his hands turned down, embracing the ground. The pale skin was drawn tight over his high cheekbones, giving his triangular face the color of a dirty drumhead. His eyes were closed from the lower lids up, like a bird's, and the grit captured in the folds of his forehead lent him an oddly pensive expression, as though frozen in mid-calculation.

Nearby was the naked man with the awful, fibrous neck wound, whose final throes I had watched a few hours earlier and over whose rigid legs I had scrambled in the dark. His staring eyes were now host to numerous iridescent green flies. As I watched, the insects in his exposed purple gullet were joined by several others, and the aggregation raised the tone of their frenzied buzzing. I quickly looked away, realizing for once and always that the food chain is, despite our linear conditioning, a circle.

Everything looked amazed and broken in the dim morning light, as the sun, hidden in smoke, tried feebly to clear the horizon like a grieving mother approaching uncertainly with her lamp. Yet something remained inaccessible about the whole scene. Battered by a hundred experiences too large for me, I began to feel an ironic calm, a lyrical sort of delirium of anesthetized detachment, which served at least to suppress compassion, and thus may have legitimized my fascination, allowing me to look as long as I wanted; but I could have been staring still, and I wouldn't have been able to accept the confusing margin between a detached limb and the rest of the body, or to reconcile the complete improbability of multiple, violent death, with its load of unlived futures consigned in a single chaotic moment to the ashes of the past. My consciousness seemed to have fled into some deep bunker of the mind where, insubstantial as a ghost, and lacking even the vitality to feel gratitude for having been spared, it now peered out as from armored slits at the wreckage that lay strewn about, bleached of all but a faint remnant of color.

I felt a vague and fleeting shame, as though seeing first porn. All the porn there is. Perhaps it was simply a trick of the mind to maintain threshold levels of shock, to protect itself from falling in the forest without an ear to hear its crash.

For some reason, a refrain from a whiny country song I'd heard in the NCO club at Nha Trang a few days before began to repeat itself endlessly in my brain. *"Our little boy's jest six years old..."* Over and over. It came from nowhere, perhaps carried in the sound of the flies, and became an *idee fixe* for some compartment of the brain which serves, I suppose, to supply captions for unthinkable pictures taken by unbelieving eyes.

Off to my right, in the direction of our southern perimeter and perched on the highest ground in the compound, a wooden water tower was pissing out its contents in ironically graceful arcs from numerous .50 caliber holes. One stream blubbered noisily onto the roof of the camp's only transport bus, which had been parked beneath the tower the evening before. The bus had been shot, too. It seemed to be kneeling where one tire was flat, and its flank was riddled with holes. Those in its windows stared back at me across the littered ground in chilling symmetry. Like crystal cobwebs, their shatter patterns gave eloquent testimony to the violence at their centers, and they stirred within me a disordered confusion of reactions. A set designer could not have placed them to better effect. I stared at the sand and thought about the harsh irony of life imitating art.

There was movement in the doorway over my right shoulder, and I spun with the weapon in a hot rush of spent adrenalin. A tall man stood unsteadily there, framed in the splintered casement. He was dressed in olive drab undershorts and what remained of a soiled t-shirt full of burn holes. It hung from him in tatters. His feet were in unlaced jungle boots, the hair on his pale legs greasy and matted. Over his shoulder, and slung in reverse, was an M-16 with the muzzle pointing down. His jaw was slack and his face was streaked with grey skin, like a diseased sycamore. The event had him, and he had it, and I felt in the instant I saw him all the world's entropy whipping through the backwash of the night in ragged strands of fatigue.

He hesitated, squinting out at the daylight, then tottered a little and blinked. He glanced over at me and through me. No one had ever looked at me that way before. His stare bonded us forever in the eternity of that moment. There were no whites to his eyes. Every capillary in his eyeballs must have exploded during the night, and the crimson-rimmed pupils formed black holes in his face into which poured all the energy from the air between us. A fat drop of sweat began to move down my left side like a spider.

Deeply alone and in silence, the man slowly, ritualistically, shook out a cigarette. With tremulous hands, he managed to ignite it using a worn metal Zippo, and then sort of slobbered it out, and it fell to the ground. He tried again with a fresh cigarette, but his hands were shaking too much for delicate work with a flame, and I rose to help him. I got it lit for him. There was a brief flicker of focus behind his blood-filled eyes, but after a few puffs the cigarette went out, and he let it drop to the ground.

"Las' week, I couldn't even spit…," he mumbled, his voice toneless, too laden with fatigue for any expression, and it seemed to come from a great distance within him. "…an' now I can't fuckin' stop."

I could think of nothing to say and returned to the haven of my bench. In a moment he joined me, wordlessly, and we sat together for some time, connected only by an accident of nationality, and watched the burning TOC before us without speaking; me with my empty Swedish submachine gun, smeared with my own dried blood, across my lap, while he stared without expression into some inner space over the muzzle of his M-16, which wavered slightly between his knees, carrying the tremors of his hands.

There was movement to our right. About 80 feet away, near a small admin office, a few medics and others began dragging dead Americans into a collection point. The corpses were being tagged and stacked like wet cordwood in a slight depression in the sand. The feet were toward us, splayed to all points of the compass, and they jostled together as each body was added to the pile. Some were barefooted, others had managed to get their boots on, and still others had evidently been killed before they could finish pulling on both shoes. Each time a corpse was dropped onto the pile, it made a sound which reminded me of large sacks of chicken feed being piled in an open-air shed, last heard when I was about six years old. Two men approached, dragging a body between them in a blanket. When they tried to fling it onto the pile, the mutilated wreckage of a man that came out just fell apart.

As the dark pile of wasted Western humanity grew, I began to feel something completely new: a sense of belonging to a species, to an integral nationality, to an unprecedentedly privileged People, who, however naive or misguided at times, were nonetheless the indisputable Good Guys. Having grown up out of the country, but with strong family ties in the United States, I had always enjoyed certain sense of objective good fortune about my citizenship but had never really felt anything like conscious, conditioned patriotism. I had consigned such feelings to that realm of simple homey virtues like unconditional loyalty to school chums and scout masters, preached by sheltered academics and unmarried aunts. Yet a sudden line of clear demarcation between "Us" and "Them" was revealed in the silent screams from that pile of dead Americans, and it came with a bonus: The Beast never sleeps. Death is random and cares not for your skills or for your purity of heart.

At length my companion broke our wordless communion by muttering, "Let's get us somethin' to drink." He made a vague gesture toward the club. I tried to say something, but my voice cracked, blanking on the note the way a pen's nib runs suddenly dry, jamming in the rut it makes. I didn't try again and rose stiffly to join him. We stepped around the bodies in front of the bench and began plodding across the sand in the direction of the clubhouse.

As we made our way across the compound, there were many places where the ground could not soak up all that the action had spilled, and we had to watch where we stepped. Bodies, mostly those of the VC, lay scattered about as though dropped from a great height, amazingly broken, most with the clothes tattered and thrown open. Among those in front of the TOC was the little man I had killed as, trapped in the firelight, he had turned to run a lifetime ago. He lay face down now, his arms trailing. The force of the bullets had blown him half out of his trousers, and nestled between the backs of his legs was a long, moist turd covered with flies. Response to impact. The sight left me with strange, conflicting feelings—disgust, renewed fear, relief, and an oddly incurious detachment.

A few of the bodies near his were still burning, and one we passed close by sizzled audibly as it cooked. It was swollen, with crisp black and purple swatches along its sides. There was a large scarlet burst-split across the back, like some evil, over-ripe fruit, from which light wisps of smoke drifted away on the morning air. The wet inner meat was still rare.

Suspended in the wire behind the clubhouse was a Viet Cong sapper who had apparently been caught while hung up in the barbs.

Something was misshapen about the image, though, and I looked again. About half the head was missing, and a pinkish-gray pudding hung out the side of the broken eggshell skull and dribbled down one arm. His AK-47 lay in the sand, its sling snagged in the wire. It was odd to actually see human brains. I suppose I had always considered them as a kind of biological-poetical figment.

When we reached the entrance to the club, my companion preceded me in by several paces. As I lurched in after him, I placed my hand on the door frame to steady myself and noticed there a deep shrapnel scar in the wood. A jagged piece of metal glinted dully in the hole near my fingers, and several strands of blond hair were trapped among the splinters.

Inside, the shadowy little room still held its characteristic smell of spills, and I fastened immediately onto the familiar scent. For a moment it connected me with a fleeting and fragmentary image of my fraternity house at college. Dusty bars of restless orange light lay across the interior, coring out the darkness from several bright bullet holes in the outside walls. Some of the chairs had been hit, but the place had come through the attack with little damage. The silent jukebox, its arching bright colors now muted and dark, seemed to cower against the wall, as though any cheerful note might break the spell and start the shooting again.

I stepped behind the bar, and my nameless companion broke the hasp on the cooler with a few well-aimed down stokes from the butt of his weapon. Mumbling something about the camp's electrical power being off anyway, he lifted the large flat lid, and we both leaned over the dark recess with self-conscious anticipation. Vapor moved inside the cooler like a restless grey cobra guarding its promising depths. We plunged our arms down through it, into the chill, and came up with two Cokes each. The colorful familiarity of the cold red cans felt reassuring. They completed an excruciating nostalgia with home, and for a moment in the shadows there, almost assumed the intensification of religious art as they presented themselves for evidence of our little sin against government property, which, considering the circumstances, seemed morally negligible.

We turned and made our way back through the strewn carnage to our bench, where we sat silently again, not knowing what to do. We sipped at the strange caramel flavor until the sun rose high enough to clear the dunes, and the moving shadow of gray smoke drifting through the broken buildings began to shift direction. The day's heat came on suddenly, and its putrid effect on the dead was almost immediate.

I began to hear an M-16 at a distance, going through clips: a few seconds to fire, ten or so to switch magazines. Gradually the sound grew nearer, and then I saw the guy who was doing it. He was stopping at every VC cadaver and letting go on full-automatic in a kind of self-appointed *coup d'grace*. Each burst was like a tiny concentration of high-velocity wind, causing the bodies to wince and shiver.

Eventually, he worked his way over by us, and I knew my education in the vale of horrors had been incomplete when I saw his face. It was flushed, mottled and contorted, as though he had it on inside out. His eyes were sunken and dark but appeared to be rolled up half into his head. His skin looked mossy and streaked with bands of red running into purple with lines of fish grey in between. He could have been a walking stroke victim. His mouth was sprung open–but he was smiling.

Later, drawn from some reverie by the growing heat, I noticed that my companion with the bloody eyes had gone. I decided to make my way back to the room and put on the shirt I had left hanging on the bed frame. When I tried to get up, I realized that my legs had swollen considerably. It had become difficult to straighten them. Painfully I got to my feet, the effort causing me to gasp in successive shallow gulps with the effort to walk. I hobbled back into the ruined doorway, fighting the nausea which had taken root in the morning's unveiling and which began to attach itself to the awful, deep stinging.

Inside the littered corridor, the morning sun lanced through thousands of bullet holes, and carried on a heady miasma of smoke, its dust laden beams sprinkled the walls and floors with irregular bright petals of light. Moving in silhouette at the far end of the hallway, two guys, clothed in fatigue pants and boots–one in a t-shirt–were stepping carefully through the debris with their weapons at the ready, checking each doorway. One of them stopped at the entrance to my room and said flatly,

"We got one in here."

"Dead?" asked the other, picking his way over to where an inordinate amount of daylight was washing the corridor from the outside.

I joined them, stepping through the doorway, to find myself back outside! The room was gone. That whole corner of the building–ceiling and walls–was missing, completely blown away, its remains scattered about the ground beyond in a fan of ruined lumber. My room had become an empty sleeve. The bed frames stood incongruously alone in the sun, counterpoised against the scene, with the shredded remnants of my shirt still hanging in place.

On the floor slab between the beds was an enormous crimson pool of jellified blood, thick and partially coagulated in the sunshine, like jam. In the midst of this lay what remained of the Ranger Captain, face down, his arm still outstretched, the fingers of his left hand still closed around the Swedish K. His entire back was an indescribable, rubbery dark confusion of exploded viscera and tattered clothing. What was left of the torn body appeared to be about half its living volume. It was wet and surprisingly dark. Bits of cloth and chunks of meat were scattered here and there throughout the deep mass of swirled blood, which along the edges had dried and cracked into a burgundy ceramic. There, floating alone like a toy boat near the far shore of this dreadful pond, was one of my shower slippers, glaring white in the sunlight against the glistening red pudding. The concrete flooring of what had been our room resounded in a soundless echo with the ghastly intimacy of his death.

"My God," murmured a voice near my ear.

The man in the t-shirt said he was a medic and asked if I was ok. I said I thought so and indicated my problem. He crouched to examine my legs, which were now streaked with unfamiliar dark colors and heavily encrusted, as though smeared with cherry pie. They still seeped blood steadily, and though both were increasingly painful, especially the right one, he tried to assure me that the wounds were probably not as bad as they looked, especially in view of the scene before us. I had to agree with him about that.

He stood and quickly looked me all over, surprising me by gently removing several wood splinters from my back. He then filled out a casualty card on me, checking the blood type on my dog tags. He handed me the card, told me to fasten it to myself, and instructed me to go back out near the bench where I had been sitting and to wait there for pick-up by a vehicle that was collecting our walking wounded for transport to a field hospital. He got the shredded remains of my shirt off the bed for me, and then I, feeling somewhat hypocritical in view of what was on the floor at our feet, turned and made my way back toward the ragged rectangle of light at the far end of the cluttered hallway.

Back on my bench, I saw that the dead around the threshold, including those that had served me during the night, had been dragged away, leaving furrows in the soft sand. The pile of dead Americans over by the Admin office was being pulled down, zipped into green rubber bags, and dragged off. I sat very still and tried to contain by gulping at the dingy air the mounting hysteria which had risen like some evil genie from the mess on the floor of my room. In an odd way, I felt I'd known the Captain, bonded somehow by mutual strangeness to this awful place, and now I came to understand the true meaning of "the quick and the dead." After all, I had been there at his terrible initial wounding, and I'd carried a large splinter from one of his bones through my ankle all night. That kind of thing can connect you to people.

A tiny silver-tinted lizard appeared nearby, one moment motionless, testing the air, and in the next, motionless again but elsewhere, after a lightning scuttle too fast for the eye to follow. I watched its occulting dashes, appearing and disappearing at its own caprice like a messenger from the supernatural, challenging me to find its meaning.

I swallowed hard against a rising impulse at the back of my throat, determined not to throw up again, as I saw stretching before me the interminable months of my tour with its implacable laws of average. Time lay heavily ahead in what seemed an endless procession, in withering contrast to the breathtaking spontaneous violence that now I knew was always on call, and for the first time, thoughts of my survival came loaded with the crushing weight of despair. The feeling of hollowness now filled rapidly with profound sadness; and something else–an unfamiliar but incontrovertible and intimate sense of loss, as though some intangible part of myself, some inner reference point, had suddenly vanished.

The feelings rose in forced entry like an unwelcome lodger, as though some parasite was trying to turn out my very being and take up the space within me where the essence of myself once had been. I could feel it lodged against my throat. I wondered how much more I could take emotionally, or survive intact, and I became very afraid that I would crack and run, letting down all the others who might have thought they could count on me.

The casualty tag I had been given fluttered against me, tugging at my attention. It was the same kind they were attaching to the dead, and it lent me a frightening connection with them. Being numerically identified among the casualties seemed to give official sanction to my vulnerability in the whole monstrous enterprise, and this, too, focused my burden of fears. I gripped the bench, trying to feel its reassurance with my fingers, and looked about me, for a while seeing nothing.

The idea that there really were people who actively sought my death was hard to accept. A whole childhood full of government propaganda films and field exercises would never have prepared me for the excruciating realization that I personally, with my small history of benign values and private manner, had somehow become the mark for violent execution by strangers. It was a stunning lesson, taught by inconceivable events, which the great majority of people, bless their hearts, never have to learn in the course of a lifetime of petty social abrasions.

I thought about how often I had heard the expression, "I'll kill you," how frequently we use threatening language in a moment of anger or disapproval; how we entertain ourselves from time to time with vengeful thoughts about those who have offended our sensibilities and who "deserve" all we can think of. Yet even on those occasions when our tormentors might benefit by a certain retribution, in the end, we are only expressing aggression in the abstract–our anger falls short of actual design. But here, the indelible reality of truly murderous intent lay all about me in a smoke-blackened jumble of coagulated dust and human ruin.

Inescapably thrust upon its unwilling participants, it now sought even from me the cost of its indiscriminate will. It had me. The Beast with dripping fangs had come forth and leapt full upon me, and I lay trapped now beneath its weight like a terrified rabbit. The effort to reconcile what I thought I knew of life brought only a lurid *pentimento* of the night's images. The pictures piled up, and I could not get beyond them. Its full dimensions were simply inaccessible to the ideological frameworks that I had inherited, and as I strained against the obstructing arm of civilization itself, I finally came to know only that the long festival of my innocence was over. This sad, insidious epiphany was childhood's end. The thought kept arriving in my brain like a telegram delivered every few minutes, and though it had nothing to offer but its integument, it broke the seal of my mind, which before its coming had seemed an insightful enough instrument, and took from me my spiritual virginity. I waited on that bench, feeling myself drawn irrevocably into a stream of immutable laws which lay beyond my comprehension, and I would rise from it with my view of the world changed forever.

My ride to the hospital came in the form of the only Jeep in camp that could still run. There were oblong bullet tears in the body, one corner of the bumper was bent up slightly, and one of the headlights had been shot out, leaving a dark socket from which its optic ganglia hung in pieces. There was a cluster of five or six bullet holes in the windshield directly in front of the driver. The overall effect of this damage was to give its approach a wry, crooked grin, which sent me a new wave of discomfort. Even the equipment was wounded– but it had a better attitude than mine.

I made my way toward it as the driver pulled up, and I eased gingerly into the right front seat beside him, careful to avoid striking my knee on the rifle rack mounted by the dash. There was one other passenger, who sat in the rear seat, cradling his left arm in a blood stained sleeve and talking incessantly to the driver. The words fell out of him like burdens at last set down, backlogged verbs and nouns of no meaning to me or the driver, who was distracted and watchful but managed dutiful listening noises. We started with a lurch and headed along our perimeter road, past breaks in the wire, as the driver scanned about for others who needed the ride. We saw no others, and as we drove out of the main gate, the wounded man seemed suddenly to swallow some new sentence he was starting and lapsed into an abrupt silence. I felt it too. Exposed now on the public road in an open Jeep, in pain, unarmed, dressed only in my under shorts and what was left of a shredded shirt, a spike of renewed vulnerability flashed through me.

We drove in separate bubbles of wordless introspection back up Highway 1 for about a mile, along the same pavement over which I had been driven, perhaps in this same vehicle, the previous afternoon, long, long ago.

The hospital was a low wooden structure that looked from the outside like a number of huts pushed together. It had a large Red Cross motif on the roof and a couple of helicopter landing pads on the ground about forty or fifty feet from the main entrance. The driver stopped in front and told me to go through the double doors and to show my casualty card to anyone inside.

I thanked him for the ride, but in turning to get out, I struck one knee against the rifle rack. Hyena pain sprang instantly through me. It pulsed in my eyes and robbed me of balance. As I swung my feet out of the Jeep, I felt the ground tilt away. Suddenly, my face was against the earth. I didn't know how it got there. I felt a line of sharp pain above my eyes and wondered for a moment if the sudden metallic taste in my mouth was brains. I was drenched in a cold sweat and trembling so violently I couldn't push the ground away far enough to raise my head.

It probably didn't last more than a few seconds, because it was the driver who helped me up, but I had passed for a while into a timeless zone in which all boundaries had shifted, and the confusion left me momentarily helpless and vulnerable to fears that I might be losing my mind. By the time an orderly came out of the building to help, I was re-oriented enough to move unassisted, though shaken and fraught with doubt.

Inside the doors it was tranquil, cool, and surprisingly modern, with smooth concrete floors and bright overhead lighting, despite the low ceilings. The antiseptic odor of alcohol and carbolic came to the nose in sculptured clarity. A short foyer with double doors opened across a narrow corridor onto a broad operating room glittering with polished steel accouterments, articulated trays, large ceiling lights, and six or eight stainless steel operating tables, grooved for drainage, like cutting boards. Chromium equipment stands supporting bottles, hoses, hooks, and knobs stood in readiness at each table, bright points of light glinting from the edges of things.

The duty staff lounged casually between the tables, dressed in olive drab, a few wearing white surgical caps with their masks hanging down on their chests. They were talking among themselves in low tones. It struck me as odd that one of them was a shapely young woman whose fatigues did little to suppress her femininity, and that she was smoking a cigarette there in the operating room.

She and one of the men looked up idly when I stepped in. I probably imagined it, but for a moment, her eyes seemed to pulse like a signal from a distant star, going from dark blue to light blue and back again. As I handed my card to a male orderly, she casually turned her attention to an arrangement of instruments on a nearby tray. Evidently I did not appear to be in sufficiently disastrous condition to merit her interest.

As I was led down a corridor to the left, I glanced back and noticed that the floor beneath the tables sloped off into drains, like the floor of a community shower. The chilling practicality of the design left a soft wound of silence upon me. The sight with its freight of implications rekindled my own sense of good fortune, but I turned away wearing my luck like a vague malignancy.

Some fifteen or twenty feet down the hallway, the orderly directed me to lie on a steel gurney for the purpose of having my head x-rayed.

"My head?" I asked, thinking that the reason for my being there should have been obvious.

"Regulations..." he began, but cut short any further explanation with the sudden roar of incoming helicopters. Through the crescendo of whining turbines and clattering blades that suddenly pounded in overhead came a man's wavering screams, carried in the engine noise on the descending machines. The orderly parked me brusquely against a wall near an outside window and raced back toward the entrance bay, as shouts and tinkling metallic sounds erupted from the O.R. The corridor was suddenly filled with yells and curses and running feet.

Two Hueys came in low and settled just outside, their engines howling and rotors beating the air, and through it all came the hysterical shrieking. The hospital doors flew open and banged against their stops as stretcher teams rushed outside, letting in a world of sound and heat, engine exhaust, dust and the smell of the earth. At least two men were screaming in wind-tossed agony as the stretchers were loaded in the buffeting downdrafts. I could barely make out a few faraway words, fragmented in the noise:

"Forget him..."

"...back for more..."

"Marine..."

"...two dead over here—"

"Here! Here! Here!," and one isolated phrase that sounded like "Truck two!"

The hospital doors flew open again as the first litter team burst in, hollering for room, and the O.R. staff began shouting instructions. I craned my neck around and caught a glimpse of a tattered arm dangling from a shapeless, jiggling hulk on the first litter. It dribbled a glistening trail of blood on the floor in which the hurrying feet of the litter bearers were spreading wet tracks across the hall. A relentless, gurgling wheeze punctuated the shouting, and the desperate repetitive intakes of breath upon which it fed sounded as though some gigantic monster had shouldered its way into the hall.

"...Uuuh! huh, Uuuh! huh, Uuuh! huh, Uuuh! huh, Uuuh!"

Immediately behind came the stretcher with a soldier whose continuous shrill screams were pitched to carry more pain and terror than I'd ever known existed. The sound of it filled the building. It was horrifying to hear a grown man wail like that, and though it was not to be the last time I would hear it, the first was enough to haunt my dreams for years.

I looked away, not wanting to see any more, but was unable to avoid hearing the crying and the frenzied shouts of the medical staff as other wounded were rushed past, loaded onto the tables, or placed on the floor over the drains to await their turn.

The steel felt cool against my back as I lay there staring hard at a water stain on the ceiling. It resembled the map of an island, complete with mountains and secluded coves. Great for anchoring a wooden sailboat, I thought fiercely. You need a classic wood boat for that sort of thing. Yeah. Gunkholing, they call it in New England. On the sunny window ledge near me lay a dead bee, capsized in the dust.

The sounds of pandemonium issued relentlessly from the unseen Operating Room: shouts and cries, the rending of fabric, high-pitched keening, and the clatter of metal equipment being moved, dropped, adjusted and discarded. I could not close my mind to what must be happening in there, nor think away the images it conveyed.

The choppers lifted off quickly, their engines in a torturous rising pitch, rattling the bottles on a shelf nearby as they wheeled away, again passing so low overhead I thought they would come through the roof, filling the world with the only sound I know that is both sharp and dull at the same time. Someone in the corridor yelled that they were going back to the ambush area for another load. The sound of the engines diminished quickly in what seemed a southwesterly direction, and I wondered, trembling, about their destination.

I must have fallen asleep, because the next thing I remember was being wheeled back down the corridor, away from the bright window. I was cold. A crisp silence had settled upon everything. It seemed to be holding even the whisper of the gurney wheels hostage against the onrush of renewed horrors. I looked up at the orderly to see if it was the same one who had shunted me there earlier. I couldn't tell. His face was foreshortened from below. The skin under his chin was pulled tight across the cords of his neck, and he was staring straight ahead, with a look which seemed to say that he, too, had passed beyond some invisible barrier and now moved in another plane, his face empty of all except a sense of something withheld.

As we trundled past the O.R., I rolled my head and looked in. All was quiet, subdued. The tables were empty and the floor was being hosed down. I didn't recognize anybody in the room, even though they must have been the same duty crew I had seen earlier. It was clear from the appearance of their smeared and spattered aprons that they had recently finished their work. I didn't see the pretty woman. These people seemed older, somehow. They moved without speaking, amid the hollow splashing sound of water on the cement. A large electric clock on the wall registered a few minutes past 10:00. Beneath one of the tables lay a single jungle boot, on its side, with a foot in it.

I was rolled into a small adjoining room. After a few moments under the x-ray cone, the orderly pushed me near a light stand with a small tray table next to it. A big man in a surgical cap which he wore somewhat jauntily, as though it were a baseball cap on backwards, stepped into the light with a nurse and began examining my legs. The tips of his pale fingers were wrinkled, shrunken, like those of a boy who has been swimming too long.

He handled me with extraordinary gentleness, though I winced instinctively at his first touch. He asked if I wanted something to kill the feeling in my legs, but the question was rhetorical, because his assistant administered an injection before I could answer.

"Thanks," I said, feeling sheepish, profoundly humbled by the effect upon me of the horrible wounds the medical staff had just been dealing with, injuries I had barely glimpsed. I was embarrassed now to present my little problems. I wanted to be cooperative but felt helpless to do anything, and in the absence of any good ideas, just tried to smile an apology, though I don't think my face moved any. "I'm having kind of a long day," I joked feebly, and then felt foolish for the remark.

A wondrous pink effusion began quickly to spread outwards from my chest, reaching to my fingertips, sensory outposts in a sea of storms. The doctor was talking to me, and by his expression, appeared to be joking, but for some reason it was in pantomime. I sensed some tugging at various places on my legs and heard the clink of bits of metal being dropped into a steel dish. The nurse's occasional comments became breathy and distant, fading in intermittent syncopation behind a tinny symphony of white noise. My arms became strangely heavy, and when one ponderous hand finally rose to attend an itch on my nose, it was too late. It dropped heavily on my chest and lay there, inert, the fingers bunched loosely. I observed this odd lethargy absently, and, with senses fusing into a glassy delirium, finally decided to worry about it later.

It was dark when I awoke with a start, under fresh-smelling sheets. After a rush of fearful confusion, I realized that I was in a bed near one end of a long ward, and as I peered into the dimness for something on which to fasten my orientation of the room, I felt by some circadian telepathy of the night that it must be around 1:00 AM. I checked under the sheets and found that I still had on the pair of G.I. underwear that I had been sleeping in when the attack had started and in which I had gone through the longest night of my life. My legs were heavily bandaged.

A small square of amber light shone through an inspection window in the door at the end of the ward, and in its dim wash I could see only the first few beds near mine. It felt like there were a hundred of them running out into the darkness, but actually there were only two rows of twenty. Somewhere among them, a voice began a wavering litany of unintelligible syllables which rose in intonation, like a question. It was both loud and small at the same time, calling in the stillness, unsettling and repetitive. I realized it must have been the sound that had awakened me. I could see cigarettes being lit at the far end of the ward. There were subdued mumbles and groans as wounded men returned to consciousness and pain.

I guessed that I was surrounded by the ambushed Marines, and that despite whatever acts of courage or circumstance had brought them here, they lay now vanquished by the long night, sampling only crumbs of rest in the intervals of fever, thirst, or pain. Yet the man whose dream calls had stirred the room seemed to sleep through it, his strange pleading like an intuitively understandable foreign language. Those of my own dreams lost there would inevitably make it through later until they took. The time would come when they'd be vivid and unremitting. I would remember other nights then and wake up half believing that I'd never really been in those places.

Suddenly, in the distance to the north, a siren began its mournful wail. "Incoming!" whispered several voices in unison as tension drew its collective breath in the room. In a few moments, muffled by distance, came the rhythmic *crump, crump...crumpcrump* of high-trajectory rounds falling into the ground. Additional sirens took up the cry progressively closer, feeding our tension, and in the palpable silence of expectation, I searched the ceiling.

Overhead, peaked rafters, painted pale green, supported a canvas roof that offered little protection from above against anything but rain. I couldn't understand why the hospital, as a repository for the helpless, was not better constructed for defense against mortar fire. Even a guy with a Going-Home wound could die around here.

The air filled with listening. I became aware of every sound. A shoe or sandal step outside, the noise of a bedspring, breathing, the faint click of joints, the tinkle of a glass thermometer in a steel tray at the far end of the ward. I felt as though I had become a limb of some large creature, linked to the others by a thin thread of noises. There was no more firing, and warily we all began to settle back into our own private misgivings.

In the silence I began to think about death. Not violent death of the sort that had assaulted my senses over the last many hours, but the natural kind–the long, slow closing of life's account, with annual payments of strength and vitality that lead ultimately to a final, flabby thump of a heart worn out, a last breath indistinguishable from a sigh. I wondered if I would ever know such a peaceful moment. In the early morning hours, when illusions wither and appalling truths open like night-blooming cereus, one's fears and longing paint themselves on shifting surfaces, leaving an exhaustingly busy canvas to fade at first light.

I came in this fevered panoply to realize the need for a different kind of bravery than that which the American paradigm has traditionally applied to war. Not the adrenalin-burst kind that takes machine gun emplacements in a wild-eyed frenzy of cardiac mania, for I could not imagine what I would do in a situation like that–it was just too foreign to my nature–rather, I came to see that survival includes the calm, enduring sort of private valor that could serve just to get you through the eerie, insidious, and cloying fearsomeness.

Marcus Aurelius wrote his *Meditations* while in a legionary camp in a gloomy Austrian forest far from home, and his ruminations there are memorable for their philosophical simplicity–for their resignation without despair. I remembered one in which he said that men should not fear death, whether there is an afterlife or not; for if there is, then we should be glad to leave this flawed world for a better one; if not, then all we do is pass into a nothingness in which we would at least be free of pain and anxiety.

These kinds of insights work nicely to humanize a historical figure–and they even serve pretty well as a talisman in the daylight, with some degree of confidence in one's visible surroundings at work–but they lose their power to convince in those post midnight hours of creeping vulnerability, when the cereus's pale petals spread and large caliber rounds begin to spill from the black bowl of the sky. Then yes, raw courage in the face of violent death is actually what's needed after all.

In the morning, a Marine Corps General came to visit his men and to decorate each with the Purple Heart. He was a short, bullet-shaped man with ruddy jowls and a brusque manner, which he seemed to have trouble reconciling with the job at hand. With him was a small staff consisting of an officious Lieutenant Colonel and two junior officers, who carried the boxes of medals and a clipboard, to which they referred for names as they proceeded along the rows of beds. They were each dressed in crisp jungle fatigues with tailored creases. Their clothing sounded like straw, and their boot soles squeaked. I wondered if starch was SOP for garrison officers in the Marines and whether it helped their postures. I found myself envying them such absurd priorities.

The General stepped among the forest of IV bottles and bandaged limbs to say a few words to each of the men who were conscious. He spoke in subdued, respectful tones, sometimes finishing with a conciliatory gesture or a gentle, avuncular pat, as though he were presiding over a dormitory of school boys, which, I suppose, many of them had been not so long before.

He terminated each interview with an abrupt gesture toward the bed, at which point the Colonel stepped forward smartly, placed a medal on the pillow, then stepped back. The little party then came to momentary attention and snapped a quick salute to each casualty before moving to the next bed.

I was struck by the gesture, particularly among tradition-bound Marines. We were somewhat more casual about the protocol of saluting in the Special Forces, but as far as I knew, the only time any officer initiates a salute to a subordinate is when the junior man wears the Congressional Medal of Honor. Even though I could measure their discomfiture, their sign of respect for what had happened to these men percolated up through my own apprehensions and was surprisingly moving. I felt compelled to look away, as though something genuinely more intimate than I knew it was were taking place between them.

As they made their way toward my end of the room, I was able to see them more clearly. Each of the officers appeared to be struggling with a crumbling objectivity, and who could blame them? The General's busy black eyes strove to restrict their attention to each of his wounded at a time, yet his self-conscious camaraderie preceded him down the aisle like an audible shadow.

They surprised me by stopping at my bed. The General stepped over and fixed me with a harsh smile. I tried to rise up on one elbow and managed a facsimile salute, but he raised a restraining palm to indicate that the rules were off for today.

"Where you hit, son?" he asked in an attractive rasping voice, measured and almost elegant, yet with the jagged edge of superior parchment—a roughness, I thought, made mostly of bourbon.

"In the legs mostly, sir," I said, trying to sound unconcerned, while showing due respect for the social chasm that yawned between us. He stared at me for a long moment, as though amused by some vague recollection.

"Hurt much?"

"No, sir, not much," I lied, pleased with my performance so far.

"Mind if we have a look?"

"No, sir."

He turned slightly and gestured to the bedding for his adjutant, who quickly stepped forward and raised a corner of the sheet, presumably to spare the senior officer's sullying his hands. I looked, too, and noticed that the heavy bandages were stained with reddish brown in places and had seeped onto the lower sheet. The fingers on the General's right hand twitched a signal, and the Colonel released the sheet, which settled gently back down, tenting my pillowed feet.

"Want a 'Heart'?" the General asked with desiccated sincerity, turning his dark eyes back to me.

"Oh. Well, sir, I don't think it really deserves a 'Heart'," I said, using his contraction for the name of the medal in the hope that it would make me sound like a veteran. He was clearly pleased with that. A thin smile jabbed at his jowls, and he turned to share it with his staff, who, sensing approval, grinned back with their faces.

"Heart!" he said with quiet emphasis, abruptly jabbing his finger at me as he stepped away. The Lieutenant handed one of the boxes to the Colonel, who stepped forward and opened it. He placed the ribboned medal on my pillow, then handed me the box and stepped back.

They came to collective attention and saluted me. I returned it, and they moved on.

When they finally finished at the last bed, they clumped back up the aisle, occasionally glancing or commenting to various men, some of whom called out to them as they rejoined a medical officer by the door. They paused in conversation with him, evidently taking their leave, while I lay there wondering if this was what it felt like to be a decorated war hero.

I glanced toward the group by the door just as the medical officer was indicating something on the clipboard. He looked up and pointed straight at me. They all looked my way. Then they looked back at the clipboard and at each other. They seemed to go into a huddle for a moment, and I detected a distinct spasm of tension across the General's back.

Suddenly, the Colonel broke away and strode back over to my bed. He drew himself up over me, and fixed me with a wintry glare, which swept down from his face in a silent avalanche of disdain. He snorted in a way I can only describe as a controlled release of something disgusting, the way polite people handle intestinal gas at the table, their faces sick with restraint. He leaned over and took the box from my hand. He snatched the medal off the pillow, then turned and walked heavily back up the aisle to rejoin the group as they all left the room, the chirp of his gleaming boots diminishing with their departure. A few of the men nearby rolled their heads and, from somewhere beyond the silence, fixed their hollow eyes upon me.

10

I awoke in the morning after a fitful night that had at last given way to sound sleep during the first grey hours of dawn. My legs were stiff from having remained immobile all night, and although they were stinging in places, did not hurt as much as I had expected. I was enjoying the prospect of spending the day in this comfortable bed with the kind attentions of the medical staff when my expectations were rewarded by the appearance of several Army nurses who began working their way through the ward, giving each man who could be moved at least a limited rub down with what turned out to be a mixture of alcohol and baby oil.

When at last one of them reached my bed, together we got me rolled over onto my stomach. She squirted the solution onto my back and began spreading it around with her hands. Though the alcohol stung a bit in the scratches and small punctures on my back, it was cool on my skin, and her experienced hands seemed to displace the sweat, leaving me feeling clean and surprisingly refreshed. She finished and offered to help roll me back, but I was enjoying the new position and the cooling sensation the alcohol left. I declined the offer and thanked her as she left me face down and moved to the next guy.

The oil and alcohol remained damp long enough to be cooled by the slightest disturbance in the air for several minutes. I decided to remember this simple remedy for night sweats. When it finally dried, I rolled myself back over as the nurses returned to offer something in the way of breakfast, which in my case was liquid. Orange juice and coffee. Since I had been given a general anesthetic the day before, I was cautioned about starting off with solid food, as it could cause nausea. Though suddenly hungry, I wasn't inclined to undertake anything that might increase my discomfort, so I welcomed the chance to prop up the pillows and sip some hot coffee at leisure.

Soon there was a disturbance at the door, and a guy in dirty combat fatigues appeared. Judging by the gestures and faint-heard syllables, it seemed he was asking about me. There was some discussion at the end of the ward, and a doctor was summoned. After sorting among some papers on a clipboard, the doctor nodded affirmatively and left. The soldier clumped down the corridor to my bed.

"Moore?" he asked.

"Yeah."

"I've come to get ya outta here."

"Whaat?" I didn't want to believe it.

"Yeah. We need ya back at the base. There ain't enough of us. We need all the help we can get for the clean-up, an' it says you're walkin' wounded."

His words settled in quickly, leaving a bruise of conscience. Several disconcerting images of further damage to my injuries flashed forward through my mind, then gave way to a slump of disappointment at the realization that "walking" was such a flexible term. I knew, though, that despite my own facts, other facts dictated that I was in no position to argue.

"Come on," he added unnecessarily, his manner flat and decisive. He had evidently been interrupted from serious work to retrieve a malingerer.

I carefully edged my bandaged legs over the side of the bed and tried to stand up. Waves of renewed pain started up my legs as the blood rushed into them, and it took a long moment to steady myself. A surge of white dots danced at the edge of my vision until the pressure in my legs settled into a rhythmic dull throbbing. At least some of the problem lay in the constriction of the windings, while both the internal and surface pain pounded outward. I felt momentarily faint and sat back down to keep from falling.

Several brown stripes stained the wrappings, and the ward nurse suggested that the doctor should have another look at the wounds before I was allowed to leave. My retriever was told to have some coffee while a doctor was called to examine me, and he accepted with barely contained enthusiasm, then returned to stand by holding the mug tightly with both hands. I noticed the fingertips under his nails were bloodless and white. His posture communicated a discomfited gratitude.

After cutting away the gauzes and looking over his work, the surgeon pronounced his satisfaction, much in the manner of a mechanic just finished with another muffler job. He resealed a few places with individual bandages, then rewrapped everything tightly, probably realizing the bandaging was going to be abused. He gave me a little plastic canister containing some pain pills along with the untimely warning that if I waited to take one until after the pain began it would be too late. He then released me to my escort with the admonition to come back for another change as soon as I could. Realizing it was likely that most of his patients never thought–or were never able–to thank him for his skill, I expressed my profound appreciation for his work on me and waddled stiff-legged out of the ward, pivoting robot-like with each step. I dreaded going back and wondered what awaited me at the base.

As soon as we stepped outside, the heat and the dazzle of morning light struck me like a fist, and I had to brace myself against the doorway for a moment to let a wave of nausea pass. I tried to suppress the idea that I was getting up too soon and told myself it was just the effect of the medication. The Jeep waited in the shimmer–a dark messenger from a host of fresh fears.

I could see that FOB 4 was still burning in the distance. From the base of the abrupt mass of Marble Mountain, black smoke rose to smudge the sky, drifting slowly to the west on the ocean breeze. The sight produced a rush of apprehension. I was to be transported back to the scene of a chilling crime in which I had been somehow responsible.

As I experimented with bending my knees enough to force the bandages to allow me to sit, the driver began a running monologue to bring me up to date. He told me they had the messhall up and running and that the Navy SeaBees had already repaired the water tower. They were starting to clear the broken lumber from some of the buildings, that he was part of an effort to dig out the TOC, which had collapsed, and there were still a few guys unaccounted for. I listened for any information of potentially mortal threat, but was distracted by the need to grit my teeth and hold my breath in anticipation of the jolt to my legs offered by each bump and rill in the road. Then he added, "They're worried we might get hit again tonight."

"What?!"

"Yeah, the fuckin' VC monks up on the mountain can see we're hurtin'."

I was not ready for that news. A new wave of despair washed over me, reviving the desperation and terror of the attack. My heart sank at the prospect of anything even remotely like it happening again. Then, with my original suspicions confirmed about the enormous rock that loomed over our compound, I understood with a chill that we, both individually and collectively, were under constant observation in the compound, both day and night. Again, I couldn't understand why the higher command would locate a camp at the foot of a VC stronghold.

I tried to sound calm when I asked, "How many of them did we get?"

"All of 'em, they think. The last two tried to get through the wire at the southwest corner after daylight. They got one inside and the last one outside, but we didn't find the body, just some blood trailin' off toward the stone cutters' village."

I was still trying to work out the implications of all he had said when we approached the camp gate. While we were still about 100 meters away, I tensed again when the air began to carry the unmistakable evidence that the clearing work was not finished. Mixed with the complex smells carried in the cinder-flecked smoke from the warehouse building was the unmistakable odor of putrefaction. There is no other smell like it. It touches with an animal fear something ancient and deep in the human psyche. It imparts a greasy quality to the air itself, and when we turned into the compound the strange, nauseating feculence became pervasive, lodging in the back of the throat. I could feel it on my skin. It rose from the ground and rubbed up against my face like a sweating animal, reawakening the clear and present horror of…when? Was it last night or the night before? For a few moments I couldn't remember.

I was dropped at the headquarters building and told to report in. I dismounted the Jeep painfully and pivot-walked inside the damaged hut, still wearing what was left of my tattered shirt and my undershorts, now stiff with blood stains and several cycles of dried sweat, while the guy who had driven me left the Jeep and hurried off to resume whatever he'd been doing.

Inside, I was told by an E-7 who was acting Top Sergeant to do whatever I could to square away any of my gear that I could salvage and to get over to the messhall and have something to eat. I'd be told what to do in the clean-up effort after that.

I left the headquarters hut and made my way down the duckboards, past what remained of the shower hut, in which I was relieved to glimpse what appeared to be about half the fixtures still intact in the undamaged half of the shed. The near side was completely wrecked, with splashguard cinder blocks caved outward, wood shattered, roof tin peeled up, and pipes contorted in the open air. It still smelled of cordite.

I continued on to what had been the corner room where I had last seen any of my gear. I began to feel a bit anxious about it. Everything I owned was in that duffle bag, and I wanted to put on some clothes and to find the .45 pistol I had been issued.

The building had been transformed. The corner was completely blown open and burned away. What had been my room was now entirely outdoors. The corridor was just a bit of flooring beneath the hanging tatters of the roof trusses. The shattered remains of the outer walls had apparently been pulled down and taken off to one of the growing lumber piles, removing any semblance of interior space and leaving the pair of metal bunk beds standing in isolation on the open floor slab, a sunny paralogical incongruence that made me wince. The emotional investment I had in that room gave rise to an odd feeling of propriety with the space, and now the bright emptiness left me feeling as though something personal and intimate lay exposed.

To my relief there, too, stood my duffle bag, forlorn and alone in the sun, still upright but shot through with shrapnel holes. With the folds at its top pulled partially open it looked a bit surprised, as surprised as I was to see that no one had taken it away. Thankfully the clean-up effort thus far had other priorities, and it had simply been left there on the slab in silent testament to other sudden absences.

In the space between the bedsteads there remained an enormous dried pudding of the Ranger Captain's blood. It had mostly crusted over and drawn itself into a horrible brown terrazzo of raised tiles, a thick craquelure puzzle alive with flies. Marooned near one edge of it and gleaming white like a distant ship in the sun, floated one of my shower slippers, derelict on the glistening red sea. A sweep of wide brown streaks curved out of the coagulation to the edge of the concrete, tracking where the body had been dragged away. On the exposed flooring beside the pool, in the shadow of the bare springs, still lay some of the parts to the disassembled carbine I had been issued.

I was stunned by the enormity of the scene's silent message, but the full meaning of it all remained just beyond my immediate comprehension. My mind kept pushing it away. The heat and the glare made my head swim, and the pain roared back into my legs. I retreated to the shade of the broken shower hut and gulped down another pain pill with a few handfuls of the dribbling water. There I tried to pull myself together before anyone noticed I wasn't working. I had to retrieve my gear and find a place to sort through it for some clothes, and I had to find the pistol. My feeling of naked vulnerability gave new urgency to finding a weapon. At the very least I needed to be armed. I went back out to what had been my bed and dragged the duffle into the shade.

The pistol was not visible anywhere in the open. I couldn't remember where I had left it and hoped I had slipped it into the top of the bag. I retrieved my shower slipper from the grip of the hardened blood. It came up with a faint crack and a mucid sucking sound, trailing a few gooey tendrils of reddish stuff. Holding it uncertainly between thumb and forefinger in one hand, I went back and heaved up the duffle with the other, then carried them into one of the more or less intact rooms. I soon found a space that did not appear to have been claimed, where sunlight streamed in through dozens of holes in the roof and walls, but at least it was more shelter than not, and it contained a bed with sheets covered by a nylon poncho liner. I decided to make it my room until otherwise notified and began to take inventory of the bag.

The pistol was evidently gone, but in the bag near the top I found my shower kit and immediately decided to take advantage of being as yet unassigned to a work detail by heading back toward the showers. The driver had said the Navy had repaired our water system, and I was anxious to get cleaned up. I didn't want to get my bandages wet, but the prospect of even a sponge bath from a broken pipe held some promise of relief in this new world of violent extremes. I hobbled back to the showers, and with slow running water and a cake of soap I got much of the engrained dirt off my face and out of my hair and washed the places the nursing staff had missed or avoided. The bandages lost their priority.

Afterwards, feeling marginally improved but with growing uncertainty about what might be expected of me once I was dressed again so that the bandages were hidden, I headed back to the room. On the way I became more aware of quiet activity around the compound. Clean-up was going on, but there were so few people to do it that the loudest sounds were a few faint voices that filtered through the hot breeze and the occasional clatter of thrown lumber. I noticed that everyone was armed, even as they worked at mundane tasks like shoveling sand and pulling boards. I was the only person I could see who was without a weapon. I felt especially uncomfortable about this, but the medication was beginning to work, and the subsidence of pain mitigated somewhat the imperative of accepting the full mandates of my situation. Follow-up attacks when the enemy has been hurt are good tactics and common knowledge, but in my enforced compromise with logic for the present, outside threat seemed to be something I had time to worry about later.

I lay on the bunk to relieve the pressure on my wounds, but soon a revived sense of vulnerability became compounded with the gauzy fear that anyone who saw me without a weapon would know that I was new, untried, undependable–at least naive. I did not wish to be singled out for any reason, and in this new reality I saw immediately that a weapon was much more than a tool of the trade. It was the essential catalytic requirement for one's survival and for the defense of all things of value, and thus it became a part of one's very being. There are no guarantees, but I had saved myself with one the first night, and the need now assumed enriched imminence in my bid for continued existence.

I had heard admonitions from veterans to protect your weapon at all times, but without the hard press of actual combat the words had contained just enough general wisdom to carry the ambiguous appeal of aphorism, just enough irony that you could choose the degree to which you would limit its meaning. But all parceling of its truth had vanished in the night for me, and being without a weapon now was a concern that took on its own mass and specific gravity. The insistent sense of fragility and nakedness had weight. It was tangible.

Periodically, there came a muffled explosion that gave me a jolt of anguish. With each I jumped involuntarily, every nerve on full alert, until I figured out that the detonations came from the fire at the warehouse, where grenades and mortar rounds were still cooking off beneath the mass of burning equipment, fallen trusses, and contorted sheets of corrugated metal roofing. I knew it would be some time yet before it was safe for anyone to go in there, and it boded ill for my chances of getting armed before the approach of another night.

The breeze struggling up from the beach moderated the temperature slightly, but the invasive odor of the dead, mixed with charcoal, smoke, cordite, and the complex smell of burning synthetics made for a heady cocktail. At least in the room, the dominant smell of splintered wood gave some small relief from the sharp odors.

I roused myself to the realization that a weapon was not simply going to materialize, as indeed it had during the attack, and that I had better do something to make myself useful. I would soon be called upon to help, and if I was going to get what I needed, I would have to rejoin whatever was left of the community. I had to get something to eat, too. I was also suddenly fiercely thirsty and therefore needed to get dressed and over to the messhall before a work detail found me lounging.

I selected a pair of combat fatigue pants from the bag and gingerly pulled them on over the bandages. The pants were intact, but loose around the waist from the water weight I'd lost since arriving in the country, probably exacerbated by whatever panic sweat I had left in the sand. My belt had only a polished brass buckle, but I was determined not to wear anything shiny from here on, and especially not in a place known in target parlance as the "center of mass." For some reason I had not been issued a "subdued" buckle in Nha Trang, and I made a mental note to add a black belt buckle to my list of needs, just under "weapon."

All but one of my remaining shirts had holes blown through them. No matter. At least I was clothed again. The boots offered their own challenge. I could get my feet into them but could not at first bend over enough to lace them, so I decided to clump along to the messhall with them open.

Back outside in the mind-bending glare, I found that I could walk fairly well with the pants on, the cinch straps at the waist band tightened all the way to keep them up. My head pounded, and each step hurt a bit, but through forced use, I could stretch the bandaging enough to take controlled steps.

A glance in any direction reinforced my sense of how lucky I had been. The camp wasn't completely ruined, but it presented an open, frowning landscape filled with bad information. The air carried a layer of gray smoke, and the sand was still littered with the detritus of violence. Stepping back on the very ground where I had passed the long night of terror filled me again with chilling images of the fight and rekindled a spasm of fear, the thing reinforced by the full extent of destruction that lay everywhere starkly revealed in the harsh sunlight. Visions of that night flashed through my mind as I came upon certain objects and spaces, yet through my medicated pain, unease and depression, I couldn't quite attach to them. Some pictures remained vague, hazy with the confusion in which they had been imprinted and seemed to hover just beyond my ability to assign them meaning, while others writhed before me with indelible immediacy.

Wherever I looked things had changed. A few buildings had burned to the ground, leaving glaring open spaces and smoke, others were shattered by explosives. Those that remained more or less intact had been shot through with bullet holes and bore the splintered scars of shrapnel. They seemed to offer a forlorn defiance of the action. Stinking VC corpses still lay swollen in the open, and there seemed to be gaps where vaguely recalled objects had occupied some corner of my memory, just…yes, night before last. Was it really that long ago? Perhaps my first experience with pain medication was protecting me from grasping the full significance of events, screening awareness just enough to conduct my passage through the ruined dreamscape.

I looked around in a daze of tentative prehension, as though I had awakened from a nightmare about fire only to discover real ashes in my hair. The sand held scraps of grey metal and strange bits of encrusted biology crawling with ants, and there were scattered patches of bright yellow, green, and red-stained ground where smoke grenades had been thrown, the spent canisters still lying at their edges. The fierce light of day kept shifting the dimensions of loss amid a small industry of contained movement at the periphery of empty spaces, where an eerily wordless attempt to draw some order from the chaos continued. People worked at the cleanup saying so little to one another that I was struck by the pervading silence of the camp. The population had been greatly reduced, and with it the amount of speech available for the dismal tasks.

There were large gaps in the perimeter wire where the recoil tension had sprung the razor loops back from the places where it had been breached. Some bodies still hung in the tangle or lay grouped around the openings. Winnowed across the open ground outside the wire was a tattered fan of jumbled body parts. Here and there among them scraps of clothing were lent an eerie and spurious animation by the sea breeze, which had the ironic effect of giving the whole scene a profound stillness. Here firsthand was impressive testimony to the effectiveness of the mini-gun fire that "Puff" had worked in so close to where I had cowered during the fight. It was said that Puff could put a round in every square inch of a football field on a single high-speed pass, and the scene that lay before me was all I needed to confirm the rumor. It was impossible to tell how many people that layered mass of butchery represented. I had not realized the full extent of the enemy's attack until that moment, and I was chilled to see the odds against me in the position I had occupied during that night should those people have made it through the wire.

A group of men with hand shovels were working along with a backhoe at digging through the mound of sand that had been the TOC, while a few of the Nungs stood guard with automatic rifles. They held their weapons at the ready, but their faces betrayed a lethargic inscrutability that did nothing to reassure me.

The fire had destroyed the hundreds of plastic sandbags that formed the bunker over whatever space was excavated into the ground for TOC operations, and tons of hot sand had been released to fall into the mysterious hollows below. Some of the radio towers had melted in place, others had fallen down completely or lay bent over and twisted, their blackened guy wires tangled in the sand.

The sun had long since begun its work on the corpses still sprawled in the warm sand. The color of the dead faces had changed from a yellow-grey to streaks of brown, to purple and even green. Some were further along. They had turned black and then to something pulpous and slimy, the skin drawn into a horrible rictus of laughter, and gazing with jellied eyes, soul-flown shells, inert, they lay utterly ruined.

A dump truck was making its way slowly around the compound, and some of the Chinese, wearing surgical masks and gloves, walked along with it in savage silence, laboriously picking up the dead sappers and heaving the bodies onto the back of the truck. Deliquescence was well advanced in most of the corpses so that the skin, hair, and stained clothes shone as though impregnated with oil. On board, two guys wearing their issue tourniquets over the lower part of their faces, bandit style, dragged them to the front and tossed them onto the tangled load. The whole operation was being carried out without directives or hand signals, as though it was a practiced routine. As the truck neared, a body was being pulled by the feet toward the jumbled pile of renitent discolored limbs at the front of the load. Its rigored forearms made a dry sandpaper sound in the grit on the hot steel truck bed before they threw it onto the pile.

Many of the burnt corpses were still scattered about where they had fallen, some still smoking, too hot to handle or so over-cooked that the limbs came off when there was an attempt to move them. Most of the dry ones had stiffened, making them easier to lift. These were the source of the heavy, greasy smell that had permeated the air on my return from the hospital. Though it was sickening, it was not exactly the sickly-sweet odor that those who've never experienced it say so simplistically. It had a rancid, cheesy quality, an insistent combination of bad meat mixed into the sour, ammoniac reek of urine and carbolic fumes, concentrated heavily with the acid rancidity that tarnished brass leaves on the fingers. It had the inescapable character of traveling in the air and attaching itself to other surfaces, clinging there like an oily film long after the source has been removed.

Yet I was oddly unmoved by it all. Perhaps I had exhausted my powers of adjustment to simply accept that the thing had happened. I could summon no moral judgment nor find a philosophical rationale applicable to this new reality. The broken buildings, the bodies, the lethargic movements of the living, all seemed to exist at some remove. The destruction maintained a kind of metaphoric distance beyond my grasp, shimmering just outside the delicate tracery of my own uncertain limitations. There were no words to describe it, no feelings to match its enormity. It just was.

The barrack building next door, some ten or fifteen yards away, had suffered the destruction of its near corner, where the roof had been shattered upwards, and the sides opened by a satchel charge. There was what appeared to be a body, or a part of one, among the shards of wood. I remembered seeing the blast happen, perhaps even causing it. The little figure that had been running with the charge that blew it up was the one I had fired at with the .45 pistol. The shot had seemed to stop him seconds before the charge detonated, and I now felt an irrepressible morbid curiosity to know if I had really hit him.

I was certain that with all there was to do in the clearing effort, any sign that I, with no visible bandages and no tools, might be simply touring the battle ground would bring unpleasant results from those who were working, so gambling that anyone who might notice would mistake movement for action, I hobbled over to get a closer look at the damage. There, under the debris, was the lower half of a small brown body. It had been blown out of its clothes and sandals, one of which, hand-cut from a truck tire, lay a few yards away. The upper part of the torso was almost completely gone, though most of the right arm lay flung at the end of a ribbon of dried skin. Just above the wrist was a tear that cupped the flesh, made by a single .45 caliber round, and the back side of the limb had been largely carried away from the gaping exit wound in a splay of purplish sausage casing that was now feeding a swarm of frantic red ants.

I felt a moment of dull satisfaction but quickly turned away from the wreckage. There was nothing to be done or said for it. "Better him than me" comes to mind, but I don't remember thinking even that. Still feeling a pervasive detachment from its meaning, I knew only, and with a sudden clarity beyond language, that he and I had shared an existential moment within something huge and permanent. I didn't wish to dwell on it. Perhaps I was afraid of other feelings that might assert themselves if given the chance. Besides, my own situation demanded attention. I was hungry and in some pain, the day's heat was intensifying, and I didn't want to be seen doing nothing. I started toward the messhall, walking mostly head down to guard my constricted steps on the uneven ground.

Then with a start I noticed one of the sappers standing against the messhall! Unarmed, I felt a jolt of helplessness, instinctively lunged to the side and almost fell. In that first instant he seemed tall for a Vietnamese, and judging by the anguished expression on his face, he was evidently in a panic of his own, eyes staring distended and mouth distorted. I couldn't understand how he had been overlooked. He seemed frozen in distress, perhaps catatonic with vain trust in the merits of remaining perfectly still. Then, just as I was about to call to the Chinese on the truck, I realized there was something unnaturally still about the figure. His color wasn't right either, his face grey and streaked like the dead. Then I saw that his feet were actually about 6 inches off the ground. I approached cautiously until I stood right in front of him.

Initially, the sight was strange and awful. Someone had hit him full blast with two shotgun loads of flechettes. Flechettes are inch-long aluminum arrows densely packed into the shells—very effective, and outlawed by the Geneva Convention for precisely that reason. The double blast had blown him off the ground and pinioned him against the side of the building. I knew about flechettes but had never seen their effect on humans, and an odd curiosity overcame my revulsion. I stepped closer.

His exposed skin was covered with the tiny Xs made by the projectiles, with little bleeding, as he had been killed instantly, though he was slightly caved in. His sallow face was pocked with dozens of little dents where each pin had gone in, giving the surface of his head a dimpled effect like a golf ball, while his hair and clothes were pinned back as though he was being held in place on the wall by a strong wind. When I had stared my fill and turned away, I continued along to the side door of the messhall, wondering slightly at my surreal indifference to this bizarre facsimile crucifixion hanging there in the morning sun. (He was eventually peeled off, though he had to be somewhat butchered down to get it all. The stain he left on the wall was still detectable there ten months later.)

The messhall and its native staff was pretty much run by a mixed-blood Vietnamese woman whom everybody called Ba Foo (Or Fu. "Ba" refers to a mature or married woman). She was large, full-bodied, and tall for her presumed nationality. I had noticed her there my first night, and though her real function would remain a mystery to me, she certainly seemed to have the local employees that we were required to hire for work in the kitchen well in hand, yelling orders in Vietnamese as they helped the mess Sergeant with the cooking, washing, and bussing tables. She seemed a bit theatrical to me, but it worked; when she spoke they jumped to it. She had evidently been around foreigners long enough to have shed her Asian reserve and was quite vivacious and easygoing with the guys, if a bit bossy.

By the time I stepped into the messhall, my hunger had edged past the need to procure a weapon, and it was Ba Foo who watched me come in and limp toward the trays. She strode over and directed me to one of the many empty chairs.

"You noo?" she asked, her black eyes pinched up in a speculative grin.

"What?"

"You noo heah? I no see you befo'."

"Oh, er, yeah," I said, finally getting her accent and the abrupt, barking speech.

She regarded me curiously for another moment, then reached out, and pinching a generous serving of my cheek with her thumb and forefinger, said, "You numba one." It was such a surprisingly homey and motherly gesture of familiarity that, despite my somber mood, I heard myself make a laughing noise out loud. Even a momentary burst of amusement served as a tonic in this domain of extravagant brutality.

"Wachu wan'?" she yelped.

"Er, breakfast?"

"You sit heah!" She pointed with emphasis at the chair. I did.

There were only a few other men at the tables, one of them trying to control a coffee mug with a heavily bandaged left hand and the fingers of the right wound together in a large lump of dingy gauze. I assumed that most of the survivors were out helping with the clean-up operations, and with normal routines discarded, the messhall was open for anyone's refreshment as needed. In his case, it served as a refuge for one who could walk but couldn't handle anything and had chosen to stay out of the way. Perhaps his hootch was gone.

Ba Foo soon returned with a real American style breakfast on a tray, then went back for coffee, which proved to be both hot and black and in which a beaded scum of iridescent grease on the surface gave evidence of the dishwashing limitations of our native mess staff. It was good, though, and I tried to give her my most beatific smile of appreciation. I remembered what I had been told about the scrounging skills of our mess Sergeant and ate ravenously, surprised at my appetite in view of the richly unsavory influence I might have expected the scenery outside to have upon it.

Looking around at the few other guys in the room, I realized I was a hopeless stranger among these veterans. No one resembled anyone I could remember as having been in the transit building the night of the attack. Of course with their drawn and haunted looks, I may have been unable to recognize even an old friend. Ba Foo, clearly someone who kept an eye on things in the messhall, did not recognize me, and I began to see that I was probably the only new guy to make it through. The only guy whose name nobody else knew. It compounded my sense of isolation but threatened whatever comforts I could conjure from anonymity.

A runner came while I was thus engaged and informed me that I should go help the guys who were trying to excavate the TOC. It occurred to me that this was the second time in less than a week that potentially prophetic news had arrived while I was trying to enjoy a meal. He told me we were missing two guys, and it was thought that one of them had been on duty in the TOC when the attack began. They weren't sure what had happened to him but were digging for any remains.

Through the windows I could see the diggers across the compound, so I knew where to go. I finished quickly and then found that the time I had spent in the chair with my knees slightly bent had stretched the bandages enough to allow me to lace the boots, but on standing realized the rest had stiffened my legs. Then, sorry to leave the comforts of food and shade, and worried that I was headed for, at best, a day of painful digging in the hot sand under the blazing sun which was bound to ruin the bandages, and at worst, possibly in for some distasteful discoveries, I went back outside to make my way over to the group.

Glare-blinded by the sand, I moved with renewed caution, feeling slightly woozy and a bit nauseated by the heat and the renewed effort. The feeling of pending malaise produced a passing wave of heat exhaustion that crested through me as I approached the machine, worried that the combined effects of the medicine, food, and heat were making me sick. It passed quickly but left me edgy and doubtful.

Taking a moment to let my head clear, I joined the small party of three guys with shovels who were sifting through the hot sand gathered in the bucket of the backhoe. They were excavating what had been a large and carefully constructed bunker of sandbags that now resembled a broad dune indented here and there with hollows where spills of sand flooded into the underground spaces. The remnants of burned sandbag walls protruded from the mound around its buried edges where one corner remained intact to a height of about four feet. There, the interlocking bags resembled dusty green cobbles from which tiny cones of sand poured from a splay of bullet holes.

The machine had just retreated with a partial scoop of sand from the area estimated to have been the entrance to the TOC. The dust that rose from the work hung suspended and carried the smell of spent explosive. It was impossible not to breathe it.

After somewhat distracted introductions all around, which included the guy who had driven me from the hospital, the hand diggers returned to sorting carefully through the contents of the tractor's latest bucket load by sliding their shovels gently into the scoop and then sifting each one back and forth like gold panners. This was clearly a more delicate operation than the presence of the backhoe had implied. I watched, not exactly sure of what to do or what to look for, as streams of fine-grained sand cascaded back to the ground from between the metal teeth of the tractor's loader.

Feeling the need to make myself useful before my preoccupations actually made me sick or someone made a crack about not helping, I reached in and started scooping an armload of sand toward the front of the bucket. They stopped me.

"You don't want to do that, man," said one of the diggers evenly. "Here." He demonstrated the scoop and sift technique they were doing at arm's length with the shovel then handed it to me.

"What are we looking for?" I asked.

"His name was Garcia. Big guy. Somebody said he was working the TOC, but we don't know. He's unaccounted for is all. Him and another guy."

I had not fully understood the delicacy of the procedure, but as usual feared that the information I might get by asking how we should go about it would not sufficiently off-set the embarrassment of revealing my ignorance of things the others might expect me to know. I took the shovel and decided to observe and simply do what the others were doing.

That load of fine sand proved free of evidence, so we all stepped away to let the backhoe operator take another run at driving the loader deeper into the mound. I was curious about the tractor. I realized that I had never before been this close to a working backhoe, and I found the movement of the lifting arms to be inordinately engaging. Perhaps my mind rushed to fasten onto it in order to escape all that had been happening, and the machine offered the novelty of a non-lethal experience that I could actually make myself understand. Perhaps it was simply that I held no particular military association with earth moving tractors. I liked the smell of its engine, and its heavy lubricants served to replace some of the putridity in the air. Whatever the reason, I found the machine to be a voluptuous distraction and took an infantile delight in watching it operate.

When it lifted the bucket and backed out, the driver shut down the machine, and in the abrupt silence that followed we set about the process of sifting the load. The sun beat down with a vengeance through a dun colored layer of lingering smoke, its glare off the sand dazzling and painful. Radiant heat from the tractor itself burned my skin. I rolled my sleeves down in an effort to divert at least some of it. It was impossible to work without squinting through slit eyes, the blare off my cheeks alone inducing a bright blindness that drained all but a remnant sense of color from the surroundings. Along with the pull of nervousness that went with being in the open, my eyes soon gave up trying, and the moving figures around me lapsed into soft focus. Although the actual work unexpectedly caused only slight stress to my wounds, they throbbed steadily, and I was soon soaked through with sweat and took my turns at the digging with a pulsing pain at the base of my skull. Whatever was affecting me, perhaps the pain or the medicine—perhaps the fact that I'd spent the past two days in a dimension wherein all sights and sounds had no precedent—it, or they, kept interfering with my ability to focus fully on what we were doing. I felt woozy and detached from the work.

After a while a few crusty balls of sand surfaced in the scoop, and although nobody thought they were significant, they were placed respectfully in a large pillowcase-size plastic bag. Further sorting revealed a scorched steel insert from the sole of a jungle boot. This evidence was greeted with a suitably contained archaeological enthusiasm. Graves and Registration were contacted on the radio, and two guys soon arrived with additional plastic bags, a rolled full-size body bag, and expectant expressions.

While the others continued to sift through the load, I stepped down to the place where the last scoop had been drawn and slid my shovel along the exposed concrete floor, deep into the sand. It felt as though it met a soft obstruction, and I pulled it out. There was definitely a lump of something organic stuck to the lip of the shovel. I took it back up to where the others were sorting and placed it on the load, where it broke open to expose a blood red center of very rare meat.

This caused a stir, and since I knew the spot, I returned to the mound. This time, I withdrew a length of scorched thigh bone, burned off black above the missing knee joint, the ball of the hip socket clutched in a large hunk of rare roast beef, bright red and stringy and cooked for so long that the bone simply came out of it and tipped off the shovel, releasing a small wisp of smoke. The size of the bone indicated a large individual, just like they said.

"Here he is!" I called, and the Registration guys hurried down to place the pieces in their bags.

"Have you got a head?" one asked. "We need a head. Without the head we can't make positive ID, and his family can't collect for seven years. Any teeth? Teeth might help."

"I think this is the bottom half." I said and drove the shovel in again.

This time it came out with a much larger chunk, quite red and wet in the sun light, and captured with it in the shovel pan was a tattered rag of burnt trouser leg that trailed forth from the sand and hung ponderously, greasy with rendered body fat.

"Man!" someone muttered. "He's been slow cookin' under there all this time."

"Yeah. I think he's about done," I said, backing off with my shoveled remnant. It was quite a large piece and was surprisingly heavy.

I placed it, too, in the backhoe's bucket. I couldn't help noting how much it resembled a dinner roast. In fact it was indistinguishable, cooked brown around the edges, growing increasingly rare toward the center. It was somewhat long grained, not unlike the monkey meat I had eaten in Jungle School in Panama, and it exactly resembled dozens of holiday meals my mother had prepared over the years. I thought about the stories of cannibalism I had read of castaways at sea and realized how close we all are to such a decision. It would be easy, I thought.

My find had focused the effort, so the backhoe was retired for the present while work proceeded with hand shovels at the face of the mound. I helped one of the Registration guys place the largest piece in a plastic bag. In the process a small piece fell away in my hand. It was warm. I examined it up close. It was light brown at one end, running to pink at the other. It looked familiar, and I thought absently, "prepared" just the way I like it.

Standing there, momentarily apart from the others, feeling this bizarre and unique artifact in my fingers, I looked out at the winnows of destruction that surrounded us and watched distractedly as the body retrieval truck ground slowly between the huts. The thought rose from somewhere that I held in my hand a once-in-a-lifetime opportunity. Even if someone saw me, who would really care? After all, we were all engaged in a sanctioned form of barbarism anyway, and there was still lots of the stuff lying around providing a host of silent testimony. While the others were occupied with the work of retrieving the rest of Garcia, I separated a tiny pinkish sliver, and numbed I suppose by an accrued inertia of horrors, lifted it absently to my mouth and closed my teeth on it. But that is as far as I could go. I couldn't bring myself to taste it. I spat it back out and looked furtively about to see if anyone had noticed. Yet I really didn't care if they had. I had just pulled myself back from the edge of another in this sclerotic black festival of brutal unknowns, leaving it forever so, and wondered at how far from the tenets of civilization I had been driven in a few short days, how my list of things that really matter had been reduced to one.

Interrupted only by a few breaks to get water from the messhall, our digging continued in the relentless heat until late afternoon. As the sun continued its slow, unremitting progress through a cloudless sky, the dust stirred by our shoveling rose fine as powder from the baked sand. I couldn't gather it in my hand, but it found its way into my lungs, nostrils and eyes, into my hair and under my clothes, where it accumulated in the sweat and stiffened the fabric with crescents of dark clay. We continued working in wordless shifts while the whole camp seemed to be smoldering in a luminous immensity, as though scorched, not by the temporal fires of men, but by an eternal flame flicked from the pitiless sky, whose slow, discrete wheel inched painfully, imperceptibly, westward.

My bandages were ruined and my sweat-laden pants became difficult to keep up without a belt. Not far away lay the unrecovered body of one of the sappers, now swollen, putrid, and curdled as spoiled fruit. It lay across its rifle, and attached to the rifle was a canvas sling, stained with a brown spill of dry blood. I went over and pulled the weapon out from under the corpse, noting with dull interest that it was a standard model 1947 AK, evidently of fairly recent Chinese manufacture, and probably built under license from the Soviets, with more external parts stamped than machined the way the Russians made them. It had rings under the barrel and stock to which the sling was attached by means of simple snap shackles, so I removed the rifle from under the mess, detached the strap and adjusted it to my waist size. It bore the rancid smell of its former owner, but clipped to itself and served through my belt loops, it kept my pants up for the rest of the day. I decided it would work until I could get an issue "subdued" buckle from Supply.

We quit digging for the day without finding the upper half of Garcia. The sand gradually surrendered other bones, burnt black and stunted, and much of the roast that had composed his hips and a leg, but not enough to enable Graves and Registration to make an unquestioned identification, a fact that remained an indigestible lump in the belly of our small success. I decided not to think about it, not to waste any more brain power chasing down irrelevant channels of morbid speculation over unequivocal events.

By late afternoon when we finally left the TOC site, much of whatever clean-up could be accomplished by hand was evident in numerous piles of lumber, bent and perforated roofing metal, and a big jumble of unusable plywood shards being prepared for burning. A large collection of the enemy's weapons was stacked outside one of the huts, and some guys working with a three-quarter ton truck were taking unexploded satchel charges and grenades out to a pile they had assembled on the beach. The Navy SeaBees had delivered some of the wood and equipment they would need in helping us rebuild, including an enormous pile of sandbags which would have to be filled. It appeared that all the corpses that had lain exposed had at last been picked up, at least from the center of the compound, though as far as I knew, we were still missing one American.

All of us were soppy with sweat and shared an advanced state of physical exhaustion by the time the setting sun, burnishing the curled strands of smoke that still drifted from the camp, began to slough out its vaporous orange shape behind the jungle to the west. The wet fatigues hung heavily on me, the loose fabric redolent with sweat, the stifling red dust, smoke, and the insistent oily feculence of the decomposing dead.

That smell would not leave. It had the tenacious properties of gas and could transfer to whatever medium would hold it. It held to the lining of your nostrils, settled into your skin, and rode in the weave of your clothes. In the months ahead, I would become familiar with it in the field, too. Sometimes, weeks later on patrol many miles away, a whiff of it would pass on the sodden air, or I'd wake in the night and it would be there, released for a moment by some trick of humidity from its indelible grasp on my web gear, awakened from its crouch in my awareness, and I would startle with apprehension that it might give away my position on the ground.

Worn down by the long hot day and enfeebled by an overload of divided attention, I made my way back to the room. Though the day so far had been light on actual violence, it was intense with bad feeling. I was haunted by fear of the implacable enemy, and distressed by gnawing, low-grade despair. I decided not to risk taking any more of the pain medicine.

Now as the shades of evening began creeping out of the feathery jungle at the base of the mountain, they brought an insidious and impotent new uncertainty. The prospect of facing another night, and still without a weapon, chilled me with renewed waves of dread that grew as early shadows began quietly to ingest fragments of the ground light.

The day's amalgamation of tyrannic iniquities and pain lay on my mind like a cold shadow, and borne on the lingering smell of the dead, it rose to reveal the singularity of its enlightening, equivocal truth. No amount of training in North Carolina or Panama could have prepared me for the experiences of the last few days. There are no classes in the psychological impact, no advance warning about the terrifying random crush of souls, and no tactical lessons in dealing with combat's legacy of self-doubt or the peculiar witches' Sabbath of emotion that brings a lasting sensitivity to irrelevant discord. There is no instruction in the excruciating reality of these intangible things, and herein my worries about the future became compounded with doubts about my hopelessly inadequate preparation.

Time now stretched before me in a tangled thicket of grim probabilities, joyless and dark, and alive with dangers. I knew now that to navigate its random declivities would require an emotional fortitude stronger than mine. The long festival of my youth was ended. I had been drawn along unseen lines of conversion into the company of fiercely altered men who were conditioned by protracted outrage to the indiscriminate demands of existence at the very edge of their mortality.

Fraught with doubts about my chances of survival, the idea of becoming a functioning member of this community was beyond my grasp. I still did not understand what these men did here, only that whatever it was had made them old. The scale of events had placed my perception in a kind of suspension, and the low-grade indifference with which I had moved through the hours since had served in its way to keep my full comprehension at bay. Yet I had already traveled far enough along the lineaments of destruction to know that I seemed able to withstand a certain amount of it, and I wondered now if the harsh sophistication of this new reality would help or hinder my capacity to cope with the demands it would make in exchange for my continued existence. Whatever lay waiting in the near future, I knew only that the one corpse I couldn't bear to look at was the one I would never have to see.

My immediate need, though, was to get cleaned up, to get out of my foul smelling fatigues. Not yet knowing the laundry situation, I decided to shower in them. I got out of the boots and padded to the stalls. The cool water arrived from the shower head like a melancholy benediction, and I reveled in it as long as I dared, soaping my clothes and releasing the bandages from my legs. After such unexpected and demanding duty, the gauze fell away in useless grey strips of rag. I tried to wash out the saturation of dried blood from the shower slipper that had been stuck in the hardened pool of blood on the floor of my old room, but all the squeezing and soaking I had time for failed to reduce the dark foam it released down the drain. I tried to scrub the blood out of the rifle sling, too, with marginal success, managing only to subdue the smell a bit. Then, after wringing out the clothes, I carried my bundled gear back to the room stark naked, indulging in a small ecstasy of air drying.

On examination I was surprised at the deep bruising that had formed on my legs. They were clouded with large purple swatches and darkly streaked contusions. There were a number of stitched lacerations, and some of the puncture wounds were drawn in like coin purses by the sutures, and though the larger tears still leaked and needed covering, it looked as though I could get along with whatever bandaging I might procure from one of the medics in the camp. I carefully drew on a dry pair of fatigues, trying to keep the fabric away from the puckered stitches.

With another dreaded nightfall coming, I decided to look for a medic and, while I was at it, to find out how to get a weapon before the onset of full dark. I still didn't know my way around the camp, and as I could see that the supply warehouse was still smoldering, I feared that Supply was temporarily out of business. The prospect of heading into another night without a rifle and ignorant of where any bunkers or trenches might be grew with the approaching gloom. It seeped through my awareness in fervent strands of anxiety.

While I was settling into dry fatigues, I was surprised to hear a few hesitant strains of music carried on the early evening sea breeze from the direction of the club house. Someone had evidently turned on the jukebox. As the beach began to give up its day's heat, the cooler ocean air was drawn in to replace it in a poignant metaphor for the paradoxical cycle of life and death. I would come to count the days of my life by the arrival of that still warm, barely refreshing buckle in the air, and this time it summoned me to the club where it seemed that a few of the survivors were assembling for a cold beer before heading for whatever fare was available in the messhall. Perhaps I could find out what I wanted to know if I went over and asked someone.

I got there to find the club was surprisingly full and lively. An enervating heat permeated the interior, still radiating down through the metal roof. Almost everyone was armed, some with pistols, others with M-16s or CAR-15s slung under their arms. When I stepped in, the jukebox was thumping out Sonny and Cher's husky lyrics to "The Beat Goes On," and the bar itself was crowded with what must have been most of the Americans left in the compound, in addition to some of the SeaBees. I recognized the Supply Sergeant who had issued me my equipment the first afternoon and went right over.

"Sergeant. John Moore. My temporary M-1 carbine disappeared. I need a weapon."

He looked at me, clearly not remembering. I couldn't blame him.

"Combat loss, eh?" he said with a wry smile.

"Yeah. Last I saw, it was in pieces."

"Well, there's lots of weapons available now," he said in a tone freighted with irony. I'll get you one."

"I don't mean to drag you away from here, but, er…when?"

This time his mouth made a quick, expressionless flat line. He glanced out at the fading light and went into business mode.

"…Yeah. Okay. We can do it now. Want a beer?"

"Sure."

We got a cold beer for me (one of the best beers I've had in my life) and another for him, then we set out across the compound as the last of the sun sank beneath the jungle, pulling the darkness after it like a curtain. The air became birdless and still, and it turned black in what seemed a single moment, allowing the glow from the smoldering supply shed to make a ruddy borealis in the smoke.

Under a bare light bulb at the hut where he was collecting whatever could be salvaged, I discovered that I had a large choice. He told me that the recon teams to which I would be assigned were carrying CARs, and there were several available.

Some were marked with dried blood on the metal or on the sling. Others showed shrapnel damage. Just as I had been bothered by the sweat band in the helmet, these pieces held a bad feeling. They contained something of that night, and I avoided them.

I soon selected a CAR-15 with a long flash suppressor that looked in good shape, and I broke it open to check the bore. It appeared little used and had a clean receiver group.

"Okay," he said, "anything else?"

He waited for me to answer, his face a stonework of high points and deep angular shadows from the single light source behind him. I hesitated to admit I didn't know where the .45 pistol was either, and reluctant to admit anything that might make me look as careless or stupid as I felt, and with a blind faith in chance that it might turn up, I thanked him and slung the piece over my shoulder, completely forgetting I needed a belt buckle too.

"No, I think this should do it. I feel a little better now."

He smiled his enigmatic smile again as he made an entry in his records. Then he handed me several boxes of ammunition.

"Let me buy you a beer?" I offered, feeling magnanimous thus newly equipped. "A man with this much firepower has to be kept happy."

He chuckled softly. "Sure. Let's go."

We went back to the club where, though reticent by nature, he explained some things about the unit that were helpful to know, including the layout, some of the history, the fact that the recon teams were named alphabetically for snakes, and that the VC made grenades and explosives out of most of the stuff that G.I.s throw away–especially drink cans—so never discard anything in a way you can't control, and always crush the empties.

During all this I came to understand a little of his quiet manner. Even his speech contained a vibrant sort of quiescence, and his silences seemed crowded with a tangible solitude. He'd been invalided off one of the recon teams with gunshot injuries and was enjoying his job as the NCOIC of Supply until his date of rotation back to the States. His strength appeared to come from interior wounds, and though the very qualities of ruthlessness and cunning, mixed with an inner reserve that comes from stunned survival, are not the qualities prized in a close friend, they were admirable in that strange context, and they made him likable, if only at a distance.

He introduced me to one of the medics, a deeply tanned E-6 with pale eyes and a voluminous blond moustache, whose fatigues were faded to an almost colorless hue. When I explained why I wanted some bandaging, he asked to see my wounds. We moved to one of he tables, and I pulled up the legs of the fatigues. He knelt down, and I noticed his scalp move as he made a quick examination. Then he asked where I was bunked. I told him, and he said he'd drop some compresses and wrapping off for me later. He was quiet, withdrawn in the way I had noted in so many other veterans, too long intimate with dangers beyond my budding comprehension, yet a hardened professional who seemed genuinely concerned, though I had the feeling his thoughts were somewhere else, manic and restless behind silent eyes.

When I left the club shortly afterwards to cross over to the messhall, I saw that most night movement between the buildings was being unconsciously channeled by available spills of light from the open windows. Most men tended to step where they could see best, and the messhall had several windows from which fell a clerestory row of bright rectangles that lay pale and distended upon the broken sand, austere and threatening in the early dark. I decided to keep instead to the long shadows, knowing that our movements could be seen from the mountain.

Once inside, out of sight of any sniper who may have replaced the bad one the guys had joked about, and at least temporarily out of whatever pattern of movement the watchers in those caves were recording, I had a large meal, gratifying primarily for its density and weight. It was reassuring to have the company of others and to be surrounded by the muted din of multiple conversations. It made me feel less alone, and with the CAR across my lap, less vulnerable.

When I had finished, I exchanged grins with Ba Foo, mouthing "You number one" and holding up an index finger as I left. She laughed. Still uncertain of how to interpret her behavior, I took her smile as a symptom of pleasure and that my strategy of trying to charm my way off some future insurrectionist's map of the camp was at least making a good start.

As I left the messhall, I saw that my shadow, framed starkly in the yellow backlight of the doorway, vaulted well out across the open ground. It shattered the brief serenity of my thoughts. Anyone who was keeping the camp under observation could reasonably be expected to watch for such signs as a gauge to time a pot shot for the moment when someone leaving a building might be expected to emerge from beneath the roof line. I now saw the presence of the bad sniper for what he probably really was–not an incompetent, but the overture to a long-term plan. He shot just to tell us they were watching and to soften our guard. He didn't need to hit anyone. That was coming. They had been preparing the big one all along.

I decided that in future whenever leaving any lighted interior, I would move quickly to one side of the doorway and, by keeping to the darkness under any overhang for varying intervals, create a delay to confuse an observer's timing before starting across the open. My initial reservations about the questionable security in this place had been dramatically validated in a festival of non-denominational terror and death, and I decided that my instincts would serve me better than the received wisdom of command protocols whenever I had the choice.

I hesitated in the darkness by the messhall and weighed the new reality of risks attending any movement about the compound at night. Weighing what the enemy had to lose by hitting us again against the success of their recent raid argued against another attack so soon. On the other hand, their Buddhist determinism leant their losses an insignificance foreign to the biblical lexicon of my own conditioning, and that thought served only to heighten my unease.

I could feel their stares on me from the smoke-dark bulk of the mountain and assumed that all movement in the compound was being noted, that even now a plan was being formulated which would correct the weaknesses of the last. I felt trapped under the implacable gaze of a thousand-year-old culture, a culture medieval in its outlook and specifically resentful of my presence. These were people who, until very recently, had existed for millennia without electricity, and to whom nightfall meant no interruption to the day. These people could move seamlessly from day to night without the psychological dependence upon artificial light that encumbered those transitional hours for westerners. The "gooks" required no such adjustment, and their vigil everywhere in the country continued without interruption at the fall of darkness.

With a throb of dread beneath my resolve, and with the heft of the dinner riding in my gut, I moved quietly along the side of the messhall, keeping to its long channel of darkness, until I reached the corner where the dead sapper had been pinioned to the wall. I didn't look to see if he was still there, but assumed by the smell that he probably was. Then I dashed through eave-cast islands of starlight shadow until I reached the doorway back at my hootch. I slipped inside in a quick convulsion of safety and went right to the room, which offered at least facsimile security.

It was not late, but the house was quiet. There were now only a few other guys bunked in what remained of the silent rooms. Each of us was alone in his own space, and as it happened, none of us was called for guard duty that night. I sat on the bed and carefully loaded four magazines with ammunition, then lay down in the exhausted after-chill of fear the way I would lie every night that wasn't spent on active alert for the rest of my stay in the country, both in the camp and on field operations–on top of whatever fabric cover there might be, or right on the damp ground, on my back and fully clothed, with the CAR-15 locked and loaded across my chest.

With darkness, all movement was replaced by apprehension. The room filed with shadows and lingering echoes. I could see a few stars through a small hole blown in the roof. Something in the jungle called three long notes, then hushed. The sudden stillness that rushed in to replace the sound brought with it a profound sense of isolation and grim expectancy. I felt entirely cut off from the known world, alone save for the unfamiliar presence of the rifle, which lay in my hands cold and heavy with the coiled weight of its enigmatic past. It seemed to hold a strange consciousness as it pressed against me like the hard bones of a sleeping predator. It was like having a pet dragon, equal parts protection and danger, and I wondered what strange magnetism it might prove to have for the writhing complexities of malevolence. It marked me now as a fighting man, while offering in the balance of contrast a silent testament to my ignorance of the rules, my doubts that I could survive the learning period, and the mysteries attending those unspoken formalities of conduct that can reveal a man's hopelessness and fear.

I felt as old as I was ever going to be, and older than recent events had led me to believe I would ever be. Thus led to make of lingering hope that I knew to be false at least a temporarily useful comfort, and feeling in the rifle the living burden of its inscrutable history, I began to wonder about the fate of its previous owner. It seemed that things often part from men less readily than a man parts from his things. Sometimes long after a person is gone, the things he owned, perhaps because of a certain emotional residuum, remain inscrutably his. People play out their minutes on the earth, but then, following that instant when death throws its private havoc over a life's loves and joys and pitches them through a sudden wall of darkness, their things continue on, passing through the lives of others, and perhaps in the process gathering still more of this oddly sentient energy.

Though over time the rifle and I would become inseparable, on this first night I felt that our relationship was conditional, probationary, as though the piece had been somehow brought to consciousness through the imponderable alchemy of deadly volition, that its sheer power to change everything brought forth a birth of awareness, and that it was I who had to prove myself to it.

After a long while the air became heavy and wet and filled with the sound of insects. I lay unmoving, listening to the night, exhausted but with my filaments stretched out into the darkness all about me like a spider at the center of his web, alert to the slightest movement. The boundary between sleep and waking became a cotton thread so tightly drawn that, too tired to stay awake and too tense to submit, I often crossed it unaware, waking in a chaos of unresolved dreams, instantly attached to consciousness.

Much deeper in the night the faint jungle sounds became fewer, clear, and quickly gone. From everywhere there grew an attentive silence. Everything seemed joined in a conspiracy to give the pressing quiet its full effect. The tension was subtle, a vibration I could feel captured everywhere in the darkness, like the inaudible cry of over-stressed steel.

11

The next few weeks were spent in restoring the compound and maintaining a 24-hour guard roster while the Seabees made impressive progress rebuilding pretty much everything except the TOC. During the day, the air was filled with the tapping of hammers and the whine of power saws. Gaps in the layout of the camp were filled with new construction as replacement hootches rose from the ground and holes in the others were closed. Thousands of new sandbags were installed high around most of the buildings, rising to the narrow screens just under the eaves, interlocked and stacked with a slightly inward slope, like fortress walls.

Tensions rose anew as the shadows grew each evening, and the Navy packed up their tools and went home. Each night the perimeter bunkers were manned with as many Americans as could be spared with such drastically reduced numbers, regardless of anyone's rank or specialty, while a rolling Jeep patrol made slow circuits inside the wire with its lights always off.

A flock of geese was brought in to serve as early warning of unusual movements and sounds. I was startled a few times to encounter them moving singly or in pairs in the starlight, but it was reassuring to hear their soft chuckling as they waddled around in the dark or nestled on the ground, presumably familiarizing themselves with the normal noises of the camp. They were fed regularly by the messhall staff, but most of the guys gave them hand-outs during the day besides, and they soon became fixtures waddling between the buildings and nesting in the shade. I liked them and made friends quickly. It seemed a good idea to cozy up to any force of guardians noted for their nervous dispositions and raucous reaction to startlement.

Replacements for our consignment of vehicles began to show up, the burned and damaged ones hauled away. The bus, with its shattered glass and many bullet holes, still ran, and after some tire repair, remained with us for the purpose of retrieving replacements from the airport. I often wondered about the psychological impact that torn conveyance must have had on the new arrivals.

A surprising discovery was made during repairs to some of the privies that were located at intervals around the perimeter and interspersed between certain buildings throughout the cantonment. These were moveable wooden "two-holer" huts placed over a pair of 55-gallon fuel drums which had been set into the ground. They were opened for cleaning as needed by removing the hut, thus exposing the barrels, pouring in an amount of gasoline or diesel fuel when the depth of their contents had reached an intolerable level, and setting the accumulation of liquefied soilage on fire. Language is inadequate to describe the odor produced downwind by this procedure, a highly unpleasant job that an elderly Vietnamese seemed to do with some degree of pride and for which he was well paid.

One of these privy huts had been the target of much gunfire during the attack, and when it was taken down for replacement, a dead VC sapper was found folded in one of the barrels, shot through the head and up to his neck in feculent excremental sludge. I watched as the swollen corpse was pulled, dribbling black lumps of slime, from the nauseating muck. I felt the back of my throat begin to open as the body was dropped and left there exposed, the distorted limbs bent into grotesque angles set by the inside curve of the barrel, and I wondered at the dedication this grisly discovery implied, that he would have lowered himself deliberately into such a place to use as a firing position. Perhaps it was simply that he, like me, had been afraid and found an unlikely place to hide. Whatever the case, the corpse now lay on its back in the sun with bloated arms and legs crossed in the air, while its obscene questions and complex meaning seeped into the sand. The barrels were fired, and as the black diesel smoke curled away, scattering insects and birds in its course, its shadow swam through the grasping arms of the solitary incongruity and moved seaward across the sand.

It was during this time that I was finally handed orders confirming my elevated security clearance to "Top Secret." Since my remnant copy of the orders that had brought me here contained a code for my security clearance, I had to assume it was Secret only, which made sense in a combat zone, but I didn't like the implication that I might be entrusted with any activity of sufficient importance to require such an exalted sounding status (only later I would learn how humble a Top Secret clearance really was) and regarded the new orders as just evidence of backlogged military bureaucracy.

Soon thereafter I was assigned as assistant team leader to recon team "Anaconda," whose hootch was the first in the row of recon huts closest to the north perimeter wire, just behind the dunes, and near the beach. I carried my gear down to the hut indicated. It seemed to have received little damage in the attack, but the completion of whatever repair it had needed was signaled by fresh paint and a high, tapering surround of new sandbags. There was a plaque bearing the name of a snake above the west-facing door, but it didn't say "Anaconda," so I trudged through the deep sand around to the side that faced the beach, and there found the entrance I was told to look for.

I knocked on the side of the hut. There was no answer from within, so I climbed up the stepped access and entered a small room with two nice bunks, one on each side against the walls. The room contained two built-in shelf systems for storage and foot lockers at the head of each bed, a row of screened ventilation windows under the eaves just above the top layer of external sandbags, and a narrow pass-though to a duplicate room on the other side of a central dividing wall. It was a duplex, the other room housing the leaders of some other team that used the entrance I had first approached. The place seemed accommodating enough, even a mild step up from the community of rooms in the transit hut I had been staying in during reconstruction.

One of the beds was made, and the bare mattress on the other announced its availability. I put away thoughts of how it may have come to be available and dropped my duffle and web gear on it.

While taking in the surroundings, I heard a footstep outside and turned to see a muscular black man about my age step in out of the glare. He had broad shoulders and a narrow waist, and he moved with a graceful shambling gait, like an off-duty halfback. The impenetrable black irises of his hard porcelain eyes seemed to take at a glance whatever measure of me he required as, with what appeared to be fleeting but ill-concealed effort, he gave me a quick smile and simply told me his name. This was Staff Sergeant Johnson, the team leader.

The worn fabric of his fatigues was faded to anemic green from heavy use and long exposure to the sun. His clothes alone announced the long operational history that had set his eyes. He moved about the room with practiced familiarity and a certain depth of command assurance. I saw immediately that, though he knew his business, he didn't like it, and he was deeply tired. He had that *feel* about him I had by now learned to expect from veterans. He exuded the remoteness I'd seen in others, born of nervous strain, of over exposure to stress. I had the feeling that he had adjusted to the responsibility of running his recon team against his own will. Despite his assured comportment, there was something missing, something that seemed to pull him back from a full commitment to the moment.

While I was sorting these first impressions, he revealed to my immediate distress that he was due for rotation back to the States. I realized that this could mean that I might soon be placed in temporary charge of the team. I wanted no such responsibility. I did not want to be in charge of anything or anybody. I knew instinctively that I was not up to the job of taking responsibility for anything in this culture of violent and inevitable consequence. I could accept being the number two guy under the leadership of someone with Johnson's evident esoteric comprehension and the experience it implied, but the idea of being the one answerable for making the right decisions under the pressure of anything even remotely like what had happened already was terrifying.

Johnson's air of worn competence, along with the fact that he was a rank above me, enabled me to cling for a few moments longer to the forlorn hope that someone with more rank and experience was actually due to replace him and that my job would be the assigned second in command. When I asked timidly what the line-up would be when he left the country, all my fears were instantly gratified by his assurance that I was that person. A wave of despair sagged through me. I couldn't believe that the military would rush someone with my utter lack of experience into such a responsible position. If they needed good leaders why not assign the new guys to teams whose commanders had several months left on their tours in which to teach their replacements?

I was convinced that I had been assigned to the wrong unit. Everything I had learned or surmised thus far indicated that whatever missions were run out of FOB 4, they were outside the scope of my training—even beyond my knowledge. I felt trapped in this harsh new imperative. I not only needed to learn quickly what was actually going on, I was in urgent need of some exotic new mental conditioning that I feared the method of and did not want.

I assumed that the attack might have opened large holes in the unit's command structure, which would explain some interim redistributions of responsibility, but from what little I had learned of its mission, the parameters of the specialty were closely guarded, deliberately held in secret, and lay beyond my uncertain grasp. I feared the job would really only be learnable in the field, and even in my limited understanding of what that might entail, any wrong decision or bad guess by me would carry irreversible consequences to life.

These worries led me to see what bothered me about Johnson's manner. The attack, coming as it did so close to his last weeks in-country, had made him nervous, had left its mark on his hard-won assurance. That fed back and made me nervous too, but for the opposite reason. What I worried about was all piled up ahead of me.

Code for the team leader's job was One-Zero, which made me the Two-Zero, and in his anxiety to turn things over to me, Johnson began his orientation, a process that commenced with informing me of that simple code designation and went on as things occurred to him for the next few weeks, but was nonetheless so comprehensive that I had trouble absorbing it all at the rate I feared I must. The attack had seared with bloody indelibility its mark upon me of what was at stake. With each new aspect of recon team work that Johnson told me about, my fears of the responsibilities that lay ahead only grew. With each thing he told me about the job, I cringed beneath the incremental burden of all that it implied.

He told me first of all to get my clothes tailored down so that they fit snugly. This would reduce the whisper the full-cut fabric made when it brushed against itself with even the simplest movement, like walking. I learned that for some missions we wore fatigues cut from captured Chinese cloth and that I needed to draw two sets of them.

He advised me to cut down the brim of my jungle hat, the standard issue olive drab head gear of the type fishermen wear. It had a wide brim that he warned would restrict my vision when, saturated with rain or river water, it would collapse around my head. (I would learn another reason later: a wide brim restricts your vision upward into the trees.) Its flat crown bore a stitched cargo ribbon all around, sectioned for the addition of leaves and foliage stems, though I had already noticed some of the men used them to display souvenir hand grenade rings in ironic parody of fishing lures.

He advised me to have a piece of day-glow orange fabric cut from the bright panels used to signal aircraft from the ground and to get it stitched inside the crown of my hat. This was for the purpose of showing the pilots, should I ever call for close air support in the field, where the good guys were. The theory was that the team would simply turn their hats inside out, and the pilots would see the bright spots of orange in the jungle to mark our positions. A simple expedient—in theory. When I asked him where one went to have these things done, he told me the maids would do it.

"Maids? What maids?"

"They'll be back. We have to hire a quota of 'indij'," was all he would say about the maids. I had the impression that, though he found their services useful, he held his own opinions about the advisability of having locals in the compound every day, and that like myself, he was not without his suspicions about the role some of these people may have played in setting up the attack.

He told me to make sure there was no serial number or manufacturer's markings on my rifle. Any such traceable nomenclature must be removed from all equipment. In addition, I should spend as much time as I needed to keep my bayonet honed to a razor sharp edge and to keep the scabbard packed with grease so that withdrawing the blade would always be silent. Then it should be worn in a convenient place on my web gear, preferably in front and inverted, the best place being the front part of the back pack shoulder strap, for ready access. None of this sounded good.

The American bayonet is short, the blade being only a little over six and a half inches long with three and a quarter inches of back blade along the top, so it is designed to function, in addition to its traditional role, more as a general use field knife. Johnson's admonitions about keeping it silent, sharpened beyond regulation standard—and especially handy—were chilling.

I still did not know exactly what the recon teams actually did in the field, though I had some vague ideas about gathering information on enemy activity through binoculars, but each of Johnson's instructions carried deeply troubling implications. I was beginning to realize that there might be rather more to recon than just scouting. I didn't like hearing about any of these things but knew by Johnson's humorless manner that I had better learn everything he could teach me as quickly as I could absorb it.

I learned about the radio frequencies we used in the field and began to study the frequency book for memory cues. He taught me the trick of folding the ribbon antenna of the PRC-25 radio all around my back pack so that it didn't stick up in the field. Fully deployed upward, it not only would catch in the foliage where it emitted a twang like a steel tape measure, a tool it closely resembled, but it marked you out to the enemy as the man connected to air support and, ultimately, to extraction. For these reasons Johnson never extended the antenna unless he could send it up along the trunk of a tree or disguise it inside some lower growth. This meant that all too often one's transmissions could not be received over the distances at which we operated, as wet foliage cut down drastically on sending range, though not quite as much on reception. Thus you could never be sure that your periodic reports back to base were being received, so if you called for extraction and the choppers failed to show, you could assume they didn't hear you at base, and then you had damn well better show up on time at the pre-arranged emergency extraction co-ordinates.

He warned me about use of the squelch knob, because you never want to make a non-jungle noise out in the field. Thus, you have to keep the squelch turned down so low that you can't hear the characteristic "tssht" sound of the transmitter and therefore have no audible indication that you're actually sending.

As the One-Zero, he said he always carried the radio himself, and despite the fact that he (and I) were both physically (and therefore visibly) larger than the Chinese Nungs who comprised the rest of our team, whenever out on operations he always walked in the center of the formation. This was the best place for the team leader in case of compromise from any direction. I began to appreciate the radio as a weapon of greater importance even than a rifle. It was a direct connection to artillery and air support, to adaptation to the unexpected, to extraction and rescue, and thus ultimately to salvation.

I learned many hand signals and some of the pidgin-English words he used to communicate with the Nungs. He warned me never to move along a ridge line or in terrain where we could be seen against the sky, to move into an RON (Remain Over Night) site through jungle that no one else can approach without making noise, and then, after nightfall, to move several yards again.

Always set out M-1 "foot" mines around your night position, and teach yourself to sleep on your back so that you will see the most whenever you open your eyes. Avoid movement at night if you can, and if you need to signal aircraft, put a flashlight up the barrel of an M-79 grenade launcher, or better, use one of the small emergency hand lights you can "borrow" from a bracket mounted just inside the doors of a helicopter. You have to be careful not to let any light strike the foliage on the underside of the jungle canopy. Not easy.

Most of these things made intuitive sense, and some I knew or thought I knew, but it is one thing to read a statement in a field manual or to hear a passing advisory remark in a classroom in North Carolina but quite another to re-encounter the information direct from a veteran who stands in living testimony to hard fact when choices are few and each of mortal consequence.

Maps, because they were made from aerial photographs, were only rough guides to your location, as the depth and layers of jungle canopy couldn't be accurately depicted from above, so the contour of the ground itself could only be estimated on the paper, making an accurate determination of your position on the ground all but impossible. To my sorrow, I would learn the importance of this ambiguity later.

Johnson told me to draw a pair of gloves and more canteen covers from supply, along with at least two dozen magazines and enough ammunition to fill them. I would need three canteens for water, and the rest of the space on my web belt would need to accommodate an additional four canteen covers as ammunition pouches, each containing six loaded magazines. He advised me to load only 18 rounds in each magazine instead of the full 20. This avoided full compression of the follower spring and increased the chances over time of uniform upward feed pressure on the ammo stack as you fired. The gloves were non-regulation, but they had them for the recon teams, not only to cut down on abrasions in the jungle, but also to conceal the natural shine on the backs of your hands. I was advised to cut the trigger finger off whichever glove was relevant.

The combined weight of water and ammo would prove initially to be a growing challenge on patrol in the jungle heat, and I would learn that the additional 25 pounds of the radio would have a protracted effect on my ability to move with stealth through the thick undergrowth.

Johnson took me over to the Nung's section of the compound to meet the other members of the team. They were "housed" near the messhall we maintained for the Nungs in their section of the camp, an area informally separated from the American portion by the row of recon huts and the network of boardwalks that connected them. I did not know what to expect. I had heard only that these men were a tribe of fierce South Chinese hill men with a long tradition of hiring out as mercenaries and that they had a reputation for efficient ruthlessness.

As we stepped into the shade under the rolled side flaps of their communal tent, I was struck by the rancid smell of *nuoc mam* fish oil, so popular in Vietnamese cooking. Like garlic, it leached out of the body in perspiration, and here it permeated the captured air with a sour, unguinous miasma that reminded me of rotting skin. I had encountered it before, but here where these men were concentrated, and so near their mess facility, it seemed to replace the air itself.

There were ten of them seated together around a wooden picnic-style table or squatting Asian style on the sand talking quietly among themselves. Johnson greeted them with some cat-cry word I didn't understand. They looked up indifferently when I heard him say my name (Sergeant Moore came back as *"Trung-shi Mo'"* by the one or two who mumbled an effort to pronounce it). A few nodded almost imperceptibly in dull facsimile of greeting and then regarded me silently with depthless black eyes in which I detected a mixture of predacious curiosity and understandable doubt.

I had no prior expectations about how they might appear but was initially surprised at their youth. The smooth skin of their faces was pared back to the shape of the underlying bone–but their eyes were old, and their hard stares soon became a physical presence, a disembodied force that quickly grew until it filled the space between us. It made me uncomfortable. Only one of them seemed to be over twenty. He, I was told, was our point man. He always held that position, a place of honor among the others. I understood why. The inherent dangers that attended the job of walking point were well known, and I could tell even then that it had aged him. I tried to smile a friendly greeting, but he just watched me with the intense, implacable gaze of the raptor. He and Johnson, despite their cultural differences, seemed to have a mutual understanding, a respect born of shared experience I did not want to think about.

Two appeared to be little more than children, and I had the discomforting feeling that at least two were real killers. I decided to say nothing, which I hoped would at least have the dubious merit of lending me some mystery in the absence of any overt signal of inadequacy.

The few faces that had betrayed a fleeting animation during the introduction quickly settled into an expressionless inscrutability, betraying nothing within. I was beset by their extraordinary foreignness to any people I had ever met, and standing among them in a vacuum created by the absence of any behavioral sign from any of them pierced me with a silent wound of profound dislocation and a sharp dread of the day that I knew was coming when I would inherit responsibility for these strange little men and their secret knowledge.

The meeting didn't last long, largely because of the language barrier, but mostly I realized, because its primary purpose had been simply to give them a look at me. The encounter served to deepen my sense of alienation and inexperience, and it hardened the walls in my prison of self-doubt among these enigmatic masters of the ancient, silent kill.

I was relieved when finally we left and made our way back to the relative familiarity of our hut, Johnson with his easy stride and happy, I was sure, to have discharged another responsibility in turning things over to his replacement, unburdened of one more thing he would soon never have to think about again, while I, pressed beneath the fierce metallic weight of the sun and freighted with my own despair, hoped that I had escaped for the present without betraying my own doubtful contingencies.

Before the SeaBees were completely finished with their work in the compound, Johnson decided to make an addition to our hootch. He befriended a few of them at the club and persuaded them to construct a grenade barrier at the entrance to the hut, which they agreed to do in exchange for a couple of souvenir AK-47s. They soon built a stout barricade wall of heavy planks which stood about two feet inside the doorway, secured at the base to the floor and at the top to a roof rafter. It thus became necessary to step around the barrier in order to gain entrance to the hut, but it also meant that a hand grenade could not be tossed directly inside the room, nor would a burst of automatic weapons fire from a running intruder likely be directed to do much harm. Hardly proof against determined effort, but a welcome inconvenience.

One day soon afterwards, I entered the hootch to discover a shy young Vietnamese woman standing in the room, her tiny hands clutching a standard American made broom. She was slight and girlish with dark eyes, inflated lips, and straight black hair that shone in the ambient window light like the promises in magazines. Her unexpected childlike presence with the over-size broom threw her completely out of context, and in the moment it took me to realize she was probably one of the maids, her small damp eyes went wide, and she fled into the adjoining room in evident fear. I felt bad for having frightened her and made the mistake of chasing after her, there to find her cowering on a bed with another young woman. The two of them clung together and stared up at me transfixed, like kittens in a box. It may have been the first time either of them had seen an American up close. We must have seemed like giants to these diminutive young people. Or perhaps they saw in me some confirmation of the racial propaganda that lives in all war zones. By smiling and using welcoming gestures, I tried to lure her back, but pursuing her into the other room had evidently confirmed her fears, so I decided to withdraw from the hut altogether and let them get along with whatever their chores might be. It seemed that these were people who had been conditioned to see the world in ways I would never comprehend but hoped that I would be able to make friends enough to at least achieve a balance with their mistrust.

I slipped back outside into the oppressive glare, and in the absence of any specific assignment to do otherwise, decided to take advantage of the general confusion of reconstruction and headed in the direction of the clubhouse, which offered the promise of something cold to drink and an oasis of humid shade. Although the ferocious afternoon sun beat its fists on the corrugated metal roof, the air captured inside the club, smelling of old spills and new sweat, was slightly less hot. A difference of even a few degrees was a relief. You could reach overhead and extend your hand into the radiant broil from the roof tin, a good twenty degrees hotter than the lower air. There were a few guys at the bar taking a break from various work details, their skin shiny with sweat. The familiar electric twang of Buffalo Springfield's "For What It's Worth" was playing on the jukebox:

Stop, children, what's that sound? Everybody look what's goin' 'round...

In view of all I had seen and all Johnson had told me, I resolved to stick with non-alcoholic drink from now on. I got an orange soda and selected a chair at one of the tables where I could sit with an unobstructed view of both entrances and enjoy holding the cold aluminum can while trying to make the fizzy sweet flavor last. I was still a bit jumpy and started at any abrupt sound—even a beer being popped open, or the scrape of a chair leg. I tried to concentrate, to sort my doubts and to discard a host of recent illusions.

Still curious about the two girls, but unwilling to add yet another irritant to my rising mountain of surreal concerns, I at first thought simply to dismiss them as not being important enough to worry too much about, though I felt sorry for how frightened they had been. I wasn't used to scaring people and had no ready formula for addressing the problem. The incident had happened, it was over in a moment, and besides, I was certain the most scared person for miles around was me, and I really couldn't see what they had to worry about.

I was trying to pass the encounter off as merely anomalous when I began to wonder if perhaps the events of the past few days had effected some change in my own outward aspect, some indication of my inner turmoil, however slight. Might I be revealing some small precursive sign, visible even to a stranger, that I, too, had come to embrace the madness? Perhaps in her flight the girl had revealed an accidental masterpiece of faint perception, fleeing the very person that I would have to become in order to survive this *ultima thule* of random violence. It was true that ever since I had first seen the camp my lessons had been crowding in like a dense pack of demons. Considering that first night's baleful introduction, still writhing with its terrors and injuries, that had ushered me into this monstrous place, perhaps she had glimpsed in me there some signature of what I knew.

My nascent enlightenment had brought into focus one clear fact, though: that here in this malevolent festival of final solutions there was but one rule–survival–though it came heavily laced with strange new conditions I had yet to learn. Here all familiar rules were held in suspension. Here there were doleful new protocols, primal and immediate, and each governed fresh dimensions of dread.

I had long held a commonsense concern about alienating anyone unnecessarily, especially foreigners who might harbor some enigmatic agenda or whose elusive subtleties of tradition invited unintended affront. I knew little about the Vietnamese and thus felt nothing against them or any of their subcultures. I had no clear aversion or animosity toward the people, and despite a host of vibrant doubts about my own future, mixed with a risen respect for the designated enemy's capacity to do me harm, I managed to retain a spark of tentative sympathy for their resentment of our presence in their country.

Although I was sorry to have upset the girls and hoped to find a way to smooth it over with them, in the horrifying flashes of that terror-riven firefight, all sentiment had been suppressed, and now whatever momentary remnants of feeling I could summon to simulate normal social formalities became secondary to an overwhelming concern for my own survival—an imperative that was growing steadily at the heart of even the most mundane daily decisions. Thus I resolved to tread lightly and wear a smile around these people who had been given official sanction to move about all quarters of the camp. No matter how pleasant and helpful they may appear to be, their presence in the compound meant that nowhere—not hootch, bunk, or bunker—would ever offer me more than spurious sanctuary.

It might be true that these two women had come onto the compound and then presumably made their way, or been conducted, to a particular assignment location without having encountered an American close up. I also realized with a start that with all the extra people in the camp—Navy personnel, temporary Vietnamese workers, and a few pallid replacements—I had failed to observe that some of the little figures in native pajama-like trousers, hunched beneath the shadow of their conical straw hats, were actually females. I wondered how, or even if, they had been vetted. I wondered if I was the only person concerned about this evident ease of access to all parts of the compound. I wondered again at all I had to learn.

By the time I finished the orange soda it had gone warm and flat, and remembering the supply sergeant's warning, I crushed the can. I had stayed away deliberately to give the girls time to do whatever they were assigned to do. When I got back to the hut, they were gone, vanished as mysteriously as they had appeared, but everything had been cleaned, the floor swept clear of the ceaseless accumulation of fine dust, the clothes on the shelves were neatly folded, including the filthy jungle fatigues that had lain in a damp pile under my bunk, now washed, sun dried, and added to the rest. Though it didn't ease my reservations about importing native workers each day, I began to see the plan had its merits.

Over the following days I learned that one of the senior maids owned an old foot-treadle sewing machine and often brought it with her for general alterations and repair work. She would set it up outdoors on one of the duckboards and enjoyed a brisk business adding unit patches and chevrons for the non-recon people, pockets, straps, stitching up rents in field clothes, and any other odd sewing work the guys needed. Due to the combined ravages of both climate and jungle operations, she usually had plenty to do in normal times, but during these weeks, with all the battle damage and the need to alter new issue, the guys kept her pretty busy, paying her extra for these chores.

I took my jungle fatigues to her and tried to indicate what I wanted, using elaborate hand gestures in combination with my limited grasp yet of the pidgin English we used with the Vietnamese. She cackled at my efforts, dropped my clothes in a pile on the ground, and shooed me away. They were ready within an hour, double-stitched, and I soon learned when I changed into a pair in order to take her the set I'd had on, that she had removed so much excess fabric the slim cut result was a bit cooler.

Although the girl assigned to my hootch remained irremediably shy and would scurry away whenever I happened to return while she was there, she slowly began to reduce the running distance until she would simply hide around the corner until I left. Gradually, though, she seemed to realize that she couldn't finish her assigned duties if she interrupted her routine to fly away whenever I was around.

Eventually she began to tolerate the barbarian's presence in his lair, although her gaze always followed me around the way a portrait's eyes pursue a tourist in a gallery. Eventually, and through continued effort, I got her to smile one day. I learned that her name was Lei Thi Hao, that she was about 20 (though she looked so much younger–unusual for a Vietnamese–that I guessed she might be lying, perhaps to keep her job), that she had a daughter, and that her husband was "gone" (not so unusual for a Vietnamese).

With the exception of a few of the SeaBees who stayed late each afternoon to enjoy the hospitality of our club and its supply of ice cubes, along with the addition of a few hard-drinking enlisted Marines from the 3rd Amtracs (our neighbors down the beach), the departure of our local help signaled the end of each work day. The sounds of construction, vehicles, and shouting gradually fell away, and in the sudden quiescence that replaced the temporary population, snatches of music from the club house jukebox rose to carry in fragmentary Morse on the unsteady sea breeze, accompanied by faint measures of ironic laughter as the shadows of evening hurried in to surround us again with their ominous silences and strange night calls.

The soft lap and hiss of surf on the beach just beyond the perimeter dunes carried none of the comforting rhythm of peaceful shores far away. Each wave muttered its mantra of warning to our inadequately defended bunkers. The whole South China Sea, so excruciatingly romanticized by novelists, became each night a dark and restless arena for speculation, offering both concealment and conveyance for the approach of an implacable enemy determined to try again.

_12_

"Pack your shit."

With those words, Johnson informed me that the day of my first field operation had arrived. I had been anticipating this news with a mixture of dread and vague curiosity for weeks, knowing that as steady progress in repairs to the camp continued the time would inevitably come when the missions of FOB 4, whatever they were, would resume. Now that the reality was upon us, all my anxiety awoke anew with a start. So here it was at last. I was to be sent forth, deprived of even the cardboard defenses of the base camp, to sortie into the mysterious hinterland, there to invite imponderable new measures of hazard.

At first, the news scrambled my priorities, and I had to get hold of myself to make logical choices in assembling and preparing my web gear and weapons. It was one thing to prepare for their theoretical use, quite another to begin the practical organization of this equipment for an actual mission that suddenly loomed, heavy with unknowns.

As Johnson began taking his gear down from where he kept it hanging on pegs he told me the operation called for our "Chinese"-made fatigues. The news that we were going out at all was ominous enough; this detail added a portentous new dimension of misgiving to the whole shadowy prospect. He threw me some "airborne" tape (actually duct tape colored a flat buff green) and told me to make sure that everything that could make a non-jungle noise was taped down, especially loose clothing, rifle sling swivels, and any buckles or metal strap ends. Even though I had taken his advice about having my fatigues tailored down for a closer fit, it was still necessary to muffle the natural rustle of clothing, especially the large cargo pockets on the pants.

Johnson told me to get ready as fast as possible even though he thought we wouldn't be going out before the next morning. This was due to the fact that the Nungs were Buddhists and as such were serious numerologists. They would not go out with an odd number of men on the team or on an odd numbered day of the month. Since that happened to be an odd numbered day, he knew we would stay on standby alert at least until morning. Then he left to inform the rest of the team and to select the ones who would be going.

When he returned, he had been to Supply and drawn freeze-dried LRRP (Long Range Reconnaissance Patrol) rations for the team, along with additional ammunition and two M-33 hand grenades each for himself and for me. He informed me that we did not issue hand grenades to the Nungs because the casualty radius of the M-33 was greater than the distance they could throw them. Then he told me to straighten a least one leg of each cotter pin that held the pull rings securing the "spoon" on my grenades and to attach them to my web gear with just enough tape or rubber bands to prevent their working loose or falling off in case we were running (running?! …Why might we be ru...?), but could be easily pulled free if needed.

The LRRP rations were in plastic bags. He advised me that two bags each, one dry, would be enough for five or six days and to open whichever one I might wish to start with and pour in a small amount of water to reconstitute just a part of the contents on the bottom. More water would make the bag too heavy, and besides, filling the bag with enough water to prepare the whole thing at once would cause the bag to swell out of proportion to its convenience and would produce too much food anyway.

Once a bit of water was in the dried meal, the bag could be kneaded to produce a mush that would be eaten in the field with my fingers. The object being to achieve a consistency that would enable me to roll a pinch of mush into a small ball so that it could be eaten quietly by hand the way the Vietnamese ate balls of rice. Then he instructed me to reseal the bag, place it in one of my cargo pockets, and tape any excess fabric to my leg. This would keep the additional weight from causing the pant leg to swing with each step, while at the same time allowing the heat of my leg to warm the contents.

I had my web gear set up the way Johnson carried his, and once he was satisfied that I was ready, with all magazines filled, gear tight, first meal prepped, and was rigged overall for silence, he announced that in addition, I was to carry the PRC-25 radio.

"Gotta get used to it," he said flatly. The man could convey a lot of perverse information with a few words.

This raised my load to something around 75 pounds. The straps bore down on my shoulders before I had taken a step. He told me to walk around and get accustomed to the weight. This effort proved the truth in all the newsreel and training film images of Vietnam in which the men always seemed to move with their bodies canted slight-

ly forward the way people walk in rain, as though they were plodding against the massed enormity of danger, heat, the sudden need to
crouch, heart ache, and a burdensome legion of private requirements
just to keep on living. Now I learned that, even if all that were true, the
characteristic angle was mostly a matter of biology, of anatomy and
the carriage required to transport all their heavy field equipment, the
posture dictated by the need to "hump the gear."

Preparation included writing down and memorizing the coded radio frequencies to be used on certain days to report our progress, plus
alternate frequencies the mere use of which would carry messages of
intelligence or for different kinds of emergencies. In addition there
were numerous letter and number codes that could be transmitted in
the clear if necessary to convey other information. I understood the
purpose for these, but the number and complexity of possible combinations was overwhelming, and in my heightened state of anxiety,
impossible to memorize, especially as most were date sensitive and
would change each day as we progressed through the patrol. Johnson
told me to keep the ones I couldn't remember written down somewhere and to literally guard them with my life. He would carry the
small ten-pound PRC-10 emergency locator radio.

As we continued with preparations, Johnson grew ominously
taciturn, withdrawing still more toward some distant inner horizon.
I guessed it was what he needed to do, and who was I to question his
coping mechanism? I went from black introspection to an almost irrepressible urge to talk, but I kept to myself, wondering what lay ahead,
worried about how I would do, yet unwilling to probe his silence with
yet another question. Besides, as long as he could cope he might be
able to keep me alive. He knew what he needed to do and doubtless knew that he couldn't really teach me everything I would need
to know. In fact, the essential information remained incommunicable
and would have to be gleaned from direct experience in the field. (After all, who could possibly have explained in advance the apocalyptic
wave that would break over me in the attack my first night here?)

As events would soon reveal, though, he had done his duty by me
as best he could in view of the unpredictable conditions imposed by
the realities of operating in the jungle. It had all made him distant and
strange. I guess it made us all strange.

Even though he didn't expect that we would be called before the
next morning, he said that being on standby meant being ready to go

at any time, day or night, until the order came. We had to sleep as best we could fully dressed and be able to get up, grab our additional gear and go in minutes. Over the hours of waiting the tension was almost beyond bearing–a living limbo of anxiety in which the leer of fate governed every leaden moment.

We took turns going to dinner in the messhall that night, one going in full gear to eat while the other stayed in the hootch with the radio, then switching. The equipment was cumbersome and heavy, but walking in the deep sand over to the messhall and back actually helped me to find an angle of least resistance to forward movement and to locate a few places where my web gear could be better silenced. I had long been aware that partially-filled canteens, whether the old aluminum type or the newer plastic issue, sloshed audibly through their covers. Mine seemed inordinately loud. When I asked Johnson if there was some trick to mute the sound, he just said that was one noise we could do little to control, that it got worse as we used the contents, and just to stay aware of it.

Then, almost as an afterthought, he passed along another recommendation: to practice easing back the charging handle of my CAR-15 until I could do it absolutely soundlessly. It would be prudent, due to the temperature and humidity variations we would encounter in the field, to do this every morning. He called it "breaking the seal" around the chambered cartridge, since the steel of the weapon itself and the brass casing of the first round could swell or contract at different rates during the night just enough to cause a residual film of lubrication oil in the chamber or on the cartridge to delay or prevent ejection, thus jamming the rifle. This, he said, was unlikely, but it was possible. Since almost everything that had happened since my arrival had been a congress of fateful new improbabilities, I was becoming conditioned to expect the greatest peril, no matter how unlikely. I immediately did as he said. The procedure had to be done extremely slowly, but with practice I managed to draw the chambered round back just a few millimeters to assure a clear fit and then to re-seat it without releasing the faintest metallic click.

That night, as we lay on our bunks in the absolute dark, fully clothed with our heads on our equipment, our faces, necks and arms smeared with two shades of green greasepaint, and alert to any summons, I realized suddenly that in all the excitement of preparation, I had failed to learn what our mission was. Feeling a bit foolish, but unwilling to live in ignorance any longer, I asked Johnson what was up for us.

After a silence his voice came out of the stillness, weary with the gravity of his long experience in this bizarre, unutterable specialty. He said that we were to be inserted in an area "near" the Cambodian border where there was a suspected prisoner of war camp in which it was believed that Americans were being held. The tinge of irony he put on the word "near" was, I felt sure, intended to alert me to which side of the Cambodian border he was talking about. I was aware of the issue of the Cambodian border, as one of our Special Forces "A" teams had recently been overrun and wiped out by a force of the enemy that had come in from the west and escaped back across the border. I had seen the aerial photographs of their camp after the fight, where the still un-recovered bodies of the Americans lay sprawled in the open and their presumed identities labeled by small peels of chart tape. We were, at least ostensibly, not allowed to pursue or even to fire across that vague international frontier.

We were to get as close to the designated area as we could and to report on anything we saw or heard, including observations about the terrain and vegetation, any trails, the nature and number of any marks on the ground or in the trees that could give an indication of foot or even vehicle traffic. In other words, we were to learn everything we could while confirming the location of any prisoner compound. He added, perhaps to ease any tension he may have detected in my ques-tion, that it would probably be a five-day milk run since I was inex-perienced, and besides, reports of alleged prison camps were pretty common. He guessed there was probably nothing there. Whatever the case, the trip promised to be a long one regardless of the exact location of our insertion point, because anyplace near the border with Cambo-dia was all the way across the country to the west.

Our elaborate preparations for unpleasant contingencies not with-standing, in principle at least, the mission sounded simple enough. We were to be inserted somewhere pretty far to the west, but it was for the purpose of seeing what we could without being seen, and once we had done that to Johnson's satisfaction—and I knew he was anxious about the imminent end date of his tour—he would call for the extraction, and the choppers would come to bring us back.

I tried to comfort myself with the fact that reconnaissance was traditionally about getting in, gathering information, and getting back out again without being detected, and Johnson had said nothing about orders regarding contact with the enemy. This was cold comfort, but at least, I thought forlornly, I was to get one operation's worth of exposure to the process before Johnson would DEROS (Date Eligible to Return from Overseas) back to the States.

Everything he had told me made sense, but the amount of new information that had to be remembered and contingencies understood was almost overwhelming. I worried that I might forget some simple but essential detail, and my fear of imperiling the team through ignorance or by some lapse in memory raised the stakes I held in the future more than anything that had ever happened to me. If something bad happened, would I panic? Would I remember the codes? What would I do if something happened to Sgt. Johnson? Would I panic and freeze? All night my mind struggled with priorities and the possibility of extraordinary events that might re-arrange them.

We passed a sleepless night uninterrupted by the mission call, but Johnson was up well before first light and told me to get over to the messhall for whatever I wanted to eat and to take care of any other "business" as soon as possible. We could be called at any time. We took care of our personal stuff in shifts as we'd done the night before, and before the first grey hint of morning, Johnson went down to the Nungs' tent to assure that they were ready.

Once all personal preparations for the day were completed, we went back to waiting. Hours passed. The day's heat rose, and we sweated in the heavy equipment, drenched in the oppressive humidity and wrung out with nervous tension. The psychological pressure of continuing standby weighed upon me. I could see it working on Johnson too, but he just said that one day of this was nothing, that the command people understood the situation and had an automatic stand-down in the event that a team had to remain on hold for a mission for four full days–96 straight, interminable hours. Sometimes the weather would not be good in the Area of Operation (AO) or in the intended Landing Zone (LZ), and then when it would clear some time later, the Nungs might refuse to go out because it was an odd day of the month, so another hold would carry the team through another night and into the next day. At last, if conditions didn't cooperate with equipment availability, or with certain Buddhist traditions, or because of bad weather or other logistical problems, the team was relieved and another team would replace them on standby alert to go in their stead.

By then, the first team would be so strung out on nervous fatigue they'd be too depleted to be effective anyway. There were times when these or other delays outlasted the tactical reasons for the operation, and the mission would simply be cancelled.

This time, though, the dreaded moment arrived in the form of a truck that pulled up beside the hootch in late morning, the signature rattle of diesel valves indicating without the need to see it that it was the unit's only deuce-and-a-half. I was already depleted and hated to hear it. I had been praying for storms at the distant LZ, wherever it was. I felt a stab of irritation when the driver then tapped out a cheerful four-note rhythm on the plaintive nasal horn that seems to be standard in all military vehicles. I wondered how many of those horns the government's contract called for each year. Too many. The sound had never bothered me before.

As Johnson assembled the Nungs outside, I struggled to buckle into all my equipment and to heft the radio pack onto my back. When I stepped out to join them, I noted that he had selected six of the guys, which meant we would be a team of eight. I nodded to them self-consciously and tried to summon a pleasant expression to cut the tension, hoping that a slight smile tinged with a wisp of philosophical resolve might convey across the cultural divide. Their eyes stared back blank as a cat's, dark slits behind the camouflage greasepaint.

We climbed aboard the truck, helping each other up, the weight of two full canteens, an additional five canteen pouches full of loaded magazines, rifle, grenades, standard web butt pack, and the radio almost overbalancing me, and we rode to the west end of the compound. There two of the aging Korean War Sikorsky S-1 helicopters I had seen before waited in the sun, tall on the shimmering tarmac with their shadows cringing beneath them. Their paint was bleached and chipped. Numerous black streaks of oil threaded from the cowl hinges and inspection ports. Today they were accompanied by two late model Hughes gun ships that appeared much smaller parked beside them wearing dark olive drab paint. None of the aircraft bore any identification markings.

The crews of the Hueys appeared to be Americans. They sat silently and impenetrable, wearing non-regulation mirrored Ray-Bans, and appeared to be keeping to themselves, aloof, while the Vietnamese pilots of the big S-1s swaggered about on the ground in their flight suits like smaller versions of their American counterparts, as though stewardship of certain flight controls translated somehow into mastery of the air itself. I had immediate doubts about being transported by Vietnamese pilots in vintage aircraft, even if they had been trained in Texas, and I wasn't in a mood that left much room for sympathy with swagger. I just hoped that, whatever their experience in the air, I would be around to breathe some of it when this trip was over.

The truck pulled up in front of the S-1s, and we jumped down. Johnson immediately began dividing up the team, assigning four each to the two big helicopters according to weapons. He wanted an equal distribution of weapons and to split the leadership, with an M-79 Grenade Launcher on each chopper, himself to accompany one, and I the other. As we climbed into the Sikorskys, the blades began to turn on the two Hueys.

Once the four team members I was to ride with were seated, I arranged myself on the steel deck in the open doorway. Thus seated, my lower utility ("butt") pack rested on the deck, and served to support the weight of the heavy radio pack. This relieved the pressure on my shoulders if I leaned back slightly.

As I settled in and watched the other S-1's rotors begin to turn, I realized that now I was really in the war. All that had happened so far had taken place "at home" on an American base or in the cantonment of FOB 4. It had arrived unbidden. But now, after enough warfare already to last me a lifetime, I was actually going "out" for the first time. It felt like I was asking for it. Out there somewhere into the Mesozoic wilds of Southeast Asia, into a mysterious wilderness, every bit of it impacted with bad feeling, and all because of some monstrous complexity of strategic reasoning which lay beyond my comprehension. I struggled to suppress my nervousness. From here on I had to be ready for pretty much anything, including the various circumstances that might accompany getting out of this dubious machine .

After a doubtful delay in getting the S-1s started, the unmuffled engines began to roar, and the long rotors began to swing past the doorways, quickly filling the open cabin with dust, wind, and noise. The whole machine began to twist and sway on its tires with the lateral torque of the blades. The wheels lifted off, both machines pivoted just above the ground, then dipped their noses and started a slanted forward climb across the compound wire, heading west.

I sat with my legs outside in the wind and watched as our shadows flailed across Highway 1 and out over a grassy marshland I had not realized lay between our base and the curtain of endless trees beyond. I had enjoyed this freedom to ride half outside while on the RECONDO mission out from Nha Trang to Entre Island soon after I had arrived in-country, but this time it made me feel vulnerable. We passed over a crashed Sikorsky S-1 lying on its side, cracked open and half buried in the green swamp. I wondered for a moment what had happened to it so close to home, and then realized I didn't really want to know. I pulled my legs in then and rode sitting on the steel floor but close enough to the door to see out and, if necessary and close enough to the ground, to jump out.

Soon I saw that the two mysterious Hughes helicopters had joined the formation, evidently as escorts, and with their arrival the whole formation climbed quickly up into much cooler air and the safety of altitude. Below us an endless arboreal sea undulated away in bleaching layers of heat mist to be lost in the hazy miasma of an indistinct horizon, while far ahead the rumpled terrain was drawn up in convergent valleys like the corner of a vast counterpane, finally to meet a lowering sky hanging worn and dreary as hospital laundry. The ocean of green was broken here and there by an abrupt island prominence that seemed to have burst through the jungle so suddenly it carried a portion of isolated forest on its head, while against its rocky base the press of trees broke in static waves. Here was a part of the world that had sustained life by its own rules since prehistoric times. As I looked out over the immense wasteland of unchecked primeval growth, it was easy to imagine that among its hidden dangers there still remained tar pits and thunder lizards.

As we made our way westward for an hour or more, I began to feel sleepy, a common nervous reaction I had often experienced myself and noted in others, too, on flights to the drop zones at Fort Bragg in North Carolina. Despite the wind and noise, my eyes kept wanting to close as my mind fled this new reality.

As I continued my private struggle to stay awake, the ground below gradually rose into more hilly country, the general undulations of its oceanic monotony giving way to a humped and gathered terrain, deeply cut with narrow, meandering cracks in which the sun flashed on coffee colored rivers, some of them nearly invisible beneath the overhanging canopy.

Some time after I noted this broken change in the ground, things began to happen. I felt a slight buckle in the air and our formation began to shift. The two Sikorskys carrying the team moved closer together, though still separated by about 80 yards, while one of the Hueys dropped down much nearer the jungle. This was for the purpose of drawing any ground fire, while the other moved to a position above us to fly top cover and to pinpoint any fire from the ground. Then the deck beneath me tilted abruptly and the formation began a long circling turn over the hills. I looked at the Nungs and saw that they were getting ready for something.

From the doorway I could see a few small clearings scattered in the hills and hollows of the jungle below. Suddenly the helicopter carrying the other half of the team dipped and began to drop toward the ground, and with another lurch and a change in engine pitch ours fell in behind it.

Well, here it is, I thought. I guess this is where the war rises up to meet me on its own terms. All my newly conditioned misgivings, doubts, and fears returned in a breathless rush as my heart rate soared again. I began to shift my weight in preparation to jump out.

It seemed only seconds later that we were settling into a small opening in the trees, the branches all around us thrashing in protest—but just before landing, the lead machine abruptly rose again in a steep bank over the trees, and we followed the maneuver. We made another false landing at a different clearing not far away, and then on the approach to a third clearing, our pilots turned around, yelled over the engine noise, and made signals for us to be ready to get out. I craned around the doorway to see the other Sikorsky actually touch down in a small field of swirling grass. Johnson and the other team members scrambled out in seconds and began running for the trees.

We were down before the other S-1 had cleared the tree tops, the wheels thumping hard on the ground through lashing waves of grass. I jumped, or rather tumbled, to the ground and immediately fell down beneath the awkward weight of gear and sprawled there gripped in a fearful, chaotic intensity of undisciplined emotion as the three other team members jumped out behind me and took off running. I caught a glimpse of them making for the trees, leaving me to struggle for control in the hot down blast and twig storm launched by the rotor wash of the rising helicopter. My rush of confusion in the noise and wind seemed to last for a long time. Finally, fueled on desperation, I managed to get to my feet in time to see the others fleeing the edge of the clearing. I started after them through the long grass that, flattened in waves by the press of swirling wind, had begun to rise again. It bowed and clashed as I hove my cumbersome burden through it, slapping at my legs as I stumbled toward the edge of the forest wall, running bent over against an expected fusillade from the trees.

I found the rest of the team in the undergrowth just inside the tree line. As I flopped onto the ground beside them, gasping, my heart pounding, ears ringing, and the blood pulsing in my vision, the others quickly spread themselves into an irregular circle, moving on their bellies to conceal themselves further on the jungle floor. Then they went perfectly still, facing outward and scanning the surrounding growth intently. I could see the procedure was familiar to them and eased myself into position, lying beneath the lower vegetation and as close to the ground as my equipment and heavy breathing would allow, not sure of what to look for but alert to any movement.

As suddenly as it had begun, all movement ceased. I was surprised at how quickly the world changed from one filled with clatter and wind to one of absolute stillness. Powdery orange light slanted down through the jungle canopy, gradually darkening until it settled upon the verdant undergrowth where we lay. Everything around us seemed suspended, still and grey as an old photograph. I smelled the damp earth beneath my chin, but all sounds lay muted beneath the constant ringing in my ears left by the helicopter engine. Indeed it was this that Johnson was waiting out as we remained there, heads up, watching and straining to see or hear anything through the numbing tympanic whine.

The surrounding forest filled up immediately with palpable danger. I saw the near impossibility of detecting the presence of anyone hidden in its endless density of growth. With my field of vision unexpectedly restricted by the voracious jumble of plant life, and my power to hear compromised as well, I felt intensely vulnerable. Anyone concealed out there close enough to have seen our arrival would know that we were at least temporarily reduced in capacity. I hoped that my more experienced team members had some kind of *modus operandi* for getting through this edgy period. The only clear option was to observe whatever they did and to follow.

The others watched the way a cat watches something, perfectly still, yet with every sense alive, watching, listening, smelling, taking in all signals, all information. I wondered if they had somehow conditioned themselves to hear through the ringing. I envied their evident ability to concentrate, to focus on the situation at hand, while my brain raced about in an effort to take in this new reality, to control my breathing, straining to hear, to fix check points in what was visible around us, and to prioritize the possible dangers it all contained. I suddenly had no idea what was expected of me, only that I had better not show my confusion.

We remained there in this state of elevated alertness for the better part of an hour past the time when my hearing began to return. For the first time in weeks I suddenly began to feel pain again from the wounds in my legs. Gradually it subsided in diminishing sharp reminders, receding beneath the mandate to concentrate every sense on our surroundings. The first sound I could identify was a sudden orchestral burst of cicadas. Soon then, the trees began to echo with the tentative cries of small birds and lizards, awakening to my dawning awareness other normal sounds of a populous jungle habitat.

At last Johnson stirred. The others looked around as he motioned for me to move nearer so he could use the radio. I crawled over, and he took the handset from me, then reached into the pack behind me, turned on the radio with a barely audible click, and I barely heard him whisper three or four phonetic letters into the mic. This was his transmission on the insertion frequency that the team was safely on the ground. Then he signaled for us to move.

Keeping low and moving stealthily, the team rose slowly and began to creep noiselessly along the jungle floor, each man scanning and listening to the surroundings intently. I was surprised at how soundlessly they could move through the heavy growth. Each of the Nungs took his position in the line behind the point man according to an order long established by the distribution of weapons. Johnson took the middle of the formation and put me two behind himself, third from the last man, but close enough to give him ready access to the radio.

We kept an interval of several yards between each man. Thus spread out, I often lost sight of the others, catching a momentary glimpse of only one, seldom more than two at a time, through the riotous jungle growth. It was a formation designed to minimize our losses should we encounter the enemy, an event that I had been told would be sudden, violent, and at very close range, so the open order of movement placed each man in relative isolation. It brought forth my sense of loneliness, never far from the surface anyway, and it made a living thing of the need for absolute silence. I watched and listened intently to everything, with every sense connected to our surroundings on invisible filaments of learning.

Entering the jungle was like stepping inside some cramped and windowless interior where the air doesn't move and the roof is always dripping. The place held an ominous silence, punctuated by strange calls that resounded through its hidden spaces. Each squawk, chirp, chuckle, or scurry carried a message I tried to understand. Some information came in the type of cry, some in its urgency, and some in the direction and distance over which it seemed to come. The humidity was almost beyond endurance. It felt as though each breath had to be drawn through warm fabric, and the energy the effort took from my body could not be replaced in the heat. Hundreds of feet above us the distant sunlight lay upon the high, interlocking roof of the forest in a patchwork of bright greens, but was filtered almost free of color by the countless layers of intervening foliage by the time it arrived at the level of the ground cover, where it lay about us in a sinister geometry of shadows.

We followed no trail. Had there been one it would have been folly to mark it with our footprints anyway. Movement was directed by gaps in the foliage where shadows passed for spaces. For both tactical and purely practical reasons, Johnson varied the pace, moving us in unpredictable starts and stops through the oppressive air that lay captured beneath the trees, the stops usually longer than the periods of cautious moves. This was not only because we could not afford to allow many minutes to pass without stopping to listen, but also because routines can soothe, can dull the mechanisms of alertness that, long overworked, seek refuge in any form of predictability, but indulging it creates patterns that are discernible to people who mean you ill.

During the stops we sat or lay on the ground watching and listening, sometimes for ten minutes, sometimes for an hour. Each time, the initial silence fell in upon us with an impact like thunder. Then, after a few minutes of concentration, the stillness would give way to stealthy, almost continuous little movements around us, which seemed to approach and recede through the pulsing in my ears.

I was drenched with sweat. The harness straps of the radio pack rubbed painfully into my shoulders, and a cloud of tiny, irritating insects kept whining around my head, plunging at the sweat that covered every exposed inch of my skin and becoming trapped in the moisture on the surface of my eyes. No amount of blinking would discourage them. On one stop, I was at last able to spread some insect repellent around the under brim of my hat–not enough for humans to smell from more than few feet away, but enough to reduce slightly the population of bugs in my eyes. Then we were moving again, sometimes walking more or less erect, sometimes on our hands and knees, at others, in a prolonged crouch made painful by the weight of my equipment, as all posture was dictated by the foliage and the load.

We moved very carefully, slowly following the passable spaces through deep swales where the growth was rampant and the ground soft and damp, and across hillocks where the dense layer of fallen things that covered the earth was drier, and the mud-powdered ground crumbled faintly underfoot. All about us the stealthy scurry of reptiles, rodents, and the hum of enormous insects grown out of all proportion from anything familiar to westerners stole through the detritus of the forest floor, betrayed by the faint rustle of leaves and other tiny sounds. In the dry places the smallest creature could make almost as much noise as heavier ones. Each faint sound, reaching up through the eerie stillness, served to raise my awareness of what might be hidden beyond my under-trained perception. It was a timeless and alien place. My anticipation and fear were nourished on constant surmise and defensive speculation. There was always enough suspicion in the air to keep me alert.

Over the course of the afternoon, the character of the jungle varied. Most of the time it seemed to exude an ominous awareness of our presence, hiding unseen dangers that flitted just beyond my perception. It enforced a compounding intensity of awareness upon me, as I listened with the whole forest cupped to my ear.

We crept through areas where the spaces appeared relatively open, like a heavily tree'd park, where the giant growth seemed somewhat discharged of potential threat despite, or perhaps because of, slightly better visibility. Sometimes these places had to be avoided, depending upon the thickness, type, and height of the undergrowth .

Often the congestion of plants on the jungle floor was so dense we couldn't keep in visual touch with each other for long periods, and during these times could navigate only by glimpses of shadow-dappled movement. When we inched through areas where the foliage cut me off from the others, a ponderous sense of isolation returned to close in around me, dark and foreboding, until all that had once been familiar about myself and the world as I thought I knew it vanished in an enclosure of massive trees hung with moss-covered vines, ghostly and still, bizarre stands of enormous green bamboo, the soft squelching mud, the deep vegetal smells, and the constant insidious approach of The Beast.

There were places that made for very hard going. The primordial jungle floor, where massive growth had flourished unrestricted for centuries, crowded the rich black earth with a vast network of interlocking roots, some lurching so far out of the ground that we were forced to crawl under them. The tangle was so congested in places that it denied any footing. The effort to avoid stumbling, to suppress any noise, even to breathe soundlessly beneath the heft of my gear, coupled with the concentration needed to constantly scan and listen to every detail of the surroundings, near and far, raised the physical demands of any stealthy forward progress to a degree that is hard to describe. The whole thing was given form and illumination, was depicted and made sensible, by the demands of unremitting vigil, born of fear and a relentless sense of vulnerability.

There were periods when time seemed to stop, when all sense of interval ceased, to be replaced by the interminable study of the trudge and placement of every step, twisting cautiously through the growth, moving so as to minimize contact with any plant life, always vigilant and conscious of the imperative for silence. With growing thirst, I fought to breathe in the exhausting heat, plagued by innumerable insects, with my temples pounding in rising nervous tension, and cut off not only from the others but from any familiar aspect of myself as well.

The effort to maintain such high levels of mortal watchfulness quickly drains the intellect, forcing it to give way to instinct. In the effort to take in all external signals and to keep processing the constant flow of new information for what to do if the enemy discovered us—or we, them—my mind raced like a machine whose governor had failed. Eventually my brain began to show signs that it had to take brief vacations from it now and then, if only for a moment. As the sweltering hours of tension continued, I would suddenly awaken to the realization that I had been fantasizing about bananas and cream, or that I had been engaging some irrelevant memory at the expense of remaining attached to the looming immutable. Every moment taught, even that of catching myself in brief distraction.

Though I knew intellectually that the jungle was neutral, that it even contained many aids to survival, and though I tried to hold tight to a vision of the environment as beautifully indifferent, there were times when it seemed to have a brooding awareness, a primeval resentment of our presence. In other circumstances the forest might have offered a fascinating nature walk, but its tangled impenetrability lives in my memory as a malevolent crucible of some half-formed intelligence seething with hostile intent. It offered some grudging protection, but I knew the bad guys were better adapted to it and better able to use it. After generations of moving silently through it, they had probably reached an understanding with it. In the deep, spooky terrain where the giant plants reined, we were the intruders, encroachers upon a profound and majestic silence, ignorant strangers to the plants' meta-sensory form of communication and to their inscrutable agenda. The rampaging growth may once have permitted the tiny human clearings scratched into its distant edges along the coasts long ago, but as I crouched there on the redolent earth among the overpowering green abundance, I had the feeling that the jungle had begun to reconsider.

It had always been such a place and would have been so even if there had been no war. It told me I was in a place I didn't belong, where things were glimpsed for which I would pay, and where things went un-glimpsed for which I would also pay, where the mystery didn't matter, and a guy could get killed just for trespassing. The forest seemed to waver between the decision to give us protection or to sacrifice the whole team to discovery by our unseen enemy at its leisure. At these times it seemed to lean over and peer down at us as though to point us out.

Each passing hour, weighted heavily with the insidious creep of doubt and apprehension, seemed to make steady withdrawals upon our balance of fortune. Every plodding step and each protracted minute of hesitation, as well as our prolonged interludes of concentrated surveillance, all seemed to peel away in thinning layers the mantle of security the forest was willing to provide, so that even as I learned the process, it served merely to illuminate further my exposure to the unknown. Time itself seemed to be drawing us forth along unseen meridians of chance toward the heart of some dark, existential postulate, be it condition or event.

We moved past huge trees that towered hundreds of feet into the distant daylight. I learned to look at them, to see movement within them and to note any contrast in color. Ant nests the size of grain sacks hung from the branches like black goiters, and vines drooped, some all the way to the ground, where they had taken root anew. Some trees vaulted out of sight straight as architecture, their long trunks rising to a distant sun-dappled mingle of fans, fronds, and sprays of glossy leaves. Some were bent and twisted into grotesque shapes in their ancient struggle with one another for the space to live, while far above, the double and triple canopy of leaves and mingled branches blotted out the sky, creating a dome of undulating light that leaked dimly upon the lower vegetation in diminishing versions of green.

Around their boles a primordial tangle of climbing vines and creepers looped into my face and snagged at my equipment with a blind, catholic tenacity. There were areas where it seemed that from the crooks of every bough flowering bromeliads and epiphytes glared an incongruous violence of color in the deep verdant world. I felt a mild flash of irritation at their cheerful little efforts and decided these varieties were probably poisonous.

We inched past fantastic pale cottony tree trunks, thirty or forty feet around, whose bark wrinkled like skin and whose trunks, buttressed in high flanges of wood, could make three high walls of a shady, loamy room where a man could easily live, or rest–or die. Here and there, gnarled branches were hung with leaves larger than a man. There were philodendrons grown out of all proportion to the common house plant, with leaves the size of umbrellas. These had to be avoided for the amount of visibility they obscured and because the giant leaves made a distinctive rubbery sound when struck inadvertently or pushed aside and released.

Butterflies, iridescent blue, striped, or clear as isinglass, threaded the jungle spaces at eye level in long nervous strings of color. We avoided towering groves of bright green bamboo with stalks thicker than my leg, and we crept past great spreading banyans, whose enormous fluted stems could have hidden the whole team and whose dense aerial root system would have trapped us. It was an alien landscape, alive with a strange, persistent watchfulness.

Eventually, the ground began to incline abruptly. We edged around the base of what I assumed was one of the hills I had seen from the air, moving cautiously upward out of the loamy black soil and massive ferns into an area of reddish clay and impossibly tangled undergrowth. By hand signals passed along our line, Johnson directed us away from any ground high enough that we might be seen against the meager filtered light that fell in tiny columns through the canopy. I guessed that he was assuming anyone who had seen or heard the helicopters might have outposts on the high ground and expect an intruder to use the easier terrain along the ridges.

We moved carefully along the hillside into a botanist's madhouse that grew in sinister stillness from a dark primordial tangle below. It crept slowly up the slope, where the knobs and knees of tree roots stood up everywhere out of the earth in grotesque attitudes, like some gathering of the demented laid suddenly bare in all their writhen attitudes of pain. Pockets of stagnant rain water captured here and there in the knuckles of limbs that clutched the earth contained the remains of dead insects, poisoned by the leach of sap. There were rodent bones scattered at their bases, too. Even the plant life in this immensely obstructive world could be dangerous. Indeed, all things plant and animal that die in the forest feed the earth, which in turn feeds the trees. The nutrients of decay become the lifeblood of the jungle itself. I wondered which, in the end, is the ultimate carnivore, man or tree. The question passed with a raking tug at the sleeve of my mortality.

A long period of deep silence was suddenly shattered by the startled squawk of a parrot—raucous, abrupt, and seemed pitched to all directions at once. My heart caught at the harsh sound, as we all dropped to the ground on breathless instinct. We hugged the earth and waited. I strained to hear any following sound, listening with my mind and with my bones. Nothing moved. After a tense 20 minutes or so, we crept on. At times afterward I had a fleeting glimpse of these birds as they flashed red and green through dusky curtains of light, but they had an uncanny ability to blend with the foliage, leaving only the orphaned echo of their flight.

All noise was dangerous, for we could not know what, or who, might have caused it. We had to assume that any enemy in the area would interpret it the same way. At any sound, especially a shift in the dense pulsing throb of cicadas, we stopped instantly and dropped to the ground. There we waited, regardless of the inhospitable nature of that particular place, sometimes for an hour or more. We listened, nerves on edge for any aberrant noise or thump of footfall that might betray itself through the background rhythm of insects, breezes in the canopy, or birds, and keeping our heads on constant swivels, we watched in all directions–ahead, to the sides, and back from where we had come.

Each man scanned the terrain and vegetation, and the movements of the least of creatures were logged into our collective cognizance until we were all federated with invisible wires of vigilance, and when we again resumed our ponderous scrabble along the slope, we crept in a growing singularity of resonance with our surroundings and with each other.

Once, we all froze at the soft poip-poip of a tree frog. It may have been quite near. I couldn't tell. Snakes, large and small, slid unseen through the surrounding ground cover, and I gradually learned to guess their size by the faint sound of their movement. Small fliers displaced the air with throbbing darts and hovers, and the echoes of monkeys screeched their warnings through the forest. All these things had to be noted, mentally sorted and catalogued for what they might imply.

The moist ground softened further. We entered a boggy region spread with ferns where we had to place our feet carefully down through the delicate lacework of fronds. My boots sank as the mud began to ooze from beneath my feet. It soon found its way through the ventilation screens on the instep of my boots, where it quickly formed a marsh in my socks. My feet became damp. They would stay that way, turning musty as with this first encroachment into my clothing, the jungle began to tighten its grip, demanding my descent to its deeper levels of discomfort.

During one of our many alarming-noise stops, I became unquestioningly aware of what a lot of insect life goes on under your nose when you've got it an inch from the earth. Though flying insects had been a plague all day, I had not given the subject of their infantry much thought until, proceeding on my stomach, dragging my body and its load of equipment along by my fingernails beneath a ceiling of philodendron leaves, entomology presented itself forcefully as a thoroughly justified science. The problem of classification alone must continue to discourage the specialists. When we stopped, my face came down near a long swath of bacon-colored ants bearing triangular bits of green leaf. They wobbled across the jungle floor in ordered lines as far back into the undergrowth as I could see. With their leaves aloft they looked like a fleet of sailing dinghies. I watched with cautious interest as long as I remained there and never saw an end to those ants or to the luffing chips of green they bore, but for the time that I lay engaged with their tiny industry, even with my brain on dull alert for events in a larger context, they provided me a respite from the world of insistent threat that I had to rejoin as the signal to move again was passed among us.

Gradually the crawl of revelation emerged from the constant arrival of hard facts. I became forcefully attuned to my surroundings to a degree I had never known before and soon began to detect things at varied distances even obliquely, usually only by their effects: shadow, movement, and faint sound. My skill grew at seeing each thing separately and relating it to the whole: a green beetle on a leaf and what it might portend, an extraordinarily tiny flower with pink and white petals, the veined translucence of a leaf. There were times when I came to see the other men as they moved through somber patches of leaf-cast shade only as fleeting shadows, glimpsed in my continuing scan of the foliage as but signs in the lesson plan, as though they were runes in a secret text I was being compelled to read.

From many unseen sources I began the slow accumulation of knowledge and meaning, but with it came a raw and pervasive unease inaccessible to words, a kind of subliminal awareness, an instinct for the surroundings that began to take root in my consciousness, not unlike an emotion. It was a *feeling* for the presence of things that lay outside the peripheral limitations of vision. Of course you have to scan, assess, and make constant minute decisions, but this is not *thinking* in the usual, methodical way. It's more akin to the development of an informed instinct.

My mind raced to assess and prioritize the implications of each tiny sound, starting with my own. I learned that, despite the degree to which the high art of moving silently can be developed, nobody can move completely soundlessly through the jungle undergrowth, especially while harnessed to a load of combat equipment. I became sharply aware of the muffled sloshing that came from our many canteens. As they gradually emptied, the sound grew louder until it seemed to fill the air and began to affect me emotionally. This was very different from the stealth depicted in films. It was even different from the patrol techniques I had learned in Ranger training and in jungle school. Here, the stakes were infinitely higher, and an elevated level of participation was required of your instincts. Mortal danger is inspiring; it awakens all the senses.

Every tiny movement launches at least a minor disturbance of the air. With concentration I could hear hints of movement in the plants, in the faint hum of distant insects, or of small animals on the ground, but this kind of listening had to be learned. I found that by forcing a yawn from time to time I could open my ears a bit more, ushering in a momentary flood of additional tiny signals.

There were times in the great vaults of stillness when I could actually hear the growth taking place–the squeak and groan of tightening vines and the creak of expansion. It could sound like a settling house, launching loud pops that echoed across broad pockets of silence. Sound served to reinforce my sense of the whole complex system as a single, conscious organism with an inscrutable intention that lay beyond my understanding, but whose life force was undeniable, sometimes overwhelming, and certainly powerful enough to make sense of the idea that it had a will of its own.

Each of my mistakes–a grunt, a stumble, a footfall too loud, uncontrolled breathing, and once I instinctively grabbed the stem of a sapling to help my balance, thereby causing movement in the foliage overhead–was pointed out by one of the team with eyes black as gun bores and a hard, silent gesture. Each became a lesson, a portal of discovery. Each of the jungle's signs I learned to interpret was a lesson in survival, but each also became a door to new dimensions of dread.

Sometimes a breeze would sigh through the upper reaches of the forest, stirring the branches and imparting a watery aquarium quality to the light, but on the jungle floor the air was always still, so still and crowded with moisture that at times I could hardly breathe. In this stagnant lower air our saturated clothes could not dry, and every cut, scratch, or insect bite quickly festered. I became wracked with a thirst that no amount of calculated gulps of plastic-flavored water from my warm canteens could satisfy. I was footsore from our slow motion advance across the uneven ground. My hip sockets ached, and under the weight of the radio the muscles in my lower back strained against the forward plod of those in the backs of my legs. The constant tug of the radio had by now rubbed my shoulders raw in its effort to pull me off the hill. Even my gloves were damp. In order to keep the sweat out of my eyes, I wrapped a cotton tourniquet around my head gypsy style and replaced the jungle hat over it. There were times when I resented Johnson for his seeming indifference to the growing weight of a PRC-25 radio over the course of four or five hours.

Between the instincts of the point man and whatever secrets Johnson held, we kept advancing through the afternoon. Sometimes we broke the pattern of listening stops with such long periods of movement that I thought they must believe that there was no enemy around at all. Other times our rests were protracted studies in vigilance. There were times when, because he heard something, or maybe just on impulse, the point man would signal an abrupt halt in place. We would remain stock still, attuned to any evidence of movement outside our own. Except for normal jungle sounds and stealthy, isolated bird calls, all remained quiet.

Gradually, the light that found its way to the jungle floor began to dim as evening settled upon the canopy, and we picked our way along in deepening shadows. Back on more level ground in a thick grove of enormous ferns, a hold was signaled again, but this time while we halted the point man went on ahead. After awhile he re-emerged from the feathery gloom and signaled to Johnson, who moved forward to join him. They spoke for a moment in hand signals and then disappeared together back the way the point man had come. Both returned shortly and signaled for us to move forward. This was a departure from our normal procedure. I didn't like it. Since every new experience from the day I had arrived in the country and each change to which I had managed a degree of adjustment had so far proven to have doleful consequences, I couldn't help wondering what new outrage this double recon ahead implied.

The smell and the quality of the air began to change. Where for hours it had been dominated by the odor of rotting vegetation, it now took on a more familiar scent: the rich musty presence of river mud and wet bark. When we stopped again, I saw through the trees the dull gleam of moving water. Johnson signaled for us to rally, and in the dim religious light beneath a cover of thick river bank growth, we formed ourselves into a perimeter.

Seeing all the others now, I was struck by how dirty we all were from the day's movement along the jungle floor. Sweat-laden clothes, dark with infusions of damp earth, and exposed skin streaked with mud aided each man's integration with the shadows as we began a wait for full darkness.

The thick dark current ran past us with a dull hiss, like poured sand. We waited. Nothing moved. We waited a long time, and the air grew surprisingly cold. Through a deeply bisected vegetal gap in the trees I watched carefully the high ground on the other side of the river, 60 or 70 yards away, as the hills became lost to the insinuating fingers of the night. It had an ominous feeling about it. Mournful, too. I don't know what it was about the undifferentiated sight of more featureless jungle that gave me the willies. Perhaps the feeling emanated from the thickness of growth there. Maybe it lay in the way the trees overhung the far bank, creating an impenetrably shadowed verge where some of their lower branches clutched the sad remnants of storm drift. Perhaps it was the fact that the rising terrain appeared to overlook our position by several hundred feet. In any case, I decided that it bore watching and wondered whether Johnson planned to turn up or downstream.

The river held the tarnished silver light of a dimming sky, prolonging visibility where we lay, but soon the darkness fell long and damp through the trees about us, and for a short while, a spectral quietude set in.

Then Johnson and the point man rose and set cautiously off in opposite directions, one upstream and the other downstream, always keeping the growth between themselves and any openings to the water. I lay exhausted and unmoving on the earth with the Nungs, listening, always listening. Soon the startling calls of the unseen birds of twilight began to echo through the jungle, uncanny and wistful, their eerie cries catching in the heart.

The ground felt cool through my sweat-soaked clothes, and I suddenly realized how utterly tired I was. My hands and thighs trembled, partly from the unremitting physical demands of the patrol with little water and no food, but mostly from the nerve-wracking vigilance. I was grateful for being in such good physical shape. I doubted that I would have been able to pull my weight otherwise.

I heard the two men returning before I saw either, feeling their footfalls in the earth and thus learning by example another reason why our progress had been so careful and deliberate. They rejoined us, conferred in whispers and signs, and then the others began to stir. Johnson came over to me and whispered that we were moving about 40 meters upstream to set up for the night, and that we would cross the river before light.

This was not good news. It caused an irregular beat in my chest that felt as though my heart thumped once and then fell over. Johnson's intention came as a disconcerting surprise, though it shouldn't have. After so many hours of concentrating upon the demands of the jungle and its ground, of trying to absorb every detail of what had happened so far, as well as cultivating the necessary insight to what had *not* happened, I forgot having seen on Johnson's map that the area we were to patrol was cut by rivers. The events of the day had crowded out any consideration of having to ford water.

River crossings were very dangerous. It meant prolonged exposure in the open, even in the best conditions, depending upon the width of the river, and especially for a man burdened with heavy gear, upon its depth. Each man would be vulnerable as soon as he emerged from cover. In addition, the current might claim anyone weighed down with equipment or who might lose his footing on an underwater snag. Entire teams had been lost to ambush in attempting mistimed river crossings.

We got up quietly. By now I was used to the weight of the radio itself, but the raw sores it had rubbed across my shoulders hampered my movement as I tried to make even a minor adjustment to ease the burning sensation of the abrasions. Loosening the shoulder straps was out of the question. More play in the straps meant more movement in the load, and the pack had to be tight should I ever need to run. There was no alternative to simply bearing it. It was the whole team's lifeline.

By the time of this last move of the day, it was past full dark. Feeling anxious about the morning, I took my place in the order of movement as we stalked carefully through the haunting splintered starlight, slipped over mossy shoreline deadfalls, and through dripping tunnels of high rhododendron-choked trees. Moving slowly at night a few steps at a time brought forth a lurid nocturnal view of the plants, causing them to appear the way I imagined a fairytale jungle to be, with impeding branches covered with flossy parasitic growths, as vines festooned with creepers and looped like bunting interlocked overhead, forming curtains of hanging leaves walled by impossibly large trees.

Someone up ahead stumbled, producing a muffled foot step–not loud; barely audible–but frightened birds exploded from the mysterious upper reaches, their cries echoing through the forest. Frogs erupted nearby with their croaks and chirps and their startling plops as they dived into the shallows. We all froze. Nobody moved for several long minutes. The blood surged in my ears. A warning to anyone for some distance around had been sounded, and we waited, listening intently. I didn't like it, and I knew the others were aware of greater consequences than I was yet equipped to imagine. The silence returned, closing in around us as suddenly and completely as before.

We resumed movement and trailed carefully on, finally settling into a fairly flat area near the riverbank, hushed and enclosed among numerous huge trees. Two of the Nungs immediately set about positioning M-1 "foot" mines at some remove around our position, while

I sat thankfully between the high flutes of a tree trunk that rose in absolute symmetry into the night like some pillar in a dark and limitless cathedral. With the weight of the radio pack on the ground at last, I eased out of the shoulder straps. Instantly relieved, I felt the blood rush into my shoulder muscles and for once luxuriated in the stinging. I pulled off my gloves, felt the fresh air between my fingers for the first time all day, unbuckled my web equipment belt, and pulled it out from behind me so that I could lean back against the radio pack.

A slight breeze off the water moved stealthily through the place, bringing a degree of relief from the stagnant air and stirring some of the broad leaves around us. I was beyond tired. My hands trembled from the long day of nervous tension and my legs from the pitching weight of the unfamiliar equipment and the demands of the terrain. As I sat there comfortably against the radio pack for the first time, protected on both flanks by the tree roots, a sense of quiet cessation had just settled upon me when Sgt. Johnson moved over and gestured for the radio. It pulled me from my momentary reverie. I twisted around and handed him the pack.

He set it on the ground, carefully unfolded the antenna from where it was tucked through loops around the pack and extended it fully, running it up along the bole of the tree. He loosened the flap of the pack, but kept it covering the face of the radio, reached under and turned it on, then putting the phone almost into his mouth the way he had done before, whispered a quick two- or three-letter report. Without waiting for acknowledgement, he turned the radio off and told me to refold the antenna and to stow the pack. In two or three minutes he had sent a status report, assuming it had been picked up. By now I was seeing the pattern of his reports and felt I knew the technique.

I felt suddenly famished, and in a sitting position for a change, decided that, the jungle alarm we had launched not withstanding, I had better eat something. I released the buttons on the flap of the cargo pocket on the side of my leg, felt for the rolled top of the ration bag, fumbled it open, and sank my filthy fingers into the soft warm mush. It was just sticky enough to be rolled into a ball. I ate about three balls of it this way and washed them down with warm canteen water. I drank my fill knowing that with my supply of Halizone tablets I could purify enough river water to refill the canteens. The night would provide plenty of time for the tablets to do their work.

The Nungs already had a system. Two of them began collecting all their canteens, and then crawled beneath the shore growth to the water's edge and silently filled each. Other than the soft rustle of their clothes, they never made a sound.

When they were done and back in position, I pulled myself through the hole in the underbrush that they had used and suddenly found myself leaning almost too far over the dark water. Even very short distances can be difficult to judge at night, and I did not expect to find we were so close to the river's edge. I almost slipped off the undercut bank into the water. This incidental mistake carried great potential danger. It startled and upset me.

I filled my canteens by feeling for the surface of the water with my fingers, then, to avoid the burbling noise that comes with holding the mouth of any bottle completely under water, I submerged it just enough to allow water to flow into the opening at the surface, grateful that the plastic helped muffle the process. By cupping my other hand around the opening to reduce the chance of small bits of flotsam being sucked into the canteen, I was able to fill both quietly–at least more quietly than the river itself.

Yet my brush with falling into the water made me realize I had got away with yet another incident that illustrated my lack of experience. It was another sign that my training, even though it was relatively extensive in the Special Forces, had been merely a pedagogical aid, whose profound limitations become all too clear when moved outside the curricular requirements of the lesson plan and into the larger context of a steaming jungle full of un-cataloged threats half way around the world. There was much more the instructors could have taught me, but they could not have covered the sheer soul-draining strain of constant sensory overload, the physical demands and the extreme isolation of these missions, and the natural difficulties of having to work out one's own means of communicating with native mercenaries.

I slipped back to my cubby in the roots, where, wrapped in one of the best items of equipment issued in Vietnam–a lightweight nylon poncho liner–with one arm through the radio pack strap, the other through my web gear, and rifle across my chest, I began a long exhausted vigil through the night. Though freighted with fatigue, I dared not surrender to sound sleep. I needed to keep my awareness on trickle charge. I saw the wisdom in Johnson's having moved our night position after that first stop at the river. If anyone on the opposite bank had been able to see us there before dark, or been alerted by the birds, we were now out of mortar range from that first location.

After a few minutes of mentally reviewing the day, trying to internalize all that had happened, I surprisingly felt the urge to urinate. I had not expected such a need in view of the profuse sweating I had experienced and the minimal amount of water I had taken during the long day. There was nothing for it but to go. I got up with care and moved quietly back through the undergrowth the way we had come. There, I got on my knees at the base of a tree and let the stream go close against the trunk to run silently down into the ground. Much relieved, I crawled back to the protection of the tree where I'd left my gear.

I could not tell if the others were sleeping. Everyone lay still and silent, visible only as dark lumps on the ground. After some time nestled between the high flanges of the tree trunk, listening to the many small night sounds and searching overhead in vain for any sign of a star through the closed roof of the forest, the darkness seemed suddenly to deepen. I wondered if it was a sign of cloud cover. It was impossible to tell, but I had the impression that there was a shift in the depth of shadows.

I was prepared to dismiss it as another characteristic of night in an Asian forest, when the jungle chorus came abruptly to life everywhere. I jumped involuntarily. Every kind of cicada, bird, insect, and species of tree frog suddenly erupted with its individual contribution–crackling and squawking, some raucous, some rhythmic or strident, some almost musical–to the mad cacophonous medley. Johnson and one of the Nungs sat bolt upright. I could make out the angle of Johnson's head, chin up and slightly inclined to the side, as he listened for a long moment. Then both men lay back down, leading me to guess that it may simply have been the change in light, or perhaps our proximity to the water, or a change in air pressure that caused the sudden explosion of sound. At least I hoped so. The cautious repose of those more experienced than I allowed me some provisional calm.

The clicking, hooting, squawking, and popping went on. Some sounded like fishing reels, some like leaking faucets, still others like tin horns. The sound at times seemed to contain pounding and gurgling, the cries varying in nature and intensity. Then suddenly it all ceased, all at once, as though on some signal. Johnson and the Nung sat up again. I tensed with their movement and, heart pounding again, sat motionless. I eased the rifle's safety switch off with my thumb and placed my finger on the trigger. After what seemed a long time, the others lay slowly back down, evidently satisfied that we weren't being approached, as a profound and ominous silence closed in around us again like an unseen fist.

Sometime after midnight, I was awakened from a twilight consciousness by the sound of approaching rain. I smelled it in the press of air being herded before a squall sweeping down from the hills upriver. It made a rushing sound like an army of whispers. The rain began suddenly, striking first the distant canopy above. Then huge drops found their way through the high cover and began plopping heavily into the surrounding foliage. They fell so hard they actually hurt. I pulled my hat down and gathered the poncho liner about me but was quickly soaked through. In moments the forest roared so loud beneath the weight of deluge on the leathery leaves around us that we would have had to shout to make each other hear. Its power was frightening. The downpour splashed so hard on the vegetation that it created a pale mist which rose all around us, obscuring visibility and all other sound. We cowered where we lay on the floor of the jungle as well as we could, and I lost sight of the others completely.

Then, almost as abruptly, the rain moved on, roaring away through the hollows of the forest, gradually fading around a bend in the river and leaving us soaked in a quietly dripping stillness filled with the smells of rotting vegetation and fresh mud. It left me settled several inches into the muck, at last so wet and filthy that it released me from all care about the last vestiges of personal comfort. It was actually liberating to reach a point beyond remedy or regard for such residual civilizing trifles as cleanliness and comfort. I was free now to concentrate entirely on whatever dangers prowled the woods. I allowed the taut spring in my mind to loosen a few coils, scrunched down into the cool mud and closed my eyes.

I must have actually fallen asleep for awhile, because I came awake instantly attached to the faint sound of clothes moving. The others were stirring, getting up, rolling their wet poncho liners tightly to squeeze out as much rain water as possible before packing them. On the jungle floor it was still dark. Veiled starlight moved past on the surface of the river. I got unsteadily to my knees, heavily sleep deprived, and buckled on my webbing. I squeeze-rolled my poncho liner and secured it with two elastic blousing straps, then strapped it in place beneath the flap of my butt pack. I hurriedly rolled another ball of flavored rice from my ration pack and ate it while checking my gear, mostly by feel. I remembered to carefully break the seal around the first cartridge in my weapon.

Johnson assembled us and by sign language indicated that we were going to attempt the river immediately. He designated the file order and pointed out a general direction for an intended landing place on the other bank. From where I stood, I could not see the location he was indicating, but I remembered from the evening before that the opposite bank appeared to be well over half a football field away, and from the direction he was pointing out, he was evidently assuming there would be some downstream carry. There were to be no more than two men in the river at the same time. That, I knew, meant the crossing would probably take longer than the remaining darkness. It would be too risky to put the whole team in the water at once, especially without knowing the conditions of the bottom or the current, or what awaited us on the other side, but it looked to me as though the last two, or maybe three, guys would be crossing in dangerously fair light. I was also afraid that, given the order of march so far, one of those would be me.

As two of the Nungs disappeared to retrieve the mines, I stepped to where I could peer through the trees. The river swirled with wraith-like mists. That could be good. It might serve to hide us. On the other hand, if someone lost his footing or was carried off by the current, it would be difficult at best to find and retrieve him. At worst, the weight of his gear would pull him under, and even if he could swim, anything from his pack that floated clear would leave a sign downstream of our presence.

Through narrow gaps in the shore cover I could barely make out the opposite bank of jungle, ghostly and smoking with morning fog, dimly revealed against the stars, a silent clamor of opulent growth crowded to the water's edge. The mists that drifted slowly up from the tangle of their branches gave the trees an ominous, theatrical look. The appearance of the place, combined with the prospect of crossing the river, underlined my misgivings about it from the night before.

The redoubtable point man entered the water first. Holding his weapon high and with his webbing piled around his shoulders, he felt his way into deeper water as we all divided our attention between his progress and as much of each shore as we could see. The last I saw of him before he disappeared into the mist, he was only up to his chest but seemed far enough along to indicate that the river might be shallow enough to cross on foot.

Johnson looked at his watch, then tapped the second Chinese, who slipped quietly off the bank and started across with gear held high, the water swirling past his legs. I tried to judge the current. It didn't look too bad near the bank, but there was no way to estimate it without being out where it counted. One at a time, Johnson tapped each of the first four men. Then it was my turn. He evidently wanted me to cross in the middle to increase the chances of getting the radio across before daylight while keeping himself and three automatic rifles to bring up the rear.

With my webbing slung around my neck and the radio on my back, I approached the bank and crouched to step in without a splash. As soon as I moved from under the growth out beneath the vestigial night sky, a sense of naked vulnerability fell in upon me, and a cold, hollow feeling of imminent danger spread across my back. I watched uneasily the heavy chocolate swirls as they dimpled momentarily along the surface near the bank, silent and profound, as though just beneath, something huge and alive had awakened for a moment of lazy awareness. I waded out, feeling exposed to a host of unseen dangers but knowing I could not show the hesitation I felt.

The surprising cold of the water shivered up my spine. The bottom felt muddy and soft but firm enough to keep a footing. The steady tug of the current pulled at my legs, and I was glad to get out deep enough so that the swishing sound of taking steps in the shallows would cease. I tried to lean into the flow to minimize any downstream set. The mists seemed a long way off, but they moved, constantly renewing themselves with the drift of the surface, and after a long time of anxious lumbering progress, I became isolated in the restless swirls where the air turned wet, and I lost sight of both banks.

It was uncannily quiet. I knew that just because I couldn't see, it didn't mean I could not be seen. The faintest hint of dawn began to fade the stars beyond the hills upriver as objects emerged uncertainly from the gloom, like remnant images in a long-faded photograph, and with it an insidious but familiar vacancy opened again within me, feeding on an irrepressible sense of being watched. I hunched my shoulders in an instinctive childhood effort to become smaller, expecting at any moment to have the silence shattered by the crack of a rifle shot from either shore.

Trapped in the general murk, I could not judge my progress or see anything below the surface. Leaves and partially submerged sticks swirled silently past out of the mist, strange artifacts from the mysterious reaches upriver. Except for the brush of water with each step, I heard nothing but a single haunting bird cry from the trees ahead.

The cold water pressed my wet clothes against me, and sending its long fingers around my skin, it gradually worked its way up to my chest. I became alarmed at the increasing depth, knowing I could not hope to swim loaded with rifle, 25 pounds of radio, plus the wet weight of the packs and webbing, grenades, and over 500 rounds of ammunition. If I were to be pulled under and shed the gear to keep from drowning, I would then be truly helpless, and the loss of anything I carried would endanger the whole team.

With every second the tension grew. My arms began to tremble with the effort to keep my weapon and as much of my gear out of the water as possible. My shoulders ached and my hands grew cold. Each tenuous footstep on the uneven bottom became a desperate gamble. Even a small log floating submerged would knock me down. Once I stepped into a hole and sank in up to my neck. My desperation spiked, but then by groping with my boot I found enough of a rise to start me back up to chest level, and pushed on, forcing my way through the water and breathing hard from the exertion and the cold.

The current became stronger against the resistance of the radio and other packs, and I lost my footing on the bottom a few times but managed to stay upright. Over time the effort, fear, and cold sapped my energy more than I'd expected. I wondered if the others ahead of me had been swept quietly away in the fog. If they made it, where did they get out? How would I find them again? I let my bladder empty again into the current.

After an eternity of struggle against the private hell of my own doubts and fears, I at last began to catch glimpses of the lower trees ahead and knew I was reaching the edge of the mist. The jungle appeared surprisingly close, and with mounting anxiety at being discovered in the growing visibility, I began to search for a likely place to pull myself out. Much of the verge was overhung with trees attached by a tangled mass of roots to their night shadows on the slow, dark water. I knew that if I pulled myself into the roots where the river had cut the bank and it was still quite dark, besides entering an area likely alive with water snakes, I would cause a lot of audible dripping in the effort to haul myself and gear straight out of the river—assuming I still had the strength to pull myself and the weight of my saturated equipment up into the limbs anyway. Then I saw a place a bit farther downstream where the bank was shelved off much lower to the surface of the river. The wet earth there was black and free of roots, and I let the stream nudge me towered it.

The upper branches of a large tree tilting out from the shore between me and the wedge of mud threatened to become an obstacle. The arch of its leaning canopy dipped into the water, where grey leaves hid whatever might complicate a passage behind the cover it seemed to offer. Fearing that staying out deep enough to avoid it might cause me to be swept past the notch in the embankment, but that heading for the shelter of the tree might get me hung up in the hidden lower branches, I was suddenly relieved to feel the bottom shallowing out. It became trashy with roots that tried to trap my feet, but it offered improved footing, so I risked backing out a step into deeper water to clear my feet and was carried through the slender top branches that trailed like fingers on the surface, their leaves trickling quietly. Once clear, I was able to push back in and to fetch the narrow muddy shingle, where I noticed there with profound relief evidence that the others had come out at this same place.

Then, in order to minimize the sound of getting out of the water, I crouched down into the river and slithered gratefully onto the wet muck. Once mostly clear of the water, and with the warm rush of blood at last falling back into my arms, I low-crawled carefully up the slimy bank. It smelled—a dark, sickly, airless stench of decay and the slow creep of centuries. Soaked and slathered with it, I stole up the bank, into the deeply shadowed undergrowth, and found a good place to conceal myself with a view out to the river.

There, with slow movements to minimize the sound of dripping from my clothes, I buckled my webbing back on and sat motionless except for shivering and tried to control my breathing while water drained from my clothes, and the river murmured past like a laborious and mournful sigh.

The others were so well concealed that I could not see them. I had to assume they were somewhere near and resigned myself to wait and to remain perfectly still, listening hard for any sound from the jungle or the river. I could not shake the sense of parlous indifference that this side of the river had given me. I didn't like being separated from Johnson and all that he knew; I didn't know what to do about rounding up the team and getting us out of there if he failed to make it across, and I had no idea where there might be other places in this wilderness that a helicopter could find a way to set down. I also didn't like our position on the slope with open evidence of our presence in the wet mud below either.

After what seemed like a long time, another of the Nungs emerged from the fog but a bit downstream of the mud bank. He saw it and used the eddies along the bank to work his way back up among the roots and pulled himself out of the water. Moving silent as a shadow he stole into the undergrowth and disappeared, leaving no sign of our presence except the marks in the mud. It was as though the jungle had absorbed him completely.

I continued to wait in the dismal pre-dawn shadow, wet, cold, and growing concerned that we had two more yet to appear, one of them being the team leader who carried both the map and the homing radio. Suddenly I became aware of a burning sensation on my side. I reached down and felt a soft protrusion under my shirt. I slowly unbuttoned the shirt to discover two slimy black leeches attached to my skin. I got out my little bottle of insect repellant and squirted it on the first, which detached from me immediately and began to shrivel, leaving a red welt, speckled with blood on my right side. I grabbed it and threw it away, then did the same to the other. I wondered if I had any more, but felt nothing, so continued to sit there watching for any movement in the river.

Slowly a vaporous grey dawn began to slop through the muggy air and over the cheerless twittering landscape like a spilled bucket of oil, eerie and devoid of comfort. The air was thick and smelled of heat and rain. Long mists still trailed downstream along the riparian defile, corralled by walls of jungle. It lay in wispy pools among the shore edge trees and moved restlessly along the surface of the brown river, gradually rising toward the paling glow of the sky in lingering tendrils, and there evaporating like steam.

As the light grew so did my anxiety. I didn't like having the team split, and I was uncomfortable having to hold this close to the river for so long. If we had been seen it would be known that we were separated and that our equipment and weapons were wet. Every passing minute increased visibility in the open. With mounting concern I began to rehearse again the emergency frequencies and to sort through a number of disconcerting probabilities.

My mind was reeling with questions about how I might improvise the team's extraction when at last I noticed movement on the water and saw Johnson, to my profound relief, waist deep and moving quietly through the broken shadows of the trees that leaned over the bank. From a smudge in the mist behind him the form of the last man took shape, with his shirt wrapped about his head like a turban and rifle held high. They, too, found the mud bank, then concealed themselves somewhere in the interlocked verdure below my position.

Johnson had been right to risk the crossing in darkness, but I knew we had been lucky, not knowing the condition of the river, and now I saw that we had started late. An hour of waiting, watching and listening, served only to inspire further misgivings in me about this side of the river. For some instinctual reason, achieving the crossing and finding good cover had done nothing to dispel my suspicions.

In the corridor of advancing light through the trees I could see the wall of jungle that faced us across the water gap. It had been a place tense with expectation and doubt, a place upon which, over the last day's interminable hours, I had exhausted my powers of observation. It had given rise to profound change and demanded that my sense of self be readjusted. Yet now it seemed somehow at rest, demagnetized of the unknowns it may have held the day before, and with little left to examine, oddly remote.

I wondered absently what part instinct might play in leaving somewhere with any real sense of place, if even in normal times it might be a function of whatever vagaries may inhabit one's capacity for observation, for sounds, and for smell. I thought about the ways this remote and anonymous jungle had revealed its singularity and its enlightening, equivocal truths, and how my condition had become the direct product of the instantaneous integration of all the forces it could loose upon me at any given moment. Whether or not it concealed the dangers we feared, the jungle would offer no down time.

Now as I sat on the damp earth in the slowly accumulating light, I began to transfer my sense of ubiquitous dread to whatever unknowns lurked ahead in the towering trees and leafy depths on this side of the river. I had not forgotten Johnson's warning about the explosive and chaotic nature of contact with the enemy on these operations, and all that I had gleaned so far from the nature of the forest and the limited visibilities its heavy undergrowth imposed made sense of his words. I prayed fervently that we would get out of there without contact. A guy could shed his whole future in this nameless place and not even know it.

I became aware of the life that a source of water attracts. Monstrous land crabs and enormous armored centipedes with dangerous pincers moved slowly in the tangled underbrush. Snakes curled stealthily beneath the carpet of fallen leaves. Birds twittered and called unseen from the trees and the open spaces overhead, and farther up the slope behind me where the air was slightly warmer, the night mists began to condense and fall back down in erratic, noxious droplets.

At length, when the early light had begun to reflect the river's surface in watery plaits under the foliage of the river bank trees, Johnson emerged from his cover and crept up the slope. I was stiff and cold, but glad at least to move, and joined the others as each emerged and picked his way stealthily uphill in flank so as to get the whole team away from the water at the same time before the filtered morning light above us could dispel the deeper shadows that still clung to the lower growth. I had spent an hour or more studying the marks we had left in the mud and was about to signal Johnson to point them out, but I saw that he knew. He turned and looked back down, studying the bank for a long moment. I could think of no way to cover the evidence of our presence without making noise or exposing someone, and so it probably was with him. Nothing short of a rising water level would erase our spoor.

We climbed on, quietly resuming the order of the day before, as the incline shouldered back, and we were able to pick our way a bit more easily through the wilderness, with me hoping for another downpour to halt the operation and flood the bank on which our signature gleamed in fresh moist ruts .

At first, sudden contrary mists formed as the early heat began to stir the moist air trapped in the river gorge. They appeared abruptly, conjured from the ground and the foliage, sometimes drifting in sinister confusion between us, reducing visibility and feeding my increasingly edgy discomfort in the uncanny silence. As the morning came on, the light filtered down through the triple canopy on mist-filled beams that struck sparkles from the dripping foliage.

Apart from having to negotiate numerous hills, this day was largely a duplicate of the previous one: heat, thirst, fatigue, pain, and constant unrelenting vigilance as Johnson varied the pace of movement. We trudged, crawled and crabbed our way through the black mire and rotting vegetation that fermented on the jungle floor in the oppressive heat. Having the experiences of the previous day to build on, I was growing accustomed to the conditions and could cope with the demands imposed upon us without living every moment on the brink of an ever-renewed void of ignorance. Although I adjusted to an expanding litany of discomforts with growing familiarity, my improved perspective simply added to the strenuous requirements of keeping all my senses on constant alert.

During the long, stifling slog through this alien botanical wilderness, time itself began to change, becoming something other than mere chronicity. It became a function of the living environment, of protracted intervals of waiting, listening, strain, fatigue and delay, all measured by the sleepless cadence of threat. There were long periods of quiet, broken suddenly by the indelible cry of a bird, the snap of a twig, the passage of rain, or most dreaded of all as it would happen, gunfire. Yet, as a matter of necessity, we also marked our progress with watches synchronized to a distant clock on a wall back at FOB 4, and the shift of allegiance between these two perceptions of time could become surreal. It was an alternate reality with its own hierarchies and values and demands. These were never spoken of, but they governed each of us by a set of rules that applied to a kind of dual citizenship in parallel realms. In this other temporal reality, I sometimes became distracted from my sense of self and began to function as though in a separate cone of ambiguity, as an interloper in some zone of altered dimension where all things moved along a separate time line, and I was merely sliding among them unseen. It filled me with an unsurpassable loneliness.

At some point it appeared that a shade was abruptly drawn across the canopy, and without warning, a heavy rain began falling in silvery curtains through the high trees. It blubbered heavily on the surrounding leaves and soon became general, soaking us anew and filling the air with its cascading sound. Johnson evidently chose the noise to mask a certain degree of uncharacteristically careless movement, and we stumbled rapidly forward through the falling water, stopping to watch and listen again only as the rain tapered off. The eerie stillness that followed its frantic passage lent a deep background of silence to the dripping foliage as we lay in the mud on the jungle floor.

As I grew more accustomed to it, the jungle's paradoxical nature kept trying to assert itself, by turns both comfort and threat. Just as it hid many dangers, it also hid us, and as visibility was seldom more than a few yards, there were times when I felt well concealed. Yet this just established the fact that the enemy, with his vastly greater experience, might be equally well concealed and very close, and in the event of either side discovering the other, automatic weapons would make it unlikely that either could escape. Even if I, or any one of us, were lucky enough to survive such an encounter unwounded, it would be difficult or impossible to elude pursuit by a determined enemy familiar with this wilderness. Suppose we were to escape but with the radio destroyed. The small PRC-10 taped to Johnson's leg could be used to broadcast an emergency frequency, but it lacked the range and voice options of the -25, and we were operating hundreds of miles to the west of any immediate help.

Thus even the radio held its irony. It could be a powerful lifeline, but its bulk could get you killed. Much of the tentative confidence I had invested in our equipment wavered, and I came to realize that it was self-deluding to think it an even bet that if you were careful enough to make optimum use of all your resources, physical, intellectual and material, you could avoid being seen in the first place. I tried to cast the net of my senses out even further, knowing that the only realistic way to escape detection was if the enemy simply wasn't around.

When at last evening shadows began to fill in the spaces around us and to obscure our footing, we came upon an area of sudden hills heavily populated by a large colony of dense bamboo groves, where throngs of enormous bottle green poles soared a hundred feet or more overhead, whose delicate upper branches feathered out to trap the fading light in a lacy collage of fine paint brush leaves. Johnson halted the team with a hand signal, and we crouched in silence to study what lay ahead.

Bamboo is an incongruously attractive plant, unlike any other in the jungle. Its polished vertebral geometry invites the eye, but bamboo was deceptive and dangerous. It appeared to offer good cover, for a mature grove is too thick to see through, and in fact, the Viet Cong were known to be able to hide in them, but our teams had learned to their sorrow reasons to avoid bamboo. Our equipment would hang up on the smooth segmented stalks, trapping a man further as he squirmed to free himself, and any disturbance at the base transferred movement up the whole length of its towering stems, causing the entire grove to sway and to knock together. The clatter and clunk that results resonates through the forest over great distances, and the agitation at their tops can be seen from far away, especially from higher ground, by which we were then surrounded. Depending upon the terrain, an attempt to move through bamboo could easily telegraph our position to anyone with field glasses for miles around.

We stopped at the edge of the grove rather than trying to get through or around this potential trap in failing light. Johnson signaled that we would stay the night. We formed ourselves into a defensive perimeter under cover of the jungle, uncertain of his plan for navigating the relatively open ground ahead. On keen alert, but knowing we would take up a new position after dark, we lay silent and still beneath the dense undergrowth without placing the mines and waited for the night.

At last the long day was closing, and I knew that, at least to a degree, the faculty of sight would soon have a rest. I welcomed the contact and the smell of the cool black earth beneath me and the rapid flight of visibility. I was footsore, aching again with fatigue; my eyes and hearing were tired from being pitted against the constant maze of tiny signals they had registered in the unsleeping contest with unseen threat.

The dank ammonium mix of old sweat and conflated soil rose from my clothes, and I was pestered with dozens of small cuts, scratches and insect bites. I could smell the rancidity of my own body. My dirty whiskers itched, and all the places where my gear rode against me burned with friction sores.

As before, after the remnants of light had soaked into the jungle floor and the cloak of night had drawn across the grove that loomed above us, the team began a long, cautious crawl several yards away through a thicket of stems and then formed a true night perimeter beneath a ceiling of large ferns. Once we were settled in place, Johnson crawled over to me on his elbows and knees to make his radio call, and the Nungs slithered silently out like salamanders to place the M-1 foot mines. Johnson assigned watch duties this time, and then, tired and debilitated, knowing I wouldn't be called for several hours and strung out on nervous tension, I welcomed the chance to free myself from the cumber of radio and web gear, to roll onto my back and to stare up at the covering of fronds that tented us on the shrouded earth. Gradually the smells and echoes of life left to its own devices for millennia awakened around us.

The chorus began soon after we had settled for the night. The massed creaking of cicadas at some distance from our position erupted from out of the general background sounds with a suddenness that startled me. Within seconds a different colony, much nearer, answered their proclamation arrhythmically, interrupting the others' pulse without pattern or sense to their thrumming stridulations. Their skipped beats, enjambments, sudden ellipses, and failed alterations jangled my nerves, as though each of those thousands of bugs was responding to separate warnings, to refinements of unseen danger, to ever renewing measures of dread, stubbornly deaf to the others, and loudly, alarmingly alone in its message.

I gripped my rifle, yawned to open my ears, and tried to focus my attention in every direction at once. The hills seemed to have drawn nearer in the darkness, and I began to wonder again if my name was churning out there somewhere in the great, faceless lottery of anonymous death.

My call for watch was a touch on the arm, but I wasn't asleep. Despite a steeply growing need for it, the stakes were too high to allow myself to sleep. While I sat quietly beneath the fronds and renewed my scan of our surroundings, I gradually became aware by a telling glossary of subtle movements in the dimness, and by the absence of any steady breathing, that the others weren't really asleep either. Our stops at night were merely rests, and the darkness did not provide sufficient protection to relax enough for sleeping. In this regard at least, my cloaked anxieties did not make me an exception. None of us ever really slept; each man's consciousness sort of hovered through the night, with degrees of practiced awareness always on alert to the world of night sounds that for the past few days I had been learning by the hour.

It's well known by anyone who has ever stood guard alone late in the night, that the grainy interweave of darkness and shadows can cause the eyes to play tricks on the imagination. It was especially true in the jungle, which in certain lights held a monstrous beauty of fecund desolation. The dense, unfettered growth formed a looming presence, especially at night. It was spooky. Indeed, the jungle was a haunted place where the vast complex of life continued day and night, for the plants never sleep. There were other times when the spectral silence of the trees seemed deliberate, and the awful quiet would swell in my head, pushing outward. At intervals during the long hours, the tiny sounds of continuing life became heightened and distorted by my charged imagination into grotesque variations of their natural causes, and they often seemed to contain the faint snaps and muffled thumps made by a person attempting to move stealthily. After all, the enemy was known for stealth, so the expectation was always there, and the imagination quickly ramps the evidence. Strange patches of bioluminescence glowed from scattered deadfall on the ground or appeared to hover eerily in the gloom between the trees.

Things that weren't really there moved, too. Sometimes tiny lights seemed to flash, dance for a moment, and then wink out. For long heart-stopping moments it could even appear that a person was standing silhouetted briefly in an open space, quite near.

Many of these illusions can appear in the filtered light of day as well, depending upon the density of growth, depth of shadows, and one's degree of anxiety–or fatigue. I already knew about the phenomenon, but this patrol had become an intensive graduate course, presenting in a constant stream of minor revelations the advantages of cold-bloodedness, of obsessive alertness to multiple details presenting themselves simultaneously—sometimes singly, sometimes in groups, but constantly—until the process of learning comes to include the very expectation of disaster.

This was no place for anyone like me, burdened with the baggage of emotion and feeling trapped in an activity where the stakes were so high that no rational person should be engaged in it at all. The marginal utility of what any of us stood to win seemed grossly outweighed by the disutility of what we all stood to lose.

The velvet murk of moonless nights on the jungle floor revealed the world the way it really is–dark, competitive, a system held in balance by the stresses of survival, where the known world, measured by clocks, seasons, the predictability of social custom, and a degree of leisure, vanishes completely, to lodge in some dim recess of the half-lit mansion of memory, distant as history.

When the earth turns its shoulder to the sun, and the sky fills with the darkness that is the natural state of the universe, Americans, who are accustomed to artificial light, undergo an idiocratic psychological retreat at the end of day. We require an adjustment to nighttime. On a primitive, immutable level, we retain a certain fear of the dark, for human eyesight is primarily designed for daylight. We don't see well at night. Ever since Thomas Edison we haven't really needed to. In true night we are at a disadvantage to creatures that prowl after dark, especially if those creatures are belligerent humans who have never lived with electricity. Night brings us an added vulnerability. At night, we become prey.

Our sense of safety depends upon a certain degree of predictability, so any mysterious sound at night, sometimes even those that would be familiar in daylight, becomes a signal from something outside the usual rules. It becomes creepy, evil, dangerous. A man posted to watch over his companions alone on the floor of an abyssal tangled wilderness deep in enemy territory must concentrate hard on sorting all sounds and upon mastering his fear.

My body hurt from the day's exertions. My eyes burned with fatigue, and when I indulged in a moment of rubbing my eyelids, the press of gritty fingers brought forth a negative image of the night's emergence, the trees standing pale and austere, the spaces between them black and impenetrable and filled with sinister mystery. Though it felt good at least to rest on the ground, I could not relax or allow my thoughts to wander. The only thoughts for a man in danger are thoughts of peril, for all else is a call to languor and perhaps to death. I was determined to become a creature of both the day and the night and in future to better mark the position of surrounding shapes while daylight still lingered.

Leaning back against the radio pack, I looked up through the dense growth, and against all odds, framed by hundreds of feet of intervening canopy, saw the solitary gleam of a tiny star, a single trembling glint of silver, impossibly remote in its passionless and unattainable serenity. After a moment I looked away to continue my scan around our position, but when I looked for it again, could not find it. It had winked but once, a fleeting talisman that whispered of disparate contingencies, of safety and of hope.

Everything appeared to close in upon me, and as the jungle put up its walls of noisy silence I had to concentrate on keeping my eyes moving, to avoid staring at any one place, and to sort through the night sounds for any that seemed to come from the ground, any tiny noise that could signal something, anything, man or beast, approaching–or that resembled language. I remained still, except for head movement, as the cold, dark hours crept on toward that pre-dawn moment when we would move and continue into the unknown.

The effort to remain perfectly still can be as demanding as the effort to keep moving. Over time, the muscles grow weary with tension, and then your first movement becomes painful. Thus, when I moved to touch Johnson on the arm at 0400 hours to begin day three, it was hard to make my limbs work. They ached with the rust of long immobility.

The team quickly and noiselessly stirred to life. I ate a few balls of rice and pulled my equipment painfully on, checked my weapon and drank some neoprene-flavored water, in the process noticing somewhat absently that my hands were beginning to follow the habitual patterns of the trade.

When we were ready, Johnson gave a hand signal to our direction that indicated he intended to give the bamboo grove a wide berth and to proceed around behind one of the hills that formed a vague caldera surrounding the shallow fern grove in which we had spent the night. We crept out of our position, taking the established order, and followed the low ground between the rises. Since any movement might alert wildlife or possible enemy trackers, once clear of the old position, we soon stopped to listen and assess our situation.

After a long vigil we resumed our stealthy progress, and by the time a grey, aqueous dawn began to filter through the growth, we were well clear of the RON site. Soon the wet, diabolical heat found its way down to the lower reaches of jungle. The air hung heavy and still, and we pushed ourselves through it until around mid day, when we stopped for a long vigil.

I was able to find a tree root on which to ease the strain of the radio on my shoulders. We sat and listened. The leaves hung in the humid stillness overhead like dead hands. All was deathly quiet, the moisture in the air probably too much even for the cicadas. Everything seemed arrested of movement. Sweat ran down my face and seeped everywhere through my clothes. I became aware of the whisper of body hair inside my shirt.

Then I heard something. Something that didn't belong. I wasn't sure at first, and yawned to clear my ears. A faint hum. Very faint. It seemed to appear and disappear, teasing along the lowest threshold of hearing. I couldn't place it. It pulsed at the very periphery of perception for a moment, reminding me vaguely of an engine one moment, and the next, some heavy insect. At first I dismissed it as anything mechanical, yet I had not encountered an insect that sounded quite like it. I signaled to the next man, but it appeared that he was already listening to it, his head cocked to the air like a dog's nose, testing the air for messages. For long moments, it was hard to decide if I was, indeed, hearing something outside my own head, but soon it became evident that each of the others I could actually see were listening too. By turning my head from side to side, I decided after a minute or more that the source was in the general direction we were heading.

A renewed alertness now animated the others. Again I had no idea what was going on, and as the others began to move in unison, I felt anew a flash of irritation at my inexperience. Up until then, my ignorance of what to expect had come loaded with the oppressive obduracy of high-stakes vulnerability, but now I was weary of it, tired of never knowing what the others anticipated, and their shared attention to this new disturbance made me angry at the successive layers of mystery to which I was being randomly subjected. This on-the-job training method had the advantage of forcing a man new to this extraordinary work to evolve his own set of priorities through direct experience, but it also meant he had to walk the cusp of mortal danger in ongoing ignorance of much for which he might have been prepared.

Within an hour of resuming our slow, methodical progress, the sound had evolved into the unmistakable hum of an engine. If our mission was to verify the existence of a prisoner of war camp, an engine to run lights or a generator would be a useful addition to any sort of cantonment, especially one so improbably remote. I wondered how it was being powered and why, whatever it was.

It occurred to me that had I not become so attuned to the sounds of the jungle, I may not have heard it at all until well after the others. Johnson had warned me long before never to make any non-jungle sound. I quietly added another object lesson to my edgy appreciation.

We crept into an area where the canopy was relatively open, where the visibility among the lower vegetation was slightly better, and with our attentiveness fueled now by the need to investigate the source of this incongruous sound, we moved quietly into a leafy hollow in which dappled sunlight flaked the jungle with vivid renditions of green.

We had progressed about half way across this thicket of newer growth, when suddenly, *Bumff*! A muffled gunshot shattered the silence somewhere ahead of us. We instantly went to ground. My heart rate soared. What was that? What was going on?! My temples pounded. My eyeballs filled with heartbeats, and in my confused desperation I swiveled my head around to search frantically through the surrounding growth for any movement. I needed to see what the others were doing, and gasping audibly now, peered around for any clue of what to do.

I just glimpsed the feet of the man ahead, his boots splayed flat upon the ground, when a second shot came from somewhere to our left, behind some higher ground. *Bumff* ! Again, the same strangely flattened report, though a bit louder. Whoever it was ahead had company off to our side who sounded slightly closer.

The team lay perfectly still. There was no more sound. Then Johnson signaled for us to move to our right. Just as we began to creep away from the direction of the shots, there was another rifle chug, this time much louder. It resounded through the trees as though reflecting from dozens of holes in the forest, and a few seconds later what must have been an RPG exploded behind me with a loud *whang!* Instantly the moist air became sibilant with flying bits of metal that pattered into the surrounding jungle, tearing into the vegetation and thudding into the trees. Something struck me in the foot, right arm, and shoulder. The impact drove my face into the black earth, and in the lost seconds of stuporous confusion before the blinding pain began to burn itself in my brain like acid, all time stopped. My zone of comprehension shrank instantly to the margin of my skin. I felt suddenly, deeply, unnaturally alone. The sensation of searing metal rods being driven into my foot and shoulder erupted through me in a flash of bright fire. There was a blur of light and shade, and the smell of the earth came mixed with iodine. Then through a delirium of dread I became aware of the frantic cries of birds exploding from the forest. After that, everything began happening with an extraneous nightmare slowness–a horrible dream state in which I was trapped awake.

Afraid to stand up, I hugged the ground and tried to squirm away from the direction of the shots. There was dirt in my mouth. My heart's output redlined, and my confused brain filled with supplications. In the throes of on-set panic, I searched desperately about to discover that none of the others had stood up or run. Why weren't they moving? I clutched the earth trying somehow to draw a carpet of safe distance toward me, and then I seemed to be swimming across the ground in a slow-motion nightmare, while forks of lightning stabbed through me. The two ammo pouches on the front of my webbing seemed to have caught on something, holding me back. I felt something release, and then began to drag myself ponderously, as in a dream, over a fantastic congestion of tree roots that could have come from the pages of a child's fairytale. Beneath them sheltered a clump of tiny toadstools, strange and solemn and leaning to show their delicate liver-colored gills. My brain fastened on them. I couldn't place the incongruous image. Was it telling me something?

I held the pistol grip of my rifle with one hand, and as the other scrabbled to drag me along the jungle floor it became the axis of all I could comprehend. Every leaf, stem, and crumble of earth that passed beneath me stood forth in luminous contrast to the ground. Then suddenly there seemed to be tree trunks close about me, my fingers fumbling in the mulch of leaf fall and dirt. With my insides creaking, struggling to keep whole, to remain sealed, I scrambled behind one of the low humps of ground we had passed through on our way in.

While a bubble of hot poison leaked within me, I strained to make my mind work, to sort out this terrifying complication. Then I realized that some of the others were tumbling over the mound, such as it was, beside me, putting at least a margin of sheltering earth between us and the source of the shooting. Johnson and the last two followed, spilling over and coming up with their weapons trained on the clearing. They each had the discipline to hold their fire, while I could see nothing to shoot at. Had I the power to make myself invisible, I would have used it all.

A lid of silence fell upon us as we crouched against the malarial black soil glacis of root-riven ground. We waited for any sign or sound of movement. Nothing happened. No one appeared. Nothing moved except the rapidly dissipating grey smoke that drifted out of a tear in the ferns from whatever had been fired at us. It rose from the quiet glade on slanted sunbeams and gathered among the tree tops in a thinning parchment haze.

After a desperate interval dense with expectancy and a crescendo of raking pain, it began to seem that we had probably not been under direct observation. There was no way to be sure, but it may have been just a lucky shot. As I was coming to realize I might live through my injuries, Johnson crept over to use the radio. His eyes were wide and hard as porcelain. He unfolded the antenna and whispered into the hand set the codes for enemy contact and for emergency extraction, in addition to some other letter combinations I didn't recognize. He whispered close to my ear the one word, "trackers." Then he pointed in the two directions the shots had come from and indicated that we had heard nothing from a third direction. Then he added, "Probably just blocking; not leading us. Keep listening behind us!"

When he crept back to his position, I noticed that there was blood soaking the back of his right pant leg. Then I saw that the Nung beside me had blood trickling out from under his sleeve. I listened with terrified intensity in every direction, but any faint sounds were drowned by the ringing in my ears.

The pain in my right foot became torrential. Something had torn through my boot just below my ankle bone, shredding the fabric, and had ripped through the top, cutting the lacings and evidently passing through the top of my foot. Blood was rapidly darkening the canvas part of the boot, and I could tell by the sop inside that the shoe was filling with blood. I had to get some tape around it to keep the whole thing from coming apart, but this was not the place or time to nurse ourselves. Something was burning into my shoulder, the muscle there too inflamed to work properly. The slightest movement took concentrated effort.

Johnson signaled us to move obliquely away from the direction of the shots, but the language of his hands seemed to indicate that we were going to cut back toward them after we'd cleared the area of the encounter. That made no sense to me. I just wanted to get out of there as far, quickly, and stealthily as our injuries would allow, starting right then.

As soon as I realized I'd be able to move, it became strictly a matter of pain. The top part of my body felt paralyzed by it. All movement hurt. Lying down had hurt, leaning against the slope had hurt, now trying to get moving hurt. Crawling hurt, and the effort to keep my gear balanced with the added pain of what was probably a shattered foot along with whatever seemed to have gone wrong with my shoulder constituted an excruciating new dimension of agony. All movement twisted its knives within me, but there was no alternative to pushing through it. Each lurching step now threw the inertia of the radio from side to side, the harness gouging into the wound in my shoulder. The effort and pain upset my stomach, but our situation did not afford me the luxury of throwing up. Besides, I was empty.

As we withdrew, the effects of the pain and the adrenalin sent me into spells of lightheadedness. I tried to hold my breath every few steps in an effort to push back against the pain, but then I seemed unable to exhale without an audible release of the pressure. It proved quieter to breathe deeply with my throat open.

Gradually I adjusted to a world of searing discomfort, since there was no time to deal with it. We were definitely in enemy territory and hundreds of miles from rescue. With multiple injuries and an unknown number of concerted enemy nearby, whatever chances remained for our salvation lay in movement. We continued our cautious plod along the back slope of ground until well past the area where we had been probed. Then Johnson signaled the point man to cut back toward the presumed area of the shot that had come from the side, in effect crossing our own trail. I finally saw what he was doing. Depending upon how long our presence had been suspected, Johnson was guessing that the trackers would not expect us to come up behind them.

We never saw them, and in our condition, didn't want to encounter such an unknown quantity, but from a position on what was probably the opposite side of where they had attacked us, we turned out again and stole away from the engine sound. Resuming a greatly elevated state of alertness, we made our way eastward for the next few hours, every step a strummed wire of pain.

Eventually, having limped and crawled some hundreds of meters from where we had turned away, and moving with fewer listening stops than we had before, Johnson came back to use the radio again. He whispered a signal into the handset, and I heard a muted voice response. He replaced the phone and consulted his watch. I didn't know who he was talking to, but was glad to hear some acknowledgement. Until then I had no confidence that our TOC had received any of his transmissions. Then he whispered that he would turn on the PRC-10 radio in about 2 hours. It was still securely taped down in his side pocket. If he removed the tape which held gathered the pleats in his pocket and thereby captured the radio against his leg, the unit would become a lose weight in the event that we had to run. If he turned it on too soon it might shorten the effective battery life.

After what seemed a very long time, he switched it on as we continued to hobble eastward. After another hour or so, when my effort to maintain a worthwhile vigil was losing the struggle with my diminishing capacity to push through the pain, we heard the faint thumps of choppers in the distance, the engine noise gradually rising to mix with the signature beating sound of the rotors. They were homing on the locator signal being broadcast from Johnson's pocket, and it sounded as though they were coming straight for us.

The sound initiated a renewed energy that passed among us unspoken, but was revealed in a rush of tiny behavioral signals which people nearing the end of any protracted unpleasantness find hard to conceal. We couldn't see the machines through the canopy, they were still too far away, and we knew that from their vantage point we were hidden deep beneath the tree tops. I wondered with troubled attention how this next event would unfold. Despite deep fatigue and pain, I had to learn how Johnson would get his debilitated team out of there.

Johnson had made good time in getting our rendezvous point as far as possible from the area where we had been compromised, and now the point man returned indicating that ahead was a large enough break in the trees for a pick-up. Johnson took out his signal mirror, and within moments the first chopper passed slowly almost directly overhead, the second going on past.

Things began to happen very fast. From the elation of hearing our impending rescue in the sound of their engines, I was now seized with new anxiety as I knew their racket would mark our position for the enemy. After three days of concentrated silence, the roar of the helicopters washed over me in a hurricane of sound and swirling scraps of vegetation.

In short order one of my primary senses became all but neutralized, and since I didn't know how they were going to get us out of there, I needed to compromise the focus of the other by dividing my attention between the wood line and the machine overhead. There was no way they could set down through the trees, and in my effort to watch everything at once, I became confused and took in little information from either.

Johnson, by now limping heavily, climbed over some deadfall and lurched into the area of most light, beneath the thinnest layer of canopy. He flashed his signal mirror up through the trees at the slowly orbiting S-1, his arm extended and turning his body to keep it focused on the helicopter, which responded by tightening its turn and coming to a clattering stationary hover directly above the trees.

In moments two long, weighted ropes dropped through the thrashing tree tops, uncoiling as they came, to flop onto the ground nearby. They had four pairs of loops tied in them, for two men each to step into one and put an arm through the other. The lines continued to collapse onto the ground until the upper pair of hand- and foot-holds came down to eye level.

As I tried to divide my attention between the surrounding forest and the crew chief leaning out of the helicopter door, barely visible above the trees, Johnson directed four of the Nungs to grab the loops.

The first two shouldered their rifle slings and leapt to the ropes, and the hovering crew chief started to winch them up. As the lower pair of holds lifted, two others got their footing on the loops, hugged the ropes, and continued up through the trees. At 50 or 60 feet above the ground, but still below the canopy, the uneven downwash on the four Chinese and their equipment compounded the momentum of their initial lunge and started them twisting and swinging wildly. One of the guys on the higher loops had to grab the other line to keep the pendulum effect from sending the lower men into the branches on their way up.

With the racket and blowing debris, I was very nervous about our being jumped while this period of deafening vulnerability was broadcasting our position. After all, despite our caution over the past three days, we had never heard the trackers until the moment they announced themselves, and we had no idea when they had actually picked up on us. They could be anywhere now, even quite close, and the team was divided with only four of us on the ground. I kept searching the area for any movement among the trees. If they were to hit us now, they might get the whole team, in addition to bringing down at least one expensive American helicopter with all its weapons and radios.

Once the first four were aboard, the ropes were dropped through the trees again, and Johnson indicated that the point man and I were to take the upper loops. I slung my rifle and got my good foot into the lower one, hooked my good arm through the upper one, and was started up immediately. As I was drawn up high enough to notice the oil streaks on the underside of the helicopter, just before I had to hug the rope to keep from being rubbed off by the branches, I looked down and saw the top of Johnson's jungle hat in the loops below me as we crashed up through the canopy. He was gripping the other rope and looking back down at the ground.

At the top, the point man transferred himself to the helicopter with the grace of a cat, while the crew chief, seeing the blood on my shirt, helped me out of the rig. I sprawled onto the scuffed aluminum floor of the helicopter, the weight of the radio capsizing me onto the deck. I felt the chopper lurch steeply into a departure turn and looked up to see that Johnson and the last man were just getting out of the rig. The chopper was leaving even before we were all secure. That was alright with all of us.

Someone helped me out of the radio pack, causing again a spike of knife edge pain in my shoulder. I then saw that whatever had cut into me had sliced half way through the shoulder strap of the radio pack, which itself was splashed with a constellation of little holes. It seemed the burdensome radio had saved me from some additional wounds.

Once we were established on the sling seats, I finally saw all of the team face to face for the first time since the day we had been inserted. It was a surreal apparition. They had been transformed–black with dirt and swollen with insect bites, festering scratches, and the remnants of camouflage grease paint. Some were stained with fresh blood, tied with dirty bandages, their jungle fatigues torn in places and caked in common with the same dried mud, which combined to give the impression that we were the conjoined segments of some fantastic lobed creature, risen from the bogs of an alien marsh world. They smiled for the first time. Johnson gave us all the high sign and a nervous, inattentive grin, but an expression of sad desperation rested momentarily in passing through his yellowed eyes. It touched some distant, familiar chord in me, and I looked away.

I leaned back against the bulkhead and tried to minimize the plunging sandpaper grind in my shoulder and the rasp of the sleeve on my arm. My right foot was a lump of lancinating pain encased in a blood-saturated, muddy boot. It did me no good to look at it. I looked instead out at the endless spread of jungle paling away into the haze of late afternoon. It seemed somehow drained of color, fading to olive grays as we climbed. I had been conveyed on a transformative journey to some sacred center filled with hardships, darkness, and peril, wherein I had been led to some uncomfortable truths of myself, more through my weaknesses than by my doubtful strengths. Now, numb with fatigue and distress, I stared dully out at the tree tops through an indelible pentimento of shifting images, and half believed I had ever really been in those places.

From the open, wind-wracked helicopter the view was wonderful in the old sense of the word. For the first time I realized the terrifying vastness of the Vietnamese jungle. Of course I had seen it from aircraft before, but then it had presented itself with a certain postcard objectivity. Now, seen from above with first hand experience of what lay hidden below, watching within it, I shuddered at my own smallness and the utter folly of trying to suppress whatever forces chose to hide there, chose to operate from its fastness and to sally forth bent upon our destruction, then to melt away again into the safety of its impenetrable shadows.

When, after some hours at altitude, we finally began the approach to the landing pad at FOB 4, I experienced an edgy mix of discomfort at returning "home." I had been indelibly imprinted with the knowledge that the base would never be a safe place to sleep, yet it held all the meager possessions of my footlocker, a comfortable bed, warm showers. It bore a now-familiar paradoxical ambiguity in common with the jungle–the web of tension between the twinned promise of shelter and peril.

13

Word was out that we had gotten into trouble and were coming in with multiple wounded. Several vehicles were waiting for us when the choppers touched down. The deuce-and-a-half to carry us back to the team area, the Colonel's jeep, and one of the quarter tons. I could see the large red cross in its white field painted on the side of the waiting ambulance's box while we were still the better part of a mile out. By then, my shoulder was so inflamed I could hardly move my upper body, and my foot could barely support the weight of the shoe, the pressure of a step, impossible. So much blood had oozed out of my boot that it left smears on the chopper's deck.

We made a spongy touchdown, and as the rotors wound down, Johnson managed to climb out by himself, but his right pant leg was saturated with bloody sweat, and he accepted help walking to the aid truck. A couple of guys helped me down off the helicopter deck and over to the truck while one of the medics checked out the rest of the team. Partly because we were so filthy, and partly because the fabric was stuck to the wounds, they just cut our clothes away and began examining the extent of our injuries there on the landing pad. On board the helicopter someone was coiling the ropes that had been used to extract us through the trees.

Johnson, one of the Nungs, and I were judged to need the attentions of the field hospital where I had been treated following the big attack, and we were immediately driven off the compound and up to the aid station. Our Nung needed to have pieces of metal taken out of his arm and back, Johnson had a deep one removed from the back of his upper leg, just under his buttock, and they took a sharp, crescent-shaped piece of shrapnel about an inch and a half long out of my shoulder. It resembled a meteorite. Several more pieces were removed from superficial wounds in my arm using a large magnet. Whatever had cut through my foot had done so without breaking any bones, though it had cracked two, and left one of the shoe lace grommets imbedded in the wound. Once my foot was cleaned up, it looked as swollen and purple as a box of plums. The deep groove that had sliced across it was stitched and tightly bandaged. I was issued a sturdy cane and told to keep my foot in a laced boot as much as possible to combat the swelling.

All our wounds had been contaminated by the dirt on our skin and in the fabric of our clothes, but the doctors said it was a good thing they had been allowed to bleed for so long, as it probably kept them relatively clean.

As even I, sadly, was once again deemed walking wounded, all three of us were released for light duty. The Nung and I were shirtless and bandaged, and Johnson's pants had been cut away. Like the rest of us, he wore no underwear, so he was issued a pair of hospital greens with a cotton drawstring, and thus attired, we were driven back to the base.

There, Johnson said we had to get cleaned up and report for the operation's debriefing. I didn't want to damage my new bandages but couldn't stand the condition I was in any longer and went right to the showers. There, the water that streamed off me was mud brown, asphalt grey, and streaked with rusty blood. I couldn't even get it all out from under my fingernails until later, but I was able to clean my scalp, shave, and brush my teeth. The warm, sudsy cascade, though burning in numerous cuts and scratches, was a luxury I couldn't have imagined just four days earlier.

Johnson and I limped up to the headquarters hut, where we entered the sanctified world of Intelligence and its multifold layers of guarded protocols. The debriefing Sergeant was pleasant enough, despite, or perhaps because of, being completely impersonal. In fact everything about him seemed to be a reflection of his closeted, air-conditioned life. His uniform was clean, the sleeves carefully rolled up to match each other. His skin showed little, if any, exposure to the sun, and as would soon be apparent, he treated his maps and photographs with an almost prissy reverence. I had the impression that both he and his office had just emerged fresh out of tissue wrapping.

He was of average height with a high arched nose, close-set dark eyes, and a narrow face, somewhat flushed, which combined to give the impression that his vision was permanently pinched to a point, as though lastingly set by habitual doubt, or perhaps by studying magic acts as a child for the secret of their tricks. With the narrow isthmus between his eyebrows scrunched into a deep wrinkle, he seemed preoccupied by nature. He was pensive and professional, and perhaps due to spending all his time marinating in "what if?" speculation, pretty thorough.

He rose from his chair when we came in, unfolding his long caliper legs carefully, one at a time, like an afghan hound standing up.

He focused his gaze upon us, then after taking us in for a moment, bestowed a sharp grin of such fierce insincerity that I thought he might bite.

"Welcome back," he pronounced through long teeth with a perfunctory regulation tone. His manner reeked of an ill-judged effort at congeniality, which may not have seemed so inappropriate if we had been allowed a little more time to recover from the events of the operation.

I had the distinct feeling that our close call in the field meant nothing to him outside its potential for contributing to some store of information, and that his opening words were no more than an enabling clause, a common pill–but with a secret potion deep inside. I felt a flash of irritation at this man and his vaguely patronizing air. My emotion was probably unjustified. After all, we had presented ourselves after medical treatment and after getting cleaned up, so other than the marks we bore of protracted insect attack and sleep deprivation, we must have appeared bleached of the blood sacrifice that, in my view, lent a certain holiness to our experience and sanctity to whatever Johnson would report.

"Now," he continued, "what can you tell us?"

I wondered if he used the collective "us" deliberately for its implication that an unseen cadre of intelligence analysts lurked just behind the walls of maps. I looked at Johnson who rose stiffly to begin our narrative of events.

Using our dirty and blood-smeared field map to estimate as best we could the team's movements from the point of insertion to the river crossing, to the area where we heard the engine noise and then were caught by the trackers, thence on to the extraction point, we related all that happened and everything we had seen. Judging by the questions the debriefer asked, he must have been taking in our testimony, but he seldom actually looked at us, which seemed to me an oversight in any intelligence debrief. Even poker players know to read the language of mannerism.

He shuffled around his map table, leaving us to feel exactly like what we were–mere servants of information–as he moved about the room and plotted our movements on projections of different scale, peering at the contour lines as though trying to squint holes in the paper. I supposed that as his job required the ability to process second-hand intelligence extracted from exhausted men who often must arrive still dazed by the portent of their own survival. It must have carried a set of frustrations of its own, but if he had shown even a slight indication that he understood the price exacted in acquiring the information, it would have gone a long way toward kindling a fully cooperative attitude in us.

After a series of seemingly irrelevant questions about the vegetation and the weather, the color of the river water and the nature of any flotsam we encountered there, he led us through the contours of the terrain and checked our report with the coordinates on his master map before at last making a noise that implied some degree of satisfaction at least with the pattern and distance we had covered.

We were not able to identify for certain the weapon that had been used against us, but we both thought it had sounded like a Soviet RPG. Nor could we be certain what exactly the engine noise was, only that it sounded like some kind of small bore, gasoline-driven machine. I supported Johnson's decision to abort the mission on the grounds that we had evidently confirmed something unusual near the area of the suspected camp and that, further, there was a reason that outlying trackers had been posted. At that point the operation had been compromised, we had wounded, and to stay would have been to risk loss of the whole team.

The debriefing Sergeant remained the captive of his two-dimensional projections throughout and stared at his papers as though trying to frown some bit of desired information into being.

"Any dogs?" he asked suddenly.

"What?"

"Dogs. Do you think the trackers were using dogs?"

This was a question I had never even considered, and like everything else I was learning about these operations, it carried implications I didn't want to think about. I looked my blank ignorance at Johnson who, always less nonplussed than I, answered in the negative.

"We're getting more reports lately of their using dogs," the Sergeant continued. "We've worked up a mixture of dried goat's blood and CS (tear gas) powder as a counter measure. You can draw some from S-4."

I waited for further clarification. None was offered. Johnson nodded and said nothing. I knew that this information would be of no concern to him. In a short while, he would never have to think about any of this again for the rest of his life.

Having exhausted our account of what had happened, we continued to sit in wordless expectation of whatever additional questions might arise from the Sergeant's sedulous perusals.

As we sat there, the sedatives I had been administered at the hospital began to wear off, and with them, my discomfort grew exponentially. I began to sweat with the effort to combat the returning pain, to find a comfortable position and to pay attention. My bandages, still wet from the shower, seeped clammily through my shirt. My shoulder ached from the shear weight of my arm, and my foot, already compressed in a stiff replacement jungle boot, became a pulsing storm of torment. I needed to lie down and elevate it. With the only table in the room full of maps, the floor offered a tempting option, but I feared the denizen of the office would think it a bit loony were I to slump carefully down and stretch out across his walking space.

At last I braced my cane against the front of the chair and rested my foot across the stick in an effort to ease the throbbing in my foot. It didn't help much but was slightly less bad, and I knew Johnson must be uncomfortable, too, as he sat skewed to his left to ease the pressure that the edge of the chair was doubtless placing on the freshly stitched wound at the back of his right leg. We began to grow impatient.

At the time it was generally known, at least in the reconnaissance and intelligence-gathering community, that the U.S. had the world's best satellite photography and were covering every square foot of Vietnam in detail from space. In addition, we had C-130 transport aircraft equipped with state of the art infrared heat sensing photography in the air every night. These planes, carrying specialists who sat facing cathode screens, could fly over an area of the jungle at a safe altitude and record the ground movements of even a single individual by his heat signature. They could tell how many individuals were on a trail, where and roughly how long he (or they) sat for a break, and whether anyone lit a cigarette or pissed along the way. With that kind of capability, I could not understand why they needed to risk sending out specialized recon teams deep into enemy territory to verify the existence of any large compound like a POW camp. Surely they could find out everything they needed to know about activity on the ground in such places, day and night, from the air. In view of this technology, I could see no reason for direct ground level verification by the old Mark 1 Eyeball, especially mine.

I didn't mention my rising distress or ask about the role of our other intelligence-gathering technology in the briefing, though as my frustration grew, so did my anger. When we were finally dismissed, I had to use the furniture to steady my progress to the door. Johnson's movements were stiff, too. He was sweating, and his leg trembled. The studious debriefing Sergeant seemed not to notice, hardly glancing at us as we left.

By the time we emerged from the hut, evening was well advanced, and the raw rock face of Marble Mountain, its garnish of mysterious thorn bushes stirring in the crevices, was deeply shadowed, and jagged fragments of the rock face jutted into the dim light of new night. To the east, a large naval vessel lay perched like a cut-out upon the shimmering grey absicca of the sea where it met the last refraction of remnant light along an indistinct horizon.

As we hobbled painfully back to the hootch, I thought again about what seemed the nearly universally needless risk of sending trained humans out on operations the ostensible purpose of which had to only to confirm what was already known from electronic surveillance. I stumbled in the sand once, and the multiple shots of fresh pain that lanced through the effort to keep my balance produced a flash of anger that motivated asking Johnson what he thought about it.

He turned and looked at me, and for the first time, I saw and understood how deeply tired he was. He swept aside a row of conjectural possibilities with his hand, and looking out through the eyes of a sleepwalker, he mumbled,

"Welcome to the 'Nam, man." Then after a few moments he added, "…We're in a book nobody's readin'."

He retreated into his former silence, and when I looked again, he was staring ahead as though amused by some vague recollection. I assumed he was simply coming to grips with the realization that he had just survived his last mission in Vietnam and would soon be on the freedom bird back home.

The need for sleep was taking me over. I would have been stumbling even without a bad foot. Johnson angled off toward the clubhouse and the hootch, but I wanted to get some dinner before allowing myself to collapse. In a sluggish daze I dragging my way toward the lights of the messhall.

Staying with my rule of avoiding the pitch of light from any windows or doors after dark, I kept to the shadows even though there was sufficient ambient twilight to see the ground and slipped into the messhall by the side door. Ba Foo saw me come in leaning heavily on the cane and waddled over.

"You wan' dinna?"

"Er, yes."

"You sit heah!" she commanded, punching down through the air with a pudgy finger at a nearby table. I nudged into a chair and hooked the cane on the table edge, amused at how like the matron in a woman's prison she might be.

She quickly returned with a loaded tray and a glass each of water and milk. I thanked her: "Ba Foo, you numba one," and I toasted her with the glass of water.

I ate gratefully, and in the process, quickly finished the milk. In order to get all its virtue from the milk glass, I then emptied the remains of the water into the empty milk glass, which naturally made the water cloudy. Ba Foo saw this and came to stand over me until I peered up to find her glaring with a practiced look of mock disdain intended to emphasize my ignorance of gastronomic refinement. Then with a theatrical flair she slammed a fresh glass of water down in front of me and stalked away. I laughed despite my mood, and some of the other guys chuckled, too.

When I finished the meal, I paused at the door and yelled across the room.

"Hey, Ba Foo!"

She turned. "Wha'?"

I grinned and held up my index finger. "You numba one, Ba Foo!"

She cackled loudly and waved me out. After that, she always seemed to watch for me and to take special pleasure in teasing me. I liked it too. It always pleased me and gave some of the other guys a needed laugh, while reinforcing my program of keeping on friendly terms with the native staff.

I had wanted to find one of the medics for a bandage change before going to bed, but instead just made my painful way back to the hootch. Johnson was already asleep, though he awoke with a start when I stumped in as quietly as I could.

I propped up my foot on a rolled blanket and lay down on my back deciding that this night I could not afford to worry about sappers coming through the wire.

The next day, after we had both slept until mid-morning, Johnson informed me that after each mission he always bought the Nungs a case of American beer as a celebration. He thought it a good idea that I should be the one to take it down to them. I shared the cost of a case of canned Budweiser, which he assured me they liked, and then hobbled down to the team's tent to deliver it.

I was met with a degree of enthusiasm that surprised me. Those who had been on the operation had evidently got cleaned up and rested since the day before, and I didn't recognize them all. They dropped much of their Asian reserve in welcoming the arrival of the beer, and with their faces ornamented by anticipation, gathered around and began opening the cans immediately.

I returned to the hootch, glad to have had a hand in doing something that pleased them and hoping I had taken a step toward forging a needed trust with them. I told Johnson that I wanted to get whatever sort of breakfast might still be available at the messhall this late in the morning, and his response was to warn me not to stay away longer than an hour. The Nungs, he informed me, share with the American Indians a low tolerance for alcohol, even the modest content in beer, and they would drink it all at once, then pass out. We had to be ready to go back and check on them before the ones who collapsed face down could smother in the deep sand. At first I thought he was joking.

After a while, we went down to the team tent together, where we discovered all ten of them virtually comatose. Sitting, lying on the ground, staggering about as in a dream state, they had escaped entirely into whatever realm awaited the benefits of drink. One was, sure enough, face down, and I rolled him over. With the sand on his face, he looked like a child covered with cake crumbs. Amid the empties scattered on their common table, there were still four unopened cans that had evidently escaped the battle of deteriorating hand/eye coordination.

Over the next several weeks the team stood down, partly to allow those of us with injuries to recover and partly because the assignment of operations was rotated through other teams. It was "good" to be back, even on the haunted ground of FOB 4, with its brooding hootches shimmering in the glare. It had the benefit at least of some dicey familiarity, along with whatever additional safety there may have been in the presence of other Americans, now mostly untried replacements. I came to realize how traumatized I'd been by the experience of that first mission. The extraordinary world of the jungle and the conditions it had imposed left me in a state of disordered alienation, yet with a constituent sense of urgency in the face of this huge and nameless presence. Perhaps it was just the loom of the war itself, the complex of constraints that dwelt within the very element in which we were all compelled to live, but it lent an unsleeping provisionalism to every aspect of my continued existence.

The harsh empirical education of the jungle was hard-earned—and permanent. Its exhausting requirement to fuse your senses with its faintest messages sears an indelible mark on the spirit while it stamps the intellect. The extraordinary effort needed to move with impossible stealth through its watchful tangles in the unbelievable heat, especially while overbalanced with some 70 pounds of equipment and weaponry and trying to learn the high-stakes catechism of everything seen, heard, or smelled, had left me with an acute consciousness of its vibrant life force. Its comprehensive dangers had already taken a lasting toll upon my sense of self worth. A man cast into that ocean of shadows and voluptuous growth was nothing but a microscopic droplet in the limitless and rapacious congestion of huge plants and the mysterious presences that dwelt within their impenetrable spaces. And most bitterly, I knew that it was all just beginning.

I had become sensitive to tiny sounds and the shifting scents that carried in the air. Now back in the compound, I could hear people's clothing and became sharply aware of the sibilant multiplicity of their footfalls in the sand or distant clumping along the duckboards. It all pointed up my own nervous tension. The orchestra of unconscious noises generated by humans in their ceaseless stirrings gave me prolonged flashes of irritation. I was glad to see the recent replacements as they moved curiously about the compound in their dark new field issue, but their presence lent dimension to the gulf of harsh experience that spread now dense and gaunt between us. It had not been long since I was one of them, but by other measures than time I had become transported to a separate dimension, a twilight realm that lay beyond the shores of their understanding.

During this time the reality of going home began to elicit moments of contained animation from Sgt. Johnson, as his personality emerged briefly now and then to blink in the sun. He began to speak of the future and referred to his home in the midwest for the first time.

He also began turning in some of his equipment, bequeathing other items to me. I inherited custodianship of his binoculars, map case, the team's recon camera, and a few other things. He even gave me two of his fatigue shirts, which had been worn, faded, and laundered free of the stifling impregnation of fire retardant they had held when new, and thus would be more comfortable than mine. I was glad to have them. Anything might help. Besides, he had survived his tour of this dangerous unconventional work, so he was lucky, and although luck and foresight are often hard to distinguish, he had bet on the correct long shot enough times in a year to be given credit at least for an unusual knowledge of form, and in the talismanic culture of Vietnam, that made even his things lucky.

One day Johnson announced that he wanted to visit what was left of the ancient citadel at the old imperial city of Hue, which was a short flight north of Da Nang, not far from the coast. I had heard of the place only in news stories. The Marines had fought a protracted battle for it a year or so before in bitter door-to-door combat. U.S. Marines were not trained for that kind of operation at the time, and over the bloody weeks of close street fighting had taken very heavy losses, heavy enough to have made prime time news back in the States—but typical of most Marine operations, they had also taken the objective. Johnson had arranged to hop a helicopter ride up there with the flight that delivered movies to the US installations, and somewhat to my surprise, he invited me to go along. There followed a day that contained events which, though perhaps not so un-expectable in places of war, have served ever since as a benchmark against which to measure such overworked terms as "grotesque," "surreal" and "bizarre."

We met the movie chopper and started north. The pilot flew up the beach, keeping well out over the water, taking no chances. I approved. After a few delivery stops at the hospitals and beach installations, we climbed into cooler air and crossed over part of the sprawling shanty outskirts of Da Nang with its dusty streets, where blasts of sunlight skipped swiftly along a patchwork of corrugated tin as our shadow swam across the congestion of tiny rooftops. Then the pilot angled inland, passing over a long area of coastal jungle growth, eventually to set down on a short strip of crumbling tarmac, where the only evidence that it might still be in use was two Cobra gun ships parked in line beside a section of old Highway 1. The Americans had built a small airport across the road from the Imperial City, but I was looking out the other side of the helicopter on the approach and did not see the Citadel from the air.

Still favoring our injuries, Johnson and I eased onto the ground. With the blades turning overhead, I leaned into the pilot's window to get his estimated time of return upon completion of his deliveries, and thus didn't take in our surroundings until he lifted off. When I looked across the road at the ruin that emerged from the jungle edge it filled me with an unexpected sense of saddening irony. Other than a few gauzy pointillist newsprint photos taken during the Marine offensive there, I had never seen a picture of the Imperial City as it looked either before or after the fighting, and thus had no expectations. Yet the forlorn sight of its reality gave me the discomforting feeling of a lost pilgrim who, after hardship and suffering, reaches the hallowed Elysium a few minutes too late, only to find the stones tumbled, their secret meaning forever lost.

It was surprisingly small for what I might have imagined any place with the exalted name of Imperial City to be. Surrounded by what was left of an impressive perimeter wall, now breached and broken, but once whitewashed to make it stand like a jewel among the press of surrounding forest, the huddled rubble within must once have held gleaming towers and tall pagodas. Now it resembled a ruined wedding cake, its tiers collapsed, walls sheared and melted by a tempest of gunfire. Every surface was porous with thousands of bullet and rocket holes. Now it was shrunken, drawn back from the vaunt of its history. Small now, and profoundly quiet.

Yet it also held a strange allure, an echo of momentous event, like an abandoned museum. Even in the harsh daylight, it resonated somehow with the sentient emptiness of a vacant theater. Yet it was a dead place. We could see behind what had once been the front gate that the earthen streets were lost in weeds and littered with the mud brick debris of fallen walls, slumped now by the episodic rains of several monsoon seasons into shapes suggesting the work of enormous insect colonies.

Johnson wanted to go in, and despite a curious foreboding, so did I, but it was posted all about with official restrictions that shouted at us to stay away, as it had still not been cleared of unexploded ordnance and forensic bits. We duly kept our distance, while the place worked its mysterious imperative upon us.

In looking around I kept thinking that one of the many characteristics of Vietnam was the lack of atmosphere in the painter's sense. There were no half-tints worth noticing, except the color of dried mud. Everywhere, both men and equipment, dressed in olive drab, stood out raw and crude in the glare of the sun with nothing to tone them down or to tone them against. Yet here was something that might once have been grand, a refuge painted to shine like a wet stone in the wilderness, protected by high walls to keep the jungle out, and now but for the islanded remnants of its plaster, worn by war almost into the ground. It was dwindling quietly back into the earth, taking with it the voices of its history and the legacy of too much attention.

Johnson had brought the team camera, so we took some pictures of the ruins and a few souvenir shots of each other and then settled down to wait for our ride to return. The flight wasn't scheduled to come back before late in the afternoon, and since we had discovered that we weren't allowed into the ruins, we faced some hours of waiting on the shelterless open of the runway. Except for the sound of an occasional vehicle passing along Highway 1, the place was quiet. A hot breeze sighed across the pavement.

However, a few interesting things did happen while we stood around whiling away the afternoon. The pilots of one of the Cobras arrived in a quarter-ton pickup and began placing their flight bags in the aircraft, while their driver stayed around, presumably to watch them take off.

While they conducted their pre-flight inspections and joked with the driver, an old civilian flat-bed truck, rusted and sagging on its springs beneath an overload of freshly-axed tree trunks, reddish and scarred and still weeping sap, came swaying precariously along the uneven highway behind us. It wheezed off the edge of the pavement just in time to give way for a convoy of ROK (Republic of Korea) Marines that roared past in dusty American deuce-and-a-half trucks, their tires singing on the hot tar roadbed.

Johnson smiled at the commotion and told me that for a long time, one of the scams that the local Vietnamese had pulled on the Americans in the region was to have an old man lie down in the road, as though injured, when they saw a U.S. vehicle coming. The Americans would naturally stop to help, and then the old guy and/or his anxious "witnesses" would claim that he had been struck by an American truck, and thus they would extort money for alleged injuries or reparations. The trick worked so often that it became a problem. That is, until the RoK Marines decided to put a stop to it. They simply began running over these people. It worked immediately. The RoKs were untroubled by moral imperatives, and there were no more hit-and-run extortion efforts. Beautiful in its irreducible simplicity.

Shortly, an old Vietnamese man with a wispy grey beard, wearing a typical conical straw hat, and leading a small boy by the hand, approached the Cobra pilots. He bowed politely to the men, and although we were too far away to hear what transpired between them, I guessed from the old man's smiles and gestures that he wanted to show the helicopter to the boy. The pilots bowed back and indicated that he could look around.

As the Americans turned back to their conversation, the old man led the boy around the machine, pointing out various things as they strolled along and encouraging the boy to reach out and feel the smooth aluminum along the boom. They crossed under the tail rotor and disappeared behind the helicopter, reappearing shortly at the nose. The scene was tranquil, and I enjoyed the way the pilots had availed themselves and their equipment to a few minutes of private inspection. Under the "chin" of the chopper's nose the barrels of its mini-gun protruded straight out, and the old man had to step around the array to complete his tour. He bent over, evidently explaining something to the boy about the weapon, then reached out and turned the barrels. In the next second, a clatter of shots shattered the silence in a single burst of noise, and the old man's body blew backwards with most of its midsection shot away, splattering the other cobra.

We all recoiled instinctively at the shock of it. The pilots rushed to the inert body of the old man, and the little boy began to wail as Johnson and I recovered and hobbled toward them across the highway. I was reeling at what we'd just seen and had no idea of what to do. Others did. The driver immediately got on the truck radio, and as soon as the two pilots realized that the old man was beyond help, one of them picked up the boy and tried to comfort him.

In a short while an American ambulance truck arrived, and the old man's body was spilled onto a stretcher and loaded through the double doors into the back. The medics, their faces set, took the hysterical boy with them, too, holding him and patting his back as his gasping screams ascended in a piercing series of emotive commas. He was probably too young to understand what had happened, but the noise and the spectacle would be enough to scar him for life.

A few minutes after the ambulance left, the pilots climbed into the Cobra and took off. When the noise and dust of their departure had settled, the silence that followed may as well have been thunder. Johnson and I stood wordlessly and alone again beneath the fierce metallic blare of the sun. The event wrenched all emotion from me. I looked over at the puddle of blood drying on the dark pavement, then at Johnson, who just spread his hands as though holding down a stack of invisible myths.

As the afternoon wore on, the hot pavement cooked through the soles of my boots. Despite the proximity of a fairly busy road, the place harbored a sense of desolation and abandonment. Much had happened here during the long battle for Hue, but all had fled, leaving incongruous icons of technology parked on the crumbling surface like footprints. The area along the verge of the tarmac appeared bereft of grass or any growing thing. Nearby, a slight depression in the ground contained a pattern of cracked earth resembling a pudding cooked dry in the bottom of a pot. I stared into it, and after a gaunt restiveness fled through me, felt nothing but the ache in my shoulder, the pain in my foot, and the hot breeze on my clothes.

In the absence of any shade, the sun was relentless. There was nothing to do but wait there in the open beneath the intractable gaze of the dead city for the unspecified hour of our flight to return. An abandoned sandbag bunker squatted nearby, its interior a shadowy sinkhole that at least promised some shade, but on inspection I found that it was full of spider webs and stank of urine. We dropped any notion of sheltering in the gloomy mildewed tomb and instead took a few pictures of each other sitting on it so that Johnson could have the film developed before he left for home.

Eventually, the sound of an approaching helicopter began thumping its faint approach in the distance. We perked up, anticipating the arrival of our ride back to FOB 4. As the machine neared though, we could see by its markings that it was not our friend with the movies.

It arrived over the north end of the tarmac at a bit over 100 feet of altitude, then abruptly cut its power for a fast autorotation descent. When it banged onto the ground, scraping forward several feet on the skids, I had a glimpse of the two men in the cockpit. Judging from the hand gestures of the one, I assumed the other was a student pilot.

The machine roared back to full power and lifted off again, did a climbing turn back in the direction from which it had come, then turned back and practiced another dramatic power reduction descent, this time striking a few sparks from the skids on an even harder landing. The helicopter, an old Huey, had evidently seen hard use. From its patches, dents, fluid leaks, and loose panels, I guessed that it was a trainer, an aeronautical vagrant in a perpetual state of mended dereliction, and probably overdue for retirement.

Johnson and I watched with interest each go-around, which the pilots seemed to have brought forth especially for our wondering attention and to ease the prospects of a bleak afternoon. As the runway here was associated with no particular base, the pilots were probably taking advantage of its inactivity to practice a landing technique that appeared to leave the pilot with only marginal control over the descent rate.

Their next landing caused a small bolt to break free and bounce along the ground. We joked about it as they lifted off again and came around for a fourth time. This time, when they struck the ground the helicopter bounced, then hit a second time, then began, somehow captured between the downwash of the rotors and what spring there was in the skids, to bounce harder and harder, locked in an antithetical emulation of gravity and lift. We could only watch in horrified fascination the men inside tossed helplessly about while the machine proceeded to beat itself to pieces. Bits of metal began to fly off. Johnson and I retreated instinctively as it flung pieces of aluminum at us.

With each bash against the ground the helicopter bucketed back and forth on the skids in a terrible jig of destruction. Within seconds, it broached enough for the blades to begin striking the ground, and broken sections wheeled away into the air. The machine, with engine still roaring, fell onto its side, the tail boom staggered up almost vertically by the force of the dying rotor stubs excavating the pavement, then fell back down, and, like a struggling beetle, the whole contraption slid to a ratcheting stop. Then it went silent, its struggle with the resolute physics of ground resonance over at last. It rocked slightly, and fuel began to dribble onto the ground.

Nothing moved. Then as we started toward it, the upper door flew open, and the pilots scrambled up out of the wreck, climbed down over the skid and dropped onto the ground. They started limping away from it, shouting for us to get back. In moments, with an almost conciliatory whoosh, the machine began to burn while the four of us stood helplessly by and watched. The pool of fuel burned so fast it appeared that the ground itself was aflame. In moments, black smoke rose into the air on a column of odorous heat vapor.

One of the pilots had injured his arm. He couldn't move it without great pain, and we all concluded that he should assume it was broken. His companion went over to the parked Cobra to see if he could "borrow" its first aid kit, but the cockpit was locked down.

What little traffic was passing on the highway behind us had gathered to watch. Someone must have reported the crash or seen the smoke, because a Vietnamese fire truck appeared some time after the flames had died down. The nose section had not burned completely, but there was little the fire crew could do. They dutifully hosed down the wreck. The water sizzled and steamed on the white panels of melted aluminum lying crinkled like foil along the bent and blackened frame. Once the pro forma sprinkling was done, the pilots hitched a ride out with the fire crew, leaving Johnson and me, once again, solitary custodians of the quiet airfield.

An inauspicious tranquility returned. The sweltering breeze carried occasional small bird cries. It chuffed in our clothes and caused pieces of torn metal in the dead helicopter to squeak faintly. Johnson and I walked around inspecting the wreckage. After all, you don't get to see something like that every day. The center section was completely destroyed, the aluminum buckled, and the transmission had smashed into the passenger compartment, but through the broken windshield the radios, avionics, and some other cockpit equipment looked salvageable. The pilot's .45 pistol was strapped to the side of his seat in a canvas holster, but I couldn't reach far enough in to retrieve it.

"Man, what happened?" Johnson muttered more to himself than to me.

"…Well," I said, after thinking about the phenomenon of ground resonance long enough to realize I couldn't explain it completely, "…I guess if you listen to Sir Isaac Newton long enough, you get subject to gravity." Johnson smiled one of the few times I saw him do so in all the time I knew him.

At last the sun began to drain out behind the mountains, washing the sky, the objects on the runway, ourselves, and the foliage with a greasy apricot glow. The air cooled quite suddenly, and we began to wonder what had happened to our ride. Cold violet-blue shadows began filling the tree line, and lighter pink tints appeared where the ridge caught the last reflection of the vanishing day long before we heard our ride returning out of the north to retrieve us from this bizarre afternoon. Our pilot settled the machine onto the ground, looked at the wrecked Huey capsized and smoking in its black smudge, and asked what we had done to it.

We took off at last and retraced the flight path of that morning. Night fell without the usual preamble of twilight despite our altitude, and we passed over the fringe of Da Nang with its warren of dim streets, tiny lights, and tin roofs, out over the dark water, and back down the coast. We landed on the warm tarmac ramp back at FOB 4 and climbed out along with the metal film canisters containing "The Sound of Music."

15

Every day that passed without a summons to another mission briefing was a gift. Each night I went to bed dreading the inevitable; each morning arrived freighted with its potential for bad news. Johnson's DEROS orders still had not come down, and thus both of us awaited them with equally profound anxiety but for dramatically opposed reasons.

The expectation wore upon both of us. Johnson had lost a friend during the big attack, which had happened on the very eve of the man's scheduled departure for the States. He had served his full tour against the unlikely odds mounted by this strange duty and had packed to leave the following morning, when a sapper tumbled a grenade into his hootch. The effect upon Johnson, as indeed upon anyone who knew about it, was to drive home the lesson that you're never safe, no matter how close to salvation it may appear, until you are truly gone. Now, as each day came and went, Johnson's control began to leak away. Outwardly, he displayed his customary taciturn demeanor, but I saw that he was becoming jumpy. Little sounds and peripheral movements revealed his simmering unease. As much as I needed him to remain at least nominal head of the team for as long possible, I couldn't understand why they wouldn't just cut him orders to leave and to wait out the final days of his tour in the relative comforts of Nha Trang, where, though still in country, he would be removed from the tempestuous fever ward of FOB 4. Besides, as I already knew first hand, a captive of nervous anxiety is of little use in the field.

At the same time I dreaded the arrival of his orders because they would signal the day I became the official One-Zero of Team Anaconda. I shrank from the responsibility and doubted that I was capable. Johnson had taught me more than I would ever have been able to anticipate on my own, but I knew that despite all the extremes we had experienced on the operation, one aborted mission was hardly sufficient experience for me to be placed in command of some esoteric directive and the lives of up to twelve men, including my own.

The wound in my shoulder, because the muscle had been torn, took a long time to heal, and the constant need to move about in the soft sand on my damaged foot invested every step with iron pain. My mobility was restricted such that carrying the weight of any equipment would have been near impossible. There were days when keeping my right arm in a sling fashioned from my issue tourniquet was a great relief, but I was reluctant to leave the hootch wearing it for the impression it might give of malingering. Better, I thought, to hide beneath the hypocrisy of toughing it out, yet I knew that whatever resistance I could muster to physical or emotional demands was just illusion, a kind of dishwater metaphorical defense mechanism composed mostly of bluff, theater, and flop sweat.

To minimize movement, I spent most of this time hobbling carefully in straight lines between the hootch, the club, the messhall, and the showers. These places offered a semblance of relief from the heat and the ever-present glower of the next operation, but I could not get used to the terror. It was not so much the rise of abject fear that can trap a person in a cocoon of lamentation, but rather the dull, inescapability of danger that loomed, like the sky itself, over everything. There could be no reprieve, for the safety of the camp itself had been compromised, and my first combat patrol and additional wounds had only served to further animate the doubt and fear that crawled continuously over me.

There were no safe "rear" areas in this zone of constant watchfulness, because no distinct border or front line marked the areas controlled by opposing forces. This was a true guerrilla war in which mortal threat filled all corners, even areas that were supposedly "ours" and were misleadingly designated so on our maps. The feeling of vulnerability was omniscient, a living force that had weight and dimension. It formed the quotidian tree rings of life at FOB 4, circumferences of threat and mood, thicker at night, thinner in the daylight, which quickly swelled into the pattern of existence there.

This time of physical healing became one of transition in other ways, one born out of the throbbing haunt of at least part-time irrationality. I gradually grew weary of unyielding tension. Constant low-grade menace is exhausting, and I slowly came to the limits of my tolerance for unavailing worry. I hated the sheer weight that the first night's attack had placed upon my consciousness and the demoralizing signature its bloody images had inscribed on all subsequent events. Its roots grew even deeper during the first mission when I had been hit a second time. Few remnants of the obsolete naivete I'd arrived with still remained. I knew now that my survival was doubtful. Thus deeply dispirited, I finally arrived at a point where I simply had to escape the pressures of insidious fear. I began to react against my preoccupation with nebulous menace—to consciously affect a reasoned balance between my hard-earned awareness of what *could* happen, and the likely perils attending my immediate situation.

These thoughts did not arrive full-blown and clear as language, rather a gradual shift of awareness began to leak through fissures in the edifice of my uncertainties. I couldn't have put it into words at the time, but through a general imprecision of feeling, I arrived at the muddled realization that once self-preservation becomes the rule, that priority can enfeeble its holder, who becomes so afraid of losing life that he ceases to use its powers, and power contracted is, in the event, power diminished.

So without a conscious decision, I began to sort and prioritize the dangers *du jour,* and thereby to reduce the waste of brain power expended in chasing down theoretical events over which I had no direct control anyway. Thus it was one afternoon that I indulged a chance of life-affirming impetuosity and made my way in broad daylight down to the beach perimeter. I climbed atop one of the sandbagged bunkers, and sat fully exposed to the watchers on Marble Mountain (but at the extreme range of a rifle shot) and attempted to renew the smudged outlines of my humanity by simply admiring the ocean for a change. There, with my artificial courage trembling painfully on the edge of discretion, I enjoyed a charmed and artless interval simply overlooking a scene that, at least for the present, appeared free of harmful intent.

The air was hot and salty, and the afternoon burned against my back as each sun-struck wave, trailing veils of sea foam, poured like liquid glass onto the beach, where it spread its frothy palms before being sucked back into the crumbling water that followed. Fleeting sheets of sky shimmered brightly along the beach in broad, shifting patterns before sinking into the wet sand, only to be replaced by the next wave in a recurring magic lantern show of light and cloud. I relaxed a little and dared to indulge in thoughts of home, with the rhythm of the waves and the wind in my ears growing soporific, like the swing of a hammock.

A pair of tall sea birds arrived and began pacing the shallows gravely with long meditative strides, their heads bowed and their shoulders hunched. They seemed preoccupied. In their philosophic elegance and imponderable reserve, they appeared the very incarnation of thoughtful dignity. It seemed to me that in most of their visible attributes they excelled the scholars and legislators whom they suggested.

Beyond the breakers, winking crescent spangles of light chased themselves around the dark surface all the way to the horizon, where I saw that the large ship stationed there before had returned. It had moved perhaps a mile closer in, clearly now a battleship poised in majestic serenity where it cut the sharp blue line of sea and sky. Just as I was wishing I had a telescope, I heard behind me the swishing sound of someone approaching through the deep sand. Johnson came up in a limping trudge with the team binoculars around his neck. He climbed up beside me, and then, positioning himself carefully on the hot sandbags to avoid pressure on his wound, leaned back on his elbows and said nothing, as though we had arranged to meet there by prior agreement. His arrival broke my reverie, but I was glad for his company. He regarded the ship evenly for several long moments, the scene requiring no caption. Even as he appeared to relax, his hard eyes held an opaque luster, like polished rocks.

"S.S. New Jersey," he said flatly, and handed me the glasses.

Through the lenses I could even see the tiny white uniforms of the sailors moving along the decks and lower superstructure.

"Wow. Big ship," I said. "What's it doing here?"

"Artillery support, I guess. Navy's gotta get their combat stars, too."

"Looks like nice, safe duty."

It did, too. Those guys out there were living free of the psychological pressure that wriggled within me. They had, from all that I heard about naval sea duty, good food available 24 hours a day; they were geographically free of attack, and most important, they lived with the luxury of predictability. They probably complained about the boredom and their repetitive duty roster, but I would have traded with any of them in a second.

Then: "My orders came," Johnson announced flatly, delivering another of his loaded three-word pronouncements. A bolt of despair shot through me as the full weight of my inherited responsibilities fell like a stone out of his casual remark, and my sense of durability, already weakened by events in general, was compromised in a second. It seemed the Unsleeping Beast would require payment for even a few stolen minutes of tranquility.

Through a sieve of bogus enthusiasm I managed a strained approval noise and slapped his shoulder. I felt genuinely happy for his sake, and profoundly envious.

"When you leaving?"

"I can't get a ride 'til the morning. Wanted to go tonight."

"Yeah. I don't blame you. Can I buy you a drink to celebrate?"

"...Uh, sure," he said with just a noticeable hesitation. "Just one. ...I ain't sleepin' tonight."

The next morning, having sat up with his rifle most of the night, he was ready, packed and, unwilling to wait for his ride to show up, out the door before breakfast to meet the Jeep up by the headquarters hut.

"Bye," he said simply. "Good luck, man."

"Thanks. Same to you."

He stood there on the steps, framed in the doorway for just a few seconds. He flexed his fingers and looked at them critically as though trying the fittings of a new implement. I had the feeling he was considering something else to say. Then he just shouldered his duffle, and thus departed a person I hardly knew, yet with whom I had shared some of the most extreme emotional topography of my life. I wondered what he might have left unsaid—some bit of advice or an overlooked tab of detail that might fit a random slot in my future. I needed to know everything he might yet have told or shown me.

In another situation, a guy that reticent might have been harder to like, but we got along well within the bizarre circumstances that shaped our association, and with his going I now faced the gaping uncertainty that would inhabit every day that I remained in the country. All that I had learned from him and all the experiences to come would be attended by an ever-renewed host of unknowns to which he had briefly held back the curtain .

Deep despondency rushed in to fill the vacancy made by his departure. I was genuinely sorry to see him go, not only for the void in leadership it created, but also because he had been the single entity in which I found myself investing a certain dependency. Then, too, with his absence came the sulfurous reality that, whatever dreadful assignments may come, I—already twice wounded and conditioned to fear shadows—was now the commander of Team Anaconda and, *force majeure*, the twelve lives that composed it.

I sat in profound isolation on the edge of the bunk for a long time, gnawing the cold bone of solitude, my head thronging with misgivings and the painful realization that, for better or worse, all decisions now really were entirely up to me. Though I could not see or feel it at the time, I had taken another unbidden step in the inevitable divestiture of privileged innocence. Whether you seek, or assume, or inherit responsibility for the lives of others, even in a backwater jungle that none of the participants really wants or has use for, you are thrust in a very real sense upon the world's stage, especially if some of those lives are nationalities other than your own.

I felt unready for the job and its freight of implications. Although I admired the professionalism of the Nungs and had learned a lot about movement by watching them, I remained woefully inferior to their knowledge and to their field experience. I worried that I may have compromised myself in some way on the patrol. I knew they had respected Johnson, but I was troubled by the profound foreignness of them. I was still separate and unproven.

The threat of imminent annihilation serves to create a kind of solipsistic bubble around the soul in which it is harder to care about others than it would be outside the realm of threat. This strange truth I had already come to know, yet for both emotional and intellectual reasons I was unprepared to accept responsibility for the death or injury of anyone who served on my side.

I thought about all I had learned from Johnson and realized painfully that the team still needed him more than it could know. At the very least he had demonstrated that I would have to learn by absorbing experience straight into the blood stream. I saw his logic in dividing the team's firepower over two helicopters for the insertion, and the way he had organized the order of movement to make optimal use of weapons in case we were to meet unhappy surprises in the field made sense. In addition I could see no immediate way to improve on his example of the amount and placement of personal equipment for weight distribution, ready accessibility, and silent movement.

As much as I hated lugging that PRC-25 radio, Johnson had been his own R/TO (Radio Telephone Operator) on most operations, and had saddled me with its heft as a way of recommending that it would always be safest to keep the radio close at hand, with the telephone hooked close to my ear. I had seen the convenience of having someone else carry it, not only for the sake of transferring its dead weight, but also because it could thus be marginally more accessible. He had only to reach into the pack on my back and switch it on, yet this meant that one of us had to move over to the other. It was easy to imagine that there might be situations that could prevent such movement. Alternatively, had I needed to use it, I would have had to take the pack off in order to get at the controls.

Although I worried that the tear in my shoulder might make it impossible for me to carry the radio if we got another operation soon, I decided that, despite its weight and the cumbersome need to take it off in order to use it, I never wanted to be separated from it in the field. In view of the unpredictable nature of conditions in the jungle, the awkwardness that came with its use would be more than offset by its accessibility. Therefore, come what may, I should endeavor to carry it myself.

The team itself was a problem. I had no idea how to assume command, or how to deploy the Chinese in case of emergency. They were very difficult to read, and I worried about the extent to which my conduct in the field may have helped or harmed my ability to gain their respect as team leader. They were well versed in their culture of mutual protection, and I had to find a way to gain a place behind the shield of that common symbiosis. Johnson had developed a functional understanding of at least the superstitious aspects of their Buddhist faith to the extent that he and the team had managed to keep each other alive, and I had seen that he had a good working relationship with the point man in particular.

Of all the discomforts that had attended the day when Johnson took me down to meet the team for the first time, I had felt most the dark scrutiny of the point man. His coal black eyes had chilled me with their silent watchfulness. His skin was marked with glassy scars from unstitched wounds and old insect bites turned septic. Perhaps it was just that his prominent cheek bones and depthless piercing gaze gave him so completely the look of a Hollywood brigand that his wordless stare was made so uncomfortable, but he had the unmistakable look and feel of a predator, the janissary of some deeply foreign vernacular, a true killer, and I had to admit I was instinctively leery of him.

There were stories that not all the Asian mercenaries who hired out to us were trustworthy, that some of the PRUs (Provisional Reconnaissance Units) had turned in the field, killed their American team leaders, and escaped into the jungle with all the equipment, leaving no sign by which we could discover the event or find the bodies. Yet there was no choice but to follow my instincts. I knew that I had to ignore doubt and shrug off the galling harness of custom if that's what it would take to affirm my position with the team, and he was their acknowledged leader. I decided to start with him.

I made, or rather, took on the decision deliberately for the purpose of problem resolution and a bid for self-preservation, not unlike the way Hamlet assumed his madness. I went over to the club and bought twelve beers, then returned to the hootch for the radio, the code book, map, a pad and pencil, and the binoculars. Thus loaded with bribes and equipment, I hobbled down to the team's tent. There I found a few of them sitting around chatting and snoozing very much in the same way I had first encountered them. Despite some marginal bonding, the product of our shared hazards on our first operation together, I felt again the huge cultural difference as my own foreignness yawned between us. Their easy communication among each other was predicated upon a background of common knowledge that I didn't have, and I had the feeling their silent mandate was a code, their stillness as they waited for me to begin, a shared secret.

I set down the beers, which produced an animated response, and called them together. The point man nodded a signal to one guy who ran off to get those who were out visiting somewhere.

The beer worked as intended, and soon the team was all assembled with a certain guarded expectation around the table. I started by indicating for each to write his name on the pad and to pronounce it so that I would have something to call them by. This they did, which showed me first of all that they were literate at least to that degree. My attempts to pronounce the names they wrote brought forth a good deal of laughter and cross talk–precisely what I had hoped. I learned that one of them spoke an acceptable mouthy combination of grade school pidgin and English, which proved, with a good deal of smiling and coaxing, quite sufficient for a stumbling translation.

The point man's name read Sy Van Nhi, a good, easy name to say, and I made a special effort to reproduce his pronunciation. Then I presented him with the binoculars and indicated that they were for his use. The effect was immediate. His eyes pulsed, and a grin cracked the masonry of his face. The others reacted too. It was evident that this simple gesture served to enhance his status even more. He handled the glasses with a surprising reverence. The others gathered around to touch them in a gaggle of excited comment and to pass them carefully around. Oddly, none attempted to look through them, as though to do so might have presumed upon the sacred responsibility just conferred upon Sy Van Nhi.

Only after they were returned to Nhi did he step out from under the rolled tent and, with the binoculars pressed against his eyes like the fists of a sleepy child, focus the lenses out at the sea. He knew exactly how to use them. Then he put the strap around his neck with all the prestige of an ambassadorial sash.

Next I got out the map, and using the marginal English speaker to translate, began explaining the rudiments of map reading. They showed an interest in it that surprised me. Among the Americans there seemed to be an unstated taboo against showing the "indij" any of our arcana, but an excessive concern for secrecy, especially when we all faced the same stakes, can interfere with optimal use of resources and thus good decision-making. I couldn't be sure of course, but in this bizarre world of operatic dangers where nothing was certain anyway, I chose to trust these guys with everything I could think of that might one day save our lives, starting with my own. It just might serve one day to get us back from the deep boonies in the event that I were ever incapacitated.

I spread the map and began by letting them get familiar with the graphic depiction of the earth's surface. Some of them showed an aptitude and began explaining the symbols to the others. We had some fun teaching each other the names for river, mountain, hill, etc. I hesitated to attempt explaining contour lines, but decided to try anyway, and was soon satisfied that at least a few of them got the concept, and I felt confident that they would pass the knowledge around. In any case, I was trying to establish a relationship within which they might feel free to ask about this stuff.

I pointed out the numbers along the top and sides of the map and explained that any position on the chart could be determined and communicated over the radio by lining them up with your position on the ground and transmitting those two numbers. (The fact that we falsified for security reasons the actual latitude and longitude on the maps that the teams carried into the field was beyond the scope of the lesson, but the principle was the same.) A few of them, including Nhi, got it at least well enough for what must have been their first exposure to this kind of information.)

The radio was next. They understood the power of life and death that it held, but because the Americans had always denied them access to it, they approached it with understandable caution, as though it were some mysterious talisman. They gathered around as I deployed the antenna and showed them how to turn the radio on, tell that it was on, and how to select the frequencies. I showed them that the selector knobs made a muted click sound if you turned them too quickly, but that done carefully, they could make changes noiselessly. Each took his turn getting the feel of the controls. Then I showed them the standard codes for certain basic things, like calling for extraction or reporting enemy contact, or (most important) reporting that the One-Zero had been hurt. I showed them the numbers as they appeared in the code book and how to transfer the information to a selection on the radio knobs.

Then I switched it on and called the provisional TOC at headquarters. (The permanent TOC was still under re-construction.) I explained what I was doing, and gave each man who wanted to try it a chance to broadcast one of the codes, so that he could hear the acknowledgement. Two held back, but as each who tried it heard the response in the handset, he beamed with satisfaction and began explaining to the others, who giggled and, as far as I could tell, discussed it further.

The meeting appeared to work. Their receptivity was an unexpected relief, and it seemed that I had achieved at least a provisional breakthrough of whatever reservations they may have held about me. When I picked up the radio and turned to leave, even Nhi conjured a quiet smile from somewhere within the dim-lit terrain of his impenetrable past.

It was evident that Johnson had never done this, and though it occurred to me that I might be overstepping a policy set by painful experience elsewhere, I decided the die had been cast in establishing an operational policy with my team, and I determined to keep these lessons going. I got back to the hootch feeling that perhaps nerve can be finessed at times after all, and hoping that *they* had the courage of my conviction.

Late that afternoon I went back to seek the company of the club, hoping to escape—at least for a while—the alienation that always stalked me. The club was loud, smoky, and full of our people, Sea-Bees, and some Marines from the 3rd Amtracs, all grasping for cheer in punishing rounds of drinks and laughter. The juke box thumped cheerfully away, trying to keep up with a rising volume of competitive conversations. I forged into the crowd at the bar and got a soda, then found a small table by the front door where I could sit in the cusp of two walls and see outside as night poured out of the sky, and Marble Mountain gradually paled away into the color of smoke. At some point I recognized the falsetto chorus of *Walk Like a Man* straining from the juke box and was amused at its irony as The Four Seasons squealed forth through the general din.

After a large dinner and some good-natured teasing with Ba Foo, I went back to the hootch. There was a western movie shown that night, and I wanted to watch it, if only to employ the time as a mini vacation from the baggage of my thoughts, but my foot hurt too much to trudge back over to the messhall area where they were setting up chairs in the sand.

Late that night I lay on my bunk unable to get comfortable enough to sleep. My shoulder hurt and my foot throbbed with the mileage of the day. From the other side of the room Johnson's empty mattress whispered of the unfathomable perils I now faced alone. My brain wouldn't shut down. It went on visiting in the neighborhoods of imagination, recapitulation, memory, and other nocturnal regions that do not quite have names. The urgent and shifting incubus of uncertainty that followed me everywhere would not let go, and I lay still listening for the distant shot that would prove the sniper on the mountain had been replaced.

I eventually gave up chasing the illusive figure of sleep and thought to go outside and sit for a while at the edge of the starlight, there to clear my head. Instead, overly attuned to the perils of chance, I continued to lie in troubled repose suffering an invertebrate paralysis of will.

At some point during the long hot night the New Jersey began firing. The signs of it arrived all out of sequence. First, the room flickered silently with the pale orange lightning of the muzzle flashes. A few seconds later the one-ton projectiles warbled eerily overhead like trains on a high metal trestle. After that the rumble of the guns rolled in from the sea. Then, following a long silence, I could hear the faintest hint of distant detonations as the rounds arrived at some far ground to the west.

16

I was carried through the next few weeks on a fragile meniscus of uneasy calm in the anticipated arrival of an assistant team leader. As I worked to gain the respect, if not exactly the trust, of the team I doubted that we'd be sent out again without a full complement, thanks in part to Buddhist numerology. Operations began coming down for other teams frequently enough, though, that I knew FOB 4 was back in business. What is now known as the Tet Offensive, which had included the attack on us the night of my arrival, was still ongoing in frequent engagements, both large and small, throughout the country, and I feared that it would get back around to me all too soon.

Some of our other teams that were back up to strength were being deployed on trail watch, interdiction, and listening missions, as well as–most dreaded of all–prisoner captures, called "people snatches." When we received orders to take prisoners it was usually to capture a specific individual. These operations were fortunately few, but "people snatches" were very difficult and extraordinarily dangerous. Any time you worked in close to the enemy was dangerous, but the effort to catch, say, a specific Chinese or Russian advisor who was likely positioned somewhere within the perimeter of a battalion, or even a regimental-sized unit, was rarely possible without highly detailed corroborating intelligence, unlikely good luck, and/or a large and costly diversion of some kind. We almost always lost our own people on a "people snatch."

A strange thing happened during this period of uneasy limbo for Team Anaconda: Another team was sent out on operation with a new replacement serving as Two-Zero. He was a nice looking, clean cut sergeant from New Jersey, recently arrived from the States and had only been in the camp for a few weeks, during which time he had presumably been given a version of the verbal orientation by his team leader that Johnson had given me.

In fairly short order his team launched on an operation. He had been assigned to carry the radio. The team got jumped by the VC its second day out and was pretty badly shot up. During the fight there had apparently been a point at which the team had no recourse but to run. The enemy had fired after them. The new guy had been saved in his panic by the radio on his back, which took several rounds, in the process knocking him down. Somehow the survivors had managed to get out an extraction signal activated on the PRC-10 emergency locator radio, and the team was, at least in part, rescued.

By the time they got back to FOB 4 the guy was deeply withdrawn into a private twilight of trembling. Able to feel only fear, he appeared locked in an emotional closet of such unendurably narrow dimensions that he could not move at all. He had to be helped from the chopper to the ambulance. Although he wasn't suffering from any serious external wounds or restrictions, he leaned heavily upon the medics, his toes dragging, bound entirely from within.

Over the next few days, the psychological effect of the experience began to tell on him. At least it appeared to. He emerged one afternoon from his team hootch and began to yell at the sky, reeling about and firing his .45 into the air and at the buildings. When he stumbled over to the area of the clubhouse he was quickly tackled and subdued, but he continued to howl and thrash about on the ground beneath his captors, his fingers tearing at the air, scratching at the cluster of invisible insects that had been waiting in the crevices of his mind.

Yet there was something so theatrical about his behavior, so classically reflective of textbook lunacy, that I wondered if we had witnessed an actual personality disintegration or whether it was all just high theater. In either case, I sympathized entirely. Of course, regardless of the integrity of the performance, it compromised his effectiveness completely, and he was sent away to some hospital from which he never returned. One way or the other, he got what he needed.

Privately, it shook me. I doubted the integrity of my own character and wondered how I might have stood up to what had happened to him on that mission. One can't dwell on such dangerous speculation, though. I forced myself to take the lessons from it and to dismiss it.

People were still talking about this event when my Two-Zero appeared in the hootch one day. Sergeant Grayson was one of the most unprepossessing Green Berets I ever saw: tall, thin, somewhat lanky, with dark unruly hair, a small mouth, which fell slightly open when his face was in repose, long neglected teeth, and an unsuccessful moustache. His full-cut garrison fatigues draped about him in folds. He did not appear to have the physique for this kind of work, but then, I didn't have the temperament, so my initial reaction was to question whether together we posed disaster for the team or, with time, perhaps a workable balance of limitations.

He seemed friendly enough. I indicated the other bed and showed him where he could stow his gear. At one point he unwrapped some unsavory and unidentifiable bits of blackened and shriveled substance and prepared to nail them to the wall over his bed. I asked him what they were.

"Ears," he replied casually, as though such touches were common in his world of interior design.

When I told him in terms he was not prepared to question that he was to get rid of them, he shrugged and did it so quickly and obligingly that I wondered if he had displayed them merely to test his range with me, or perhaps because he felt a sufficiently grisly artifact would demonstrate a desired effect of his recent duty. Whatever the reason, I was not going to allow him latitude to compromise my well-being, such as it was, nor to do anything that might upset the Chinese. Besides, regardless of his reason for it, anyone who would keep such gruesome souvenirs, even for a minute, required some serious re-orientation.

Now that I had an assistant team leader, ready or not, I feared that operational orders could arrive any day. I hoped of course that Command wasn't that desperate to demonstrate our readiness, but still I began Grayson's lessons the first day, explaining the layout of the compound, what kinds of operations my personal experience had revealed that we could expect, and that regardless of orders, my priority was always to save the team. Any behavior that might compromise that one singular goal would not be tolerated regardless of the mission. I did not tell him my suspicions that the ground teams were redundant, simply that I would not spend lives for the kind of information we were equipped to get. Then I told him about the big attack, so that he would understand that many of the teams were short on experience due to losses and that the event had produced an attitude adjustment among the survivors. The former complacency appeared to be gone, but what implications this change carried for the rest of us was still open to speculation, none of it comforting.

Over the course of the next week or two I gave Grayson everything Johnson had taught me, in addition to what I had learned in the field. He had a brassy vitality that I came to like, and he proved to be both attentive and cooperative. In addition, he harbored a secret kindness that I did not expect, while his husky voice carried a graceful facility with profanity. I found his lack of introspection and insight remarkable, though he gradually revealed things about himself, but dispassionately, as though everything behind him was one long, flattened dead road.

He wasted no time in drawing enough extra magazines to fill four canteen covers, got his clothes tailored down as instructed, practiced with the radio, and was soon at least as materially fit for whatever might come as could be expected.

I wondered if all this quiet industry was being noted at HQ, or if perhaps I might be able to keep our growing state of readiness percolating just below their line of vision. If an operation under my command was inevitable, I wanted more time to work with the Chinese and also to heal. Besides, any delay in orders meant an opportunity to build confidence in Grayson and to observe what he might be able to bring to the team, which meant incrementally greater service to my stated purpose of avoiding loss. It also served to secure my authority, even if it was secretly made of straw.

I explained to Grayson my efforts to educate the Nungs in the use of our equipment and the reason for risking such a departure from what appeared to be custom. I wanted him to understand that my intent came from an evaluation of likely developments in the field based on direct experience, that the Nungs had shown themselves to be experts in the jungle and far more adept at movement than we were.

When I took him down to meet the team for the first time, I cautioned him to keep quiet, to reflect a degree of reserve that might appeal to their cultural reticence, and to smile whenever I did. As expected, most of the team regarded him with little outward sign. They sat wordless and watchful, like a living chunk of chaos pounded into silent being, the way they had when Johnson had first introduced me to them. I was actually glad to see them close down on Grayson too. He would have to earn their respect, and by now I understood that the reward would then be mutual.

Lei Thi Hao, our little maid, was initially as afraid of Grayson as she had been of me. His appearance so alarmed her that it set back the fragile bridge of trust I had been building with her. I could not tell by the way Grayson looked at her what his attitude toward Vietnamese women was, or if he shared my reservations about native workers in the camp, but I made it clear that she was a sweet person, good at her job, and that anyone who upset her or did anything to disrupt the guarded confidence with which she now went about her sweeping and laundry duties would not only upset me but would damage to the whole giddy structure of the indigenous employment program.

She watched his movements warily, keeping her small round face and damp eyes turned toward him whenever he was in the room. All expression would drain out of her eyes the instant he glanced in her direction, turning them blank as slate. It reminded me of the way the cold gaze of a portrait seems to go vacant the moment you turn. I watched the uncanny timing of this nervous interplay for a few days, partly to see how Grayson would handle it. Then, both for her sake and as word to the wise, I revealed to him her weakness for Coca Cola.

I soon learned that Sergeant Grayson and I shared a mutual interest in chess, a game at which we proved so equally inept as to be well matched. He had a cheap plastic set, much damaged by life in a duffle bag, but its board was so badly warped as to be unplayable. He found an old meal table frame somewhere, fire damaged but useful, and from the SeaBees I scrounged a nice piece of plywood on which we drew a chessboard using a black laundry marker, and with it replaced the top of the table. Some of the game pieces were so badly broken that not much more than their bases were left, so we fashioned little signs with the names of the missing pieces and glued them to the available bases using chunks of C-4 explosive kneaded with wax scraped from discarded radio batteries. Thus the game provided us with a conduit for getting to know each other as well as a medium for mutually speculative insight.

It was during a game we were both losing that I received by runner a call to report to the HQ hut. I didn't think at first that it could be a mission so soon after the arrival of the team's Two-Zero, but went with the runner, who claimed not to know why I was being called. Of course in this world of stratified secrets, no one ever seemed to know the reason for anything, so I just followed along, quietly loading up with tendentious reservations.

The briefing removed all doubt: a Navy jet, hit by a surface-to-air missile over the North, had come down in the jungle just south of the DMZ. The navigator in the back seat had managed to get out, but no one had seen the pilot's parachute. I was to take the team into the crash site to recover whatever confirming identification we could find in the wreckage.

A marginal advantage of this mission would be that such places were usually quite remote (though I had already been wounded in a place that was supposedly quite remote), and besides the lack of reported enemy activity in the region, sites that had seen great violence were generally regarded as taboo. It was not that nobody ever ventured into them—in fact, depending upon how difficult it was to reach them, aircraft crashes were often scoured by both sides for any useful artifacts, from batteries to aluminum, hand weapons and ammunition to scraps of insulation—but it was true that isolated areas of great conflagration or group death were often simply avoided, just for their bad ju-ju. Presumably due to this common knowledge, the briefer, not knowing what a tangle of nerves he was addressing, tried to assure me that we would probably have the place to ourselves and that the operation was routine. As much as I would have liked to believe him, I suspected that he was patronizing me, and knowing that even catastrophic crashes could offer rich opportunities for scroungers, I chose to ignore his assurances.

I was given the relevant section of map with altered co-ordinates, assigned the codes and frequencies to be used, and told we had the afternoon to draw the supplies we needed. Since the next morning would be an even-numbered day of the month, I knew we had to be ready to board the choppers before sun-up. Weather was expected to be good. I requested a second copy of the map, which I told him was for Grayson to conceal.

This left me with almost too little time to invest my customary worry in our prospects. As I walked back to the hootch to alert Grayson and the team, I started through a mental list of required supplies. First, not knowing how much of the pilot we might find, I decided to take all ten of the Chinese. An intact corpse could require up to four of us to carry the corners of a body bag, and these four would need to be spelled pretty often, so the carry team had to be doubled. That would leave only two other guys, besides Grayson and myself, and they would be needed for defense should we get jumped with other hands full. Despite some concern about exposing my own shortcomings to the entire team at once, should I commit some error on this job, I felt that taking everybody would teach both the Chinese and ourselves the most about each other in the shortest time.

I sent Grayson off to Supply with a list of our requirements, including one body bag, while I went down to alert the team. Shortly before dinner we assembled back at the hootch where I distributed ammunition, including extra grenades for Grayson and me, and five days of rations. I gave the second copy of the map to Nhi and showed him the target area, thus proving my word to him, then went over the radio codes with both Grayson and Nhi, showing both in which pocket I would always stow the code book and in which the map. I explained to Grayson that I would keep him abreast of our movements on the chart and showed him the symbols I would use to mark our progress.

I wanted to bring two M-79 grenade launchers with us. Nhi knew better than I which of the team were best with that weapon, so he would assign them. If we were to be operating in or around an open area of the jungle, the M-79s would be more effective free of intervening trees should we need them and were a bit easier to carry than a rifle in the event that we didn't need them.

I concluded my briefing with a point that had been bothering me ever since the mission with Johnson: I had not liked the sloshing sound of several partially emptied canteens as we moved through the jungle. In fact it was at times the single loudest noise we had made. From now on the team would share just one canteen at a time, passing it around on hand signals as needed. This would not only reduce to one the source of this challenge to our essential need for silence in the field, it would keep us all aware of just how much water we had among us. After a moment's consideration and the exchange of some invisible signal that I sensed had passed between them, the Nungs nodded agreement, a small but important response to my first independent directive.

Breakfast was to be laid on for us at 0300 hrs, and we were to be ready for pick up at 0430. There were no questions or clarifications. The Nungs never seemed to need answers. They accepted all developments with impenetrable resolve and simply rose without a sign and retired to their tent for the night.

After trying the radio pack, I realized that my shoulder hurt too much to enable me to carry it, so I told Grayson that at least for this mission, he had better use the afternoon getting used to its weight. I spent the time studying the map and memorizing frequencies.

It was impossible to sleep that night. As we lay in our bunks, I explained everything else I could think of to Grayson based on my limited direct experience. A profound solitude seeped in from the night to fill the spaces in the darkened room, as the prospect of the next day's events seemed somehow to have isolated the hootch in some provisional dimension separated now from all life in the rest of the compound. A vibrant silence crowded the stillness between my words, arresting them as though they were spoken in a vacuum, heard by no one. If Grayson knew this was to be my first operation as One-Zero, he said nothing, and I didn't tell him.

Unbidden thoughts and images, feeding on a meaty helping of doubt, rose to form a sentient structure in my mind. Although composed only of imagination and unsaid words, which should have passed on leaving no trace in the living world, they came at last to stand over me in the darkened room, a bodiless yet ponderable being. My wounds all began to hurt again at once. The Beast that found me the first night in camp and had prowled with gaunt restiveness all ground since, now waited, licking its paws in the dark den of tomorrow, a living force of incomprehensible magnitude.

In the blue waking hours before dawn we rose for final preparations, assembled by the hootch, and were met and driven to the chopper pad. There we climbed off the truck to await the arrival of the helicopters. They were a little late, but the signature beat of the heavy S-1s soon came in from the north. How different I thought the sound was when they were coming to take you out on operation than when they were approaching in the wilderness to bring you back.

I used the remaining minutes before their arrival to divide the team for each aircraft, making sure that we had an even distribution of automatic weapons and an M-79 on each in case one were to go down, or were to encounter a hot LZ (Landing Zone). I took the radio to have with me in the lead helicopter and quickly reviewed with Grayson what he should expect as soon as we hit the ground and that he should be ready to take the radio at any time after we landed. Then I posted him to the second chopper.

As we lifted off and turned northwest, the dawn began, glassy and pink and stained in its lower reaches just above the carpet of trees by a gelatinous band of pale smoke, a layered capture of haze, like the held breath of the forest itself. In minutes the sun rose, dazzling with its instant fire and searing the skin on my face as it bored a hot yellow core through the open helicopter. The air cooled as we climbed, but that did nothing to ease the oleaginous pour of the sun.

The bowl of the sky turned a deep blue, arching serenely over the confection of light that dusted the treetops below. In other circumstances the view from that lofty perch in the sloping morning blaze would have been spectacular, but instead, as the ocean of trees passed ominously beneath us, still and menacing, I rode on the metal deck, humbled by doubt and leached by leaden despair. While trying to keep a neutral face for the sake of the others, I mentally reviewed every likely scenario that might greet our arrival, and some that were not so likely. The sharp backbeat of the blades overhead became a numbing dirge for the legion of fears that tramped through my brain.

When the pilots eventually alerted me of our approach to the crash site, I leaned out to make as much of a survey as our speed and altitude would allow of the target area. We flew over a long brown scar in the jungle where pieces of metal lay glittering like the track of a spent tear. I tried to assess the surrounding terrain and to estimate (just guess) ways to approach the clearing. Of course the ground itself remained hidden beneath the canopy of trees. Close to the west was an area of thick jungle interwoven with deep pocket gorges from which ghostly mists fumed upward. I didn't like the look of it. The clefts were choked with towering growth, impenetrable, brooding, and seemingly capable of hiding anything.

I was relieved when the helicopters sheared away, banking to the north, and soon an old B-52 strike appeared ahead. It had blasted a staggered line of huge craters for several miles trailing eastward through the endless blanket of trees. The holes in the forest were wide and deep enough to hide a sequence of false landings with ease, though many reflected the sky from seep water that lay pooled at their bottoms. These would reduce our options. There was no way of knowing the depth of the water or if the area was under observation, but the number of opportunities these bowls of exposed earth offered would at least make it easier for the pilots to get in and back out and would make it difficult for anyone watching to tell exactly where they might have unloaded.

As we dropped toward the pattern of blown earthen holes, I was glad to be moving away from the dark rifts, but as the ground rushed toward us, I realized that even if we got out in one of the closest craters, it would take at least two, probably three, days to work our way back to the crash site. The chopper tilted sharply, and I braced myself in the door, trying to divide my attention between observing everything I could outside while keeping an eye on the pilots for the signal to jump out. Control cables groaned and creaked. Through the floor plates I felt the strain and the twist in the fuselage as the sound of the blades increased pitch.

My innards went light as we swept over the tree line and settled abruptly into one of the craters. As twigs and clods of earth tumbled in the roil of loose dirt that fled across the ground beneath us, I was surprised at how devastating the bomb damage was. Enormous trees had been blasted into the air and thrown outward, leaving the edge of the red earth crater fringed with their woven carcasses like a scorched basket, while the higher banks bristled with shattered roots that hung in the air like frayed rope. The hole was deep enough to swallow the whole helicopter and perhaps three more abreast. The blast had excavated the earth so far below the level of ancient growth that it would take human lifetimes for the forest to recover. The sides were cut with hundreds of last year's rain courses, and at the bottom was a sump of reddish ground water. It was hard to estimate by the slope of the walls how deep it was. The pilots hung us there for a moment before roaring out and hopping over the intervening isthmus of shattered trees to settle in a second crater.

Despite the fact that this one was also flooded at the bottom, I got the signal from the pilots that this was the LZ, and we got ready to jump out. I scanned the wood line quickly, flipped the safety off my weapon with my thumb, and leaned out to watch that the other helicopter followed our pattern. When we splashed down to the hubs in a wash of muddy water, it settled like a giant grasshopper into the pond behind us. I slung the radio pack over my good shoulder, and we scrambled out, jumping into the shin-deep water, which fortunately was standing in clay. I caught enough footing to run out of it and into a furnace, as the other guys splashed past and began clawing their way up the earthen sides of the crater toward the trees. I hesitated in the downwash long enough to see that the rest of the team got out of the other aircraft. In seconds the rotor blast kicked up enough swampy water to soak me to the waist. With the last man out, both machines pitched forward and made for another crater, roaring away to a bogus landing to the east. We had unloaded in less than 10 seconds.

I scrambled up the bank after the others as fast as possible to get out of the open. The tangle of roots near the rim was harder to get through than it had looked from the bottom, and by the time we got among them we were blocked by an impenetrable maze of destroyed trees, their trunks embedded with ballistic stones and plastered with dried mud. It looked impossible to get through them, but driven by the absolute need to get under cover, we found several small gaps in the congestion of roots, through which each of us was able to crawl singly into the splintered branches and to pick his way to a place tented by broken tree limbs several yards down the outer slope of debris. There we assembled in a makeshift perimeter. We lay faced outward, once again on full alert for movement until our hearing returned.

I checked around at the team, relieved that we were all together and no one seemed to have been hurt during the insertion. So far, so good. We were already so muddy we blended into the terrain. Nhi and I exchanged a signal then returned to our vigil, scanning for any movement and trying to hear. Except for the constant ringing pulse in my ears, all was still. The saturated air was heavy with the smell of exposed heartwood, the churned earth, and burned vegetation. I lay as flat as possible on my stomach and held my mouth open to quiet my heavy breathing and waited for the moment when I could inhale through my nose again without making a sound.

In spite of the weeks of worrisome anticipation, this day seemed to have arrived with unnatural suddenness, and now I was trapped in this terrible situation by an accident of rank and timing. There were others with me, but the feeling of utter isolation and abandonment was hard to suppress. A ripple of panic slopped through me. The unnerving magnitude of my responsibility haunted the unpredictable outcome of open possibility. Not all of the war's miseries were external events. The kind of work in which I was ensnared was a Russian doll carved from increasingly dense layers of clear and present danger, and though not always certain, always there, either just out of sight or crouched within, clutching at the mind. At the center of the doll, even for the wary, was a black void called oblivion. I made tight fists to force the trembling from my hands.

Despite the nervous excitement and fear at being left again out in this impossibly remote wilderness with its strange, hostile consciousness, there was no alternative but to subordinate my doubts to the urgent need for reading every detail of our surroundings. This was truly no man's land, a place where death was always watching, never tiring, never sleeping. Out here there were no rules, no territorial claims, just a trackless and mind-boggling riot of primordial growth beyond the reach of timely support and capable of hiding an enemy within scant yards in any direction. People had been sent into it only to disappear without a trace–not even a whispered syllable over the radio.

I forced my attention through the screen of these dark possibilities to accept the fact that I had nonetheless been propelled across some existential line that separated the tidy theories of command from its raw, unbidden reality and that I had to begin sorting the immediate alternatives we faced. It didn't matter that I wasn't up to the job. I was responsible for the conduct of the mission, and like it or not, I was already trapped in the process.

I knew from the first mission with Johnson that nothing was quite as it seemed. Here, where the creepers and lower foliage filled the surrounding spaces, there were places of unlit menace that blotted out all but dim refractions of the sky. The jungle here was devoid of the bird cries that I had been able to hear even through the ringing engine sounds the first time. It was more than silent. It was a crushing vacuum of stillness, a quiet that roared in my ears. I knew we had to move soon, but gripped for the moment in a violent dead zone between action and reaction, I couldn't sort out the alternatives to make a decision. At least, judging by what I'd seen from the air, I had some idea of the heading we needed to take back toward the gash in the forest. I resented not having a starting position fix and just hoped I could function without revealing my inexperience. I had to act the part. For all that the others knew, I had done this kind of work before.

The jungle here was thick. Under the high canopy it was like being under water, where two hundred feet down in the airless preadamite soup, all was dark green with the surface shimmering faintly far overhead. Around our position all was dark and jumbled with thrown trees, upon which fell occasional still pools of filtered sunlight. In places the huge trunks were draped with flowering vines, and the lower growth that had escaped the rain of debris from the 1000 pound bomb blasts was a forest itself, full of loamy shadows and choked with huge glossy leaves, some larger than tables. Absent my inner turmoil, the scene was almost peaceful. The busy, fiery flowers on the jungle floor gave a sense of tropical stagnation, a thwarted luxuriance doomed to live and die with no notice other than our own. I had the feeling that something serenely gloomy was hidden beyond, an Arcadia of mortality, but though the vegetation would make silent movement very difficult and slow, it could also provide us with good ground cover. I mentally added a day to reach the crash site.

While we lay there waiting and watching, I decided to start by trying to determine as near as possible where we were. I eased out the map and unfolded it slowly. The contours that identified the location of the deep rifts I'd seen from the air were easy enough to identify, but I didn't know how far from that clearly identifiable place we actually were, because the map had not been marked to show the bomb strike, which of course any aerial photograph of the area taken in the past several months would have revealed. I was angry that it had not been depicted.

The code word for a B-52 strike was "Arclight." Arclight strikes were so destructive that they were understood to be cleared with any U.S. units running long range reconnaissance missions into or near areas of known bombing targets. The mission briefer at FOB 4 should have known about the raid that had created these craters and so designated them on the map. It was a huge oversight that would have been of enormous help in pinpointing our insertion point and therefore in providing a progressive estimate of position, as well as some gauge of how accurate the contours might be. I looked around for some general idea of the slope of the jungle floor, but the growth obstructed my view too much to suggest a correspondence on the map. I made a provisional guess and marked it.

At length, I heard a faint bird call and realized my hearing was coming out from under the fading assault of the engines. I got carefully to one elbow and reached into the radio pack. I felt the detent on the switch as I turned it on, put the phone almost in my mouth, and whispered the code for insertion, then turned it off hoping intensely that the small shriek of energy it launched would be received back at the base. I hoped the pilots would report where they had actually dropped us.

The others heard the movement and began to stir quietly. I slid the radio pack to Grayson, who sat up and slipped his arms through the straps. I then crawled into the center of our little ring and indicated for Grayson and Nhi to close in. I showed them my estimation of our position, running my finger out to the margin at the top and to the side of the map so that Nhi could see the pair of numbers designating my mark on the paper, but indicated to them in hand signals that I wasn't sure of it. I showed my estimated heading to the target site on the map and then pointed for the benefit of the whole team. Everyone nodded that he understood, and there appeared to be nothing in Nhi's library of instincts to disagree.

Not far away lay an enormous downed tree. In falling it had torn through its neighbors, opening a long gash in the canopy and crushing the lower growth into a thick tangle of bent and broken branches. Except for the additional yellow light that fell through the rift, the tree offered good cover as long as we kept to the difficult congestion of still-foliated limbs rather than the easier progress offered by the long bridge of its trunk. I indicated the narrow burrows beneath it where the trunk was supported by its broken limbs, and the others acknowledged.

Preparatory to moving out, Nhi scanned in the intended direction with the binoculars for what seemed a long time. Using binoculars within the close press of the jungle may seem pointless, but they were very handy for revealing tiny movements, slivers of things hidden in shadow, and textures that do not match their surroundings. This phase was critical, as the noise broadcast by the helicopters made the insertion and extraction points the most critical. They could magnetize a place.

With a sign from Nhi, we assumed our pre-arranged order of march. With Nhi taking the risk of his customary position out front, I placed myself in the middle with Grayson and the radio two places behind me, an M-79 near the front in third position, and one near the back in tenth place. Despite my anxiety to get away from the insertion point, we began to move very slowly, crouched and wary, with Nhi setting the pace of frequent listening stops, and varying the duration of both movement and rests. He knew his business, and I found that my feelings toward him had oscillated into a kind of warped affection.

The ground here was softer and much wetter than the region along the Cambodian border where we had been inserted before, and we soon encountered areas of squelching glutinous mud that sucked at our boots and made silent moving difficult. All morning, sweltering in the torturous humidity, we crept or belly crawled through swampy glades saturated with a profound and watchful silence. The stillnesses were not at all peaceful. They looked back at me with a brooding and vengeful aspect. An occasional breath of hot air sighed through the dense growth to stir the hanging epiphytes and cause the lobes of giant philodendron leaves to waggle in our faces as though waving goodbye.

Too soon exhausted by the sheer weight of the air and the concentration required to assess every obstacle for a noiseless way to get through or past it while harnessed to the cumber of our gear, we had to fight off the constant assault of insects. The sweat feeders and blood suckers that landed on the skin could not be slapped away for the sound it risked, so they had to be rubbed off, pinched to death, or snagged in flight and crushed–usually after the fact.

We were often startled by harsh, fervent bird notes that flew out of the towering hardwood stands like sparks from an anvil, and we ducked beneath giant vines with leaves large as awnings flourishing in cynical fecundity, watching, always watching and listening for any sight or sound that didn't belong. Each step had to be taken with concentrated care, especially where the jungle floor was littered with the chance fall of loose-packed leaves and rotting moss-backed logs, some populated by incongruously bright flowers among the interlaced ferns and ground creepers.

We entered a boggy area of straight green tree trunks with dark ferny corners and speckled shade, where the steaming ground itself held a Mesozoic quality, like some timeless Carboniferous swamp where prehistoric saurians lurked in feigned sleep. Here the ground became a tangled carpet of sturdy procumbant vines whose heart-shaped leaves and rigid stems grabbed at our ankles. To snag a foot on one was to send a message along the entire tendril into the unseen depths of the undergrowth.

Trees trampled each other in torturous confusion, with trunks and limbs interlocked in a voracious mangle seeking vestiges of filtered light. There were pale stems, gnarled and choked with creepers, that clung to the bark sucking at the moisture captured there, while others, determined choking vines that seemed to crystallize the remorseless competition by starting up the tree trunks as a natural means of reaching for light—but in growing, gradually wrapping and tightening, eventually strangling their host, stealing both its life and its place in the forest. It was all overwhelmingly new, raw, and weird–a natural battlefield in itself, where the unsleeping struggle for life was the preoccupation of every living thing in it–reason enough for a respectfully soft tread, not to mention the likely presence of a determined enemy .

Some trees, delicately fluted, rose straight up without branches for a hundred feet or more, spiraling slightly as they went, sometimes with a slight swing or curve in the bole that gave the tree a look of tension and muscularity, like a bent bow. Between the larger ones, thin saplings that had seeded in the warm decay of leaf mold and rot shot upward, leafless in their haste, toward the light. Occasional sunny patches of bright papery green hosted dragon flies that jerked about in the stillness where the contrast hurt my eyes. It was a restless and terrible place, hot, full of bright color, and deeply foreign. Had I been able to see these surroundings with dispassion, I may have appreciated the forest's majestic indifference, but I could not afford a moment of relaxed vigil and saw in the strange and magnificent plants only their ominous capacity for guarding secrets, for harboring danger.

My nervous system began to merge into the jungle's mesh of sounds, smells, and other nameless stimuli, the thrum of adrenalin and the prescience of trouble and thus to move on an urgent current of instinct. Over enough hours the strain of constant anticipation bestows a degree of perception, at times almost prophetic. I began listening to my inner voice without realizing the origin of certain feelings or suspicions and made quiet decisions to signal a move or to remain still in response to subliminal tremors in the ether. I could not escape the feeling that the jungle was not merely a vast assembly of individual plants, but a gigantic singular consciousness wherein I could feel underfoot its breathing and the subterranean thud of its heart. The team, as before, began to cohere within the forest's omniscient will, moving in response to the slightest signal from me, or a sign from Nhi.

In the afternoon, after hours of silent slogging, as we eased in turn over a fallen log that lay greasy with old rainwater and slick moss, I suddenly felt a premonition–a stir in the mix of sensations given off by the forest. I couldn't account for the source, but some prescience of change prickled a warning through me, and the instant I became aware of the shift the entire team halted and went to ground as one. We crouched dead still and on full alert for long minutes. Nothing happened, but the feeling would not leave. We waited. Insects buzzed across the deep silence. My temples pounded in the vibrant stillness.

Then I heard voices. I went rigid with tension. In a few minutes a line of five men appeared, walking noisily toward us through the shoulder-high lower growth–a patrol of what appeared by their uniforms and pith helmets to be North Vietnamese Army regulars (NVA) approaching from our right. They were chatting amiably, muttering in their nasal triphthong, with rifles carried casually across their shoulders or slung on their backs, clearly not expecting their enemy to be anywhere around. I held my breath as they neared, closing obliquely with our heading. They were moving effortlessly enough that they had to be following a trail.

They continued directly toward where the forward part of our team lay hidden, and I realized in a spike of emotion that they would pass between my position and our first two or three men. They got so near I could smell the rancid combination of their body sweat and *nuoc mam* fish oil. Then they walked right through us, not 10 feet in front of the Nung who lay just ahead of me, and continued on. Through a narrow aperture in the vegetation I watched breathlessly as each man passed. Their khaki uniforms were dirty but otherwise appeared to be in good shape, and each was well equipped with the latest Soviet AKs and webbing. Their presence here surprised and worried me. These were soldiers of the regular North Vietnamese army, not VC, not the shadow army of local farmers during the day and guerrilla fighters at night. These guys were part of an organized and much larger force, and they were not known to be operating this far south–or east. They were pretty far from home. I wondered how they had been transported, or if they had walked all the way down from the North. It was still Tet, and our units in the south were on alert for further attacks, so it was possible that we had encountered a small party from a much larger infiltration. If that was so, we had probably crossed with a group somewhere behind the lead element, because they were walking too casually to have been the advance party, even on ground they believed was secure.

We lay in silence for a long time while I tried to sort through the implications of their presence and braced myself for more of them. We held position for most of an hour, then, in the absence of any sign that others were coming, we began to move again. In a few yards we came across their trail, a narrow moist black pathway through the jungle, full of footprints indicating heavy use by single file foot traffic in both directions. I halted and took a photograph of a clear print made by a sole cut from a truck tire. Even supplied with footwear by the Chinese and the Russians, many of them seemed to prefer the homemade open sandal with tire tread sole.

I noted with relief the absence of any crossing prints, which meant that Nhi and the two guys who had been cut off with him had hopped across it, leaving no sign of our own, just moments before the soldiers cut through our silent formation. Nhi must have come upon the trail, and realizing the implications of so many fresh tracks, did not halt to pass the word back, but kept moving in an effort to get us all across.

I stepped over the muddy path and signaled those behind to do the same quickly. Once across, we kept moving as far as we could to put distance between ourselves and the trail. We soon came upon Nhi and the others and stopped to regroup and to check the compass. It had been a very close call. If luck is the residue of design, then our deployment in open formation when trying to move through doubtful terrain had resulted in spectacular luck. A matter of mere minutes made all the difference in our escaping notice.

As shadows in the lower growth began to deepen, I knew we needed to find a RON site before it became too dark to set up for the night with any idea of our surroundings. When we finally came to a place open enough to organize a defensive position, the growth around us was so thick that it seemed impractical to use Johnson's trick of moving again after dark. Our position had the advantage of being enclosed by such thick undergrowth that no one could approach without making noise, and a well-placed mortar round would just have to be risked. I chose not to chance any farther movement that day and signaled the stop. Besides, I was exhausted and emotionally drained. The Chinese appeared tired, too, as far as I could read their perennially placid expressions.

I signaled Grayson to move up, deployed the antenna, and transmitted the codes for RON. I tried to find the code for having sighted the enemy but couldn't read it in the dark and decided to report it the next day. Besides, it occurred to me that were I to report enemy activity in the area, someone might order an air strike without our own position being known. Then I re-stowed the antenna carefully around the outside of the radio pack and checked to see that Grayson was holding up okay. From what I could tell in the fading light, his adrenalin levels alone were probably sustaining him through the weight of the radio, the stifling humidity, and the enormity of our isolation.

With hand signals I set the order of watches. I knew that none of us would actually sleep, but with twelve of us, each would only have to be on official watch for 30 minutes. Thus caught between the urgent need to see and the blind security of the dark, we settled into the crowded moon-dappled growth for the night. I indulged in two pasty balls of rice and some gulps of warm water, then lay down on my back in order to begin the long night in a position that enabled me to see the most of all that surrounded the botanical confines of our little nest. A well-placed mortar round could take us all out, but I knew we were well distant and concealed from the trail we had crossed.

I could not get over our brush with the enemy. Besides the real danger of being close enough to smell them, something about the encounter continued to elude me. Anxiety at having been that close dripped steadily inside me like a glass tube dispensing acid. It ate away at my organs of comprehension. There was something very troublesome about the casual way the five soldiers had walked and about both the existence and condition of the trail. What were they doing around here and why were they moving so carelessly, unless... unless this was *normal*? Suppose there was a network of those trails in this area, a major infiltration system, and that we had been either deliberately or inadvertently dropped in the middle of it. It began to make frightening sense, and our ostensible mission of recovering the remains of a Navy pilot suddenly seemed to be a sham. But then, a cover for what? Could it be that we were inserted in this dangerously populous area simply to verify reports of enemy foot traffic heading south? If we were actually on a trail watch, why wasn't I told? If the whole operation was that clandestine, what other reason could there be for cutting the team leader out of the information loop? Could this have anything to do with the failure to depict the Archlight craters on my map?

These and other angry thoughts of how I might be able to find out more about the way our own intelligence system worked kept me on alert long after I had tired of sifting through alternative hypotheses about the next day. For all I knew, large numbers of enemy "gooks" were bedded down all around us. If so we were in an extremely precarious position. We had been extraordinarily lucky so far, but if indeed we were not alone here, as a party of twelve we would have great difficulty sneaking noiselessly through the dense vegetation that surrounded our present location when we resumed in the morning.

Apprehensions churned within me all night, bringing forth an intense awareness of all sounds, smells, and subtle shifts in air temperature. I had already learned, and the events of the day had reinforced, the fact that the presence of truly mortal danger has a way of awakening the soul. It makes things vivid. When you're really afraid for your life, you see things you might never have noticed before; you pay attention to all the little signals, the messages that the world has been sending all along. Herein lies the paradox, that proximity to death brings a corresponding proximity to life. Neither is comfortable or pleasant, not even the insight gained in this great truth, but both coexist in dour embrace.

After awhile, the restless dark deepened with cloud cover, and within moments the night sounds began with a suddenness that I was learning to expect, although I had to wonder if the chorus had been triggered by movement. There was a curious rhythm in this area of the jungle where additional moisture in the ground seemed to have drawn more life than in other places. It was as though we were trying to rest on the floor of a vast nightmare engine room that was working toward some set purpose. There rose a permanent regulated background of steady cries as though we were in the presence of heavy machines. Electric cicadas and an endless variety of frogs laid measures of sound across the tightly drawn earlier silence, monotonous and impersonal, with no waver, no end, and no discernible beginning.

Fearing that they would cover the sound of someone attempting to approach, I tried unsuccessfully to comprehend the complex, illusive tempo of these noises. I knew there was information in it that carried some obtuse significance, information about movement and survival that I was simply too inexperienced to understand, just as the sequence of purrs and hums has familiar and telling connotations for those who control complex machinery. It throbbed methodically in the blackness. Every now and then a distinct cry or movement in the branches close at hand, immediate and intrusive, cut through the symphony in a startling confidential stroke and with dominating urgency. I kept my eyes rolling and my finger on the trigger, and in this way, with mortality screaming through the walls of the jungle, the cold hours crept on toward the dawn as we huddled on the soft jungle floor.

At last, with the accompaniment of the barest suggestion of wooly light in the lower growth, the machinery wound down, and small, familiar sounds crept into a pre-dawn silence. I knew the others guys were awake, but no one stirred as each of us spent a few minutes reading the surroundings. Suddenly the stillness was shattered by loud thrashing and screeching that exploded from the trees just to the north! Instantly we all came to in a flurry of alarmed paralysis to meet whatever it was. I searched in desperate confusion for the source of the racket. As it grew louder and closer, I realized it was echoing from high up in the trees. It turned out to be a large troop of howler monkeys migrating rapidly through the canopy and screaming at one another as they leapt through the interconnecting branches. They passed noisily overhead and quickly disappeared in fading raucous to the south.

With my heart pounding in the silence that ensued, I sat back down, temporarily enfeebled by the backwash of adrenalin. We exchanged uneasy grins, but for men already keyed up on nervous strain, it had affected us all profoundly. Then I realized that the animals' urgency could mean they were fleeing something or someone. In that case, anyone else within hearing would have been warned, too. We had to move.

We listened for any sound that betrayed movement. Then we silently assembled our gear and began a meticulously slow and watchful belly crawl along the damp ground until I was satisfied that the whole team was well clear of the RON site. About an hour later the undergrowth opened enough for easier movement, and we began to make better time, though always accompanied by the creeping dread of things unknown. Because of our brush with the enemy, the jungle seemed restless with their shadows.

Keeping an eye on the compass and adjusting Nhi's heading from time to time, we progressed through another torturous day of insects, debilitating humidity, and exhausting caution. By late afternoon we had crossed no other trails, and my suspicions that we had been sent to a known traffic area on some disguised agenda began to ease.

We were moving unusually well through high protective undergrowth when we came to a gentle downward slope, a shallow cleavage in the earth which held closely-spaced trees. The largest trees grew in the deepest part of the cleft, indicating an ancient water course, perhaps now underground. The place "felt" neutral. It was quiet with few bird notes, pristine and demagnetized somehow of the forces that prowled the area of the bomb strike and the trail we had crossed the day before. The map showed a pinched progression of contour lines in an area that seemed approximate to my estimate of where we were. I couldn't be sure but marked it as a provisional dead reckoning check of our position at the end of day two.

By now we were almost unrecognizable, matted with earth and sludge-brown mud, tired and much depleted by the cumulative effects of nervous strain. The ground felt like a good RON and offered the trees that would disguise the antenna which I wanted to deploy fully to transmit our progress report. The thick foliage would reduce my radio signal, but at least it was dry. Wet foliage closes a damp fist around transmissions, absorbing the effort.

I called a halt for the night, and the team moved silently into a perimeter that made for limited but sufficient fields of fire. In among the dense trunks of large trees, it would be all but impossible for the enemy to direct accurate fire into our position, so I signaled that we would set up without the customary move after dark.

The Nungs set out the M-1 mines, and we pulled into our defensive circle, grateful for the rest. I sensed that the Chinese felt the benign quality of the place as well. They seemed to relax where they lay on the ground sharing the mysterious redemptive quality of adversity overcome that can engender an almost mellow gratitude for seeing the end of another day. I felt it too, and again dirty beyond caring, rewarded myself with a bite of half-melted chocolate and some welcome gulps of sour water.

I was deeply relieved that we had not seen any other trails and that the going had become slightly easier as we got farther south toward our ostensible goal. I moved over to Grayson who had slipped out of the radio pack and was sitting against a tree, his dirty face gouged with misery. His black whiskers, the mud, and the dark greasepaint smeared on his face contrasted with the bright blood in the rims of his eyes to lend him a look of advanced fatigue. I could smell him, an odor rich and heady, like burnt yeast. Of course, if I could smell him so could the enemy, but we all stank, and there was nothing we could do about it.

He gulped deeply from the shared canteen—too deeply for a guy who might have another two or three days out here. I conjured a quick confident smile–at least that's what it felt like–and gave him our "Indian" sign for two more days by traversing an arc over my head with two fingers and bringing them to rest on my left forearm. He nodded unhappily.

I pulled the radio antenna out of the keepers around the outside of the pack and extended the metal ribbon up along the southeast facing side of the tree, silently clicked the radio on, and whispered the codes for RON and estimated position, then clicked off immediately. Again, because I could not be certain of what discovering the enemy's trail had meant, and because I still held residual doubts about the reason for this mission, I decided to keep quiet our encounter with the enemy until the debriefing when we got back. There were good reasons to report such an unexpected event right away, but some instinct prevented it. I stowed the antenna in case we had to move in a hurry during the night.

It was almost dusk, but on the jungle floor all brightness was gone from the few breaks in the canopy, and it was full dark in minutes. I ate two balls of mushy rice and took a careful look around the team to assure myself that each man had cover and access to narrow openings between the trees before taking my own position, lying on my back with weapon and eyes up.

After a few hours the earth began to release its moisture. A thin mist arose in the swale where we were camped. I could feel it more than see it. It breathed against my face like a mournful sigh. I welcomed it for it brought a darkness I had never experienced before, a blackness that seemed impervious to light. It was so powerful that for a few seconds I had the superstitious fear that if I switched on a penlight, the night would rush in and devour the tiny beam, then engulf me with it, extinguishing any trace of my presence. I suppose these thoughts were conditioned by the relentless hours of vulnerability, but the feeling was real.

Nothing bothered us during the night. The odd sense of security the place had given me paid off, and we continued unmolested on our heading toward the crash site before the ferrous hint of dawn could leak down to the jungle floor. Gradually, faint miasmic spills of pale light drew the muddy green botany from its bleak patches of uniform grey as we crept and stopped, crept and stopped. We had needed the night of relative calm after the close call and the hard going of the previous day, and despite the dirt, constant hunger and raging thirst, and the cumulative effect of fatigue and sleep loss, the team moved well through the shadowy green flourish of veined and glossy foliage, steep gullies, and tangled hillsides of the third day.

I was struck with how conditioning by cautious advancing through constant danger can have the effect of molding separate individuals into a single mentality, with common instincts and shared reaction times, not unlike those in birds and schools of fish. Often when I decided privately that it was time to stop, or to move again, the whole team would do so without any signal, seemingly in direct response to my thoughts. Perhaps we were all simply learning to react to the same set of subconscious signs from without; perhaps I was experiencing some new horizon of the mind, ripe for study. It might have been a resurgence of an ancient instinct shared by prehistoric hunting parties, awakened now by nervous strain from far back down the stems of Darwinian logic, or maybe it lived only as an extension of my charged imagination. Whatever it was grew from our collective need to survive, our parceled experience of fear, and the unspoken knowledge that the hunters are also the hunted. It worked through us and for us like a force field of awareness as real as the earth itself, sound, or light.

The swale in which we had spent the night brought us up to rolling terrain, heavily treed, but with reduced ground cover. Here the canopy was so thickly layered that little light made it far enough down to support large-leafed ground plants. They were plentiful but did not produce the enormous umbrella-like leaves common elsewhere that reduced visibilities but helped us to remain hidden. Noting the change, we slowed our progress, and instinctively began to crouch in a forward lean the way people do when walking in rain.

We plodded on through the relentless heat. Troubled by doubts about the accuracy of my dead reckoning, I fought to maintain a sense of our progress despite the need for constant change of pace as dictated by the terrain. This need to vary the pace, the uneven ground, the burden of movement, the mandates of silence, and the heavy, vegetal capture of oxygen made me dizzy. I found myself setting meaningless goals: holding my breath for two paces, then releasing it noiselessly for two paces as long as I could keep count; marking the passage of seconds with my heartbeats, then drawing disproportionate comfort from the achievement–and always, always scanning, listening, smelling, sensing.

In the afternoon, as we traversed in deepening shadow a broad slope where the congested trees soared from the ground at an angle of about 45 or 50 degrees, a shift in the light foretold the hurrying night. The light withdrew as though sucked from the air around us. This was sometimes a sign of approaching clouds, but looking up through the lacy triple canopy several hundred feet above, I saw only the pin-pricked light upon the roof of the jungle fading to an orange blush. We had little time to set up for the night, and I didn't like the prospect of staying for long on a hillside. If we passed an uneventful night, it would at best be uncomfortable, and in the event that we might have to run, there would be only one quick direction for escape, which any attacker could reasonably predict.

We halted so I could check the map for any level terrain, but it appeared that if we were anywhere near where I thought we were, there was none depicted. Of course all my dead reckoning had been compromised at the start because the Arclight strike where we'd been dropped off had not been indicated. I couldn't match the terrain we were in now with any contours on the paper. I knew the map's contour lines could not be accurate, depending as they did upon estimates based on aerial photography, so as far as the cartographers knew, if the tree tops were level or sloping, the ground beneath them was too. My instinct was to continue on the estimated heading I had calculated at the start, but the reality of the ground didn't match my projected line of advance.

Then things began to change. Nhi crept in with a jagged fragment of aluminum. I examined it and realized it was flush-riveted aircraft metal, torn like construction paper, pale green on one side with a small patch of light grey paint on the other. Even though we had come in search of a plane crash, I was struck by the incongruous presence of such an artifact in this wilderness. Like a twig found floating on the ocean, it was a sign of proximity, and I looked up. High overhead some broken branches hung withering in the shadows. Nhi and I then scouted a short distance ahead and saw that to the southeast a patch of reluctant grey light spilled through a thin place in the upper canopy. It was marginally brighter there, though the late hour rendered all light and shadow ambiguous. If it was an indication of broken tree tops it could mean that we were nearing our objective, though the character of the jungle ahead gave no other sign. I didn't think we were any-where close enough to the penciled mark on the map that designated the crash site, and in the absence of any corroborating symbols on the paper that might confirm my progression of estimates, I despaired again of my navigation and decided there was too little light left to find a more level place to RON anyway.

We got ourselves in between the trees as before and set up our defensive formation. This time, after full dark, we moved about 30 yards farther down slope and nestled in among some close-growing tree trunks with our mines out. Because of the slope, only a few guys found more or less level benches of ground where years of run-off had compiled earth dams among the roots, and they were able to get into prone positions. The rest of us settled into pockets formed by the downward spread of roots that gave us some visibility outward, while those against the trees at our feet could scan the terrain above our po-sition. It was not comfortable, but the size and proximity of the trees gave us a measure of protection that helped to off-set the discomforts. We were close enough in our circle to alert each man for watch with a simple nudge.

As the hours passed the night was strangely quiet. It seemed that everything around us was holding its breath, awaiting some unknown event. I couldn't escape the feeling that this elemental place had something to tell me. My jungle lore, though strenuous and without joy, was slowly improving, but while I held quite still and listened in solitude among the enormous plants as the shadows darkened around me and the wind stirred the high canopy, the sheer magnitude of the living forest overbore me. It had the power to enthrall, to enlighten and to frighten, to teach and to disturb. It made me feel crushingly insignificant. I wondered, as so often before, how I had come to be there. It all seemed so sudden.

I was beyond tired and almost completely overcome by a desperate need to sleep. Despite a conspiracy of the senses, I fought to stay awake. The sheer weight of bodily fatigue alternating with an emptiness in my brain threatened to close my eyelids down, against all effort. Sleep tried to take me over, to turn out every vestige of consciousness and to occupy all the places within me where once sentience had lived. Every slight movement–checking my watch, shifting my weight, pinching the poison from an insect bite–seemed an affront to the common store of awareness. I shifted to place my spine against a painful knuckle in the tree that would serve the need for staying wakeful.

Sometime after midnight the sky began to flicker in eerie morse. Silent flashes fled through cloud banks low to the northwest. After awhile a warm rain began. It approached with a sound like pouring sand. It seemed long minutes after rattling upon the trees high above us that it began to find its way down to the ground, falling through the swaying foliage in enormous blobs, delivering a shine to the leaves even at night and a glossy blackness to the ground, where it landed like scattered applause, made little streams in the soil, and pooled beneath us where we sat in the capture of roots. All the elements seemed roused by the change, leaving no place unexposed. It reminded me that there was a time not so long ago when man knelt in dread before nature's moods.

About two hours before first light the rain passed on, out of the hills and away to the east, leaving us soaked and shivering. It revived me and brought the taste of mud, dirt, and the greasepaint into my mouth. It released the ammoniac smell of my filthy clothes, and soon I could smell the warm jungle fug from the others, too. We all smelled as strongly now as the fishy NVA we had seen the first day. My wounds ached, my scalp and whiskers itched, my eyes burned, and my skin stung from dozens of scratches and insect bites.

The saturated air continued to surrender its moisture as I sat motionless in my mud puddle peering blearily into the night, searching through a fog of delirium for any movement or for any change in depth perception that would signal the first grey hint of dawn. Drops of water trickled from leaves and along the grooved stems of the lower growth. Rivulets that channeled through the layers of vegetation descended noisily to the jungle floor, soaked further into its rotting carpet, carrying the fetid humus of dying things into the levies where we hunkered at the base of the trees. The air was thick with the pungency of oxidation, leaves, and earth—a rain-pounded compost mashed into fertilizer for vegetation already grown monstrous. The jungle breathed out in wisps of restless mist that drifted ethereally upward, imparting a ghostly movement, like the first flutter of the forest's waking eyelids.

My stomach growled, and when I snaked my fingers into my leg pocket for a pinch of rice, I was inconvenienced to discover that the rain water had conveyed a measure of gritty mud into my food pouch. I ate it anyway.

When at last the darkness began to give way as a dim and hesitant light seeped into the trees, but before we could see clearly, we rose stiffly and retrieved the mines. I signed to Nhi to strike a course toward the place where we had seen light leaking into the jungle the previous afternoon, and, soaked through with rainwater, we abandoned the muddy pools and began creeping in a more easterly direction. Movement brought a second wind and rekindled alert mode, but I was dangerously tired and moved through the morning with the hope that we were actually approaching the objective instead of tracking some somnambulistic abstraction born out of growing fatigue and uncertainty.

About midday we began to see a lot of daylight through the trees ahead. Above us, some of the trees had been broken off, with many branches hanging and others on the ground. The ground smelled faintly of kerosene. We came upon other pieces of metal and soon began to smell burnt vegetation. I was greatly relieved, but watched with dull, isolated attention the unfolding evidence that we were approaching the site. I realized that I had guessed us to within about 150 meters of the place. This meant of course that we had found it, but it also meant that my estimate of our start point could be fairly closely established in the debriefing to come.

Sunlight now lay just beyond the broken trees. Overhead the tops had been sheared off at a progressively steeper angle until the shattered stumps were only a few dozen feet high. Spills of sunlight began to fall upon the foliage around us, and then ahead through the tangle I began to see a nightmare of destruction and churned earth. The air was heavy with the scent of broken wood, chlorophyll, and burnt vegetation seasoned with the sharp oily redolence of kerosene and smoke.

When at last we crouched near the edge of the brown gash in the forest, I saw that there had actually been little post-impact fire. The aircraft had hit with little, if any, fuel in the tanks, though evidently enough remained in the system to have ignited the area of initial impact. I guessed that the pilot had been dumping fuel or the tree tops had breached the tanks. The wreckage was strewn away from us in a long jumble of broken trees on a roughly southeasterly heading. It lay on sloping ground–something that I had not realized from the brief fly-over sight of it I'd had from the air and did not expect.

We had come out just to the west of the point where the aircraft had first entered the trees, with slightly higher terrain to our right. I wanted a better view of the site before committing any of us to the open, and it appeared we might be better positioned to assess things if we moved to the higher ground. We retreated into the cover of the forest for several meters and began working our way around the clearing, keeping well back from the light.

After an hour of this cautious avoidance, we arrived at what appeared to be the highest point of land surrounding the crash. There we set up, and I signaled that this would be our RON. It was past mid afternoon, and I didn't want to approach such an exotic artifact without a long and careful watch, nor did I want to risk venturing the team into the open more than once. I also didn't want to spend what was left of the day and the night in close company with whatever remains of the pilot we might be able to recover.

We formed our defensive perimeter while Nhi and I traded use of the binoculars to scan every detail of the wreckage and as much of the limited immediate area around it as could be observed from our elevated position. The destruction was beyond what I had imagined. I had never seen such a thing. The massive incongruity of it seemed to lend it a prolonged release of life, as though somewhere within the terrible scene this extraordinary machine, lost to its intended element, had not given up. It lay horribly broken and saddened, yet brooding in defeat. It spent all first thoughts on appearance. Had I not known the general configuration of an airplane, it would have been impossible to identify a single piece of the distended tangle that lay scattered through the trees in front of us.

There was at least a portion of the vertical stabilizer visible on which, through the lenses, I could make out a partial number. For the rest, I could only guess that it hit the tops of the big hardwoods and broke into pieces that jammed into the ground and impacted more trees, until the remaining structure had simply tumbled into smithereens. Judging by the length and shape of the tree damage, it appeared that the aircraft had arrived under some control, but striking the trees had destroyed its last vestige of lift and sent it careening into the jungle with enough forward momentum to tear out about 100 meters of dense forest, smashing into the ground in a smothered fury that seemed barely contained in the hole it made. We had labored our slow and arduous way to this lost place not really knowing what to expect, and now it lay before us in monstrous stillness.

We watched and waited. The place held an ominous tranquility. A deathly quiet seemed clamped upon it. No birds called; no monkeys screamed from the surrounding jungle. There was no breeze, and nothing moved. I motioned a query to Nhi if any of the others wanted to look through the glasses. Grayson and two of the Nungs took a look, although the two Chinese were hesitant and held back after a cursory peek. I made a mental note that we could use a second pair of binoculars and two additional compasses, one each for Nhi and Grayson.

As the shadows of evening began to deepen around us, Nhi, who had maintained a concentrated vigil on the site with the glasses, stirred and tapped me on the shoulder. He handed me the binoculars and pointed to something moving through fading sunlight on the other side of the wreck. I focused through breaks in the trees and was shocked to see a large tiger. It was majestic and frightening, though in a detached sort of way, as though I was seeing it in a travel film. It was a danger so exotic and unexpected that I couldn't for a moment or two accept that a wild tiger was just eighty or so meters away, separated from us for the time being only by the motionless air. It appeared to be testing the air, then it turned, silk footed, and silently moved its muscular coat back out of the light. I was intrigued but very relieved to see it retreat into the trees. It could probably have covered the distance to us in well under a minute.

Since this was an addition to the uncertainties that threatened our welfare each night, I signed to the others, to mixed reactions. The news energized us all, and though it didn't help our mental strain, it did much to rekindle our wakefulness as darkness closed around us. There was no sunset. All color just seemed to fall out of the sky in seconds. I transmitted a position report and the codes for RON and "objective reached," and then with barely enough visibility to find our way, we moved a little farther along, keeping the wreckage in sight, and set up for the night.

I believed from the outset that we were being sent to find something that would have created a clearing of some size in the jungle. Accordingly, I had the two M-79 grenade launchers brought along in anticipation that, if we found the place, we would have to leave the protection of the trees to accomplish any sort of retrieval. As it happened, the crash did not clear much beyond the immediate impact area, yet there lay a rent in the forest before us where enough trees had been torn away to form a dangerous aperture of light, and openness. As darkness filled in the clearing, I deployed the two Nungs with M-79s on the wreck side of our position, where the weapon could be used to best advantage, down slope and outward from the congestion of trees. The rest of us took our positions for the night behind them, knowing that we were sitting on the rim of an artifact that held enormous attraction for the bad guys. Though rags of fatigue clung to us like damp cobwebs, the tensions of the long night passed like a troubled dream, without incident—or rest.

We were up before light and, leaving two riflemen and the two M-79 men at the RON site to cover us, now faced the prospect of leaving the protection of the forest for the exposure of the clearing. We stole forth hugging the jungle floor. Even after the hours that we had studied it carefully through the glasses, the pieces of wreckage surprised me by their mass. The aircraft had been made out of large components, which even driven partly into the ground, still rose in places well over our heads. A concretion of torn vegetation and burned earth had been compacted so hard into some of the pieces that it could not be scratched away with a fingernail. It smelled of petroleum smoke, fresh turned earth, and hydraulic fluid.

To begin our search for any remains I divided the eight of us according to our distribution of weapons. Although I favored the far end of the site as most likely to hold whatever could be identified as the cockpit, I went with those assigned to the initial impact point first, where I had seen numbers painted on a fragment of the tail. While stepping quietly among the detritus of crumpled and broken metal, I was surprised to find that there were parts still giving off heat and releasing tiny localized wisps of smoke.

As visibility improved I saw that it would be one of those hot, very still days when the sun would not emerge to break the spell on the petrified scene. The overcast looked high, but it was sliding rapidly eastward, which meant that whatever was pushing it was coming from the west. That could mean a quartering headwind for any aircraft dispatched to locate us. I hoped we would find what we were looking for soon, giving the helicopters the majority of the day's light and no weather delays in coming to get us. It was early enough that I had hopes of calling for an extraction soon. That would give them plenty of time to organize it and get us out of there before the return of darkness.

I finally made my way to the piece with the numbers. It included a portion of the leading edge of the vertical stabilizer which still pointed more or less forward. I couldn't tell if this meant it had been torn from the top of the fuselage in the early or late instants of the crash. It didn't matter now. I copied down the only four legible digits. There were others, but the metal was torn, and I could not find the relevant missing part(s?). I made what observations I could without knowing the aircraft type while working forward through the spread of junk toward where I expected to find the final resting place of the cockpit.

There were places in the wreckage that held the familiar putrid smell and the sound of flies, but we found nothing. Whatever forensic biology there may have been was buried too deeply in the wrenched and folded metal to enable us to reach it. No matter how much the Navy wanted identification, I was not about to move anything that would emit a non-jungle noise.

As we inched our way along the devastation it was hard not to think of the pieces, thrown as they were into the grotesque postures of their destruction, as the remains of a living thing. I felt a growing sadness that such an achievement should have fallen so far from home, its instruments winding down in the sudden stillness of the jungle floor with nothing else to report, there to be consumed by the vast and indifferent forest, eventually to host the nests of birds and the dens of serpents, yet all soon reclaimed by the creeping fingers of voracious growth.

Near the end of the tear in the woods, I came upon a fragment of the pilot's flight helmet and a piece of the seat. I could smell faintly the bad meat, but none of us could locate any of what we had been sent for. I turned back and then recognized a contorted portion of the instrument panel, which still held a few avionics, overlain by other junk and mostly buried in the plowed earth. A bit further into the tangle that had been somewhere near the front of the airplane I saw an object that, by its color and texture, seemed out of place. It contrasted in some existential way with the material surroundings, and I approached a bit apprehensively.

There, trapped beneath a fold in the metal, was a hand. A dismembered left hand, partially decomposed and bloated almost beyond recognition for what it was, the pale fingernails bloodless and grey. Flies seethed about it in their frantic myriads. Their constant whine should have alerted me, and I couldn't understand how I had missed it before. There was very little dried blood at the exposed bones of the wrist, which probably meant either that it had been torn away after death or had simply been consumed by insects.

At first I didn't want to touch it and was about to ignore it as simply a gruesome indication of our proximity to the cockpit, but then I noticed a dull glint of gold entrapped in a swollen finger. That was important, as it was probably inscribed, but to find out, I would have to remove it. I ducked under a flap of aluminum, scattered the flies, and pinching the hand between thumb and forefinger, brought it out. For some reason Nhi watched attentively as I placed the nauseating thing on a piece of broken branch and unsnapped my bayonet sheath. I pressed the blade into the slimy skin. The cut squirted a gangrenous auburn syrup. I had to swallow the rock that perched in my throat before bearing down on the blade, but the joint separated more easily than expected. Then, holding my breath against the smell, I pulled the finger out and the putrid flesh slipped off the bone like pudding. I wiped the ring on my clothes and slipped it into my pocket.

With that, as far as I was concerned, our mission was completed. Graves and Registration always preferred to have a head for positive identification, but all they were going to get was the ring. I hoped it would at least provide sufficient proof of death for some sympathetic Naval officer to authorize release of due benefits to the pilot's family. In the meantime, my priority shifted to getting us out of there.

I signed for Grayson, and while he rested the radio pack on a piece of the wreckage, I took advantage of the open to extend the antenna fully. I called for immediate extraction and sent estimated coordinates.

Between that and my message the night before that we had reached the objective, they should be able to find us—assuming they had received my transmissions at all. They had, after all, flown right over the site the day we had been inserted. I allowed myself a certain tenuous hope that since they had already charted this place, they'd come soon. If they didn't come for us before dark, we would have to spend another sleepless night on site. I assumed that anyone with experience working the TOC back at FOB 4 would know that having reached the objective the day before, the team would be ready and anxious to get back as soon as even marginally possible. The yearning to be out of there rose within me like the pang of hunger.

We moved back into the cover of the woods and set up to wait for the sound of the choppers. A few guys ate a bit of their reconstituted food, taking large gulps of water. I felt suddenly famished, but I knew my rice supply tasted like mud, and my fingers smelled of death, so I ate some chocolate, and after a few hours of growing anxiety, switched on the PRC-10 emergency location radio in my leg pocket. It had limited battery life, but I decided a quick test was in order. Besides, all signals would help, and I could nurse the power by switching it off. Any attempt to locate us would need it to home on our hidden position as they got close anyway.

We maintained a sharp defensive strategy while we waited, with the grenade launchers alert to our open side and all automatic weapons aimed around our position. We could not let up our ordeal of constant vigilance, for it was entirely possible that if the enemy had been observing the site all along, they would wait in the expectation of bringing down a helicopter when it tried to extract us.

The day ticked tediously by. Noon passed, then two more hours, three, and the afternoon light began to shift. Nothing stirred to break the deathly quiet of the crash site; the woods around us seemed devoid of any birds or ground dwellers. I had growing fears that either the people at HQ had not been receiving, or for some logistical reason were unable to scramble the rescue team, which should have been standing by–even if they were standing by the bar–since the day before. In a spate of contained anger, I reached for the radio determined to risk another message, this time with the squelch knob turned up enough to give at least an audible signal that the radio was indeed sending. Just then, the faint beat of helicopters began teasing the air way to the east.

Enlivened by anticipation, I checked in my side pocket to make sure the PRC-10 was transmitting. As the sound of the choppers grew, I signaled the sequence of our move back toward the wreck, anticipating the order of departure when the helicopters arrived. Then, keeping under the cover of the lower growth, we moved out. I tried to time our arrival at the clearing with the landing so the choppers would have no delay on the ground. There was room for one helicopter at a time to set down near the area of initial impact where the most trees had been shorn off or knocked down. When we arrived back at the crash, I deployed the team in the shadows at the edge of the ground cover and alongside the half-buried pieces near the tail section.

When the first Huey came into view, I flashed it with my mirror and was immediately relieved to see it swing toward us and begin orbits of the clearing. The big Sikorskys followed, the first descending right at us. In the wind storm of its arrival, I grabbed the radio from Grayson and yelled for him to run for it. I waved for the next five Chinese to follow him, including one of the M-79s. They all rushed the open door and clambered aboard in seconds. I signaled the pilot, who lifted off in a deafening torrent of blown chips and flying vegetation.

The second Sikorsky was down before the first had wheeled away. I followed the last five Nungs, and with a leap from the ground to the tire, slung the radio pack on board and was on the metal floor with one hand on the precious radio and the other gripping a seat stanchion as the deck tilted sharply, and the ground began falling away. The pilots wanted out of there as much as we did, and in their steep climbing departure, we had to hold on to keep from sliding back out the door.

The helicopter kept a gratifying angle of climb as we lurched to an easterly heading in the cooler upper air. I remained on the deck and rolled to sit back against the forward bulkhead. After watching the trees recede, to assure myself that we were actually getting out, I looked up at the Chinese. They were grinning. My skin was so caked with dried greasepaint and dirt, I couldn't tell if my face moved, but I gave them a tired thumbs up. For just a moment, I felt a splinter of the great burden of my responsibilities lift ever so slightly, but weightless as a sigh.

From the safety of altitude I glanced back outside at the roof of the jungle as its mournful grandeur receded beneath us. Suddenly the whole scene began to pull away in another sense. The edgy anabasis in which we had slogged through the grueling days and sleepless nights tethered to the wild scenery by such bizarre requirements for survival, began to seem distant and surreal. Even in those first minutes of the flight, surrounded by the affirming painted faces of my companions, everything below us seemed to recede into a fading patchwork of vague mental snapshots. We had been plucked from an otherworldly place so far from the tenets of normal life that, even through the flood of relief that rushed in to replace my exhaustion and fear, the sea of distant trees that rolled beneath us defied me again to believe that we had really been there.

Back at the base we were met by the medics, who asked if anyone was hurt and looked us over quickly for any unusually suspicious infections. We were advised to report back to them for disinfectant swabs after we got cleaned up, and getting cleaned up was for me an absolute priority. My skin felt suffocated with mud and sweat and the salty concretion of fear.

I proceeded directly to the hootch and unloaded all my filthy gear onto the floor. Everything in the room was exactly how I'd left it. It surprised me. After the long days and endless nights of nervous tension on patrol and the constant effort to analyze unknowns, to sort and prioritize dozens of possibilities that by their nature defy predictability, seeing the small organization of familiar objects again placed them for the moment outside my hard-earned adjustment to another scheme of things. Even the chess pieces remained in their squares on the table where we had left them, mute testimony to a mad confidence in chance.

I spent a long time in the hot shower, feeling the constant sting of numerous cuts and insect bites, while trying to scrub the dirt from under my fingernails. I also did what I could to clean the gold ring. It still stank. I saw that it was indeed inscribed inside, but the engraving was too small to read, even with the aid of some contrast provided by a dark substance that remained captured in parts of the script and that resisted washing with soap and water.

Afterwards, I took Grayson with me to the debriefing. I warned him that this, his first mission, had been on specific orders to bring back whatever we could of the pilot, at least to confirm as well as possible his fate, but I held private suspicions that, in this business of constantly shifting uncertainties, truth was a perishable commodity. This didn't mean that we should not be forthcoming in the debrief, but as, for reasons I thought were good, I had already elected not to report our encounter with the NVA at the time it happened, I could foresee that events might sometimes require other compromises in reporting the degree to which the unexpected might affect our ability to fulfill the assignment.

I did not tell him of my ambivalence toward the debriefing Sergeant, but suggested that he wait to be asked anything before volunteering any of his own experience on the mission, because the debriefer had a demonstrated preference for his maps over the condition of his sources.

When we entered the hut, the Intelligence Sergeant greeted us with one of his inattentive politician's smiles and indicated the chairs. We sat.

"Well now," he began, winking with his voice.

I made an effort to put aside my instinctive dislike of his manner. I had to make an accurate report, and I had to admit I envied the air-conditioned isolation of his job, since it prevented his direct exposure to the demands and the risks of the one I had been given. I got up, and using my field map with all my hand notations, pointed out the estimation of our insertion point, while making politely clear my feelings concerning not being told beforehand about the location of the Arclight strike craters where we had been dropped off. His attitude betrayed nothing.

When I told about crossing paths with the NVA, he became quite interested. This aroused my original suspicion that they knew about the enemy's presence in that area. I described everything I had observed about their clothing, weapons, shoes, and casual movements. I turned over the camera, which contained the photos of their footprints, and indicated on the map where I had figured the point of crossing to be.

He then became quite pointed and wanted to know why I had not reported the enemy encounter right away. By now I had thought about that very point for several days and had concluded that I should indeed have taken the first opportunity to call in enemy contact, and I was prepared for the question.

First of all, knowing that the NVA is a large body, I had no idea how large a unit the ones we saw actually represented. We waited there, with the team split by their trail, long enough to satisfy me that they had been only a small party, but in order to avoid unnecessary risk to the team, we got as far away as possible as quickly as movement on your stomachs through an area occupied by the enemy would allow. This meant no immediate opportunity to even operate the radio. Certainly firing on them, even if we silenced them all, would have alerted whatever accompanying forces remained concealed by the dense vegetation in the area and would have risked losing the whole team as well as compromising U.S. presence in the area. I told him that if we had lost the team, he would have probably concluded enemy activity there, anyway, which was all I could have transmitted given the limited information provided for by our codes.

Most importantly, I told him that because I had not been briefed on the presence of the Arclight strike, I reasonably concluded two important things: first, that since the bomb strike had been ordered at some point in the recent past, it made sense to conclude the raid had been because NVA activity in the area was known, and that secondly, further to not having been told of the strike location–the coordinates of which our Intelligence had to know exactly from aerial photographs–I had to consider the possibility that we had been deliberately sent out without being apprised of known enemy trails in the area as a kind of bone-headed effort at obtaining corroborative information. If that were true, I concluded that Command regarded the team as expendable, and in that case there was every reason for me to expect another bomb strike on the area, even while we were still out there, as HQ would have no way of knowing how fast we were moving except by once-daily position reports. He listened expressionlessly and said nothing. I expected at least a jovial denial.

I went on to report every detail of our experience, all I had observed of the crash, and what speculative conclusions I had been able to draw from the condition of the wreckage. I handed him the ring, and then finished by emphasizing that it was only by shear dead reckoning that we came out anywhere near the objective, because our start point, thanks to not knowing about the location of the Arclight raid, had necessarily been pure guesswork. Surprisingly, that got no reaction. It seemed that he was completely ignorant of conditions in the field, of the extraordinary difficulty of navigating through a jungle environment where its sheer unpredictability was continuous.

After an effort to match my check points with their corresponding locations on his larger scale maps and trying to fit our RONs onto his records by back-tracing the locations from the known crash site to that of the NVA trail, he seemed satisfied, although it was difficult to tell because whenever he studied his big map, his speech lost all intonation and inflection. His few remarks were nominal, words dragged along the voice box floor. He asked little beyond what I had observed of the enemy, then asked if Grayson had anything to add. He didn't.

From there, he asked a lot of seemingly irrelevant questions about the flora and the troop of monkeys whose passage had so scared us the morning of the second day. I could only guess by his reticence that such information might provide clues as to the season and whether the animals were local to the area. I was able to answer most of his questions about the vegetation because every leaf and vine out there could have hidden a host of dangers, and the effort to see through, under, and around them had left many species permanently imprinted on my memory.

When we left the hut, Grayson asked, "What now?" I told him that as far as I was concerned we had earned some time off. I told him about the team's beer tradition and then left him in the club while I picked up a case of beers and headed down to give them to the Chinese.

I arrived at their tent to discover that I had inadvertently scored some points with Nhi. He had seen and understood the symbolic purpose of retrieving the pilot's ring. As Buddhists, the Nungs believed in the importance of being buried at home with their ancestors, and barring that, to have personal possessions or artifacts returned as surrogates for their spirits. He had explained what happened to those who had not seen the recovery of the ring, and when I arrived with their beer they gathered around and patted me gently on the back, repeating "Trung Shi Mo!" with approving smiles. Some held out the little gold Buddha effigies they wore about their necks, others indicated their ring fingers so that I would understand what they were saying. Even though I had felt compelled to retrieve the ring against my will to even touch it, I was very happy to feel their approval and decided just to bask in the credit. It would pay dividends in the coinage of respect when future chips were down.

They pressed one of the beers into my hand, and we all shared an incomprehensible toast, one of the most rewarding of my life. Immensely relieved, glad of their approval and facing some time off now, I left in an elevated mood and, ravenously hungry, made for the messhall, knowing I would have to come back and check on them in an hour or so to roll one or two over for the night.

While I was enjoying an enormous dinner, I was surprised by the Intelligence Sergeant, who brought his tray over and sat across from me. His entire demeanor was different now. He was friendly and personable away from his office and seemed genuinely interested in hearing about my experiences in the field. I immediately began to re-evaluate him. After a friendly exchange, he leaned in and told me that my report of seeing NVA the first day out, the description of what they wore, and the photos of their footprints, had been big news to 5th Special Forces Command, who had no idea of any enemy activity in that region just south of the DMZ. Infiltration had been suspected, as this was still Tet, but the question of where it was happening had until now, been unknown. The fact that they were NVA meant that it was a large scale effort. That the men I had seen were not on their guard implied they had been in the region for some time.Tthe Sergeant was very pleased.

Apparently, my report served to tie together certain other strings of information gathered from sources elsewhere, and he expected that we were likely to be commended for it. That was mixed news. I did not want to be singled out even in a good way, especially as it could result in even more unpleasant assignments. I just hoped to live out my tour as anonymously and invisibly as possible.

I was glad, though, to hear about the success of our report. It served to justify, at least partially, what we had been sent out to do, and it dispelled my suspicions that the team had been used in a way that smelled to me like willful and unnecessary risk. Whatever tiny slot in the larger picture our snippet of information might serve to fill, the important thing to me just then was to learn that the team had not been sent out on some false directive. I decided to let the question of the Arclight strike go for the present, though it still bothered me, and asked instead if the ring had been returned to the Navy. He said that the Navy had been informed of its recovery and that it was being dispatched to them as soon as the command bureaucracies involved would authorize handing it over to a liaison officer, or that perhaps the pilot's squadron would send someone to get it.

I knew in theory how the cords of information were gathered by the Intelligence analysts and how such webs of inference were woven, but their exact methods and conclusions were not aligned with my "need to know." I only wished I had one of their jobs in a nice air-conditioned hut instead of crawling miserably around in a sweltering bug-infested crucible of prehistoric life packed with danger, disease, and rot.

17

Despite the time I had spent at FOB 4, I still did not know many people there. Because of the devastation of the big attack my first night in the camp, most of the personnel were strangers not only to me but to one another, and many replacements had arrived during the time I was preoccupied with learning the layout of the place and the nature of its operations. Then, after being wounded on the first mission with Johnson, I had tried to minimize moving around much and, other than the messhall for meals and a few visits to the club, stayed pretty close to the hootch at the lower end of the compound.

There was another, somewhat awkward, reason: The main business of the place centered on the operations of the recon teams and the processing of information they brought in. Consequently there prevailed an understated deference toward individual team leaders. At least from a social point of view we were symbols of the central mission—the personification, so to speak, of its mysterious operations. I saw now that this had been the reason for the subtle change in attitude I had noted during in-processing whenever anyone read my orders, and even here at the heart of the whole dreadful enterprise it seemed that the team leaders were at least lightly dusted with its mystique. I suppose there were those who saw certain advantages in this kind of attention, but I was reluctant to socialize enough for others to glimpse the utter fraud that struggled to remain hidden within me.

Besides, with the base now largely restored, most of the popular gathering points–the club, team huts, messhall–were clearly visible from many points on Marble Mountain, and I assumed that they had all been freshly sighted in from up there. I soon learned that indeed, while I was away in the field, the casual sniping had started up again on movie nights. Incredibly though, people were still treating the "bad" shooting as a joke, although we had now given a nod to the danger by maintaining a listening post on the summit of the mountain, manned by components of the recon teams. I couldn't see what good that was expected to do. Although I had never been up on the mountain, if the rumors were true that the rock was honeycombed with caves—some large enough to contain Buddhist temples and all known now to be occupied from time to time (if not all the time) by VC—I could see only disaster for any of our people deployed up there. The taper of the mountain to a stepped point at the top made it unlikely that anyone on the summit would be able to see over the shoulder of its slope, which meant they would be unable to report the origin of any sporadic shot from farther down the side of the rock, while each day left them vulnerable to attack by an enemy equipped with hand grenades and known for stealth, especially at night.

I found the whole idea offensive, not only that we were not given permission to clear the mountain of VC, but that our immediate Command continued listening to MACV HQ in Saigon on the subject. Besides, the unique geological problem made it extremely doubtful that a small "listening post" at the top would achieve anything. I stared at the face of the mountain, scouring every bush in every crevice for any evidence of a crack or an opening. There were none visible. I asked how we were getting our people up there and was told that they had been flown up and inserted by chopper at first, but that now they were being relieved on foot every few days by means of a path that snaked up the back side of the rock from the Vietnamese stone cutters' village at the base of the mountain on the other side. I just didn't want to believe that after everything that had happened, our Command was willing to risk the likely consequences of such an ill-conceived decision; but as usual, decided that they must know more than I did and simply filed it away as yet another unexplained detail on the monument to our vulnerabilities.

Soon enough our team's turn for lookout duty on top came around. We were to be up there for two days and two nights in a position that I was informed was in a narrow confine of boulders. I drew supplies, including extra M-33 grenades and two phosphorus grenades. Phosphorus grenades were truly deadly weapons. On detonation they launched a spectacular blossom of white-hot bits that seared their way through human tissue, continuing to burn even inside the body. They were larger than the M-33 and considerably heavier. The natives could not throw them far enough to escape the blast, so if we had to use them, I thought they would probably be more safely thrown over the cliffside where, at the very least, they would make such a show that everyone below in FOB 4 would instantly know that something important had justified their use.

I selected five of the Nungs, counting Nhi, so that we'd be a team of six with a pair of binoculars. For this local mission, we filled our packs with C-rations for two days. [C-rations were (are) concentrated tea, coffee, cocoa, a can of Spam or something that was supposed to be a ham omelet, mystery meat, some bland tasting crackers made of wheat concentrates, and the like, all packed into individual tins and packaged in a thin cardboard box about 3"x 7". The cans were not labeled, so you never knew what you were getting until you opened them with the little P-38 can opener included in each package. Sometimes you'd get lucky and discover that one of the tins contained fruit cocktail, a prize worth hoarding.]

Once equipped, we sat and waited for the old Deuce-and-a-half to collect us. I hated the waiting. Soon we were driven out the main gate, then turned south on the baking hot road for several hundred meters. We turned left again onto a hard-packed dirt road that led into a small neighborhood of surprisingly well-built single story houses clustered in the shade of trees just on the other side of the mountain. In fact, a few were built right against the base rocks, incorporating the mountain itself as a wall. A few sullen Vietnamese emerged from their doorways to regard us with wordless intensity. They were doubtless counting us and noting our weapons. Their looks confirmed to me why the village was suspected of being a center of VC sympathies. As we jumped down from the truck, it was easy to see that, VC sympathizers or not, the natives resented our presence deeply.

I liked the relative cool of the area beneath their tall trees, where the ground had been worn clear of any undergrowth and visibility was good. Little tufts of grass and brave clumps of wild flowers here and there hung bent in the dusty shadows, lending the place an incongruous hint of forlorn domesticity. From the native point of view the community was ideally situated–shaded from the sun, cooled by sea breezes, and at the foot of an endless supply of the material from which they carved their livelihood. Before the Americans came, they must have enjoyed unrestricted access to the sea, too .

The road continued on through the settlement and out to the beach, where I knew from having seen it from the air, that it led to the tents of the Third Amtrac's U.S. Marine base, a location I liked even less than our own. Why would U.S. Marines set up in a location that required access and egress through any native village, especially one of widely doubted allegiance? I was anxious about our trek to the top of Marble Mountain but glad that we would not have to traverse through the whole village.

Between some fallen boulders fringed in bushes we found the entrance to the foot trail leading to the top of the mountain. It began among some large base rocks where much of the stone had been harvested over the years by the cutters. We started up in single file behind Nhi, moving as quickly as the steep incline allowed, often pushing off the lower stones and grabbing higher ones to leverage ourselves upward along the well-worn path. I didn't like the vulnerability invited by the fact that we had to sling weapons in order to use both hands for climbing. There were places where the bushes encroached on the path, offering good cover to anyone above—places where a burst of automatic fire or a couple of grenades sent tumbling down would have quickly wiped out our entire little party of six.

When at last we emerged unmolested into the little clutch of outcroppings at the summit, I was struck by the spectacular view. There is an odd feeling of power that resides in high places. I could see for miles off to the west across the endless waves of treetops in their limitless expressions of green. Up the coast to the north, the sea, soundless in the distance and flashing like broken mirrors, washed listlessly the long crescent of China Beach and its miniature tents where some of the medical staff were out swimming. I focused the glasses on them and saw a few of the nurses relaxing on their beach towels, poured out like honey in the sun. Beyond lay the tin roofs of Da Nang's toy houses, and farther, the shimmering concrete runways of the airport. To the east the blue South China Sea stretched across the curvature of the earth in the direction of freedom, far from the talons of The Beast. The USS New Jersey floated in the cerulean vastness like a forgotten matchstick, robbed of its power by this insolent trick of perspective. I allowed myself to see the wider scale of things for a short while and to appreciate the pristine majesty of the country's terrible beauty. Yet all of it soon began to glare back, brooding with bad feeling. It seemed to resent even a few moments of unguarded appreciation.

Below us, over the shoulder of the mountain, what I could see of the FOB 4 compound appeared very small, its gleaming little roof planes no more significant than some artifice on a tabletop train set. I had been right about the limited use of this location as a listening post or a lookout. The mountain's crest rocks obscured more than half the view of our camp, leaving completely unobservable that portion of it most within a rifle shot. The shots fired at the movie crowd could not have come from here on top. This argued for an enemy observation point farther down. To the southeast, though, I could see over the trees to the whole of Third Amtracs' beach compound.

We quickly set up for the night where we could crouch in the limited spaces available among the rocks. The ground around the man-sized stones was littered with the crushed C-ration tins of previous occupants, and the place smelled of urine. American-issue footprints covered the area, so I could not tell if any of the other kind had been made between our patrols. I turned on the radio and sent the on-site code, and we settled in to listen and to watch for any movement. We were actually fairly well protected from direct fire by the large number of boulders cropped about us, but we were open to the sky, and the effect of a mortar round or well-placed grenade would have been made even worse by the rocks themselves.

That night a bright moon rose into the clear night, a bomber's moon, soft and saffron misted to look at, but it bathed the backs of our hands and the rocks of our little aerie in a flood of harsh pewter light. The deep shadows of our every movement fell sharp upon the ground and leaned upon the rock faces in defiant facsimile of any effort to remain still. Far below, rectangles of yellow window light fanned across the open spaces of FOB 4, the American bases to the north twinkled with scattered lights, and at the far end, the city of Da Nang was a constellation of tiny points of light wavering in the night heat. Way off to the west, across the moonlit forest, yellow lightning pulsed beyond the black cut-out of the horizon. Through the binoculars long tendrils of mist captured in the distant flashes swept southward below the clouds. Some, swollen at their tops, appeared to support like ghostly pillars the lowering bulk of a storm, while through rifts in its arches, slabs of moonlight fell between the columns, down upon flickering patches of jungle. I was glad not to be out there, wherever it was.

In the morning, after a balmy, uneventful night, the blazing copper eye of the sun burst over the horizon like a shout. The temperature shot up 15 or 20 degrees in seconds. We cowered in what little rock shadow we could, but it soon shrank to nothing. Since the enemy—assuming the caves were occupied—could not by now have failed to know about our outpost, I saw no reason to broadcast radio reports in code or to refrain from whatever small sounds might accompany opening and heating our rations.

We made a small stove from an abandoned tin can and placed a hunk of C-4 explosive in the opening. When lit by a match, the C-4 burns intensely for several seconds, plenty of time to heat the contents of a little C-ration can to boiling, and it makes very little smoke. In this way we made hot coffee, and those who wanted to could heat each meal by simply pinching off another piece of the explosive. Even bland food is enormously improved by heat, and thus the tedium and preoccupation with the dangers that accompanied our posting were temporarily somewhat relieved.

About mid-morning, while scanning about with the binoculars, I noticed a foot patrol leaving the compound at Third Amtracs. The tiny Marines were split into two columns, one on each side of the dirt road, with a leader out in front, as they made their way toward the stone cutters' village. I focused in on them, and noticed that the leader's fatigues were darker than the others. From this I concluded that he was fairly new to the country. The sand was blowing sideways across their course, and had it not been for that, I might never have noticed the danger that lay hidden in the road ahead of them. Like a rock just beneath the surface of a stream, the moving sand revealed the tell-tale "v" signature of the pressure-sensitive triggering prongs of at least two heavy land mines.

I got immediately on the radio and called HQ to call Third Amtracs and halt the patrol. I did not know the frequencies used by the Marines but assumed that we were coordinating our excursions to some degree, and that somebody at our base would know how to call them. I kept the radio phone to my ear and went back to watching the patrol as it approached the mines.

Nothing was happening to stop the men on the road. My anxiety soared as I watched helplessly the growing inevitability.

They were mere yards from the little "v" marks when the man in the middle of the column with a radio antenna protruding into the air from his backpack raised a hand and evidently called something to the leader. The leader stopped the patrol, and his Radio Telephone Operator ran up and passed him the hand set. I watched the drama unfolding through the glasses, as the leader put the hand set to his ear under the rim of his steel helmet. Then he leaned forward as through peering ahead, said something else into the radio phone, then motioned for his R/TO to resume his place in the column. I expected at that point to see the leader call an about face or to walk back through the men and call for the patrol to follow him back to the camp. Instead, he raised his right arm into the air, and with a classic John Wayne "wagons ho" gesture, started them forward again. I couldn't believe it. In six or seven paces the tension through the glasses was so great I could hardly hold them steady.

Suddenly there was a flash in the ground, and a large geyser of sand erupted beneath him, separating his legs and sending the scraps of his body, weapon, and gear tumbling upward. The men near the front were blown backward, some to lie still. Others scattered, dove to the ground, or ran away from the explosion. The remnants of the leader fell back to the ground at about the same time that the distant sound of the detonation reached me. I could only stare unbelieving through the lenses as the little figures tried to collect themselves. Soon an ambulance truck emerged from their compound. Stupid.

The next day we were told that we were to be relieved. We collected our gear and made our way back down the difficult pathway among the rocks to meet the truck. We found it parked in the shade of the trees, the driver having a casual smoke in the open cab with his feet up. The whole village felt different now, openly hostile and glaring, but the driver's thoughts were evidently elsewhere, oblivious both to the sound of our approach and to the palpable menace that soaked the air around him. He was surprised when I told him to get us the hell out of there immediately.

Back at FOB 4, it felt as though I had just completed a refresher course on the insecurity of our position. The contained relief I allowed myself to feel at returning intact from the field was tempered again by the cloying unpredictability of living at the base of that mountain. I couldn't understand why neither we nor the Marines had secured the mountain or cleared the stone cutters' village before locating bases at these demonstrably indefensible thresholds. We had only come through the big attack because of air power, and it had just been dramatically demonstrated that the Marines could neither access nor leave their base without passing through a community that was openly hostile to them. Perhaps, I thought, the Marines welcomed in some odd way, the presence of this threat. I had often overheard visitors from Third Amtracs bragging in our clubhouse about the number of men the Marines lost in various engagements, as though their losses lent the living a sort of spurious nobility, the fairy dust touch of survivor magic. Perhaps their training taught them more about frontal assault and fatal gesture than it did about being spared, or perhaps Marine Corps tradition requires an occasional lunatic dance on the lips of mortality to animate their tradition of fearlessness. Maybe it was simply that larger losses enriched proportionally the quality of one's day-to-day survival, with its attendant euphoria providing an irrepressible need to talk.

None of it made sense to me, and not only because in Special Forces philosophy open engagement was to be avoided if possible, but also because my own experiences so far had produced a profoundly humbling need to employ my faculties in cutting back the despair, to set a wedge against the bitterness, the fear, and the impotent gnawing resentment. Dwelling upon our dead served only to animate The Beast, stirring it into menacing propinquity.

There was a new arrival at the club that afternoon: a loud, pink-skinned blond Staff Sergeant named McKibbon, who—he informed us proudly—had just been kicked out of Officer's Candidate School for disciplinary reasons, but he had completed enough of the course to be released back into the pool of enlisted ranks as an E-6. He was personable, very funny, and the force of his personality soon captured the attention of everyone in the room. It was hard not to like him, even though his sense of humor bordered dangerously on boorishness. He had been assigned to one of the recon teams, though he seemed a bit physically large for the job. I guessed he would probably lose 20 pounds or more fairly quickly anyway.

A few days later, I was sitting in the messhall around mid-day, when I was joined at the table by two guys I didn't know. They were scheduled to go out shortly on operation. As we spoke, the one nearest me, a short man somewhat older than me with black wavy hair and a squarish jaw line, asked me to pass him a serviette. I had never heard the word before and asked what he meant. He smiled and said he was Canadian and that was their word for napkin. As I passed him the napkin dispenser, we began to talk. He identified himself as a mercenary who, though a Corporal with us, had been a Major in the U.N. forces. Working with US Special Forces and Bolivian guerrillas, he had been with the party that had trapped and killed Che Guevara a few years earlier. In fact, he had been the one who identified the body. This was interesting information, but before we could get any deeper into the subject they got the call to "mount up" and had to go. I wished the Canadian good luck and went back to my lunch.

The next morning word came down that one of our teams had run into big trouble. The R/TO had gotten out a desperate call that the indij had turned on them. The bodies were being brought back that afternoon, and the Colonel wanted the whole camp to turn out to meet the choppers.

Accordingly, we assembled on the landing pad at the appointed time. The mood was somber but nobody seemed to know what to expect. When the aircraft approached the Colonel stepped out from somewhere in the crowd and took a position in front. Two machines landed. With the helicopter rotors swinging slowly overhead, some guys began to off load six body bags. The Colonel called us all to salute as the bags were laid out on the ground in a line. He then ordered them to be zipped open, and when each had been folded back like lapels and the contents within revealed, he suddenly lurched toward the nearest. He dropped to his knees, and between some indecipherable animalistic noises, began addressing the bodies as though trying to rouse them from sleep. He moved from one to the next, speaking to them, asking them questions, and slapping at them companionably. He kissed the dead faces, hugged them, and grasped their hands in his. He seemed to have entered a private world of theatrical grief. It was disturbing to watch, like an under-rehearsed play. Even weird. I thought perhaps it was a deliberate performance intended to communicate to the rest of us how much he cared about his men, but it was conducted with such an element of self-conscious zeal that at least its outward aspects seemed entirely bogus. A few of us were exchanging quizzical looks by the time he reached the last rubber bundle on the ground.

Then he rose and gave a short speech. His eyes would not settle. They dodged about erratically as he admonished us all to be ready to make a similar sacrifice, as surely many of us would be called to do. He may have been trying to inspire us with his confidence and trust, but his words had the opposite effect. This was not a time to tell your people they were going to die too, especially in this particularly uncontrolled and gruesome way. It was the fate of which the recon teams were always conscious anyway and against which we struggled to neutralize our fear, to sanitize the unknowable. We did not need a venue like this to be reminded.

If he had dwelt entirely on the sacrifice these men had made, he might have come closer to his intended point, but as he continued I came to realize for perhaps the first time that just because someone is in a position of authority it doesn't mean he is immune to madness. My questionable first impressions of him were dramatically reinforced by this outrageous show. I would have preferred to think that he was simply a bit clumsy with public speaking and engaging in an ill-judged effort to demonstrate some version of leadership, whereby he was inadvertently revealing his dismay at life's ferocious indifference to the drums of his ambition, but I soon came to the conviction that he had long been campaigning tirelessly on behalf of error. He may have been unstable to begin with. Perhaps it was a response to the pressures of his job, where everyone—both commander and commanded—lived in a world of trickling unknowns in which all decisions, judgments and conclusions were uncertain, speculative, all information incomplete, and careers rose or fell by the subtleties of conjecture. Perhaps he was haunted by some fork in the path of his life taken long ago, and he was struggling now unconsciously, probably with the very lives of his men, to retreat from a foothold in the madhouse. I stood there sweating quietly, breathing in the lifeless air beneath an acetylene sun, listening without conviction to this monstrous performance and watched all the destiny drain out of him.

I looked around and saw that if I had correctly guessed the purpose of his demonstration, his words had fallen wide of their intention. Most of us looked decidedly uncomfortable with the whole thing. It wasn't just the gruesome display of our compatriot's remains. That was bad enough, but most of us had seen such things before. What turned the afternoon into a lost crusade was the lasting damage worked into the air between us and the Commander by the insidious fingers of doubt.

Then, after successfully creating a mood like one of a yellow jaundice ward on the banks of a swamp, he stepped aside and ordered us all to pass in review of the bodies. We dutifully lined passed. At first I could tell only that one of them was McKibbon, the new guy. His face was undamaged, but much of his shirt had been shot away, revealing that the exposed skin of his chest, belly, and sides was torn with numerous bullet holes which had not bled. They had been fired into him after his heart had stopped, an alarming testament to the fanaticism of the shooter. Killed on his first mission, his skin, pale as veal, had not had time to tan.

Next to him was a corpse I could not at first identify, and from its small size assumed was one of the indij. It was blackened and greasy. Then I realized with a shock that it was so short because the head was missing. All that remained at the end of the trunk was a mangled flap of dark skin that had once contained a skull but now hung like an empty sock. There were slits in it where the eyes, the nose openings and mouth had been, from which a fragment of the right mandible with a few teeth protruded. Much of the left side appeared to be missing, and it had a small patch of moist, wavy black hair. With a start I knew who it had been–the Canadian of the serviettes. The other four bodies were very badly shot up and disfigured—all that remained of the native mercenaries who presumably hadn't turned, though someone near me expressed doubts about one of them. It was strange how dark the skin of all the corpses but McKibbon's had become.

When we were finally dismissed from the ritual, I noticed that the Colonel was already gone. I imagined him throwing up in the officers' shower. The images of the bodies continued to haunt me. Again, the message they pleaded was, "put yourself in my place"–a condition my new job made perilously intimate. I didn't know how many had gone out on this trip, but the profoundly lifeless objects lying in those open bags appeared to be the work of at least two men with weapons on full automatic.

Despite his bombast, I had liked McKibbon right away, the Canadian too. The Canadian Corporal was experienced in conflict and probably understood the risks, but McKibbon had been sent out and "greased" before he had even a chance to learn just what we were doing. Their characters, personalities–whatever you call that mysterious and volatile spark of nature that makes us human–had appeared and then vaporized in an instant, like drops of water on a hot griddle. Yet despite the horrible appearance of the cadavers, I was strangely unmoved by it all. Their sudden absence had changed nothing for the rest of us, other than offering another deposit on our investment of doubts. Now, despite a twilight sort of memory of their personalities, we were left to continue inching along the brink of our own extinction while the world continued indifferently on without them, as though they had never been. Thus it would be, too, for each of us. The war was slashing apart the delicate tapestry of such tenuous companions as my own reticence allowed. We had all become marginalized entities in this place, abandoned probes into a realm unknown and connected to our memories of society only by a thick cord of longing.

A thunderous wave of apprehension washed through me when the next operational order came, and with it the realization that Command had not forgotten about me after all. Skulking about, keeping a low profile by minimizing daylight movement in the camp and attending only a few of the almost nightly movies, had evidently failed to achieve the desired measure of invisibility. In fact, as I was told in the briefing, I had been singled out for this one. It was to be a road watch across the Laotian border on the complex of heavily trafficked jungle tracks known collectively as the Ho Chi Minh Trail.

Even though the Trail offered its own set of risks to insertion and extraction of the team, at least this was to be strict reconnaissance and not an interdiction mission or a "people snatch." By now, everything I'd heard about people snatch missions had corroborated the warnings Sgt. Johnson had made clear, so my renewed anxiety over another mission was marginally leavened by the fact that whoever had selected my team for this one had not asked for the dangers that attached to prisoner captures.

There is a region about 120 miles almost due west of Da Nang where the border with Laos bulges into South Vietnam in a large salient visible only on maps but fringed to the west in photographs by the occasional delicate tracery of a meandering mud road. We were to set up along the infamous trail concealed wherever we could find a place from which we could take a running two- or three-day count of all foot and vehicular traffic.

In the briefing, Grayson and I were shown several aerial photographs of the trail which revealed that, even the day following an accurate B-52 Arclight strike on the road, gangs of hand shovelers enabled the trucks to keep rolling by the simple but labor intensive expedient of clearing back the blown earth rim of each impact crater where it affected the road. Thus the transports, both motorized and those drawn by animals, just drove down into the bomb craters and back out the other sides, continuing south with whatever they carried. Our high-tech interdiction was doing some disruptive good, but appeared to be effecting little more than a temporary deterrent, an inconvenience that simply delayed for some hours the continuing supply and deployment operations out of the north and into the tri-border area of Laos, Cambodia and South Vietnam.

From the unbroken canopy of jungle in the pictures I could see no place where the team could be inserted and said so. I was told we had been doing this enough that the pilots knew where to land. I didn't like the implications of this precedent, of anything that implied an operational pattern and its attendant predictability. I decided the only recourse was to place some reluctant faith in at least that portion of the whole doubt-ridden system that left control of our particular fate up to ourselves.

The briefing ended with the surprising information that I would be given a flyover of the proposed insertion area the next day. Having gained helpful perspective on the AO that actually resulted in the success of the mission by flying over the crash sight on our last operation, I wondered why flyovers did not appear to be standard operating procedure, but knew that even if I asked there would be no satisfactory answer.

Accordingly, the following morning I was driven over to an air station near China Beach, where a large number of helicopters were parked along both sides of a runway paved for small fixed-wing aircraft. There I met the pilot of an Army 0-1 "Bird Dog." He was a tall, good-looking poster boy-type Warrant Officer a few years older than me, and although he presented the very picture of competent authority in his one-piece olive drab flight suit with its zippers and oddly angled cargo pockets, I detected in his manner a vague reservation, a degree of controlled reluctance, and his dark eyes were cold like oil.

He picked up his white helmet with its sun visors, checked an enormous wrist watch that resembled an alarm clock with a belt, and we strode out into the igneous glare of the sun to where the plane rocked gently in the hot breeze that raked the tarmac. The doors on both sides of the cockpit had been removed, exposing the entire interior of the plane, so I saw that it would be a breezy ride. He caressed the air with the back of his hand in a gesture for me to climb into the rear seat and made sure I was securely buckled into the seat parachute. He then plugged the rear seat headset into the plane's intercom system and climbed into the front seat, his weight causing the light aircraft to lurch.

Once he was buckled in, he switched on the intercom. It made an intimate metallic click in my ear. He started what amounted to his pre-flight briefing:

"Can you hear me okay?"

"Yessir."

Then after a few standard instructions about adjusting the volume control and the fit of the headset, he asked,

"D'ya see that joy stick on the floor between your feet?"

I looked down and saw a spare aircraft joy stick secured flat to the floor in a pair of pressure clamps.

"Yeah."

"Okay. Now, see that socket below it?"

I looked again and saw through a small opening in the floor there was a kind of universal joint into which the U-shaped base of the stick evidently fit so that the back seat passenger could control the airplane from there, although it wasn't obvious just how the stick might fit into it.

"...er, yeah."

"Alright. Now if anything should happen to me, you take the stick out of the floor clamps and put it in that socket. Pull it back, we go up; push it forward, we go down; left is left and right is right. Got it?"

"Er..."

"Now, when we get hit (*When? Not if?*), you'll feel the whole plane jolt. I'll tell ya' if we have to jump. The pilot's the last to leave the ship, but if I say 'Go!' and you say 'What?', you'll be talking to yourself. Got it?"

"...Um..."

He started the engine. It sent a shudder down the fuselage, and we taxied down to the opposite end of the runway while he talked over the radio to Control, and I watched the passing ground reflecting off the underside of the wings where four small-bore rockets rode on wing-mounted racks close inboard on each side. I had always wanted to take flying lessons but had never ridden in a single engine plane before and so looked forward to the flight with curiosity tempered by my customary reluctance to attract the notice of fate.

We climbed out sharply, reaching for altitude beyond rifle range, and turned west over the wilderness. During the flight, the niggling sense of doubt I had first detected in the pilot's demeanor was confirmed when he told me that he had been shot down once already. It was clear he didn't want to repeat the experience. He didn't explain how he'd been rescued, but I thought that at least on this flight we might be flying at a higher altitude than we may have otherwise.

Below us the featureless jungle terrain revealed nothing helpful. Even when we had worked our way over to the border, remaining high, I could see only an intermittent crease in the tree line to the west marking the cut of the trail itself, I saw no place for the team to be inserted. We received no ground fire, and as we turned back, the pilot said he wanted to fly a bit farther south to a place where there had been trouble in the past. That sounded to me like a place to be avoided even at altitude, but he altered course staying at least high enough to frustrate small arms fire from the ground.

Soon a massive stone outcrop rose almost vertically out of the jungle. It had an island of forest on top with a long spine that sank gradually back under the sea of trees to the east. It seemed to be a good observation position for anyone on the ground, as it looked out over the endless canopy through an arc of roughly 100 degrees for miles.

My speculation about it was interrupted by another click. "Here it is. We've taken ground fire from this place before. Hold on."

With that, he tilted us abruptly up into a wingover, rolling almost completely inverted, and as I hung from the belts with my eyeballs pulsing, and the ground ahead of us spun upside down, he fired a pair of rockets that erupted from the wings with twin loud bangs! and streaked away at the ends of long snaking trails of hypnotic white smoke toward the cliffs below, where they converged at a point in the shadows under the verge of trees in a burgeon of flame. Then he rolled back level, only to pull into a tight climbing turn to come around again.

He repeated the maneuver, firing off another pair of rockets on two more passes, and though I was nerve-thrilled by the spectacle and the g-forces, it seemed that anyone on the ground in that place would by then be annoyed enough at our lingering overhead to launch whatever form of retaliation they had at hand. My instincts were all for getting out of there. Apparently, his were too, for he pulled sharply away with a pair of rockets still on board, presumably in case they might be needed on the way home.

On the way back at 1500 feet, we flew over a scar in the jungle that contained an old abandoned runway, the pavement a puzzle of cracks in which the vegetation had returned with a violence of energy, impatient to conceal and reclaim all traces of men's feeble scratchings at its belly. A few broken buildings slouched beside it, peering out from beneath the trees with smoke-blackened windows. The pilot told me it was the ruins of an old Special Forces A camp that had been overrun some five years before. Skewed off the runway, bleached and partially overgrown, its sharp lines melting into the grasp of surrounding jungle, was a disabled C-130, limp and broken in the trees with much of its upper surface paint weathered away. The pilot explained that the aircraft had been trying to rescue the Special Forces team when it was mortared on the take-off roll. Before anyone could escape the crash the VC had come in and killed them all. He said he sometimes flew by in tribute because the guys were all still inside, that no attempt to retrieve the bodies had ever been made.

As we passed over it I could see even from our altitude that the cargo door at the back of the C-130 was still down, a dark opening to the silent mystery of its interior. It was a spooky, poignant sight, a strange and profoundly disconcerting little smear in the vast and hostile jungle, visible only from the air, isolated far beyond practicable access.

Farther to the east and closer to the relative safety of the American presence on the coast, the pilot indulged his love of aerobatics with a series of loops and aileron rolls. It was fun, not only because of the unusual experience, but also because they revealed the pilot's more relaxed confidence, and the certainty it implied of our arriving back safely.

Once on the ground, I thanked him, and one of the clerks at the station called FOB 4 to send someone to pick me up. The flight had been an education in a number of ways, but none of which served its purpose. I arrived back at the base tired and no better informed of our LZ or the AO in general than I had been before.

That afternoon I initiated our preparations to go. This time I drew two extra compasses, one for Grayson and the other sneaked to Nhi. I also picked up two cans of the mixed CS powder and dried goat's blood, just in case of trackers using dogs. I was instructed to carry a supply of sabotaged Soviet rifle ammunition, code named "Eldest Son," in case we should happen upon an enemy supply dump or a cache hidden along the trail, so I added a Chinese-made bandolier of compromised Russian AK ammo to my load. Our Intel people had substituted C-4 explosive for the powder in this ammunition, and if we were to encounter one of the many ammo bunkers known to be scattered in the jungle along the trail, we would try to insert the bandolier into their stockpile. As soon as an attempt was made to use it, the explosion would destroy a rifle and probably the shooter, too. Thereafter the entire contents of the bunker from which it had been drawn became compromised, and the enemy would have to destroy it all.

I really didn't like the idea of being sent out to a place where the enemy was *known* to be operating in numbers. So far I'd been dispatched to areas where the enemy *might* be, was even very likely to be, but now we were headed deliberately into their traffic. If we were discovered, there would be no escape. I was still haunted by the image of the dead Special Forces camp I'd seen from the air, and the prospect that now loomed before us boded ill for a quick extraction. Despite the lingering pain in my shoulder, I wanted to keep the radio nearer than would be possible if anyone else carried it, much to Grayson's secret relief. This time, I selected four of the Nungs, so six of us went on standby dressed again in our Chinese cloth fatigues.

We were held up for most of two days by bad weather in the area of the proposed LZ, so when we finally flew out following reports of clearing conditions to the west, it was in the debilitating aftermath of a 40-hour standby alert. I was tired and tense before we even left. After a long, nervous flight, a shift in engine tone foretold our descent. I looked out to get some idea of the area and to search for any openings in the trees. If there were any gaps or breaks in the canopy with unusual shapes from the air, I might be able to use them as reference points when calling for the extraction when (or if) that might be. Ahead and off to the left, a bit to the south, white-topped clouds with the rain wrung from them were breaking up over the jungle, but the uniformity of the canopy gave no signs.

As it happened, the insertion down through an abrupt and tiny opening in the trees went without a serious hitch, both helicopters letting down and racking out in turn. As before, when we leapt off the choppers, I was immediately pulled off balance by the heft of the radio and the pain it reawakened, but I was glad to have it with me, even in the dash for cover. We assembled on the jungle floor for a long precautionary time, watching in perimeter while our hearing gradually returned. I was especially anxious to be able to hear. There were bad stories about being around the trail, and I wished with impotent religious fervor, not to become a featured player in the next one. As I heard the choppers depart I wondered again if this would be a bad place, the wrong place, maybe even the last place, and whether they'd made a terrible mistake this time.

I could not tell exactly how far from the trail we had been let out but estimated that cautious progress to the west for about two days, maybe three, would bring us close. The jungle here was thick, limiting visibility to just a few yards. I lay there feeling thin and fragile, taking in the saturating strangeness of the place, which felt no less than before. Instead, it fattened and darkened in accumulating alienation. The oppressive tropical sun back-lit the canopy above in luminous green, tenting the lower growth with deep shadows that gripped narrow shafts of light in which thousands of tiny insects darted and swirled. Despite my long acclimatization, the heavy sultry air among the trees was breathless and seething. It felt like hot silk, while the radio exerted its own weight upon my effort to draw each breath. Parasite ferns nested all around us in clumps of humus rotted into the massive tree trunks, and leaves shaped like enormous demon's ears wagged lazily in our faces, nudged by the hot, torpid air. Dark roots lurched from the damp black soil like huge gnarled fingers grasping for a hold on the surface. Everything seemed to be growing with a savage violence.

In the penumbral shadow world beneath the great trees, life teems in a tensely abstract fashion, not unlike that in a great city, where creatures who co-exist in close quarters move among one another on incomprehensibly separate agendas. Sometimes their lives intersect briefly with painful consequences, but most often, everywhere just want to be left alone. The force that crosses this line most often are the insects whose mindless courses fill the air and whose instinctive response to body heat is voracious and inescapable.

Here the high moisture content in the rot of the jungle floor kept the ground alive with movement. The undergrowth twitched as small serpents, enormous insects, and land crabs scuttled away, launched by our sudden trespass upon their frenzied errands. It was all alarming, the menacing menagerie seeming to justify the irrational conviction that some determined beast may lurk nearby. I tried to keep calm, for not only did I not want to be bitten, I was so attuned to any motion that even the natural inhabitants of the ground could startle up a hot rush of adrenalin, and each little surge left me incrementally depleted.

In scanning about, I looked overhead and noticed that a gossamer lace of spider web pearled with dew drops netted the gaps between several lower growth stems. Then suddenly my whole body whipped taut when I saw that it sagged beneath the stealthy tread of its large, wooly architect. I had never seen a scarier spider. To me it looked like a fur-bearing softball mitt, and it spiked my anxiety to crawl out of there before the thing could drop on one of us, especially me.

It was, though, a useful sign of what to expect of the terrain in which we had been deposited. If an insect of any kind could grow to such a size, it meant there was plenty of food for it, which in turn meant moisture, and therefore it was likely that we would encounter soupy ground.

At long last, I saw that the others were responding to the little sounds I was beginning to hear. I signaled for us to move at least far enough away from the spider web for me to unlimber the radio and send our insertion confirmation. We low-crawled beneath the ground growth for several yards, then stopped long enough for me to make the transmission. Once the radio was re-secured I checked the compass, showed Nhi my intended number, and indicated to the rest of the team our rough direction. I looked back at the spider with relief. It must have been disappointed.

The going was exceedingly slow, the jungle impeding both movement and visibility, and the effort it exacted, too soon exhausting. I was drenched in minutes, swallowing dryly, with my vision obscured by sweat that coursed into my eyes and mouth. It tasted vaguely metallic. Although keeping a fairly close order, we were soon spread out far enough that I lost sight of all but the man ahead and the one behind me. The ground was moist and spongy with a damp carpet of dead leaves and the rotting remnants of long-fallen branches, through which rose bright green ferns and thousands of tiny seedlings. Hardly any earth was visible through this blanket of malodorous rotting things where the foliage provided its own soil.

Up to a height of twelve feet or more a dense undergrowth of saplings and palms of all kinds–office plants allowed their full expression–hid the roots of the giants, and out of this wavering sea of dimly illuminated groundcover rose straight upwards, with no apparent decrease in thickness, countless tree trunks for a hundred and fifty feet and more before they burgeoned into a solid ceiling of dappled green which almost entirely closed out all but a secondary version of sunlight. High above, where the monstrous stems spread into branches, fantastic hanging gardens of mosses and ferns formed a drapery of parasitic creepers, some bare and intertwined like ropes, others, thick as a man's thigh, occasionally broke into huge ribbed leaves large enough to shield two people from a heavy rain. Everywhere vines and their attendant creepers hung straight down from the heights to the ground, where many had taken root again and looped themselves from tree to tree like the jumbled rigging of wrecked ships.

We moved slowly through this wilderness, often crawling on our stomachs, for two and a half days. During this time, as the effort to move, the constant nervous tension, and the temperature sapped our strength, the heat stalked the spaces between the trees like a living presence, hugging us, and the damp ground drew energy from our bodies each night. I began to develop a dull apathy to the relentless conditions, an entirely temporary but recurring indifference to what-ever impending doom might lie in wait somewhere ahead.

There were times when odd words or images filtered up unprompt-ed from the chambers of memory–a snatch of song or verse would throb with the pulse in my ears, a headline, a half-remembered event, or some quotation–in a kind of surrealistic bubble which declined to burst. All such thoughts were rooted in experiences far removed from our situation, all doubtless symptomatic of the mind's effort to escape the reality, yet under them all remained the inescapable mandate to remain alert, to keep watching and listening for any tiny sign that something did not fit the patterns of sound, movement, or smell.

None of it let up at night. The voracious presence of a countless-in-sect chorus filled the arboreal canyons with their deep reverberations, masking all but the most proximate sounds. Croaking and chuckling, creaking and ticking, unidentifiable shrieks, hoots, and grunts, often repeated from different places, now close, now far, the continually shifting noises echoed among the trees against a deep background of steady sound. Then a sudden, momentary silence would cut through the noise, and I would tense with alarm, only to hear the symphony begin again. Sometimes the torpid moisture of the night carried an errant hint of fragrance, a strand of floral perfume which wafted for a moment atop the dank redolence of jungle rot to sweeten the shad-ows with sad and unnamed blossoms that must have been shed in the dark, for I never sensed or saw them during the day. I lay upon the damp ground and listened intently for any sudden shift in the pattern of sounds, craning my ears for signals, sorting for disruptions, alert to any coherent sign of formal possibilities, and rose before light each day sleepless and strung tight on nervous energy.

On the afternoon of the third day we happened upon an anomaly. Hemmed among the bases of several large trees, we encountered a collection of withered branches with graying leaves. The pile didn't fit its surroundings. They were not random deadfall and lay together more or less aligned–and the stems had been cut. We stopped and lay still, listening to the twittering silence of the forest for a long time. Nothing moved. At last Nhi rose from the undergrowth ahead, peered around through the lower vegetation, then turned and signaled to me. He moved stealthily toward the pile. I rose and followed, circling out to keep separation and to flank the structure.

Heart pounding, I flipped the safety off as we split and approached the drying camouflage from two sides. Overhead the canopy was closed, which made the attempt to cover whatever this was a curious effort. Nothing stirred within the pile of branches. Trying to swallow my gasping, I remained low, braced for surprise. A quick look back showed me that the remainder of the team with Grayson had spread out and were keeping good cover, watching all around, not just in our direction.

Gradually Nhi and I closed on the strange pile. He eased a branch away, revealing an entrance to an underground munitions cache bunkered with musty sandbags. It was a partial dugout overlain with logs and then disguised with cut branches that had since been neglected long enough to dry. That indicated the site had not been tended in perhaps a week, but I could see nothing that hinted at the pattern or schedule, if any, of its use. Although some of the ground around the entrance had been cleared and trampled in places, there were no discernible footprints and no useful signs on the pressed vegetation. Evidently no one had visited this place at least since the last rain. It was eerie and profoundly uncomfortable to be in the presence of so much of the enemy's equipment. It held their presence strongly and seemed to stand in surrogate of their imminent arrival. With growing anxiety that we might be compromised while we lingered over this important discovery, I gave up trying to puzzle out the implications of the cache's neglect in the face of this opportunity to sabotage the supplies within and get away.

I got Nhi to remove the bandolier of "Eldest Son" ammunition from my pack and, careful not to leave a boot print anywhere, leaned into the low entrance. Though not deep, it was musty and dark, and it smelled vaguely of gun oil, muddy earth, and the ubiquitous rancidity of the enemy's presence–*nuoc mam*. Several wood crates rested on a rubber tarp which had evidently been placed to repel moisture from the ground, and another tarp covered them. I could not read the nomenclature stamped on the boxes, but thanks to the universal use of the numbering system, I recognized the designation for caliber. If they weren't using these boxes for something else, then each contained standard AK ammunition. I was also concerned to see several U.S. ammo boxes, too, probably stolen or captured. For a fleeting moment I thought to take one or two of them back but decided that they were probably being used here to store AK ammo. Besides, the collapsible handles on the top of U.S. ammo boxes always rattled–something we could not afford–and they held enough that the contents would be heavy, so I decided not to take any with us.

I reached in and carefully lifted the lid of a wooden case containing rifle ammo and added the bandolier of sabotaged bullets to the contents. I folded the corner of the tarp back the way it was, and Nhi replaced the covering branch. As far as I could tell, we had left no trace.

Nhi and I returned to the team with an elevated awareness that this little cache was an indication that we were nearing our objective. My anxiety, already gorged on the discovery of the ammunition, now burst forth with a sense of looming hazard. All my senses filled with the stealthy belly-down crawl of peril.

In about an hour I glimpsed sunlight through the trees ahead, an opening in the jungle. We stopped and listened. Nothing. After another 30 meters or so of soft-footed progress, it was clear that we were approaching a wide gash in the forest. We had come upon sloping ground, higher on our right, and from our left we heard the quiet trickling of a stream. We waited. I thought that in view of the light ahead and the higher terrain to our right, we should move upward. If this was the actual edge of the Ho Chi Minh Trail, and if it presented any choice of concealment, I did not want to be on the same level with the road. I wanted to be in a position were we could look down on it. If we were detected, at least any pursuers would have to start by climbing uphill.

We moved to the right into an area of large trees growing so densely that it was hard to find enough space to lie down between them. The luxuriant, tangled undergrowth around them made for a pestilential and sinister bower, but it provided good cover. I crept in, eased over the roots to what by now was clearly the very edge of some opening, and then looked down upon the infamous muddy Trail itself.

It was streaked with the water-filled ruts of tire tracks and almost uniformly cupped with foot prints. I was well concealed behind the growth at the edge of what I saw to be a natural rise that had evidently been an obstruction to the builders of the road, and though there was a partial cut bank below, the trail had been cleared to go around its base in order to avoid unnecessary excavation, thus creating a short loop that made of the promontory where we lay a wooded peninsula affording a limited but extended view in both directions.

Here it was. I was looking at the renowned highway used to supply the VC in the south and to transport the NVA all along the western border of South Vietnam. I had heard it discussed and even crudely depicted for years on the nightly news back in the States, and even President Johnson had talked about it on nationwide television. Since arriving in-country, I had seen aerial photos of its activity, bomb damage, and monsoon washouts, and I had heard hair-raising stories of our intelligence-gathering and interdiction missions gone wrong in places along it. Suddenly I couldn't remember how I had come to be here from so far away.

We set up for the night in our position on the high ground, and I transmitted our RON and "objective reached" signals then settled in to observe and remember anything about the location that might be useful in affecting an escape. Visible on the opposite side of the road, about 60 meters or so off to our left, was one of the many bunkers varyingly spaced for miles along both sides of the road. It was a fairly large example of guerrilla engineering, a cross between an excavation and a beaver dam, made of logs, mud, cut branches, and gabion baskets of stone and earth. It was known that foot traffic fled into these makeshift bunkers when an American bombing raid was coming.

All was empty and still but for the bird calls in the jungle. We waited out the afternoon, listening for any non-jungle sound, hearing only the strange hoots, barking and mellifluous songs of the birds. My mind raced with possibilities as I tried to sort the likely scenarios of our being discovered from the merely more-or-less possible ones.

As darkness descended on the scene, Nhi, who had been lying nearby, rose stealthily from the ground. I wondered what he could be up to, and for a desperate wire-strung few moments remembered what happens when the indij turn on us. I lay still, expectant, and watched with mounting alarm as, keeping to the shadows, he quietly moved to the other Chinese and collected several of our M-1 foot mines. Then he stole down the slope to the very edge of the road. I didn't know what he was doing. My mind raced with panicked possibilities. Had I misplaced my trust? He might be giving up the whole team. Even if he was up to something else he might be spotted. It would compromise the whole team, and I had no idea how we could ever be pulled out if that happened. Trying to escape and evade in a shooting retreat through the jungle at night didn't even bear thinking about. He disappeared in the undergrowth at the edge of the road for a long time. None of the others stirred. I saw no movement and heard nothing from where I had last seen him. Several long minutes passed. Then he suddenly emerged from cover into the starlight and scampered barefooted across the road to duck into the black hulk of the bunker. With the exception of one step, he leapt from puddle to puddle on the road. After a short time he reappeared carrying only the horseshoe safety clips from the mines, retraced his steps across the road and shortly, to my unutterable relief, came up beside me with his boots on again, silent as a shadow. He held up the clips to show that he had buried the mines in the bottom of the bunker. This would serve to compromise the bunker, and over time as word spread, perhaps others, too. I allowed a smile to slip out to Nhi, squeezed his shoulder and went back to listening.

We were positioned miles beyond the alleged limits of the American presence in Southeast Asia, well beyond rapid or even acknowledgeable assistance, and so far our mission had accomplished two opportunistic acts of sabotage but had nothing to say for its official purpose, which was to make a traffic count on the Trail.

We lay there all the next day. Splinters of sunlight moved slowly through our position as the afternoon wore on. Then, late in the day, the heart-stopping grind of engines began to approach from the north. We tensed with expectation, and I involuntarily scrunched farther down into the ground. I pulled out the camera, and soon two old Russian-made trucks appeared, sluicing through the furrows. They lurched noisily past, dusty and covered with dried mud that looked as though it had been deliberately smeared on the upper surfaces by hand. They laced the air with exhaust smoke, their squeaks and mechanical lumbering suddenly offensive in the pristine wilderness. They seemed an odd representative for the vaunted volume of traffic that had so rutted the road. I managed to get photos of both and noted the time of day. That was it for several hours. The jungle sounds returned, but the trucks had reawakened my bleak dismay that the enemy was indeed smellably close at hand, and we were far beyond any hope of timely rescue.

As darkness came on, my anxiety rose, as always. Our discovery of the ammunition cache, the Trail only yards away, and our proximity to known enemy activity, all combined with the loss of visibility to become a conscious fear that wrapped around me like another skin. I tried to conceal from the others any sign of my growing discomfort by keeping my face down or turned to the road. After months of practice at hiding all semblance of emotion, I was getting seasoned, scared but in marginal control as long as nothing happened, but I still didn't trust my involuntary "tells." I put my head down that night wondering vaguely if this would be the end, if I would pull up the night's darkness like an existential quilt to wake up dead and at peace evermore.

During the night, real road traffic began. Trucks crested the hump below us and whined by, feeling their way along without lights and accompanied by intermittent groups of foot soldiers. In the starlight it appeared that some of the individual infantrymen carried rocket rounds in slings on their backs. There was a certain amount of talking and laughing among the walkers, but the motor traffic drowned out what little could be heard. I could not have understood what was said anyway, but I guessed that a few of the Nungs might be able to make out some of their words. I was listening for tones, as that might suggest attitudes, even states of health.

At one point, six trucks groaned slowly past, pitching on the uneven surface, and two or three companies of men walked with them. I counted the men as well as possible, but some passed on the opposite side of the trucks. Nor could I tell what the covered trucks were carrying. They might well have been shuttling troops who traded off with the walkers.

One man stopped not far away and squatted beside the road. Some of the others laughed as he left a watery deposit, but none stopped before he was able to move on. I wondered if it was a sign of sickness in their ranks or simply that he was a part of a group under urgent orders.

The last of the night traffic passed and quiet returned well before first light. I had kept notes during the night, but without light, had written many of my estimates down in large print, which I now saw were scrawled across several pages of my little notebook. As I was going over the figures to clarify the writing, I suddenly heard a faint, non-jungle tinkling and clunking sound. It was coming from the road a short way to the north, the direction the traffic had come from. We all tensed again immediately. I strained to hear, and as the sound grew slowly louder, peered up the road to see what was coming.

In the early gray light all color was muted, the open spaces only marginally paler than the vegetation in which we hid. Below us the dim sky lay streaked in the ruts. All remained still, but my heart thumped as the strange clattering grew closer. Then we saw him.

Ambling along alone, his feet squelching in the mud of the road, came a lone NVA soldier carrying a long pole across his shoulder. At each end of the pole hung a large cluster of 20 or more metal canteens which clattered as he walked. He must have been the lowest rank-ing or least popular guy in the company to have been dispatched to retrieve water for so many. The water weight alone would have been quite a burden on such a small person for his trek back. I took this as an indication that the unit he belonged to was not far away and that it did not have a water truck.

Then I remembered that we had heard a stream the day before. Af-ter the man passed our position, I signaled Nhi and the team to follow. We lay still until he was far enough in the direction of the stream to be well out of hearing, then I rose stiffly to my knees, and we quietly moved down the slope.

At first, I thought only to observe, to learn what we could from whatever he was doing, but a chance to grab a guy who was so obvi-ously alone soon appeared. Nhi signaled that he wanted to snatch him. Suddenly my mind raced with the implications of a capture. We were not supposed to try for a prisoner without first getting permission, as such attempts were so risky, and a radio call was out of the ques-tion. In order to capture him, we'd probably have to wound him first, which could be noisy and in any case would slow our retreat, and then I didn't know how we would get him back through three days of eva-sion and perhaps pursuit.

I decided there were just too many risks to Nhi's plan, that we should lie low until the little man was gone, then begin our trek back for extraction. After all, we had so far gotten away with what we'd been sent to do, and I had no interest in lingering a minute longer than we had to for any reason. Then, just as I raised my hand to signal Nhi to forget it, the little man stumbled into full view through the trees. He dropped his cluster of canteens beside the stream and knelt over a small pool with his back to us. He was muttering to himself, as I would probably have been in his place. He was unarmed and distracted.

While I was still trying to signal, Nhi drew his knife, and quick as a cat, he and one of the Nungs jumped the man. Nhi pressed the man's head into the ground with a hand over his mouth while he made a neat incision along his side, slicing right through the helpless little man's shirt in a single quick jab and draw. They hurriedly bound his mouth with a tourniquet tied tightly around his head and pulled him away from the stream. He made muffled noises but was so terrified that he soon stopped struggling. It was done so quickly and silently that it took me a moment to realize they had thought to wait until he had laid down all the canteens—and that we had a prisoner.

They pulled him to his feet. Nhi whispered something into the wild-eyed soldier's ear while pressing the blade of his bayonet under his chin. Whatever he said seemed to inspire immediate cooperation, and we set off immediately eastward through the jungle, away from the Trail and to the south of the route we had taken in. I did not want to cross again with the cache we had found on the way in.

We moved fairly steadily for the better part of an hour as the light improved, which brought us, by my estimate, about 200 meters or more from the road. It was still early, and I guessed that if our prisoner had been sent out on his water mission entirely alone, it might take a little more time before he would be missed. I couldn't be sure of course, but I had been living for so long now on the serrated edge of a world in which nothing was ever certain that this guess would have to serve.

With Nhi on point, the job of keeping a close threatening presence on our prisoner went to the one who had been in on the capture. He kept a hand on the poor man's shoulder and prodded him a bit with his knife every now and then, even though the captive gave every indication of doing whatever we wanted in order to avoid being stuck again.

He was quite young and obviously terrified. That was okay, as it assured his cooperation, at least for the time being. I watched him carefully, knowing that any attempt to break away would mean his life at the hands of the merciless Nungs, for whom I now held robust respect. As we continued I saw that his side was bleeding badly, and under the constant pressure to keep moving he was beginning to weaken. He'd been trembling almost to the point of incapacity from the beginning, but now he staggered noticeably.

I signaled for a halt, and as the team crouched on alert, I moved up to the prisoner who lay pressed to the ground by his keeper. I gave him a slight smile and patted him on the chest. He stared wildly up at me, securely gagged and chuffing short breaths through his nose, probably never having seen a white man before, especially one painted green. I lifted the bloody tail of his shirt. The wound was messy and bleeding steadily, but he was so dirty it was hard to tell if the cut was clean.

I got out a first aid pack and sprinkled some sulfa powder into the cut. I got a gunshot wound bandage on the opening and tied it off around his waist. His eyes followed everything I did. He flinched when I stuck a morphine surette into his leg and squeezed the ampule into him. I gave him another reassuring pat then signaled for us to proceed.

The next time we stopped I used the radio to call for extraction and to transmit the code for "wounded" and "prisoner," two signals that should get immediate results. This would prove to have unexpected consequences.

We progressed slowly, but with the expectation that we may be followed, somewhat faster than we had moved going in. I wasn't comfortable with the pace our prisoner necessitated. When we stopped for the night he behaved as well as could be expected. I knew he was in pain, hungry and thirsty, but we dared not remove the tight gag for fear we would yell out. I decided that once he was back at our base, treated and fed, the combination of his fear, the newness of his situation, a good meal, and the attention he would get from the medical staff might serve our intelligence-gathering interests well.

Once we were in position for the RON I gave him another shot of morphine. By then, if he thought about it at all, he may have realized that for better or worse we were his best hope. The dose of morphine was calculated for an American, so I guessed the drug would probably knock him out for the night. At the least it would keep enough of his pain at bay to keep him sluggish and quiet.

During the morning of the second day of egress we heard the muffled shot of a tracker behind us. We stopped instantly and went to ground. My heart rate spiked. The last time I had heard that sound I had got hurt and near panicked out of my wits. After a few minutes there was another shot, behind and off to our left. I couldn't think how any trackers could have got on to us, since our departure from the area of the Trail had been during such a quiet time. Perhaps our prisoner's unit had sent him some help with the water after all and discovered signs of a struggle in the mud by the discarded canteens, or maybe some outlying patrol had picked up our movement as we withdrew in greater haste than normal. I couldn't figure it since I knew we had maintained good silence discipline. Perhaps they knew only that there was movement, not the cause.

Then I heard the yip of a dog, followed by a third shot behind and to the right of the first. This meant there were at least three people tracking us and at least one dog. Not good. We all noted the direction of each sound and knew that we were being triangulated, though so far the direction we were heading was open.

I don't do good work when I'm scared. Trying to make my fingers work and mind racing, I removed my pack to get out a can of the blood-laced CS powder, which I managed to sprinkle liberally along the ground behind us. I humped back into my pack and kept dribbling powder as we continued eastward, progressing as stealthily as six people leading a drunk could move with automatic weapons in pursuit.

We heard a few more ground shots, but they didn't seem to be much closer. We could not afford to slow down. After another half hour or so, the sudden agonized howling of a dog echoed through the jungle from somewhere behind us. It was a horrible sound, filled with yelps and sustained screams brought to abrupt silence by a single rifle shot. In the stillness that ensued I calculated that when the dog encountered the first of the powder, they must have been no more than 80 meters behind us. Way too close.

We continued on, although I was churning with an effort to sort through our limited options in case those following were to close with us. I thought of adopting a zig zag course but rejected it on the grounds that it would shorten the distance between us. I thought about simply stopping and waiting to ambush whoever appeared, but realized that just because we'd heard three shots didn't mean there were only three following. We were moving pretty quietly and the undergrowth was very thick, which gave reason to think that any trackers might not be sure what they were onto. Then I thought we should move in an open "C" pattern like the one Johnson had used when we'd been flushed before, but I couldn't be sure how many might be pursuing us. I could thereby be leading us into a large unit that may not be moving in trail but spread out.

I realized there had been no more shots after we'd heard them shoot the dog, but did this mean they'd given up the chase? Keeping

alternative hypotheses constantly in mind—although vital to the intellect and a constant companion to pursuit of my degree in Philosophy
at the University of Virginia—can lead to the fatal flaw of indecisive-
ness in a combat leader. I had to forcibly push alternative possibilities
out of my mind when weighting likely courses of action on the part of
the enemy. My academic training in giving equal weight to theoretical alternatives was sometimes debilitating–an options catatonia–and
in wild desperation, I fear that more than once I made an impulsive
choice, throwing my life and those of my men to the fate of blind instinct. Fortunately for us all, my instincts on this day were generally
good and amply buttressed by the experience of the Nungs. In this
case it just "felt" right to keep moving east, so we did.

We varied the pace so often that anyone coming from behind
would likely give himself away during our stops in time for us to give
first response. Yet no one came. The trackers seemed to have given
up after what happened to their dog, and we continued on depending
primarily upon the compass and the places where the growth allowed
us to pass in silence.

Still, the fear of that pursuit rushed out of the jungle and put its
whole mouth over me. It sank its teeth into my brain, into the ancient
lizard part that predates reason and conjecture. The need to keep moving and to get us out took me out of my head and to an extent out
of my body, too. I began to see myself from slightly above and to
the right, over my own shoulder. The space between any sheltering
growth and the trackers behind, between subject and object, suddenly banged closed as sudden reserves of adrenalin somehow became
available as though from some outside source, pumping up and putting out until it washed over the fear, and I became lost floating in it.
Death by drowning.

I switched on the PRC-10 locater radio in my pocket for a few
minutes every half hour as we moved. At last, toward the end of our
second day of flight, desperately tired and still haunted by the possibility of pursuit, we heard and then saw two helicopters orbiting
about a half mile away, ahead and over to our left. It looked as though
they were indicating a direction for us, luring us to a place where they
could make the extraction. They circled and stopped, hovering for a
moment then circling again, the way a dog tries to get you to throw
something. We immediately headed toward them with the PRC-10 on.
If we were being chased, the presence of the choppers would surely
indicate our position, but it meant fire support.

These helicopters were not the Sikorskys we were accustomed to seeing. They were Hueys and wore no visible markings. As we closed and there was no point in worrying about any soft noise the radio might make, I turned it on and switched to the agreed frequency for the pick up, broadcasting in the clear our approximate position from them. The call back said they were over an old bomb crater and would wait.

As soon as we broke into the partially overgrown clearing, one of the Hueys dropped down into the opening to take us out, its door gunner braced at the M-60, while the other flew top cover in tight orbits overhead. I was very concerned that we were still being followed, and if so, the presence of the helicopters would by now have removed all doubt as to where we were, while at the same time enriching the target.

Nhi, with one of the other Nungs and I, tried to keep an eye on the woods behind as I signaled for Grayson and the others to start into the clearing to anticipate the touch down. I wanted to minimize the choppers' vulnerable ground time. My skin crawled with a sense of our vulnerability, and my mind pleaded with clasped hands for us to be out of there.

I saw our prisoner recoil, almost falling in the wind below the sinking helicopter, an object he had probably never seen up close. The others grabbed onto the poor horrified and half-drugged soldier in preparation for loading him aboard, when suddenly the sound of the rotors changed to a loud crackling intermixed with the steady *whop, whop* of the blades. I saw immediately what was happening. The pilot was too close to the verge of trees. His blades were chopping into the branches, launching sticks and fresh leaves into the vortex. In seconds, whole clumps of branches began swirling into the air as the rotors began to disintegrate at the tips. The pilot made a desperate attempt to get out of the situation but over-corrected.

Everything seemed to move in slow motion then as the tail rotor swung into the trees. The door gunner, with his clothes pressed by the wind, was knocked down and almost fell out. I was on the radio directly underneath shouting a warning into the hand set when, with a sudden lurch, the helicopter stopped flying, tilted and fell. I instinctively dove for the ground, and the machine crashed onto its side right beside me. The last thing I saw before flinching my eyes closed was one of the blades swing down out of the sky and stop against a fallen log by my head.

I opened my eyes as though from a dream and stared for a moment unbelieving at the surface of the log that had saved me. In a momentary struggle to reassemble my wits, I stumbled to my feet afraid now of post-impact fire. I was still gripping the radio telephone hand set, but its wire swung in the air, torn free of the radio. I tripped over the log, fell down, then crawled around to the other side of the wreck to find that Grayson and the Nungs as well as the prisoner were unhurt, although badly shaken, especially the little NVA who was trembling uncontrollably as though in the grip of a seizure.

As we all began to collect ourselves, and the pilots crawled out of the cockpit, I began to check for injuries. Our situation had in seconds gone from serious to disastrous. The helicopter door gunner had hurt his arm, which soon appeared to be broken, and the pilots were bruised, scared and angry. This greatly complicated our problem. As far as I knew, air crew were not trained for the ground, were now out of their element, and were suddenly my responsibility. Not knowing how much they might know about conditions in the field, I had to assume they were at least temporarily disoriented and therefore to a degree helpless. We had injuries to them, a downed aircraft full of expensive and salvageable equipment that had to be protected as well as possible by my exhausted team, and we now had no workable radio.

Then I remembered the PRC-10 in my pocket. It was still transmitting the homing signal but was now very weak on dying batteries. For all I knew, we had advertised our position to the enemy about as clearly and loudly as possible. Fortunately the other chopper had seen it all and called in support, which began to arrive about half an hour after I got the flight crew integrated into our perimeter. The pilots were armed with .45s, better than nothing, but neither of the machine guns on board the wreck could be used. The one on the crash side couldn't be retrieved even if it was still good, and the one on the high side was jammed into its mount and could not be brought to bear on the tree line. I don't remember thinking clearly about any of this–just functioning barely on a confusion of fleeting visual clues and the voracious consumption of our odds by the crash and its inhabitants.

To my wondering amazement and considerable anger, when the support arrived it wasn't used to extract anybody, not even the wounded crew, but rather to drop a demolition team who set about trying to blow up the wrecked helicopter. >From another Huey they repelled into the clearing like participants in a Special Ops recruitment poster, and they began scurrying officiously about as though it was up to them to save the situation, and quickly got to work by misusing detcord in a fruitless effort to blow the rotor stubs free of the hub. It seemed to me there were plenty of priorities that came before destroying the sufficiently wrecked equipment–such as getting injured people out of there–but if they were determined to disable their equipment first, why not the weapons and electronic stuff on board? In any case, even I knew that detcord was not the correct explosive for cutting through the honeycomb structure of helicopter blades, but it was also true that judgment and a sense of measure often disappear from those giddy with authority, especially if it's mixed with the fear of being caught after dark in an unfamiliar wilderness full of unseen dangers.

I mentioned my doubts about their methods to the downed pilot, who simply sat wordless on the ground rubbing his leg. He looked cankered, crabbed in black thoughts, glowering at the ground. His rage was palpable. Understandable, for it must be aggravating to lose an expensive helicopter, especially through pilot error, and thus to complicate the rescue effort, not to mention whatever disciplinary recourse awaited him back at his mysterious unit. Then of course his mood made him useless, too.

The light was beginning to fade. This meant that nightfall would bring other complications to our situation, and I didn't need any of the helicopter people, whom I presumed had little if any experience in the field at night, making noise, jumping at night sounds, or drawing down on our water supply.

Just before dark, other choppers arrived that lowered rescue baskets for the first crew, then yet another extracted the incompetent demolition crew. When it became evident they planned to leave us– the whole reason for the mission in the first place–still alone on the ground, I was furious. I let the last man know we still had a prisoner, were low on food and water, and had no radio. Somewhat to my surprise, a radio, though not a trusty PRC-25, was lowered to me before the last machine departed.

I was still angry, but once resolved to another night, realized that, on balance, we were probably better off relieved of the burdensome strangers and their odd priorities. I was sure they had no experience of the overwhelming need the jungle imposed upon one's ability to remain silent and alert, and in addition, their departure meant that at least some of our people now knew exactly where we were. We could anticipate rescue in the morning without being held responsible in the meanwhile for the lives of the first attempt.

In the sudden stillness after their departure, we had no choice but to prepare for another night on the ground. The black hulk of the downed machine lay silent nearby. Such things were attractive targets for a culture schooled in scrounging, so we were further stuck with the allure a far-from-completely-stripped treasure trove. Still, I did not want to move from the additional cover the wreck itself might provide us in the night. We had two claymore mines with us, and I found two more in the wreckage. They would not protect the clearing completely, but they might serve to tilt the odds, to neutralize a small party of pursuers, especially when backed by our other weapons.

We set up in a crescent using the wreckage as a part of our cover to await the fast-approaching night. While I was preoccupied with worries about possible incursions we might expect during darkness, the Nung near me reached over and tapped my shoulder. I looked over. He indicated that the man at the end of our line wanted to show me something. I shifted my attention to another of the Chinese, whose eyes were rigid in the fading light. He pointed into a stretch of ground that resembled a portion of a long-overgrown trail. There, about ten feet from him in the open, and in complete contrast to all colors around it, was a giant fiery orange centipede. The man smiled weakly and silently drew his finger across his neck. The message was clear.

There is in most of us an unused deposit or residuum of awe for certain outlandish things, like volcanoes, earth quakes, forest fires, and the octopus. We read about these things in our early youth (and later in books of the 19th century when awe was cheap) when images conjured by their descriptions fed a fear of living confrontation. To these I must add the giant centipede. This one was as splendid and frightening a specimen of mirapod as I ever want to see. Bright orange, whose articulated shell was segmented into bilobal sections that stretched well over a foot, and with a body thick as pairs of golf balls, with enormous pincers to the fore and myriad legs moving slowly like the oars of a galley, it was a genuine monster. They were rumored to be very dangerous, and this one was probably lethal, for all centipedes are poisonous to a degree, and if size was anything to go by, this thing packed a man-killing dose.

In any case, the Chinese clearly knew of its reputation and showed it. I indicated for him to murder the thing. I saw that he had every intention of doing just that but was waiting for my permission to move. While I wondered briefly if this was a sign of respect, he rose quietly and drew his knife. Approaching from behind the creature, and while still far enough away from it to imply that he knew it could react, he stabbed forth and cut down through its body in two places, the crunch of its carapace loud in the stillness. The pieces writhed and curled. I noticed that the cut took a lot of pressure. The problem now was trying not to think that, where there is one, there's likely to be another somewhere unseen and nearby.

As the skin prickled at the back of my hands and neck, I instinctively drew in my legs from the undergrowth. Quietly, stealthily, imperceptibly, a fresh fear of the coming night crept into my mind. We were settling into a wild place, a place that had been the scene shortly before of so much heavy activity for so long that we were highly likely to be discovered by any of the enemy who had been tracking us earlier, and we were now huddled in fading light among killer insects.

After building rapidly in among the trees, darkness joined the sky in minutes. Everything became abruptly quiet and motionless. Not even the birds had returned after the mechanical racket of the afternoon frightened them away. Quietly, Nhi and I got up and collected the claymores. We crept out to place them at the edge of the trees, across the roughly circular clearing from our position, facing each into the forest. By starlight we attached the ignition wires and led them back to the team's position near the wreck, placing all the trigger devices together. This meant the wires were draped across the clearing, and thus also across the fallen trees and irregularities in the ground, so the team knew not to enter the open space for any reason, not even in stealthy search of a private place for a bowel movement. I thought it likely that if we were still being followed, anyone who might chance to emerge from the shadowed tree wall during the night would probably trip one of the ignition wires, thus at least giving some early warning.

Gradually, the night sounds resumed, which I took as a sign that all was undisturbed across from us. There followed a long night during which none of us slept. I checked on our prisoner several times. He remained gagged, and I was sure he was helpless with fear, hungry, and probably in a state of advanced thirst, but I dared not release any of his restraints. I gave him a soft pat each time, convincing myself that any small kindness might pay dividends in cooperation when he was finally turned over to his interrogators, but I was increasingly anxious to have us all out of that place for numerous new reasons, not least of which was the fear that he might die on us. He was clearly in the throes of an entirely new experience, and I worried about the combined effects of fear, bleeding, and privation.

First light the next morning revealed that we were all still in the same place, and no one had been attacked by a centipede during the night. Relieved for the present, I ate a few balls of rice from my pocket, then transmitted that we were still waiting at the extraction point.

I held serious doubts about the unit that had been dispatched to get us out. I had not recognized their helicopters, couldn't interpret their unmarked flight suits, and I didn't like their strangely uncommunicative attitudes. It seemed that, whoever they were, saving us was secondary to something else, and I wondered what they, or our own people, would do to get us out today. I couldn't understand why our own people had not come to get us in the first place.

Before long, we heard the faint rotor thud of helicopters, more than one, and this time accompanied by a heavier beat and deeper engine noise. I could not see them through the tree cover, but again began preparation to leave and assigned the guys who would go out first in the event that we were dropped the McGuire rig.

Soon the choppers appeared through the trees, and I was surprised to see that one of them was a giant Sky Crane heavy lifting helicopter. It eased over the clearing staying high, its 100 mph down draft sending the treetops reeling. It moved to one side while another Huey came in just above the trees and began lowering four men on ropes. As soon as I realized what was going on, I disconnected the claymore triggers and let the ignition wires droop.

These new arrivals, barely acknowledging our presence as before, set about attaching large canvas slings to the downed helicopter. Then the crane descended like some enormous nightmare insect, its rotor disk darkening the sky, and dropped a cable which they attached to the straps, as we crouched warily in the tortured vegetal tempest and tried to protect our eyes. As soon as they were done, the new arrivals jumped off the wreck and moved aside. The crane took up the slack, lifting the damaged hulk off the ground. It swung awkwardly out and up, rising back into its element, but dead now, its incongruous shape limp and powerless in the straps. It took some of the earth and tree branches with it.

Then the Huey returned for the sling men. I yelled through the wind and engine noise to ask when we were going out, and the guy said he thought it would be "soon." The white-hot anger and frustration I felt at that point came dangerously close to breaking down my ability to make decisions.

Not long after the Sky Crane and its attendant minions were flown out, and about the time our hearing recovered, two more unmarked Hueys showed up and, as expected in view of the initial debacle, dropped some looped ropes along with a single lifting harness. We were familiar with the method, but I worried about our prisoner. I put the woozy little man into the harness and strapped him in with his own belt while Grayson and two of the Nungs took the other loops. They were lifted clear.

As a second chopper came in overhead, I reattached the claymore triggers. Nhi and the last remaining Chinese took their places on the ropes, then I stepped into a loop, and as we lifted off, I drew my legs up to make sure I was well clear of the backblast from the mines and pressed the firing handles on all the claymore triggers. They went off, and the vegetation below lurched with the lethal fan of their steel pellets, both before and behind them. I dropped the triggers so that I could hold onto the rope and tried to make myself small. The claymores should have taken care of any unseen watchers.

Apparently these choppers did not have winches, except for the one harness into which I had strapped the prisoner, and as we cleared the treetops, I was glad to see that he was being retracted into the lead helicopter. We were thus flown hanging by our ropes through the sky, but not eastward as I expected. The Sky Crane with its load hanging like a dead grasshopper beneath it was rapidly disappearing to the east, but instead we were diverging to the north in the direction from which all the extraction activity had come.

After what seemed like half an hour of this, we approached a small mountaintop clearing where a helipad and a few small buildings were grouped beneath a large antenna array. As we were lowered, I noticed that the chopper pad was nicely paved. It was probably because the landing space would become mired during the monsoon season, but it seemed an almost delicate affectation for such a tiny and isolated installation.

The air was much cooler here. A welcome breeze rustled through the surrounding forest and pulled gently at my clothes. Its view over an endless verdant wasteland to the east was spectacular. After freeing ourselves from the ropes, a thin, balding radish of a youth with silent watery eyes and new, unmarked fatigues appeared and directed Grayson and me toward one of the buildings, while the Nungs were shown to another. I stepped in to protest, but the wordless man blocked me and just pointed to the doorway he had indicated earlier. I watched until Hhi and the team disappeared into the neighboring hut and added to my growing list of resentments about these people, whoever they were, the way they presumed to split my team like that. While trying to shake the circulation back into my hands, I determined to find out what the hell was going on. Who were these anonymous, well-equipped people who so clumsily intercepted my extraction call, took away my prisoner, and treated us with such avuncular indifference?

Inside, we were offered some coffee by a short but stout middle-aged man with a ruddy, deeply lined face. He wore a shoulder holster that contained a non-regulation 9mm Browning High-Power over a standard US combat jacket but with jeans and civilian sneakers. I accepted, gulped at the porcelain mug gratefully and indulged my suspicions by observing him carefully. He invited us to sit in chairs that faced a desk behind which he settled quietly into a chair of his own. His movements were careful and deliberate, like someone recovering from an operation.

Once seated, he fidgeted about the surface of the desk, touching things, rearranging, smoothing papers, weaving about himself a mysterious invisible order. The desk was standard issue US government gray steel and largely covered with neatly stacked papers, a pair of trays containing more papers, and a few artifacts: an M-79 round serving to hold down one corner of a rumpled map, and its counterpart, a rock that appeared to contain flecks of gold. Behind him leafy branches outside made dark watery patterns upon broken Venetian blinds hanging askew, admitting crooked triangular stripes of light through which the shadow of his head moved. I couldn't quite place Venetian blinds in my experience of the day.

During this period of wordless settling in, Grayson and I exchanged a quick surreptitious glance, and I helped myself to a look around the room. The office was fairly neat and, possibly because of the altitude, free of the customary cloying red dust that filters onto the surface of everything else in the country. It was a great relief to be out of the jungle and free of its threats, even if we'd been engulfed by yet another foreign situation, but it was personally discomfiting to sit there. The room seemed to cringe as Grayson and I, in full combat gear, sat in rancid juxtaposition to its orderliness, filthy and filling the space with our jungle funk. It was all highly irregular.

Finally our host looked up, turning his riven attention directly upon us. He appeared considerably older than I would have expected of someone posted to such a remote installation, and I wondered if the grooves in his face were the product of other forces than age. With his rough hands joined like clamshells on the desk, he regarded the two of us silently for a long moment. His hesitancy seemed busy with hidden reserves of judgment and secret purpose, and I assumed he was orchestrating the delay as an effort to gain some psychological advantage from the poignancy. I felt only irritation at the presumptuous manner of our treatment, mixed with gratitude to be at last out of the field. At that point it didn't matter what he might have to say..

Then his thin mouth stretched across the face in a slow, cheesy rictus that stabbed at his jowls before he spoke. I noted that he failed to introduce himself, though he knew our names. Despite his attempt at smiling, I felt that the mind behind the stolid vacuous face with its weary blue eyes lurked cold and formidable. Though his manner remained detached, when he spoke his voice rang deep, and the words came fluidly free of harshness, like the sound of water running under a fresh cover of snow. He began a series of questions about what we had seen of the Trail, with particular interest in the vegetation.

He wanted to know if a certain kind of tree was growing in the area we had been in, and had either of us observed any of a certain kind of berry that grew in thick clusters high in the trees. He asked if there were any monkeys in the area, and if so, were they eating any of those berries?

I spoke for both of us, and after weaving a garland of vagaries intended to hide the fact that I really couldn't remember all that much about the types of trees in the region, while at the same time trying to give him something I thought he wanted to hear, I became increasingly irritated by this line of seemingly irrelevant questions and told him so. I had conducted my customary scan into the trees overhead for snakes and what glimpses the canopy permitted of the sky for changes in the weather, but if this type of botanical information was so significant why had I not been alerted to look for it before going out to risk our lives on some other directive? I was familiar with the appearance of many varieties, but did not know their scientific names and was certainly capable of making such additional observations in detail if it was important. I couldn't reconcile the extraordinary trouble and cost in damaged aircraft and misplaced expertise this man's unit had undertaken to get the answers to such simple questions, especially without giving former notice of their interest, and it would have been a hell of a lot easier simply to send someone over to FOB 4 to sit in on the debriefing. Before I finished I began to wonder if we were on the same side.

His walnut face, which until then had worn the kind of canted, alert expression of someone always on the lookout for something that hadn't happened yet, registered a moment of disapproval, but he said nothing. I wanted to get back to our base, have a shower, brush my teeth after a tense week in the field, and put this whole exhausting experience behind me. This interview just added to my feeling of being hopelessly trapped between bureaucracies in a realm where nothing was ever certain and where clandestine agendas mostly produced a cross-fertilization of ignorance.

He rose after a silence, went over to the door, and stood for a moment in the long quadrangular light, his elbow against the jamb and his head resting on his forearm. I couldn't tell if he was merely tired, exasperated with my answers, or perhaps about to say something clarifying. Finally he told us that our prisoner would be taken care of (whatever that meant), and the rest of the team and I would be flown back to FOB 4 shortly. He invited us to have some more coffee, and then pointedly suggested that I tell my debriefer back at our base as little as possible about this mountaintop interlude. I thought that very strange.

I thanked him for the coffee, and we stepped back outside, which probably did much to clear the breathing air in his office. I wondered if he had any idea how much more cooperative I would have been if he and his people had treated us with anything other than their vaguely elitist superiority. The Nungs appeared from the other hut, but I searched their inscrutable faces in vain for any hint of what had happened with them while Grayson and I had been in with the boss. I felt better as soon as we were reassembled.

This whole detour was so irritating and inexplicable I began to realize that, as much as I detested it, I was learning my job with a growing strength of resolve made holy by blood sacrifice, and despite my struggle with fear, the relationship I was forging with the Nungs meant I was better able than any other living soul to judge the balance of risk to value for myself and those who had to depend on me. Neither this anonymous interloper, nor anyone else, was going to interpose their agendas on the risks my little team had to undertake in the field.

We were loaded again, minus our prisoner, this time inside two of their unmarked Hueys, and flown back to FOB 4 in relative comfort. The interior of the machine in which I rode was cleaner than I was accustomed to, the inside paint less chipped, and the corners free of impacted red dirt. We rose off the mountain into the electric flames of a long-ray tropical sun setting beneath such brilliant layers of wispy cirrus that in another place and time might have changed the way I thought about color. About a mile away, a localized rain was falling, its veils bent and bright orange in the splendid evening light. I estimated dully that we would pass it in about three or four minutes. The effort to calculate it made me aware of my extreme fatigue.

Below us spread the misty undulant forest, fading into a barrenness of color off to the east. Its meaning kept shifting. One minute it was a desperate place for an emergency landing, and then it seemed suddenly a world apart, not the same jungle that had held us in such fearful mystery for so long. From above, its surface touched with the fingers of peach-tempered mist, it all seemed peaceful and benign, transformed as though risen from the pages of a fairy tale.

Several times in the fading carnelian light that washed through the open doors of the helicopter I glanced over to find the Nungs looking at me. I tried to smile and looked away but wondered at their stares. It was unlike them in their silent composure to make prolonged eye contact. Did their dark eyes contain fear? Resentment? I thought it possible that this operation and its unexpected interlude on the mountain had introduced them to some unprecedented protocols, something to which they were unaccustomed and didn't like. That was certainly true for me. I worried, too, that they believed I had called for this departure from their expectable routine, and that perhaps I had something to do with splitting the team when Grayson and I were taken into the office. I couldn't be sure how they were reading the signs but feared I may have failed them in some way and would not be able to explain that I hadn't known what was coming either. I wondered about the mysteries of their culture and worried that I might have missed some signal from them. It mattered enormously what they thought of me. Perhaps they felt I had deceived them, that the mission had been about something else. I wouldn't blame them. By now I doubted the purpose of the operation, too. The possibility saddened me, for I needed their respect. I hoped I could make it up to them with enough beer.

I stared out at the dying light and felt the crushing weight of living in a world not of my own making. I could extrapolate, draw conclusions upon little evidence, much fiction, and a certain blind instinctual faith, but I could never know the truth of any situation, the value of the action, or the desirability of the consequences. I despised the not knowing, the never being told the whole story, and I had come to hate and fear all surprises. I had done, and thought vaguely that I would likely continue to do, things in the name of duty that I did not entirely agree with and dreaded with cold fear. I told myself the limit would be when some basic moral principle of my own was compromised, but circumstances continually pushed that threshold farther out. In the meantime, I would survive for this hour, this day, and for as long as I was able on a thin thread of serendipity and blind happenstance.

A great preponderance of sleep began settling over me despite the chill of altitude. My nascent acceptance of the job not withstanding, I remained a frightened neophyte at this awful work and felt the weight of my responsibilities and failures pulling me into a void with no end. I felt deeply weary of the uncertainty, the constant worry, and of my ever-renewed confusion at all that had happened, that indeed was ongoing, wherein any one event would change a man forever. I longed for any peaceful interlude, for any kind of tranquility that wasn't just the absence of threat. I wanted only to surrender everything to it before facing anymore the Orwellian grope through all the coming days and months; but I had to fight it off. I had to stay awake, stay alert, do the thinking, stay alive. It was a mad irony that I was even there, but the joke lay in the blackest corner of fear, and we might all die in its silent peals of existential laughter.

We arrived back at FOB 4 after dark. Though I assumed that we had been extracted by whoever these people were because we had reported a prisoner at a place relatively convenient to their base, it was general knowledge that unmarked aircraft of any kind belonged to the "spooks." If the walnut guy with the shoulder holster didn't want me to talk about our diversion to the mountain top, why would they fly us right into our own home base in their "sterilized" equipment, even in the dark? It didn't make sense; but then, very little did.

When we landed, I was so beaten down with the combined effects of physical exhaustion, relentless fear, and humble wonder, that

I didn't give much thought to the fact that, strangely, no one was there to meet us. This was exceptional. A small reception group, which usually included at least two medics and the ambulance, always met the teams when they returned from the field. Every team needed some form of medical treatment each time. I assumed dully that no one had been notified of our arrival. So as the helicopters took off, sneaking clamorously away into the darkness, we started our weary trudge toward the recon huts which lay at the far end of the compound. It was just another unexpected development in the stream of surprises that had trailed us ever since we left, when? Six days ago? Seven? I really couldn't remember.

Someone on duty at HQ had evidently heard the unscheduled arrival of the choppers and started down to the pad in a Jeep to see what was up. He was surprised to encounter us, to confirm who we were–prodigal sons shuffling up the perimeter road–and immediately piled all six of us into and onto the Jeep. When he dropped Grayson and me at our hootch, where normally we would all have unloaded together, I asked him to take the Chinese all the way down to their tent.

Grayson and I got cleaned up, which revived me temporarily, and were debriefed that night. I told everything about the prisoner and the circumstances of his capture, the trackers, the cache, trail traffic, and the whole debacle of our unexpected extraction by the strange helicopters. I told also about our meeting on the mountain and made it clear that I wanted to know what was going on. I knew I would get no answers, but at least it was an opportunity to lash out at this world of relentless guesswork, the hateful cloying uncertainty, where the results of our risks were seldom known, and where nothing was predictable but mortal danger and the insidious depletion of one's personal reserves of humanity through constant low-grade fear.

With a small grin at one point, even though I had given Nhi full credit for the capture, the debriefing sergeant muttered something about my being a risk taker. No one knew better than I how untrue that was, but at least "risk taker" sounded better than "reckless, impetuous fool" or "providential coward."

When the meeting was finally finished, the sergeant said simply, "Okay. Good luck." The words were delivered automatically and flat side up, as a way of dismissing us, as empty and meaningless as "so long." He didn't seem to get that those of us being sent into the field were engaged in a shatteringly intense personal struggle with a range of mortal dangers, and whether it was rational or not, we invested the idea of luck with a desperate reality: in the timeless effort to transfer even a little power, there were guys who wore religious medals, carried talismans, believed that certain articles of clothing were inhabited with fortune, had ritual moves, or kissed their thumb knuckles smooth. Not even the inscrutable Nungs were immune. Each wore a little gold effigy of Buddha around his neck in the uncomplicated belief that it would protect him. (Their belief was so certain, that when one of them was killed or hurt, the others claimed simply that his Buddha wasn't as strong as their own.) Men in conditions of protracted uncertainly could not help themselves from reaching out for even phantom versions of security. Very few were free of it, and although the sergeant's carelessness lent him a certain gargoyle charm, it was an indication that his air-conditioned map room insulated him from the vibrant reality in which his fellows dwelt. Perhaps the room itself was his talisman.

In a few days, my worries about the Nungs were put to rest when I was surprised to be invited to have dinner with the team. I went down to their area and joined them in their circle on the ground around a large bowl containing a rich mixture of rice and various meats of mysterious origin. They were all in good cheer, and according to their custom, each served the man on his right, a tradition that hinted openly at the value they placed on community. To my surprise and unsteady delight, my bowl included both a foot and the head of a chicken. I had been briefed months earlier on enough Nung customs to know this was an honor. The feet or the head of the chicken was served to the guest of honor, but I had not been told what to do with either in the unlikely event that it happened, and never thinking that I would be confronted with the situation, I hadn't asked about the protocol.

Here I was, unexpectedly invited to join them, and now confronted with the challenge of being served both the foot *and* the head. I decided there was no choice but to plunge in. I laughed in appreciation, took out the head and put the whole thing in my mouth. The appreciative bubble of laughter that burst from them indicated that such extraordinary indulgence was not customary, but it was clear that they all got a real kick out of the performance. After a few moments sucking ostentatiously on the chicken head, I settled down to dinner, using the least-bad English speaker to translate my feelings of deep appreciation and respect for them all. Together we made a large dent in the

Vietnamese *paella,* and I left after dark with a feeling of complicated warmth toward these strange little men, along with diminished doubts about the way they had looked at me on the flight back.

A few days later I was informed by our debriefer, again in the messhall, that our prisoner had proven quite cooperative and had delivered unexpectedly useful information about his unit and its purpose, composition, and destination. The importance of this was undeniable, and it was suggested that I should be very pleased and was likely to be commended. It sounded to me, though, like our serendipitous capture had given the wrong people my name.

Later still, months later, I was to learn that the CIA had developed a high-density microphone that could pick up with unprecedented clarity the sounds within an impressive distance of its position and transmit them hundreds of miles. They planned to use these mics on the Ho Chi Minh trail to send back the sounds of all traffic, including speech, which our analysts could process while sipping coffee in their safe TOCs and mobile radio shacks, thus incidentally reducing the need for putting eyeballs on site far out in the Mesozoic boonies. They had found a way to disguise these listening devices to look like the berries we'd been asked about, and they could be placed by the simple expedient of dropping them into the trees from aircraft and allowing them to hang in clusters that appeared quite natural. The trouble was that monkeys liked to eat those particular kinds of berries, and the spooks didn't want the monkeys to eat our microphones.

Years later I read that a zoologist was consulted during this clandestine program. His role was to identify any fauna of the Indochinese region that might activate acoubuoy microphones. In this version of the story, the zoologist declared that he knew little of acoubuoys but noted that the ones he was shown had red protuberances that were sexually stimulating to a local species of monkey. Hence, he explained, the command center at Nakhom Phanom should know that the air strikes, which in the early stages of the project were intended to be triggered automatically by acoubuoy transmissions, might be responding to lascivious monkeys rather than to North Vietnamese formations moving south.

This footnote makes the old quotation about the fool who tried to hustle the East all the more apt. If the walnut man had simply smiled and said to me that, believe it or not, there was good reason to ask his questions, I would have been happy to give the subject more thought, and possibly even been willing to keep quiet about our conversation on the mountain. *Sic Semper Tyrannus.*

Rumors had persisted ever since the big attack my first night at FOB 4 that we were to be hit again. Due to the way in which we rated intelligence, giving a figure of merit to both the magnitude of the threat and to the dependability of the source, some of these warnings were ignored, and some, due in part to the numbers, resulted in our going on special alert for a night or two.

A few days after we returned from our Trail mission, a threat that Command believed serious was declared, and the camp went on full alert. During the afternoon, however, a runner brought me the news that long-overdue orders had come in for me fly to Kontum in the central highlands, several hundred miles to the south, in order to attend One-Zero school. In view of the experience I already had in running Team Anaconda, this seemed a bit late. Evidently an application had been put in for me during the recovery period after the big attack, and since the military's wheels grind exceedingly slowly, the orders had only just come through. But orders are orders, even obsolete ones, and I was to be ready to leave first thing in the morning.

At least, I thought, it offered an excuse to get away from this place for a few weeks. I might even learn something, especially as I had been pulled out of RECONDO School in Nha Trang shortly after arriving in-country. I set about packing for two weeks. It wasn't likely that Grayson would be sent out in my absence, so I knew that the guys would have at least fourteen days to relax, except for any periodic alerts like the current one. The time could be a reprieve, but who could know?

The growing number of these alerts had occasioned the excavation not far from our team hootch of several shallow slit trenches in the sand, each sized for one man. They were just deep enough to prevent the sand from filling them back in, and were close enough to the hootches that in an emergency, a guy could throw himself into one and by lying flat, could be at least partially concealed just below ground level.

Concern over an imminent attack was serious this time, and most of the day was spent with preparations to defend the camp. Ammunition and additional grenades were loaded into the watch towers, inspections of the perimeter wire were made periodically throughout the day, trenches were dug, weapons checked, and magazines loaded for a fight. I did not know how I could ever make it through another attack like the last one, and as evening came on, I became increasingly anxious.

It looked to me as though, one way or another, we would be up all night. With any luck, I would have to stay awake through the night and all of the next day as well. I was getting acclimated to a certain amount of sleep deprivation, but it was not easy to keep functioning adequately when every hour made steady withdrawals on my reserves. Functioning at peak was a bygone idea.

At dusk, when many people were taking positions around the perimeter bunkers and trenches, Grayson declared his intention to remain on the floor in the hootch doorway. I decided to lie down in one of the slit trenches outside. That way, on my back, I would see 180 degrees from the north perimeter wire to the sandbagged walls of the large 81 mm mortar pit that dominated the lower part of the camp, nearby on my left. If nothing happened I'd at least have a view of the stars, and if an attempt were made on the wire in our section, I'd be, though somewhat exposed, in a reasonable firing position with good visibility all around.

Up until then I had resisted the use of any chemical assistance in keeping awake, but in view of what the night and next day might bring, I fished around in my issue of pills in the first aid pack for one the right color, swallowed it with warm canteen water, took up a bandolier of magazines, and shortly after dark, went out to one of the marginally deeper man holes. There I lay down with my rifle across my chest, first round in the chamber, and thumb on the safety.

The night was clear and calm, the sand in the hole retained just enough solar heat from the day to be in comfortable balance with the sea air. Perhaps because of the tension throughout the compound, all was quiet. No noise came from the club or the messhalls. Every now and then, I could hear muffled laughter coming from some guys inside the mortar pit. With a heavily bagged off-set entrance, they were pretty well protected in there against any but indirect fire and were thus about as well-situated as anyone—unless of course a mortar round, even a small one, were to fall inside the pit. One's sense of security was always a compromise and often depended upon a degree of self-delusion.

As the early hours slipped by, the only thoughts that would come were about the magnitude of events since my arrival. The baleful, contiguous presence of the images cast such a shadow over everything in my life that had gone before, that few of the things leading up to it all seemed now to have made it inside. The pictures just stayed there, stored in my eyes, crowding out reflections of my former life, and I had trouble making all the segments fit. It was just as well. Reminiscence is distracting. It can cause hesitation, and hesitation can be dangerous.

I watched the night progress as the bowl of stars tilted slowly past. At the edge of the hole, bobbing slightly against the sky, was a small clump of grass and a single little wild flower, complacent, insistent and heedless of human fury and stupidity. I wondered how it had come to be there in the furnace of daylight temperatures on this beach. While I was letting my attention wander, thinking distractedly that nature was profoundly reactionary in its blind attachment to the *status quo*, an arc of sparks crossed the sky overhead. It took a second for me to identify it as the trail of a Soviet RPG.

In a hot flash my whole body went instantly tense. The grenade fell somewhere off to my left, and judging by the dulled sound, went harmlessly into the sand. Instantly, sporadic rife fire crackled along the north perimeter. People at the wire began shouting. I peered over the edge of the hole and saw several long bursts close on my right, the muzzle flashes illuminating someone firing through the wire.

A flare rushed into the sky with a sound like a faint sneer, leaving a sheaf of spangles to wither quietly in the air. At the top of its arc, the parachute opened with a pop, and suddenly all exposed objects, people, and huts leaped from the dark into its harsh incandescence, spanceled to long swinging shadows. To my immediate right an AK opened up with short bursts. There, a lone bare-legged sapper, too intent upon firing at the hootches to notice me, ran through a flickering bar of the flat silver light and continued past, his foot steps thumping in the sand. I couldn't understand how he had got inside, but I instinctively thumbed the safety off, sat up and fired a quick two-second burst at him. He looked over, stumbled for a second, but kept going, running toward the mortar pit. Then, on some errant impulse rooted somewhere beyond conscious access among the deeper instincts of self-preservation, I suddenly realized I was running after him, sprinting as fast as possible in the soft sand with the bandolier slapping against me. In a strained, unfamiliar voice I yelled to the guys in the mortar pit, "In the pit! Sapper coming! Don't shoot; I'm on him, I'm on him!!"

He ran through the harsh light of a crude Buddhist shrine the Chinese had set up in the middle of their compound, a tacky affair made of brightly painted rocket ammunition crates containing an effigy, joss sticks, and, most stupidly of all, a 100 watt light bulb that launched its glare across the ground, illuminating most of the Nungs' section. It would show me too if he turned. I fired again as he ran through its fan of light to disappear into the darkness beyond, his heels flicking sand. I couldn't believe the Nungs had left that light on during an alert. It fed my anger, and in a blind fury as I ran past, I knocked the whole structure to the ground with the rifle butt.

Without the glare of the shrine, I glimpsed the sapper duck into the secondary messhall for the indij. He was quick as an animal. All I could think was that he had to be stopped. I got to the door in seconds, fired a burst through the screen hoping to keep his head down in case he had stopped just inside, then dove through the flimsy door frame and onto the floor, where after a disoriented moment, I managed to roll to one side. He fired wildly from the darkness somewhere deeper in the room, the muzzle flash dancing in the blackness and the bullets splattering into a forest of inverted chair legs on the long community tables. Splinters of wood trickled down. I could hear his empty casings clattering onto the concrete floor and guessed that he was moving toward a side door near the far corner. Desperate with angry panic and with my eyes tearing, I crawled across the filthy floor to a large stone cooking area near the center of the room, rancid with *nuoc mam* oil and food spills. From there, I fired two or three single shots low across the floor hoping to get them past the table legs that flickered in the shots. He yelped, then fired a long burst which crashed into a wall of woks that hung over my head. The woks exploded with shocking metallic clangs and, blown from their hooks, began falling onto me in a terrifying and painful clatter. It shocked me. I had no idea of what was happening. It scared and angered me and left me shaking.

Through the chair legs across the room, I just caught a glimpse of him against the starlight of the side entrance, and as he made a lunge for the screen door I stood and fired directly at his silhouette. He either fell or launched himself past the doorway opening.

Instantly everything went quiet. I couldn't see clearly what happened, the muzzle flashes from my own weapon leaving colored glyphs on the darkness. In the abrupt stillness of the big room I heard only my own heavy breathing and the ringing in my ears.

I did not pursue. I knew I would be vulnerable coming outside through that door, and the whole thing had left me terrified and depleted. Gasping and dizzy, I couldn't move. The adrenalin wash had me. The sudden chase, the desperate running firefight, and the paralyzing clamorous cascade of metal cookware onto my head and back had cost me any will to continue. I sat down amid the fallen woks, with my back against the stone firebox, voices in my ears, eyes too wet to see clearly, chest heaving, my lungs burning in the rifle smoke and sour fish oil smell, just relieved to be alive.

It seemed to take a long time for me to summon a coherent thought, and as awareness gradually spread, I realized there was no more shooting outside. Guys were running about in the dark, and there was some yelling, but no sounds of weaponry. Shaking, I got to my feet and stumbled unsteadily through the fallen pots to the front door. The screen was broken and holed. I pushed open the remnant of the frame and stepped back outside, weak-kneed with temples pounding and breathless in the aftermath. I felt emotionally drained, unsteady, and enfeebled by a bleached vacancy that had opened within me.

A confusion of people were running around everywhere, poking rifles into the shadows and probable hidey holes. Still trying to sort out what had happened, I started back toward the hootch. My legs felt heavy, each step a minor effort. I went past the tumbled shrine I had knocked over, its boxes and effigies on the ground and forlorn garlands of plastic flowers strewn on the sand. As I approached the mortar pit, one of the guys stepped out and asked, "Did you get him?"

"I don't know. Maybe."

When I arrived back at the hootch, Grayson said it looked like it had all been just a probe. A few sappers had penetrated the wire on the north side, and word was we'd killed them all. I wondered about the man I'd chased into the center of the compound. I thought he'd at least been hurt, but I felt so abstract and insubstantial that I had to trust that someone else would finish him.

Then, quite suddenly, I was pulled from numb reverie by an unexpected priority. It erupted with an unmistakable gurgling in my gut and told me I might have taken the wrong kind of pill. There followed a blossoming urgency to get to the latrine.

After a disconcertingly explosive experience in the latrine, I went over to the messhall, knowing I'd need something to eat before a long travel day. I was shaken and not very hungry, and a bit worried at the persistence of the sensation in my lower tract.

While I nibbled hurriedly through a fragment of toast and some coffee, I watched out the window as two guys dragged a sapper's corpse past the building. It was greasy and bare-legged and had turned dark with bullet wounds. I heard them say they found it by the side entrance to the indij messhall.

20

At Da Nang airport I boarded a C-47, the military version of the venerable DC-3. It was configured, for a surprising change, with forward facing rows of passenger seats, airline fashion, and wore an air of dignified, if worn and slightly impatient, resignation. I was surprised to be reminded of the cramped passenger space. With the insistent discomfort in my plumbing, I took an aisle seat in expectation that I might need to get up and use the little room at the back at some point.

Sure enough, even though I didn't think there was anything remotely solid left in me, the pressure continued to accrue until, some time into the flight, the discomfort reached the critical point, and I had to get up as expected. I rose and headed back down the aisle with a pressing deadline.

Fortunately, the bathroom was unoccupied, but when I lifted the seat, I discovered that the aircraft had no holding tank. The commode simply led straight out the bottom of the plane through a short length of pipe filled with the noise of the engines, with the sunny Vietnamese countryside sliding past the wind-sucking hole at the end. Not the most comfortable perch, but the accommodation left no alternative. I spent a miserable hour or so making a highly personal contribution to the air, sweating despite the cold of the little room, and felt safe to come out only upon noticing by pitch and throttle changes that we were about to land. I got back to my seat feeling weak, quite sleepy, and worried that the problem still did not seem to be over.

After landing, the group to which I found that I was attached was loaded into an open truck and driven off the airport and into foothills. Some miles later, while grinding up a jolting mountain road, we passed a dusty American infantry patrol, moving wearily along the shoulders, their dark figures marked out in stark contrast against the powdery earth. Some peered up with looks of silent tolerance and misery from beneath the rims of their helmets as we drove by, raising more dust.

We disembarked at a place where the road widened among a remnant ridge community of broken houses whose windows were open wounds in walls that were pocked with a confluent rash of bullet holes. The little buildings crouched on the spine of the mountain wore looks of saddened surrender. Having been ravaged and abandoned by the humans, they were now about to be embraced from behind by the wilderness. The fighting here had been fierce, and the signature its damage left upon the houses still resonated in the stillness. Fresh from a firefight just the night before, I found the scene too vibrant for comfort.

It was cooler here, the thinner air slightly freer of the ubiquitous jungle smells that had become so familiar to me over the months, even though the trees pressed forth all around. For several minutes we waited near the truck, not knowing where we were supposed to go or to do next. Hoping to improve my mood a bit by indulging in the view offered from such a high vantage point, I stepped away from the others to stand near the edge, where one of the ruined houses raised its pitiful masquerade amid a fringe of rusting tin cans and layers of dried trash that lay compressed like leaves in a drain at the base of the walls. Bullets and shrapnel had perforated its thin construction through and through. The weathered exterior plaster showed a radial path of splinters from the burst of a rocket-propelled grenade, the pattern cross-hatched with grey fragmentation cracks. I peered inside. It was empty and dark, with trash scattered on the earthen floor, but light filtered through from the many holes in its exterior walls, projecting a frieze of wavering shapes inside made of wind-stirred tree shadow, while small birds flitted through the empty sockets of the blown windows in busy glimpses of color.

However, the darkling panorama out to the west beyond the house offered none of the solace often found from high overlooks. It was deeply depressing. The sky hung low, the color of old meat, while lightning prowled behind the distant hills, pulsing in eerie silence. I knew too well the saturating strangeness of the conditions out there, the dangers hidden within it. The ominous landscape fell sharply away behind the broken houses, where it contorted into erratic mountain ranges, rumpled valleys, and deep jungle ravines that paled gradually away into a gloom of haze. It was perfect guerrilla country, and with the coming dusk, ghastly mists were fuming out of the valley floor below, ingesting light. I knew by now that I would never get used to the visceral spookiness of that terrain. Its secrets didn't lessen with exposure; they just darkened and fattened in accumulating alienation.

Soon the lead elements of the patrol we had passed arrived too and halted in the dead village. The dusty men fell out into the ditches in elaborate postures of exhaustion. From what I could overhear, they were to await extraction by air. I wondered at their lack of noise discipline and seemingly careless exposure on an open road. With darkness fast approaching, and their LZ little more than a foothold on the narrow road just down slope from the ruins, I wondered if they would get out at all that night.

After awhile our escort arrived. We shouldered our packs in the dying light, and followed him in single file out of the village and along a well-worn jungle pathway to arrive shortly after dark at the mountain camp that would serve as our training base in Kontum. By that time my next bout with the problem was pressing. Not only the pressure itself, but the effort to contain it was painful, and I arrived at this new place with growing fear that my sweating and constant urges might be symptoms of something worse than full blown diarrhea with its implications for fever and dehydration.

We found the American cadre surprisingly inhospitable. They showed us to our barrack somewhat dismissively, making it clear that it was for transients, and left without the common courtesy of pointing out any local facilities. They clearly resented the presence of strangers, and among other restrictions to my lasting resentment, would not permit us to use the U.S. latrines. When I mentioned my problem, I was directed instead to a remote and crudely-thatched open latrine built for the Vietnamese.

There was no lighting, so I felt my way along a double row of raw, sash-milled uprights in the darkness. These proved to designate facing pairs of slightly swamped concrete platforms with sump holes in the middle, over which one was expected to squat. In my seriously liquefied condition, I could not have used one without soiling myself, my boots, and pants, so, muttering curses at my countrymen for their discourtesy, I groped frantically in the dark until I contrived a way to keep my clothes separated from the slab by balancing on the narrow edge of a low wicker splashboard that fronted each stall, and then, holding on to two rough-sawn upright boards to keep from falling backwards, surrendered miserably to gravity for the rest.

If the place had been attacked just then, I would have been helplessly trapped in the combined assault of both internal and external forces. The extreme discomfort of that unfamiliar and primitive facility lasted all through the time allotted for our dinner that night, and although I had to contend with other priorities than hunger, the experience served to animate a vibrant resentment of our host cadre. I made a terrible mess of the slab, I'm sure, but in the absence of any lighting, could not tell or even see, so doing anything to clean up after myself was also impossible. I regretted leaving things the way I had to, but again, nature made most of the rules that day, and I returned to the American barracks tremulous, wet with sweat, and feeling slightly faint, but with an attitude toward the stunningly trivial enmity of the people who ran the place that I was unable to shed throughout the entire course.

Afterwards I located the U.S. showers, though, and assuming they were restricted, too, I chose to indulge myself in a long one, fully prepared to tell anyone who dared question my presumption exactly what he could do with his objections. I was very tired, had killed a man the night before, and been suffering in lower tract *extremis* ever since. If one of the self-righteous bastards who lived here tried to deny me a shower, he would be outnumbered by my resentment alone.

The shower improved things, and on the walk back to the barrack to which we'd been assigned, I noted that all the buildings clung to the shoulder of a sharp ridge, giving them a commanding view of the surrounding jungle but confining the compound to a long, narrow perimeter. The slopes were very steep, which might deter an attack on foot, but mortar fire seemed a likely effective alternative. The nearest rising terrain was certainly close enough to support an attack by mortars.

The rest of the garrison was watching "The Sound of Music" somewhere. I could hear bits of the familiar strains but, still worried that my gut might not last through it, I continued my private recon alone. The moon had not risen, but the starlight made the hills silvery like the sea and intercut with deep shadows. Perhaps the relative brightness made them seem closer. The fish belly leaves at the top of the jungle caught the pewter light of the sky, sharp like the spines of grasses, reflecting a steely sheen on black oil. Somehow the greater visibility and the odd color made them more mysterious. I decided to re-gauge their distance in the light of day.

I did not know any of the others in my group, but after we had bedded down, the first night revealed that some of them were experienced. Troubling scenes told with disturbing effect on their nervous systems, as some relived them in their sleep. Muttered oaths, an isolated cry of defiance, curiously intermingled with snatches of prayer or scripture combined with my own now-habitual fears about the enemy's mastery of the dark to keep me awake. Their utterances reminded me of the black soldier who stalked the aisle between the bunks in the transit tent my first night in the country. I lay there on dull alert listening expectantly to the jungle night sounds.

At last, through the long hours of darkness that followed, punctuated by familiar cries from the trees, I began to realize to my profound relief that I was at last recovering from the combined alchemy of the previous night's firefight and the pill. Each time I awoke from what shallow rest the unfamiliar surroundings allowed, I could tell that the affliction was finally withdrawing. By the time some raucous parrots had me up before dawn, I knew that the ordeal was over. Feeling thus improved and hungry, I joined the other newcomers for breakfast

We entered a long common room built over a steep jungly hillside. It smelled of coffee and commanded an extensive view over the trees to the northwest. It felt the way I imagined an African safari club might–not a bad spot to start each day. Many of the sullen cadre were there, too, and among them I was surprised to recognize a sergeant I had known at Fort Bragg in North Carolina.

This was S/Sgt. Massey, whom I liked. He held two Silver Stars, was demonstrably brave, and maintained a dependable sense of humor, but I remembered that he was afraid of cows. Like many other urbanites both black and white, he reserved a steady mistrust of large animals. Once on a night jump in the hills of Georgia, I had left the plane right behind him and came down in a family's watermelon patch near where he had glanced off a cow. He and the cow both panicked, and in the confusion they ran into each other, and the cow stepped on his hand. I always assumed that the reason we got on so well after that was because he knew I held his secret. Now here he was, sitting across the long table near the opposite end. I got up, walked around behind him, and gave him a peck on the top of his head.

"Sergeant Massey," I said. "Boy, am I glad to see you! I came all the way to Vietnam just to kiss your bald spot."

He turned slowly and looked up at me with one of his dark smiles and growled, "Hey, you see a boy aroun' here, you jus' walk over and slap him."

It caused some scattered laughter around the table and may have helped some in reducing the tensions imposed by our arrival, for it launched numerous smiles on both sides–but the test would come later. We were soon led off to begin the training, and I never saw Massey again. I've often wondered if he survived the war and what he might be doing today.

My knowing one of the cadre appeared to give me some discomforting status with the other transients, some of whom looked to me at various times with questions about what to expect. I had no idea, but soon began to expect very little.

In the first place, I began to suspect that the instructors, of whom there now appeared to be two, had less field experience than I did. At least they had little of the kind and duration that we were running up north in I Corps. There was little classroom work, and most of that was conspicuously free of actual practical instruction. It was heavily theoretical, and I began to wonder if the instructors had been flown in from cushy assignments in the States specifically for this "school." When I asked questions based upon my own direct experience, they just glared at me in irascible speculation for a few moments and left me to process my lingering doubts through anything else that might appear on the curriculum.

Our training patrols were also of dubious benefit. It soon became clear that one of the reasons the school was located in this part of the central highlands was because, despite heavy fighting around the immediate lower terrain in the past, this place had not seen much enemy incursion for some time. It was considered tamed, or at least a place where the American presence was dominant, which may have explained some of the attitude we encountered among the base personnel. Whether or not any of them had actually played a hand in pacifying the area, they must have felt entitled to a certain inherited complacency. Whether they wished to acknowledge it or not, this was still central Vietnam, and though the Americans occupied the high places, they had to leave the security of their bases and come down through a potentially hostile native population in order to go anywhere, and that included our daily forays into the field.

I was further disconcerted by the fact that we were transported down from the ridge to our areas of field training in open trucks on public roads. The vulnerability this imposed was tangible. In addition, the terrain selected for the training was considerably more open and flat than I was familiar with, and we were taken through it on our training patrols with a lack of caution in movement that I assumed was correspondent to the greater visibilities. This was pure carelessness as far as I was concerned. Moving in open country eased the need for absolute silence, but it did nothing to reduce the imperative for constant vigilance, and in my concentration on our surroundings I often missed whatever words of marginal utility the instructors put forth. We moved noisily through the scrub, where the tramp of my companions' feet, the dust, the brush of their fatigues, and the sloshing of their canteens, kept me increasingly on edge.

Some of the other guys wondered at my discomfort and said so. I soon learned that they had no experience in the kind of work for which the exercise was supposed to be preparing us, and I overcame enough of my sense of inadequacy to fill in some of the shortcomings in our instruction—everything from "breaking the seal" in the mornings to the merits of various escape and evasion patterns, getting their clothes tailored down, and the importance of resting face-up at night. I told them about frequent yawning to open your ears and about reading the insect sounds. It seemed that none of these small life-saving tricks of the trade were known to the instructors. They never mentioned them.

There were a few hardened veterans in the group who sensed that this was grade school for "newbies." They were easy to identify. Most were probably a bit younger than I but with all the youth sucked out of their eyes and the fundamental iridescence drawn from their skin, even though we were all tanned. They were people whose lives seemed to have backed up on them, and there was the now-familiar sense about them that told they were not going to wait for any of it to come back. There was a tough, but blank, resignation in their faces, and they, like me, were probably just as glad to be away from their customary AOs.

There were also others who, though evidently some time in-country, were being introduced to long-range reconnaissance techniques for the first time. I wondered how many of them had volunteered for this kind of training–for operations ranging beyond timely support, where nothing is certain, and where, if they survived their first LRRP mission, they would find that levels of information were also levels of dread.

I decided to keep my reservations about the usefulness of the course quiet and simply watch and listen to everything. I might just learn the one essential thing that proves to make all the difference some day, and besides, as long as I was in this place, I was away from a region under daily threat of enemy activity.

I was surprised to discover but hesitant to admit that I, of all scared people, had a certain edge in experience that soon emerged in the course of events, and served to break down some of the initial reserve between strangers, as a few guys, sensing the porous instruction, began to ask my opinions. One of them was a corporal named Snow, from a "leg" infantry unit. Snow was a poet, full of good humor and with an unusual flare for rhyming. He was the master of an involved comic rhetoric that enabled him to express his moral indignation and still keep a worldly wit. He read some of his comic poetry to us in the evenings. It was genuinely clever and original, though he sometimes mispronounced some fairly common words. (He pronounced "hearth," for instance, as "heerth." In a private moment I once asked him if he had grown up in a house with a fireplace, and he said no. There were other words too, but he was so personable and creative that his pronunciation seemed less important than his original use of language.) I liked him and worried for him in whatever assignment awaited him back at his unit. He just didn't seem the type for long range operations; but then, I wasn't either.

One of the guys in the training was local to the host unit. I never learned if he was actually part of the cadre, but he was certainly known to them and was always with us, often functioning as a kind of assistant to their efforts in the field. He was stocky, with an incipient gut, dangerously talkative and an insufferable braggart. He was called Collins. Three-quarters of what he said was simply untrue, and the rest was clear nonsense. He strutted about in almost comical self-awareness, and he pontificated loudly and irritatingly on two subjects: a violent objection, punishable by numerous threats of retribution, to any criticism of the singer Barbra Streisand, with whom he was somehow obsessed; and secondly, the claim that he had killed 95 VC and wouldn't leave the country until he had killed an even 100. (Of course he had no control over when he left the country, no matter where his other fantasies took him.)

By now I had spent enough time with real killers to know the difference, but if he was in fact a man who by temperament was capable of doing real harm, he was now in circumstances where he could pursue disaster virtually unimpeded, and he was the kind of person who would always be a danger to those with him. Maybe he was just a leftover high school bully who had finally been put in a place where he could enjoy freedom from restraint, but as far as I was concerned that meant the mechanisms of his untidy passions made him a person who would be enormously improved by death.

To the amusement of some of the others, I began to refer to him as the "Killer of Kontum" and spoke in his hearing about violence bred of thwarted idealism and the possibility of links between obsession and impotence. I doubt if he ever got it, but he knew something was wrong and gradually developed a singular resentment of me. His suspicions gave me full control of our encounters and provided me with the few entertainments I was able to glean from the school.

As our field experience expanded, I was introduced to some strange conditions. At one point, we were trucked to an area where, after slogging through muddy streams and generally wet conditions for two days, we entered an area of knee-high grass. Notably there was no discussion beforehand about how one approaches such terrain or deploys for its hidden dangers, we were just led straight into it.

The men started high-stepping awkwardly like short-sighted people wearing unfamiliar bifocals. I followed along and soon noticed that the ground was becoming spongy and wet. Saturated mud crept over my ankles, and soon we were all wading waist-deep in standing black water. It continued deepening until we were all in a chest-deep swamp, surrounded by water-dwelling trees, and well above our ammunition belts in the dark water. During the endless slog through these conditions the whole afternoon we were about as trapped as I could imagine being. We moved through island patches of dense growth where gaunt trees stood dead, enshrouded by creepers. The banks were low and crowded with tree stems. A thick wall of dark forest pressed forth in all directions, fading together in the captured haze of each bend and lagoon. We had been led into nature's version of a slum.

Little islands of thick growing swamp grass rose in tufts throughout, many solid enough to support one's weight, and whenever we took a break, some of the guys tried to climb up on them to get out of the water. I found that I could back up to some of them and kind of hump my butt over the edge to lie back with my lower legs still submerged, but in this manner at least my upper torso and its gear had a chance to drain. This was also the only way to gain access to the sealed food pouch in my pocket without filling it with swamp .

When at last I saw the instructors hanging their web gear in the branches of trees, I realized the game plan was for us to stay in the swamp all night. I was lucky enough to find a grassy tussock large and dense enough to lie back upon, and although my lower legs and feet would hang under water all night, I had no choice but to put thoughts of snakes out of my mind and tried to get as comfortable as possible.

Eventually the customary chatter of the men around me died down and the moon rose, spiking the water with the splintered shadows of trees, its light reflecting on the dark surface like the flash of knives in a cave. For a long time the only sound was muffled voices from the guys who had not yet been taught to listen. Suddenly the tranquility was shattered as though by prior arrangement, when a hundred species of frogs exploded into song, burble, poip, and clack in a mind-wracking symphony of such diversity and unexpected density that the source of any individual voice was impossible to distinguish. The sound filled my senses, even seeming to vibrate the air. I wondered how to tell if the chorus was a warning. Were there messages in it that one could learn, or would alarm come in the form of a sudden, terrible silence? An occasional desolate, discordant shriek from somewhere high in the trees would silence them for a second or two, then the concert resumed. The cadre mentioned nothing about these signs.

I couldn't remember if the instructor set a watch schedule for the night. I wasn't called. Perhaps he stayed awake. I certainly did. Shortly before dawn I got up stiffly on my elbows and looked around. The place lay beneath a pale stain of mist wherein the weakened moonlight was held suspended just above the surface like a vaporous dust. The men were in grey heaps all about on the grass islands, some sprawled, some drawn up like piles of discarded clothing. No one else moved, though I could smell cigarette smoke. My submerged feet were numb, and I worked my toes in their boots to restore circulation. When I pulled my knees up to get my heels against the edge of the tuft, the dripping sound broke the silence like a waterfall.

It was a new experience of a different sort of landscape, one I would never have allowed a team to enter. The vulnerabilities it imposed were not worth the knowledge of how to move through it. It would always be worth a few extra days crawling around such a place in hostile territory rather than risking everything from snakebite to envelopment.

Back at the barracks the next night, when two of the guys pulled off their saturated socks, the soles of their feet, or parts of them, came off with them. All the calloused portions of their feet had been softened, in effect rotted, by long confinement in the water. They were temporarily crippled—perhaps lucky, as it would take weeks, if not months, for the tenderness of their inner dermal layers of skin to harden enough to enable them to walk normally again, not to mention the risk of infection. *Hors de combat,* they were for a time ineligible for field operations. It also meant they would not finish the course, but in view of the quality of instruction, I considered that of minimal consequence.

My feet were white, doughy and soft from their days and nights too long compressed into wet boots, but thanks partly to long toes with good separation, they remained intact. The raised shrapnel scars across the top of my right foot were ridged and appeared crumbly like feta cheese. They were still tender to the touch, but the doctor had done a good job.

On one of the last days of this training, as we faced the prospect of returning to our respective units, the group was loaded again into the back of two deuce-and-a-half trucks, where we stood closely packed for a trip out to the field. As our progress along a rutted road shuffled us like crackers in a box, some of the guys started good-natured complaining about being treated like cattle. They began to moo.

As a kid I had always enjoyed riding in the back of pick-up trucks, but things had changed. My tension had risen as the deadline for returning to FOB 4 loomed. In addition, I did not like being exposed in these open trucks, especially when two vehicles loaded with troops offered such ripe targets. I took a position at the side rail of the second vehicle, prepared to leap out if necessary. Contributing to my irritation was Collins, who rode at the back, and as usual, was holding forth to no one in particular about his lethality.

The tires of the truck ahead made pinwheels of flickering mud as it passed through a shallow ford. Then we crossed, where the slow water shone like oil in its colors and mended itself behind us before the run-off from our tires had even finished draining back. Then, just as I watched the water heal itself, looking for any signs it may hold in its color and movement, or any foot prints in the mud, we lurched to an abrupt stop.

We were stopped on a road in the open, yards from a running stream that appeared to be supplying the sole water source for a nearby village. There was little cover for some distance around, but we were well within range of small arms fire from some houses on one side and trees on the other. I went on instant alert. Some of the others did too, but as there was no outward sign of danger, most just milled and muttered. Gradually the tension began to run in quiet contagion through the others.

Just as I was preparing to jump over the rails, Collins started in again with his enthusiasm for closing with the enemy.

"Shut up, Collins," I said.

"Who said that?" Collins couldn't see me for all the intervening heads.

"I did, you drawn up little creek fuck. If you don't shut up and keep your eyes open, you're too stupid to live."

This broke the tension with enough general laughter that it disarmed Collins, whose bluster had, presumably up until that moment, bought him a certain immunity from direct confrontation. He was unaccustomed to it, and his imaginary sense of self-worth took another bruise a few minutes later when Snow's voice, from somewhere in the crowd, said,

"You know, that Barbra Streisand is one horse-faced woman."

I looked over at Snow who began winking at me with such conspiratorial vehemence that I feared he would do himself an injury. Back by the tailgate Collins began to snort and struggle, but the guys hemmed him in so that he couldn't turn. He stifled an oath when someone else said,

"Yeah, man. Nasal, too."

"And cross-eyed!" from someone else.

It was fun to watch Collins in his porcine struggle, but our general amusement interfered with my effort to concentrate on what seemed a risky predicament. I pushed my way to the center of the crowd, got his attention, pointed directly at him, and said slowly with all the others as witness,

"Collins, don't…you…move."

This was one of the few times in my life I have ever confronted another person in direct personal standoff. It was evidently a new experience for him, too, and he went silent, clearly unprepared for the assembled feeling against him. Thus we chipped down a pompous ass while serving at the same time to drain some of the tension from an inexplicable halt, which continued unresolved. For the benefit of those who hadn't noticed, I pointed out the proximity of the village and the fact that we were a fat target, sitting stationary within small arms range from two directions. Some of the others joined me in refocusing their attention outward to the perimeter of the truck. Still, we waited.

Shortly an old Vietnamese woman with a bundle on her head came along the shoulder, making her way toward us through the spiky growth that verged the road. Experience with the fanaticism of sappers had conditioned me to mistrust any Vietnamese carrying a package. I climbed over the rails and dropped to the ground on the other side of the truck just in case. Some of the guys began to tease her, and to her credit, she teased back in the universal pidgin that always seemed to make do in such exchanges.

I went up to the driver's window only to learn that he could not explain this ill-conceived halt in the open either. I told him I didn't like it, and he surprised me by saying that he never liked this road. In the back of the truck one of the guys began to offer the woman money for "boom-boom." It probably started as a joke. She refused, and angrily, by the volume of her response, but he persisted, upping the price. In a few minutes she was persuaded, and the guy jumped off the truck and took her behind a small clump of bushes.

The absurdity of the event was striking. A few months earlier I might have found the whole transaction utterly repellant, but by now I was well aware of what poverty had done to some of these people and just dismissed it. For many, want and privation had become an attitude, an ingrained sense of impoverishment and emotional drain. Their resentment contained a combination of anger, depression and apathy, and over time had become a way of life. Though this event was distasteful, the woman would probably be able to feed a family of five for a week with what she had been induced to "earn" from him.

Then, just as abruptly as we had stopped, and just as inexplicably, we started again. I leapt back up the side of the truck as the guy who had been with the woman ran out from the bush to be pulled back aboard the other side.

"Little jumpy, aren't you, Sarge?" said someone.

"Yeah," I said. "I am."

Unlike most of my fellows in the course, I knew what sort of work I would be returning to, so when we were graduated it was with a dubious sense of achievement that I bid Snow and a few others good-bye and left the uncertainties of Kontum for renewed emersion into those of FOB 4.

A few days after getting back to FOB 4, I was called up to the HQ hut where I was informed that special orders for me had come in while I was away. With them came a new Department of Defense military I.D. card. This one was printed in red, and it came with the directive that from now on, even on errands to the PX in Da Nang, I must always be armed. I was told this was what came with being "tapped" by the spooks. This was a development fraught with unspecified and uncomfortable implications, and it came with all the disconcerting baggage of having been singled out again, no matter what the reason. Like so many other surprises, it was at best an ambiguous contingency, while the conditions it required certainly made no secret of the secret.

21

The next operation was to be an interdiction mission into the tri-border area where Cambodia, Laos, and South Vietnam come together in a jungly confusion of deep, eerie ravines, shattered mist-bound hills, and bad reputation. Thanks to the stories I had heard about it, a hot charge of remorse shot through me with the news, and I listened with dry-mouthed apprehension to the assignment as estimates of my survival suddenly revised horribly downward. We had lost entire teams in the region, and it was a place most of us held in special dread.

While preparing for it I became fouled in fear, doubt, and recurring waves of sheer emotional exhaustion. In my case the popular belief that experience with terror makes you braver did not apply. It may be that being afraid all the time equips you in ways to hide your fear, and I did what I could to conceal any outward sign, forcing my concentration onto the details of equipment prep, radio checks, and memorizing the schedule of emergency frequencies, but I felt sure the others were able to intuit the symptoms and to smell it on me—the ancient odor of animal flight sweat. It was a miserable time. Before it yawned a pit of likely misfortune that cancelled all expectations of alternative futures.

We waited, equipped, painted, and on full standby all through the first day and night for the weather in the area of the objective to clear. The next day it was still socked in and anyway was an odd numbered day of the month. The third day was still mercifully rainy in the designated AO. Just how merciful I would not know for another week or so.

During the third morning, as I was silently whispering into the Great Ear for heavy rain to keep falling out there, I was called up to the HQ hut. With soaring misgivings pushing through the emotional fatigue of such a long standby, I trudged up to the Command building, only to be told that orders had come in for me to proceed alone as soon as possible down to Special Forces HQ in Nha Trang. Nobody knew why; I was just supposed to get ready to be driven to the airport right away.

I went back in the glow of reprieve, yet uneasy about this new mystery, and gave the happy news to the team that we were canceled. Another team was assigned our operation while I hurriedly packed a few things. I dutifully strapped on my reissued Model 1911 .45 pistol and checked that the spare magazine was loaded. The Jeep came by for me and I was driven to the airport, where, with the unfamiliar weight of the pistol on my right hip, I boarded an unmarked black C-130.

The forward portion of the fuselage was packed with large wooded crates containing machinery. There were a few ammunition and smaller cargo crates strapped down in front of them and a dirty field-worn Jeep with a dusty canvas top was secured amidships. To my surprise there were a few civilian Vietnamese sitting in the sling seats, including some children and their mothers, who bore looks of resigned misgiving. The women in their dresses and pajama pants seemed out of place in the spare mechanical interior. I wondered if their unease simply told of first flight jitters, or if their careworn faces reflected the generations of internecine warfare and an endless intrusion of foreigners like me. When I stepped in from the glare I nodded and smiled to them, receiving no detectable response, though their small black eyes tracked me like gun bores as I crossed to take a seat along the port side near the Jeep.

The flight was waiting for the last of its load before taking off for a long round-robin flight down the length of the country by the inland route and then back up the coastal route where I would get out, I knew, late in the day. I realized that in the hasty departure I had failed to bring anything to read and resolved to entertain myself, perhaps by counting rivets, to a long day.

The last of the cargo finally arrived. A Deuce-and-a-half backed up next to the loading ramp, and a fork lift removed two wooden crates. These proved very quickly to be a pair of poorly sealed coffins containing, I was told, the bodies of two indij killed the month before and only recently recovered. Returning them to their villages was part of our psychological warfare program to recruit the Buddhist natives, as being able to make good on the promise of returning bodies to rejoin their ancestors was something the enemy could not do.

The swollen crates were soon strapped down behind the Jeep by a loading crew that hastened back outside. The boxes leaked a horrible burgundy fluid from their seams, and as soon as they were placed aboard, the heavy stench of putrefaction quickly filled the air inside the airplane. In minutes it permeated all fabric in the way it has of seeming to attach upon every surface in a greasy unquinous film. There is no other smell quite like it, and it shares with oil the characteristic of remaining long after the source is removed, clinging to skin, hair, and living in clothes long after washing.

The engines were started, and the crew chief raised the ramp a foot or two off the pavement but kept it open for the taxi as long as he could. The women produced handkerchiefs or used their dresses in an effort to filter the smell. As we bounced over the pavement joints, each little jolt sent a small spurt of sickening brownish fluid out between the planks of the coffins. Then, on the take-off roll, the stuff coursed rearward in the cargo grooves of the deck. When we had climbed to altitude and leveled off it began to return forward, finding its level somewhere beneath the Jeep. The air vents did little to keep the smell at bay.

Thus we proceeded during the day. With each landing, the fluid ran forward beneath the crates, and with each takeoff, it dribbled back toward the ramp so that no length of the flooring was free of it. With each landing the crew chief opened the ramp as early, and closed it again as late, as he could.

The civilians disembarked mercifully on the third or forth landing, but we carried the boxes on through the afternoon. At one point I thought that if I couldn't escape it, I might be sick, so I got up and climbed into the Jeep. Even though the old Jeep was tied just in front of the coffins, closer to them than where I had been sitting, the vehicular smells of dirty grease, dried mud, and fire-retardant chemical treatment in the jungle-saturated canvas Jeep cover served to keep the insistent stink of rotting corpses sufficiently at bay to get me through to the landing, somewhere in the south of the country, where the coffins were at last unloaded. I got out with them just to breathe the outside air until it was time to take off again.

We finally landed at Nha Trang late in the day, where I found that a Jeep and driver were waiting for me outside the little terminal building. I was glad that transportation had been provided, but a bit uneasy at the special treatment. What was going on? Was I being reassigned? Did this have something to do with my recent brush with the dark forces on the mountain top? Might there be an emergency of some kind at home? I had no idea.

When I was delivered to Headquarters and reported in at the designated office, it was near the close of the working day. As I saw people leaving their offices, I was reminded of the garrison lifestyle I had forgotten existed. My uneasy curiosity about the new orders was deepened by the careless air of presumed security that was everywhere obvious. People went about unarmed, dressed in starched fatigues and boots polished to mirror the sun. They walked casually through the open areas in talkative groups, keeping to the sidewalks and duckboards. Their speech was too loud. The whole base, every building I could see, was within easy mortar range of all that surrounded it. Yet it exuded the same sense of lazy confidence I'd encountered at FOB 4 that first disastrous day. I couldn't suppress the expectation of imminent catastrophe. With the skin on my back squirming, I hurried into the designated building and reported in. A clerk looked over my orders and disappeared into the back offices, leaving me still mystified.

A minute later my friend from that first night in-country, Steve Anderson, came grinning from around the corner with his hand out. He had shaved his head and grown a large handlebar moustache since I had seen him last. The look served to increase his extraordinary likeness to the actor Keenan Wynn. He said he knew all about my orders but that the first order of business was a drink at the club. Thus still in the bureaucratic dark, we left the offices together and started across the compound.

As soon as we were alone, he disclosed with delighted conspiratorial drama that he had cut my orders himself. He just wanted to see if he had enough power as one of the head clerks to pull a guy off combat duty! After a moment of stunned speechlessness while I absorbed the full implications of what he had done, I surrendered to the first full-bodied laugh I'd had since arriving in the country. He was almost as pleased as I was, but I knew no one could possibly understand my relief at being removed from FOB 4 at just that time. I didn't mention anything about the operation I had been slated for but simply luxuriated in the way fate can suddenly drop a stone in the river of care. We joked about his administrative powers while he showed me to the room he'd arranged for me in one of the concrete buildings normally reserved for officers.

I claimed the bunk by depositing my bag and pistol belt on the mattress, and thus unencumbered by the weight of the side arm, proceeded with Steve to the main clubhouse I remembered from my transit stay all those months before. It was clear that Steve's jovial personality had fed delightedly at the trough of good living at SF HQ. He had gained a little weight, and it soon became evident by the people who stopped at our table to say something to him that he had friends throughout the ranks. I guessed it was because he had learned to work the system and had developed the right contacts for the purpose of getting certain people things they wanted. He had become good enough at his job to have achieved a useful level of respect, immunity from restrictions against the unconventional slant of his mind—and clearly, freedom from scrutiny over personally cutting orders to extract a friend from highly classified work near the DMZ.

Although I was still a bit jumpy at the noise and crowd inside the club, that night marked my first tenuous relaxation in the months since I had last seen this place. It didn't take long to notice there were even a few women at the bar, one in particular, a gorgeous Eurasian with a Playboy Magazine centerfold figure. She had green, slightly almond-shaped eyes tastefully lined, blondish hair which she wore shoulder length, and a modest sort of western-style summer dress, not at all flamboyant, but that could not hide her shape. Steve explained that she was a famous prostitute, conceived during the French occupation, who had sort of adopted the Special Forces as her market, although there wasn't always a charge. She spoke a delightfully accented English, and from where we sat, apparently enjoyed real friendships among the bar crowd. She seemed to have perfected a subtle balance between her natural allure, a demure ability to listen, and genuine good humor. It was fun to watch the way crescents of light in her clothes clung to her contours and to be reminded that a world in which certain forms of the pleasures she represented still existed.

Steve and I went to the messhall for a good dinner, after which he suggested that we walk the short distance into the town of Nha Trang, which was accessible from the rear gate of the HQ compound. I did not think this a great idea. Being on foot in the warren of streets and native dives that appear to grow like toadstools around large U.S. compounds seemed an unnecessary risk. Steve assured me that it was perfectly safe, that he went into town all the time, that there was a nice USO not far away, and besides, he had made some Vietnamese friends there. So, with my reservations on simmer for the moment, we walked past the guard at the back gate and onto a broken road that in about 50 meters led into the border shanties of Nha Trang.

Ahead, a Southeast Asian town rose from the ground into a hodge-podge of single- and two-story frame and masonry buildings speckled with pools of fierce electric light through which moved figures on bicycles while others sauntered among the shadows. Everything looked blown through smoke. A tinny mix of native music and American rock and roll carried forth on greasy air from the lazy commerce of numerous bars. Females of domestic reputation lounged upon the balconies with faces done up in indigo, gaudy as the rumps of apes, and they peered from behind their fans with a kind of lurid coyness like transvestites in a madhouse. On the sidewalks several Americans in faded olive drab towered over the native white shirts and slender ao dai dresses that shimmered in colorful contrast to the muddy and trash-strewn street. The air smelled of joss, mud, urine, rotting vegetables, and all of whatever the standing puddles contained.

As we made our way through this alien landscape I felt increasingly obvious, like some kind of specimen under glass. It seemed a dangerous place, full of sidelong resentment, and still unused to the new directive that I must be armed at all times, I realized I had left my pistol behind. We were away from the security of the compound, unarmed, and surrounded by a density of sullen natives who looked just like the enemy.

We stopped in the USO, a tall, harshly lit cell hung inside with bare bulbs and nearly empty except for a few Vietnamese men playing pool with two American soldiers. Morbid rock music fell forlornly from speakers mounted high up the patched plaster walls, competing with the quiet click of the balls. Ceiling fans stirred the air so slowly that flies hitched rides on their dusty blades. There were a few young Vietnamese girls in attendance behind a small bar area, but their professional smiles failed to mask the listless depression in their eyes. We didn't stay.

The neighborhoods improved as we strolled deeper into the town and farther away from the businesses that depended mostly on trade from the base. Here it was possible to glimpse an occasional scene that seemed to reflect a marginally higher degree of Vietnamese life. Though the smell of refuse persisted, there were fewer foreigners like ourselves, restaurants offering views of the street held customers seated at tablecloths, and there was some traffic in cyclos and motor scooters. Western products were displayed in shops still open to capture some hours of business after the heat of the day, and here, as in the world over, the better class of women clattered noisily along the street, their feet tipped like arrowheads. Their eyes swept the ground before them with a mix of curiosity and indifference, somehow taking a fragment of extra time to add speculation to hesitation, and with the absolute assurance of being seen.

After a short tour of less well-lit side streets, during which I grew increasingly nervous, we decided to head back to the compound by way of a house where Steve wanted to stop. I wanted to get back through the compound gate and behind our perimeter as soon as possible, but decided that I would stay with him, where at least the prospect of being inside some house seemed less risky than wandering alone back to the base.

We entered a street that seemed a cut above the rest of the town. The houses were better maintained, and the street was relatively clear of refuse. Above, a cuticle of light winking through the leaves of a large banyan tree became the flowering nimbus of the moon, nearly full. Its pale opalescence winked across our clothes as we entered the dappled shadow of the tree. Just beyond was a masonry house behind a steel fence that stood in the moonlight like a parade of starved soldiers.

"Come on," said Steve in a stage whisper. It seemed he had hidden some doubt as to the location. "This is it."

He swung the metal gate open with a hesitant familiarity, rather like an uncertain scoutmaster, and I followed his long moon shadow across the ground with an attitude of reserved curiosity, feeling a bit superfluous, like the dot at the end of a question mark.

The entrance to the house was through a moon gate, wide and crimson, like the lacquered nostrils of a Chinese dragon. We stepped through and stood for a moment blinking in the harsh light of what seemed to be a mockup of some western-style living room, sparsely furnished with heavy easy chairs covered in green vinyl, their curved chromium armrests reflecting dingy overhead fluorescents. In fact, all the few furnishings stood in grim reminiscence of an American bus station of the 1950s. Pale green walls mottled with mysterious stains stared back blankly, and from somewhere, the toneless tinkling sounds of native music struggled through the heady sandalwood incense, that hung protectively about, layered in the wet air like mosquito netting.

It was still. Suspended. The only other occupants of the quiet room were two disheveled privates from some infantry outfit, evidently stoned, in dirty fatigues and wordlessly smoking cigarettes. Both were slouched in low chairs against the opposite wall, facing the entrance. Each regarded our arrival through reddened half-lidded eyes with what I took to be a version of suppressed defiance. I looked at them evenly for a long moment, causing one to shift his weight defensively. It released a loud farting sound from the vinyl upholstery. I dismissed them as a couple of typists from some clerical pool, but their sullen presence was dimly threatening, and it made me uncomfortable nonetheless.

I still didn't know why we had come to this place, but the sense of waiting for something pervaded the room, and I was glad for the diversion of Steve's personality. He was going to have to wait in line, but in the meantime, he could run interference.

We helped ourselves to some chairs, and just as we sat down a middle-aged Vietnamese woman breezed into the room with a flurry. She was dressed in a plain shift, but trailing a colorful diaphanous scarf whose floral pattern fluttered in the air behind her like seagulls in the wake of a ferry. She was a floating opera of cackling delight.

"You come now!" she screeched at the first of the privates, as she grabbed him by the arm and pulled him brusquely up from his chair. His eyes darted confusedly, searching for a place to stub out his cigarette. "You come now! You nex'!" She appeared to take no notice of Steve or me.

It dawned upon me what was going on here as she nudged the boy toward the inner door, her body swaying attentively and her hips shuffling in haste. In her high triphthongal diapason, she yelled something to a girl through the inner wall, and was answered with a few shrill syllables from the adjoining room, as the previous customer brushed past them, self-consciously straightening his clothes. The two men avoided looking at each other.

The woman came right back after delivering the private to the inner doorway, obviously delighted with the evening's growing volume of business. She made a grand show of welcoming Steve, who appeared to be a favored customer. After some laughing, patting, and teasing with Steve, her eyes quickly shifted to me in glittering anticipation, reference business being always a measure of one's commercial success.

I signaled no, and Steve explained that he was the only customer. Instantly incredulous, her face fell open like the claw of a steam shovel. So much for oriental inscrutability. It was evident that she could not believe it. Her reaction was genuine and so comical that I felt myself being taken up in the lurid miasma of oddball humor that was beginning to pervade the situation. Unwittingly, I seemed to be introducing this pleasant-faced woman to an unprecedented possibility.

"You no want boom-boom? ...Whassa matta?...you no like?"

We all looked at each other with half smiles in a three-way Mexican stand-off, each waiting to see if another would offer an explanation. Steve began to giggle.

She leaned over my chair as though to better study some scientific aberration. I peered warily back in the enforced proximity, feeling momentarily trapped in a vacuum of unassailable impulses. She smelled faintly of lilacs, mixed perhaps with linseed oil and camphor balls. Her tanned face, under a streak of greying hair, was somewhat flabby for a Vietnamese, and it held two black eyes that seemed trapped in a spiderweb of weary lines. Her eyelashes, uppers and lowers, were so gathered with mascara that she appeared to be looking at me through bottle caps. She studied me for a moment with real curiosity, then suddenly shot her hand down between my legs and grabbed me with the speed of a conjurer.

"You like boy, mebbe?" she snorted as I yelped and batted her hand away.

"No!" I said with horrified amusement at both her boldness and the absurdity of the notion. The three of us laughed, and even the sullen young soldier by the wall grinned crookedly for a moment before his faced collapsed back into a rheumy red stare.

She looked up and abruptly changed the subject.

"You want beea?"

Steve, grinning broadly, ordered us a couple of beers, and she turned to get them, shaking her head in mocking wonder.

The sound of springs and a certain animal culmination, began to rise from the next room before she returned with our beers. I noticed that the wall separating us from the "service" room did not reach the ceiling. It was simply a cinder block blind which rose to within a few feet of the ceiling and ended some three feet from the far wall to form an entryway, though there was no door. To enter the other room, one simply walked around the end of this divider. All conversation and other noises issuing from the inner chamber, were clearly shared with anyone sitting in the outer room. This arrangement lent the place a homey informality which made me smile.

Our Mama-san quickly returned with two green bottles of local Ba Muoi Ba beer, her excitement renewed by the imminence of a new shift inside. She began herding the remaining clerk toward the opening at the end of the wall, where they were greeted by epithets from the previous customer. He evidently felt rushed. I remarked to Steve that the business seemed to enjoy a healthy turnover, and he assured me that it was still not too late to change my mind. I took my first sip of Vietnamese beer and understood immediately why people joked that it was brewed from embalming fluid.

When our hostess returned, she tried once again to promote the services of the house to me, by assurances that the stock was both healthy and talented. She knew this because they were her own daughters, and furthermore, they were "No too ole'!" ranging in age from 14 to 16. I thanked her, as though declining a helping of petit-fours, and indicated that the beer was quite enough to keep me happy.

Steve's turn soon came, and he stepped behind the wall, where he continued his conversation with me until his words blended hollowly with those of the young girl and the harsh enthusiastic notes of her attentive mother. Apparently, he was an important enough customer to require the ministrations of the older woman as well. In the few moments of relative quiet which followed, I was left alone to relax in the chair and to speculate that the only universal laws are paradox, humor, and change.

My ruminations were quickly dispelled by an eruption of laughter which came over the wall in an explosive mixture of all three voices. Steve's deep, bombastic guffaws were all but drowned by screaming nasal peels of glee from both women. Whatever was happening behind there was obviously a great delight for everyone involved. Gasping for breath between his long heaving laughs, Steve finally croaked out, "Hey, Moore...get in here! You have to see this!"

So, accompanied by a crescendo of sound from the women, I got up and rounded the corner. The pure, exalted absurdity of what I saw next remains suspended as a bright fantasia of hilarity, thus far unequaled in the course of my sometimes rousing life:

Steve, roaring with laughter, was lying on his back in the middle of a slightly sway-backed double bed, fully clothed, including his boots. Suspended above him was the girl, jack-knifed into a large brown basket with a circular hole cut out of the bottom, through which her narrow buttocks protruded like a pair of quarter moons. Her bare legs were draped over the rim of the basket and her small hands gripped the wicker between her knees. The entire contraption was suspended from the ceiling above the bed by a double block and fall, which led to a cleat affixed to the wall near the doorway, where Mama-san controlled the tether. Filling the air with peals of laughter, the woman was lowering the girl onto Steve's large pink erection, which, with a howl of cheer from the girl, went home, sending a shimmer up the ropes. As the skillful hostess leaned slightly on her end of the line, causing the basket to rise and fall an inch or so, Steve began to spin the whole bundle, making of the girl a giggling, rotating lighthouse of smiles.

I began to laugh so hard I lost my balance and had to sit down. I could not get my breath. Tears filled my eyes, as finally, for the first time since arriving in-country, I felt myself yielding to all the fear and anxiety, all the sanguine guesswork of youth, the vague hopes and the silliness; surrendering all to the novelty of being alive and impressed by the urgency of tremendous trifles.

When this wonderful event was concluded, and we were all four spent—or at least laughed out—Steve, ever the diplomat, demonstrated the reason for his favored status in the place by asking the Mama-san if he might sample one of the other daughters as long as he was there.

Both the Mama-san and the girl, who was trying to extricate herself from the basket, now capsized on the squeaky bed, seemed pleased with his appetite. He was quickly escorted outside, through a side door, and along flagstones to an apartment at the back. Even as I began to question why it had all seemed so funny, I wondered what additional novelties the place might hold and followed his progress along the side of the house, still clutching my ceremonial beer.

The woman rapped on a door and barked something through the open transom. In a moment she was answered by a small voice, which stepped out into the dim exterior light in the form of a thin teenage girl, rubbing her eyes, not with her fists, as I'd seen other kids her age do, but with well-manicured nails. She was draped in a light colored ao-dai, ankle length and slit up the side. She took Steve inside with a speculative glance back at me, possibly gauging her energy requirements.

I sipped from the warm bottle in silence and listened to the crickets, while through the transom came the muted, repetitive vocalisms of mutual effort. In short order there came a distinct grunt of finality from Steve, followed by what sounded like a small bucket being pulled out of the mud. He emerged from the doorway in a few moments with a moist "Aah," smacking his lips in parody of a gratified gourmet and absently smoothing the front of his pants.

He was followed by the girl, who appeared barefooted and clad only in a pair of bikini panties.

"You nex'," she said, beckoning with her tiny arm.

"Come. I give numba one boom-boom you."

"No, thank you," I told her gently.

"You come...You come now!" she persisted, beginning to frown.

When I said no again, an honest bewilderment flicked across her brow, and I felt, rather than saw, the moment it was replaced by uncomprehending anger. She stared at me, her slender body framed in the black doorway. Her thrusting pair of heavily-ringed nipples regarded me sorrowfully, like spaniel's eyes.

Steve and I said goodbye cheerfully, but she had been insulted and would not be mollified by words. As we picked our way along the flag stones toward the street, she screamed pidgin-English obscenities at my back from the darkness for as long as we could hear her.

We walked in silence for some time, and after a while I said, "Well. What else is there to spend it on but whores and toothpaste, anyway?"

A damp breeze, smelling of vegetation, sighed out of the north, and its warm breath wrinkled a large luminous puddle, making of the telephone lines reflected in it illegible black zigzags.

After a thoughtful pause, Steve replied to nobody in particular:

"Booze, tattoos, and shit medicine."

It was after curfew when we arrived back at the compound gate. The guard didn't want to let us in. We tried to appeal to his sympathy, but he had his orders and told us we'd have to spend the night in the town. About the time I was tempted to pull out my new ID card to test its secret powers, Steve started to sing Barry Sadler's "Ballad of the Green Berets" to the guard.

"Fighting solders from the skies...."

"Okay, okay," said the guard. None of that...Jeez."

He unlocked the gate and let us slip through a narrow gap, back onto the base. I was glad to be back inside and thanked the guard, who just said not to break the curfew again.

Finally back in the room where I'd left my stuff, I noticed that my clothes still smelled faintly of the two coffins on the plane and decided that I'd take a shower before getting into bed. I stripped down, got a towel from a rack in the room, and stepped outside again, just as the wonderful Eurasian whore and an American Lieutenant, both stumbling drunk, came around the corner and made their way into the room next to mine.

Later, after returning from the showers, I climbed into bed, grateful to be able to sleep behind cinderblock walls for a change. Some time after allowing myself to drift away from full consciousness, I heard the woman leave the room next door, laughing about having to go to the bathroom. She thumped against the wall outside, evidently feeling her way unsteadily toward the latrine.

Soon she came shuffling back, but didn't go quite far enough. She lurched into my room and fell across the bed. She hit her leg on the bed frame, which seemed to sober her enough to launch some choice expletives and to understand she'd gone through the wrong door. I helped her to her feet and pointed her down to the next room, toward which she staggered off, smelling sweetly of liquor and jasmine perfume. Such was my brush with celebrity.

I stayed in the relative safety of the HQ compound for three or four days, the duration of my orders. During this time I answered Steve's questions about conditions in the north, the big attack back in August, and how far we had to operate from any American control. I shared my worries about the odds, that two of our team leaders had been killed since I had arrived and two more had been medivac'd out of the country. He reminded me that I could buy some time away from there by putting in for R&R.

Perhaps because of my festering preoccupation with the daily requirements of survival, the idea of putting in for R&R had not even occurred to me. Steve reminded me that everyone was entitled to at least one R&R and that if I applied, he might be able to arrange for us to take them at the same time in Hong Kong. It sounded like a great idea, and when I left to fly back up to Da Nang, we agreed that I should put in for the leave right away so he could try to coordinate them.

When I returned to FOB 4, I learned the team that had gone into the tri-border area in our place when I left for Nha Trang had disappeared. The day after insertion they had failed to come up on the check frequency. Numerous fly-overs had failed to pick up any signals or find any sign of them.

The news was announced to me in the plain language of fact. I tried to show the grim face of expressionless resolve that all the veterans wore, but inwardly I was struck hard by the substitution, by the agency of fate. I was chilled by a cold sigh from the pit, the black void into which we were all falling, piecemeal and in small groups. I tensed against a sudden rush of trembling which overtook my joints when I allowed myself to think about the imponderable improbables that had joined once again to preserve me somehow from that yawning, lubricious chasm.

22

Soon after returning, my name came around again on the roster for a night of guard duty on rolling patrol. Each team leader, along with other NCOs, pulled all night watch in the Jeep on a rotation schedule. It was not unpleasant duty. There were times when I looked forward to it as a substitute for my growing insomnia. You drove slowly throughout the camp by starlight with lights off, checking by moonlight the wire, each of the guard towers, and the guys on watch in the perimeter bunkers. It was usually quiet, the loudest sounds being the whisper of waves on the beach and the muffled Jeep itself. It was a kind of lone time, and some nights the sky filled with a flung lace of stars. Since I couldn't sleep anyway, my turns at the patrol gave me something to do that might also make me the first to know of any trouble, so I never objected and occasionally even took the duty when one of the other guys on the rotation was sick or just didn't want to give up the sack time.

This night I was to be accompanied by a major whom I did not know. He was new and had been sent to FOB 4 on some temporary assignment. He soon proved to be a man easily startled and fueled by prodigious incompetence.

Just after dark I got into the Jeep and drove over to the HQ hut to pick him up. He appeared, breathing excitedly, with all his insignia of rank carefully taped over, heavily decked out with a side arm and a fully loaded M-16, wearing his steel helmet and flak jacket. Though helmets and flak vests were standard issue, none of us wore them because of their bulk and weight. In fact, I used my vest exclusively as a pillow on my bunk. This was the first time I had seen anyone on the base actually wearing one. He was overweight, not too much for a garrison field grade officer, but certainly overly pudgy for anyone who could have qualified for Special Forces.

I introduced myself and stuck out my hand, saluting being a custom universally ignored among us. He admonished me for not saluting him. Surprised, I apologized dutifully and assured him that no disrespect was intended. After we exchanged the important saluting ritual in the near pitch dark, he settled into the passenger seat with a clamber of adjustments to his load of gear, I eased the Jeep into low gear and pulled slowly and quietly away, resigned to spending a whole night with an officious jerk. He had probably never been assigned to any kind of guard duty before in his life, and it soon became clear that he was disconcerted at the prospect and quite nervous.

We ground slowly along the perimeter road as I tried to keep the whine of low gear and the hum of throaty combustions under the hood to an absolute minimum. It was a fine, clear night, calm and quiet but for the soft thump and swish of waves that came from the beach and with a bright enough moon that an attack upon us would have been foolish. Though I chose to live with the assumption that an attack could come at any time, experience told against such attempts on clear nights, and besides, it was an odd numbered day of the month, and the enemy were Buddhists too. I had not heard that the VC held the same superstitions as the Nung's, but it seemed reasonable, unless of course their hatred was greater than ours. Then I remembered hate had indeed trumped numerology when the big attack had come on the 23rd of the month...

These thoughts were interrupted by a single squawk from one of the geese along the southern perimeter–sharp against the steady pulse of background sounds, but common enough most nights. The major jumped in his seat, his eyes round and white as marbles in the starlight.

"Wha'–! What was that?!" he almost screeched, his voice fluted with fear. He pulled the charging handle on his M-16, mindlessly ejecting the live chambered round, and in a frantic effort to stand up, swung the barrel wildly about, more or less in the direction of the call, but once passing the muzzle across my face. I batted the rifle away.

"Whoa, sir! Hold on! …We'll drive over there and see what's up."

He didn't seem to hear me. He sat rigidly in the seat, mantled in fear and desperately scanning the night, with one hand white on the dashboard grip handle, the other on his weapon, finger on the trigger.

We ground slowly around the perimeter road until we arrived about where the noise had come from. I asked the guys in the closest bunker if anything was going on, and both said no, that a few of the old geese were just strutting around outside the wire.

"There's always one needs to be the stud duck in the pond," one of them chuckled.

"Okay," I said. "Keep an eye out. You never know what it might have sensed." I added that for the major's sake, but I was much more concerned about his nerves and feared that he might panic at any time and begin firing wildly.

The rest of that night passed without further incident, except that I had to push the muzzle of the major's M-16 away from me several times and to ask him politely more than once to hold his weapon facing out his side of the vehicle. He was a man thrown completely out of his element and lost in his fears. I had to admit a grudging sympathy for him beneath my disrespect, for I knew all too well how he felt.

Happily, he chose to leave the patrol early. I was relieved to drop him back at his hut several hours before daybreak. He caught a heel and stumbled awkwardly when trying to dismount the Jeep, the clunk and squeak of his equipment offensive in the stillness. He tried to recover his dignity by bidding me good night in a tone of voice adjusted for authority and calling me "Sergeant" with deliberation.

I expected him to stand for a moment in anticipation of a parting salute, but he turned abruptly and waddled away through the sand toward his hut. I couldn't help thinking of him as completely hollow. He was built robustly enough, but I imagined that inside there was just an empty grey space with nothing in it but frustration and fear; no real force other than the dangers his emotions posed for others, just a tensed configuration, like a three-dimensional diagram of stress. I was relieved to see him go. It was more comfortable (and secure) doing the rounds alone after that.

Some weeks later, I returned from an operation to learn that the fumbling major was gone–sent on a speaking tour. Having no direct experience of a subject on which he was qualified to speak, I concluded that it was a cover story. Then I learned the inciting incident had been a night patrol that he had sent out without coordinating it with our QCs. The Nungs on our southern perimeter saw movement and opened up on our own Hatchet Force. Little harm came to them, thankfully, but a stray bullet entered the head of a Marine on guard duty over at Third Amtracs, killing him. At least one other Marine was hurt.

These things happened. They're not the sort of incidents that make it into even the opposition press at home, but at least this one got rid of the erstwhile major. We had more than enough threat to life on the perimeter without him, and I am certain that right up to the point when he was reassigned, an ecumenical fear for his own life was so consuming that it protected him from understanding what it did to others. He had been borne away from FOB 4 on a crest of enthusiasm among the survivors, haloed, I'm sure, in a mist of his own desperate illusion.

Shortly after my patrol with the major, team Anaconda was sent out again. This was to be another interdiction mission, slightly north of the dreaded tri-border area where one of our teams had recently been sacrificed to an operation initially assigned to me. It wasn't to be in the same region but close enough to crowd everything else from my consciousness.

A recent battalion-size engagement with the NVA had resulted in the loss of a man with a Starlight night vision scope, and the Americans had withdrawn under fire without being able to retrieve the body or the scope. Since an air strike had been called in to finish the NVA, it was hoped the remains had been destroyed along with the scope, but they wanted to be sure. The important thing was to retrieve the scope, or whatever might be left of it, before the enemy could find it.

Night vision technology was still new, and the scopes in use at the time worked by gathering available light from the night sky. They worked fairly well, certainly well enough to make it important to keep the instrument out of the hands of the enemy.

We flew out to the west again, while I sat in the open doorway in order to see all I could of the land—any rivers, breaks in the endless knap of trees, or any promontories—by which to orient an unassisted escape in case we were compromised on the ground. I had learned to see more, to better gauge the probable contour of the ground, but it was always mostly conjecture, guessing down through a continental featurelessness that cannot be imagined by anyone who has never seen it. This time the shoreless botanical ocean that lapped beneath us mocked my effort.

Having learned little by the time we over-flew the brown scar in the jungle that marked our objective, I had then to contend again with those chilling squads of fear that invariably welled within me as the chopper began its descent. Since we did not know what, if any, investigation of the site had been (or was being) conducted by the enemy, and due to the paucity of insertion points in the area where the battle had taken place, we could not be landed at the site itself, or even conveniently close to it.

This time we had to rappel hurriedly down through the trees while the choppers hovered, which as far as I could see, meant that we were clearly showing our insertion point to any observer. Our only clear option for eventual extraction would be the objective itself–a large scar in the landscape I had seen from the air. It looked to be about four or five miles away, which further raised the stakes of its timely discovery. If we all made it down without mishap, it would be a long slog at the pace we had to move, perhaps as much as a week.

Once settled on the ground we crawled slowly, cautiously, for three and a half days southwestward, creeping stealthily toward, what? I didn't know enough. We were making for a place that had been ravaged by an air strike. We were supposed to scour a large area of wilderness burned by napalm and otherwise in unknown condition for an object about 4" by maybe 18", which was possibly mounted on a rifle. The odds against our finding it amid the destruction lay beyond reasoned calculation, and if the bad guys knew about our objective they were very likely looking too, assuming they had not already captured it. The whole operation seemed hopeless, and although my feelings about pointless risk were by now familiar, they did nothing to lessen a sense of the dangers assembled in places of known interest to the enemy.

There was another feeling too, an oppressive, generalized perception of endlessness, a distortion of reasonable expectations, constantly reborn from integrated layers of threat that seemed to drag on in a ceaseless drudgery of re-emergence without resolution. Nor could I escape the feeling of entrapment between the colliding agendas of disparate bureaucracies and their inexplicably correlated vagaries, wherein the high art of stealth for days on end in a stifling jungle, and its costs in time and emotion, simply raised the price of any interim conclusions I could draw from available evidence, while no resolution ever seemed to come, and the reward for survival was just to be sent out again.

The sense of expectancy was a conditioned impulse that gradually, little by little, bogged you down. There was never any feeling that you were safe and none that some dependable outcome would result. Quite the contrary. The reward for sharpening your jungle skills, for training your senses and forcing an inner resolve kept receding, and slowly the notion that the iniquity was provisional gave way to the feeling that it may be endless. Nothing could be conclusive for there was no grip, no evidence, by which a leavening realization could be seized. The feeling, once acknowledged, spread like a gray leprosy, and it left me crawling on the jungle floor with the last remnants of my initial belief that I might survive unraveling in a tattered weft of abandoned hope.

A warm rain soaked us briefly on the fourth day, adding to the misery of our condition and reopening old chafing wounds under the pack straps across my shoulders. We were hot, dirty, thirsty, and now, between the dripping vegetation and mucid black compost of the jungle floor through which we had to move mostly on our hands and knees and to belly crawl, our fatigues were saturated with rain water, ammoniac sweat, and wet earth. I strained to listen for any sound of movement while tiny insects whined in my ears and plagued my eyes.

The tangled undergrowth made for extremely slow going. We were forced for much of our progress onto the ground itself, creeping like animals among the stems and roots to keep below the congestion of vines. I did my best to scrape the mud from the closure snaps on my ammunition pouches and other equipment, washing my fingers when I could in the run-off from the leaves.

Just before evening came down, the jungle began to reveal signs of having been recently disturbed. It was strange to see such evidence after the deep sense of isolation and abandonment that our days in the wild had imposed. There was a freshly broken stem here and there, torn leaves, trampled ground cover, and occasional projectile injury to the trees. It was impossible to tell who or what had caused the damage. It could mean we were approaching the objective, or it could be signs of some other engagement entirely. We might have come across the path of enemy movement made by a body of men who could still be close by.

We went on increased alert, the whole team just melting soundlessly into the shadows, where we lay listening and watching for any movement. As we waited the shadows deepened. The light that filtered feebly through the canopy quickly withdrew to make room for a thick, viscous darkness.

We stayed where we were, enclosed by large trees, and formed ourselves for the RON on wet ground. I wasn't looking forward to whatever we were likely to encounter, if indeed what we had seen so far were indications that we were nearing the objective. I knew we would be subject to the risks that attended our last operation to open ground, with little likelihood of recovering a lone Starlight scope in whatever remained of a deep jungle air strike that had happened some five days before. I worried about how much time we would have to spend in such a place of likely interest to the enemy in order to do a sufficiently thorough search for me to answer the questions I'd be asked in the after-action report.

I ate a ball of gritty rice and tried to plan through all the unknowns, but there just wasn't enough information. I settled into the mud for the night, sending the filaments of my attention outward.

Around us the leaves dribbled from the recent rain, the droplets falling in loud splats and then trailing off in blubbering runnels. It was familiar on one entirely physical level, but even as my understanding of the jungle grew, I knew that I would never come to truly know it. Even after days of fearful observation and the studied movement that it demanded, I knew I was really only seeing its surface. It always withheld the essential nature of its moods, day or night, light and shadow. It's difficult to put into words that hugely metaphysical quality that it whispers to you in a voice too vast and deep for human hearing the full history you think it tells.

The fresh moisture had released a complex of smells that rose as darkness fell. The strong odor of rot in the damp earth intensified, but there soon seemed to be the breath of other things carried on the muggy air. I sensed burnt vegetation and turned earth, a hint of cordite, and then–the unmistakable sickly eminence of death. In the gathering gloom, I had seen no sign of a clearing ahead, but I could hear the Nungs sniffing and realized that we had all picked up on the evidence and knew we were near the site of something bad.

The complex salad of rancid odors grew as we worked our careful approach the next morning. Grayish light through the trees ahead soon gave way to open sky and a great sagging canopy of coming rain, plump and low. As we emerged, beneath the clouds was revealed a landscape of the Last Judgment. It required a long minute to grasp the scene and the implications of what it contained. The earth was churned, torn, scorched, layered over with still smoke, and strewn with the blackened remains of dead humans. Parts of bodies protruded from the furrowed ground amid the skeletons of shattered trees, some shivered off at the base of the trunk, many others with a single grotesque and hopeless branch left. Nothing moved. The place still radiated heat and had been swept clean of living things by a tempest of orchestral death. There were no birds. Even the air was stilled.

Dull points of light glinted weakly throughout from a rain of empty aviation cannon brasses and the torn metal of burst napalm containers. Numerous oblong craters of different sizes reflected the sky in standing brown water through a thin pall of gray smoke that fed upon scattered wisps drifting forth uncertainly from different places, some from the bodies, a few of which still cooked. The putrid, all-pervasive smell of rotting meat hung over everything.

We waited a long time, taking in the devastation and watching for any movement. Then, keeping under cover, we skirted with great care about half the clearing, surveying the destruction from different vantage points and gradually coming to believe that we were, at least for now, alone there.

Such places were taboo to both sides and with good reason. In addition to the horrible collection of violent deaths, swarms of disease-bearing flies that arrived to feed together on both the living and the dead were a strong deterrent. In addition, air strikes on collected infantry produced an omnipresent blanket of putrefaction that saturated every breath. I began to think that these things would probably serve to make it a fairly protected RON site, at least discouraging of enemy incursion. I tied my tourniquet around my nose and mouth, bandit-style, the earthy smell of the fabric delivering some relief from the rotten air.

Yet the scene held a morbid fascination. There were long minutes when I couldn't tear my eyes away from it. It gripped my attention, insisting that I look. It wanted me to take it all in, make it a part of my living consciousness and of whatever might remain of my own uncertain life. Even in the thrall of its present evidence I found it hard to imagine the full horror of being on the receiving end of a napalm attack. I thought how the sacrifice of another people for one's own strategic aims was a fearful thing indeed when one was down here among those being sacrificed. I felt an intense surrogate kind of fear of what I was seeing, as though just looking might somehow connect me with this kind of violence. It was notably reminiscent of old sepia photographs of the terrible devastation on the Somme and in Ypres at Passchendaele in WW I, but here, it was the religious intensity of the smells that animated such a garbled and poignant fascination.

Nearby, a tangled row of roasted corpses, busy with flies, lay thrown together, their swollen trunks like burned sausages, and among them was a severed head that faced us with its strange half-lidded look of grotesque *ennui* into which the features had dried. It seemed to whisper that the facile recourse to violence that our technology has introduced to the 20th century experience had given us a new Dark Age.

The ground had been so churned by the air strike that it was difficult to tell where the American ground force had been positioned. We had to locate their old line if we were to have any chance of finding the scope. Judging by the angle at which most of the craters had been made, it appeared that the aircraft had come in from the north, the same direction as we had. This meant that the Americans had probably not been at the southern end or our planes would have been firing toward them. I had to guess that any signs of the U.S. position would have to be some distance back from either the northern end of the clearing or from the east or west sides, assuming the aircraft had been called in roughly parallel to the friendly front—a pure guess. Everything was so torn up that it was very hard to tell anything certain from our limited perspective. If I was guessing right, though, the bodies we encountered near the northern end seemed out of place. This indicated the limitations of my guesswork and that we had most of the perimeter to explore, possibly leaving only the southern edge, and that would take much more time than I wanted to linger in this dreadful place. I didn't like the prospect. The going promised to be difficult work.

The others by now had wrapped their faces in tourniquets, and thus struggling through the sickening air, we continued making our way around the site, adding to our defensive scan a search of the ground for any abandoned U.S. equipment, dropped gear, rifle brass, signs of the firefight and withdrawal. We found nothing, not even burned rifle brass. I guessed that either we had worked our way down the wrong side, or the Americans had been farther away than I assumed, or perhaps they had withdrawn before the air strike, and evidence of their position had been obliterated in the wreckage of the site.

By late afternoon we had crept, stumbled and crawled with great difficulty all the way around to the southern end of the burn, which I had speculated initially to have been the most likely position of the enemy. The few artifacts we collected had indicated no pattern. Just at the edge of the trees, we came upon an impact crater that had thrown up a pile of ejected earth near the base of a half-burned tree. There, in a hollow at the top of the little hill it made, sat a dead Vietnamese machine gunner behind the ruins of his weapon. The top of his head had been blown off and the brain pan was full of rain water. We stopped to rest here as the trees were particularly dense, and we were all exhausted. I relieved myself of the radio and propped it at the base of a tree. Because this location was slightly higher than the rest of the site,

Nhi and I risked exposure by crawling up the back side of the blast mound to scan the open area with binoculars.

Except for the air bending in heat vapor, nothing moved anywhere but the insects that darted against the dark wall of the jungle. As we continued to wait and to watch the stagnant surroundings, we began to amuse ourselves by idly trying to flick pebbles into the corpse's head. Every now and then one of us would be rewarded by a satisfying little *plerk* noise from the target pool.

After a time, as we continued trying for greater accuracy, it dawned on me what I was doing. How, I wondered, had I come to this? When did the line begin to blur between the person I had been and the one who was here now whiling a few distracted minutes in this macabre little game? What were the steps by which I had come into this shadow world where the quick and the dead exist in such intimate embrace, where the dead might offer themselves for a moment of quiet amusement? Had I really closed off my capacity for horror to the extent that I could so parcel my attention for greater threats; and then: what part of my mind was able to stand apart from this moment to pose the question? Perhaps I had simply wanted to do something harmlessly entertaining, some brief activity I could actually control, and thus enjoy a fleeting illusion of power over all that was frightening, unseen and dangerous.

I had been pushed progressively nearer some metaphysical brink than I ever expected to go, had crossed an un-sensed boundary where the seed of personality had become lost in the cumulative nature of lethal congruences and incremental austerities. Much later, I would come to realize that, however childish I might remain, actual youth had been pressed out of me in those dark, interminable hours and over the months of baneful operations in that malignant and endless wilderness.

These thoughts were suddenly arrested by a sound, a faint noise more felt than heard, little more than a scurry in the mind. I stopped and strained to hear. Nothing. Nhi went rigid too. After a few cavernous moments of whispery insect sounds, it returned. This time, it burbled hesitantly on the stagnant air as nothing more than a tiny, plaintive bleat, almost like something newborn far off, but too veiled by the dense vegetation to judge the distance.

With that, we both jumped, instant voltage. It could have been some kind of animal voice; I couldn't be sure. In any case it filtered through the normal jungle sounds like a scratch on the silence. The team behind us tensed, and two of them looked off to the left. It sounded as though it might have come from that direction, and for the moment their stares seemed to endorse the instinct. My temples pounded in the charged uncertainly as we waited, urging our senses through the stillness. I forced a yawn to clear my ears. It could have been the muted croak of some small burrower or a tree lizard. Sometimes even burned or rotting vegetation would expel a release of gas with soft, eerie sighs that could haunt the sanctums of the forest in the night and leave a man huddled in his poncho liner on the ground trembling in a private hell of fear and longing.

Then I heard it again. A thin, wavering cry rose and fell, barely audible, a twisted thread plucked from the sleeve of silence, little more than a tentative assertion in the negative of the day. It died once more, leaving no echo, only a kind of soundless mimicry of its quaver, the empty shadow of a noise. I still couldn't tell what we had heard. Apart from its strangeness, I wasn't sure in the silence that followed if we had heard anything other than perhaps a bird. Parrots could sound unnervingly like the cry of a child. Except that the Chinese, by the tenor of their stares, had obviously been alerted to something they couldn't identify either, and they didn't like it. They were strung taut.

Alarm raced through us all in a bolt of morphic resonance, and Nhi and I slipped back down the muddy berm into the shadows. I thumbed the safety off and signaled for the team to spread out, assigning one to watch out behind us in the opposite direction. We began to creep through the palpable stillness in the direction of the strange mewl, keeping low to the jungle floor and with all receptors on full alert. After covering 30 meters or so of torturous movement through the tangle of downed trees and twisted undergrowth, another cry tugged again at the fearful quiet. It was close. We stopped. Listened. Then we saw it. About 15 feet away lay a body on the ground in burned clothing amid a swarm of flies. It twitched, and we drew down on it as we approached.

He was in the tattered remains of American fatigues, the scorched fabric greasy and dark with old blood. He had been shot and burned, his skin horribly discolored, red veined and purpled, and there were places where it had peeled from his limbs in dried sleavings. Had I known him I would not have recognized the damaged face. His eyes were sunken, the lids drooped at different levels, and what little awareness remained in them seemed to have receded far beyond the threshold of sanity. With him on the ground, blackened and muddy, was the rifle with the Starlight scope.

Here was what we had come for with such tremendous odds against finding anything. This poor guy had probably been sent forward at night with the scope, and his buddies, perhaps having heard the shot that wounded him, and unwilling or unable to send out a patrol to find him the next morning, had withdrawn in the desperate confusion of the air strike without him. Wounded, perhaps before the pull-out, and without medical attention or food for all this time, he must have realized at some point after the terror of the napalm drop that he had been abandoned, yet had somehow managed to drag himself to this lost place. I hoped for his sake he was not aware, but our presence over him with our weapons made the last of his misery, for his eyes flicked at us, he gazed vacantly for a moment, then a dark leer of madness set his face, his arm made a strange embryonic gesture, and his head dropped back onto the ground. His mouth stirred and released a sound, a burble of noise for which there is no word, just a soaked orphan of the alphabet. He tried to roll over and was dead. I could tell by the way the body seemed to subside, as though something had been let out of it, that he was gone. Perhaps on some level he had been waiting for the moment when his friends would return.

We quickly gathered up the scope and pulled the body to a sitting position so that I could get my shoulder under it. The slumped weight was greater than I expected and the cold skin greasy. I staggered up with it and we moved back through the heavy pestiferous air to our position just inside the tree line. The corpse was a gruesome burden, creepy and hard to balance, until breathless and near collapse, I got back to where I could set it down beneath the half-burned tree by the dirt mound. Some of his skin had stuck to my equipment. I sucked at the muggy, death-laden air, and with my vision swimming and the ventricles pulsing in my chest, realized that I was probably suffering a loss of strength from the initial stages of malnutrition. I had to sit down and put my head between my knees to arrest the dizziness.

I can still feel him there across my shoulders. Once you've carried a dead person, I guess he'll always be there, riding with you. It's true, almost unbearably so, that close exposure to the dead sensitizes you to the force of their presence. That day, I think we all felt the weirdness of finding him and realizing the strange circumstances of his being in the place he had crawled to in his terrible pain and unthinkable despair. Now at least he was past hope, past care. Had he lived, he would probably have been doomed to wait out his existence in some VA hospital, a deranged husk, with burned skin tightening, encasing his body in a slow prison of integument.

I took his dog tags and a few incidentals from his pockets. I checked the scope. It was damaged beyond use, but at least we were able to recover it. I wondered what would happen to the poor guy's company commander when it was learned that we found his man alive.

I turned on the radio and sent the codes for extraction, giving as our location the site of the objective. By then, it was too late in the day to come for us, so I also sent that we would RON on site. Lastly I transmitted the code for one dead, hoping the implication this carried for the team itself would produce an emergency launch for our extraction first thing in the morning.

We were all at the end of our strength. I was shivering with fatigue and nervous strain when we set up for the night and, as usual, suffering the debilities that are the inevitable price of sleep deprivation. I was not at all sure how I would hold up through another day in the grim authority of this place where quantum death, the muddy stench of rot, and the insidious pervasion of finality commanded the senses.

Awaiting extraction from the field was always strenuous. Because of the need to turn the squelch control on the radio so far down, I was never sure my messages were getting through. Worse, this time we were deep in wet vegetation, especially bad for signal strength, although any jungle will cut the range of transmission. I ran the antenna out into the open edge of the burn, hoping to send in relatively unobstructed air, but there would be no sign of success until we might hear the faint beat of the big Sikorskys thumping slowly nearer in the distance.

Low clouds brought an early end to daylight, and sudden rain swept in through the trees to usher out the last of it. We covered the pitiful corpse and its weight of sadness with a rubber poncho, which rattled in the fall of rain most of the night, lending the quiet thing beneath it a discomforting voice. It demanded of us the attention it had been denied. None of us slept.

Back at FOB 4 at last, I was beset by a growing awareness that each day and each mission peeled away the incremental layers of probability, eroding further the likelihood that I would survive. As time went on, the declining balance of chance had given birth to an incipient fatigue that grew within me like a virus, a steadily-bleeding wound of the spirit that exacted daily withdrawals upon my diminishing store of vitality. Recurring flurries of pain from my wounds were a constant reminder that I had somehow survived a series of assignments with such remote chances of success that it seemed my very existence was entirely tenuous, a wraithlike improbability suspended between impossible contingencies. I was a marginal being held upright merely by an increasingly fragile assembly of biological coincidences, and my boundaries of perception often seemed blurred. I often felt as though I was moving through time only by some fateful oversight, muddling through without credentials, hovering always between life and death, stealth and discovery, between the marginal security of American technology and the isolation of operations beyond any timely application of its advantages. In this world of bleak uncertainties the margins of reality shifted constantly.

My wits had been greatly sharpened by the hot chemistry of worry and protracted fear, but at an exhausting cost in fortitude. Constant alarm had given me a potent kind of mythic intuition, that could not now be dialed back or turned off, for the conditions that made it necessary were relentless. Depending upon where I was at any given time, the conditions never went away; they simply modulated. I had become nervous, jumpy at small sounds and changes in the air. I was now one of only three team leaders who had survived four operations, and I could not see how I would much longer survive this kind of work. I felt The Beast approaching, as though I were being watched from across a room, a room with few exits, the most likely of which opened to oblivion.

In the meantime I looked forward to a respite of what I expected would be about a week of down time between operations, and I wanted to do whatever I could to make the most of every hour. In an urge to do something impetuous and life-affirming, to escape the oppression of my thoughts, I decided to go down to the beach, out past the thousands of sand bags that comprised the roofs of the bunkers drifted in their sensuous plastic undulations along the dunes of our eastern perimeter.

It seemed a long time ago, and under another name, that I had loved swimming in the ocean, and on this hot afternoon the idea of getting in the water held an especially voluptuous appeal. To feel the wet sand under my bare feet would be a relief. For that matter, just sitting and listening to the ever-renewed birth of waves might summon a flight of memories on which I could be borne away, at least for awhile.

Thus closed tightly in a preoccupied silence, I arrived there and was surprised to discover a happy crowd of both Chinese and Americans playing in the surf. The waves were higher than usual, and were arriving in steady intervals with an almost mathematical precision. They looked perfect for body surfing, and though no one seemed to be riding them, some 20 or 30 guys were splashing about, many floating on their issue inflatable air mattresses. I immediately went back to my hootch and stripped down. At the bottom of my footlocker I found a pair of long-abandoned undershorts, grabbed a towel, and ran back to the beach.

The water temperature was perfect, slightly cooler than the air. I waded out and soon got several good, long rides into shore from where the waves were breaking. It was fun. Most of the guys were just bobbing in the waves or letting the water push their air mattresses around. Several Chinese were in the water, too, but they were keeping to the shallows close to the beach. Only one other guy was a body surfer, and between us we began to attract the attention of the Chinese who had evidently never seen anyone do it before.

I tried to teach them by demonstrating how they could launch themselves ahead of each roller for short rides while staying in shallow water by pushing off the bottom with their feet. Some persisted admirably in trying it, but most of them just laughed and splashed about in the spent waves like children, or sat in the foamy run-off grinning and pointing as I allowed each wave to carry me right up onto the beach. It seemed to be a day of celebration with so many of us in the water, splashing each other and leaving the war to itself for an hour. I surrendered to the whole experience.

Suddenly, the two Sikorskys roared in, sweeping low overhead, and banked so sharply over the outer breakers their blades cleared the water by mere feet. With great skill, but hair-brained expertise, the two pilots brought the big ships to a hover over the spot where most of the swimmers on air mattresses were congregated. Then, with the noses held high and tail rotors down in the wave troughs, they danced the machines gently up and down to avoid the tops of each successive wave, while using the main rotor wash to blow the air mattresses out from under the swimmers. It worked. In the swirling launch of spray, several air mattresses shot out from under their riders and became airborne, wobbling through the air and then tumbling across the sand. I had never seen anything like it. I watched in horrified fascination, expecting any second to see a wave catch one of the tail rotors and bring the massive clattering machine down on a lot of guys in the water. The pilots looked down and laughed out their windows while the swimmers showed a mix of fist-shaking anger and outright amusement.

After the success of this game, the choppers straightened up and left to over-fly the camp and land on their pad beyond the hootches. Several guys down the beach got out of the water to retrieve their mattresses, while I continued to indulge myself in one of the few truly recreational times I ever had there, enjoying both the water and the delighted appreciation of the Nung audience.

Some of the Chinese were in the water among us when I happened to glance to my left to gauge a coming wave and saw two Chinese together preparing to jump up as it passed. Suddenly one of them froze, his shoulders hunched and arms bent. A look of pained surprise flitted across his features, and he pitched forward into the water. His companion screamed and fumbled in the water to drag him toward shore. The Chinese on the beach became animated in seconds. The body was dragged onto the sand, dead.

From down the beach someone yelled, "Sea snakes! Sea snakes!" and people began frantically emptying onto the beach. I didn't know what a sea snake was, but it didn't take long to connect all that was going on, and I headed for shore. As I plowed through the water, a small wave smacked me from behind, and I looked down to see two bright green streaks slide past me, just inches away. They could have been snakes or seaweed—just green stripes in the curl of the wave. I didn't know what they were, but the color was good enough for me, and I redoubled my surge for the shore.

The young Nung was dead, surely killed with great suddenness by something in the water, and a many-legged gaggle of his friends began carrying his body off the beach. In less than a minute the water became deserted, and all joy evaporated from the day.

I didn't know if sea snakes, whatever they were, could crawl up out of the water, and as I walked warily back toward the opening in the wire that let into the compound, I watched with curiosity for any serpentine wriggling or flopping in the crumble of frothy run-off, but nothing did. In just moments there were only a few guys left on the beach, all moving away from the water, some cursing with mechanical passion. The Nungs had disappeared, and the last Americans were collecting their towels and errant mattresses and walking solemnly away. I had grown so accustomed to the violent acts being committed by human agency as to quite forget that there are other orders of misfortune, other thresholds of pain.

I lingered a few minutes until the beach was cleared. The waves continued to rub against the shore, collapsing rhythmically onto the sand, quickly obliterating the congestion of frantic footprints where the body had been retrieved. The water soon repaired the beach, erasing all signs of our having been there, restoring its preferred order and leaving all unchanged: sunlight, dusty sand, the slap and hiss of the waves, the cry of a seabird.

Beyond the breakers the blue surface sparkled as ever in the sunlight, its broad smile turned suddenly sinister. It was different now. Its spurious invitation, like everything else in the country, had risen to attack us without warning, and its message was the same everywhere: *do not presume; do not relax.* Yanked back from the forbidden brink of an hour's inattention by the unblinking eye of perilous encounter, I was plunged even deeper into the gloomy hopelessness I had tried to escape. There would be allowed no time-out from this place.

As I made my way back to the hootch and a shower, drugged by renewed despair, I began to feel a sharp burning on my skin. It rapidly grew worse and soon erupted into a galaxy of red welts that wrapped from the center of my chest, under my right arm in a speckled crescent of inflammation, and ended somewhere near the middle of my back. Over the next few days it continued to bloom, becoming rough with tiny bumps, many of which soon became blisters like those produced by poison ivy. The medic told me it looked as though I'd been brushed by a jellyfish tentacle, and he gave me a salve to smear on it, but the stinging continued to grow for several days, becoming so severe that I couldn't stand to touch it, even to apply the medication, and it was seriously painful to wear a shirt.

After the pain subsided, and I was able to begin breaking the blisters in the shower water, the welts and most of the redness faded, yet not completely. Long afterwards, my skin remained discolored along the crescent and never tanned evenly. (For years a small patch of those blisters would erupt anew in the center of my chest with each seasonal change–the first day each Spring hot enough to induce general sweating, and the first days of each Fall when I would begin layering my clothes with a sweater. It took years, but the seasonal recurrence gradually faded. I never have learned exactly what hit me that day.)

A period of relative ease came that week. The skin problem had at least the happy consequence of making me *hors du combat* for a string of uncomfortable but welcome days, and I was relieved of the duty roster for field operations. A few guys even said it was unlikely that I'd be sent out again, since I had already run four operations, and that seemed to be the magic number, beyond which we lost so many people that Command was taking surviving team leaders out of the rotation after four. Like most rumors about relief and happy resolution, it proved to be pure myth, but even though I half-suspected it was nothing but smoke, I grasped the mirage and invested it with childish hope just the same.

While on this temporary suspension status, I recieved orders for R&R to Hong Kong. Steve had come through. As usual with orders, there was no lead time, and I was to get going. Not really knowing what to expect, I saw only that this promised to be a chance to leave the country for a whole week. I had seen pictures of Hong Kong, and knew only that it was a crowded, bustling Asian city with enormous tenements, iconic junks on the waters of the harbor, and narrow streets bannered with indecipherable signs–National Geographic stuff.

We were required to travel in khaki (Class A) uniform, of which I had only one set, now somewhat mildewed in the bottom of my footlocker, its brass insignia dulled by humidity and confinement. I had no civilian clothes to change into and no idea of what to wear for a week in a new place or what conditions to expect at the destination, so I simply discarded such questions and borrowed a small parachute equipment duffle from our unit photographer. I put a few toiletry items in the bag and changed hurriedly into the wrinkled travel uniform with its tarnished doo-dads and put on the signature green beret in time to be driven to the airport, only half believing it was happening. I was curious about Hong Kong and glad to be getting out, but the skin on my side was a constant nuisance, I was slightly unnerved by the suddenness of the orders, and I felt conspicuous in the unfamiliar clothes.

After another long-round robin flight down the country, I rendez-voused with Steve at the Nha Trang airport for our flight to Hong Kong. The brass on his starched Class A uniform flashed in the sun. He was visibly excited, his ideas full of tender mischief. By contrast I was still numb, not entirely comprehending this rapid turn of events. I felt like what I was–a refugee from another world, a reality little comprehended even by headquarters personnel.

During most of the flight I sat and stared around the civilian interior of the aircraft trying to recall how long it had been since I had last seen such a place. Steve was full of plans to do and see things he'd been told about, while I quietly tried to retrace the steps that had brought me through the months since I had arrived in Vietnam. Being transported away from it, even temporarily, turned the reverse optic of memory upon events that were blended into a nightmare swarm of dread imagery, events of such extraordinary magnitude that they seemed to exist in some other dimension illusive of chronology. I had trouble sorting them all. I tried to anticipate the richer colors of Hong Kong, but the anxiety still had me. It formed a dark background that kept insinuating its fingers into the promise of this brand new experience.

Many of the other passengers gabbled animatedly among themselves about the pleasures they anticipated awaiting them in Hong Kong. Others sat wordless, staring vacantly, their eyes empty of youth and dulled by fatigue beyond caring. Perhaps they believed they had already died in combat and were being conveyed to a kind of happy hunting ground. It felt like that to me.

The descent into Hong Kong was a rare experience in flying, and when I noticed how close the tenements were passing by the wingtips, I craned across Steve in the window seat to watch our approach. In order to land at Hong Kong the pilots had to turn sharply within the confines of surrounding mountain peaks and fly an approach that took them right down among the buildings of the city, an exciting experience for someone unfamiliar with its challenges. I watched with growing anticipation as the pale blue harbor with its steel shipping and traditional junks rose in the window, and buildings slid past just outside.

When we stepped out of the plane I was struck by the coolness of the air. I breathed in the smells of the busy harbor and heard, for what seemed the first time in my life, the sounds of traffic. The noise remained subdued despite its capture in the surround of mountains, but the steady oceanic roar on my jungle-trained ears was exciting and disconcerting at the same time.

Steve had the foresight to have made reservations for us at the Merlin Hotel on the Kowloon side of the harbor, and after a brief lecture by an American military official with a cushy job about behaving like ambassadors while there, and warnings about venereal disease and public drunkenness, none of which amounted to instructions I needed, we set off in a taxi.

I became quite nervous in the car as we made slow progress through the crowds of pedestrians. I asked that the windows of the cab be rolled up. Steve looked quizzically at me, and we settled on having them open at the top just enough to prevent the ingress of a hand grenade. I felt a little better but was relieved when we were finally delivered to the entrance of the Merlin. The cab stopped near a line of colorful rickshaws parked, traces down, across the street, their diminutive "drivers" standing together on the curb smoking and watching the hotel entrance with predacious speculation.

We discovered that the Merlin Hotel was located very convenient to the harbor, and it offered great views of Victoria Peak and the Hong Kong side to those guests lucky enough to be housed at the front of the building. We were shown to a room on the side overlooking a crowded little street, but the view didn't matter.

We needed to change into civilian clothes. Steve had a small supply of his own, and it was early enough in the afternoon that stores, including tailors, were still open. Steve, again demonstrating his deserved reputation as an efficient clerk, had the name of a tailor just around the corner from the hotel, and said it was one of the reasons he had selected the Merlin.

After dropping our bags in the room, we went back downstairs, out the main doors, and proceeded around the corner, up Johnson Street. We found the small tailor shop just yards up the street and stepped inside. The little tailor, laughing delightedly, approached us with both hands. In his stiff, fitted clothing he appeared the archetypal Hong Kong merchant, with a spine that had a built-in calibrator that seemed to know instinctively just how far to bend the back on a scale divided into fine shades of respect. He was very personable, chatty, and set about the business of accommodating us with practiced professionalism, scooping the air in welcome as he ushered us into the shop. He was amusing, and I liked him right away.

He set to work immediately, grinning and barking orders to an assistant as he measured, He demonstrated an easy familiarity with fitting westerners, who must have been outsized for most of his patterns. He bubbled with mouthfuls of gallant compliments as he worked. I was measured for four shirts, two jackets, and two pairs of slacks, the total cost coming to an amount in Hong Kong dollars of something less than the cost of a single jacket in the States. Steve ordered some shirts, a turtleneck sweater, and a suit to add to his ensemble of escape clothing.

The perpetually smiling tailor finished quickly and promised that I could have at least one change of clothes in an hour. Steve laughed at my astonishment, and we headed back to the bar at the Merlin to await our new wardrobes. I was sure the war in Vietnam had indirectly provided many welcome contributions to the tailor's business. I was glad for him. He had learned to shed his Asian reserve for western customers and had adopted a sales attitude both inviting and entertaining.

In the piano bar downstairs back at the Merlin, we met a rather morose ex-pat American writer of middle age who dressed with calculated carelessness in bohemian black and who remained anchored, pleasantly drunk with notebook in hand, to a stool positioned in the curvature of the piano. There were a few well-tailored international Asian businessmen chatting quietly, and three friendly British couples who proved to be schoolteachers brought from England and Australia before the government had made apartment flats available for them to live in. For the while they were being housed at the Merlin.

I would learn over the next few evenings that all but the Asian businessmen were regulars, and we would spend many hours enjoying the teachers' conversation and piano music, while the writer regarded us all blearily, seldom adding a word. He probably told himself he was observing life for his book.

We made friends with the teachers right away. They were surprised to discover that Steve and I were both university graduates and quite capable of keeping up with their literary and historical references. In Britain, most educated people who join the army become officers, thus we proved to be anomalies. One diminutive lady with tired eyes of an arresting pale shade of blue and whose wavy hair, the color of cigarette ash, was parted unfashionably down the middle, played softly on the piano as we all engaged in a discussion about the long-scheduled, now imminent, return of Hong Kong to the mainland Chinese.

"Oh!" the pianist suddenly declared, apropos of nothing while she continued to play. "Of course. That explains it. You have conscription in the States, don't you? This pulls people from all walks of life."

She had a clear, open sort of face, unobstructed by guile, where every shade of feeling floated like the shadow of clouds along a grassy field as her fingers danced among the keys. I could not remember the last time I had heard a piano played, and the sound kept drawing me away from an interesting talk with her husband about the coming changes to the colony. He was fortyish, balding, with a sparse, sandy moustache: a pleasant-faced historian who was quick to express his worries about the fact that the latest Chinese textbooks being sent in preparation for returning control of Hong Kong to the mainland Chinese already contained propagandistic mythology to cover the truth about the atrocities of the Red Revolution.

I very much enjoyed the subsequent evenings filled with conversation and amateur piano music so unexpectedly beautiful that at times it almost seemed like a reproach in the smoky warmth of the crowed little room. I sympathized with these pleasant, well-read British people who had come all the way from their homes to spend up to two years living in a modest hotel on behalf of the hopeful and uncertain effort to educate young Chinese students in maintaining the infrastructure of free enterprise and an accurate version of their history after the communist Chinese were scheduled to take over. One couple had children at school in England whom they had not seen in a year.

That first evening, though, Steve, who had civilian clothes, decided after a few drinks to explore the city. I returned to the tailor's and was pleasantly surprised to find my shirts and pants ready as promised, along with initial cuts on the two jackets, ready for the first fitting. I collected the finished items in a neatly-folded paper package and returned to the hotel to try them on.

It felt good to get out of the musty khaki uniform and to find that the new things fit perfectly. The thin cotton shirt felt soft, its light oxford weave barely brushing my fish wound. Thus decked out in fitted finery, complete with my tiny initials embroidered on the shirt as a bonus from the tailor, I stepped out into my first evening in Hong Kong.

The air was fresh and cool. Lights were winking on aboard the ships in the harbor. The departing sunset was streaked with orange and pink behind the mountains, while a pale wispy grey weft of dying cirrus faded above the city. Victoria Peak stood black as a cutout, like crumpled butcher's paper back-lit against the feminine colors, and there was a thin line of bright silver where the ridges intersected the sky.

Keeping at first to familiar ground, I turned again up Johnson Street. Beyond the tailor shop, near the top of the street, was a nondescript three-story building bearing a sign which said in English over Chinese, Chanticleer Restaurant. From its awning-covered rooftop where yellow lanterns flickered, came the sounds of laughter and the tinkle of glass and utensils. I felt invited.

I went in and climbed the stairs, not knowing if I could make myself understood, and was relieved to be welcomed at the top by an impeccable maitre d' who spoke clear English and ushered me to a small table near the parapet that overlooked the street. The table was covered with a clean white cloth on which burned a small candle lamp that cast a pleasant watery light across the fabric.

When the menu arrived I searched in vain for anything I recognized, even in English. Then I saw among the mysterious soups, borscht. I had never had borsht but least the word bore a marginal familiarity, and besides, I was in a mood to try something new. I was asked if I'd like it with the sour cream. Not knowing why or what the sour cream option implied, I said yes, and when the dish arrived, it was so good that I sat there that night in the open air under the dreamscape of soft flickering lanterns and finished two more large bowls of plain old beet soup—one of my life's more memorable dinners. The waiters were amused, but I bought them off with a generous tip.

Afterwards I walked down to the harbor to smell the sea air and to take in one of the most famous ports in the world. Unused to bright lights after dark—indeed, uncomfortable within the range of any light at night—I found the whole scene dazzling. The shore lights cast glittering trails of copper coins across the water, neon advertising flashed bright declarations into the night, and the lemon-colored light of countless apartment windows stacked together into the sky, rising in ordered geometry into the surrounding hills.

The famous silhouettes of Chinese junks ghosted silently between cargo vessels as they continued their unloading trade after dark. The drape of lanterns at waterfront restaurants lined the harbor like strings of pearls. From time to time the shadow of an unlit sampan glided noiselessly across the shimmer. Movement on the water was silent and unhurried. The scene was tranquil, but beneath it pulsed the hum of the city.

I began to let down a little, to feel the fist of tension inside ease its grip as I relaxed into this unfamiliar freedom from the laws of inevitability. I indulged in an enjoyment of the activity, but soon began to feel vulnerable again, too long distracted from the old imperative. I felt compelled to keep checking over my shoulder, for what, I didn't know. So I moved over to a building front and stood with my back against it. That felt better, more secure, and I remained there for several minutes watching the Star Ferry approach from the Hong Kong side, all lit up and crowded with passengers. It reversed engines, churning the water noisily, then drifted gently into its slip nearby, nudging the fenders and disgorging several dozen shoppers and commuters.

This was the main conveyance for crossing the harbor. The Star Ferry Company maintained steady service between Kowloon and Hong Kong proper. A ticket was just a few cents, so, on impulse, I decided to ride it across and back. I bought a ticket, walked aboard, and took up a place on the starboard rail.

The trip across was fun. The air was cool against my face, and when we were about half way across I felt as though we were moving past a towering forest of floating buildings, steel ships whose dark bulks soared up into the starlit sky, their huge anchor chains, smelling of sea life and rust, rising mysteriously from the depths. We passed one fairly close by from which a skein of grassy marine growth hung below the waterline, where a small ecosystem flourished and schools of tiny silver fish flashed below the surface in the refracted lights of the ferry.

When we docked on the other side, I walked up the gangway and got back in line for the return. On the new starboard side this time, I saw the whole bowl of the city as it wrapped around the harbor, the lights of floating restaurants, and its famous bobbing necklace of moored sampans. It seemed like a fantasy taken from travel posters.

Back at the hotel I checked in the piano bar and had a beer with the group, then went up to my room for the first sound sleep I'd had in months. Steve was out somewhere, already burning through his week. After a hot shower I slid into the sheets with hungry gratitude, rubbing the soles of my feet on the crisp cotton fabric. I wondered idly about what the next morning would bring, but soon drowsiness closed down upon the vivid new images with an oblivious embrace.

The startling cry of dawn came on so suddenly I leapt to a sitting position in a panicked jolt of confusion at the unfamiliar surroundings.

It took a breathless moment to remember where I was and to identify the shuffling sounds of traffic beneath the window. I looked around the room in grateful relief. Steve's bed had evidently been occupied for a while, but he was gone. I flopped back down on the pillow and slept again until midmorning.

I couldn't remember ever sleeping as soundly as I did in that hotel. That first morning set a standard for the whole week, during which I slept until mid to late morning each day, usually waking to find that Steve had already left. In fact I saw little of him the whole stay. Each day I awoke feeling that the sleep I indulged was at the cost of living. I had little expectation left of surviving my tour in Vietnam, and fought to ignore the fateful algebra of balancing any waking opportunities presented in the safety of Hong Kong with the diminishing prospects of life that awaited my return. Yet I couldn't help it. Each morning I slept through the pre-paid hotel breakfast and had to content myself with the coffee and rolls that were available all morning, although I found them to be as luxurious as a full-course, five-star meal. I tried to memorize every moment.

Hong Kong was a living bazaar in which everything seemed to be for sale and the price ever-negotiable, where masses of people filled the narrow streets, hemming in the motor traffic, bobbing in and out of the shops. Other than a bit of walking around amid the commercial marvels of free enterprise gone wild, I spent a large part of each day riding back and forth across Hong Kong harbor on the Star Ferry. I let the cool air of the boat's movement play over me and tried to program every sensation into my memory. I watched the shipping and the busy competition of sea birds and stared down into the pale green water as the refracted sunlight angled past in the wake. Gradually the welts and infected jungle scratches on my face and hands began to heal.

Once or twice I disembarked for a walk around Hong Kong itself, and one day Steve and I visited the China Fleet Club together, where my wondering eyes led me through its many departments, stunned by how inexpensively famous name products could be purchased and shipped. It offered an interesting contrast to the variety and cost of products available in American PXs. The British seemed to appreciate their armed services, and this store was one way to sweeten overseas duty in the Far East.

Initially overwhelmed by the magnitude of choice, I soon selected a stereo amplifier, reel-to-reel tape player, speakers, a good pair of opera glasses, and a small Minox spy camera. These things I shipped, courtesy of the club, straight to the States, where they were to wait for me, to hold my place as hostages to my survival. They seemed to give me a foothold on the future, although in the alternative event, I knew my parents, my brother and sister, would find them useful..

The Hong Kong side also held the famous Cricket Club, an intriguing place whose gleaming white colonial architecture crowned the gentle sweep of manicured lawns, but where the mysteries of long tradition remained barred to those without a member's invitation. I would have loved to see it but feared that even in the unlikely event that a British Naval officer encountered at the Fleet Club should prove to be a member and offer me a visit to those hallowed smoking rooms and verandas, I would probably be found speaking too loudly, or I might stumble into a tea trolley. I had to be satisfied just to have seen the landmark building.

Later in the week I ventured up streets that climbed farther away from the tourist neighborhoods that ringed the harbor and into the realm of towering apartment complexes that the British government had to build—indeed were still building—to accommodate the Chinese who had fled the Red Revolution as well as the quota of immigrants drawn by the long-range magnet of free-market living. The school teachers had told us about the bodies that came down the river from mainland China during the purges and were still sometimes found floating in Hong Kong harbor.

Here the congestion of apartment blocks was more dense even than Manhattan, where the wider streets of New York created more space between the structures. The population density here seemed incalculable, oppressive, and it served to explain the housing shortage that kept our teacher friends confined to the Merlin for the foreseeable future.

In the middle of Kowloon is a terrible neighborhood with an infamous reputation. The teachers warned me to steer clear of it, but I came upon it by chance. Made of hand-built plywood hovels congested around narrow dirt pathways and enclosed by a high fence, it was known to be an impenetrable haven for every kind of criminal, sneak thief, murderer at large, and international pirate who could make his way to refuge there. I discovered one of its entrances quite by accident and was struck by its contrast with the modern concrete and glass towers just across the street.

At its edge, the huge slabs of the modern city seemed to slant suddenly backwards, as though the architecture had been reined in sharply on the brink of perdition. The charging city stopped short at the edge of a vast pit, where everything lay low and strangely hushed. Nothing moved among the squalid hovels, not even birds. It looked as though it had been pounded into the ground by the affects of weather and stagnation. The crowded warren of shanties squatted irascibly in the mud, glaring at one another across a central street of packed earth. It seemed still as death until I noticed a few thin columns of grey smoke that managed to escape from scattered cooking fires. The whole wretched husk of squalor appeared to have been constructed piecemeal of found lumber and tin thrown together in an excavation for buildings that never went up, resulting in what appeared to be a junkyard for discarded building materials. To enter the compound, one would have to step down several feet below the paved street, as though leaving the surface world for one of the outer pavilions of Hell. It was eerie. It felt distinctly resentful, and after an indelible stare, I turned and hurried away from it, fleeing toward the protection of the new buildings, totems of my own tribe, with their reassuring walls.

I felt foolish for having stumbled so carelessly upon such a notoriously dangerous place and continued walking rapidly along the empty streets after dark, partly to put distance between myself and it, and partly to increase the chance of finding alcoves and corners from which to watch in case I was followed.

I walked through the light spills from balconies barred across by the shadows of handrails set so low and far apart that they seemed to measure the space rather than to cage it. From them came the sounds of mah-jongg tiles clattering on tabletops, heard everywhere through open windows and from all stories above. The noise was captured between the buildings where it echoed and rang like tap dancing. It was reaffirming, carrying implications of family life and a degree of normalcy in contrast to the place I had fled. Mah-jongg, I learned, is a national obsession, and families played it every night–not surprising, considering that a huge percentage of the population were refugees from mainland China, where literacy was held suspect, and thus a quiet evening spent reading, unlikely. I never asked how it is played but admired how beautifully the ivory pieces were worked in every shop where the game was for sale.

On this night I was especially relieved to get back to the piano bar at the Merlin and to find the usual crowd, with Steve ensconced upon the sofa with a beautiful hand-carved ivory chess set with large pieces he'd bought that afternoon, inviting all comers. The pieces were of greater interest than the progress of the game, but people were more engaged with drinking and talking than playing chess anyway. The nightly atmosphere in that smoky little room was dependably congenial, and where I looked forward to it each night, this time it became a haven, a retreat from my discomfiting explorations.

The writer was there, as usual, hunched over the piano like a charred bird, his dark wardrobe and notebook apparently little more than props. He hardly ever spoke, though he seemed to be listening through an alcoholic haze to all of our discussions. Whether his regular attendance was for the company or for the booze I couldn't tell. His brooding presence bothered me a bit. Perhaps the notebook provided him with a form of justification for I never saw him write anything down. He seemed out of place and a bit foolish, like a bag of tools left behind when the curtain rises on a stage set for romance. His manner seemed deliberately posed, cultivated as a mantle of lone creativity, as though he held an image of himself carried forth from the beat generation of the '50s, and now his faded attention was guessing its way into a new age.

Something like sorrow, but sillier, seemed to have loaded his eyes in a way that made them hang heavy and hopeless in his mallowed skin, and when he did speak he had a deep, melancholy intonation with the perpetual character that people's voices assume when a dead person is lying somewhere in the house. I once tried to tease him into conversation by observing that work was the bane of the dreaming class, but he just stared back at me with piercing eyes. I'd read enough novels to know that my own eyes were darkly glowing.

The English were well aware of the unpopularity of the Vietnam War with the American people and asked how, since our government changes every four years, the war could be continued in opposition to mass expressions of public outrage for so long. I could only tell them that it was pretty unpopular with me, too. In addition, I thought it naïve to assume that the more people involved in any political process, the more democratic it is. Power gravitates to the special and the organized, as too often against the general interest, and this meant that Steve and I, as well as the thousands of other guys, were being dispatched halfway around the world to throw away our lives at the arbitrary will of the state. I added with bitterness that even a cursory reading of history teaches that the greatest mass murderers have always been people's own governments. It was muttered casually, but it met with snorts of approval and ironic laughter, and I found myself set up with another drink. It was one of those odd moments in life when you find yourself the unwitting author of an unexpected effect upon others, people whose very existence until a few days before was unknown to you. I graciously permitted them to use my voluptuous insight upon their students.

Yet most of our conversations ranged over lighter pastures, with happier ideas, where remembrances and stories often went unfinished in the crosstalk and laughter, like spokes on a rimless wheel, ending in air. It was fun to feel the compatibility across our related nationalities, and I felt envious of the security they had in their futures. They were living in the hotel only temporarily, true, but they did not face the fatalistic uncertainties, the desperate unknowableness of every day, every hour, to which I would soon return.

Those evenings in the piano bar of the Merlin Hotel stand out in stark contrast to the rest of that year. Each night I went up to the room gratefully reassured that I had not traveled so far from the tenets of civilization that I couldn't enjoy the companionship of such open people. Each night I slept soundly, leaping awake into the next morning, my head heavy with the weight of unremembered dreams.

As the number of days remaining in this brief vacation diminished, my anxieties returned, and a gaunt restiveness began to inhabit all my efforts to avoid thinking about going back to the war. I tried to imprint every impression of Hong Kong, while at the same time recognizing that I had to re-arm my defenses.

The week seemed to end almost before it began, despite the fact that I spent almost all of each day in quiet, reserved activity, simply walking, riding the ferry back and forth, and waving off street hawkers. Occasionally, I would see Steve in the traffic, leaning back importantly in the seat of a rickshaw with arms crossed while an aged little man, gripping the forward extreme of the hand traces and almost counter-weighted off the ground, struggled to hurry with his charge through the crowd. I wanted to ride in one, too, but just couldn't bring myself to have one of these little old men pull me around. I knew it was denying them their livelihood each time I turned down their solicitations at the rickshaw stand, but I just didn't want to look like one of the barbarians who tried to hustle the East.

The last two nights I slept fitfully, loaded again with emotional baggage and haunted by a thousand ill-remembered events whose effects still remained. During the day, with all its color, bustle, and noisy distractions, images of the war scurried through my mind weighted with chains, arriving unbidden at odd moments while I was trying to concentrate on something–anything–else, triggered by the most commonplace smells or sounds, and effectively robbing me of the last tenuous days.

25

The trip to Hong Kong may have been a welcome respite, but it made coming back all the worse. Fear is a natural defense mechanism, ready and necessary, but in normal times it sleeps unmolested, sometimes for years. Then its awakening can be brutal. It can be teased awake by incidental happenings, or it can be shocked from its slumber by events of such magnitude as to program your entire future. Months of low-grade threat interrupted by prolonged seizures of intense apprehension, and bursts of sheer terror can leave a lifetime imprint upon a person's nature.

I re-entered life at FOB 4 with renewed trepidation, my doubts given form by the balance of contrast with my glimpse of life outside the country. It wasn't just the fear of specific possibilities, or even the renewed necessity to revive my hard-won instinct for the compass of surrounding threats. In addition to the whole monstrous enterprise, I had developed a phobia for Vietnam itself. The cumulative effect of long exposure to unpredictable hazard, lack of sleep, and responsibility for other men's lives rushed fearfully back in, animated by an irrepressible sense that the scales of chance had tipped, and my time was running out. The odds against making it through whatever lay ahead seemed insurmountable.

I learned that in my brief absence another of the One-Zeros had been killed, and the photographer whose equipment bag I had borrowed for the trip to Hong Kong was lost in a helicopter crash. He had been just two days short of his scheduled return to the States. Had I not been wounded, and were I not so fraught with reasonable doubt about my abilities, I may have taken this news with the sort of fatalistic resolve that got us all through such things, but with my growing nervousness fighting to reconcile all the evidentiary indications that I would die in the country, and probably soon, it caused me a spate of trembling. I hugged myself to stop it.

I realized I should never have taken R&R. It had weakened me. It had exposed me to a voluptuous world in which people led normal lives, and the reminder crippled my power to come back from it. An iciness raked my skin, and I knew I would be unable to function unless I could find a way to suppress the fear. I had to make a deliberate attempt to bifurcate my rational life from the actuarials by creating an existential disconnect between what I knew I had to do and the probabilities that attached themselves to the doing. The Beast had my scent this time. I could feel its breath.

While trying to readjust during those first days back I received orders for promotion to Staff Sergeant E-6. When I had first joined the military, that rank had seemed so high up the scale as to be unobtainable during a single enlistment and so had not been worth even thinking about. Yet I had been functioning in the rank ever since taking over the team, and now that I had been officially promoted it seemed incidental, an unfelt achievement, like a birthday. I was glad to have the recognition, as rank is so important in the highly stratified life of the military, and it meant a little more pay, but it did nothing to ease the weight of responsibility or to thin the legions of hazard.

Thus it was when we were sent out again a few days later. Trapped once more in the hot grip of malignant anxiety, I tried to hide the unsteadiness in my hands as I selected the team for this one. I even put on my sweat-stained patrol gloves when I went over to the Nungs' tent in an effort to cover my fingers while I designated the guys and the weapons we'd need for the operation.

As though our other missions had not been bizarre enough, this one would bring about a truly eerie encounter. The next day we were dropped into the wilderness along the spine of the country on an interdiction and trail watch. This meant the strong likelihood of enemy contact. Not good. We were to locate an obscure trail, not visible from the air, where Intelligence reported we were likely to encounter an NVA movement of U.S. prisoners. We were to report on if, when, exactly where, and how many. Although we were to avoid contact with the enemy if possible (standard admonition), just to be safe, I planned to set up our watch, assuming we were successful in even locating the trail and if we could find the right conditions there, in a position that lent itself to conducting an ambush. This was not ambition on my part, in fact, quite the opposite. The disposition of assets required for a successful ambush coincided with optimal coverage of the target area and maximum concealment.

Ambushes were dangerous affairs, due to the great difficulty most people have in remaining quiet for the long periods of patient vigilance they required. (If you have to pee while lying in ambush, you can't get up. You can't risk disturbing anything in the absolute need for motionless silence, including whatever living things have settled into your presence. You just have to lie there and pee.)

Further, it is crucially important that an ambush be sprung in a place from which there is no escape for the target group, a condition the terrain did not always allow. I wanted intensely to avoid contact, and the best way to increase the odds of that was to set up in exactly the sort of terrain and cover conducive to ambush. If we found that Americans were being conducted by a small escort, it seemed that since we were to be monitoring the trail, wherever it was, we would probably find that we needed to be close enough to it that conditions might make it possible to spring an attack to free our guys.

If the escort group was too large for me to be sure of a successful ambush, which meant killing *all* of the escorts, or if the enemy was interspersed with the prisoners, then we would just take the count and try to get out once they passed. Both alternatives required that the terrain would hide us, present us with at least an adequate view of the trail, and allow us to escape undetected. If we could find a way to free any prisoners, I would need a plan for escaping with them in company, depending upon how many there were and what physical condition they might be in. I also needed to estimate in short order, if we attempted to take them, how much transport and what kind we would need to be sent for extraction. These were a lot of unknowns.

Each of these operations was a first. You can try to tell yourself that you're growing jungle wise, that you're getting "used" to it, but the only things these missions had in common were stifling discomfort in the extraordinary heat, dirt, relentless nervous tension, the insistent presence of mortal danger, and the maddening loom of uncertain outcome. The enemy was everywhere, the nature of the terrain, despite its outward appearance of unending sameness at times, was uniquely demanding on each trip, and even those conditions changed with your every movement. Therefore the conditions in which you might encounter the enemy kept changing. Every move, almost every minute on patrol, forced you to readjust your priorities and expectations, and to continuously reevaluate the implications of what you could see, hear, and smell. The process was exhausting and debilitating in the extreme, but jungle operations cut no slack. The price of survival was constant vigilance. This meant vigilance with all five senses—and sometimes, as we were about to learn, a sixth.

This time we made the drop and spent the first night after insertion on the loamy jungle floor in a place fairly free of ground cover, within a grove of enormous hardwoods. They were so big they obscured the visibility around us, and despite the slim gaps between them, provided considerably more protection than the shadowy groves of giant philodendron that grew sprinkled with quiet petals of filtered sunlight along the random dew lines permitted by the high canopy. Here, the earth was black and moist and smelled strongly of the slow accumulation of centuries.

The first night was long but uneventful. The usual ebb and flow of night sounds remained free of alarmingly abrupt changes. I had the feeling that we were truly alone. That in itself was good, but whenever the comfort of knowing we were well positioned came over me, it arrived mixed with the cold loneliness of having been abandoned in one of the world's deepest, most impenetrable wildernesses. As usual before dawn, I lay on my back wrapped in a poncho liner and a mix of conflicting emotions, finger on the trigger, listening, listening, listening, and waiting for the first grey hint of morning.

Night comes in many shades. I stared up at the pre-dawn version of darkness held captive in the impenetrable gloom of the upper forest. It seemed to give, not so much the suggestion of light as the sensation of coming change, something sensed in the back of the mind, like the first breath of autumn. Tiny ground dwellers stole past, barely audible in the black stillness.

My consciousness, dulled by the long hours, was just hovering between sleep and a catholic awareness of tiny sounds and small movements around us, when the night was suddenly torn open by an eruption of sound and fury that might accompany the end of the world! The deep stillness was shattered by a mighty incandescent sphere that flashed beyond the trees like a sun, and in seconds a shock wave slammed through the forest with the speed of thought. A hot wall of air littered with torn vegetation, tree branches, and flung birds hit us, lifting me off the ground. It must have thrown me over, because I became aware of looking mindlessly down at the ground as it came up to my face, and suddenly we were all cowering in the convulsed earth, hands over our ears, as cataclysmic thunder overwhelmed the world, raining a mass of torn branches, shredded scraps of vegetation, and earth down on us.

The horrifying sound rumbled off rapidly through the forest, echoing in the hollows, and behind it a bitter, carbonized smoke rolled along the jungle floor. All our heads came up at the same time. We looked around wild-eyed in the stunned silence that fell in upon us after the bank of heat passed through. At first I feared we had been discovered and expected another explosion. Perhaps they were ranging on us. Then it seemed that the magnitude of the detonation was too great to be employed against a little team like us. Besides, I couldn't understand how any projectile of that size could have been directed at us, even if our presence was suspected. It didn't make sense. Where could such a launcher be located?

We waited tensely, expectantly, hugging the earth for several long seconds, bracing for more. More what? I didn't know. My ears rang beyond usefulness, and then I thought to get to the base of the nearest tree. I began to crawl toward whatever protection might be provided from a repeat of this unknown fury. We all got our backs against the roots of the massive trees and waited as a slow dawn sent its fingers down through the upper branches.

Whatever the explosion was, it shocked the forest into profound stillness. It may have killed most of the small wildlife. In the darkness I smelled the smoke, along with chlorophyll and fresh wood.

Gradually my hearing returned, though at first I could detect only the closest sounds, the rustle of clothes, breathing. After awhile, a faint blush of sunlight thickened to a dingy glow roiling high in the canopy, full of ash and the charred ghosts of leaves that drifted silently onto the ground cover about us. At length I turned on the radio and reported the event.

There was no repeat of the thing, and all remained quiet. Eventually, a few bird calls returned, but they were distant. We resumed our belly-level progress toward the location of the trail as depicted on the map, but with a renewed caution intensified by nervous confusion and the lingering feeling that the morning's wake up call might actually have been intended for us. It didn't make sense, but we couldn't ignore the possibility. Besides, the protection we had enjoyed from the trees now seemed compromised. We moved cautiously out of the area with a sense of having been bruised by some terrible outside power that could reach us even within the bower of our careful obscurity.

The going was slow and difficult. We were plagued by insects, and I swallowed dry as long as I could stand the thirst. We stopped during the hot mid-day stillness and waited, listening. The jungle seemed breathless, arrested of all movement in the stagnant air. All life, even the insects, seemed to have reached a point of sudden stasis, where all things were held abrogate until we might break the spell by resuming our careful creep along the jungle floor, noiseless, avoiding the touch of any living thing.

Toward the end of the day we entered an area of rolling ground congested with small twisted shade dwellers, tangled vines and black earth. It was a dark, unwholesome place. It felt hostile. Great stifling webs of vegetation spread over the ground and crawled up the giant banyans, forming enormous green cones of leaves overhead that resembled backlit versions of circus tents. It was a creepy place that made me feel enclosed—and that meant trapped, trapped along with any unseen dangers that were in there with us. Moving silently through this kind of growth was all but impossible, and we advanced with painful care and deliberation, quietly clearing tangles and snags from each other's gear.

The ground eventually opened into a shallow depression with a low wooded ridge off to the right, about 30 meters to the north of our position, impenetrable thicket to our left, and enough congestion ahead that I knew we couldn't move in it without slashing noisily at it. It was a quiet swale in the normal undulation of the jungle floor, but its serenity held an edgy restlessness for me. I couldn't see how far it went, due to the obscuring growth, and I looked toward the ridge as the way out of the bowl. This was the moment when the operation turned strange, uncanny.

As I looked to the right something awoke within me. Some instinct sent a shiver through my skin. It cut instantly through my concentration. I tensed immediately, and we stopped. I checked the others and saw right away that the Nungs had gone on heightened alert, too. That clinched it for me; something was wrong, and yet I had seen and heard nothing. There were no outward signs. For some reason the place had an oppressive, malignant quality I couldn't quite define. There was something else, too, although it wasn't until much later that I could name it: its vibrant silence contained a kind of separate awareness that was not unlike the feeling of being watched. It was sourceless and intensely unsettling.

I fought down the panic, subverting into a shift in our direction. Darkness had begun to insinuate through the trees when I signaled a move to our right, off the easier jungle floor onto the slope, taking care to remain below the ridge line where we might be seen against the fading slivers of sky that fell like a woolen backdrop behind the trees. The slope was thick with undergrowth, and by crawling slowly through it, we made a preliminary RON site at a place where we could not be approached without hearing the effort. The fear that someone was aware of our presence gripped me like a fist. Yet still there were no outward signs.

The slope wasn't steep, but it was high enough to overlook the area we had left. As we went to ground to wait for full dark, the eerie watchfulness of the place grew. There was still nothing visible to give us the creeps, and in the darkness there was nowhere to turn, but my instincts were confirmed by the nervous intensity in the others. The Chinese peered into the gloom, their expressionless black eyes shiny and unblinking. Grayson looked worried, too, probably sensing the general feeling that passed among us in subliminal telepathy. No one had said a word or made a signal, but he had learned to watch the Nungs.

After dark we crept very slowly about 30 yards farther along the shoulder of the slope and then set up for the night. The Nungs put out the M-1 foot mines and then we drew in and waited for something to reveal itself, but the strange watchfulness of the place had us all. I signaled for us to form a tight circle on our backs and to hold hands. That way, besides seeing the most, anyone who suspected anything during the night had only to squeeze the hands he held to alert the whole group.

No one slept. I hovered through the night in terrified expectation of being set upon at any moment. But the long hours passed without event. Before first light, exhausted with nervous tension, we took in our mines and moved over the crest of the ridge and down its other side. We crossed a narrow grassy swath that resembled an old road-bed, then climbed another natural embankment and ducked into a wall of high razor grass.

As we entered the grass, I suddenly felt better. The feeling of being observed abruptly lifted as suddenly and inexplicably as it had come upon us the afternoon before. I saw that the Nungs were relaxed, too. They traded little smiles of relief, the intensity of their stares subsiding noticeably, as though their eyes had been dialed back.

We moved a little deeper into the rasping blades of elephant grass and stopped. Hidden in a kind of nest that we pressed into the tall stalks, we could just observe through a curtain of green slivers the open cut between ourselves and the little ridge where we had spent the night.

After a period of cautious observation, I felt confident that we weren't followed and signaled a break where we were. We stealthily pooled our freeze-dried coffee, tea, and chocolate powders, and using a wad of more-or-less smokeless C-4, cooked up an instant black energy brew that we passed all around. It made me feel better and seemed to animate the others. It was a celebration, just as though we had escaped some known danger. After awhile, as nothing had stirred beyond the grass, and the insect sounds were steady, we moved off.

We were unable to find the trail. It evidently wasn't where it had been depicted on the map overlay, or was possibly no longer in use. Though it might not appear in aerial photos depending upon the angle of the sun when the pictures were taken, it was entirely possible that it lay now obscured in a bend away from our position—or that our intelligence was simply wrong. The open ditch-like depression we crossed just before entering the grass was clearly not in use as a trail.

After another day of fruitless search, we were all weary, filthy, hungry, and dangerously dispirited. I felt it and could see it in the others. Our strange night on the slope had taken an emotional toll on the whole team, and we were in no shape for any encounter with the bad guys. I called for an extraction.

Back in the debriefing at base a day later, I told about the big early-morning explosion and was informed that we had been five miles from an Arclight strike. It was incredible to me that a detonation that violent had taken place so far from our position. I had never heard of a single-bomb Arclight strike. Maybe they had them, but my doubts about being told the truth came back, mixed with an unholy resentment. Although I was glad that the sergeant felt moved to supply me with some kind of answer, even a less than completely satisfying one, instead of retreating into one of his mysterious studied silences, it brought back my former suspicion about the coordination of 1000-pound bomb strikes while people like me were supposedly known to be out there. I wondered, too, if this might explain the loss of some of our teams, but I didn't say anything, just pretended to accept the story. After all, even less likely things were true.

Before Grayson and I left the map shed, though, I decided to risk telling the sergeant about the strange feeling that had affected us all the night we spent on the slope. I had been hesitant to mention it, but it was clear that all of us had sensed something, especially the Nungs, whom I always credited with superior instincts. When I told my version of what had happened, and Grayson corroborated it, the sergeant surprised me by showing interest. He asked me to show him on the map where we had been. I indicated the place as well as the inherent vagaries of such maps allowed. He took my dirty field map and transposed the operational coordinates over to his master sheet. Then he opened a chart drawer and got out another map in a different scale. He studied the two together for a minute or two while Grayson and I exchanged speculative looks. I wondered uneasily what to expect.

Finally, the sergeant made a little sniffing noise through his nose, then turned to us and said,

"That's very strange. You said that after you moved off the ridge you crossed a low grassy area?"

"Yeah. Yeah we did."

"Could it have been an overgrown road?"

"Er, well…yeah. Yes, I suppose it could have been a section of old road. We only saw a small portion of it in darkness and just moved across for cover. In the morning it just looked like an overgrown ditch."

"Well, if your positioning is accurate, you crossed a road where a unit of the 1st Cav was ambushed and wiped out a few years ago."

A whelm of silence burst within me. If it was true, we must have walked through a place where the past had some kind of sentient hold on the present. We had felt the residual essence of a place where the past shaded perceptibly into the present, where a brooding sense of tragedy still pervaded, left by an event of such intensity that it remained somehow incompletely diffused, captive perhaps of the living trees.

Yes, I thought, even less likely things were indeed true.

26

Some of the recon guys had somewhere found two pairs of narrow gauge railroad axles attached to steel train wheels that could actually be used for weightlifting. They had built a workout bench and had it set up on the duckboards between the recon hootches, where I found them a few days later hefting the wheels around to the approving fascination of the Nungs. The wheels probably weighed something over a hundred pounds, too much to be lifted by the little Chinese, but impressively wieldable by the Americans.

I delivered some of my clothes that needed repair to Ba Thong, the aged crone who pumped away on her sewing machine treadle on weekends, always out in the open, where the blaze of the sun so heated the machine's flywheel that she had wrapped it with tape, a solution she seemed to find preferable to setting up shop in the shade. She had placed her machine in the sand near where some of the guys were lifting the train wheels and performing feats of strength for the Chinese, who sat around them on the ground the way they positioned themselves at the movies. After delivering my tatters to Ba Thong's pile, I strolled over to watch the workout. A few of the guys seemed to have some experience with weights, but most were just clowning for the Nungs.

Having worked with Olympic weight sets all through high school and college, I decided to try my hand. I went over, braced my back and picked up the makeshift barbell. It felt strange to be lifting actual railroad wheels, but it proved to be possible, so I just continued the lift up over my head in a straight press. There was a muted chorus of approval from the Chinese, who always reacted emotionally to any kind of entertainment. It was one of their unexpected charms, considering their definitive cold-blooded approach to combat patrols. I continued with some curls, then a set of bench presses, all to the great amusement of the Chinese, who laughed and clapped and muttered punctuated observations. They were always responsive at the movies, too—just the kind of audience that film producers and stage actors hope for. The short-coupled axle wasn't that unwieldy, as workout equipment can be, but it was satisfying to perform reps with it, and we all agreed that the look of the train wheels lent a bit of drama to the whole affair, even for us.

Ba Thong, with whom I had developed a teasing relationship over the months, watched too, and cackled in her toothless high-pitched laughter to see us lifting this unlikely object, an exercise I felt sure was outside the native experience and probably outside their understanding. After all, why would anyone do such a thing anyway?

When I finished, I walked back past Ba Thong at her machine, and she turned her deeply grooved, laughing face to me and said, "Trung Shi Mo', you numba ten!" and then chuckled delightedly at her teasing insult as she turned back to her work.

This was a typical crack. The numerical rating was universally applied to both people and objects, as well as to pretty much any situation, and the scale was very simple: something was either "number one" (good), or "number ten" (bad). It made for a clear and easy way to communicate degrees of approval. However, there were no gradients in between; something was either number one, or it was number ten.

"Ba Thong," I replied, "You numba five!" and I held up five fingers. This set her off on a wet cackling jag that almost alarmed me. Calling her number five seemed to introduce the old lady to an entirely new concept, and in her paroxysms of snorting laughter, she almost lost the tenuous perch her bony hips had on the little sewing stool. It pleased me to make her laugh. She was consistently cheerful, and I liked her. She always did good work on her machine for the many repairs the jungle made necessary to my clothes, and I always overpaid her for the pittances she charged.

The workouts soon proved to be an outlet for my fear and frustration, and I began then to use those train wheels for hard workouts, usually alone and late at night in starlight, since I couldn't relax enough to sleep anyway. It was something I could do without disturbing others, as dropping the wheels after each set made no more than a soft thump in the sand.

A few days after discovering the potential for exercise offered by the train axles, I encountered a few of the guys in the club house who had been responsible for having "commandeered" them. They were discussing an additional plan for our amusement. They wanted to replace the camp's daily import of maids with prostitutes. That way, they reasoned, they could make more efficient use of the work force by combining certain services. They guys had invested some time at the bar in congratulating each other on the brilliance of the scheme, which to my surprise, they discussed seriously.

When they asked what I thought of the plan, I told them it was stupid, stupid and dangerous. It was evidently not what they wanted to hear. I pointed out that they were inviting both health and security problems by bringing such an element into the camp, and that besides, as far as I understood it, housekeeping and whoring were two different specialties with few crossover skills.

I dismissed their notions as drink talk but learned a week or so afterwards that they had contrived to get the experiment started. Using their sense of humor, they had probably managed to sell the idea for a trial to the employee liaison officer. Although it was all good natured in the beginning, it wasn't long before some of the guys began to get sick; of course their hootches were never cleaned, and their laundry service disappeared. I didn't like seeing those women around the compound and told our maid, Lei Thi How, not to let any of them near our hootch.

In a few weeks most of the schemers had contracted some disease, those who had not got scared, and all had become disillusioned with the lousy service. I doubt if the Colonel knew about this effort in advance, but when these guys began reporting in with mysterious symptoms, he ordered the new women off the base immediately.

I never heard of what, if any, disciplinary action was taken against the men who concocted the plan, but I did learn of other consequences: Southeast Asia is a world leader in unknown strains of disease. At least one of the guys had amused a crowd in the club by placing one of these women on the bar, and then on a general bet, demonstrating one of his techniques to the gathering. Everyone chipped in to watch and by all reports had a great laugh, but the guy contracted some kind of unknown flesh-eating disease, and when I left the country a few months later, he was still quarantined in a Japanese hospital with the lower portion of his face rotting away. The medical staff had still not isolated the strain that was causing it, but from the description of his condition as reported to me, he didn't have much reason to live anyway.

I could never reconcile that kind of stupidity. It's a form of temporary insanity, I suppose, a conditioned response to violence and the uncertainty that just won't end. Perhaps, like the rest of us, they had been pulled from some degree of fidelity to their values and, wrung through a crucible of moral challenges, had retreated into the private regions of some immutable winter, where strange winds howled through the conscience. I liked a few of these guys pretty well, and I knew the harebrained plan was just a way of escaping–all just supposed to be in good fun. But they lost sight of the lesson: *do not presume; never relax.*

For some reason, this was a period of lull in our operations. All but one of the recon teams was at "home" at FOB 4, so there were more people than usual in the compound. This meant more defensive fire power if needed, but it also meant that we made for a target-rich environment for the invisible watchers on the mountain. Accordingly, a period of lazy intermittent sniping resumed from somewhere high on the mountainside, sending a few rounds whining harmlessly overhead as people gathered in the open almost every evening to watch a movie. As before, there didn't appear to be an effort to hit anyone, just a reminder, a calling card from Charlie.

During this time a tall sergeant with sun-bleached blond hair was assigned to FOB 4 on temporary duty for reasons I never learned. He did not like the fact that we were being fired on, even poorly, any more than I did. By now I was as used to it as most of the others, and though I was leery of what it might portend, shared their amusement at the new guy's epigrammatic swearing.

One day he accompanied a few other guys in the Jeep on an errand up Highway 1 to the large American PX located in a compound north of us, just outside Da Nang. On the way back, they came across a large 155 mm "Long Tom" mobile artillery piece, just parked on the side of the road. The 155 was a massive long-range gun mounted on multiple axles and a large number of tires. There was no driver or gun crew around. The new guy knew how to drive the gun, so they stopped, he climbed up into the cab and started it up. He "borrowed" this monster and drove it down the road and onto the FOB 4 compound.

I first noticed it when I heard the unusual engine sound and looked up to see the huge barrel of the gun loping gently on a cloud of dust as it crested the high end of camp. He roared into the recon hootch section and stopped, then elevated the barrel and traversed it to aim at Marble Mountain.

It was a great curiosity, and a lot of us gathered around laughing at the audacity of stealing such a thing. We climbed up to explore it.

I had never seen one of these giant guns up so close and was curious about the aiming controls. Sitting in the firing seat and sighting along that enormous barrel that darkened the sky felt quite empowering.

Before long the gun's owners showed up in an advanced state of unrest. The driver and his commanding officer and a Jeep-load of MPs, having seen the barrel protruding over our roof tops from some distance down the main road, came swerving along our perimeter road trailing a great genie of dust. It didn't take long for them to see that their weapon was unharmed and was actually the centerpiece of some broad amusement, not to mention the object lesson it made for leaving such things around with the keys in them. Shortly afterwards, the bounty of our club bought us forgiveness enough that they agreed to leave the gun parked where it was until the next day. That night there was no sniping from the mountain.

The next operation came down at a time when, after five months and some weeks, I had the unsettling distinction of being the longest-living team leader, having survived two more operations than any of the other One-Zero at the time without being killed, lost to the jungle, or invalided out of the country with wounds or a bloodstream full of exotic microbes. I don't know how it happened, other than the sheer luck of escaping encounters with the enemy despite a few operations that placed the team very deep in bad-guy territory. With our recovery of the Navy pilot's ring and the Starlight scope, the prisoner capture, and then being tapped for work with the super spooks—all events in which I had been the helpless plaything of blind chance–I became gradually aware that people were treating me with a subtle, somewhat tentative and vaguely exclusory sort of camaraderie. It seemed that an entirely undeserved reputation had devolved upon me, and considering how this sort of thing often played out in the military, I knew it boded ill for the future. It enlarged the burden on my diminishing prospects of survival and raised the stakes for trying to hide the solitary tumults in my heart.

Eventually the distorted favor that came with survival returned in the form of an operation that was so dangerous and frightening that most of my memories of it come from the perspective of a place above and slightly behind my right shoulder, as though my mind had caught its sleeve in the effort to flee.

At this time in 1968, Senator Ted Kennedy—who throughout his long career seldom missed an opportunity to demonstrate his problems with analytical thought—began getting press time by repeating the North Vietnamese claim that we were bombing non-military targets around Hanoi. In this way, he presumably sought to gain votes among his constituency in the state of Massachusetts, a region by some measures, notably even more distant from the fighting than Washington.

For reasons that remain obscure, the White House decided that direct ground-level reconnaissance was needed to counter or confirm the blithering Senator's claims. Again, this was information readily obtainable at the time by state-of-the-art cameras we had mounted in aircraft, not to mention satellites. It was entirely unnecessary to send some poor scared guy deep into the North to make corroborating observations in person, an explanation I would have been happy to express to the President in person, leaving for Washington right then.

When I was called in to be briefed for the operation by a stranger of unknown name and rank who insisted that I report to him after dark while the movie was on, I was appalled. I couldn't believe they were actually going to dispatch one of our teams that far into the North, and least of all, mine. The idea seemed so far outside even the pliable limits of rational thinking, as well as beyond the realm of my experience in particular, that I had trouble absorbing all the briefer told me. I listened dry-mouthed, swallowing hard while he laid out the purpose of the mission, which, though detailed in operational facts, managed to elude clarity of purpose. It seemed that to have been singled out for such a job meant I had been graduated to some additional level of trust, but since by chance or design the reason for the operation remained unclear, I decided to risk their misguided confidence and pointed out the oversight. The briefer's face clouded. Then he added with a kind of lubricious unction that my name had come up in White House intelligence briefings. This was a distressing surprise. It was evidently intended to carry implications of honor and privilege, but of course it had the opposite effect. It terrified. I wanted no part of cynosure, and it carried dreadful implications for the cavernous bicameral minds that attempted to run a war from far-off Washington. I joked feebly that it would be better if *his* name came up in White House briefings. He proved humorless on the point.

Almost every aspect of this operation required a great extension of all support and communication elements. The physical distances would greatly expand any reaction time for mobilizing an extraction. Radio range would require an intermediary contact to pass along any message I might be able to get out. That would at the very least create a delay, and in any case introduce an unpredictable additional step, a chance for failure over which neither my radio nor the TOC operator at FOB 4 had control. There would be no hope of timely rescue or support, as any on-site air activity would in itself not only compromise the mission but give away our future capacity for such deep-penetration activity, assuming the enemy was not aware of them already. It was certain that if we were compromised on the ground, we would all be lost. Dread had fed my suspicions to the point that I even feared they were conjuring a deliberate sacrifice.

With mournful resolve and a heavy sinking in my chest, I selected the six best of the team and pulled together the other preparations to go. The news was so ponderous, the magnitude of the enterprise so bold, that I couldn't wrap my mind around all its implications. Finally I decided that, with a few contingencies, it had to be treated like all the other missions, in which our daily operational decisions had to be focused on whatever signs of danger appeared in the immediate situation. In other words, literally one step at a time. That would be paramount, the alleged purpose of the mission secondary. I would be prepared to abandon the effort if things looked unlikely at any point. I would not risk the lives of the team for an objective that even someone as low in the pecking order as myself could see was of unlikely value.

I took the list of frequencies and drew brand new batteries for both the PRC-25 and the emergency PRC-10 radios. Then I drew a second PRC-25 for Grayson, so that we would have two primary radios. I also drew another .45 pistol. I told Supply I wanted it as a backup, but I issued it to Nhi. Judging by the reaction of the team to this gesture, it made him immortal. We were all to wear the Chinese cloth and, as usual, to carry no identification. As was by now our established custom, we would keep strict water discipline and maintain our policy of sharing a single canteen at a time.

Most of my memories of this mission are like images caught in a flash with all the hard shadows left in. A photographer came to get some shots of us individually as we waited for the choppers to show up while I went through last minute radio checks. We had never been photographed before, and I didn't know what to make of it. Since nothing about this operation was good, I decided that getting pictures of us just before a trip so far out beyond support was a bad sign too. Why would they want a photographic record this time?

I took a long last look around the hootch, letting my gaze dwell upon various familiar objects in a vague effort to imagine what it would be like to see them again after the ordeal and then to recall what it had been like to perceive them through the prism of its expectation. I wondered if I'd ever see them again and who might inherit them.

We left about mid-afternoon a day later, a team of six. We flew up the spine of the central highlands in two of the unmarked Hueys, with two more flying top cover. After some hours of relentless jungle scenery rolling beneath us as though painted upon some enormous slowly turning drum, we came down in a jungle clearing where a few other helicopters sat parked under the trees. I was unfamiliar with these other aircraft, but they looked to me like Russian machines. We got out, were given some sandwiches, peed, and transferred to the strange, somewhat tinny foreign-looking choppers with their sparse, industrial interiors. We took off again, and after another hour or so descended through the closing twilight to be inserted in the jungle at map coordinates that indicated we were about six miles west and south of Hanoi itself. Except for the use of foreign equipment, the insertion had followed familiar procedure, and there was nothing notably different about the terrain or the jungle itself. Yet the knowledge of how far we had come and how deeply we were trapped in enemy territory, made everything *feel* very different. Once again I was beyond the limits of my experience and could not reassure myself that what I thought I knew would help this time.

After the helicopters left, I didn't know what to expect. I struggled in a private sedulous despair that threatened to take me over as we lay on the lightless jungle floor waiting for our hearing to return. At least, I thought, we're so far into enemy territory that they are unlikely to be watching for us. It was a small point on which to fasten a crumb of encouragement, but it was something. The whole situation remained surreal. We had been in these conditions before, just never so far out of touch, so far into the belly of the Beast. I tried to put the distance in its place. After all, barring our getting somehow compromised on the ground, if the spooks could put us in, they could supposedly get us out, although if we were discovered this time there would be no extraction.

Night soon closed around us. The extreme humidity held the scent of turmeric vegetation and coated my skin like honey. We set up our perimeter for the night and waited for the faint morning twilight to bring enough visibility for us to make some decisions. I sent the insertion signal, and we settled into a tight perimeter of watching and listening. I rolled a sticky, amylaceous ball of dirty rice flavored vaguely with anchovy and swallowed it whole. It might have to do for the whole next day.

Our situation was so bizarre that I couldn't completely shake my preoccupation with the distance we had come, and I struggled with a persistent suspicion of abandonment to treat the whole thing like our other missions. Even though we had been inserted far beyond quick rescue on those operations, too, there was something about knowing help had been a matter of hours away—even if those hours amounted to more than 24—that seemed to justify a fatuous sense of security and that made our present situation so different.

Just as I had realized on the mission with Johnson, there was no way to prepare someone psychologically for a first step into such unknowns. The minute-to-minute practice itself, never quite comprehensible, becomes an open-ended gamble in which decisions are driven by immediate priorities encountered in the field. Thus the stated mission quickly becomes secondary to bare survival. Most of the important things cannot be taught in advance, and you force yourself to continue by unwanted calculation against greater loss and always hoping you've made the least-bad choice, from which those who emerge are all more or less wounded.

In the vague outline of things revealed at first light, I saw that we were on the north slope of gently rising ground. I climbed into a tree and, peering through the branches with binoculars, saw that we were in a position with fairly good visibility over lower ground to the east and the north in the direction of the objective.

I allowed myself to wonder about the odds of success if we just hid out for several days here at the insertion point and then called for extraction, but I knew there was nothing for it but to start moving. I signaled for launch, and we ducked into the wall of leaves and crept all that day and the next with my nerves stretched like thrummed wire. By the end of the third day we could see the lights of Hanoi at night.

Our continued movement had to be guided by the assumption that they had patrols out as well. According to our information the country skirting the city in the direction of our approach consisted mostly of rice paddies. This proved to be true except for the anti-aircraft batteries which were part of the city's belt of defenses. Some were hidden in the jungle, where we came upon one, and then a second, on the fourth day. We heard the voices of the gun crews and smelled the heavy lubricants—and their latrines—long before we saw them. With my heart pounding so hard I could barely keep the camera steady between held breaths, I managed to photograph the guns and their indolent-looking crews, and we crept stealthily on. It scared me to get so close to them. We were mere yards away, hidden in the growth that crowded up to their gun pit. Some of the gunner's shirts hung on branches of the very trees that sheltered us. To get the photos I had to creep in too close to breathe. The slightest noise–a cough, a stumble, a single slap at an

insect–could have alerted them to our presence with disastrous consequences to both sides..

Our orders were not specific as to what we were to report other
than a BDA (Bomb Damage Assessment) on the outskirts of the city—
another strange aspect of this assignment—but it was another of the
vagaries that I had come to expect from the people who had conceived
this operation. Since the city itself was a military target clearly visible
from the air, there was no reason to get too close, and I decided that we
would confine our search for bomb damage to whatever outlying farm
houses and paddies we could observe from a "safe" distance.

We encountered a huge network of dykes that contained paddies
and reservoirs to the south and west of the city. They stank in the
heavy air saturated with the hothouse smells of vegetation and mud,
and they presented an enormous obstacle to a foot patrol, since I did
not believe that it would be safe to cross the network of narrow land
bridges they seemed to offer. To leave cover and venture into the open
was out of the question, and any attempt to cross over them at night
would risk revealing our movement against the night sky reflection
in the waters. We had to change direction and make our way around
them to the west. It would add two days, possibly three, and the same
coming back—assuming we would be coming back—but there was
no other choice if we were to get the information.

Hours later, long after dark, frog calls rang from the paddies and
ditches with the urgency of unanswered telephones. Their chorus
would have covered the tiny sounds we might have made, but we
could not risk moving in such darkness, especially near houses where
the farmers were likely to have dogs. We halted and set up, the Chinese drifting in their silent movements like ghosts. I spent the night
hours listening to the sounds and breathing in the effluent of whatever
things lay festering in the bilges of the capitol.

Several times in the process of our long circuit we came near outlying hovels which I manage to photograph, complete with the families that occupied them. Life seemed normal enough for them. I don't
know what I expected, but encountering these scenes of rural domesticity surprised me. The children looked like those in poor countries
everywhere with their stick limbs, dusty hair, and eyes downcast.
They entertained themselves with small objects and moved among
their mothers like sidling shadows. It was difficult to imagine their
futures, but I could not afford the effort to think about them beyond

whatever I could learn from direct observation, for they were merely obstacles to our situation.

We kept to the jungle, slowly and silently working our way around the city to the north over the next days, circumventing the AA gun emplacements and crossing all roads at night. We watched using two pair of binoculars to shorten distances I didn't dare attempt the risk of exposure that closer observations required. We took many photos of the rice farming and a few water buffalo, making sure that some of the pictures included the city's outlying buildings for verification. In fact, life on the outskirts of the enemy's capitol seemed quiet, far from the war, captured in a bubble of ironic serenity. We watched and listened as the AA gun crews teased the women working the rice fields. We were close enough to smell their cigarettes–and discards. We kept going, ever alert to any movement or sound that didn't fit, always aware of the need to keep a back door open as well as the jungle would allow, and always under the oppress of imminent discovery.

We did see one area where there appeared to be some bomb hits just outside a rice farm. There was blast damage to the tree line, and the earth there, blackened and raw, held several round water-filled craters, some interconnected along the ground near a field of paddies. It looked as though one of these had broken an earthen berm where some of the water had drained out, but it had been repaired. I photographed it, too.

We came upon a section of road where a group of armored vehicles had been attacked from the air and were lying tossed together on a section of moonscaped road. One truck had been ruptured by a direct hit that blackened the steel and forced the sides out like metal sails, perforated by a thousand holes through which the sunlight flared quietly. Yet all of this was open to the sky and would have been easily seen, even with very high altitude cameras. Again, I couldn't understand why we had been sent in for this. Why had they undertaken this risk?

By the seventh day we were exhausted from the unremitting nervous pressure, and were all getting low on food. My fatigues stank, heavy with sweat, and we were each caked with mud. The radio hung on my back with the weight of another person. My fatigue pants were badly torn, having given out at the knees, and I had to tie them to my legs to keep them from flapping. The oppressive risk, the knowledge that we were expendable, and my nagging old suspicion that we might even be engaged in a deliberate sacrifice, had built until it became a living presence with substance and dimension of its own.

Finally there came a moment, a quick stirring of awareness, like sensing a change in the season by some breathless flush of air, when I knew instinctively that we had passed the delicate balance point between pressing on and survival. Our luck could not hold much longer. I decided that we had seen enough. I did not care if we returned to be admonished for failing to observe more than we had, so long as we returned. Despite a provisional adjustment to the growing imminence of doom, my questions about the decisions that lay behind this assignment had grown into scrupulous anger. I just picked a moment and signaled that we were done.

With that, one of the younger Chinese looked at me and smiled a broad, tense grin, his full lips parting to expose slightly splayed teeth lined with a yellowish mulch over which his upper lip was drawn. His face was scratched and bitten, the marks inflamed with the irrepressible infections that inhabited all our abrasions. He was the picture of all that seemed wrong with the risks we were engaged in as well as living evidence that we had stayed long enough. All of our faces necks and arms were stitched with scratches and swollen with insect bites. Dry leaf dust coated our faces, clung to the camouflage grease paint and had accumulated in black deposits along the creases of our skin. We had sustained to the quintessential point of no return the balanced imbalance. I could see nothing that we could learn in this way that wasn't already known, especially when weighed against the consequences if the team were compromised. It was time to get out. I was so exhausted by the conditions and the tension that I dreaded the demands of even our withdrawal.

We began the long, arduous trek back toward the higher ground that contained our two alternate extraction points. We circled back wide of our inbound track, and the eight additional days it took to get there became an anabasis of pained fatigue and delay, but it was distant enough that even if Russian helicopters were to be observed from the outskirts of the city, they (or at least their purpose) would likely be misinterpreted.

Each day was a slog of excruciatingly slow and cautious movement on constant nervous alert, weighted with the unrelenting ropical heat, constant attack by insects, rasping thirst, and the growing imperative of unseen mortal danger. Every passing hour reduced our chances and each held prolonged moments when I thought I could not continue another step without a sip of water. Somehow each one passed. My saliva diminished until my gullet became dry and sticky. My neck and then my whole scalp pounded with the effort to press on. The shoulder straps of the radio pack rubbed my skin raw, and it had begun to fester. I fought to keep my mind from drifting, awakening to the desperate reality every few moments, only to confront another crisis of thirst that had to be suppressed. Every obstacle presented by the jungle degraded further our diminishing capability, corrupting our capacity for parceling the group's collective resources, and with our steady degeneration, I knew that we had become unfit for any encounter with the enemy.

When at last we found ourselves approaching the general area of our insertion over two weeks earlier, we were on our last legs. My breath came short and painful, and with temples pulsing, I had been swallowing dry for two or three days and nights. When we weren't actually crawling on the ground, the guys walked with the ponderous pushing steps of deep fatigue. Yet we could not let up. Any sound unnatural to the jungle could give us, or the enemy, away. The resultant encounter didn't bear speculation. Those killed might be the lucky ones. The fatigue, the heat, the constant fear of encounter, and the enormous likelihood of discovery, thirst and hunger, had depleted us all. Even Nhi showed signs of the pressure. I saw his anger and frustration burning through the fatigue in the hot globes of his eyes. He well knew where we were, and he didn't like it either.

At last we arrived at a more or less defensible place in the jungle near enough to one of our designated alternate extraction points to conceal us while providing a view of an opening to the sky through which the helicopters could get in. We found a well-covered area nearby where we collapsed into a defensive perimeter, and I called for the pick up. A convective breeze sighed up the slope, but the air was still so hot and close it lacked all power to refresh.

We spent that night and most of the next morning on the jungle floor, unmoving except for quiet repairs to clothing and adjustments to gear, uncertain of rescue. Some shared the last of their food, and we passed around the remnants of our water. When I sent my second canteen around, it came back empty. The weight of the PRC-10 radio swinging in my side pocket had gradually torn my pant leg almost completely around, and I was in the process of taping the cloth directly to my leg late that afternoon when, with unutterable relief, I thought I heard the faint thump of the helicopters. The others sensed something at the same time. Their heads came up, and their eyes began to search up through the canopy. I left off the taping and switched on the locator.

The Russian helicopters arrived overhead, and we were quickly pulled out by a wordless Caucasian crew. I didn't know who these guys were. Their uniforms were unmarked, but at that point I cared only that they knew their jobs. I didn't recognize any of them from the insertion crew, and nobody said a word to us. We were all so dirty, debilitated and tenuous that we said nothing either.

The trip back was a long retracing of the route in. At least it seemed to be. I could not keep my eyes open for all of it, but each time I managed to look out we seemed to be flying south over the central highlands. Eventually we landed at the mountaintop base where we had changed helicopters before. During the brief layover I was offered some coffee which I gulped so fast it burned my mouth. It revived me a bit, though it was flavored by the grit in my teeth. Our transfer to the waiting American Hueys for the leg back to FOB 4 was delayed. The pilots were there, but the whole operation seemed to be held in suspension while they stood around checking their watches and the sky. The team collapsed on the ground, and I fell into a dreamless sleep. Eventually we were roused and loaded into the Hueys. It was evening. Thus we arrived back at FOB 4, no doubt by plan, well after dark.

The trucks met us as we stumbled out from under the turning blades. The choppers lifted off immediately, banking back to the northwest and switching off all lights. I looked around at the familiar scene with a strange detachment. My legs trembled with fatigue. Even the Nungs, worn beyond their customary jungle proficiency, staggered sideways, moving uncertainly, like antique machinery. My web gear pulled so heavily on me I didn't want to attempt the climb into the back of the truck. I just stepped onto the running board and held onto the outboard mirror frame for the ride down to the recon huts. My eyes kept trying to close.

Except for the guys who met us and the silent presence of the night patrol jeep, the camp slept. I staggered into the hootch with Grayson behind me. Seen through the haze of my fatigue, the little room took on a momentary surreal quality, and I realized that throughout the time we'd been gone, I had harbored the suppressed belief that I would never see it again. So relieved and so filthy I didn't want to sully my bunk, I just dropped my webbing, lay down on the floor, and plunged into a deep and pathological sleep.

In the morning I awoke with a jolt of anxiety, immediately attached to what might have happened while I was unaware. Grayson was asleep face up on his bunk, breathing with a faint clacking sound from deep in his throat as though a ratchet were being wound to unbearable tightness inside him. He still wore his webbing, having fallen from consciousness before he could get out of it.

My thoughts turned to the dreaded debriefing that lay ahead. I worried about what I might not have been told regarding the real reason for the operation and was concerned that my report would bring about once and for all the ruthless exposure of my ignorance and my unsuitability, perhaps through some lapse or perceived malfeasance, for these kinds of jobs. I tried to comfort myself with the idea that if it happened, it might excuse me from further duties, perhaps even land me in a safe prison, on the grounds of an insufficiency of military fiber, or maybe just a want of Green Beret professionalism.

I was restless with constant worry and exhausted by the months of uncertainty, while in the background hummed an unremitting silent rhythm section of abject fear. Each completed operation, each return to the dubious security of FOB 4, was a small victory weighed against the war's pitiless indifference, but each one stretched the elastic of my capabilities increasingly taut, and each release revealed it to have grown a degree more slack. I knew that soon I'd have no more. It is not in the nature of roulette to allow the gambler to keep winning, and given the time remaining in my tour of duty, I knew the wheel was still turning.

I trudged to the showers to wash and shave off a dirty two-week growth in the warm cascade. The hot water burned in the many infected scratches on my skin, but it revived me, and after a change into clean fatigues, I felt much better. Grayson was stirring by then, and I told him he didn't need to come with me up to HQ if he didn't want to, which he didn't. I went over to the messhall for a quick coffee, but found that I needed several glasses of water with it. Then I headed to the briefing hootch anticipating a large breakfast afterwards.

To my surprise, the debriefing went exceptionally well. I was relieved that they seemed happy with my report, and I was assured that the photographs I'd taken were being rushed to Washington. The meeting was unexpectedly short and informal—suspiciously so in view of the alleged magnitude of the operation and the huge risks we had taken.

Afterwards, that in itself seemed strange, too. Since we'd been sent out with orders essentially just to look around, I couldn't understand the excitement over the photos, which I assumed to be of limited intelligence value. I wanted to know why we'd ever been sent in the first place but did not expect to find out. Gradually, though, I learned some things that enabled me to venture a guess:

Our debriefing sergeant, who had been a source of minor leaks to me a few times in the past, told me that not long before, while I had been away in the field, General Creighton Abrams, the overall commander in Vietnam at the time, had shown up at the gate to our compound. All pressed and starched in his polished Jeep, he demanded to see our facility, but he was denied access on the grounds that he did not have a "need to know." He had not taken the news at all well. I remembered hearing something about the incident at the time, but it had sounded so unlikely I had dismissed it. Now, though, it began to make a kind of bizarre sense.

The incident could probably have been handled more diplomatically, but there was no historical love lost between Abrams and the Special Forces. Gen. Abrams was a famous tanker with a well-deserved reputation, having distinguished himself as a thirty-year-old Lt. Col. in Gen. Patton's relief of the 101st Airborne at Bastogne in 1944; however, like many senior WW II-era staff officers still in service as late as the Vietnam War, he was a man whose ideas about strategy and the deployment of resources had been developed during another type of war in an entirely different theater of operations— and perhaps importantly, a different generation. Not only did conditions in Vietnam fail to lend themselves to the use of tanks or even to large-army maneuvers, but Abrams was a thoroughgoing, by-the-book, conventional thinker who mistrusted, and by all accounts eventually came to despise, unconventional operations, along with anyone who functioned outside traditional regulations. Of course, as experts in unconventional warfare, the Special Forces came in for much of his execration.

In fact, it was well known that since he had taken command, Special Forces casualties had greatly increased, and it was thought at FOB-4 that he was deliberately ordering unnecessarily risky missions for the FOBs in order to make the case in Washington that the Special Forces had become obsolete, citing the latest figures as an indication that their mission in Vietnam had been compromised.

In view of our recent Hanoi mission, it seemed there may have been some truth in this story. It was certainly an operation of questionable value. Then there was the surprising enthusiasm for my after-action report and the almost gleeful receipt of the photos, which were being rushed off to Washington. It made sense to think Abrams' appointment as overall commander had been a purely political one in view of his long service, and I could understand his resentment of us, even if he hadn't been rebuffed at the gate.

It began to make sense to think that the supposed need to answer Senator Kennedy's ravings had been a cover, when what was really intended was for me to come back with ground-level photos and a personal report to prove Special Forces capabilities to the President, countering the efforts of the Abrams camp. That might also explain the photos taken of us before we left. They would presumably contribute to a White House briefing on the whole operation.

I was never told this, nor was I ever given a satisfactory explanation for the mission, but this makes the most sense in view of these other little-known facts, especially when, a few weeks later, I was informed that the unit was going to be awarded a citation from the President. This happened at an awards ceremony held in due course at FOB 4, in which I was given a few decorations, and the assembled company was informed that we were all entitled henceforth to wear an additional Presidential Unit Citation above the right breast pocket of our class A and other garrison uniforms. Needless to say this dealt another severe blow to my quest for anonymity.

28

It must have been obvious to the debriefing sergeant that I was growing nervous and irritable beyond the point of continued usefulness in the field. To my grateful surprise, he recommended me for another R&R. By then it was around the middle of December, and he suggested that it might be good for me to spend the holidays out of the country. I told him that it would be good for me to spend *any* days out of the country. He added that with only 60 or 70 days to go before my entire enlistment was up there was a good chance that I would not be sent out again after my return. This was great news, if only suspended on the strings of hope. I had suffered too many disillusioning moments to accept it completely but jumped at the opportunity to leave the country again.

This time I decided to apply for Hawaii. The idea of spending an entire week simply sitting on a beach in the shade of some coconut trees carried a certain sybaritic appeal. Orders come through within a week, and I was soon back at the airport, this time with the little equipment bag I had inherited packed with my new custom-cut Hong Kong civilian clothes.

There, in the crowd of guys being sorted according to flights, I found that a senior sergeant had been bounced from a previous flight to Hawaii, where he had planned to meet his wife. He was waiting now in a state of ascending agitation for any space available. Apparently he and his wife had been planning their rendezvous for a long time. He had applied for his leave for that particular week, and she had flown to Hawaii from somewhere in the continental US to meet him for Christmas, but now some administrative screw-up had risen at the last moment to threaten their plans with collapse. With each departing Hawaii flight, he was losing time with her, and I could see in his face that he was feeling every moment of it.

The plane I was assigned to was full, with no stand-by space. I didn't really care so much about the coconut palms or where I went, as long as it was far away, so I gave him my seat. It was touching to see his gratitude. He outranked me by three grades, but he wrung my hand with tears in his eyes. I missed my family hugely but had spent these months conditioning myself not to think about them, to convince myself that my other life was over. I had no girl friend, no emotional ties to a woman that he did, and his unabashed expression of sentiment sent a mixed *frisson* of regret through me, although touched with relief that no such tie burdened my singular need to survive. A flight with space available was leaving for Hong Kong in another hour or so, and I happily transferred to it.

That night, back again at the Merlin Hotel, I went right to the piano bar and was delighted to find that some of the English teachers that Steve and I had befriended were still there. One couple had left for permanent housing, but another still hung out in the bar where the American writer also lent his saturnine presence. My reunion with the teachers, who now seemed like old friends, was a happy one, and we bought each other a round of drinks. The writer, however, was able to control his enthusiasm.

This second week in Hong Kong was almost a duplicate of the first, except for the bright seasonal decorations in the streets and stores. I did little other than walk around indulging myself in the life force of the city. I bought a set of hand-carved dice from an old man who had cut them from ivory scrap and filled in the dots with red nail polish. That was the extent of my purchases in this Mecca of free enterprise.

The week passed in a kind of dream state. I had become so conditioned to the expectation of death that each day's experience seemed provisional, filled with sights and sounds borrowed against some separate legacy. I was content to ride the Star Ferry and to sit on the quay for hours just watching the harbor traffic. Once I ventured over to the Hong Kong side and boarded the strangely-angled funicular train for the straight pull to the top of Victoria Peak, there to look around at the rugged coast and the distant commercial ships captured like toys among the cloud shadows on the sea far below.

Only a few hours flight time from the war, it was indeed another world. To be transported so quickly out of the rage and deposited in this separate reality was somehow harder to grasp this time. Before, there had been distractions to this odd sense of displacement. I had been with a friend, and everything had been new. This time, alone with my thoughts, the trip seemed more like a recurrent dream, complete with a dream's miracles.

Under a sky of clouded steel the wind chuffed and nudged at my clothes, birds wheeled and settled and chirped faintly in the shrubbery of the little mountaintop park. The peak with its nodding flowers and panoramic views held a vivid palliative amelioration I did not want to leave. The silver patchwork sea below receded toward a dark horizon until, blurred and pale as an aquatint, it disappeared beneath the sea-borne clouds and into the mists of distance. I could feel an enormous presence out there, something palpable yet lightless and huge. The monsoon season would be here soon. The smell of it was in the air, like the sense of a thing just out of sight, just beyond a bend.

Seeing the sea from such a height and from such a famous notch on the rim of Asia brought home its rich paradoxical nature. The sea has always been both barrier and gateway at the same time, separating yet connecting remote regions of the earth, in this case both barring and conducting the British influence to a harbor so distant from 19th century England. Like an army or a crowd, an ocean is multiple—an unsleeping power, often releasing its force in terrible storms, yet it can soothe, even heal. It moves, yet is constant. It's dense and cohesive, but you can easily put your hand into it. It is said that all life emerged from it, and if so, it is the image of stilled humanity, for all life eventually flows back into it.

As I tried to shake off the truth that the misty 900 mile bastion was also a bridge back to the fury, the canted rail car arrived behind me and deposited a young Asian couple who stepped out of the narrow doors holding hands. They walked together to the edge of the little park and stared out over the sea, instantly in thrall of the spectacle, perhaps even joined in the strange power it held for me. After a minute or so they approached shyly, and evidently speaking no English, offered me their camera and asked by gesture and self-conscious smiles for me to take their picture. When I indicated a suggestion for them to pose on the Hong Kong side, rather than the shimmering but feature-less sea side, they moved accordingly, and with their smiling faces together, I snapped two shots of them with the blue-green harbor and sprawling bright city arrayed distantly around its shore behind them in a scene that spoke more clearly of where they were than would a seascape. They grinned and bowed their thanks, then crossed back to the sea side. There they took a few close-ups of the flowers but then returned to staring once more out to the east. It left me wondering if they had really wanted their picture with the open sea behind them in the first place.

When I boarded the train for the trip back down the mountain, the couple was still there, looking out over the water. I enjoyed the glimpse they had given me of their affection. The molecular power of the ancient human mandate to reproduce had generated a contagion of warmth that touched me unexpectedly. They had stirred a vague and sleeping hopefulness, but I left with a lingering unease that I had forever failed them with the camera.

On Christmas Day I went to the phone banks at the post office to book a cable call to my parents in London. Fortunately, the wall displayed a row of world clocks, showing times in several capitol cities around the globe, which saved me the trouble of calculating the difference in hours across the International Dateline. Christmas morning always starts early in our family, so I took a mathematical risk and timed the call for 6:30 or 7:00 in London.

It was strange, almost surreal, to hear the familiar voices of my parents, brother and sister, faintly but clearly in the handset, sounding as though through a garden hose. It served to remind me of who I was and filled me with poignant memories of all the years we had been together in all the countries we had been fortunate to live in as my father was transferred internationally in his work. I pictured so clearly each of them at home around the phone. I knew where in the room they were standing, and I could hear in my imagination the faint early morning traffic sounds in Knightsbridge. I knew the corner where the Christmas tree stood and remembered all the old broken ornaments my mother had carefully preserved through the years to hang again with the good sides out.

I spoke to each of them in turn and reminded them, along with myself, that I was now counting the time remaining in weeks instead of months. I quickly changed the subject from anything that might tempt me to linger on such prospects. I wished them happiness, told them I missed them and not to worry, and suddenly the call was over. I was back on the other side of the world alone with a phone in my hand.

It had been good to speak with them and to have had even a brief flight of fancy, but I needed to get over the sentiment, as I knew that all too soon I would be back in conditions that would make of it a liability. The hotel was planning a Christmas celebration, and I assumed my greatest chance of getting a facsimile version of my family traditions at this time of year lay with the English people in the piano bar.

I headed back to the Merlin in anticipation of some champagne and traditional holiday piano music. The streets were busy with shoppers and festooned with holiday decorations, some Christian, some

Chinese variations on the theme, all cheerful and bright. Here, too, Christmas was a special time. Regardless of religion, the adaptive Chinese saw an excuse to borrow a good time from the Barbarians of the previous century. Even the Father Christmas/Santa Clause tradition had found a fit with the Chinese lore of *djinns* and rascally spirits that enter your house at night.

As a warm and cheerful oasis, the piano bar did not disappoint. The 25th was well underway in Europe, but here people were just getting cranked up. I found a deep contentment, enriched by its transience, in simply sitting on the lumpy sofa with the pudgy school teacher while his wife played traditional carols on the keys. We talked about history, the differences in the ways this time of year is celebrated across cultures, including our own, and other subjects that mattered far less than the pure exalted uniqueness of being in that little room with those individual people at that particular time.

The champagne provided by the hotel was plentiful, and before long it revealed its effect all around, and I suppose in me as well, for my thoughts turned morose. The fear that I might not be alive in a week's time began to force itself into the room. It began to insist on a place at the table, leering through the veil of laughter and candle light, demanding that its frightful probability be included at the party. I knew that if it was to be, these kindly people would go on with their lives unknowing. Humans eventually all sink down, fall over and die, and the bleak and shrouded earth goes trundling on, trackless and unremarked on its path through the ancient dark beyond.

In an effort to withdraw before I became noticeably maudlin, I eased off the sofa and went quietly up to my room. There I lay on the bed listening to the street sounds. Weak light fell through the window and draped across the sheets to lie congealed in dim geometry upon the carpeted floor. This would be my second to last night in Hong Kong, and though my mind thronged with misty hopes and fears, I wanted to stay awake, to savor every moment. I knew that in another 48 hours my memories of being here would seem as remote and insubstantial as dreams.

The day I left felt like a death sentence. I looked around the hotel lobby, noting the design in the carpet and the gleam of the wood paneling, then all the sights on the way to the airport, the buildings stacked against the mountainsides and the junks in the harbor, believing that I might never see such things again. My English friends had all been at work when I checked out. I had not said good bye nor told them of the date I was scheduled to leave. I wondered if the American writer was sleeping it off or perhaps actually using his solitary daylight hours to write something.

There was an American warship in the harbor, the USS Hugh Pervis, grey and threatening, yet incongruous and somehow neutralized by the busy urban surroundings. The close presence of the peaceful city seemed to rob it of its purpose, placing it out of context, like a wheelbarrow in a salon. The name of the ship was oddly familiar. Then it clicked. A close boyhood friend of mine had taken his NROTC cruise on the Hugh Pervis years before while he was a student at Yale, and the memory suddenly whipped through me with a painful ecumenical poignancy. When your life itself is uncertain, any pleasant memory from happier times, hopes or desires that are predicated upon your survival, can writhe and contort themselves in the mind until pressed down with the firm hand of resolve.

Arrival back at FOB 4 late in the day showed a painfully familiar compound. I felt a residuum of detachment from the place and had to forcefully accept that I was back. I was glad to find, though, that Grayson had applied for R&R, pending my return. I was delighted, for Grayson deserved some time off, and mine made acceptance of his application likely. Most importantly, his timing implied benefits to me. Not only was it unlikely that I would be sent out again with my Two-Zero away, but a quick calculation showed that by the time Grayson got back from his leave, there would only be about five weeks remaining until my enlistment was up. Happily, there was a certain leniency to short-timers with respect to field operations at FOB 4. When a guy got down to just a matter of weeks before his DEROS date, Command usually found a way to assign him duties within the camp until it was time to leave.

I went up to the Command shack and pushed for Grayson's leave, sighting the fact that I had been given two R&Rs, and Grayson deserved a break because he had been on every mission since he'd arrived. This may have given the impression that I had a certain avuncular concern for the welfare of my second in command, but I was thinking less about the debilitating effect of Grayson's prolonged field duty than about the declining balance of time that would remain for us to be sent out again by the time he would get back.

In due course his leave was approved. I relaxed a bit in his absence, indulging an edgy confidence that my operational days might be over. Despite the months of conditioning to disillusionment and despair, I allowed myself to glimpse the coming end of my responsibilities. Reasons to hope were in the air: Grayson would be away until I had only a bit over a month to go on my entire enlistment, some of which would be needed for out-processing; I was the senior surviving One-Zero, having run more missions than any other team leader as chance would have it–and the monsoon season was approaching. Over the past few weeks the weather had begun flirting its promise of downtime, and already one of our teams prowling out on the Laotian border had barely gotten back ahead of rains that arrived with such fury all air operations were brought to a stop.

In a few days the rains began their clockwork arrival at almost precisely the same time every afternoon. Fairly heavy but of short duration, it drummed on the metal roofs of the hootches, everywhere releasing steam from heat stored in the ground. Everyone warned that the rains would become stronger over the next several weeks, sometimes building into ferocious storms. This curtailed all operations for us, since we depended on aircraft for insertions and retrieval of the teams, and aircraft needed better conditions. Weather did not stop the bad guys completely, but heavy rain made life in the field so miserable that it even slowed them. It caused weapons to rust in a matter of hours, fabric to rot, and fungus to take root beneath your clothing.

Each day I thrilled to the rumble of approaching thunder and the smell of the coming torrent for the promise they bore of down time. With astonishing suddenness the sky to the west turned black every afternoon, exploding upward as though sprung from the earth itself into fabulous heights. The massive cloud sucked up bits of debris and scraps of paper high into the air as, flickering with swords of light, it advanced upon us like a living thing. Wind-blown sea birds lurched sideways overhead, crying in the gusts like lost cats. Then the falling water arrived in a heavy rush like a deep breath. The noise soaked through me in a torrent of welcome change.

As predicted, these squalls gradually built into protracted storms of increasing strength. The light would change as the sky quickly turned a brassy brown, and a sudden wind would strike the hootches with such force the buildings lurched. The rain rushed in sealing off all visibility of anything outside except a deluge of water that came by like a solid object. The first time it happened I stood powerless in the leeward doorway of the hootch, fascinated at the spectacle and tinged with an ancient timidity at the display as odd shadows fled through it. Inside, beneath the metal roof, the roar of water and the clatter of things lofted against the outer walls made speech at any volume practically impossible. Sheets of roofing cartwheeled by. Tons of sand flew past in horizontal tendrils and swirled around the corners of the buildings while smudges of stuff tumbled across the ground or fetched up against standing obstructions, captured in place by the air pressure. Some of the plywood hootches began to undulate, and one started showing glimpses of daylight at one corner before the wind subsided. Inside ours, papers and other loose objects swirled in the suction. I once stuck my arm out from under the eaves and had to force it up against the downward drive of the rain. I actually lost sight of my hand in the amazing aerated deluge.

Most of these storm systems subsided quickly and passed out to sea, ending as abruptly as they had arrived, leaving the compound littered, roofs dribbling, and the ground grooved by wind. Drifts of sand sloped up the sandbags while scraps of cloth and tattered plastic wrenched and fluttered captive in the barbed wire. The storms left behind a dripping world where constant run-off glittered in the sudden pewter light as a pale and cowed sun re-emerged to launch clouds of wraithlike vapor from the ground to drift away like an army of retreating ghosts. The air smelled of wet sand and mildew.

Another reassuring surprise appeared at this time. The film star Martha Ray arrived at the compound on one of her celebrity tours and mixed with the guys at the club for a few days. Decked out in combat fatigues, she had adopted the Special Forces as her pet unit and spent some time in the country visiting various SF installations. She was a bubbly presence in the club and easily made herself part of the company, drinking, laughing, and cussing with the best. I got to speak with her only briefly. It was fun to address the famous face and to find in her a Hollywood celebrity that, at least in our bizarre circumstances, seemed genuine. She flashed like a beacon in the darkness. With her there, it almost seemed for a brief while that we weren't.

As one of the small fry subject to the impenetrable whims of colliding bureaucracies, I did not know, and my aggravated resentments would not let me see at the time, that most of our seemingly unnecessary operations were to varying degrees justified as parts of a larger strategy. Years later I would read about some of the decisions taken behind the curtain, some of which would indeed confirm my suspicions, others less so, but at the time, I was so desperately afraid that I was going to be sacrificed to the war, and without good reason, that I saw only lame-brained motivation and garbled Service pride behind my orders.

It was with my customary doubts on low simmer that during this time of increasing weather, I was called up to the HQ hut. These summonses never failed to give me a sinking feeling. The little building always breathed out an atmosphere of perplexity and foreboding. I'd been told, though, that the super spooks had a decoration or two for me, so this time I went over half expecting a quiet little awards ceremony such as there had been in the past.

I reported in and stood wordless again before unfamiliar countenances that regarded me across an impenetrable chasm, grim with purpose. The central figure was tall with an illegible expression, though a quiet demeanor, slim and wiry, with a head that pointed not at the top but at the bottom, being broad in the forehead and sharp at the chin, like a "yield" sign. His receding military cut was shorn from tight, curly hair so that the brush effect sloped rearward toward a slight fullness behind the ears, lending him an impression of airless forward speed. Whatever my vague expectations had been, he announced flatly that I had another operation.

The news burst upon me in meridian perfidy. For a moment I couldn't believe it. As he continued speaking, and I grasped what was actually at stake, the room emptied of air and my tenuous augurs for the future vaporized in seconds. I broke out in sour perspiration as the fear took me over, dislodging my last glimmer of foredoomed hope and filling me with a formless night. Everything that had ever defined me as a person simply drained away at the sound of a few words.

At that moment, as though to put proof to my scrambled expectations, it began to rain. It rattled heavily on the metal roof like dropped birdshot, shifting the light in the room and stirring watery shadows on the maps like a shimmer of tears.

There was a moment when I actually allowed myself to believe they were joking, a kind of ribbing from the secret handlers before producing my DEROS orders. But as the terrible truth sank in, a withering stone of hopeless dismay rolled into the hollow that had opened within me. Everything I could think of argued against another operation: the rains, Grayson's absence, my short time until DEROS, as well as my bizarre survival so far beyond the statistical limits that governed our operations. As the sheer weight of it all pressed down upon me my wounds began to ache again, and I had to hide my hands behind my back in case the mavens saw the trembling.

I stood there in the little room only half listening to the operational orders with this congestion of secret grievances writhing within me. I had never seen any of these men before, yet I had again been singled out to serve as the hapless trifle in a game the meaning of which would remain obscured by their multifold layers of hidden power.

I wondered who were these people, really. To what extremes of the horrid and the insuperable must they go in their need for ever more excess before they might experience a thrill of disgust? How could they contemplate a launch in this weather? What could justify it? I realized how deceptively I had allowed myself to take courage from the rains and the short calendar and now had to confront the fact that I was truly done, burned out. For months my emotion-driven desire to *get* out had been subtly kneaded into a growing psychological need to *be* out. I had come to a point beyond my tolerance for risk. Strung out on dread, profoundly sleep-deprived, and long past the odds, I could not understand why they couldn't see it. It was probably true that they simply didn't care.

Could it be possible that they meant to arrange for my disappearance because of what they assumed I might have figured out about the Hanoi trip? It was another of those frightening moments when I felt pinned like a specimen at the foot of the immutable layers of control above me and tried pointlessly to look up.

This time I was told that a regiment of NVA was moving south, trying to take advantage of our reduced air activity in the wet weather. They were believed to be advised and accompanied by a Chinese Colonel. We wanted a position report on them and, if possible, a head count. In addition I was to capture or kill the Colonel.

So here it was. A dreaded people-snatch—and from the middle of a large-scale unit. This was not good. I knew for certain I was not up for it. With my whole family history fleeing through me I examined the map and noted the approximation of the enemy location, the estimate of their size, and presumed direction of movement. The rest of the map designating unknown territory seemed to grow and swell around the tiny marks until it made of them an insignificant smudge near a crease in the paper. The spreading geometry of the page itself showed our utter insignificance.

With a harsh grin intended to pass for encouragement I was congratulated on the detail included in my previous reports. Here, as though I needed to be reminded, was terrible confirmation of the daedalian reward for collateral success. As far as I was concerned, the negative odds were stacked so high that survival was the only significant achievement. If you happened to bring back information that others could use, so much the better, but it was merely an addendum to the real accomplishment.

As usual I tried to hide my doubts and fears beneath a strained attempt at humor, but it had no more effect upon them than it had on me.

"Will there be services?"

The yield sign's face betrayed a momentary facsimile grin, so fleeting as to be barely noticeable, the only change being a brief alteration in the geometry of his mouth, like a twitch. The rest of his face remained unmoving, utterly expressionless.

Of course I knew that direct close-range observation could yield much useful intelligence about troop condition, weapons, state of equipment, and possibly even the nationalities of any advisors who might be in company, but it seemed to me that if they had some idea of where a unit this large was located, they could remove the threat with a single Arclight strike. After all, the details of their conditions wouldn't matter if a bomb strike of that magnitude was carried out. Any few survivors would be shocked permanently stupid, beyond the realms of sanity. I knew not to ask if anyone had thought of such an expedient, but I had experienced reasons for doubting that Arclight Command was well coordinated with our long-range operations on the ground, so I ventured to ask if any bomb strikes had been ordered on the target group during the time we would be out there. I hoped this would demonstrate that I had some awareness of the bigger picture and at least introduce the subject of alternative solutions. After a telling little pause, someone said simply, "…No." The word hung in the freighted air as though some disembodied voice had spoken it from the very center of the room.

As the briefing continued I saw all that I had experienced–the pain, the risks and fears, the acquired talent for seeing and hearing patterns in the intense green turmoil of jungles in three countries, and the learned ebullition of abstract reasoning for contingencies–was all to be thrown away on this last gamble. The briefer's voices continued, but by the time they had finished I perceived only white noise. When finally the Yield, or one of his sinister accompanists, pronounced with universal military finality, "Understood?" from somewhere far away, I heard my mouth say, "…Yes, sir."

I would have to return later to the HQ hut for details and a sterilized map, but while those things were being prepared I left the terrible little room and headed down to the indij tent to alert the team. So, I thought, this was how it was going to end for me after all. I told myself that at least there were others on the team who could work the radio, but I knew that if we were compromised that far out to the northwest, there would likely be no poignant last report, no record of what happened. We would simply disappear, like so many others.

I wondered how many years it would be before my parents could collect whatever meager benefits the government deemed a life was worth. I couldn't imagine what it must be like to lose a child, even a grown one, but I was intimately familiar with the silent howl of immutability that surges in when a sentient being is killed, leaving only a mist of fading memories bereft of context. My parents would grieve for a while, but they were intelligent, educated people quite capable of recognizing a situation over which they had no control, as well as the futility of investing lasting emotion in whatever childhood images might cling to fading photographs. Besides, I had a brother and sister who would fill any interim hole in the texture of the family my absence might create.

I managed to shake off these morbid thoughts with the need to plan for the operation. I still had to make the decisions about organizing and drawing equipment for the operation. By the time I arrived at the Nungs' tent, all my hopes for a future had faded, receding as though drawn silently away on a piece of concealed stage machinery. The future had ceased to exist. The idea of the mission swam through my mind as though it were already in the past, lived somehow already, the way one emerges at times from dreams. The feeling suddenly returned of having become in some way transparent, insubstantial—the same sensation that had overtaken me following that first firefight back in August—and I watched myself through other eyes begin the motions of preparation, groping along the checklist, assembling gear, as though what was left of my former nature were no more than an afterthought, lolling in a vague and shimmering timelessness.

I knew that Nhi would show little, if any, reaction to the news, but this time we would need one of his Chinese to carry a second PRC-25. It would be heavy on his small frame, but the unusually wet weather would have a negative effect on all radios, and I wanted a back-up unit. I was so fraught with doubt that we would get away with another operation I wanted every hedge I could think of against the odds. Since Grayson was away, I had to select from the smaller men, and I worried about the choice.

Fortunately, the Nungs saw responsibility for the radio as an honor. As I'd learned, within their culture, one who is entrusted with specialized equipment was given elevated status on the team, so I was pleased that there were several volunteers for the job. Even though I had continued to give them each lessons on how to use it, I chose the one who spoke the best English, just in case. Since I could not account for all the possible hazards to our survival the weather might bring, I gave the radio to the one who was most likely to make himself understood in sounding out the code words through possible static. He wasn't the most confident operator and still seemed to regard the instrument as wizardry, and he happened to be one of the smallest physically, but he was my best bet on getting a message through if something incapacitating happened to me.

Since the rains along the coast arrived at about the same time every day, I expected that morning would be the time for our ride to the helicopter pad, but of course this didn't account for the fact that the rains were coming from the west and needed several intervening hours to sweep eastward. I paid several visits to the weather briefer's office and in the course of these learned that many of the rain storms were local to discrete areas and some actually formed in the temperature gradients east of the Central Highlands. In other words, the weather might be clear enough for operations at one time and within an hour or less become completely untenable. This random birth of local squalls was not good news. Each leg of an extraction flight would take longer than the birthrate of such storms.

There was a glimmer of hope implied by the possibility that the aircraft might be able to fly around local conditions and maintain visibility, but it was clear that our prospects for a quick extraction were poor, and we faced even more unpredictability than usual on the ground. It meant that even if they could insert us into the intended AO, the weather might prevent even an unopposed extraction well beyond the duration of our supplies, even if the pick-up point itself were clear. I decided to draw extra rations in the event that we got stuck out there in a place safe enough to hole up for a few extra days. I expected that our movements would at times be helped by the rain, but that we would be soaking wet much of the time—and certainly muddy. In addition to the rain itself, the drenched foliage would drastically cut our transmitting range. I hoped fervently we would encounter nothing that required an urgent call.

Since conditions were so stacked against us this time, I made the private advance decision that, should we be successfully inserted, we were not going to move around much out there. If we didn't sight the enemy, so much the better, for I could not stop the invidious pressure in my mind of knowing I'd long outlived the arithmetic of survival. This one was stretching the texture of shear fortune past the rupture point.

That night in my bunk was long and sleepless. It passed in an unusually profound cathedral quiet. From time to time as the air shifted, the faint sound of aircraft scratched distantly at the weft of silence, then faded back into the stillness, leaving long intervals in which I could barely hear the mournful whisper of waves on the beach. I stared at the gloom and listened to the darkness, trying hard to memorize these last hours.

When at last a miasmic grey light began to filter into the room I got up, already tired, drugged by hopelessness and the enervating inescapability of it all. I looked sadly around at all the things in the hootch and wondered about their continued existence after I was gone, but I couldn't quite grasp the concept. It was a passing illusion quickly lost in the middle distance of errant notions that lay behind such a massive cloud I couldn't see through it.

Outside the door in the dusky light the Nungs began to shuffle into quiet assembly. They, too, were withdrawn and sullen, their eyes cast down. They seemed reproachful. I was with them, whatever they felt. We were all staring into the empty eye socket of death.

The flight out to the insertion point was short, only 100 miles or so, the beat of the rotor blades louder than usual in the heavy moisture-laden air, and we were put down into the jungle just to the southeast of a moving rain squall. The choppers lifted out just before the rains swept in, assuring that we were soaked before we even started.

We lay beneath lower vegetation in the cool mud listening through the dripping foliage as my senses again filled with the jungle, its smells, its sounds, and its uncountable versions of green. When full hearing returned, I propped the radio under the umbrella of a large philodendron leaf and sent the insertion code, though with serious doubt the message would escape the wet conditions.

According to the map, soon so damp that it sagged from my hands like cloth, there was a large open area about four miles to the northwest. It was depicted as a plateau shaped like a large hand, with steeply declining terrain falling between the "fingers" all around in a series of narrow forested defiles. It lay roughly in the direction I had been told the NVA unit was progressing. I decided to begin moving toward it. Open terrain would increase the chances of successful radio transmissions while the higher ground might afford us some visibility over distance. The whole thing was a crapshoot, but at least such a distinguishable map reference, if confirmed, would provide me with specific coordinates, and keeping a calculated distance from such a feature meant I could maintain a more accurate than usual sense of where we were. In the end, it might also prove to be a good extraction point that would be easy for the pilots to find in reduced visibility. These all seemed good reasons to verify it.

Each man took his position in line according to his weapon. M-16s at the front on point and at the tail, M-79s inside each of them, with automatic rifles and radios in the center. We carried extra grenades and smoke signals. Already wet in the steaming air, we began to ease with animal stealth slowly through the leafy undergrowth. As usual, heavy ground vegetation hindered all movement but made good cover. As always, though, it served both sides, so it made for an extremely cautious advance. We could not afford a moment's complacency.

We stuck to our system of varying periods of movement and stops, always watching and listening through the dripping vegetation. As the ground soaked up the rain, it became soft and began to sigh beneath our feet, so we had to change the way we moved to avoid the sucking, sticky sound of each step.

A high-voltage pulse pounded in my ears with the heat and the exertion required for each step, the effort to process each sound, and to push through my fear, to access the instinctual animal within, the creature who had so far gotten me through. My mind raced continually to distill each tiny sound, every smell, to find incongruities in the open spaces through the leaves, and to keep my weapon ready, while at the same time guarding against the haunt of irrationality, the tendency to oversubscribe possibilities spawned in the den of my own dark doubts.

Our instincts dwell beneathe layers of inhibitions, social codes, bridled emotions, inherited wisdom, and feats of mental dressage. All this must be abandoned for movement through a hostile environment. It's not easy to do, but it comes with bitter experience, and the catalyst is fear. The neutrality of the primeval jungle itself gives way to the dangers hidden within it, and any hesitation born of social conditioning could get you killed. This time, my mental attitude was complicated by the fact that I had managed in Hong Kong to escape the crushing quotidian anticipations of the war and had returned to allow myself to find within the events of several careless days the seeds of hope, and they had worked within me like a drug, lulling for a time my deeper expectations.

That night we formed our perimeter in wet loamy soil. Not real mud, but duff wet enough to make its way through our clothes. It was clammy, but it served to darken our clothes, forming damp surfaces for real mud to cling. Thus we moved the next day with additional camouflage. Each day we became encrusted with more soil until each of us was pretty much the color of the ground. The green greasepaint on our faces, renewed each day, was a good match for the vegetation, and by the third day, we looked like creatures risen from the floor of an unplumbable wilderness. With increasing discomfort, we blended ever better.

Each night I sat awake and listened. Sometimes a rain came through. The branches above us would sigh and creak, the mantle of leaves rustled and clattered in anticipation, and then the rush of rain on the canopy would launch a fresh cascade of heavy drops down through the layers to splat noisily upon our hats and clothes. In the morning, the sunlight on the roof of the forest made the space overhead reminiscent of certain fierce churches, all spikes and shadows. A thin rind of rust began to form on our rifles, and each morning I used the early light to rub mine down with an oil-soaked corner of my tourniquet.

On the fourth day we encountered slightly rising ground and denser growth. Any change deserved study, so we stopped to analyze our surroundings for a long time, noting variations, the type and size of the plants, distribution of the larger trees, character and color of the ground, and not least, the smell of the air. If this was a sign that we were nearing the plateau I expected to find, then I had a pretty good idea from the map of where we might be, but as there was no daylight leaking in through the lower vegetation from any direction to indicate an opening beyond the trees, I concluded that either we weren't especially near the objective feature, or it made the reason the jungle was thicker here. Both could be true, as run-off from higher terrain stimulated heavy growth in lower lying areas.

As evening shadows rose to meet us in that curious way jungles have of growing dark from the bottom up, we moved onto relatively dry ground. It was slightly elevated from the surrounding soil, and we found it less sloppy to sit or lie upon. Ahead of us a dull sunset filtered through a group of enormous trees that stood upon a low embankment where the ground seemed to have been drawn up by the grip of their roots. Their knobby fingers gathered the folds of earth like the fringe of a carpet. There was something oddly expectant about the way the trees grew here in almost ordered symmetry. Like giant sentinels they rose together as though barring the way, their regimented order awaiting some unheard signal to step aside and reveal what lay beyond. They stood with unsettling purpose across our course. I was grateful for their shielding presence, though, and decided to wait for better light to work our way around or through them. We stopped for the night at their feet and curled into our perimeter.

After a time, while we sat perfectly still taking the measure of the sounds around us, a slice of moon climbed into the night sky and winked in its slow progression through the umbrella of branches. I could barely make out its signature through tiny porcelain cracks in the canopy. It shone in dim, penumbral reluctance, grey and still upon the shoulders of the lower growth leaves, deepening the shadows beneath them where we lay gathered in our circle. It made our position dark and small. This time I felt secure enough not to move to a second RON, and I waved off Nhi's hand signal query. He nodded agreement.

In the deepening dark the big leaves took on a scared-sheep look the way they seemed to herd themselves together in the half light. They had a human look, too, the way they stood crowded up close to one another. It seemed almost as though they expected trouble, as though something had warned them that they might be destroyed, or left behind and forgotten. Even as I looked, I thought I saw them huddle just a fraction nearer together. In the darkness the water drops that still fell from the foliage seemed louder.

At night, deep in the field, darkness always took advantage of tension and frayed nerves to enter into a conspiracy of the senses, altering the margins of things. All dimensions lost their outer realities. The ground before me often seemed to move at night, and here even the flora closed in. Gradually the forest stilled, and the night leaked its heat. Around 3:00 in the morning a rain shower passed by somewhere to the south.

At long last in the early grey of first light the faces that had leered at me during the night simply dissolved, fading into the withdrawing shade as the mere tricks of shadow they had been. I ate a ball of rice, transmitted an estimated position report, and checked the compass against my estimated position. Our heading would have to take us through the regiment of trees and the wild congestion of their roots. I saw no feasible way around them.

We started by climbing onto the bank of earth the big trees had drawn forth and began a careful plod through the maze of roots. Eventually we emerged into an area of rumpled ground that continued the gradual incline we had entered the day before. Footing became difficult as the ground separated itself into distinct water-carved rifts. It made for challenging footing and confirmed the presence of steeper ground ahead.

Around midday I sensed distant thunder, more felt than heard, a low grumbling too distorted by our position on the floor of the forest to estimate its distance. The light among the trees dimmed with its customary abruptness. Up through the canopy I saw vaulting slate-colored clouds, and an electric tension built in the air. It would only be a matter of minutes before the voltage discharged itself in pounding rain. We halted, and I searched about in the undergrowth without success for any place that might provide us with some extra cover. There was none. Suddenly a deafening rumble crackled through the air directly overhead. The air pulsed with the sheer volume of its reverberation. Even though I expected it, the shock caused my heart to spasm in a moment of atavistic fear, as the jungle was struck by an enormous fist of deluge. The trees themselves recoiled at its impact. It roared upon the canopy, drowning all other sounds. Violent winds rocked the trees. They swayed and knocked together, launching terrified birds that cried out and darted through the trembling growth in flashes of color, as a shower of leaves, then whole branches, began to fall on us. Rain rattled loudly on the giant elephant ear leaves that rattled and twisted in the lower gusts, and we were instantly drenched.

Although the downpour would cover our movement, we couldn't see well enough to stir. We simply cringed on the liquefying ground beneath its awesome force. In moments, the jungle floor was cut by violent rivulets that poured through our position carrying sticks, the detritus of the ground, and a porridge of mud. There was nothing to do but cower in the water and hope the tempest would pass without injury to any of us. It had to stop if we were to be extracted.

On the coast, from where our extraction would be launched, the weather was usually clear by nightfall. I saw that most storms arrived from the west, and we were now some 100 miles or more west of the coast. The arrival of this cell appeared to comply with the pattern, as it hit us about the middle of the day. This meant, though, that the afternoons were likely to be a problem for a pick-up from where we were, since the weather evidently took most of each afternoon to travel the distance from our present AO to the coast. A typically widespread downpour to the east of our position, moving slowly on typical winds, would intercept the course of our escape and could cut our chance of rescue by at least six hours each day. Therefore, I thought grimly, any event that might call for an emergency extraction had better occur in the morning..

Monsoon conditions effectively reduced to a few hours a day the likelihood of our being brought out at all during this time of year. In my depressing calculation, the nights at least offered brief windows of opportunity for rescue; however, the difficulties of attempting an extraction through a hole in the trackless jungle in these conditions after dark didn't bear thinking about. On the other hand, if we were to find that the plateau depicted on the map was there and of the size depicted, we stood a chance of foul weather rescue from that place.

At last, with the tail of the storm still rattling down through the vegetation, we got cautiously to our feet. We took stock of ourselves in the mists that condensed among the leaves, enshrouding our cover while dense silvery drops fell through the open spaces, smacking loudly into our clothes and dribbling off the larger leaves in blubbery runnels. I was soaked. My clothes clung to me, and my web gear was heavy with the weight of rain water. Each step now had to be taken more slowly to minimize the squelching sound of pulling our boots from the fresh muck.

We started again. The storm had altered the ground dramatically. Peering through the condensed air I saw that the washes were generally aligned in the same direction, which was further evidence that we were approaching higher ground. This could be a good sign as far as finding the open plateau was concerned, but I worried that its estimated location, even its very existence, had become a fixed idea for me. I began to fear that in my determination to lead us to some symbol on the notoriously untrustworthy maps, I may have overlooked some alternative, some other land feature where we might be more sure, safer, better able to determine position or to call for support. The place loomed ahead in my imagination like some citadel, some ancient hill fort. In fact, if the bad guys saw it on their maps, then it seemed reasonable to expect that they may have already prepared it for defense. They might even be there. For some reason I had not considered that possibility before. I became doubtful anew and discouraged.

Perhaps, I thought, my imagination was getting the better of me, but I had to remind myself that we were deep in untrodden wilderness and of the immediate priority of searching the ground and the vegetation for any sign: a foot print, broken twigs at shoulder height, low-lying cut brush that was a little dry, such as the enemy used to disguise "tiger trap" pits–man traps dug deep enough to assure that a person falling into it would become skewered on sharpened bamboo *punjis,* there to twitch out the last moments of life in unimaginable pain, like some grotesque specimen pinned in the shadow box of an insect collection. If that happened, there would be nothing any of us could do, and the body would have to be stripped of gear if at all possible and abandoned after we had done whatever would be necessary to silence the screaming.

We entered an area of enormous hard-mud ant hills that rose from the undergrowth in contentious black castles. They stood in silent defiance, wet and harder than clay, randomly deployed across our course and glistening like metal splinters of sunlight. We stopped and listened. All was silent and unmoving except for a vaporous steam writhing through the undergrowth and drifting past in cooling veils of moisture, chased closely by the ponderous and inescapable humidity that clamped to our wet clothes in added weight. In the silence I could actually hear the tiny scrabble of the ants nearby. This was not a place to stop for long. Something in the treetops shrieked a desolate, discordant warning of our presence, but afterwards the silence filled itself back in, leaving only the steady sound of dripping around us.

We pressed on, weaving our way around the ant towers, finally arriving at a place where I could see daylight leaching through the trees ahead. Here there began an unmistakable slope up and out of the forest into open air. We halted to study this change.

Nhi and I went forward and crept up the slope where we saw that the forest opened to reveal a field of tall grass. A little way farther, and the thick, wet selvage of undergrowth crowded into sunlight. From there we could see that the surrounding jungle walled the edge of the meadow. There it stopped so abruptly that the trees appeared to be caught off balance. Sure enough, here was the plateau–or at least a plateau–pretty much where there ought to be one. I allowed myself a moment of hopeful relief. If nothing else, this meant we had a readily-identifiable extraction point. Open sky through the trees on our left, indicated that we might also be able to use the site for the command it appeared to hold over much lower terrain to the south. The more I studied it, the more it seemed to conform to the depiction on the map, but from where Nhi and I crouched in the grass I couldn't see enough to be sure.

It was odd to be out in the open blinking in the harsh late afternoon sun, but the fact that the trees met the field with no gap of scrub between meant that we could enter the open terrain without exposing ourselves unless we stood up. It looked as though the rest of the team could line into the grass, simply exchanging one form of cover for another. I didn't like having the team split. If anything happened I wanted our firepower to be concentrated, so after satisfying ourselves that the place appeared deserted, I signaled the team to come up.

Together we stood just inside the tree line and looked out over the plain. This had to be the place I had seen on the map. The fresh rains were tinting the grass with new growth, while the old growth stood stiff and pale about three to four feet high. Across the top of the grass I could see the leafy crowns of trees crowding the narrow washes that fell away to the south between a series of narrow peninsulas. This confirmed that the meadow, emerging from the edge of the jungle eighty yards or so to the north, spread into several finger-like plateaus, just as shown on the map. For the first time I knew exactly where we were.

We all started into the grass, keeping good separation. An explosion of yellow butterflies burst from the long sedge and trembled away in a frenzy of sunny color. They almost made me smile as I angled over to the edge of the closest "finger" and confirmed that, by virtue of the land falling sharply away beyond, we were on a promontory. I confirmed the contour lines on the map while Nhi scanned the spectacular view with his binoculars. From here, any movement of a large body of men in the jungle below might easily be revealed in the tops of the vegetation, especially if they were undisciplined in jungle movement, or if they felt secure enough to move unguardedly. I had learned on that first operation with Sgt. Johnson not to touch anything, not to grab any branches or saplings to help with footing, not to do anything that might stir the overhead growth whose stems both hindered progress and concealed your position. Now here we were, sitting in an ideal place to observe the object lesson.

The tufted carpet of unbounded wilderness that spread below us had the tumultuous appearance of other jungle wastelands I'd seen in other lands, but their incomprehensibility lay simply in their density and seeming endlessness. They had never seemed so vibrant with ill feeling as this, so impacted with a steady sense of conscious intent.

I had no idea where in this Gordian prehistoric frontier we might intercept even a very large contingent of NVA soldiers. The misty view to the south simply showed how hopelessly vast this deep and tangled wilderness really was, and besides, I wanted fervently to avoid any contact with the enemy anyway. There's nothing like a high-angle view of the area you're operating in—even a large city—to show how unlikely it would be to find a specific objective anywhere in it. The perspective reveals, too, how profoundly insignificant any person is in such an endless twittering wilderness.

Beneath my relief at having navigated to this place with its distinctive shape so easily identifiable from the air, was a growing concern for where the NVA might actually be. We were on a good Landing

Zone, and I wanted to stay close by, but I had no idea if the bad guys were ahead of us to the west, still somewhere in the jungle north of us, or if they were already past this point, hidden in all that mysterious low country beyond the precipice. There was nothing in the character of the surroundings that gave any indication of a probable, relatively unobstructed passage for a large body of men, either onto this plateau or through the wall of densely growing trees that bordered it.

Through the remainder of the fading afternoon we rested at the edge of the long grass, meticulously studying the jungle around us but especially below us to the south where there was greater landscape. We saw and heard nothing unusual, although for awhile our attention was commanded by a group of large black birds resembling buzzards in their lazy circles over a point in the distance.

I could think of nothing else to do. The whole operation seemed a needless wild goose chase in the first place, and now, looking over the motionless square miles we could see from this position just pointed up the futility of it. Besides, I was growing, if at all possible to exceed previous levels, increasingly risk averse. I was going to be ending my tour in Vietnam within a matter of weeks and was feeling unjustifiably dispatched back into the craw of hazard anyway.

I played with the idea of simply waiting here on the edge of this open place for a few days and then calling in for extraction. We were on good ground at a specific map reference and in the best spot any operation had presented me for transmitting. In the event that some movement should reveal itself while we just waited and watched from this vantage point, I could report it, but it seemed unlikely: any large unit making its way south would find this promontory a major top-ographical obstacle that would have to be circumnavigated to gain access to the lower terrain to the south—not a dead end perhaps, but at least a geographic nuisance around which it would be difficult to navigate a large body of men and maintain unit integrity.

The sun melted into the hills scrawled with jungle to the west, and when the sky was still washed with a pale and fading pink like a dying gas flame, I decided that we should move farther into the grass and away from the edge of the precipice. Always conscious of escape options, I didn't feel that the precipitous ground to the south offered a chance of escape or evasion without broken bones and the risk of losing the team's cohesiveness. My instincts whispered that it would be safer to retreat to the cover of the jungle for the night, but we were muddy and wet, and I thought that, at least for a few hours, we might find the deep grass more comfortable than the saturated jungle floor. The grass provided some cushion against the ground, and if the night remained clear, we might be able dry out some.

The weather had faired off clear and appeared at least temporarily stable. Since we as well as all our gear were still damp and clammy as the night closed around us, I signaled a move back toward the middle of the field, where we set up our customary defensive posture in the tall congestion of long-leaf grass. It was open to the sky, which was mildly disconcerting because it made me feel exposed, but everything was still, and the position was much drier than the jungle floor.

I took off the radio and sent a quick RON signal and the position, then, keeping the handset close to my face and an arm through the shoulder strap as I did every night, prepared to lie more or less comfortably in the grass. The others lay spread in a circle of which I was farthest to the south by a few yards.

I was searching the sky for the evening star when there came a faint syllable, fleeting and lost. It cut for just a moment across the insect noise. At first I wasn't sure of what my ears were telling me, but I looked around and saw that the others heard it, too. We lay perfectly still and listened. Then the silence was fragmented by the unmistakable muffled sound of approaching human voices! Alarm resounded through me like surf in a cave, and the blood flooded into my head. I was still in the first hot jolt of disbelief when there was a subdued laugh and the clink of equipment. It came from the tree line just to the north of our position. Then, clearer snatches of speech and tramping feet. I smelled sweat and fish oil. I craned to peer through the stems of grass, and in minutes, a large body of NVA emerged from the trees, talking casually, weapons slung, moving noisily with no reason to make a secret of their presence. They passed close by us, and then on some tinny shouted command, began deploying around the promontories at the southern edge of the field. I was stunned into brainless alarm. We were suddenly deep in a Wagnerian chorus of shit.

I held my breath as a small-frame man in a uniform I could not identify passed nearest us. By his position beside the main column and the shape of his hat, I took him to be an officer. They appeared to be in battalion strength, perhaps three small companies. I couldn't be sure but estimated maybe 150 to 200 men. Most carried Russian A-Ks, and I counted three machine guns. There may have been more, but by the time I could get my mind wrapped around the need to make such observations, many of the soldiers had passed. At last the end of their column tramped by, everyone—luckily for us—keeping to the same path.

By the time they were deployed around the field, we were almost completely surrounded, enclosed on three sides, and too close to risk even small movements. They were setting up in all directions around us, except, guessing by the sounds of their voices, for a gap to the north where they had come out of the trees, but they continued encircling our nest in a closing horseshoe that tightened by the minute. I expected that any second someone, a rear-guard straggler perhaps, would come straight at us, cutting across the field to report in.

I was almost frozen with fear, locked in a fever of mindless expectancy. I had no idea what to do. I couldn't get my brain to fasten onto any course. It reeled in a terrified paralysis, fumbling through a useless liturgy of vacant notions in a tossed thought salad as I struggled with the hysterical calculus of the condemned. My head pounded and my heart beat against the ground so hard it became painful to lie on it. I was sure the others could hear it. I felt things open and close inside me as my mind lay cowering in a room full of closed doors.

Each of us lay still as masonry. The last NVA arrivals trampled down a grassy bed for the night quite close to us, perhaps 50 feet away. There was absolutely nothing I could think of to do, to tell the others to do. It was my fault entirely that we had been caught like this. I felt foolish, stupid, and angry–and doomed.

At last I forced myself through enough of the panic to realize that they may be leaving an opening in their perimeter to the north, a short distance off to my right, where they'd entered the field. I couldn't organize my thinking, but I fixed on the conjectural gap as something that might be important, or maybe useful, or at least possible, if I could just make some kind of sense of it. I could acknowledge the possibility but couldn't think of what to do about it.

Suddenly I had an urgent, irrepressible need to pee. There was no recourse but to let it flow right where I lay, without moving. I could not have held it back. I prayed the enemy wouldn't smell it.

While I struggled through my terrifying paralysis of will, the smoke from cooking fires began to drift across the field and into our little circle. Full darkness came mercifully quickly, and the enemy became talkative. There were occasional bursts of laughter, and judging by the swishing sounds of movement through the grass, there was some visiting back and forth across their perimeter. I hugged the ground in spiraling fear and prayed that no one near the open end of their formation decided to cut across the field. We were trapped, and it was only a matter of time, perhaps just minutes, before they knew it.

I could think of no way for us to escape to the north. We were too close to them to risk the sound of any movement in the grass and so badly outnumbered that even misdirected fire from that many automatic weapons was too much to risk. Even a limited dragnet would be likely to run down any of us who might make it to the trees unwounded. Perhaps if we waited until 2:00 or 3:00 in the morning, we could slither out singly, but if we woke any of them or were spotted by a guard, we would not be likely to escape.

At last I decided our only option lay in risking a radio call while the battalion was still noisily settling in. I slipped my hand under the flap of the radio pack and nudged the knob until I felt the detent, and it came on. I put the handset inside my mouth as far as I could and still be able to pronounce words, and began an airless whisper broadcast in the clear, "Get me out of here! We're in the middle of a battalion size unit of NVA! Get us out!" Then I sent the coordinates and the code for an air strike request on the plateau at first opportunity. I had no idea if the messages got through, and after some seven interminable hours of cringing in the darkness, sent it again at 2:00 AM.

There was nothing we could do but stay where we were and lie perfectly–absolutely–still through the endless night, balanced on a knife edge of detection. Any small sound could have given us up: a cough, a snore, a fart. Or, one of the enemy might get up at any time to relieve himself and stumble onto us. It was the single longest night of my life. Any movement excited the grass to some small degree, and so we remained throughout the night so still that all through those hours I never heard a sound from the others, even though the farthest one from me lay only about 20 feet to my right. Except for being able to smell them, I could have been utterly alone.

At the bare suggestion of first light I thought I heard a moment of aircraft sound. It was just for a second, unsteady and far away, faint as a moth at a night window. There was nothing unusual in hearing aircraft at any time, but with no confidence that my pleas had gotten through, I instantly fastened onto the uncertain buzz with a maniacal hope that I had been heard after all, that the sound was somehow connected to us. The conviction grew uncontrollably, struggling up through a thick layer of anxious childlike need for it to be true. I strained to hear. For a few moments the uncertain hum seemed to grow, and with it my rabid anticipation leapt like a tethered dog and raced to the end of its lead, only to be jerked up short as the barely-audible noise receded into the early morning silence, taking with it my misplaced hopes. A crushing despondency collapsed back upon me, free-falling back into the iron core of unleavened dread.

Our chances of getting out of there were immeasurably low, but we had to do *something*. The troops would begin stirring any minute, if some weren't awake already. There had been no audible talking among them all night, and through the limited visibility allowed by the grass I had seen no cigarettes glowing, so had no idea if they had even felt it necessary to post sentries. I tried to tell myself that their sloppy order of march on arrival, their quick disposition along the rim of the cliff, and the fairly hasty way they had prepared for the night, were all indications that they had been very tired. I was only guessing and knew it. There was no justification for making assumptions about them.

I remembered that the ground we had covered on our approach to the plateau had risen gradually, steepening abruptly at the tree line. It was thickly foliated, but not so much as to have prevented our moving through it much faster if we had not been proceeding so cautiously. That drop-off offered only a theoretical notion of escape, but we all knew that ground, and if we could get back there somehow, it meant we would have to make a dash for the edge of the field where we had first come out of the woods. It was all panic reasoning with nothing but vain desperation to connect the fantasy of re-crossing the field with any expectation of surviving the effort.

We had to start immediately, before the soldiers were fully awake, by tossing grenades into their line and running for all we were worth back toward our original entry point, shooing at everyone we saw. Since I could throw the farthest, I decided to start by hurling an M-33 as far toward the cliff edge as I could. With luck, it would cause a distraction toward that end of the field and might give us whatever time the shock could buy.

I eased a grenade off my webbing and reached through the grass to the closest one of the Nung. I indicated to pass the grenade signal to the others. They all knew that it was now or never, and each, moving carefully so as not to disturb the grass, got a grenade ready. I gripped the spoon tightly against the grenade, straightened out the bent arm of the retaining pin and carefully pulled back the ring, easing the pin out of the catch.

All of a sudden the airplane engine noise returned, shattering the silence and approaching very fast! I froze in unbelieving comprehension as two long bursts of .50 caliber machine gun fire cut through the thunderous crescendo in a rain of bright tracers that streaked into the startled troops, followed by two A-1 Skyraiders that roared in echelon low over the trees, their wing tips streaming vapor trails in the heavy air. A wall of heavy slugs tore up the earth in fountains of dirt and clumps of grass, ripping into the ground and exploding the brown uniforms, while the hot brass casings rained painfully down on us. I could hardly believe it.

The surrounding troops began to leap from the ground in their sudden panic and confusion, many torn by the heavy bullets. Clods of earth tumbled into the sky, and men were already screaming when I yelled, we jumped up, threw our grenades into them, and started running for our lives back toward the edge of the woods. Galloping through the grass in a delirium of shooting, with my eyes flooding I fired without aiming at every up-turned face that appeared, back and forth in short bursts, leaping across the meadow in the longest strides I could manage, wheezing hoarsely and breathing in ash-dry gulps.

The pilots had found their marks, and the uniformed figures were taking it bad. I was vaguely aware of odd bits flying into the bitter air around me in the deafening confusion–clumps of grassy dirt, people, bits of gear–gook compote. It felt like the end of everything in the world. The figure of Nhi suddenly appeared from the smoke and dust to my left, running several paces ahead, while two of the others were off to my right. Everyone was shooting on the run.

Suddenly my clip was empty. I checked impulsively over my shoulder through the noise and sour smoke, I suppose to see if the others were following, and in that surreal second glimpsed a "fast mover," an F-4, streaking in above the trees with a long napalm canister falling away from it. I saw an image of familiar figures bounding through the grass behind me, shooting off to the sides, but I called instinctively through my confusion for them to run anyway. The air pulsed, the ground seemed to shift. There was a sound as though the whole earth gasped, a moment when all color dimmed to a grey sodium wash. Then the world around me seemed suddenly plunged into momentary darkness, before the trees ahead flashed brilliant orange, and I had a fleeting sensation of weightlessness as a searing furnace wave struck me in the back and sucked away the air. I lost traction and almost fell. My eyeballs pulsed outward, and I couldn't breathe. I felt my lungs collapse as I began to drown in a super-heated vacuum. The exertion demanded large gulps of air, but something was terribly wrong with my breathing. A painful constriction gripped my chest, my vision closed in, and I plunged ahead hoping to last enough steps just to outrun the sticky globs of flaming jelly. My lungs burned, and my vision had dimmed to a grainy image of a leafy gap between two trees when I was hit by a gale of dusty oxygen and got slammed with a hot shallow breath.

Bullets filled the air, crackling and whirring around us. With the edge of the jungle just yards ahead and my vision only beginning to clear, the little officer in the unfamiliar uniform suddenly popped up in front of me. He stared wildly at the conflagration behind me, his orange face distorted in an eerie rictus of terrified disbelief at the erupting world of horrors he saw in the fire. On some maniacal impulse, I reached out as I ran past him and grabbed onto his clothes, yanking him off his feet, and pulled him with me as I launched into the woods.

I fell, dragging the little man with me as we tumbled down the slope. I was vaguely aware that some of the others came crashing through with us, but I was scrambling to keep hold of the brown uniform in a mindless frenzy that became as good a substitute for knowing what to do next as any. I only knew we had to get out of there as fast as possible, and I pulled the man to his feet as I followed the others in our frantic retreat through the undergrowth while bullets whined through the trees and smacked into the branches, snapping twigs and leaves. Most of the shots were over our heads and random, whipping past all around us without pattern. I couldn't understand how so many of the enemy could be in pursuit. I looked back when a second jet came through, and the flames roared anew, the jellied fuel leaping behind the blackened silhouettes of the trees. A fearful greedy crackling ate up the silence of the forest. Birds called in panic, darting erratically through the smoke. I could see no one moving against the fiery glare of the burning grass, where orange flames were spreading to the trees, racing up the creepers and crackling in the upper growth. Smoke issued from the standing trunks, whipped around by a hot wind that charged past us toward the harsh light, tugging at me like the breath of an oven.

Through rifts in the roof of the jungle I glimpsed an enormous black cloud of smoke burgeoning into the sky. Already a dark pall of grey ash had entered the upper canopy where the curled remains of roasted leaves lurched back and forth in the tortured air currents. I could smell burning vegetation mixed with the chemical odor of napalm, heavy smoke, and burning flesh. The screams were dying, smothered in the storm of flames.

The man I had attached myself to suddenly flew into a full-blown animal panic, screaming and thrashing violently. I fought to contain his flailing arms, his kicking and twisting in his battle to get free. Fortunately he was smaller than I, but his mortal terror gave him physical powers equal only to those fed by my own fear, and the grapple quickly began to sap what was left of my adrenal energy. I tried to keep my hand clamped tightly over his mouth to stifle his guttural howls, but he bit me, and that actually made me for the first time more angry than scared. I slugged him hard, but it only stunned him enough to let us stumble a short distance farther..

By the time I had dragged him back among the field of giant ant-hills, the structures constricted our movement further, and his contortions pulled me down again. I realized we could not continue with him as a prisoner of opportunity. We had to leave him, and not knowing how many of his men might be closing in upon us, I did not want to risk a shot. The terrifying situation had nearly exhausted my powers of adjustment, and with no more thought about it, I pulled out my bayonet and, struggling to control him from behind, tried to stab him in the chest, but the blade was stopped by his webbing. I tried again, this time jamming the knife into his side, but as I pushed it in it scraped against a bone. The feel of it scuffed up through the handle and into the bones of my hand. It sickened me. He convulsed and went fiercely rigid, with mouth agape in a silent scream and bulging eyes. Then the body subsided as though the air had been let out of it, and I let it slump to the ground, where it lay in sudden terrible stillness. With my comprehension reeling, chest heaving, and pulse throbbing loud in my ears, I stared incredulously at the oddly familiar handle of my knife protruding from the side of the corpse. It didn't look real. All sound and movement disappeared. I became suspended in a timeless bubble of stillness. The contours of reality felt as faint as a tracery of fine lace through which I could have floated away irretrievably.

As I watched the body lose its color, I thought vaguely that I should get the knife back and to keep moving. When I bent forward to grasp the handle, the back of my throat suddenly opened, and I threw up the meager contents of my stomach, mostly a hot flux of acid. It spilled across his uniform in a queer baker's glaze that left me momentarily depleted and unbelieving.

A bullet fippled past and the sound jerked me back to an awareness that shots were still crackling through the flames and chirping by around us. The rounds were probably just cooking off in the ammo pouches of the victims, but their lethality wasn't reduced just because they may not have been aimed. As I glimpsed the remnants of the team disappearing into the trees ahead the first clear thoughts I'd had since the aircraft appeared began to jell out of the confusion: I didn't want to be left behind, and the dead officer might be important. I began to explore the officer's pockets. They contained a tightly folded map, a small note book that appeared to contain code and word information, an identity card, and a small Chinese pistol in a leather case. There was also a worn sheet of paper, smudged with dark creases marking its many folds. It bore what appeared to be Chinese writing on both sides. I hurriedly fumbled them all into my own pockets, pulled the knife free with a difficulty that surprised me, and set out to follow the team, leaving the body staring up among the extravagant mud towers, where I'm sure the ants made quick work of the soft parts.

With bullets still singing through the foliage overhead, I began to run between the ant towers in an instinctive crouch. Fatigue, lack of rest and unrelenting fear can sometimes bestow a kind of hysteric sensibility and an instinct for the slightest danger. For a long lucid moment I seemed to have enhanced senses and perfect vision. I saw everything in detail; heard every breath and felt every footfall in the soft earth as I weaved, felt the tug of my clothes and the brush of the ferns. I was moving with perfect balance, the weight of the radio for a change lending forward momentum to my escape. Ahead I clearly saw Nhi kneeling and waiting, scanning the area through which we had come. The earth beneath the ground cover was just soft enough for good footing, and I was quickly closing the distance to Nhi's position when a large fudge-colored chunk exploded from a nearby anthill, and two simultaneous wires of pain lanced into my hip and right buttock. I didn't understand what had happened and stumbled forward another three or four steps before I felt the jolt of a contraction in my leg and fell heavily onto the ground in confusion. I instinctively scrumbled around for the problem and found that my pants were torn, and my hand came away painted with fresh blood.

Nhi and one of the others appeared over me. They grabbed my arms and dragged me farther into the undergrowth. They helped me up and then got under both my arms, and with surprising strength, took much of my weight as the rest of the team reformed defensively around us, and we scrabbled crab-like through the jungle. I was so confused by the pain and the fall I lost perception of what was going on and watched with wondering incomprehension as the vegetation rubbed past. I'd evidently been hit by something, but I couldn't focus on what was happening. I had felt no forceful impact and couldn't understand why I had fallen down. Then a deep, penetrating burning sensation overtook me and bloomed within my groin and right hip. A tingling numbness stole the feeling from my right thigh and lower back, as though parts of me were suddenly falling asleep.

By the time we arrived back at the row of large trees where we had spent the night on our way in, Nhi must have called a halt, for I became vaguely aware that we were taking cover in the roots behind the earthen bank. I was stupefied, so weary and pained, so empty of everything but being alive, that it took several long moments for me to come to grips with our situation. I was surprised to discover the knife still in my hand. It was already sticky with blood. There was a lot of it on my right hand, which shook so violently I could hardly get the blade back into the sheath. Fearing the worst, I took in a quick inventory of the team and was amazed and deeply relieved to find that we were all still together. I guessed Nhi had seen to that while I was preoccupied with the little officer. Nearly everyone had been wounded in some way. Two had much of their clothing burned off their backs, and their skin was badly blistered. One, naturally dark, had wet patches of what looked like bloody suet showing through the burn holes in his shirt. Two had been grazed by bullets and were bleeding steadily; another had a bloodless injury to his ankle, a break or possibly a sprain, but flesh wound or sprain, we would not be able to move any faster than our slowest man, and it began to appear that I would be the problem. We were a mess, badly reduced in capacity.

I discovered that I still had the radio with me, although I had been unaware of its weight since we had first leapt up from the grass. I put it aside and lay back heavily against the bank and tried to examine my wounds. My pants smelled of urine, and the rest of me reeked with panic sweat. With trembling hands, I felt cautiously around for the source of my own bleeding but could not find the one that had entered the inside of my leg. The one that hit me in the hip had torn a gash in my pants, but the entry wound seemed small for the amount of pain it delivered, even though it looked by the blood flow, and felt, to be deep. With my racing heartbeats it was leaking a lot of dark blood. Then I noticed a clean bullet hole through the right pocket of my fatigue shirt. It had cut through some of the papers I had taken off the officer.

My hands shook with a life of their own, but I got the trusty tourniquet wrapped around my leg as well as I could, and then tied it off, placing a strip of padded gauze from my first aid kit between my legs and around my waist to keep the knot in place. I seemed to hurt everywhere, with a burning sensation inside my hip and deep within my lower mid section. My jungle hat was gone, and I realized that the back of my head felt sunburned. It hurt to the touch, and I could feel that some of my hair had been singed away. I couldn't recall much of what had happened, even though we were still within hearing of the shots and the terrible fire. I tried to put the sequence of things together, but only fleeting disjointed images tumbled through. All the connective events were gone. Probably just as well, I thought. There were new agendas to think about, and I groped for the elusive clarity I needed in order to continue.

We took care of each other's wounds as well as we could by pooling our first aid supplies, while my mind kept retreating to wonder at our survival. I managed to break open an ampule of morphine and jabbed it through the pants into my leg to ease the pain. I gave two more to Nhi for the two guys who had been hurt the worst. In my depleted condition, the drug soon took effect.

I checked my watch; tried to focus on what it meant; and was surprised to see that it wasn't yet 5:00 in the morning. Events had so crowded my mind that I had come to believe the dim light we entered in the trees to escape the firelight had meant the close of the day. The whole thing, from the first appearance of the aircraft to our headlong flight into the sanctity of the woods, was probably less than a full minute, though it had felt much longer. In our mad dash across the field to escape both the napalm and the enemy, each second had dragged past in a surreal nightmare of interminable images, separated by fleeting glimpses of the enemy, the grass, and the fire. From then to the little man's frenzy and the stabbing was perhaps another three minutes, maybe more, perhaps less. I don't know how long I lingered over the body, but from then to the moment I was hit, and then to our present position, was probably the better part of, what? Maybe five minutes? Three? Fifteen? Perhaps twice that. I couldn't seem to do the math or summon from the swirling imagery the awareness to guess, and even our now-familiar holding position by the root berm seemed like a memory stolen from a stranger.

When the hands on the watch face indicated 5:00, I still couldn't quite slot the information into the scheme of things. It took a moment to realize the sun had not even cleared the surrounding hills. This meant that we had the whole day to get away from this place and to search for an area from which we could be extracted. The distinctive plateau behind us would have been an ideally open place to bring in helicopters, and the dark smoke would mark it well, probably for several days, but I had no idea what was back there or how many of the NVA might still be alive. In any case, the scene was one I wanted to avoid enough to risk a doubtful and pain-fraught search in the opposite direction.

I checked over the radio and found that it was useless. There were two holes in it. It would not turn on, and the handset was missing. I signaled to the Nung carrying the back-up, and he crawled over wincing with injury. His clothes were tattered, and I saw by the raw burns on his arms and legs that he must have been some distance behind me, but it looked as though the radio itself had given him some protection from even worse injury. He must have been in great pain. He trembled and was breathing in rapid shallow gasps as we looked the equipment over. The pack was scorched beyond further use, but there were no outward signs that the radio casing had been hit. I switched it on, and to my inexpressible relief, it worked. I got the ribbon antenna unfurled and broadcast the codes for multiple wounded, including the One-Zero, and for our intended direction of movement. Assuming they received, that would alert them that we were alive but had injuries of unknown severity, and I hoped that they would contact a rescue team to be ready on short notice. Since I had transmitted in my call for help the night before that we were in the middle of the enemy, I hoped they would reason that we were in pretty bad shape, especially after whatever the pilots may have reported. Bleeding doesn't stop just because extraction might be on its way.

We had to move on, not only to find a place to be taken out, but the sooner we started the sooner we would learn just how incapacitated we really were. Before we could start, a sudden shower struck the canopy and started falling through the foliage in heavy drops, soon filling the spaces around us with a fine mist and soaking us in a few minutes. We continued treating each other as well as we could and bandaged the worst cases with wet dressing. I sat on the ground and watched with numb detachment as the rain released anew the smell of urine in my pants, and my blood ran into the mud. I realized that the rain might put out the grass fires behind us and turn the smoke white from whatever else was burning. I could no longer smell it so strongly, so guessed that the squall had changed the wind direction, but my brain failed in the effort to sort through any implications such a change might have for us. The convective wind currents had subsided, too, gasping more quietly now, like a child at the end of its tantrum.

When we could see to move, and the constant spatter of drops would still serve to cover any small sounds we might make, I signaled for us to move out. We transferred the good radio to my holed pack, and I abandoned the dead radio at the base of the dirt berm where I had been sitting. Nhi helped me to my feet. I stood unsteadily for a moment and found that the feeling had partially returned to my right leg. I turned to Nhi, put my hand on his shoulder and looked gratefully into his impenetrable eyes, which in turn regarded me steadily from behind the line of raindrops that spilled from the brim of his jungle hat. I tried a small reassuring smile, though I couldn't feel my face move, and nodded my gratitude. After a moment he surprised me by allowing the bare shadow of expression to pass behind his eyes, but he knew as well as I did that we were acknowledging our survival prematurely, and the moment withdrew as subtly as it had appeared. In less than three seconds the killer re-emerged.

Though the mere effort to stand caused severe trembling, I had enough muscle control to hobble so long as the morphine held out. From what I could tell, walking was very difficult, initially barely possible, for at least two of us. We were crippled. Everyone but Nhi seemed to be hurt someplace, though I could never tell with him. He was a stoic's stoic. All movement aggravated my bleeding, as evidenced in the soaked fabric of my makeshift truss. Despite the dose of morphine, the pain in my groin was unprecedented. I had never experienced anything like it, and it propagated alarmingly fast, insistent and demanding, its message carried in every heartbeat. Yet it had to be overcome, no matter what, though each effort to take a step sent electric spikes through me. It fought my concentration.

The guys who were burned must have been in a torment of contained agony. Yet nobody uttered a sound. We had to remain on alert just as we always did, although some instinct told me that we were probably moving away from the only threat in the region. Despite the destruction behind us, there were too many unknowns for us to move in that direction.

We made frequent stops, and while two kept watch, the rest of us adjusted each other's bandages and reapplied such medication as we had to ease the pain. After a few hours, when my own distress had grown to the point where it became a priority, I gave myself another shot of morphine, but I tried to go as long as I possibly could without it. In my reduced capacity I had to lean more heavily upon Nhi's skills, but it required all the jungle lore I had accumulated over the long months in-country to continue the scan and to make decisions while pushing through growing despair and an absolute fog of pain. Each step had to be planned so that foot placement was as noiseless as I could make it, each shift in balance calculated. I began to drift in and out of a vague nubilous semaphore of awareness.

I grew woozy with the constant effort to function through the festering in my body. I had never known such physical pain. It was so encompassing that it affected my ability to think, to make decisions. I had to force my concentration on the single imperative of getting us out. My hands shook uncontrollably, and tremors travelled up and down my whole corpus. I took in gulps of air and held them in an effort to push down the distress. It was a form of breathing that helped suppress the vocal sounds that demanded release through the tartarean pain, and mixed with periodic attacks of free-ranging shivers, I despaired of how long I could last. As the hours passed, I felt my energy draining away, my endocrine system shutting down. I was beset by a strange lassitude of clogged cognition. Waves of confusion flowed through my consciousness, sometimes cresting in a moment of complete darkness. Awareness would return just before—and a few times just after—I fell. Any effort at movement reached new portals of pain, but large movement would be necessary to get myself and the others out.

Both the morphine, which helped to increase my tolerance for the pain, as well as the struggle to keep alert when its benefits began to wear off, had the combined effect of clouding my mind, sometimes causing my imagination to wander, and at others, offering up to my wondering attention a pageant of fantasy objectives. I began to feel chilled, which I guessed was the result of fatigue and blood loss. I tried to tighten the makeshift bandaging, such as it was, but found it hard to control my hands. Great concentration was demanded of the smallest effort at taking care of myself. I wondered if I was dying.

In the afternoon we arrived at a gap in the tree cover that, though located on a slope and too small to land a helicopter, was wide enough for us to be dropped the McGuire rig that had brought us out after my first mission with Sgt. Johnson, a lifetime ago. Though far from ideal, the site was a feasible compromise for an oblique extraction up through a crack in the canopy. Though the narrow opening in the forest favored the hillside, it offered a chance for us to be lifted clear if the pilots swung us out at a climbing angle once we were secure in the loops. I tried hard to visualize how the site would appear to the pilots from above. The prospect was discouraging, but I knew we couldn't push much farther through this wilderness in our condition, and it was too likely that we would not encounter another break in the canopy, even as unpromising as this one, for a greater distance than some of us could walk. I just prayed that it would work. None of us wanted to spend another night in the field in our condition if we could possibly get out before nightfall. Through the opening in the tree cover I saw that curtains of rain hung in a sky dark as dishwater all along the misty southeastern horizon, and my heart sank at the prospect that they could delay, or even prevent, our rescue.

We set up a perimeter, deploying poncho liners for the guys whose burns would otherwise be in contact with the dirt. I transmitted a best estimate of our position and sent an urgent call for extraction, adding again the code for multiple wounded and also the codes for the rig and winch. That way they would understand that at least we believed each of us had the strength to come out that way. We settled under cover and waited. If we had to spend another night out here, at least we knew that we were at a serviceable extraction point. I saw that we were not capable of much more movement. The others were visibly tired, something they seldom before had shown, but now they were hurt also. We had all been through extreme demands upon our abilities, and we were in growing need of medical attention. I doubted that we could pass another test of our capacity for remaining quiet in this situation of rapidly diminishing options. Most importantly, I did not think that we could effectively defend ourselves.

My pants leg had become a coagulated gruel of blood and earth and so saturated with bleeding that I feared another night on the ground might draw ants–some we'd seen were quite large. I was still haunted, too, by a vivid memory of the giant orange centipede that had rowed into our perimeter on a previous mission, and now I worried that I might be luring something that took even bigger bites than a whole brigade of ants.

We lay there near the clearing for almost three hours before I began to hear the faint, thrilling signature throb of approaching helicopters. My expectations leapt instantly, and after an initial attempt to get my fingers to work, I groped out the PRC-10 and switched it on.

Soon two of the tired old oil-streaked S-1s arrived and tilted into steep orbits overhead. Relief poured through me like a warm cascade of flat soda, without any charge of adrenalin. In a delirium of advancing pain and numb relief I got to my feet in the confusing down draft. While the wind tore at my clothes, I gestured toward the hillside gap so the Crew Chief in the door above the trees could see that once on the ropes we were good for being pulled clear of the overgrowth if they swung us out from the clearing and over the hillside drop.

Two bundles of rope fell from the first chopper, uncoiling with pre-knotted loops for two guys each. I wanted the worst wounded of the Nungs to be sure of getting out, so I signaled for them to grab the loops, and they, along with two others, were started up as the machine tilted away over the trees, winching them off the sloping ground and safely inside while making room for the second aircraft.

Then the second helicopter swung into a hover directly overhead, but on looking up I saw that it had no winch rig outboard of the open side doors. This meant flying back on the ropes. No matter. We were getting out. I just hoped I had the strength to hold on.

They dropped the two knotted ropes, and I signaled for Nhi and the Chinese who had carried the PRC-25 to leave me the radio and take the two upper loops. I was worried that I didn't have the strength to handle the additional weight of the radio but was certain the little Nung did not. I wanted to be able to drop it if I had to, so with the rifle sling around my neck, I hooked one arm through the strap on the radio pack and slung it over my shoulder as the helicopter backed off enough for the last two loops to clear the ground. Then the last Chinese and I made for the ropes. I hopped as well as I could with the weight of the radio and got my good foot, the left, into the lower loop, then laced my arm through the upper loop as the machine continued its lift, up and away from the hillside.

We came abruptly off the ground and swung free, out over the drop-off, where the treetops fell rapidly away beneath us. The tone of the blades pitched louder as the pilot began a rapid climb. My innards sagged heavily; the burden of gear tried to pull me downward, to tear me out of the loops and send me back down through the air, plummeting to the far canopy and into the abyss from which there would be no return. Ever. I embraced the rope for all I would ever be worth and prepared for a long, torturous ride in the storm-force wind.

The two ropes began to swing wildly apart and then back toward each other as the helicopter corrected its drift and turned eastward. As our two tethers swung towards each other, Nhi, who was hanging onto the upper loop of the other rope, made an attempt to capture the top of my line to arrest the erratic swing. If the pendulum effect continued, we could collide and knock someone off. Besides, it was one of the techniques required in riding the McGuire rig while suspended, because such sway beneath the helicopter can also affect the machine's weight and balance in flight. He wasn't able to capture the line above me but managed to grab it long enough to slow the swing. The next time we crossed, all of us were able to catch each other's lines and to hold them together until they stabilized in the ram effect of the air.

As we climbed to a safe altitude above the jungle and began to accelerate, the wind caught the radio pack and tried to tear me out of the loops. My strength was down, my right leg was hanging useless in the wind, while the left began to tremble under my own weight combined with almost 100 additional pounds of equipment. The air very quickly turned cold. I had an issue carabiner with the coil of rope I always carried but was afraid to change the grip I had on the rope to try to snap myself in. I decided just to hold on for dear life and hope not to pass out during the hour or so the flight would take.

We soon closed in on a rain squall that lay across our flight path and flew straight into it. The rain slammed into us like a wall of sand, stinging every bit of exposed skin and soaking through the windward side of my clothes. It added enormously to the force of the air itself, and my efforts to hang on drained all the blood from my hands as well as the arm I had through the upper loop. I tilted my head down to shelter behind my arm and let the sleeve take the main blast, closed my eyes and tried to tell myself that this had to be my last operation, so don't fall out. As my limbs went numb I lost the sense of how well I might be gripping the rope. Whenever I risked opening my eyes in the ballistic water, I obsessed on the weave in the rope. I stared at it, concentrating on every fiber, watching the raindrops in their haste to spring back from the sides. It became the meridian of all focus, a line of demarcation along which I poured my concentration, and the world on either side faded away into dark grainy hemispheres of irrelevancy.

By the time we flew out of the rain I was shivering in spasms with the cold and growing light-headed with fatigue and the relentless fulgurant burn of whatever had shot me. A dull, insensate paralysis took me over, my muscles frozen at the angles of my death grip on the rope. From what I could see of my right leg, which angled somewhat behind me in the wind, my jungle fatigues were saturated and dribbling fresh, bloody rainwater. I wondered distantly if I had enough blood left to make it back. At some point I passed beyond the world of lancing pain and care, into a dimension where the whole universe appeared as a vast slowly turning vortex of oceanic dark away to my right, spreading in silent concentricity and featureless of object or light, where along its depthless penumbral edge I moved somehow on ever-diminishing threads of consolation.

Something pulled me back from this vision? place? perhaps a change in the air, for it suddenly became warmer, and I opened my eyes to see that we were much closer to the trees and descending. When at long last Marble Mountain rose against the sea ahead, and I could see the landing pad at FOB 4, I had to fight the desire to loosen my grip in preparation for landing. I clung to the line, even as the helicopter slowed and began its descent to a hovering stop directly over the pavement. I watched in hypnotic fascination as the ground rose to meet us.

When my feet touched the ground I looked over and saw the other chopper was already down, and the medics were unloading the guys who had been burned. Then I found that I couldn't open my hands or get my arm out of the loop. The guy above me on the rope was just over my head when I finally pried my fingers open and freed my left foot from the loop. I tried to step back to get out of the way but caught a heel in the gathering tail of rope on the ground. A sharp knuckle of pain bolted through me, and I stumbled as the full canted weight of the radio pulled me backwards. The rope on which I had been transfixed for so long and the tattered figure upon it, with one muddy boot groping for the ground, became strangely illusive, drifting away. I had a glimpse of the dirty underside of the helicopter, and then the evening sky sort of smeared around behind me, and my vision, fringed with a grainy corona of darkness, began curiously to fade.

The next thing I remember was being jostled on a litter in the back of an open Jeep. There was a guy next to me with his arm across my chest to keep me on the stretcher as we bounced over the grate at the main gate. He was holding a plastic pouch containing clear liquid over me. Tiny points of tarnished light winked in the contents. There was something vaguely familiar about it. There was recent rain in the air, and the sky was whorled and dark, like an endless bruise. The pavement smelled wet. Then a rhythmic scallop of telephone lines began dipping past like the hem of an invisible awning. The Jeep halted with a jolt, as though it had run into something, at a place where a pair of floodlights laid a lake of harsh illumination all around us. I have a hazy memory of being carried into the same hospital entrance where I had been taken before. Then there were other faces around me.

When I woke again, so woozy and vacuous I couldn't focus at first. I was between clean sheets in a quiet ward. I wasn't at first able to remember how I got there, but with a rush of relief, I thought I recognized it as a place where I might at last be able to indulge the urge to sleep. It was dark, and I could feel an enormous bundle of cloth bandages wrapped between my legs and around my hip like a pillow. I felt clean and wondered idly how that had happened. Somewhere a generator hummed. It was all distantly familiar, but the meaning remained evasive, swirling lazily to the surface and then sinking shyly away again before I could grasp it. then I recognized the ceiling rafters, and instantly the effusion of comfort gave way to the vulnerability of paper-thin walls and canvas roofing. Then another bubble of vague care. Yet it was all so peaceful I decided that I should ask somebody what was going on. It would be interesting to know. Maybe later.

30

The next time I came aware, it was lighter in the room. I noticed my surroundings and experienced a quiet thrill to think that I had actually survived what just *had* to be my last mission. The count of days remaining eluded me though. I knew only that I was, in the vernacular of the craft, "short." I felt no great pain, although I found that stirring in the bed was difficult due to the bulk of the bandages around my middle and between my legs. I dared allow a constrained thought that the real challenges were at last behind me.

The hospital staff was attentive and solicitous, for which my gratitude sometimes overwhelmed me. I struggled to relax into their care but found that I could not surrender my constant assessment of options should the place get mortared. I knew by the misty state of indifference that seemed to cloud my mind that I was being sedated, but the feeling of helplessness kept me fighting feebly against it. When not entirely under the influence of the drugs, I fell into the kind of rest I used in the field, a kind of semi-conscious hovering through the night, a floating or drifting, in which my mind kept working on some level so that I could ask myself if I was sleeping even while I dozed, yet acknowledging every noise above ground, every distant explosion, every tremor in the ground or the floor, and cataloging the specifics of each without waking. There is no pleasure in this kind of rest for it is not sleep, but it was a habit, a commodity, and it got me through the long months.

For some reason my throat was very sore, and it hurt to speak. The nurses in their whispering jungle fatigues seemed to check on me often, for I would awaken to find that something had been tucked or adjusted around me, and once or twice I woke up to the sound of someone walking away. The surgeon came by a few times too. He was a good-natured man with a narrow, starved face, whose forehead held a deep line of anarchy. His lower eyelids sagged ever so slightly, betraying an ancient weariness. He could have been the model for a martyred saint in a Spanish painting, but he teased easily with the nurses in a dry, pleasant voice and made light of my condition, sparing himself from the old joke:

"...and as far as I'm concerned you still can't play the piano."

He explained that I had evidently been hit by a ricochet, and the bullet had split, sending most of it into my hip and a piece of its metal jacket into the back of my leg, beneath the buttock, to lodge in my groin. The cladding piece had penetrated an area of soft tissue so deeply they had gone in to remove it from the front. In effect, between the wound and the surgery, I had been pierced clean through. Cored. That explained the bulk of bandaging. I told him I felt so packed with wadding that if he discovered he was missing some implement that might rust over time, this might be a good time to retrieve it. He gave a throaty sort of ventriloquist's laugh that spared any unnecessary lip movement. Then the flat line of his mouth jabbed deep parentheses into his tawny cheeks. As he turned to leave he told me to mind my own business and go to sleep.

In this way I lingered in chemical twilight, mostly silent and alone, sometimes in a cottony roseate febrility. I had time to think, to recall much that had happened. I thought about the little wooded pocket where we had been ambushed on my first patrol with Johnson. It summoned ghost pains in my shoulder and foot. I remembered vividly the whole experience and thought of the oddly random selection of lost and anonymous places where it is said that men choose to end their lives. I thought of all the close calls: the big attack my first night; being called down to Nha Trang by Steve, just for a lark as it happened, only to return to the news that my replacement and his whole team had disappeared. Getting away with the first prisoner, the unlikely recovery of the wedding ring, the mad coincidence of finding the Starlight scope, learning that another One-Zero had been killed while I was in Hong Kong, and finally, not only surviving the latest operation, but the sheer chance that we had been sent into a region that contained such a singularly identifiable position on the map for pinpointing an air strike call–the only thing that, though we were caught on the edge of its fury, could have saved us. Truly, coincidence gives accident a necessary place in the record of events.

I tried to sleep, but what I got instead was a dazed cycle of bits and pieces of worry, yearning, kaleidoscopic images of vivid but pointless memory, a descent to the edge of dreams, and then back around again. Remembering that night in the grass woke me several times a night, and even during the day it would send an involuntary shiver through me, sometimes violent enough to cause the bed to squeak. The awesome power of the napalm, far worse than anything the Lord ever put down on Egypt, danced insistently behind my eyes through the trembling silhouette of smoking trees.

I thought of all those people we had killed on that grassy plateau, and I wondered about the body of the man I had stabbed. I still saw it clearly, staring up through the towers of the ant colony–a quick departing glimpse indelibly printed on my memory, perhaps forever. I wondered how many years it would take for all traces of the body and of the radio I had left behind to disappear completely in the jungle's voracious reclamation. Conditions in that wilderness could destroy hardware while it was still being used, and all organisms that died in it were immediately set upon and recycled back into the living. Thoughts of both the dead man and the mute 25-pound instrument in which I had invested such love-hate regard drew upon me like a precipice.

I could never have imagined the prodigal intimacy of my kinship with death brought by those missions. Until we are overwhelmed by its profusion, death carries meaning as a special event–a moment to which we attach a host of emotions. It has long served philosophers and poets with colorful speculation in the warmth of their lamps, but death on the scale I had seen–indeed had induced in the case of the air strike–renders the search for meaning a pitiful exercise. When your identity group is more dead than living, the significance of life becomes the question, for it is life that is transitory–and, as I now knew well, very cheap.

One day two officious strangers arrived to hear my after-action report. Still tired, dopy from pain medication, and deeply survival raptured, I was able to recount little more than the main points of what had happened. Only much later was I able to begin recalling events in detail, but for the moment the men seemed satisfied with vaguely sequential highlights drawn forth from a pharmaceutical haze with the edges all smoothed off. I told them about our arrival at the grassy plateau and the RON; my confusion during the air strike; how I'd had to "grease" the prisoner, and how Nhi had saved me and got us all to the first waypoint. I gave them what I could remember of the escape, and how it must have been Nhi who had kept us moving toward extraction, as I could remember only versions of tilted images, the pain, and the times my face came close to the ground.

They said they had debriefed Nhi already. I wondered when they had done that and realized I had no idea of how long I'd been in the hospital. When I asked they responded simultaneously in an under-rehearsed comedy of misinformation.

"Three days–".

"–Five days".

There followed an awkward moment of declining buoyancy in which it became evident that there would be no explanation for even this weightless question. They offered a tight, perfunctory congratula-tion which, despite the formulaic words, I took gratefully as a form of template acknowledgement. Then they got up and left, muttering breathily to one another in tones that diminished with distance. While they were there they had maintained, as these people always did, a gulf of superfluous mystery between us, and now that they were gone, I was left to wonder if I would ever again have to be debriefed by anyone about anything.

Grayson and some of the guys from FOB 4 surprised me with a visit, too. Symptoms of relief at having missed it all animated Gray-son's face and garlanded his voice when he asked questions about the operation and answered mine about his serendipitously-timed R&R. I was happy for his good time in Bangkok, knowing he would likely soon be inheriting the burdens of Team Anaconda.

I was struck by the attentions of the other men who came. Over the long months in-country my private campaign to avoid notice had developed into something of an obsession. This entirely delusional preoccupation with obscurity had often allowed me to keep an out-ward appearance of sociability as circumstances required while func-tioning within a solitary bubble of withdrawal. Over time, this need had served to create the equally false corollary assumption that I must exist outside the others' customary purview. Of course, in such an elite unit, this was actually a potentially dangerous fantasy. Their visit was therefore entirely unexpected, and I was both pleased and touched by their support.

They told me that at long last I was being taken off field duty until DEROS, and furthermore the scuttlebutt held that I was to be impres-sively decorated for the captured information they had retrieved from the fatigue pants they'd cut off me, in addition to calling in an air strike on my own position. This last point was information overload.

The events all sounded so deliberate and purposeful the way they told it. It had not occurred to me until that moment that what had happened would be interpreted in such a way. They were giving me credit for acting with forethought. They didn't seem to understand about the heart-stopping terror, the numbing confusion, the thoughtless blind instinct for flight—that in truth everything I could remember doing was just a tearful whimpering cry for deliverance. It did appear that I had called in the attack on our position, but I hadn't thought of it *their* way; it was just that the obstruction to our escape happened to be all around us, and my frantic efforts with the radio were no more than a last desperate plea by a terrified groundling mindlessly frantic for rescue. I had been a tiny confused bubble in a sea of torment and fear.

With a surge if gratitude and admiration I told the guys that the real work had been done by Nhi and the team. The Nungs had not panicked; they had pulled me out of there despite their own severe burns; and they had kept moving in disciplined silence all through the agonizing retreat in spite of their debilities and obvious pain. I still couldn't believe the sheer weight of improbabilities that had attached themselves to my luck, and besides, I thought it was better to serve as panegyrist to the worth of others—especially as the Nungs were unlikely to get the recognition they deserved—than to be dawn into an account of my own deadly blunder.

It was all so odd. Is this what it felt like to be a war hero? I could not remember ever thinking about that before, but whatever I might have assumed, this was not it. Hero. An action word. Even the masculine-specific sound of it held disturbing implications of brave deeds and noble self-sacrifice, of behavior so far from my nature that I came to realize I really didn't understand what it actually meant. I could see all that had happened to me over the months only through a filter of intense dread and stark blinding fear, only through a protective gauze of disbelief and mindless impulse extorted from animal fright, with no plan, no confidence in outcome, no leadership assessment of alternative contingencies, often wrung from such numbing doubt that I still could not permit myself to venture near the impatient void of speculation about it.

Over time I had many occasions to extend my list of humbling reasons never to play "what if." Yet my mind persisted in leading me back across the fearful landscape of memory. There were moments when, lying there in the clean sheets, the sensation returned of doubting I had actually been in some of those places. Some images appeared bleached and colorless. Occasionally a trail of emotion would lead back to an event impacted with such bad feeling that it would evade recollection and vanish at the threshold on a shiver. The most available recall was mostly about the movement, the cloying imperative to keep moving through the fierce watchfulness of the jungle as the endlessly wild topography changed, and never allowing the mission to assume a greater importance than getting the team out alive. There appeared long gaps in the images that played through my mind, blanks in the parade of recollection that would only return in vivid troubled dreams and, years later, in memories triggered by seemingly irrelevant incidents.

On another visit to the hospital the guys produced several beers smuggled in a first aid bag, and with a tentative sip out of sight of the staff I realized it was the first remotely alcoholic drink I'd had since Hong Kong, which seemed to be most of a lifetime ago. I couldn't finish the beer, but the gesture made one of those moments in life that one carries forever.

The staff began to treat me a bit differently too, apparently having heard mutterings of this rumored decoration. I had a number of service and action decorations already, commendations that had come down through either the Army Special Forces or the Spooks, and though I was proud of the recognition, as it leant me a certain ironic gravitas within the unit, I still cringed at the attention. Up to now, commendation had meant reputation, and I'd been trapped irremediably in a situation where reputation had only resulted in more dangers. Now, though, with a nascent expectation of the future, I was beginning to sense the merits of the rumor.

I enjoyed the cheerful deference with which even the strangers in the hospital began treating me and felt a yet tentative but growing confidence that I would not be sent into the field again. My enlistment would be up soon, and it was becoming clear that my injuries would assure my uselessness until then. I decided to relax into whatever benefits might come to those real heroes into whose towering, silver-lined shadow I was evidently being consigned.

There were additional ironies that accompanied award ceremonies. We knew that medals were often given out as part of an unspoken publicity effort to send heroes home to a population widely opposed to the war. Families and communities at home take pride in the boys who return with evidence that they did well, even in a bad and little understood conflict on the other side of the world. Yet these symbols can be self-serving, too, for they enhance the reputation of the combat units where the recommendations are generated in the first place. Of course certain decorations have to be approved higher up the giddy structure of command, but a volume of awards naturally translated to a unit's reputation for achievement. By the end of course, I was immensely pleased to have the recognition, but medals can carry secret ambiguities that place conditions on their meaning, and in my case, they came heavily freighted with cowardice and fear.

Despite the bloody lessons of history, the military's traditional view of a fighting man still places him in a visionary concept of warfare distorted by notions of chivalry and a certain romance. Such ideals are given shape by colored ribbons and have been for centuries. In medieval times, though, they had a much better system. Conspicuous achievement in battle often resulted in the King's grant of titles and lands that provided a lifetime of passive income. Nice.

My thoughts about this came not from any disrespect for genuine heroes and men of achievement in the face of mortal danger. We had plenty of those in the unit. I knew them, and it was because of them that our award ceremonies were usually for multiple acts of conspicuous bravery. Being around these men always intimidated me. I held them in humbling respect out of excruciating personal familiarity with the conditions they had surmounted, coupled with the painful knowledge that I had groped through my assignments by sheer chance, survived so far by the serendipitous intervention of blind fortune, and had stumbled against my will into circumstances that had been generously exaggerated in their reporting by my superiors. The fact remained that I was merely a product of desperate fortune.

31

By the time I was released back to FOB 4, it looked as though I could expect my DEROS orders soon, and as I could walk only with difficulty, I felt increasingly safe from further field operations. I had been disillusioned on this point before, of course, and had learned never to assume, but this time I was truly incapacitated for the demands of the field. I returned conspicuously on crutches to be mildly, but happily, discomfited by many expressions of congratulation, which I accepted with hypocritical gratitude.

Stepping back into the hootch for the first time, I saw that someone had heaped my filthy web gear in a pile under my bunk, and with it was the blood-stiffened tourniquet I had used to bind myself up in the field. It had hardened into the crumpled shape it had taken when discarded by whomever had removed my stuff from the landing pad. It seemed a gruesome artifact for someone to have saved, and I picked it up with the idea of just throwing it out. It retained the rigid shape into which it had dried with my own blood. Yet it had served me well. This simple, faded green triangle of cotton was one of the most versatile items of equipment we had been issued. It had served variously and faithfully as kerchief, sweat rag, headband, gear oiler, sling, bandage, tourniquet, and general wiping cloth. I decided to keep it. After a good soaking in cold water followed by soaping in the shower, it was cleaned of its gore and, except for the quiet resonance of strange history it retained, returned to its former state of faded, innocuous green cotton cloth. I have it to this day.

At the club I was offered more drinks that day than I could have handled and managed to get out by buying everyone drinks in thanks for all they had taught me. There was general good natured agreement on that point while I sneaked away with two cases of beer and a bottle of Scotch for the team. I was anxious to reward them, and though I worried that I might be overloading their capacity for so much alcohol, I hoped the generosity would be appreciated. Grayson, who I was glad to see had been cultivating his relationship with the Nungs, had to carry the beer. Together we went down to the Nung's tent, and I presented them with the booze. The result was predictable with much cheer and celebration, and later that day we had to go back to make sure they were all okay.

I wanted to do something special for them, though, despite the success of such simple rewards as drink. I asked at Headquarters if there was any way to have them decorated. I explained their extraordinary field discipline and how they had come to my aid and dragged me out of imminent danger despite their own wounds; how they always waited for my signals and always served to advance the operation despite all conditions, fatigue, and injury. I explained my certainty that it would mean a great deal to them to be recognized by the same standard we used to commend ourselves, and how it would serve to secure their loyalty.

The request was denied on the grounds that we had no policy on commendations for the Nungs. I departed the office leaving the strong recommendation that we develop a policy of reward in addition to the money that bought their service. I tried to point out that the team regarded US equipment with great respect, even with a certain awe, and that I had proven their ability to use it. Partway through this heartfelt appeal, I realized I was talking to myself.

I left the HQ hut determined to see that my team got their hands on something that would indicate my sense of their worth. At the time, the Americans were issued lightweight pullover windbreakers in black nylon. They had the multiple benefits of being good-looking civilian-type jackets that could be folded into a very small bundle, and were quick-drying, but I never saw anyone wear one, even in the monsoon season. The only time I tried mine on it proved immediately, due to the character of the synthetic fabric, to be too hot. For some reason, though, everyone wanted one. I, too, liked mine even though I never used it.

I hobbled over to Supply and made a moving appeal to the supply sergeant for an issue of ten nylon jackets to give to my team. He took some persuading, but in view of my experience with the team and, incidentally, my "heroism," he relented. However, he said we still had not received our full complement of the jackets since the supply warehouse burned down in the big attack back in August. They were warehoused somewhere in-country and due, he assured me, any time. Then he added that I should be ready to turn in my weapon in the next day or so.

My reaction to this news was unexpectedly ambiguous. Despite the months of daring to dream that the day might come when I would still be alive to turn it in, rather than a day when it would be picked off me, now that the time might actually be here, I didn't want to part with it. It had become an essential–a living organ of my daily life and the tensions of each night, through the relentless crucible of field operations, heat, rain, and uncountable portals of pain. It had taken on an intimacy I could not define. I had become used to its heft and the reassurance in its pistol grip. What tenuous levels of confidence I had been able to muster in the field had come from the feeling of it in my hands. I had cleaned and cared for it, and in turn, had become convinced that it had cared for me. It is hard to explain to anyone who has not experienced it the symbiotic sort of attachment a person can develop for a weapon in those circumstances. It's the kind of affection you can feel for a blood relative.

I began the process of turning the team over to Grayson and told him I thought it a good idea for him to support Nhi's leadership among the Nungs by making a show of respect for him in front of the others. Nhi was good–better than we were–and as far as I was concerned, had more than proved his worth many times over, but dragging me to cover on our last operation had secured him once and for all. I suggested that as soon as Grayson was made the new One-Zero, he should find a way to use our equipment for rewarding them and gaining their trust: to keep up the radio lessons, and make sure Nhi kept the binoculars. I told him about the jackets and asked him to keep checking with Supply to make sure the team got its issue if the consignment came in after I was gone, which now seemed likely. Grayson appeared ready—at least better able—to take over the team than I had ever been.

While waiting out my last few weeks I was put in charge of running the projector for our almost-nightly movies. It was something I could do without much physical strain, although it involved a lot more walking and moving about than was comfortable. The films provided intervals of relaxation from full-on alert mode, despite the occasional teasing whine of a high round from the mountain and the fact that The Sound of Music came around for about the seventeenth time. The job was fun but included the responsibility for driving our Jeep off the compound and down Highway 1 for the few miles to the Special Services office to pick up any scheduled film canisters that were not directly delivered by helicopter. However, after the first attempt to drive, I found that I wasn't healed enough for jouncing along, working the clutch and shifting gears.

Thus I was assigned a driver, which lent me an amusingly marginal layer of status, a fact that made us both laugh. I may have been the only Staff Sergeant in the whole army with his own driver. He was good company and made his respect for the recon guys obvious.

Once, though, he broke the spell by asking me what I had done for the commendation which he had heard was now confirmed. With his question the hypocrisy that lodged in the complex of emotions I carried rose anew. I could not think of an answer. He deserved one; he was interested and wanted to know. I waited, but nothing came forth. I tried to speak, if only to fill the gap with a listening noise. Finally the best I could say was, "…I don't know. Survive, I think. Just outlast the chances somehow."

I told him not to believe the rumors of rapid approval for such a decoration, not only because of what I knew about the actual events, but because it was a general truth that, even though the recommending unit might puff the citation language and press for early confirmation, citations at the level of these rumors took months, sometimes even years, for a decision to percolate down through the tentacles of the bureaucratic octopus. Privately I knew that no saffron exaggeration could do justice to the intensity and complexity of emotions that were the legacy of my burden of fear—that I might not ever outlive all its affects. Whatever subtleties of exaggeration might have crept into the official report, it seemed that rumor was at work amplifying events to further distortion.

There were several replacements in the camp. Their recently-issued fatigues were stiff and dark in the harsh light, their skin ruddy with new sun. I noticed them pointing me out with small gestures and looks of edgy speculation. A flash memory flew through my mind of the red-eyed recon leader and his Asian team that I had seen camped between the vending machines in the Philippine airport terminal all those long months ago. I recalled with a shudder how remote they had seemed from any reality I could have imagined at the time, and now I saw in the eyes of the fresh new men a similar clutch of uneasy conjecture and realized the wheel had come full round. I almost smiled at the contrast I must have presented to them—the veteran with his sun-bleached clothes stained with earth, dried blood, the ghosts of gun oil spills, and hasty medication—and the tangible aura of mystery that attaches to those who return from the haunted regions of our imaginations. I recognized in them the terrible question, but for a long moment couldn't recall the steps by which I had evolved into an object of such discomforting attention. I allowed myself a blush of gratitude, though, that the price of this difference appeared increasingly to have been paid in full.

The day came when I was ordered to turn in my CAR-15. Except for brief intervals spent in Hong Kong and the hospital, I had not been separated from it day or night since the day it was issued to me. It had gone for months without being fired and had worked each time I needed it. I had lavished attention upon it, cleaning it regularly, breaking the seal each morning, and doing whatever I could to protect it from the rain and keep it clear of mud. I had developed a genuine companionability with it, the kind of affection that aficionados of other mechanical things like cars and motorcycles truthfully call love.

I've often thought of that little rifle over the years since and wondered where and in what form it might still exist.

Of course I was thrilled with the implications of finality the order to turn it in carried, but I wasn't prepared for the sharp reality of actually giving it up. On my walk over to Supply I wondered how I could go on without it. I tried to think of ways I could keep it, take it home with me. Upon arrival at the Supply building I pled with the sergeant to let me keep it until the last hour before I left. He said he had his orders, too. Then, after the long moment it took to hand it over, I felt in its abrupt absence naked, extraordinarily vulnerable and a little off balance. I told him it felt like I was out in public conspicuous as red pajamas.

As I left Supply and started back to my hootch with the intention of strapping on my .45, which was still required by my Spook minders anyway, I was startled by what sounded like a grenade explosion from high on Marble Mountain, followed immediately by the pop-pop-pop-pop of an M-16 and a short chugging burst from an AK. I dropped instinctively to one knee and fell over in trying to turn toward the sound. The dying echoes seemed to place noises quite high up, perhaps near the place where we maintained our occasional outpost at the summit. The supply sergeant and I exchanged a look, and as I flattened myself against the hut, he stepped out to join me for a better look.

There was nothing to see but a remnant drift of brown smoke from near the top of the mountain. I didn't like it, but the shooting had stopped as abruptly as it had begun, and there was no more noise. None–not even the startled chirp of a rock bird–just a thick silence, dense with expectation. It was a bright clear day, the mountain stood quietly, the bushes clinging to its crevices nodding complacently in the sea breeze, but there was always a menacing discomfort about the interval of dead silence following an exchange of gunfire. It hung in the air like an unanswered question.

I didn't know the current schedule of our outpost at the summit, and the Supply sergeant couldn't confirm that we had anyone up there. Just in case, though, I asked for my rifle back at least until my last day, but he said that in anticipation of my coming over to turn it in he had already logged it and didn't want to re-do his records. In the scheme of things, re-doing his records didn't sound like an irredeemable rupture of protocol to me, but he was a friend, so I let the question go and limped back to the team hootch to put on my .45. That made me feel less vulnerable.

Despite the strange disturbance on the mountain, things returned, albeit a bit disquietingly, to normal. The firing seemed to cause no additional activity in camp, so with a degree of passing concern for the fact that I had heard an AK, but with no specific orders or need to be anywhere in particular, I decided to make my way down to the bunkers along the beach. They were farther away from the mountain, out of easier rifle range, and provided a slightly better view of the mountain top. If there really was to be nothing more from the exchange we had heard, so much the better, but if the shooting was a precursor to something more, I thought that a guy with my mobility problem would be best off near the refuge of a stout bunker. Besides, I wanted to indulge my conditional freedom from combat operations with a visit to the beach.

I climbed painfully onto the hot sandbags and tried to enjoy a view of the water while keeping conscious of the mountain. The sea was calm, and lazy waves broke gently on the shelf of the beach, leaving areas of wet sand exposed by the withdrawing tide shining glassily their brief time in the sun. I tried to release myself to the view of the sea and the restful rhythm of the water, but I could not suppress the feeling that the exchange of fire on the mountain meant something important, that something bad was building in the silence. We knew the mountain was frequented by VC, but this daylight exchange of fire was something new.

A seagull swooped in and swaggered along the water's edge, leaving arrow-points in the grey sand. To the north toward China Beach, distant figures wavered and swayed in the heat mirage, sometimes appearing to separate into segments, then to rejoin, only to wallow anew, at last emerging as solid forms resembling strange water birds breast deep in the silver haze.

After a while I heard one of our trucks start up and head loudly out of the compound going up through the gears. That was unusual, too, but all else remained quiet, and the beach was tranquil. I was stretched out on the bunker in the on-shore afternoon breeze with my head propped on a sun-baked sandbag and trying to indulge the voluptuous prospect of leaving FOB 4 when it occurred to me that I was lying in the exact place I'd been with sergeant Johnson the day he announced that his DEROS orders had come. It made me smile. That had been a good day for him. The synchronicity was amusing, but it made me feel old.

The sea was an ample viscously glistening space. It stirred nervously in the foreground, gradually assuming a uniform texture with distance until it met the sky in a hard, unbroken line at the rim of the world. I tried to think of what it would be like when I was finally over that horizon and back home, but somehow the reality of it remained out of reach. I remembered Johnson's reticence in talking about his prospects for going home when we had sat together here, and I realized that it may have been simply because he, too, had been drawn so far from the customs of civilization that he could not penetrate his own conditioned defenses enough to glimpse what lay beyond the wall. Perhaps he could not, or dared not, attempt to accept whatever truth might remain of the life he had left when he was sent here.

My own yearning was oddly unfocused, animated more by the prospect of getting out than by any clear image of what it might be like to actually *be* out. What would it be like to live free of the trammels of full-time caution, where moment to moment decisions had to be filtered through one's personal defense mechanism, and all sensory signals analyzed for their promise of harm? I just couldn't remember. The images were there, but I could not summon the feelings that would give the memories life, and so could not even "versionize" what to anticipate.

After a while I heard our truck returning to the compound. It was moving slowly in a low gear and sounded labored. Then I became aware of increased activity behind me and turned to see some guys arming themselves and running between the hootches. This did not bode well, but I needed to find out what was going on. I climbed down off the bunker and headed back toward the recon hootches.

Grayson told me that the outpost on the mountain had been probed and it looked as though the relief team of indigenes had been hit by claymore mines while they were waiting in the deuce-and-a-half for the team they were relieving to come down. The initial report was that the whole relief team had been killed, including the American driver. The truck had been towed back in and was over by the supply building.

This was exactly what had disconcerted me about that outpost duty. It was necessary to enter the stone cutters' village, a place known to be in sympathy with the VC, in order to start up the trail on the back side of the mountain, and the trail itself was such a hard climb that, while on it, either trying to work your way up through the rocks or stumbling down its narrow ledges, each man was vulnerable from the time he left the village until he was established among the boulders at the summit, and even there, the rocks would increase the effect of an incoming hand grenade or RPG.

It was soon rumored that an old woman and a twelve-year-old boy she had trained approached the loaded truck while they were parked beneath the trees in the village. The two held claymore mines painted to look like Polaroid cameras, which the size and shape of the mines vaguely resembled. They got close enough unsuspected to place the mines against the side of the truck and detonated them. In the process they destroyed themselves, but they succeeded spectacularly in shredding the bodies of the twelve guys in the back of the truck, thus wiping out our entire relief force in a horrible blood bath–literally.

Armed only with a pistol as activity grew in FOB 4, I made my way slowly back over to Supply. I didn't at the time fully understand what was going on, but guys were saying that we were finally going to do something about the VC presence in the caves of Marble Mountain, and if we were planning anything that might invite response from the mountain, I wanted my CAR-15 back, even if I had to sign for a different one.

A Cobra helicopter from a neighboring air unit showed up overhead and began to orbit the mountain, its blades whacking at the sea breeze in sharp cuts as the pitch angle changed. It fired a short burst into the side of the mountain then angled sharply away. Activity in the camp was building rapidly. Guys began running past me, putting on their webbing. Someone said that the Colonel had finally decided to attack the mountain and worry about permission from Saigon later—a decision I for one welcomed as the first positive command decision I had heard since arriving here some 10 ½ months before. An extended patrol was forming up near the Supply hut to scale the mountain from the beach side.

With a roar the Cobra appeared from behind the mountain, swung into a hover, and began pouring mini-gun fire into a hidden cave entrance high up on the eastern face of the rock. I looked up at the whirring sound of the firing and watched with delight as the bright red tracer stream poured into a clump of thick scrub. A glittering cascade of spent brass casings rained down from the chopper. Suddenly a billow of smoke and rock dust began rolling out from behind the bushes. It looked like evidence of a secondary explosion from inside the mountain. I hoped so.

Soon additional helicopters appeared and began an all-around assault on the mountain. Their engines roared overhead in a wavering symphony as they found targets of opportunity among the higher crevices and their spent casings scattered into the compound. I had to get under a roof to avoid them. Then I saw that we had foot patrols working their way along the hidden ledges that the enemy had been using, and I watched as the first of many phosphorous grenades was thrown into an unseen opening. It exploded with a muffled thump somewhere inside, and its insidious white fingers of smoke burst out in a fan of deadly bright-tipped arcs.

A full-blown firefight quickly developed as it became apparent that the enemy had an enormous store of ammunition hidden in the caves. Their return fire was heavy and damaged several helicopters, though none were brought down. More helicopters showed up, as additional air units joined the fight, landing on our pad to re-arm and re-fuel. They brought over their own fuel trucks and armorers. It appeared that the mountain's reputation as a VC stronghold was general knowledge, and installations from all around were sending units to join in on the kill.

Casualties from our own people on the mountain began to come in as some of the walking wounded made their way back down, but we knew that we had some dead. I watched as one guy worked his

way onto a narrow ledge beneath a shallow overhang where he became trapped, unable to move forward or back as his position was
visible to the enemy. He saw that he was in a cross-fire and hesitated
for a moment of indecision. He was looking back at his closed line
of retreat when they shot him the first time. He jerked and staggered,
dropped his weapon and fell with his hands clutching his face, trying,
it seemed, to withdraw into the world behind his fingers. The enemy
could evidently still see where he fell because they continued to shoot
at him all afternoon. In the echo of the hollow rock his voice took on
a rangy metallic anxiety each time he was struck, as though he were
speaking out of a mechanical diaphragm. The sound was haunting. I
couldn't understand why they didn't leave him alone. They must have
realized he was helpless and probably dying. He was certainly no longer a threat.

At last, so late in the day that I almost forgot the initial incident,
and long after the constant roar and crackle of the fight had become
general, I heard a single shot that cracked out in a momentary lull in
the shooting. It was followed by a babble and a scream, a nauseating
howl in a queer bleached voice that might have been a man, a woman,
or a monkey. A white sound as featureless as water, and after that there
were no more cries from his place on the ledge.

I watched in helpless fascination as the fight grew into a pitched
air-to-ground battle, augmented by our own ground patrols who made
their way into some of the caves and set off grenades to neutralize
the enemy, along with colored smoke canisters to reveal to the pilots
where the camouflaged cave entrances were. The choppers circled and
fired prolonged bursts at targets I could not see from the ground until
they ran low on fuel or ammo, when they would break away from the
action and land for reloading.

The defensive fire from the mountain did not seem to diminish all
afternoon. It wasn't as heavy as ours, but appeared to be consistently
accurate. As darkness come on, the local air sorties continued uninterrupted. Strangely the fighting settled into levels of activity far enough
overhead that life in the compound began to return more or less to
normal. I went over to the messhall, where I dined beneath the roar of
helicopters. automatic fire, and the rattle of empty casings bouncing
onto the roof.

The enemy was too distracted to bother with shooting into the
camp, and life on the ground for those of us not involved became one

of spectatorship and trying to make ourselves heard over the constant din of the fight. I felt a bit guilty and helpless but had to admit that I was grateful for having been invalided out of the action, especially so close to the time I should be leaving.

It wasn't smart to wander around in the open, even though relatively little ordnance actually fell into the compound. A few stray rounds sang in and struck the roof tops or tumbled into the sand, but as I would discover later, at some point during the afternoon, an RPG or a small mortar round fell through the roof of our hootch and exploded, setting fire to a section of floor and one wall as well as to part of my footlocker. It apparently burned itself out, but I didn't find out until later. I left the messhall and went over to the clubhouse.

I got a canned fizzy something and pulled a chair over to the doorway of the revealed in hut and sat a bit back from the opening to watch the action in comfort. The occasional muffled explosion heard through the deafening ballet of helicopters, and the subsequent issue of dark smoke revealed in the muzzle flashes from unseen openings on the mountain indicated that we were getting into the caves and blowing things up somewhere in their deep corridors.

With the arrival of full dark, the spectacle took on another character as the bright streaks of tracer fire—red inbound and green outbound from the rocks—stitched up the night. Darkness brought a reduction in pitch as the ferocity of the shooting tapered off somewhat, but it continued with a kind of steady intermittency, probably because we had managed to kill most of them and to destroy much of their cache. Return fire from the mountain was clearly diminished.

Guys coming off the mountain, dirty and stained with combat, wild-eyed and remote, reported breathlessly that the whole mountain was honeycombed with deep caves, some of them containing spectacular colorful pagodas and old shrines carved from the rock. It appeared that with a steady food supply, the caves could sustain and conceal a large population indefinitely. These were the people who had been looming over us my entire time at FOB 4. It was about time we were finally doing something about it. It was an example of the ironic nature of the whole war, that the enemy was always camped right on the doorstep of our secret operational headquarters, biding their time until they felt things were ripe for vengeance. They had selected by unfortunate coincidence to take their revenge my first night in the place, and now, on one of my last, they had provoked something that was beginning to appear as a final solution to our ignorant Good Neighbor policy.

Finally Puff the Magic Dragon was brought in. I had last seen "Puff" work when it had come to our rescue during the big attack back in August. A basic C-47 flare ship mounted along the fuselage with up to twenty Vulcan mini-guns, each capable of firing 300 rounds a second of 7.62 millimeter ("mike-mike") Gatling style. When Puff was working everything else seemed to stop while a solid stream of bright red poured out of the night sky. Every fifth round was a bright orange or red tracer, and from the ground, the sinuous ribbons hosed gently up and down or right to left, then would suddenly dry up between bursts, vanishing from the air to the ground like a solid object. A few seconds later the sound of the guns would cease, too. It was hard to believe that anyone on the receiving end of such fire power could survive.

The Marines' nickname for Puff was "Spooky," a good label. Several Marines had joined the fight during the day and a few of them were drifting in and out of the club as small units were gradually relieved from the action. As we stood together watching the terrible hypnotic beauty of the C-47 squirting its colored streams into the mountain, one of the Marines standing nearby muttered, "Spooky understands."

Things wound down during the night. Most of the aircraft retired as return fire from the mountain tapered into silence, broken afterwards only by occasional muffled explosions which attested to the continuing efforts of our ground units to blow up the facilities deep within the caves. I finally wearied of the spectacle and headed over to the hootch and bed. That was when I discovered the fire damage to the hut. Someone had put out the fire with a quantity of water which had not fully dripped through the floor. I went to bed on heightened expectancy in a balance of probabilities with the smell of burnt plywood and a view of the night sky through the hole in the wall.

The mopping up operation, punctuated by muffled explosions from inside the mountain, went on until about mid-morning the next day. At first light, though, the evil rock stood silent against the stars, its face pocked and spalled in pale splotches. Grey smoke drifted in ghostly tendrils from numerous unseen crevices, but otherwise all was still, and except for sporadic dull detonations, the strange quiet that always moves in to replace firefights prevailed.

While the camp pulled itself together again, and the night patrols came in for breakfast, I went back over to Supply to see if there was anything I could do to incite my friend, the sergeant in charge, to nudge the system for my team's jackets. The night's action was likely to have produced requirements for new requisitions anyway. There I noticed that the truck in which our outpost relief team had been ambushed was parked nearby.

At first, when I saw a leg draped over the side, I assumed that some guys from the night patrols were taking a break off the ground. Then, as I approached, I could see that the right side of the truck was badly blown in, the olive paint shattered off the bare metal, and the seat back strakes were splintered away. The leg remained very still. The canvas cover over the cab hung in tatters. Then I saw that there were some indistinguishable lumps heaped on the splintered seats. The reality dawned on me when I smelled it and heard the flies, but I was not prepared for what it contained.

On some notion that this matter should be attended to, I went over and unlatched the tailgate. When it fell open, I had to jump back to avoid a massive gelatin of partially congealed blood, a thick burgundy pudding containing boots, hands, partial human limbs, and scraps of equipment, that slopped toward me and oozed heavily off the steel deck. It fell onto the sand with a moist sucking sound in huge lumpy blobs, splattering my pants with its sticky, fetid gore. I reeled back in horror at the slaughter and stumbled in recoil from the scarcely believable damage done to twelve human beings by two claymores.

So this had been the villainy that finally triggered our Colonel's long-overdue decision to take the matter of the mountain into our own hands, repercussions from MACV Saigon be damned. I had never seen anything like it. I could only turn and walk away, leaving the terrible contents of the truck bed and its cloud of flies to slide slowly down and dribble piecemeal onto the ground. Even if the truck could be hosed out and the bed replaced, I knew that it would never be used again. It was as much an irreparable combat loss as any GI killed in action. Even if restored somehow, it would always be inhabited by an insidious, ghostly animism. You could feel that sort of thing.

The camp recovered quickly this time, as there was little material damage, although we lost some people on the mountain, the truck, and the patrol it had held. A morning or two later things were pretty much back to normal. A runner showed up at the hootch and said I was wanted at the HQ hut, and expecting that it might have something to do with my departure, I accompanied him back to his post. There I was amazed to be handed orders promoting me to E-7. I was told good-naturedly that it was calculated to be an incentive to re-enlist. At the time, the military offered a generous monetary re-enlistment bonus and an additional bounty that seduced many into extending their tours in Vietnam. Had I considered for a moment doing so, I would have been paid considerably more in bonuses than I had earned in tax-free combat pay, jump pay, and hazardous duty pay for the whole time I'd been in the country, in addition to the fact that I had apparently been made the youngest Sergeant First Class in the Army. It was clear that if I were to give the military more time, I was on a somewhat fast track. Now that I was feeling safe from further field duty, I was happy with the recognition but knew to keep quiet about my plans.

It was then explained that there was to be an awards ceremony the next day, and I was to receive decorations for the last mission, but that the Big One had been downgraded a notch by higher command for three reasons: what had happened had not been witnessed by a field grade officer, the engagement was not considered large enough, and most importantly (but unofficially)–I had remained alive. Even the Executive Officer had a share in the ironic laugh about that one. I was grateful for the commendation, though, and glad to see growing light at the end of the tunnel. On the whole, I was coming out of this thing in pretty good shape after all, the biggest prize being survival. My desire to be out of the country had continued to grow exponentially, devouring each day now that I was primarily occupied with departure duties. Each twenty-four hour period was made the more vivid by the times before when the end had appeared to be in sight only to be snatched away by another operation.

The next day we were duly formed up under the hot morning sun, and several of us were given medals. Such ceremonies were fairly common and were conducted with a degree of informality that would probably have surprised members of conventional units. Medals were pinned, salutes were exchanged, and we all adjourned to the club as quickly as possible, as much for the shade as for the cold drinks.

Then the ultimate reward–the unreachable star–came in the form of my DEROS orders. I was told to be ready for the Jeep to take me to out-processing at an American compound a few miles up the road, where I was surprised to learn how much of my stuff, including an unused pair of new jungle boots, I was allowed to keep. Half joking,

I asked the guy who was going through my duffle if I could keep my .45, and for a moment he seemed to consider it. He started to suggest a way I might be able to conceal it, but then he chuckled and said, "Nah. Better not." I've always wondered what he had in mind.

Back at FOB 4 I turned in the pistol at last, packed my duffle, and said a few good-byes. I was informed that there was a new regulation that allowed those who wanted to opt out of wearing their Class A uniforms for the flight home to do so, and as my Class A uniform had been pretty well ruined by the musty conditions in my footlocker over the months–which included mildew, smoke, organic mold, and fire–and as I had no desire to draw another set or waste any time trying to polish the collar brass and other metal insignia, I happily chose to travel in my combat fatigues.

32

The next morning I shook hands with Grayson and wished him luck. I meant it too. The Jeep came, and I set out for the airport on a trip I had long ago despaired of ever making. At Da Nang airport I boarded a round-robin flight that would retrace the route down the spine of the country as far as Saigon, then back up the coast to Nha Trang.

Deep into the afternoon that day, back at Special Forces HQ with its air of confident disregard, mowed lawns, and the hum of window casement air conditioners, I wasted no time getting my orders checked and then went to look up Steve. I found him at his duty station behind a tabletop financial district of stacked papers. I had naively assumed I'd be continuing on out of the country that night and wanted to tell him goodbye, but he informed me that I'd probably be held there for a few days, so I might as well relax and enjoy the time. He recommended that I spend the rest of the day at the beach, and we'd meet after his work hours. In the meantime he'd take charge of my duffle while he arranged better accommodations for me than the transient tent.

I didn't like the news about a delay, but his suggestion of the beach sounded almost fun, except that in order to get to the beach I'd have to leave the compound and make my way along the dusty public road I had last seen my first days here months before. It would mean a tedious little hike, but I felt adventuresome enough to try it. Before leaving my duffle with him, I fished out a pair of issue underwear to use as a bathing suit, though it meant digging down through the whole contents of the bag to find them, to the amusement of some of the other guys in the office. On the way across the compound I slipped into the transients' latrine and put the shorts on under my fatigues. It felt confining to have underwear on again after so many months. They were hot, and the gather of cloth between my legs made me feel oddly conspicuous.

By the time I had hobbled as far as the gate a dull ache pulled so hard at my hip socket that I had to stop and rest. Beyond the gate I moved through the ubiquitous miasma of risen dust, red in the filtered afternoon sunlight, and past the street vendors openly hawking their contraband. The crowds and the openness were nerve-wracking.

On arrival at the beach I was surprised at the large number of Americans sunning themselves on the leather-brown sand or playing in the water. I was further confused to see that a few guys even had surfboards (where did they come from?) and had to wonder if this might be a sign of how little there really was for people to do at Head-quarters.

Nearby on my right the jungle crowded onto the sand, leaning forth as though to remind the carefree swimmers of where they actually were. The trees formed an interlocking border of undercut roots where the spent waves rubbed and gurgled hollowly, while the beach curved off to the left around a low promontory that had once been the playground for a row of crumbling hotels. I found a place somewhat removed from the others, there to assess things a bit before committing myself to the water, but as soon as I sat on the hard packed sand I realized I needed the rest, to simply sit and stretch out my legs. Soon, though, the feeling of being exposed to observation on the open beach became too discomforting. I was supposed to be relaxing, luxuriating in the private thrill of escape from FOB 4, but couldn't escape the feeling that I was teetering on the edge of something.

I decided that taking a swim would provide me with more cover, and if I kept my boots on it would afford an opportunity to rub the dried jungle mud off them, too, but then decided that the sight of anyone in this place walking into the water with boots on would bring attention. So in the interest of invisibility I took off my boots and socks, pants, and combat tunic and made a little pile of them. I immediately felt naked and vulnerable. If I'd had a pistol belt I'd have put the weapon on even to swim. The skin on all but my jungle-scarred forearms and hands was pale compared to the tanned and well-fed staffers who had long been earning their combat pay gamboling like hillside lambs on the beaches of Nha Trang. My white feet with their long knobby toes and lurid pink shrapnel scars appeared like strange fantasy objects on the dark sand as I stepped self-consciously toward the water.

The bay proved to be warm and shallow for a long way out, with a hard sand bottom the color of river mud. The water felt good even though the salt content caused some of my insect bites and scratches to sting. I tried to hide myself along the periphery of the swimmers and bobbed uneasily in the gentle waves while trying to imagine what the sad beachfront hotel buildings must have been like when the city had served the French as a seaside resort in its former life. Their empty windows and deserted balconies, moldering quietly into ruin, stared blindly out across the beach, the echoes of their past unheard even among the Vietnamese, few of whom were likely even to remember. Their presence on the beachfront held an oddly poignant reminiscence for a time I had never known, yet a place I could hardly wait to flee. Even the laughter of the guys playing in the water echoed from the trees in ironic contrast to the weeping concrete. Despite my deeply conditioned dislike of the country, alloyed now with the imminent thrill of leaving it, the scene had a mildly depressing effect on my effort to eke forth an hour of pleasure.

A slight offshore gust brought a hint of rain. I was facing out to sea but sensed instantly the shift in the air and knew what was coming. A dark shadow lanced with orange sunbeams rose suddenly behind the buildings to sweep the shore, and with a loud rush rain fell hard for a full minute or two. Most of the swimmers, taken by surprise at the sudden change in the weather and presumably afraid of getting wet, charged out of the water in a comic flurry and began gathering up their towels and beach paraphernalia. I remained in the dimpled water enjoying the show through the grey curtains of rain and then swam over to the shallows beneath the dripping trees to watch it pass. The shore was soon almost empty. I wallowed there feeling the spent waves slop across my back and watched them unfurl against the beach. Steve had again proved correct. The unexpected rain had brought a peaceful interlude. I enjoyed the solitude it provided in clearing the beach and wondered what it might have been like to serve out my time in Vietnam with a job that prioritized the luxuries of headquarters duty such that I might give up a swim to keep my beach towel from getting damp.

I enjoyed having the water to myself, but the empty beach turned against me in lengthening shadows as the evening came on, and I got out to recover my little heap of clothes. I drew damp fatigue pants on over my wet skivvies, then climbed out onto some tree roots that overhung the water to dip my feet free of sand before trying to pull on my socks and boots. Then, wet but cooler, came the long limp back to the security of the compound.

I remained in Nha Trang for two more days anxious to leave, but so numbed by disappointment and conditioned to unpredictability that I passed the time in semi-detachment from the scenes around me, while restless doubts that my release would actually happen continued to creep through me. As darkness fell the first night I became uneasy and told Steve that I wanted to spend it in one of the perimeter bunkers, a prospect he found highly amusing. He agreed to accompany me, and after lending me his standard-issue M-16, which he had never handled the whole time he had been in the country, we repaired to a concrete-reinforced bunker on the western line of defense. I thumbed the first round out of the magazine to test the spring tension, pocketed the bullet, and pulled the charging handle to chamber the following round, while Steve watched bemused. Then I climbed down into the shelter, and while I kept nervous vigil over the open ground beyond, Steve sat out in the open on the roof in a folding chair he'd brought along for the occasion, smoking joints and joking deep into the night. He finally got up and went off to bed, leaving me, acutely conditioned by vibrant expectancy, to watch all through the silent hours the tranquil starlit paddies beyond the wire, anxious lifeguard to a deserted shore, alone with the tranquil sounds of night.

Orders arrived a few days later for me to board a transport down to Saigon for the flight home to the States. I said good-bye to Steve without ever telling him that he had been the unwitting instrument of my salvation all those months before. We promised to stay in touch, and I heaved my duffle into the back of a Jeep for the next leg, a drive back to the airport for a flight to Saigon, for another out of the country.

At Tan Son Nhat Airport in Saigon I joined a large group of men who drifted and stirred through the departure concourse in the manner of basking sharks. Most were dressed in shades of green for one of the first flights to the States from Vietnam after the requirement to travel in Class A uniform had been dropped. Thus I was to fly back to the States in the fatigues I had worn in the bush. In fact, I had on the stained and faded tunic with the bullet hole through the pocket, torn there on that last operation and poorly stitched up by Lei Thi Hao—a good laundress but an indifferent seamstress. I was glad not to have to bother with the tropical Class A with all its required insignia and ribbons, but my jungle clothes felt suddenly out of place in the open spaces of the terminal, somehow provisional.

There were still many guys in khaki with all their brass gleaming beneath the terminal lighting, but most were dressed as I was in olive drab fatigues. Special Forces were required to wear the green beret, though, so as I stood around waiting for boarding orders in the milling crowd, I only gradually became aware of the subtle effect of my conspicuous head gear.

Despite the air conditioning in the terminal building, the beret felt hot and unfamiliar on my head after so many months in a jungle hat, but the furtive looks it drew from many of the other men reminded me that it carried a certain mystique. I was reminded that Special Forces at the time were enshrouded with rumor and enigma that, over the interminable months of survival priorities, I had almost entirely forgotten. Our missions in Vietnam were generally obscure to conventional operations, and though widely rumored about both in and out of the military, those of the FOBs were quite simply Top Secret. The relatively few in Special Forces who became CIA contracts as I had, functioned still deeper in the fathomless realm known vaguely as Black Operations. I suppose we had been case-hardened into a kind of individualized knitting of mutual reliance and stubbornness in the face of mysterious, and often famously dangerous orders, from which rumor and reputation had leaked, thus acquiring the image of a clannish and impregnable society of specialists, a body enigmatic.

I had not had occasion to look at us from the outside before and felt again my conditioned aversion to being noticed. Even among these men who shared my desire for transport out of there, such glances carried a sense of separation that our mutual expectancy failed to neutralize. Besides, I was so humbled by months of tension that I simply wanted to disappear.

There were only two other Green Berets in the crowd, and we soon gravitated together. In talking with them, I learned that one had come in from a remote A-team somewhere in the central highlands and the other had spent his year in a headquarters company after an early wounding in the field. Though they had little knowledge of the FOBs, they knew of them, and as we had field experience in common, we soon felt ourselves to be somewhat apart from the rest of the crowd.

There was another subtle difference: We were unconventional troops with a separate chain of command. We had become used to living comparatively free of the sometimes blind and unreasoning authority that bound conditions in conventional units. We may have been subject to greater risks or not, but we had at least escaped a certain rigid hold on precise molds of conduct, however traditionally justified. We knew it, and so did many of the others there. They reminded me of the similar glances of deference that I had received from time to time during the years before, when the eyes of strangers had taken in my uniform and then filled with a kind of anxious curiosity. After a while I almost allowed myself to enjoy the whispering attention, for by now I had been steeped in magnitudes of "otherness", and if it bought me a certain air of mystery, so much the better. I would enjoy the few moments of conditional privacy that came with the distinction it provided.

From speakers hidden overhead, a worn recording of Scott McKenzie's *If You're Going to San Francisco* played through a scratchy hiss, barely audible through the general murmur of the men. I had to smile at the song's naïve suggestion "to wear some flowers in your hair" as I looked around at the grim-faced people in the room. Many wore expressions of worry, some hardened into lasting woe. Some gabbled with boyish enthusiasm, but others had the look of truly brutal men, coarsened far beyond normal limits, who stood quietly now at the end of a hard-labor prison term.

There was evidently to be no debriefing or official readjustment procedure; we were simply to be loaded and evacuated, cargo like any other. In the meantime, we–the livestock of the military–had been herded into a commodious holding pen to await selection. The men were generally subdued, the din of their conversation about like that in a large restaurant, although occasional individual boasts of the pleasures and conquests that awaited the voice once he was "back in the world" emerged from the sea of words before sinking back into the general drone.

"Back in the world." That was the way we all thought about anyplace outside the country. That was the real world. The surreal miseries of Vietnam, with its astonishing heat, fearsome novelties, and endemic hostility were so unlike anything we had known before that the country seemed indeed a place unto itself, a fantasy realm, conjured of evil intent, and then set aside to boil–and to consume.

The men began to stir as word was passed that we were to listen for our names to be confirmed for the boarding manifest. The crowd fell into a vibrant silence. A few officers were called first, and then the general boarding began alphabetically. There was an occasional whoop or spontaneous expletive as the tinny voice made its way down through the names, as one lucky GI after another stepped forth and joined the growing line. I waited in a private anxiety of faithless anticipation for the "M"s, more than half expecting that my name would not be there. When in due time it was called, I was almost surprised to hear it. A long empty second dragged past before I thought to call out, "Here."

In a bubble of existential wonder that this moment had actually arrived, I joined the long line. After an officious corporal directed me to place my parachute equipment bag carry-on in a special wooden template to make sure it wasn't too big, something that struck me at the time as supremely petty ("chickenshit" to use the universally flexible military adjective, adverb and noun), I was cleared to step outside onto the glaring concrete ramp to follow the guys from the first half of the alphabet on their walk out to the aircraft.

The plane that waited there in the sun was a civilian airliner with the letters ONA painted on the side: Overseas National Airways. The high boarding ladder faced the sun, and blinding light blasted from the edge of each aluminum tread. The metal radiated waves of heat from the steps, and the handrail up each side was too hot to touch. When at last I stepped into the shade of the cabin I was surprised to be welcomed by a crew of luminous flight attendants in crisp airline uniforms. They were evanescent, glowing with the virtue of personal care products I had long forgotten as they smiled in cheerful welcome. A nostalgic hint of floral perfume stabbed me with a flash of wistful sentiment as I passed by to find an aisle seat toward the middle of the plane and on the left side, so that I could stretch out my right leg to change the angle of my hip as necessary during the long flight. I sat quietly on the surprising upholstery while the seats all around filled up.

When at last with a sharp pneumatic gasp the door was closed and latched, shutting out the insidious creep of hot Vietnamese air with its weight of random malignancy, a scattered cheer went up throughout the cabin. Air conditioning began to spill from the vents in a visible mist that roiled in the overhead, but I sat silently attuned to every mechanical sound, unable to shed my well-trained doubts and half-expecting to hear a bang on the door from one of the spooks, come to recall me.

Intellectually, I knew I was sitting in an airplane, the longed-for freedom bird, the outbound tunnel. Yet the full delight to which I should have been able to surrender remained elusive, shimmering just below my full comprehension. Perhaps the long months of indelible phenomena and paradox had fused together to condition such a level of hopelessness that by the end it drained the moment of its thrill–even of its truth.

When the engines spooled up and we began to taxi, I still wondered if it might all just be a tease of fate, if something would yet prevent my getting out of the country. The Captain's voice came through the intercom welcoming us on board and delivering a brief address in which he gave us what sounded like heartfelt thanks for our service in this godforsaken place. It had not occurred to me that I had been involved in something that might ever draw an offer of gratitude. His voice was calm, conciliatory, and his words touched me surprisingly. When at last we lifted off the ground, I still couldn't shake the feeling that The Beast had not intended for me to escape, that I had somehow slipped past the intentions of the universe, and that the long arm of retribution would yet reach out for me, even into the sky.

We landed in Japan to refuel for the long hop across the Pacific. They allowed those who wanted a stretch to leave the plane, but we had to remain confined to the cantonment where the plane was being serviced. I had never seen Japan and chose to step out. Outside, the air was deliciously cool and misty. I went down the boarding steps and stood on the pavement nearby, breathing in the freshness. The air smelled of wet grass.

Although it wasn't raining at the airport, the pavement was damp, and dark grey clouds were gathered all around, restless and heavy with promise. There was something benign about them; they lacked the aspect of furious intent that the monsoons in Vietnam had brought. I had grown to hate the rain in Vietnam for what it did to my skin, my clothes and equipment, and especially my weapon. It exacerbated all health problems, and it placed fearful doubt upon a timely rescue for anyone caught in the field. On the other hand it served to curtail most operations for a time, so rain in Vietnam was not a neutral occurrence. One way or the other we all carried an emotional investment in the rain. Yet here the prospect of showers closing in the middle distance with sunlight rimming the clouds was drained of foreshadow and passive as theater, even metaphoric.

There was a modern terminal building nearby to which all the other guys who got off headed, presumably to avail themselves of the lures offered up to tourists everywhere, but as we were only to be there a short time, I wanted to stay outside where at least I could experience Japanese air. There was nothing of particular interest to see, just the area where the plane and its contents were hemmed in by the building and a surround of high cyclone fencing. I wondered at this apparent restriction. I had read of the traditional cultural isolationism of the Japanese and assumed it might be related somehow to that, a descendent of old barriers, but it could also have been some policy imposed by American authority. Maybe they were afraid of desertions. There had been some unsanctioned absences by guys who, having been exposed to Asian culture for the first time, decided they liked it enough to escape into it, and also by others who feared the now well-known incidents of misguided reprisals against returning veterans by angry war protesters at home.

Anyway, the reason for confining us to this remote corner of the airport didn't really matter. As much as I would have enjoyed a day or so to see the place, I had seen enough airline terminals to prefer biding this short time outdoors where the air smelled floral, the sky was free of helicopters, and at least some small corner of Japan was visible for a little while.

The long flight across the Pacific that followed with nothing to see outside from an aisle seat brought forth a tumbled mental landscape of painful reminiscence, happy anticipation, and anxiety about a future that might contain new rules for one whose values had been inexorably tempered into unrecognizable form by laminations of outrageous fortune. Everything that had happened since my arrival in Vietnam had been conditioned by the unexpected. Events both great and small had broken through the seal on my mind with persistent and audacious improbability, allowing no room for moral inertia, no reason or recourse for justification, and too little time to learn. Living always in the shadow of death had evoked a truer estimate of its meaning and, in the end, had enriched the value of living. I was rushing now eastward through the night, speeding toward a place where such verities were likely to be under-appreciated, worn smooth by the walls of domesticity–happily so to be sure, but I worried about the invisible chasm that might ever yawn between me and the priorities of those whom I loved.

Between periods of sleep, I woke with a flash of panic in the strange, dim-lit surroundings of the plane, then sank into a complex of reservations. I suppose my feelings were not entirely unlike those of a pregnant widow, whose anticipations of pleasure and reward are suddenly compromised and muted at great personal cost, who faces now a future where the rules have been changed.

I was anxious to leave the military and to get home...to what, I really didn't know, for I feared instinctively that things might be different, or that my perception of the icons of a former life might have become lost in the long storm of fervent priorities, but I was in a rush to be reunited with what I remembered. I wanted to flee what I could of my dark and ponderous new sophistication, to indulge in the safety of my family and to recapture that roseate life. I had lost about 20 pounds in the Asian heat, the stress and the fear and even wondered idly if my civilian clothes still fit.

For some reason one of the hostesses came by my seat repeatedly during the flight and crouched down to talk to me. Not having been so near such an attractive woman in years I was grateful for her attentions but couldn't understand why she singled me out. Perhaps she hadn't. She may have simply been exercising her professionalism on a randomly-selected seat number, but during these visits over the long hours she came to ask a number of personal questions with what I took to be genuine curiosity, and she shared some hints about her own life. Sometimes, kneeling there in the aisle with the dim night cabin lighting in her hair and her face in deep shadow, she lapsed into moments of wistful reflection, as though in recall of something deeply guarded, or perhaps to offer some gentle reveal that had been allowed to escape the weft of her private reservations, before which any words I might have thought to say would have lain forever abrogate.

She was very pretty. I liked the line of her cheek, her curbless modulations, and the flecks of color in her eyes. She spoke naturally, with none of the insipid professional cheer such women are trained to present in simultaneous welcome and defense. I wondered if her guarded smile might have been cast up with the flotsam and broken planks of a lost ship that had struck something greater than itself and sunk within her long ago. I could smell the fresh scent of her hair. It reminded me of something all but faded away, and a buried teenage yearning stirred within me to simply reach out, to draw her femininity against me and whisper in her shell-pink ear of the ancient mandate, to tell her we owed ourselves the exploration of our happy congruence; but I could only sit there in my primeval twilight and struggle to summon words that might balance the urgent algebra of our small talk. To have told her these thoughts would have sounded at best naive, the words leached of their intention by inanition and wonder, at worst, lost to invidious solecism. Yet the fact that I could feel anything at all bestowed a soft benediction on the moment.

Despite the attraction, I found it difficult to talk to her, to contribute my part to our little exchanges. I could think of little to say, for there was nothing in recent experience I could summon in support of normal pleasantries. I didn't want to talk about the war or risk revealing anything about myself that might frighten her off. I heard the clumsy effort in my responses, which seemed to come from somebody else entirely, some other me, groping like a mole for the light. They were inept and muddled with moody adverbs that rose to cast their solemn shadows over her piquant cheer.

The trans-Pacific flight was as long and only slightly less tedious than I remembered the flight over to have been, the main difference being that a non-threatening future lay in promise beyond the night. I had long hours to review my life and the barely-credible escapes that had brought me to this point. Between the periodic seat-side visits, I sank back into contemplative solitude, my thoughts interwoven with the steady lull of the engines.

At last a grey morning began to tint the windows, and people stirred stiffly with the change in light. Then, some time after a coffee service, the sound of the engines softened as we began a descent. The energy level throughout the cabin rose instantly and all at once, as though by some ancient tribal telepathy. People came awake and sat up. An impenetrable nacreous mist had been moving past the windows ever since first light, but suddenly we broke into a bright gap in the clouds and found ourselves surrounded by high snow-covered Alaskan peaks with tall pines mantled in white drifts. It was stunning, pristine and beautiful, like a Christmas card from the world itself. The noise that burst from the men was indescribable: a choked explosion made of cheers, gasps, laughter, some applause, and spontaneous weeping. An insistent lump rose to lodge in my throat at the sight and would not subside. The massive slopes outside passed so close to the wingtips they might have appeared from a fairy tale, and the glistening, surreal scenery blended so fittingly with all the interminable months of groundless hope that the mountains seemed to shoulder their way into my dream, there to stand in living testimony to my tattered longing.

Later, there was more applause when the wheels bumped the ground at last, but by the time we taxied to a stop a strange quiet had descended upon us like a sealed lid. When the door was finally opened we rose and crowded into the aisle. The air was electric with anticipation, but there was little chatter among the men as we shuffled forward. Through the bobbing river of heads, I lost sight of the hostess who had befriended me and just surrendered to the acumen of the press for the exit door.

At last I stepped into cold air. It carried the scent of recent rain and chilled instantly through my worn jungle clothes. I breathed it in. On the tarmac ramp lay puddles full of silver sky, and darkling mists hugged the far mountains, a scene voluptuous with unspecified promise. In the distance beyond the airport buildings the snow-laden slopes of Mt. Rainier rose through a grey drift of layered clouds.

In the fresh cold and the strange, pure air free of jungle smells, I became conscious of the incongruence in my faded tropical clothes, clothes in which for months I had lived such extremes of emotion, their purpose now suddenly obsolete, and realized there were still dried chunks of black Vietnamese mud caked in the lug soles of my jungle boots. I was bringing the wretched place back with me.

I filed down the ladder toward the pavement, adding my own to the heavy clatter of many footfalls on the aluminum steps, though in a daze of uncertainty, trapped for the moment in some conflicted space between paradigms, still unsure and still connected to the torturous primeval wilderness that crowded my mind. For a second I was afraid that when my foot touched the ground The Beast would shock me from this rosy daydream and yank me back across the world to awaken on patrol in some remote corner of jungle, trapped in its unending despair. Then, at the bottom of the ladder, I bent down to touch the pavement with my hand. I was back in the States at long last, and though yet on unfamiliar ground, I began to feel the first tentative touch of its coalescent promise.

Ahead lay an unknown interval of out-processing, the resumption of petty military protocols that had been dispensed with in the combat zone, and more flights–home, across the country, and thence across the Atlantic to London. I looked forward to it all as the closing act, but anticipating the journey across the shoulder of the earth that still lay ahead served to tease the grip of the recent past and kept at bay a full appreciation of being home, of awakening completely to the impossible dream. As we were herded toward the terminal building I surrendered to whatever final logistical requirements there would

be with the exhausted patience that dwells in the aftermath of conditioned unpredictability. At least for the time being I was still a wry
exile from a time when fundamental concepts like truth and freedom
had different meanings.

Across the ramp, contained by wire fencing and guarded by two
or three MPs, a thick assembly of GI replacements stood ready to
board our aircraft for the flight to Vietnam, a sad testament to the
rate of attrition. It appeared that the turnover was an oiled machine. I
felt a sudden desire to warn them, to tell them that if they kept their
heads down and their eyes and ears open, they would be all right. I
knew in my heart that it wasn't really true, but in their eyes looks of
rue and of uncertainty beckoned for some message of reassurance. I
crossed toward them, only to be stopped by one of the MPs, who told
me politely but firmly enough to make his orders clear that I needed
to rejoin my group and not speak to the new men. I've wondered ever
since what the authorities feared a guy fresh back from the slaughter
might have told them. The truth? There wouldn't have been time even
to begin.

EPILOGUE

The events described here happened over forty years ago, yet many hold a baleful grip upon me still. At least half my years since living them have been spent in the quiet effort to forget, but at last, under pressure of repeated suggestion from my friends and relatives to write about them, I began the effort some fifteen years ago to put into words an account of even those events that live deepest in the heart of that darkness.

Many of these experiences sensitized me enormously to what it means to be a person, yet it has taken this delayed process of summoning them from the dungeons of the irreparable to awaken parts of the message. The full curriculum has lain suppressed for years, hidden beneath discomforting images. Just as I believe that a fifty-year moratorium should be placed upon naming buildings and parks after dead politicians until history has given us some perspective upon their achievements, so too some of the lessons of Vietnam, both personal and national, have benefited by their time in the shadows.

In addition to the troubled dreams one might expect to find in the long shadow of such experience, my journey through the process of deliberate recollection has led me to discover with what surprising detail the archive of memory can summon the immediacy of extraordinary events, and with what tenacity long-past experience engrained with emotion can cling to one's values, hidden just behind the parade of daily events, even decades later.

Much of it lives on in a state of suspended animation, like a darkness standing always at the window, silent, quietly inquisitive. Often a memory will drift up entirely out of context, pause for a moment showing the pale of its lazily beating fin, then sink back down without breaking the surface. Tiny signals in the form of sounds, smells, glimpses, or remarks overheard, can summon a moment of recall. Sometimes the memories chill. At other times they serve to put some interim priority in perspective—sometimes even to my social or professional detriment—but they always inspire the thrill of gratitude that I am still here. Writing about them has revealed that those events have been at least indirectly responsible for years of emotional reaction to petty things, whether flashes of unreasonable anger or bursts of inappropriate laughter, and I fear they have also dealt an insidious hand in my failures at the game of romantic love. The fingers of mortal fear are indeed long, and even its wondering stepchild—the ineffable charm of simply being alive–can assert an undue influence years later upon seemingly unrelated events and upon certain choices that one may learn too late have been misunderstood or misjudged within the snug parlors of society, where walls are worn smooth by the consensual protocols of domesticity. Perhaps, now that they have been recorded, some of the memories revivified here are free at last to go.

In retrospect I may not have had to keep myself on such unrelenting alert while at FOB 4 during the times between operations. It meant being deprived of the rest that such intervals were supposed to provide, and that long before the end I was both regimented and overborne by an advancing state of mental and physical depletion. That indenture carried on into the years afterwards and affected my sleep for more than a decade.

Yet the experience engendered a shadowy kind of sophistication too. It revealed how psychologically dependent we are upon even our subliminal expectations of the short term future: what to expect of the next five minutes, the next hour, what we'll do at the end of the day. Without some degree of confidence in our control of the minutiae of daily events as we go about the humble business of creating our lives from moment to moment, the future ceases to exist altogether. We are cast adrift in an existential dead sea where all knowing lies hopelessly in the past.

However, being thrust into an unrelenting athanasian limbo of strain for so long has served to make constant vigilance a way of life, an appreciation of living itself a kind of religion, and instilled in me a life-long awareness of my surroundings that has paid dividends in judgment and situation analysis ever since. It gave birth to my profound distrust of government, a regrettable but commodious indifference to most people, an iron loyalty to those with whom I am cast emotionally, and perhaps most importantly, it has served to greatly reduce the number of things that I judge to be worthy of worry.

ABOUT THE AUTHOR

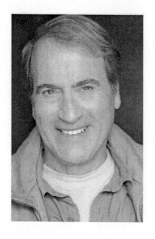 John Rixey Moore is an actor and writer. He has been a contract player on several TV soap operas and the on-camera announcer in over 460 network commercials, competed internationally for several years on the U.S. Bobsled team in the 1980s, served as boat tune-up crew and sail advisor for the America's Cup, and sailed a 73' trimaran across the Atlantic from Plymouth, England to Newport, Rhode Island in 1976. He has flown his Beech Bonanza across the United States some twenty-three times and built a home-made car out of parts scrounged from wrecks and yard sales (with a bit of reluctant professional help) which he has driven across the US twice so far.

He can be seen from time to time on The History Channel being interviewed on the crop circle phenomenon and on the subject of UFOs. An amateur historian, he enjoys walking ancient sites in Europe and maintains an extensive collection of antique books and household displays of medieval weapons. He lives in the Los Padres National Forest of Southern California, where he paints and enjoys firing his collection of antique cannons.

To contact: www.johnrixeymoore.com

Other Books by
Bettie Youngs Book Publishers

On Toby's Terms

Charmaine Hammond

On Toby's Terms is an endearing story of a beguiling creature who teaches his owners that, despite their trying to teach him how to be the dog they want, he is the one to lay out the terms of being the dog he needs to be. This insight would change their lives forever.

"Simply a beautiful book about life, love, and purpose."
—**Jack Canfield, compiler,** *Chicken Soup for the Soul* **series**

"In a perfect world, every dog would have a home and every home would have a dog like Toby!"
—**Nina Siemaszko, actress,** *The West Wing*

"This is a captivating, heartwarming story and we are very excited about bringing it to film."
—**Steve Hudis, Producer**

ISBN: 978-0-9843081-4-9 • ePub: 978-1-936332-15-1 • $15.95

The Maybelline Story

And the Spirited Family Dynasty Behind It

Sharrie Williams

Throughout the twentieth century, Maybelline inflated, collapsed, endured, and thrived in tandem with the nation's upheavals. Williams, to avoid unwanted scrutiny of his private life, cloistered himself behind the gates of his Rudolph Valentino Villa and ran his empire from a distance. This never before told story celebrates the life of a man whose vision rocketed him to success along with the woman held in his orbit: his brother's wife, Evelyn Boecher—who became his lifelong fascination and muse. A fascinating and inspiring story, a tale both epic and intimate, alive with the clash, the hustle, the music, and dance of American enterprise.

"A richly told story of a forty-year, white-hot love triangle that fans the flames of a major worldwide conglomerate."
—**Neil Shulman, Associate Producer,** *Doc Hollywood*

"Salacious! Engrossing! There are certain stories, so dramatic, so sordid, that they seem positively destined for film; this is one of them."
—*New York Post*

ISBN: 978-0-9843081-1-8 • ePub: 978-1-936332-17-15 • $18.95

It Started with Dracula

The Count, My Mother, and Me

Jane Congdon

The terrifying legend of Count Dracula silently skulking through the Transylvania night may have terrified generations of filmgoers, but the tall, elegant vampire captivated and electrified a young Jane Congdon, igniting a dream to one day see his mysterious land of ancient castles and misty hollows. Four decades later she finally takes her long-awaited trip—never dreaming that it would unearth decades-buried memories, and trigger a life-changing inner journey.

A memoir full of surprises, Jane's story is one of hope, love—and second chances.

"Unfinished business can surface when we least expect it. *It Started with Dracula* is the inspiring story of two parallel journeys: one a carefully planned vacation and the other an astonishing and unexpected detour in healing a wounded heart."
  —Charles Whitfield, MD, bestselling author of *Healing the Child Within*

"An elegantly written and cleverly told story. An electrifying read."
  —Diane Bruno, CISION Media

ISBN: 978-1-936332-10-6 • ePub: 978-1-936332-11-3 • $15.95

The Rebirth of Suzzan Blac

Suzzan Blac

A horrific upbringing and then abduction into the sex slave industry would all but kill Suzzan's spirit to live. But a happy marriage and two children brought love—and forty-two stunning paintings, art so raw that it initially frightened even the artist. "I hid the pieces for 15 years," says Suzzan, "but just as with the secrets in this book, I am slowing sneaking them out, one by one by one." Now a renowned artist, her work is exhibited world-wide.

A story of inspiration, truth and victory.

"A solid memoir about a life reconstructed. Chilling, thrilling, and thought provoking."
  —Pearry Teo, Producer, *The Gene Generation*

ISBN: 978-1-936332-22-9 • ePub: 978-1-936332-23-6 • $16.95

Blackbird Singing in the Dead of Night

What to Do When God Won't Answer

Gregory L. Hunt

Pastor Greg Hunt had devoted nearly thirty years to congregational ministry, helping people experience God and find their way in life. Then came his own crisis of faith and calling. While turning to God for guidance, he finds nothing. Neither his education nor his religious involvements could prepare him for the disorienting impact of the experience.

Alarmed, he tries an experiment. The result is startling—and changes his life entirely.

"In this most beautiful memoir, Greg Hunt invites us into an unsettling time in his life, exposes the fault lines of his faith, and describes the path he walked into and out of the dark. Thanks to the trail markers he leaves along the way, he makes it easier for us to find our way, too."

—Susan M. Heim, co-author, *Chicken Soup for the Soul,*
Devotional Stories for Women

"Compelling. If you have ever longed to hear God whispering a love song into your life, read this book."
—Gary Chapman, *NY Times* **bestselling author,** *The Love Languages of God*

ISBN: 978-1-936332-07-6 • ePub: 978-1-936332-18-2 • $15.95

DON CARINA

WWII Mafia Heroine

Ron Russell

A father's death in Southern Italy in the 1930s—a place where women who can read are considered unfit for marriage—thrusts seventeen-year-old Carina into servitude as a "black widow," a legal head of the household who cares for her twelve siblings. A scandal forces her into a marriage to Russo, the "Prince of Naples."

By cunning force, Carina seizes control of Russo's organization and disguising herself as a man, controls the most powerful of Mafia groups for nearly a decade. Discovery is inevitable: Interpol has been watching. Nevertheless, Carina survives to tell her children her stunning story of strength and survival.

ISBN: 978-0-9843081-9-4 • ePub: 978-1-936332-49-6 • $15.95

Living with Multiple Personalities

The Christine Ducommun Story

Christine Ducommun

Christine Ducommun was a happily married wife and mother of two, when—after moving back into her childhood home—she began to experience panic attacks and a series of bizarre flashbacks. Eventually diagnosed with Dissociative Identity Disorder (DID), Christine's story details an extraordinary twelve-year ordeal unraveling the buried trauma of her past and the daunting path she must take to heal from it.

Therapy helps to identify Christine's personalities and understand how each helped her cope with her childhood, but she'll need to understand their influence on her adult life. Fully reawakened and present, the personalities compete for control of Christine's mind as she bravely struggles to maintain a stable home for her growing children. In the shadows, her life tailspins into unimaginable chaos—bouts of drinking and drug abuse, sexual escapades, theft and fraud—leaving her to believe she may very well be losing the battle for her sanity. Nearing the point of surrender, a breakthrough brings integration.

A brave story of identity, hope, healing and love.

"Reminiscent of the Academy Award-winning *A Beautiful Mind,* this true story will have you on the edge of your seat. Spellbinding!"   **—Josh Miller, Producer**

ISBN: 978-0-9843081-5-6 • ePub: 978-1-936332-06-9 • $15.95

Truth Never Dies

William C. Chasey

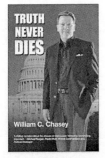

A lobbyist for some 40 years, William C. Chasey represented some of the world's most prestigious business clients and twenty-three foreign governments before the US Congress. His integrity never questioned.

All that changed when Chasey was hired to forge communications between Libya and the US Congress. A trip he took with a US Congressman for discussions with then Libyan leader Muammar Qadhafi forever changed Chasey's life. Upon his return, his bank accounts were frozen, clients and friends had been advised not to take his calls.

Things got worse: the CIA, FBI, IRS, and the Federal Judiciary attempted to coerce him into using his unique Libyan access to participate in a CIA-sponsored assassination plot of the two Libyans indicted for the bombing of Pan Am flight 103. Chasey's refusal to cooperate resulted in the destruction of his reputation, a six-year FBI investigation and sting operation, financial ruin, criminal charges, and incarceration in federal prison.

"A somber tale, a thrilling read."   **—Gary Chafetz, author, *The Perfect Villain***

ISBN: 978-1-936332-46-5 • ePub: 978-1-936332-47-2 • $24.95

Out of the Transylvania Night

Aura Imbarus

A Pulitzer-Prize entry

"I'd grown up in the land of Transylvania, homeland to Dracula, Vlad the Impaler, and worse, dictator Nicolae Ceausescu," writes the author. "Under his rule, like vampires, we came to life after sundown, hiding our heirloom jewels and documents deep in the earth." Fleeing to the US to rebuild her life, she discovers a startling truth about straddling two cultures and striking a balance between one's dreams and the sacrifices that allow a sense of "home."

"Aura's courage shows the degree to which we are all willing to live lives centered on freedom, hope, and an authentic sense of self. Truly a love story!"
—**Nadia Comaneci, Olympic Champion**

"A stunning account of erasing a past, but not an identity."
—**Todd Greenfield, 20th Century Fox**

ISBN: 978-0-9843081-2-5 • ePub:978-1-936332-20-5 • $14.95

The Morphine Dream

Don Brown with Boston Globe
Pulitzer nominated Gary S. Chafetz

An amazing story of one man's loss and gain, hope, and the revealing of an unexpected calling.

At 36, high-school dropout and a failed semi-professional ballplayer Donald Brown hit bottom when an industrial accident left him immobilized. But Brown had a dream while on a morphine drip after surgery: he imagined himself graduating from Harvard Law School (he was a classmate of Barack Obama) and walking across America. Brown realizes both seemingly unreachable goals, and achieves national recognition as a legal crusader for minority homeowners. An intriguing tale of his long walk—both physical and metaphorical.

A story of perseverance and second chances.

"An incredibly inspirational memoir." —**Alan M. Dershowitz, professor, Harvard Law School**

ISBN: 978-1-936332-25-0 • ePub: 978-1-936332-26-7 • $16.95 US

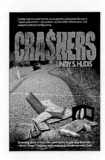

Crashers

A Tale of "Cappers" and "Hammers"

Lindy S. Hudis

The illegal business of fraudulent car accidents is a multi-million dollar racket, involving unscrupulous medical providers, personal injury attorneys, and the cooperating passengers involved in the accidents. Innocent people are often swept into it. Newly engaged Nathan and Shari, who are swimming in mounting debt, were easy prey: seduced by an offer from a stranger to move from hard times to good times in no time, Shari finds herself the "victim" in a staged auto accident. Shari gets her payday, but breaking free of this dark underworld will take nothing short of a miracle.

"A riveting story of love, life—and limits. A non-stop thrill ride."
—Dennis "Danger" Madalone, stunt coordinator, *Castle*

ISBN: 978-1-936332-27-4 • ePub: 978-1-936332-28-1 • $16.95

A World Torn Asunder

The Life and Triumph of Constantin C. Giurescu

Marina Giurescu, M.D.

Constantin C. Giurescu was Romania's leading historian and author of the seminal *The History of the Romanian People*. His granddaughter's fascinating story of this remarkable man and his family follows their struggles in war-torn Romania from 1900 to the fall of the Soviet Union. An "enlightened" society is dismantled with the 1946 Communist takeover of Romania, and Constantin is confined to the notorious Sighet penitentiary.

Drawing on her grandfather's prison diary (which was put in a glass jar, buried in a yard, then smuggled out of the country by Dr. Paul E. Michelson—who does the FOREWORD for this book), private letters and her own research, Dr. Giurescu writes of the legacy from the turn of the century to the fall of Communism.

We see the rise of modern Romania, the misery of World War I, the blossoming of its culture between the wars, and then the sellout of Eastern Europe to Russia after World War II. In this sweeping account, we see not only its effects socially and culturally, but the triumph in its wake: a man and his people who reclaim better lives for themselves, and in the process, teach us a lesson in endurance, patience, and will—not only to survive, but to thrive.

"The inspirational story of a quiet man and his silent defiance in the face of tyranny."
—Dr. Connie Mariano, author of *The White House Doctor*

ISBN: 978-1-936332-76-2 • ePub: 978-1-936332-77-9 • $21.95

Diary of a Beverly Hills Matchmaker

Marla Martenson

Quick-witted Marla takes her readers for a hilarious romp through her days as an LA matchmaker where looks are everything and money talks. The Cupid of Beverly Hills has introduced countless couples who lived happily ever-after, but for every success story there are hysterically funny dating disasters with high-maintenance, out of touch clients. Marla writes with charm and self-effacement about the universal struggle to love and be loved.

ISBN 978-0-9843081-0-1 • ePub: 978-1-936332-03-8 • $14.95

Trafficking the Good Life

Jennifer Myers

Jennifer Myers had worked long and hard toward a successful career as a dancer in Chicago, but just as her star was rising, she fell in love with the kingpin of a drug trafficking operation. Drawn to his life of luxury, she soon became a vital partner in driving marijuana across the country, making unbelievable sums of easy money that she stacked in shoeboxes and spent like an heiress.

Steeped in moral ambiguity, she sought to cleanse her soul with the guidance of spiritual gurus and New Age prophets—to no avail. Only time in a federal prison made her face up to and understand her choices. It was there, at rock bottom, that she discovered that her real prison was the one she had unwittingly made inside herself and where she could start rebuilding a life of purpose and ethical pursuit.

"A gripping memoir. When the DEA finally knocks on Myers's door, she and the reader both see the moment for what it truly is—not so much an arrest as a rescue."
—Tony D'Souza, author of *Whiteman and Mule*

"A stunningly honest exploration of a woman finding her way through a very masculine world . . . and finding her voice by facing the choices she has made."
—Dr. Linda Savage, author of *Reclaiming Goddess Sexuality*

ISBN: 978-1-936332-67-0 • ePub: 978-1-936332-68-7 • $18.95

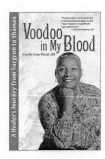

Voodoo in My Blood

A Healer's Journey from Surgeon to Shaman

Carolle Jean-Murat, M.D.

Born and raised in Haiti to a family of healers, US trained physician Carolle Jean-Murat came to be regarded as a world-class surgeon. But her success harbored a secret: in the operating room, she could quickly intuit the root cause of her patient's illness, often times knowing she could help the patient without surgery. Carolle knew that to fellow surgeons, her intuition was best left unmentioned. But when the devastating earthquake hit Haiti and Carolle returned to help, she had to acknowledge the shaman she had become.

"This fascinating memoir sheds light on the importance of asking yourself, 'Have I created for myself the life I've meant to live?'"
—**Christiane Northrup, M.D., author of the New York Times bestsellers:** *Women's Bodies, Women's Wisdom* **and** *The Wisdom of Menopause*

ISBN: 978-1-936332-05-2 • ePub: 978-1-936332-04-5 • $21.95

Fastest Man in the World

The Tony Volpentest Story

Tony Volpentest

Foreword by Ross Perot

Tony Volpentest, a four-time Paralympic gold medalist and five-time world champion sprinter, is a 2012 nominee for the Olympic Hall of Fame

"This inspiring story is about the thrill of victory to be sure—winning gold—but it is also a reminder about human potential: the willingness to push ourselves beyond the ledge of our own imagination. A powerfully inspirational story."
—**Charlie Huebner, United States Olympic Committee**

"This is a moving, motivating and inspiring book."
—**Dan O'Brien, world and Olympic champion decathlete**

"Tony's story shows us that no matter where we start the race, no matter what the obstacles, we all have it within us to reach powerful goals."
—**Oscar Pistorius, "Blade Runner," double amputee, world record holder in the 100, 200 and 400 meters**

ISBN: 978-1-936332-00-7 • ePub: 978-1-936332-01-4 • $16.95

Amazing Adventures of a Nobody

Leon Logothetis

From the Hit Television Series Aired in 100 Countries!

Tired of his disconnected life and uninspiring job, Leon Logothetis leaves it all behind—job, money, home, even his cell phone—and hits the road with nothing but the clothes on his back and five dollars in his pocket, relying on the kindness of strangers and the serendipity of the open road for his daily keep. Masterful storytelling!

"A gem of a book; endearing, engaging and inspiring."
—Catharine Hamm, Los Angeles Times Travel Editor

"Warm, funny, and entertaining. If you're looking to find meaning in this disconnected world of ours, this book contains many clues."   **—Psychology Today**

ISBN: 978-0-9843081-3-2 • ePub: 978-1-936332-51-9 • $14.95

MR. JOE

Tales from a Haunted Life

Joseph Barnett and Jane Congdon

Do you believe in ghosts? Joseph Barnett didn't, until the winter he was fired from his career job and became a school custodian to make ends meet. The fact that the eighty-five-year-old school where he now worked was built near a cemetery had barely registered with Joe when he was assigned the graveyard shift. But soon, walking the dim halls alone at night, listening to the wind howl outside, Joe was confronted with a series of bizarre and terrifying occurrences.

It wasn't just the ghosts of the graveyard shift that haunted him. Once the child of a distant father and an alcoholic mother, now a man devastated by a failed marriage, fearful of succeeding as a single dad, and challenged by an overwhelming illness, Joe is haunted by his own personal ghosts.

The story of Joseph's challenges and triumphs emerges as an eloquent metaphor of ghosts, past and present, real and emotional, and how a man puts his beliefs about self—and ghosts—to the test.

"Thrilling, thoughtful, elegantly told. So much more than a ghost story."
—Cyrus Webb, CEO, Conversation Book Club

"This is truly inspirational work, a very special book—a gift to any reader."
—Diane Bruno, CISION Media

ISBN: 978-1-936332-78-6 • ePub: 978-1-936332-79-3 • $18.95

The Search For
The Lost Army

The National Geographic and
Harvard University Expedition

Gary S. Chafetz

In one of history's greatest ancient disasters, a Persian army of 50,000 soldiers was suffocated by a hurricane-force sandstorm in 525 BC in Egypt's Western Desert. No trace of this conquering army, hauling huge quantities of looted gold and silver, has ever surfaced.

Nearly 25 centuries later on October 6, 1981, Egyptian Military Intelligence, the CIA, and Israel's Mossad secretly orchestrated the assassination of President Anwar Sadat, hoping to prevent Egypt's descent—as had befallen Iran two years before—into the hands of Islamic zealots. Because he had made peace with Israel and therefore had become a marked man in Egypt and the Middle East, Sadat had to be sacrificed to preserve the status quo.

These two distant events become intimately interwoven in the story of Alex Goodman, who defeats impossible obstacles as he leads a Harvard University/ National Geographic Society archaeological expedition into Egypt's Great Sand Sea in search of the Lost Army of Cambyses, the demons that haunt him, and the woman he loves. Based on a true story.

Gary Chafetz, referred to as "one of the ten best journalists of the past twenty-five years," is a former Boston Globe correspondent and was twice nominated for a Pulitzer Prize by the Globe.

ISBN: 978-1-936332-98-4 • ePub: 978-1-936332-99-1 • $19.95

The Tortoise Shell Code

V Frank Asaro

Off the coast of Southern California, the Sea Diva, a tuna boat, sinks. Members of the crew are missing and what happened remains a mystery. Anthony Darren, a renowned and wealthy lawyer at the top of his game, knows the boat's owner and soon becomes involved in the case. As the case goes to trial, a missing crew member is believed to be at fault, but new evidence comes to light and the finger of guilt points in a completely unanticipated direction.

Now Anthony must pull together all his resources to find the truth in what has happened and free a wrongly accused man—as well as untangle himself. Fighting despair, he finds that the recent events have called much larger issues into question. As he struggles to right this terrible wrong, Anthony makes new and enlightening discoveries in his own life-long battle for personal and global justice.

V Frank Asaro is a lawyer, musician, composer, inventor and philosopher. He is also the author of Universal Co-opetition.

ISBN: 978-1-936332-60-1 • ePub: 978-1-936332-61-8 • $24.95 US

516

Bettie Youngs Books

We specialize in MEMOIRS

. . . books that celebrate

fascinating people and

remarkable journeys